ENCYCLOPEDIA OF
FRONTIER AND WESTERN FICTION

ENCYCLOPEDIA OF
FRONTIER
AND
WESTERN
FICTION

Jon Tuska and Vicki Piekarski

EDITORS-IN-CHIEF

McGRAW-HILL BOOK COMPANY

New York   St. Louis   San Francisco
Auckland   Bogotá   Hamburg   Johannesburg   London   Madrid
Mexico   Montreal   New Delhi   Panama   Paris   São Paulo
Singapore   Sydney   Tokyo   Toronto

Thomas H. Quinn and Michael Hennelly were the editors of this book.
Christine Aulicino was the designer. Thomas G. Kowalczyk supervised the
production. It was set in Caledonia by Santype-Byrd, Inc.

Printed and bound by R. R. Donnelley and Sons, Inc.

ISBN 0-07-065587-1

Library of Congress Cataloging in Publication Data
Main entry under title:

Encyclopedia of frontier and western fiction.

  Bibliography: p.
  1. American fiction—West (U.S.)—Biobibliography. 2. American fiction—
West (U.S.)—History and criticism—Dictionaries. 3. Western stories—His-
tory and criticism—Dictionaries. 4. West (U.S.) in literature—Dictionar-
ies. 5. Frontier and pioneer life in literature—Dictionaries. 6. Authors,
American—West (U.S.)—Biography. I. Tuska, Jon. II. Piekarski, Vicki.
PS374.W4E53 1983   813′.0874′09   82-14831
ISBN 0-07-065587-1

123456789 DODO 876543

Dedicated to pioneers of the past, present, and future

CO-EDITORS-IN-CHIEF

Jon Tuska

Author of numerous books, many of them devoted to Western fiction and film, the most recent of which have been *The Filming of the West* (1976), *The American West in Fiction* (1982) and *The American West in Film* (1983). Together with Vicki Piekarski, he co-edited *The Frontier Experience: A Reader's Guide to the Life and Literature of the American West* (1983). He wrote, produced, and appeared in the ten-part series, *They Went Thataway* (1970) for PBS, and was special film consultant for *Images of Indians* (1980), also for PBS. He is on the adjunct faculty at Lewis & Clark College in Portland, Oregon.

Vicki Piekarski

Associate editor and contributor to the Close-Up on the Cinema series consisting of *Close-Up: The Contract Director* (1976), *Close-Up: The Hollywood Director* (1978), and *Close-Up: The Contemporary Director* (1981), she is also co-editor of the *Frontier Experience: A Reader's Guide to the Life and Literature of the American West* (1983). Together with Jon Tuska she is at work on *Native Americans: A Reader's Guide to the Life of and Literature about the American Indian.*

CONTRIBUTING EDITORS

Robert E. Briney

A noted critic of popular fiction, contributor to the *Encyclopedia of Mystery and Detection* (1976) and *The Mystery Story* (1976), he is also the editor of *The Rohmer Review*, a professor of mathematics, and a department chairman at the Massachusetts Institute of Technology—Salem.

John D. Flanagan

A historian of Nineteenth-century United States and Europe, presently associated with the Bonneville Power Administration.

Deane Mansfield-Kelley

An assistant professor of English at the University of Texas—El Paso and a student of American literature, her doctoral work was devoted to a study of the Indian woman in American letters.

John Milton

Western poet, biographer, professor of English at the University of South Dakota, editor of the *South Dakota Review*, and host for a PBS series of interviews with noted Western American authors, he is also the author of a critical study, *The Novel of the American West* (1980).

Jack Nachbar

Editor of *Focus on the Western* (1974), co-editor of the *Journal of Popular Film and Television*, he is also a professor of English and popular culture at Bowling Green State University.

Priscilla Oaks

A professor of English at California State University at Fullerton, and a field editor for the Gregg Press' Western fiction re-issue series, she was formerly teaching American Studies at Fudan University in Shanghai, China.

David Wilson

Research editor for the *Close-Up on the Cinema* series as well as a contributor, he is presently at work on a historical account of the motion picture stunt and special effects industry.

CONSULTING EDITOR

PHOTOGRAPHER

C.L. Sonnichsen

For more than thirty years a professor of Southwestern life and literature, author of numerous books, the most recent of which is *From Hopalong to Hud: Thoughts on Western Fiction* (1978), past president of the Western Writers of America, senior editor of the *Journal of Arizona History*.

Stephen Wagner

Photographed all illustrations not otherwise credited.

PREFACE
by Jon Tuska

In assembling this encyclopedia, the editors have followed Aldous Huxley's advice in his essay, "Books for the Journey" (1925). "It should be a work of such a kind," Huxley wrote, "that one can open it anywhere and be sure of finding something interesting, complete in itself, and susceptible of being read in a short time." Even should one not take it traveling, these are good attributes for an encyclopedia in one volume to have.

The dictionary of the *Encyclopedia Britannica* defines a Western as "a type of fiction or motion picture using cowboy and pioneer life in the Western United States as its material." That is as good a definition of the Western as perhaps there is to be had, provided, however, that we expand it to encompass frontier fiction of all kinds if set on the North American continent. The earliest example of frontier fiction the editors of the present encyclopedia have chosen to cite is *The Pioneers* (1823), the first of the Leatherstocking tales of James Fenimore Cooper. While with some justification *L'Heroine du Texas* (1819) by "F---n M. G---n" might be cited as the first Southwestern novel, it was written in French by a young man about whom, other than his initials, very little is known. Therefore, for our purposes, we have chosen Timothy Flint's *Francis Berrian* (1826) as the first Southwestern novel whose author has been included.

I must stress that the *Encyclopedia of Frontier and Western Fiction* is a reference work. Its primary objective is to convey factual information. Only in the final summing up for each author is an effort made to place his or her work in comparative relationship with the main body of frontier and Western fiction. This summing up, however, is not intended to be literary criticism. As far as the editors are concerned, literary criticism is a matter of subjective opinion—no matter how clearly formulated the aesthetic principles from which it is derived—and therefore essentially different than information of a factual nature.

Yet I should like to say a few words in general about how I believe Western fiction ought to be approached critically here, where it belongs, by way of a preface. Aristotle demonstrated long ago in the *Poetics* that the most viable form of literary categories are those determined according to structure, then content, and finally style. In dealing with Western fiction, in order to circumvent the ancient aesthetic debate between formalism and realism, I would opt for a concept of historical reality as the basic standard of value and the content of a Western fiction would be distinguished on the basis of its deviation (and the way in which it deviates) from this standard.

"Historia scribitur ad narrandum non ad probandum" [history is written for the purpose of narration and not to give proof] Quintilian wrote, and I do not believe that it should be any different in our day. Historical events cannot be recreated empirically. They can only be recreated by a process of inference according to logical principles, ideally taking into account all available evidence and *never* to prove or disprove some thesis or interpretation. ". . . The art of the historian," Morris R. Cohen wrote in *The Meaning of Human History* (LaSalle: Open Court, 1947), ". . . is something that involves literary skill but, even more, an imaginative capacity for seeing threads of connection between historic facts and significant issues." He developed a model for the historian: "The ideal of an imaginative reconstruction of the past which is scientific in its determinations and artistic in its formulations is the ideal to which the greatest of historians have ever aspired." I would call such a model an historical construction. It is the recreation, as closely as possible, of a former reality in terms of what that reality was for those who were then living and perceiving it. The questions to be asked at this stage of historical inquiry are of this order: Is all the available and pertinent evidence fully taken into account? Are the determinations such that they can be verified by the known historical data? Are the data themselves reliable? Is the construction based on the evidence logically consistent with the evidence and, internally, as a construction? How valid are the inferences and can they withstand logical scrutiny? Finally, the historian must be willing to admit that this historical construction is at best only probable and provisional.

Only once all this has been done ought ethics—the

rational examination of human behavior patterns in terms of their effects—enter upon the scene. If an historian is going to evaluate a past reality in ethical terms, it must logically come after that reality has been recreated by means of an historical construction and the historian, in making such evaluations, is best advised to be straightforward as to just what ethical standard it is that he is using.

When it comes to Western fiction, I have found, employing this standard of historical reality, that there are three principal modes: the historical reconstruction, the romantic historical reconstruction, and the formulary Western. Now, it should go without saying that no critic is really qualified to evaluate historical fiction of any kind—including Western fiction—unless he knows enough about the historical period, the place, and the people involved to know the difference between historical reality and fantasy. Too much criticism of Western fiction—and Western films—has been written to date by critics who have not known the difference and it has resulted only in confusion at worst or, at best, to invoke the French term, *jeux d'esprit*, flights of fancy.

The difference between what I term an historical construction in Western history and what I term an historical reconstruction in Western fiction consists in this: An historical construction, ideally, should contain no statement not necessitated or supported by the factual evidence whereas an historical reconstruction, because it is fiction and not history, can embellish the details based on the evidence *while it cannot at any point contradict the factual evidence.* It was acceptable for Leo Tolstoy in *War and Peace* (1862–1869) to "interpret" the personalities of Kutuzov and Napoleon—and those personalities did change as the novel passed through its several drafts—but he could not have Kutuzov win the battle at Borodino. No more and no less can an author of Western fiction write an historical reconstruction in which the known facts of Western American history are deliberately distorted or violated.

Yet, although varying in degree and purpose, this is precisely what happens in the other two modes, the formulary Western and the romantic historical reconstruction. There are, in fact, two very powerful links between these two alternate modes. They both distort factual history and they both share a reliance on the structure of romance. Romance, as it was first developed by the Greeks, consists of an ἀγων (agon), or conflict, followed by a πάθος (pathos) in which the conflict is brought to its conclusion, and ends with an 'αν-αγνώρισις (anagnorisis), or a recognition. There is an optional middle term, a σπᾰραγμός (sparagmos), or a mangling. In the basic Perseus myth, the typical romance structure reveals a helpless community ruled by an old and ineffectual king. The community is threatened by a devouring sea-monster and, in order to propitiate the sea-monster, the community regularly offers up a human sacrifice. Perseus, the hero, comes upon the scene just as the king's beautiful daughter is about to be made the next sacrificial victim. Perseus defeats and slays the sea-monster in combat, winning, as his reward, both the princess and the kingdom. A *sparagmos* episode may be included, in which Perseus is mangled in the course of the combat. The *anagnorisis*, or recognition, in the Perseus myth, as is also the case in the formulary Western where the hero vanquishes the villain or villains, is—in Virgil's words—*"deus dabit his quoque finem"* (a god will put up with only so much of such things).

The romantic historical reconstruction retains the structure of romance, but in addition, in the anagnorisis, offers an ideological interpretation of human history. Whatever occurs in a romantic historical reconstruction occurs for *ideological* reasons and is never merely the result of the interaction with the land or between peoples, as these phenomena have happened in history or as a consequence of character.

I regret that I cannot further develop these concepts, but the reader interested in pursuing them is referred to my three-part essay, "The American West in Fiction," which appeared in the May, June, and July/August, 1981 issues of *The Round-up*, the house organ of the Western Writers of America, and the General Introduction to my anthology of Western fiction, *The American West in Fiction* (New York: Mentor Books, 1982). Also, in the lengthy biographical and literary history of the Western fiction section of *The Frontier Experience: A Reader's Guide to the Life and Literature of the American West* (work in progress, 1983), Vicki Piekarski and I have traced the growth and development of all three of these modes throughout the history of Western fiction as well as surveyed most of the literary criticism which has so far appeared that is concerned with Western fiction.

Western fiction, in my view, has only progressed beyond being a "minor" literature where it has addressed actual human experience and real human conflicts. We cannot persist, as the characters in George Orwell's *1984* (New York:

Harcourt, Brace, 1949), in constantly rewriting our history to suit the fashion of the moment, as is done in so many stories set in the American West, as if history were nothing more than the handmaiden of wish-fulfillment. I believe that the purpose of Western American fiction, as of all art, is—to paraphrase Dr. Samuel Johnson—to prepare ourselves better to understand life or, when that proves impossible, at least better to endure it.

I would only add to the foregoing one final suggestion, one based on Mary Austin's essay "Regionalism in American Fiction" which first appeared in the *English Journal* in February, 1932. Ms. Austin counselled that she would require two factors to be indispensible in a regional story. The first of these is that the region itself must be an integral part of the structure of the story, either as a character or as a prime mover of the plot. The second is that the story must be *of* the region, and not just about it. These factors, when combined with historiographic accuracy, are invariably found in the best examples of what I term the historical reconstruction.

If the historical past does have something to teach us, and I believe that it does, and if we are willing to learn from it, then the Western novel and story may well be the ideal literary form through which our American past can be evoked vividly and painfully—painfully because it was mostly painful. The story of the American West, truly, has nothing to do with heroes and romance; it is rather a question of human endurance in the face of tragedy and defeat. But in tragedy combined with human endurance, in spiritual resilience in the face of disaster, as writers since Aeschylus and Sophocles have known, there is the potential for human nobility. Most of the best fiction about the American West is about *man in Nature*, not the denatured, mechanical, sterile world that has come increasingly to serve as a backdrop for human activity in other kinds of fiction. Indeed, in finding some good in our American past, albeit in these more realistic terms, we might well entertain some hope for the future. In this way the American West remains what the Native American always thought it to be; the land beyond the setting sun, the Spiritland. The Delphic γνῶθι σεαυτόν [know thyself] is deepened and broadened by the new experiences on a new continent; our collective idea of humanity is strengthened through a more truthful understanding and assimilation of our historical past.

xii

AN INTRODUCTION
by Vicki Piekarski

"Forget what you think about it and tell how you feel about it," Stephen Crane once advised a young, aspiring author. This is sound advice for all writers. I have devoted the last several years to thinking about the Western and its multitudinous facets. I would like now, with the reader's permission, to explore some of my feelings about the subject.

I must confess that when I was young I did not spend my afternoons watching Western movies at a local theatre nor on television. This is an odd confession to make—perhaps even un-American—since I am co-editor on this Western encyclopedia. However, I found Western films inane because of their predictability and their black and white philosophy of good versus evil. When I did upon occasion watch a Western, more often than not I would side with the underdog.

In the Seventies my work brought me in contact with many of the Western films I had so diligently avoided as a child. I met a number of people who had been involved in the production of Western films. I began to feel that Westerns were an unavoidable part of my life. A. B. Guthrie, Jr. has written: "Each passing generation of actual inhabitants loses the West, and each succeeding one rediscovers it." My discovery came a little later than it does perhaps for most, but it did come.

At the inception of the Western encyclopedia project, I volunteered to research the women Western writers in addition to the male Western writers I chose, so I was enthusiastic since I am extremely interested in women writers. Because of my unfounded assumptions based on the Western films I had screened, I was rather skeptical about the quality of Western fiction. I was also overwhelmed by the number of Westerns extant. I began an intensive reading program of the landmark and influential Westerns in addition to reading the works of the specified authors I had been assigned. My assumptions proved to be completely erroneous. Western literature—for indeed much of it must be considered *literature*—has very little in common with Western films.

I am sure there are those who would disagree vociferously with me. Some might even go as far as to say that Western fiction has nothing to offer, whereas Western films are a legitimate form of artistic expression. After all a sufficient number of Western films, particularly those directed by John Ford and Sam Peckinpah, have a loyal cult following and have had a significant influence on films both in and out of the Western genre. However, I believe that the majority of feelings about Western fiction, both among the public and the *literati*, are based, as were mine, on false assumptions, the source of which have been Hollywood's film and television "*odeurs*," not because they have read a sampling of the genre.

Indeed many Western novels are formulary. They are built around standard cliché-ridden story-lines and are peopled with invincible heroes, unscrupulous villains, and beautiful, virginal heroines. However when the great drama of the American West is dealt with in plain human terms it becomes an important and *necessary* addition to a representative national literature for the United States as Western writers Mary Austin and Vardis Fisher pointed out years ago. Dismissing Western literature as low-brow fiction, or even "trash" as I have heard it called, is dismissing a significant part of America's history as well as its present and its future.

The detective genre which portrays generally the corruption of mankind at a very superficial level, where one man—the detective along with perhaps a faithful companion—can make matters right, commands a devoted audience in the public community and a surprising amount of prestige in academia. Yet, Western fiction has been relegated, in the aggregate, as a body of fiction read by cowboys, remedial, and/or slow-witted readers. A personal experience will substantiate this unfortunate state of affairs. In addition to reading Westerns and Nineteenth-century women writers, I read books on psychology. When I began frequenting a local new and used bookstore I would quite often purchase, in addition to a number of Westerns, a book or two on psychology. Months later I became acquainted with two of the people who worked at the bookstore, a man and a woman. They both confessed, on different occasions, they were puzzled by my acquisitions from their stacks. Not only did they view me as a cowgirl with a neurotic problem in search of home-grown analysis, but they also projected into my dress a "Western" flair. I did not, and do not, wear cowboy boots and I still wear the same clothes I did when I originally visited the bookstore. Yet they believed I dressed differently then, than I do now. This may seem unusual, but I feel it is typical of the way the general public views Western fiction and the people who read it. Psychologist C. G. Jung has written in "Images of the Unconscious" (1950): "The persona . . . is that system of adjustment or that manner by which we deal with the external world. Almost every occupation or profession has its characteristic persona. . . . The danger is only that one will become identified with his persona, as sometimes the professor with his textbook or the tenor with his voice. . . . One is able to say with some exaggeration: the persona is that which a person essentially is not, but rather what he and other people wish him to be."

Americans love heroes and find comfort in the belief that one man alone can change the course of everyone's life and solve their problems. (This fact is particularly evident every four years when presidential election time rolls around.) And, I think it is safe to say, despite the stigma surrounding Western fiction and the image of the Westerner, that the "persona" of the entire American people is that of a self-sufficient, unconquerable, yet mythical Western hero as embodied in the late John Wayne. Americans like to project this image and in turn it is projected on us by people of other lands. When I was in France a number of years ago, a John Wayne Western was being aired in a "prime time" slot. In talking with a number of exchange students from various countries at a local university I was told that their image of the United States and of Americans was based entirely on films they had seen in their homelands. Those films were usually Westerns starring John Wayne.

For the majority of Americans under 30 the names William S. Hart, Tom Mix, Buck Jones, Tim McCoy, Ken Maynard, and Gene Autry hold little significance. That is not the case for millions over 30. In addition to watching a great number of "A" and "B" Westerns, I have read about the lives of the screen cowboys, heard numerous stories about them, and was lucky enough to meet one and spend some time talking with him. What I find distressing, even frightening, is that a great number of the movie cowboys tried to become the image they portrayed on the screen. I have watched Buck Jones dash across the screen fists clenched, brow wrinkled, teeth gritted with such forceful determination a great many times: I wonder how much influence his career as a Western hero had on his actions on that fateful day in 1942 when he rushed into the Cocoanut Grove conflagration to save a friend. If it is true that the movie cowboy image colored and shaped the lives of the men who depicted the Western hero, what did it do to the millions of young, impressionable children who saved their pennies each week for the Saturday Western matinees? We certainly need our myths as all people do. However, at what point do these myths become harmful?

I cannot answer this question. I do not know if at this point in time anyone can. However, it is my feeling that the Western film has been more instrumental in shaping the attitudes of American men, and to a lesser extent women, than any other genre. And yet, the books written about Western cinema—there are a great many of them—retell the plots, record the facts and figures, tell about the lives of the people involved in Western productions, and, ultimately, if you will, take a jaunt down memory lane. This on-going nostalgic affection for the Western has culminated in recent years in not only books of reminicenses but also in memorabilia shops, Western film societies, and annual Western film festivals where thousands of people congregate to watch old "B" Westerns and rub elbows with the surviving Western players.

Feminist Simone de Beauvoir has written in the third volume of her autobiographical tetralogy, *Force des Choses* (Paris: Librarie Gallimard, 1963): "I had picked up a taste for Westerns from Sartre in the old days. Above all the rest I preferred [John] Huston's *Treasure of the Sierra Madre* [Warner's, 1948]. . . . But Gary Cooper in *High Noon* [United Artists, 1952], Marilyn Monroe in *River of No Return* [20th-Fox, 1954], and the violence of *Shane* [Paramount, 1953] had also held me breathless. . . . But most of the time the Americans were now spoiling this sort of film by working the same old political 'message' into them all. A hero or heroine, sometimes a child, would have an almost neurotic repugnance toward violence; for an hour and a half, sometimes two, the wickedness of the 'bad people' would fail to have any effect on this attitude; suddenly, at the last moment, to save a friend, a fiancée, a father, the main character would kill. The audience then returned home convinced, it was hoped, of the necessity of the preventive war." The Women's Movement has heightened the awareness of millions of women throughout the world. Women are questioning not only their own life-styles, but the way they have been depicted in history, fiction, and in film. Enlightened and often angry books on the subject are being published. The two most popular books written about the role of women in films—Marjorie Rosen's *Popcorn Venus* (New York: Coward, McCann, 1973) and Molly Haskell's *From Reverence to Rape: The Treatment of Women in the Movies* (New York: Holt, Rinehart, 1974)—fail to attain the insight Beauvoir has on the Western. However, women are questioning the influence and impact that films have had on their lives and society at large. It is my hope that men will soon begin to challenge the stereotypical roles men have been forced to try to live up to because of the thousands of Western films cranked out by the Hollywood "dream machine." Like women, men need to revolt because after all even John Wayne wasn't the John Wayne he portrayed on the screen.

I am not one of those people who look only toward the future convincing myself and everyone else that the past is past and has nothing to tell us. However, I believe that our attachment, our affection, for the West has been displaced. The West was populated by all types of people, from every walk of life. It was not peopled with heroes and villains. The real heroes were ordinary men and women who built homes for their families and worked the land. Their trusty companion wasn't a six-shooter, but rather the tools of their trade. The "villains" were societal outcasts and refuse, the wanderers, and the most treacherous of all, the greedy big business men who wanted to rape the land of its resources. For the vast majority the West represented a second chance in life and freedom. It was not a stage where heroics were acted out for the benefit of future-generation audiences. The West was in the words of A. B. Guthrie, Jr. "the adventure of the spirit." Many were called, many followed, some succeeded, and many failed.

There are many books in the world of Western fiction that tell the story of real people who went, or might have gone, West, that deal with the human condition and depict the spiritual struggles of men and women. These books deserve recognition. Had I not been given the opportunity to work on this Western encyclopedia, I would have continued in my assumptions, out of ignorance, that all Western fiction featured larger-than-life heroics. I would have been wrong.

This is not to say that the well-written formulary novels

written by Western authors like Luke Short, Ernest Haycox, Max Brand, Lee Hoffman, and Ann Ahlswede do not serve a purpose. They too are worthwhile reading for those who enjoy intricately plotted stories with intriguing characters. Many formulary Westerns transcend the ordinary adventure tale for they depict the moral ambiguities of humans and society as a whole. They are not necessarily just novels loosely put together by action sequences in which good conquers evil that serve as pablum in our troubled times.

There are other books that I feel deserve to be considered classics of American literature and should be taught in schools. Several of the works of Mari Sandoz, Elmer Kelton, Mary Austin, Vardis Fisher, Edward Abbey, Benjamin Capps, et al., are lasting stories that capture their respective periods in American history both realistically and poignantly. The works of these authors and many others in the Western genre portray people struggling, loving, working, searching, celebrating—in one word, living.

The West was, as hundreds have already written, many things to many people. Much of the world of Western fiction recreates and breathes life into that unfortunately distorted part of our history. It is the intention of the editors and all the people who have contributed in one form or another to this Western encyclopedia that Western literature be re-evaluated and recognized as a significant and necessary asset of our national literature. This encyclopedia is a pioneering effort, the first step towards that recognition.

There was an old phrase in the West when someone respected or genuinely liked another. He or she would say, "They'll do to take along." American literature, in its relatively short history, could do worse than "take along" the works of authors who have contributed important and lasting books in the Western genre.

There are five articles in this encyclopedia other than author entries to which the reader's attention is called. They are: "Historical Personalities," "House Names," "Native Americans," "Pulp and Slick Western Stories," and "Women on the Frontier."

In giving the title of a book in the text of an entry, it is followed, if it was published in the Nineteenth century, by only the year of publication, e.g., *The Pioneers* (1823). If it was published in the Twentieth century, the title is followed by the city, publisher, and year of publication, e.g., *The Virginian* (New York: Macmillan, 1902). Generally only one-word identifications have been used for publishers, as in the case of Harper's instead of Harper & Brothers or Harper & Row. The same procedure has been followed with regard to film producing and releasing companies, as in the instance of Warner's instead of Warner Bros. or Warner/Seven Arts.

Motion picture references give only the releasing company and year of release, e.g., *The Virginian* (Paramount, 1929). When the producing company is other than the releasing company, the releasing company is still the one given, e.g., *The Virginian* (Preferred Pictures, 1923) which was produced by B. P. Schulberg Productions. Only director credits are given with motion picture titles, e.g., *The Pioneers* (Monogram, 1941) directed by Al Herman.

All references to book titles in bibliographies are given by year only, e.g., *The Virginian* (1902). All such years of publication, whether in the text or the bibliographies, are to the year of first publication, whether as hard-bound or paperback original. Where possible, title changes have been noted in the bibliographical section following the title by which the book was first known. The Copyright Act of the United States of America permits a book to change title only once before it loses its copyright protection. Short stories in book collections are noted [short stories] after the book title, as are [short novels] following the book title. All pseudonyms for authors in the text have been given an alphabetical reference listing with a referral back to the author's real name, even if he is not known at all by that name. However, when a particular author is referred to in the text of an entry other than his own and is best known by his or her pseudonym, the pseudonym is used for comprehensibility and for the sake of ready identification, i.e., "Dwight Bennett Newton was influenced by Max Brand" rather than "by Frederick Faust writing as Max Brand." When a name is familiar to the reading public as a pseudonym used by a number of different authors, it is included alphabetically in the text with a reference to the entry for "House Names," e.g., Peter Field, Jack Slade, Jonas Ward, etc.

Since this encyclopedia is concerned primarily with entries for authors of fictional works, only a very few non-fictional authors have been included—authors who have written *no* fiction whatsoever, e.g., Theodore Roosevelt—and these only because of their influence or impact on Western fiction. While full responsibility for inclusion or omission of any individual must rest with the co-editors-in-chief, nonetheless a list of potentially suitable names was broadly circulated among many of the more noted authorities on Western American literature, among Western authors, and among readers and collectors of Western fiction. Those who have been excluded from the encylopedia were those either rejected by this panel of experts, or authors about whom there was insufficient information available from which to prepare an entry. Where possible, when an author has written a small number of books, an effort is made to mention all of them within the text of the entry, and where this has been done no bibliography is included. Short stories *not* collected generally receive no mention. Also, wherever possible, the editors have cited book-length biographies or critical studies about a particular author. All bibliographical references are further confined only to an author's *Western* novels and story collections in book form—as the term "Western" is defined in "A Preface" by Jon Tuska.

For further recommendations and critical writing on virtually all aspects of Western history, Western fiction, and Western films, it is suggested the reader consult *The Frontier Experience: A Reader's Guide To The Life And Literature Of The American West* (Work in progress by Jon Tuska and Vicki Piekarski).

All the bibliographies and filmographies may not be complete. They are only as complete as they can be as a result of checking the listings of books copyrighted in the United States and included in the *National Union Catalogue* against lists supplied to the editors by the authors and/or the authors' agents and estates. The same was done with motion picture derivations, radio and television adaptations, or original screen stories: they are as complete as the information available. If an omission has been made, the editors would appreciate a communication to that effect addressed in their care to the publisher of this encyclopedia and inclusion of any such additional title(s) will appear in future, revised editions of this volume.

Self-Portrait by Edward Abbey

Abbey, Edward (1927 —) Contro

versial author of fiction and non-fiction books dealing with the preservation of the wilderness of the contemporary American West, born at Home, Pennsylvania. Abbey, the son of Mildred Postlewaite Abbey and Paul Revere Abbey who taught him "to hate injustice, to defy the powerful, and to speak for the voiceless," was raised on a farm in the Allegheny Mountain region of Pennsylvania where he received his early education. From 1945–1947, Abbey served as a rifleman for the U.S. Army stationed in Italy, an experience which Abbey claimed made him an anarchist. His fascination with the Southwest began in 1944, one year before he graduated from high school, when he hitchhiked to the Pacific coast. In 1947, he enrolled at the University of New Mexico in Albuquerque where he received his Bachelor's degree in 1951. His summers were spent visiting and exploring the various terrains of the Southwest. His writing career began while he was at the University of New Mexico where he edited the student literary magazine, *The Thunderbird*. He was awarded a Fulbright Fellowship in 1951–1952 and spent most of the year in Edinburgh and later traveled through Europe for three months before returning to the United States in June, 1952. He attended Yale University for two weeks upon enrolling in their graduate school as a philosophy student. Abbey tried for one year, as he would also do in 1962 and 1964, to live and work in New Jersey as a factory worker, social worker, and technical writer. With each attempt, however, Abbey became more repelled by the sterility of Eastern existence and industrialized society.

Abbey returned to the Southwest where he continued his graduate studies at the University of New Mexico, the same year his first novel, *Jonathan Troy* (New York: Dodd, Mead, 1954), was published. An *Erziehungsroman* (novel of education), the protagonist, Jonathan Troy, a boy raised in Pennsylvania, is drawn to the West, which for him represents freedom from the suppression and corruption of the East, much as it did for Abbey. In 1956, the year of the birth of his first child by the second of four wives, Abbey received his Master's degree in philosophy and served his first term with the National Park Service for which he would continue to work on and off for the next fifteen years. He published his second novel, *The Brave Cowboy* (New York: Dodd, Mead, 1956), which subsequently was revised in the Ballantine and University of New Mexico editions due to several minor errors which Abbey felt needed to be changed, and it was made into a successful film, *Lonely Are the Brave* (Universal, 1962). *The Brave Cowboy*, subtitled "An Old Tale in a New Time," is concerned with Jack Burns, an anachronistic cowboy who prefers the wilderness to the city and his horse to an automobile, who in his alienation from contemporary society attempts to save his friend, Paul Bondi, who was jailed because of his lack of cooperation with the Selective Service. Although the plot is somewhat formulary with its share of stock characterizations, it is unique for its notion of a traditional Nineteenth-century hero living in the modern day West, a literary *tour de force* which few writers, save Max Evans (q.v.), Robert Easton (q.v.), and Elmer Kelton (q.v.) have attempted seriously. Abbey combined what he admired most about the old West with what he admired about the contemporary West and in the process raised some important questions concerning freedom and progress. Abbey called *The Brave Cowboy* an anarcho-Western as he did his third novel, *Fire on the Mountain* (New York: Dial, 1962), which is based on a real person, John Prather, a New Mexico cattleman, who fought the government in its attempt to take his land which it wanted to include as part of the White Sands missile base. The story is told from the point of view of the grandson of the protagonist, John Vogelin, who refuses to leave his ranch and comes to question man's relationship with the land. At one point in the story John Vogelin says, " 'I am the land. . . . I've been eating this dust for seventy years. Who owns who?' " Abbey's disgust and frustration with big government, big industry, and the failure of technology to fulfill our needs are important themes in his fiction and non-fiction. *Black Sun* (New York: Simon and Schuster, 1968) an unrealistic love story, and *The Monkey Wrench Gang* (Philadelphia: Lippincott, 1975) followed. *The Monkey Wrench Gang* is set in the Colorado River region of Northern Ari-

zona and Southeastern Utah—Abbey's favorite region—and deals with the adventures of four unlikely characters who go about sabotaging various governmental and industrial projects.

Abbey has won praise from such authors as Larry McMurtry (q.v.) who called him "the Thoreau of the American West" as well as from such scholars as C.L. Sonnichsen. In an Introduction to the University of New Mexico Press' re-issue edition (1978) of *Fire on the Mountain*, Gerald Haslam said of Abbey that he "wants us to stay in touch with the forces of Nature that spawned our species and that continue to give us life. His books explore people and places at war with this country's continued attempts to subdue Nature, with development, with 'growth for the sake of growth,' which, he points out, 'is the ideology of the cancer cell.' " Abbey spoke for the voiceless who are concerned about the wilderness and how important that wilderness remains to our mental and physical well-being. Labels such as ecologist, conservationist, anarchist, naturalist, philosopher, propagandist, and hippie of the wilderness cult have all been attached to Abbey because of his outspokenness on the subject of the American West, but "if a label is required," he said in his Introduction to *The Journey Home* (New York: Dutton, 1977), a collection of essays, "say that I am one who loves unfenced country. *The open range*. Call me a ranger. Though I've hardly earned the title I claim it anyway. The only higher honor I've ever heard of is to be called a man."

Lonely Are the Brave (Universal, 1972) based on Abbey's *The Brave Cowboy* was directed by David Miller.

For further information on Abbey's

work see *Edward Abbey* (Boise: Idaho State University Press, 1977) by Garth McCann.

Adams, Andy (1859–1935) An author noted for his knowledge of the cowboy way of life and his ability to capture the natural language and humor of the working cowboy, born on a stock farm in Indiana. Adams grew up with two brothers and six male cousins from an adjacent farm so that, from youth, his life seems to have been a very masculine one. He had little formal education, and although he attended several three-month sessions when he was growing up at a country school, he preferred outdoor pursuits. Adams' father raised horses and cattle for sale and Adams began his experience with cattle there. However, his father was very stern and Adams left home at the age of 15, seeking adventure in the Far West. By 1881 he was working in a lumber camp near Newport, Arkansas, and he traveled from there to San Antonio, Texas, where he went to work in the shipping yards of Smith and Redmon. Among his duties there was collecting horses for shipment up North and he spent some time on the trail driving horses to Caldwell, and Dodge City, Kansas, going through Indian Territory. Adams made his last drive in May, 1889, when he took some cattle, including some of his own, on to the Cherokee Strip. Although he did make several trail drives, most of his experiences were vicariously accumulated from talking to cowboys and cowmen from Texas and Kansas. He made lasting friendships with Frank Byler, Jr., J. Frank Dobie's (q.v.) uncle, and Charles Siringo, author of *A Texas Cowboy* (1885).

In 1890 Adams moved to Rockport, Texas, to start a feed and seed business. After staying there for four years, he went broke and moved on to the gold fields of Cripple Creek, Colorado. After Cripple Creek, he settled in Colorado Springs where he remained for the rest of his life. Although he represented himself in Colorado Springs as a "mining broker," he never actually did much buying or selling. Instead he saw a performance of Harry O. Hoyt's play *Texas Steer* in 1898 and was so displeased with its portrayal of Texas cowboys that he decided to write his own play. In this way Adams came upon his true profession; he became a writer.

Adams' play, *Corporal Segundo*, was not a noteworthy dramatic endeavor, but in it his ability to reproduce cowboy language and for storytelling were evident. In 1901 Adams sold his first short story, "The Passing of Peg-Leg," to *Frank Leslie's Popular Monthly*. A year later *Leslie's* bought a second story, "A Question of Possession," based on an incident that Adams had witnessed while a member of a posse in the Cherokee Outlet. It presently occurred to Adams that his own experiences and memories of what others had told him could provide him with unlimited material for his fiction. The problem with writing from experience, however, was that the real life of the cowboy and cattleman did not always match up to the wild and wooly image of the Westerner portrayed in the dime novels that were then in their heyday. It was said of Adams that he wrote fiction so that it read as fact. He gave the reading public what seemed to be verisimilitude; yet the public preferred more obvious fabrication. Nonetheless, he did realize that the cowboy's life was long hours, hard work, and good companionship, but it was not all heroics, gunfights, and blood in the street, as the public seemed inclined to think. To the end of his life Adams still said, "I have always contended that fiction can be written as convincingly as fact."

To be sure, Adams' creative writing appeared so factual that his book, *The Log of a Cowboy* (Boston: Houghton Mifflin, 1903), considered by many to be his masterpiece, was even thought to be an autobiography. The book centers around a trail drive in the year 1882 from the Rio Grande to the Blackfoot reservation in Northern Montana. It is the story of fifteen cowboys, exclusive of Don Lovell, the owner of the herd who only meets intermittently with the herd at various points along the way. Tom Quirk, a newcomer, acts as narrator, while Jim Flood, the foreman, directs the drive. During the course of the novel, the group must cross swollen streams and face quicksand, stampedes, rustlers, Indians, and the dangers of whiskey and women in the cowtowns. All of these obstacles are overcome by little use of violence and much use of sound trail sense that comes as a result of experience. It is evident that Adams debunked successfully the stereotyped portrayal of the cowboy while his trail-driving group is, thereby, made no less interesting.

Adams' later novels, *A Texas Matchmaker* (Boston: Houghton Mifflin, 1904), *The Outlet* (Boston: Houghton Mifflin, 1905), *Reed Anthony* (Boston: Houghton Mifflin, 1907), *Wells Brothers* (Boston: Houghton Mifflin, 1911), and *The Ranch on the Beaver* (Boston: Houghton Mifflin, 1927) all deal with some aspect of the cattle business. His anthologies, *Cattle Brands* (Boston: Houghton Mifflin, 1906) and *Why the Chisholm Trail Forks* (Boston: Houghton Mifflin, 1956), are particularly good collections of campfire tales.

In an introductory note to *Cattle Brands*, Adams wrote: "A hard day's work or a reminiscent night may be recalled in its pages, wherein the characters around the fire were the men who redeemed the Lone Star State from crime and lawlessness. The cowboy may be met in his own salon, with his back to the wagon wheel or his head pillowed in a saddle, looking up at the stars. In fact, all the characters met in these brands were men—nothing more, just men." Adams rebelled against dime novel stereotypes, but it might justifiably be claimed that he introduced his own unique kind of romanticism into his tales, related by analogy, if different in substance, from the romanticism of Owen Wister (q.v.) or Zane Grey (q.v.)

D.M.-K.

A good biographical and critical study of Andy Adams is Wilson M. Hudson's *Andy Adams: His Life and Writings* (Dallas: Southern Methodist University Press, 1964).

Adams, Clifton

Adams, Clifton (1919 —) Author of skillfully written formulary Westerns, born at Comanche, Oklahoma. Adams attended the University of Oklahoma and was in the U.S. Army 1942–1945, attaining the rank of Sergeant and receiving five battle stars. His hobby of collecting books relating to the Southwest developed simultaneously and led him to spend years compiling a bibliography, devoted to indexing this entire area of fiction and scholarship.

The Desperado (New York: Fawcett, 1950) was Adams' first Western novel and, subsequently, he went on to write several Westerns under his own name as well as the pseudonyms Matt Kinkaid and Clay Randall. Although he never achieved the polished precision in traditional formulary Westerns that Ernest Haycox (q.v.) or Luke Short (q.v.) did, Adams does belong classed with a middle group of such writers, e.g., Lewis B. Patten (q.v.) and Giles A. Lutz (q.v.) who were more competent in terms of structure and characterization than such pulp-oriented Western storytellers as Nelson C. Nye (q.v.) or Walt Coburn (q.v.). Adams' best novels are those he wrote in the late sixties, especially the two which won Spur Awards from the Western Writers of America, *Tragg's Choice* (New York: Doubleday, 1969) and *The Last Days of Wolf Garnett* (New York: Doubleday, 1970). Perhaps Adams' finest qualities as a Western novelist are the sensitivity with which he depicted his female characters and the vividness with which he described the harshness of frontier life.

Clifton Adams' Western novels under his own name are *The Desperado* (1950), *A Noose for the Desperado* (1951), *Two Gun Law* (1954), *Gambling Man* (1956), *Law of the Trigger* (1956), *The Race of Giants* (1956), *Stranger in Town* (1960), *The Legend of Lonnie Hall* (1960), *Day of the Gun* (1962), *Reckless Men* (1962), *Hogan's Way* (1962), *The Moonlight War* (1963), *The Dangerous Days of Kiowa Jones* (1964), *Doomsday Creek* (1964), *The Hottest Fourth of July in the History of Hangtree County* (1964), *The Grabhorn Bounty* (1965), *The Most Dangerous Profession* (1967), *A Partnership with Death* (1967), *Tragg's Choice* (1969), *The Last Days of Wolf Garnett* (1970), *Biscuit-Shooter* (1970), *The Badge and Harry Cole* (1971), *Hard Times and Arnie Smith* (1972), *Hassle and the Medi-*

cine Man (1973), *The Hard Time Bunch* (1973), *Shorty* (1982).

Adams' novels as Matt Kincaid are *Hard Case* (1953) and *Once an Outlaw* (1970).

Adams' novels as Clay Randall are *Six Gun Boss* (1952), *When Oil Ran Red* (1953), *Boomer* (1957), *The Oceola Kid* (1963), *Hardcase for Hire* (1963), *Amos Flagg— Lawman* (1964).

Films based on Adams' Western fiction are *The Desperado Silver Mine* (Allied Artists, 1954) directed by Thomas Carr [based on *The Desperado*], *Outlaw's Son* (United Artists, 1957) directed by Lesley Selander [based on *Gambling Man*], and *Cole Younger, Gunfighter* (Allied Artists, 1958) directed by R. G. Springsteen [source unknown].

Ahlswede, Ann (1928 —) Author of three distinguished paperback original Western novels, and artist, born at Pasadena, California. Ahlswede was educated in California and at an early age discovered her father's library which included the classics, detective stories, and Westerns. She chose to read the classics and Westerns and saw similarities between the best of each.

Ahlswede's first published Western novel was *Day of the Hunter* (New York: Ballantine, 1960) and she followed it with

Hunting Wolf (New York: Ballantine, 1960) and *The Savage Land* (New York: Ballantine, 1962). Her short story, "The Promise of the Fruit" (1963), was included in the anthology *The Pick of the Roundup* (New York: Avon, 1963). After the publication of this story, Ahlswede became a professional artist, working in both representational and abstract art.

In *Day of the Hunter,* Ahlswede explored the idea of racial prejudice by focusing on a mixed-blood's search for the murderers of the couple who raised him and their daughter to whom he was engaged and who, in turn, is hunted, being the "logical" suspect for the murders because he is a "half-breed." *Hunting Wolf* is another revenge story, this time about a protagonist, accompanied by a young woman and a boy, searching for his pregnant Navaho wife whom he refuses to believe is dead and who has been kidnapped by four saddle tramps.

Dr. Cicero Smith, a mountebank of questionable reputation, is a recurring character in Ahlswede's novels who serves as a sounding board for her protagonists when they reach an inevitable confrontation with themselves about their reasons for living. Ahlswede's most powerful novel, *The Savage Land*, is a study in defeat which examines the tenets of social Darwinism. This pursuit story focuses on Tully Davis who becomes a convenient victim used by predatory and exploitive townspeople of a small California desert town when they need a suspect for the murder of a drunk perpetrated during the commission of a bank robbery in which Tully is involved at first but from which he tries to withdraw once he realizes he is to be framed for the whole thing. The novel is memorable for its desert scenes, particularly a sand storm reminiscent of Dorothy Scarborough's (q.v.) *The Wind*

"Blue Day" by Ann Ahlswede

(New York: Harper's, 1925). Few authors have depicted greed as a cold deliberate emotion as well as Ahlswede did and in the pessimistic *The Savage Land* she used the book's Western setting to make a major statement on the lack of justice and the ineptitude in the American legal system. Few women have been able to write formulary Westerns well; yet both Lee Hoffman (q.v.) and Ann Ahlswede can be considered notable exceptions to this. But it must needs also be stressed that, in doing so, Ahlswede, unlike Hoffman, had to exceed the rigid limitations of the formulary Western, especially in *The Savage Land*, and that her protagonists are in no sense conventional.

Allen, Henry Wilson (1912 —)
Author of both historical and formulary

Western fiction under the pseudonyms Will Henry and Clay Fisher, born at Kansas City, Missouri. Allen attended Kansas City Junior College after which he left Missouri to travel throughout the West, working at odd jobs. Once in Southern California, Allen found employment as a loader for a moving van company and worked in horse barns in the San Fernando Valley, pitchforking manure and hot-walking polo ponies. For a time he was a columnist for the *Sunset Reporter,* a newspaper published in Santa Monica. In 1935 he went to work for an animation film company, Harman-Ising in Hollywood, as a story man. After two years of this, Allen went to work for Metro-Goldwyn-Mayer as a junior writer in the short subjects department and worked there under contract for $250 a week for nine years. He married in 1937 and continued to take numerous trips throughout the West.

When the M-G-M job ended, Allen tried his hand at writing Western fiction, although previously he had read very little of the fiction published in the field. *No Survivors* (New York: Random House, 1950) was his first novel, published under the name Will Henry. It is an historical novel featuring historical personalities as minor characters and a central character, John Buell Clayton, and several others, who are fictional. While other Western authors as Oliver La Farge (q.v.), Harvey Fergusson (q.v.), and even Edgar Rice Burroughs (q.v.) had occasionally given intelligent portrayals of Native Americans, Henry Allen from the start set out to characterize Native Americans as an integral part of his fiction. "I treasure the Amerind," he once remarked, "for his unassailable ideals, his passion for personal freedom, his fierce pride, sturdy honor, vast dignity, his inalienable right to remain aloof and hold beliefs which are his without intruding upon the beliefs of his fellow, so that in the end he finds all of his marvelment, all of his physical being and all that is his of senses and soul and the final grand astonishment of breathing life given over in gratitude to *some* Maker for this priceless gift of his presence here, and for the fruitful Mother Earth upon which to live out that wondrous gift."

The pseudonym Clay Fisher came into existence when Random House's Western fiction editor, Harry E. Maule, rejected Allen's second Western novel, *Red Blizzard* (New York: Simon & Schuster, 1951). The story, reminiscent of Frederic Remington's (q.v.) *John Ermine of the Yellowstone* (New York: Macmillan, 1902), is quite grim, concerned with a mixed-blood who is totally ostracized by both Indian and white culture, although the latter exploits his abilities as a scout and his understanding of Indian ways. In view of Maule's attitude toward the book, Allen's reaction, natural perhaps under the circumstances, was that he must be able to write two totally different kinds of Western novels without being absolutely certain as to just how or why one was distinct from the other. Every time Maule would reject a novel Allen would submit, it became a Clay Fisher. The dichotomy, if it reflected anything, was at first more or less Harry E. Maule's taste, although in time Allen himself came to regard the split this way: "I think it safe to say that the principal separator is a matter of attitude on the author's part. Clay Fishers may indeed be based in as heavy a bit of history as any Will Henry but generally the Fisher book will take a lighter viewpoint, tell the tale with less restraint, go at it in, if you will, a fundamentally simpler way." Actually, there is often no essential difference between the two.

In general, many of Henry Allen's novels deal with the failure of the frontier experience, the greed, the rape of the land, the genocide, novels which end tragically because, in the case of the history of the American West, tragedy often was the historical outcome. Betty Rosenberg in her Introduction to the Gregg Press re-issue edition (1978) of *From Where the Sun Now Stands* (New York: Random House, 1959) wrote: "The information . . . for realistic and honest novelization of the Indian wars was available. Lacking was a novel-reading audience willing to accept tragedy in place of romance. Such an acceptance would force the reader to recognize that Indian cultures and ways of life are sophisticated realities and their destruction wanton evil; that the invaders' Manifest Destiny was a blatant hypocrisy, an excuse to cover the theft of land and commercial exploitation; that missionary activities were a tool of subjugation; that the imposition of an Anglo culture upon the Indians was an unwelcome curse."

From among the Clay Fisher group, *The Brass Command* (Boston: Houghton Mifflin, 1955), which deals with the 1878 trek of the Cheyenne Indians as does Mari Sandoz' (q.v.) *Cheyenne Autumn* (New York: Hastings House, 1953), and *Yellowstone Kelly* (Boston: Houghton Mifflin, 1957), "a fictional romance" about scout Major Luther Sage Kelly, treat their subjects seriously and maturely. Of the many formulary Fisher novels, the two featuring a Franciscan priest, *Apache Ransom* (New York: Bantam, 1974) and *Black Apache* (New York: Bantam, 1976) are superior to most of the more mundane formulary Westerns of other writers such as Lewis B. Patten (q.v.), Giles A. Lutz (q.v.) and Ray Hogan (q.v.).

On the whole, however, under either name Allen's heroines tend to possess almost unbelievable beauty and amount to little more than male fantasies. He was capable of creating a fictional character who is truly terrifying, as Fragg in *Summer of the Gun* (Philadelphia: Lippincott, 1979), and yet, when he wrote about an historical personality, as in *Reckoning at Yankee Flat* (New York: Random House, 1958), where he could have used such a talent for characterization in depicting Henry Plummer, Allen proved to be too intimidated by his historical subject and satisfied himself, if not his reader, by confining himself to quotations of eye-witnesses to describe Plummer. It is this circumstance of being intimidated by historical sources which, at times, lessens the effectiveness of his fiction, but in Allen's best novels, and above all in the Will Henry novels, *From Where the Sun Now Stands*, *The Last Warpath* (New York: Random House, 1966), and *One More River to Cross* (New York: Random House, 1967), the view of history is internally consistent and the total effect is commensurately impressive.

Henry Wilson Allen's Western novels as Will Henry are *No Survivors* (1950), *To Follow a Flag* (1952) [alternate title: *Pillars of the Sky*], *Death of a Legend* (1954) [alternate title: *The Raiders*], *The Fourth Horseman* (1954), *Who Rides with Wyatt* (1954), *The North Star* (1956), *Reckoning at Yankee Flat* (1958), *The Seven Men at Mimbres Springs* (1958), *From Where the Sun Now Stands* (1959), *Journey to Shiloh* (1960), *San Juan Hill* (1962), *The Feleen Brand* (1962), *The Gates of the Mountains* (1963), *MacKenna's Gold* (1963), *The Last Warpath* (1966) [short stories], *One More River to Cross* (1967), *Alias Butch Cassidy* (1967), *Maheo's Children* (1968) [alternate title: *The Squaw Killers*], *The Day Fort Larking Fell* (1969), *Chiricahua* (1972), *The Bear*

Paw Horses (1973), *I, Tom Horn* (1975), *Summer of the Gun* (1979).

Allen's juvenile novels as Will Henry are *Wolfeye, the Bad One* (1951), *Orphans of the North* (1958), *The Texas Rangers* (1958), *In the Land of the Mandans* (1965), *Custer's Last Stand* (1966), *Sons of the Western Frontier* (1966) [short stories].

Allen's novels as Clay Fisher are *Red Blizzard* (1951), *Santa Fe Passage* (1952), *War Bonnet* (1953), *Yellow Hair* (1953), *The Tall Men* (1954), *The Brass Command* (1955), *The Big Pasture* (1955), *The Blue Mustang* (1956), *Yellowstone Kelly* (1957), *The Crossing* (1958), *Niño, the Legend of the Apache Kid* (1961) [alternate title: *The Apache Kid*], *The Return of the Tall Man* (1961), *The Pitchfork Patrol* (1962), *The Oldest Maiden Lady in New Mexico* (1962) [short stories] [alternate title: *Nine Lives West*], *Outcasts of Canyon Creek* (1972), *Apache Ransom* (1974), *Black Apache* (1976).

Allen's juvenile novel as Clay Fisher is *Valley of the Bear* (1964).

Films based on Henry Wilson Allen's Western fiction are *Santa Fe Passage* (Republic, 1955) directed by William Witney, *The Tall Men* (20th-Fox, 1955) directed by Raoul Walsh, *Pillars of the Sky* (Universal, 1956) directed by George Marshall [based on *To Follow A Flag*], *Yellowstone Kelly* (Warner's, 1959) directed by Gordon Douglas, *Journey to Shiloh* (Universal, 1968) directed by William Hale, *MacKenna's Gold* (Columbia, 1969) directed by J. Lee Thompson, *Young Billy Young* (United Artists, 1969) directed by Burt Kennedy [based on *Who Rides With Wyatt*].

Allen also wrote the teleplays for the following episodes for television series: "The Hunting of Tom Horn" for *Tales of Wells Fargo* (NBC, 1959), "A Mighty Big Bandit" for *Tales of Wells Fargo* (NBC, 1959), "Sundown Smith" for *Dick Powell's Zane Grey Theatre* (CBS, 1959).

Arnold, Elliott (1912 —) Author of historical Western fiction born at New York City. Arnold pursued a career in journalism before he joined the U.S. Air Force in 1942, where he served in the European theatre of the war. After his discharge, Arnold moved to Arizona and, while there, wrote *Blood Brother* (New York: Duell, Sloan, 1947). It is concerned with the friendship between Apache chief Cochise and Indian agent Tom Jeffords, and Jeffords' love for and marriage to Apache maiden Sonseeahray. To be sure, Cochise is romanticized, as is Sonseeahray, but the novel features one of the few sympathetic portraits of the Apaches to emerge since the days of Edgar Rice Burroughs (q.v.) and Will Levington Comfort (q.v.) in definite contrast to the stereotyped blood-thirsty savages so typical of formulary Western fiction. Once *Blood Brother* was adapted for the screen under the title *Broken Arrow* (20th-Fox, 1950), Arnold prepared a specially abridged edition under the same title for juvenile readers. Subsequently Arnold wrote two more novels with Western settings, neither of them quite as successful, *The Time of the Gringo* (New York: Knopf, 1953), a story of the conquest of New Mexico by Anglo-Americans reminiscent of Harvey Fergusson's (q.v.) novels, and *The Camp Grant Massacre* (New York: Simon & Schuster, 1976).

D.M.-K.

Broken Arrow (20th-Fox, 1950) was directed by Delmer Daves.

Arthur, Budd. See Shappiro, Herbert Arthur

Arthur, Burt. See Shappiro, Herbert Arthur

Arthur, Burt & Budd. See Shappiro, Herbert Arthur.

Arthur, Herbert. See Shappiro, Herbert Arthur.

Atherton, Gertrude (1857–1948)

Author of fiction set in the Spanish period in California, born Gertrude Horn at San Francisco, California. Atherton was educated in private schools in California and from an early age dreamed about being an author. An elopement with her mother's boyfriend, George Henry Bowen Atherton, delayed her literary career, although against her husband's wishes she wrote secretly. When he died in 1887, she was free to write, giving her children over to the care of her mother-in-law.

Atherton made the mistake of writing too many books, many of them carelessly, both fiction and nonfiction. She remains best known perhaps for her book *The Conqueror* (New York: Macmillan, 1902), a fictionalized biography of Alexander Hamilton which was one of the first biographical novels ever written and which sold well over one million copies after publication. She wrote until her death in San Francisco from a stroke after having become an advocate of an artificial rejuvenation clinic. She received three medals from the French government for her war work including the Legion of Honor, two honorary degrees, and the city of San Francisco presented her the Gold Medal on her ninetieth birthday.

Although Atherton used numerous locales, to which she had traveled, as the settings for her stories, she almost as often made use of her native state. Her romances set in the Spanish period of California are: *Los Cerritos* (1890), *The Doomswoman* (1892), and *Rezánov* (New York: New York Authors and Newspapers Assn., 1906). Her short story collection, containing tales of old California, *Before the Gringo Came* (1894), which was later re-issued in a revised and enlarged edition under the title *The Splendid Idle Forties* (New York: Macmillan, 1902), is probably her best California book. Jack Schaefer (q.v) once stated that "... there are some flashes of gold in the pages," and compared Atherton's short story, "The Vengeance of Padre Arroyo," to O. Henry's (q.v.) best work.

Atherton wrote an autobiography *Adventures of a Novelist* (New York: Liveright, 1932).

Austin, Frank. See Faust, Frederick.

Austin, Mary Hunter (1868–1934)

Naturalist, essayist, author of Western fiction, and non-fiction, born at Carlinville, Illinois. Austin was educated in local schools and received a Bachelor's degree in 1888 from Blackburn College in her home town. Because already at the age of 7 Austin had decided that she would someday write, she surprised many when she studied science and mathematics in college. Her response was that she could best study literature on her own. Shortly after graduating, she moved to California with her family when her father homesteaded near Bakersfield. Austin made friends with several workers on the vast Tejon Ranch near the family homestead and from them she gathered much of the background about California and its inhabitants that she would later use in her writings. After failing the qualifying teacher's examination twice, Austin tutored children in the vicinity until her marriage to Wallace Stafford Austin in 1891. The marriage ultimately ended in divorce due to Wallace Austin's financial failures and the birth of a mentally retarded daughter.

After the success of her first non-fiction book, *The Land of Little Rain* (Boston: Houghton Mifflin, 1903), Austin moved to Carmel, California, then fast becoming an artists' colony where she met Jack London among others. Five of Austin's nine novels are set in the West. Her first, *Isidro* (Boston: Houghton Mifflin, 1905), a romance set in the mission days of California, depicts the role of the Roman Catholic Church in a far different light than does Helen Hunt Jackson's (q.v.) *Ramona* (1884). Austin's sympathies clearly were with the Indians and she showed the often violent repercussions which resulted from the restrictions placed upon them by the missionaries. *Santa Lucia, A Common Story* (New York: Harper's 1908), *Outland* (London: John Murray,

1910) written under the pseudonym Gordon Stairs, and *The Ford* (Boston: Houghton Mifflin, 1917) are also set in California. In the two latter novels Austin voiced her dissent concerning the invasions of communities as Carmel by commercial interest groups. In 1925 Austin moved to Santa Fe, New Mexico, and there she remained in her adobe home, Casa Querida (the Beloved House) where, incidentally, Willa Cather (q.v.) would finish her Southwestern classic *Death Comes for the Archbishop* (New York: Knopf, 1927), until her death from a fatal heart attack. The commercial development of Carmel had driven her away and, attaching herself to New Mexico, she did not want to see the same thing happen all over again. In 1927 she was involved in the Seven State conference on the water diversion problems posed by the then proposed Boulder Dam project. In 1933 she received a Doctor of Letters degree from the University of New Mexico. At the time of her death she was working on a new novel.

Austin wrote thirty-two books and over two hundred essays in her lifetime. She was very outspoken and knew many of the prominent intellectual figures of her day, among them Henry James, Joseph Conrad, George Bernard Shaw, and H. G. Wells, this last considering her the most intelligent woman in the United States. Austin wrote numerous essays on the role of the writer and the meaning of regionalism in fiction. Austin believed there were two requirements before a novel could be considered regional: 1.) the region, as a character, must be an integral part of the story; and 2.) the story must be of the region, not about it. She observed that a sensitive author cannot avoid expressing regionalism in his writing since the author's environs are a generating source for his art.

Austin often digressed in the course of her novels to relate her personal philosophy. This was her major flaw as a novelist; whereas her short stories are more tightly constructed. Her short fictions were collected into five volumes and remain her finest achievement as a fiction writer. She was also fascinated by Indian culture and folklore and wrote two stage plays based on the remote past of the Southwestern Indians, *The Arrow Maker* (1911) and *Fire* (1914). Both were written in a poetic rhythmic style reminiscent of Indian verse and *The Arrow Maker* is, in fact, one of the few dramas of Indian life with Indian characters to have had professional performance on the American stage.

She was a feminist and promoted women's suffrage and birth control, having become convinced at an early age that conventional marriage for many women could only result in the destruction of one of the partners. Also, as Vardis Fisher (q.v.) would later, Austin chastised the narrow view of New York critics whose tendency to ignore non-New York writers infuriated her. She believed that Western American literature had many riches to offer and that this had to be recognized before the United States could be said to have a truly *national* literature.

Although critical opinion varies immensely on Austin's ability as a writer—some claiming she possessed genius but no talent; others contending that she had talent but lacked genius—she certainly deserves more recognition that she has so far been accorded. Her contributions to Indian lore, folk literature, myths, and the oral traditions of the West have a lasting quality as does the vision embodied in her best work of the possibility of man living in harmony with Nature and not obsessed merely with the conquest and exploitation of it.

Mary Austin's Western novels are *Isidro* (1905), *Santa Lucia, A Common Story* (1908), *Lost Borders* (1909) [short stories], *The Basket Woman* (1910) [short stories], *Outland* (1910), *The Ford* (1917), *The Trail Book* (1918) [short stories], *Starry Adventure* (1931), *One Smoke Stories* (1934) [short stories], *Mother of Felipe and Other Stories* (1950) [short stories].

For further information see Mary Austin's autobiography *Earth Horizon* (Boston: Houghton Mifflin, 1932), Thomas Matthews Pearce's *Mary Hunter Austin* (New York: Twayne Publishers, 1965), and Jo W. Lyday's *Mary Austin: The Southwest Works* (Austin: Steck-Vaughn, 1968).

Averill, H.C. See Snow, Charles H.

B.,M. See Faust, Frederick.

Ballard, Todhunter (1903–1980)

Prolific author of formulary Western fiction under several pseudonyms, among them Parker Bonner, Sam Bowie, Brian Fox, John Hunter, Clint Reno, and Jack Slade (see House Names), born at Cleveland, Ohio. Ballard obtained a Bachelor's degree from Wilmington College in 1926, studying engineering, and his first two years, following graduation, were spent as an engineer with F. W. Ballard and Company in Cleveland. In the years that followed, he was employed by a variety of magazines, newspapers, and, occasionally, film studios, and in 1942–1945 he worked for Wright Patterson Field in Ohio as a member of the production control staff in the maintenance division. In 1936 Ballard was married to Phoebe Dwiggins who, Ballard claimed, collaborated with him on all his books.

Ballard's first novel, *Say Yes to Murder* (New York: Putnam's, 1942), was one of ten murder mysteries he wrote under the name W. T. Ballard, a series which continued until 1967. His first Western novel, *Two Edged Vengeance* (New York: Macmillan, 1951), was written and published under his own name. Ballard became so prolific at writing Westerns that he felt obliged to adopt several pennames. It was under the pseudonym Clint Reno that Ballard began writing a Vigilante series, beginning with *Sun Mountain Slaughter* (New York: Fawcett, 1974). Writing under the house name Jack Slade, Ballard actually created the Lassiter series, beginning with *Lassiter* (New York: Belmont Tower, 1968), to which, among others, Ben Haas (q.v.) contributed an entry. Ballard also created the Ben Gold series about a Jewish storekeeper in Denver, Colorado, which began with *Go West, Ben Gold* (New York: Paperback Library, 1974), written under the pseudonym Clay Turner.

Ballard was a skilful formulary writer, albeit more often imitative than original. The Ballard Westerns of the 'Fifties and 'Sixties, such as *Blizzard Range* (New York: Popular Library, 1960), tend to imitate the theme, familiar from the fiction of Ernest Haycox (q.v.) and Luke Short (q.v.), of the weary hero and the romantic conflict between two women. His later Westerns followed the contemporary generic trend toward multi-volumes about a series hero. During his career he contributed over a thousand stories to various magazines along with motion picture treatments and television scripts. His novel *Gold for California* (New York: Doubleday, 1965) won a Spur Award from the Western Writers of America.

J.N.

Todhunter Ballard's Western novels under his own name are *Two Edged Vengeance* (1951), *Incident at Sun Mountain* (1952), *West of Quarantine* (1953), *High Iron* (1954), *Guns for the Lawless* (1956) [with James Charles Lynch], *Showdown* (1957), *Trailtown Marshal* (1957), *Roundup* (1957), *Saddle Tramp* (1958), *Trouble on the Massacre* (1959), *Trigger Trail* (1960), *Blizzard Range* (1960), *Gunman from Texas* (1960), *Rawhide Gunman* (1960), *The Long Trail Back* (1960), *The Night Riders* (1961), *Gopher Gold* (1962), *Westward the Monitors Roar* (1963), *Gold in California* (1965), *The Californian* (1971), *Nowhere Left to Run* (1972), *Loco and the Wolf* (1973), *Home to Texas* (1974), *Trails of Rage* (1975), *The Sheriff of Tombstone* (1977).

Ballard's novels as Parker Bonner are *Superstition Range* (1952), *Outlaw Brand* (1954), *Tough in the Saddle* (1964), *Modoc Indian Wars* (1965), *Town Tamer* (1968), *Borders to Cross* (1968), *Applegate's Gold* (1969), *Look to Your Guns* (1969).

Ballard's novels as Sam Bowie are *Thunderhead Range* (1959), *Canyon War* (1968), *Gunlock* (1976).

Ballard's novels as Brian Fox are *A Dollar To Die For* (1968), *The Outlaw Trail* (1972), *Apache Gold* (1976).

Ballard's novels as John Hunter are *West of Justice* (1954), *Ride the Wind South* (1957), *Badlands Buccaneer* (1959), *Marshal from Deadwood* (1960), *Desperation Valley* (1964), *Duke* (1965), *The Man from Yuma* (1967), *Plunder Canyon* (1968), *Death in the Mountain* (1969), *Lost Valley* (1971), *Gambler's Gun* (1973), *The Burning Land* (1973), *The Highgraders* (1974), *This Range Is Mine* (1975), *A Canyon They Called Death* (1976).

Ballard's novels as Clint Reno are *Sierra Massacre* (1974) and *Sun Mountain Slaughter* (1974).

Ballard's novels as Clay Turner are *Give a Man a Gun* (1971), *Go West, Ben Gold* (1974), *Gold Goes to the Mountain* (1975).

Ballard's contributions to the Lassiter series and other Western novels under the Belmont Tower house name Jack Slade are *Lassiter* (1968), *Bandido* (1968), *The Man from Yuma* (1968), *The Man from Cheyenne* (1968), *Sabata* (1970).

Although he contributed significantly to motion pictures and television, only *The Outcast* (Republic, 1954) directed by William Witney [based on *Two Edged Vengeance*] gave him a screen credit.

Ballew, Charles. See Snow, Charles H.

Barker, S(quire) Omar (1894 —) Western poet, humorist, fiction, and nonfiction author, born in a log cabin at Beulah, New Mexico. Barker was educated in public schools in Las Vegas, New Mexico. In 1917–1919 Barker was in the U.S. Army and served with the American Expeditionary Force in France where he attained the rank of Sergeant. He received a Bachelor's degree in 1924 and an Honorary Doctor of

Letters degree in 1961 from New Mexico Highlands University. Before embarking on a literary career, Barker worked as a U.S. Forest Ranger, high school teacher, and high school principal.

Having been raised on a small mountain ranch, Barker decided to write about what he knew best: cowboys, cattle, and ranch life. He began contributing stories and verse to Western pulp magazines in the early 'Twenties and subsequently contributed to practically every Western magazine ever published. Between the years 1929–1956, Barker and his wife, Elsa, also a writer, operated a small ranch in the New Mexican Rockies. Their brand was the "Lazy SOB."

Barker's only novel, *Little World Apart* (New York: Doubleday, 1966), a story about a pioneer family in New Mexico, is partly autobiographical. His short stories tend to embody authentic portraits of ranch people and cowboys in which humor is emphasized. "I consider the story of the oldtime cowboy as a folk hero, a proud traditional *legend*, not a myth," Barker once stated, and he also considered the cowboy ". . .a horseback man of courage, hardiness, personal pride, loyalty, and inimitable wit and humor, whatever his faults and vices." *Born to Battle* (New Mexico: University of New Mexico Press, 1951), a collection of short stories, incorporates these ideas, as do two of Barker's short stories, "Trail Fever" and "Outlaw Trail," contained respectively in *Branded West* (Boston: Houghton Mifflin, 1956) and *The Saturday Evening Post Reader of Western Stories* (New York: Doubleday, 1960).

In addition, Barker wrote five books of Western poetry, nine adventure stories for boys in the *Bret King of Rimrock Ranch*

series under the house name Dan Scott, and edited two Western Writers of America anthologies. Barker's stories appeared in over sixty anthologies; he won numerous awards during his career, including three Spur Awards; and he was the only author honored while alive by the National Cowboy Hall of Fame in their Famous Western Writers category.

Barr, Amelia Edith (1831–1919) Author of fiction in the American Southwest, born Amelia Huddleston at Ulverston, Lancashire, England. The daughter of a Methodist minister, she was educated in private schools in Northern England and she taught in a private school herself until her marriage in 1850 to Robert Barr. After her husband's woolen business went bankrupt, the couple immigrated to the United States, settling in Chicago, Illinois, where Amelia opened a school for girls. Her outspoken husband soon made an enemy of a powerful local politician and they fled the city, eventually arriving in Austin, Texas. After her husband and two sons died of the yellow fever in Galveston, Texas, Barr at 38 years of age moved to New York City where she took up writing in order to support her surviving daughters. She contributed more than 1,000 articles and poems to various religious publications over the next decade and published her first book in 1875. In her later years Barr lived on Long Island until her death from cerebral apoplexy.

Barr's novels with their sentimental plots, strong religious coloring, and vivid characterizations were once widely read. Particularly noteworthy is her *Remember the Alamo* (1888), a regional novel based in part on the battle of the Alamo, focusing on the loyalty conflict of Anglo-Americans and Mexicans. In it Barr boldly stated her opposition to the role played by Roman Catholic clergymen and, in fact, a priest is a villain in the novel just as is the case in Mayne Reid's (q.v.) *The White Chief: A Legend of Northern Mexico* (1855) and Augusta Jane Evans' *Inez* (1855), the latter also set in San Antonio during the revolution. Barr's autobiography, *All the Days of My Life* (New York: Appleton, 1913), remains worthwhile reading and is probably more likely to be enjoyable to a modern reader than most of her fiction.

Barry, Jane (1925 —) Author of historical Western fiction, born at New Baltimore, New York. Barry, who was educated in New York, began her writing career working as a reporter for the *Coxsackie Union News* in Coxsackie, New York, from 1946–1948. She served as editor for the Coxsackie centennial edition in 1950–1951 which won an award and for the *Green County Examiner* in Catskill, New York, from 1952–1953. She published her first, main-stream novel in 1955.

A Time in the Sun (New York: Doubleday, 1962) was her third book and is one of the few fictional works where a white woman by choice marries an Indian—in this case an Apache with Mexican blood. Barry, who included much information on Indian culture in the story, treated the Apaches very sympathetically, a trend which began in the 'Forties in books such as *Blood Brother* (New York: Duell, Sloan, 1947) by Elliott

Arnold (q.v.). As in most novels written about intermarriage between Indians and whites, however, the marriage is cut short by the death of one of the partners (the husband in Barry's book).

Included among Barry's subsequent novels are two more books set in the West: *A Shadow of Eagles* (New York: Doubleday, 1964), a romantic story in which she explored the struggles of the dying Spanish aristocracy in Texas, and *Maximilian's Gold* (New York: Doubleday, 1966), a story which deals with the lust for gold and which is dedicated to J. Frank Dobie (q.v.) who introduced Barry to the legend that served as the basis for the story—a cache of gold buried in Texas following the execution of Maximilian. This latter book has been compared to B. Traven's (q.v.) *The Treasure of the Sierra Madre* (New York: Knopf, 1935) and includes some of Barry's best character creations, such as the aging adventurer Jake Starke who sees the advance of civilization in the West as an end to an exciting and independent way of life.

Baxter, George Owen. See Faust, Frederick.

Beach, Rex (1877–1949) Best remembered for his stories set in Alaska, Beach was born at Atwood, Michigan. The Beach family, seeking a warmer climate, traveled by boat with several other families to Florida where they became "squatters" under the Homestead Act on a deserted military base near Tampa. Beach entered the prep department of Rollins College at Water Park, Florida, in 1891 where he continued until 1896. Having set his goal at becoming a supreme court justice, Beach went to Chicago where he attended the College of Law while doing odd jobs for his brothers' law firm. In 1898 he joined the thousands of gold-seekers headed for Alaska, making it only as far as Rampart City. For three years Beach worked various mines in Alaska until, at 24, he returned permanently to the United States, taking up a job as a firebrick salesman in Chicago. When he heard from a chance acquaintance that there was money in stories about Alaska, he decided to write of his own Northern experiences. Beach placed his first story with *McClure's*, receiving $50, and thenceforth continued to turn out stories from his "fiction factory," as he called it, while pursuing his job as a salesman. His first novel was *The Spoilers* (New York: Harper's, 1905) and it deals with the greedy land speculators in Alaska, which subsequently became a constant theme in Beach's fiction and was the subject of articles he wrote such as "The Looting of Alaska" (1905). At the time *The Spoilers* appeared in a book edition, Beach's serial *Pardners* was running in *McClure's,* which has led to some dispute as to which was written earlier. The "love interest" in *The Spoilers* is supplied by Cherry Malotte, a character based on the famous courtesan of Virginia City, Nevada, Julia Bulette. Malotte makes her second appearance in Beach's *The Silver Horde* (New York: Harper's, 1909), another Alaskan tale set in and around the salmon fisheries of Bristol Bay.

Beach soon came to dislike the label of "Alaskan author" which was being attached to him, so he began writing stories set in other parts of the world. *The Ne'er-Do-Well* (New York: Harper's, 1911) was based on experiences Beach had while traveling around the Isthmus of Panama; *Heart of the Sunset* (New York: Harper's, 1915) is set in Mexico during the Pancho Villa era; and *Flowing Gold* (New York: Harper's, 1922) is a novel about the discovery of oil in Texas. This effort at variety notwithstanding, Beach periodically returned to his Alaskan settings in such novels as *The Iron Trail* (New York: Harper's, 1913) which is about the building of the first railroad in Alaska, *The Winds of Chance* (New York: Harper's 1918), and in several of the short stories in the collection *The Goose Woman and Other Stories* (New York: Harper's, 1925).

In 1917, while continuing his literary production, Beach started his own film company, basing his first film on his novel *The Auction Block: A Novel of New York Life* (New York: Harper's, 1914). He was the first author to include a clause in all his contracts about film rights and this ingenuity at business was also reflected by the success he had as a film producer in his own right. During his lifetime, fourteen of his novels and sixteen of his original scripts were brought to the screen by himself or by others.

Although he continued to write, Beach's later years were principally devoted to agricultural experiments in Sebring, Florida. In the mid 'Thirties he lobbied to get back the mining rights to Glacier Bay National Monument in Alaska which he was convinced would provide jobs and income for Alaskans. Suffering from inoperable cancer of the throat for the last two years of his life and also going blind, Beach shot himself.

Dubbed the "Victor Hugo of the North," Beach showed Alaska in his fiction to be an extremely cruel and hard country. The wealth of information included in his novels and stories was based on his own encounters with the elements and a wide assortment of interesting characters. His use of dialogue and tall tales make his fiction seem authentic, while in reality they are highly romanticized "he-man" narratives of the Northwest school which also includes such authors as Jack London (q.v.) and James Oliver Curwood (q.v.). Beach wrote of his own work and a writer's responsibilities in his autobiography *Personal Exposures* (New York: Harper's, 1940) that "however fertile may be his inventive genius, it seems to me that he owes it to his readers to respect the realities of his environment and if he proposes to make use of facts he should see that they are accurate. All of which is perhaps another way of saying that I'm a sort of longhand cameraman."

Films based on Rex Beach's Northland fiction are *The Spoilers* (Selig, 1914) directed by Colin Campbell, remade under this title (Goldwyn, 1923) directed by Lambert Hillyer, (Paramount, 1930) directed by Edwin Carewe, (Universal, 1942) directed by Ray Enright, (Universal, 1955) directed by Jesse Hibbs, *Pardners* (Mutual, 1917) [director unknown], *North Wind's Malice* (Goldwyn, 1920) directed by Paul Bern and Carl Harbaugh [source unknown], *The Silver Horde* (Goldwyn, 1920) directed by Frank Lloyd, remade under this title (RKO, 1930) directed by William LeBaron, *The Iron Trail* (United Artists, 1921) directed by William Neill, *A Sainted Devil* (Paramount, 1924) directed by Joseph Henabery [based on the short story "Rope's End"], *Flowing Gold* (First National, 1924) directed by Joseph De Grasse, remade under this title (Warner's, 1940) directed by Alfred Green, *Winds of Chance* (First National, 1925) directed by Frank Lloyd, *The Barrier* (M-G-M, 1926) directed by George Hill, remade

under this title (Paramount, 1937) directed by Lesley Selander.

For further information on Rex Beach see his autobiography, *Personal Exposures* (New York: Harper's, 1940).

Bechdolt, Frederick Ritchie (1874–1950) Author of both formulary and historical Western fiction, born at Mercersburg, Pennsylvania. Bechdolt was early interested in the American frontier and in military history. He went West when he became a student at the University of North Dakota in 1892–1895 and was graduated from the University of Washington in 1896.

Bechdolt began his career as a newspaperman in 1899 and with *The Hard Rock Man* (New York: Moffat, Yard, 1910) made his appearance as an author of fiction with a Western setting. Bechdolt's next two books were non-fiction, gleanings from his extensive travels and the interviews he conducted in the Western United States, *When the West Was Young* (New York: Century, 1922) which is centered around historical incidents and personalities, and *Tales of the Old-Timers* (New York: Century, 1924). *Giants of the Old West* (New York: Century, 1930), also non-fiction, furthered this tendency, but with *Riders of the San Pedro* (New York: Doubleday, 1931) Bechdolt returned to fictional treatments. By the time he came to write *Bold Raiders of the West* (New York: Doubleday, 1940) he was able to interweave historical events from the Civil War with a somewhat formulary Western plot.

Frederick Bechdolt's Western novels are *The Hard Rock Man* (1910), *Riders of the San Pedro* (1931), *Horse Thief Trail* (1932), *The Tree of Death* (1937), *Danger on the Border* (1940), *Bold Riders of the West* (1940), *Hot Gold* (1941), *Riot at Red Water* (1941), *The Hills of Fear* (1942), *Drygulch Canyon* (1946).

Thieves' Gold (Universal, 1918) was directed by John Ford [based on the short story "Back to the Right Trail"].

Bellah, James Warner (1899–
1976) Author of Western fiction, born at New York City. Educated first at Wesleyan, Bellah was graduated from Columbia University in 1923 with a Bachelor's degree. He was a Second Lieutenant during World War I in the 117th Squadron of the Royal Air Force and, after the Armistice, served with the rank of Captain in General Haller's Expedition for the Relief of Poland. Bellah worked in advertising in New York City 1923–1925 and simultaneously taught English at Columbia. He served as a special correspondent in China in 1927–1928 and in Europe in 1928 for *Aero Digest* and in 1929 went to the West Indies and Central America for *The Saturday Evening Post*.

During World War II, Bellah served in the 1st and 80th Infantry Divisions and on the staff of Admiral Lord Louis Mountbatten at the headquarters of the Southeast Asia Command as an American officer. He saw combat service under General Stilwell, General Wingate, and Colonel Philip Cochran in Burma and emerged from the war with the rank of Colonel, honored with the Legion of Merit, the Bronze Star, the Air Medal, and the Commendation Medal.

Bellah's first novel was *Sketch Book of a Cadet from Gascony* (New York: Knopf, 1923) and indicated his preoccupation with military subjects which would inform much of his subsequent fiction. It was not until after World War II that Bellah began writing memorable series about Fort Starke during the Indian wars. The stories were published in *The Saturday Evening Post*, which had a long-standing policy against showing the Indian point of view. This scarcely hindered Bellah, however, since he was primarily concerned with glorifying the role of the American military. In his story "Spanish Man's Grave" reprinted in *Reveille* (New York: Fawcett, 1962) Bellah described what for him was the essential dramatic *tour de force* of his fiction: "Your first man dead in violence is a sick thing in your mind, for many suns and many moons, until the others fade its picture into shadow. But you never forget the first white woman you see that the Apaches have worked over." Bellah's novel *A Thunder of Drums* (New York: Bantam, 1961), which was subsequently brought to the screen, opens with an identical incident. Yet, despite his ideological distortions of Native Americans and the Indian wars, his stories are in many cases sufficiently well written to deserve being treated as literature.

Most of Bellah's stories and magazine serials were never collected into hardbound book form, although several, such as the *Reveille* collection, were published as paperback originals. John Ford particularly admired Bellah's stories and of his cinematic Cavalry trilogy, *Fort Apache* (RKO, 1948) was based on Bellah's story "Massacre," *She Wore a Yellow Ribbon* (RKO, 1949) was based on the stories "Big Hunt" and "Command," and *Rio Grande* (Republic, 1950) was based on "Mission With No Record." All four of these stories are to be found in *Reveille*. Ford's *Sergeant Rutledge* (Warner's, 1960) was based on an original story by the same title written by Bellah and Bellah received credit for his work on the screenplay. Bellah also was credited for co-script on Ford's *The Man Who Shot Liberty Valance* (Paramount, 1962), based on a short story by Dorothy M. Johnson (q.v.). In 1961 Bellah was given the *Time* award for the Best Western of the Year, that being *A Thunder of Drums*.

Bellah's short story "Command" was requested by the State Department for translation into Thai for the "This is America" program. Bellah also wrote the dialogue for the official U.S. Navy documentary, *This is Korea!* (Republic, 1951), also directed by John Ford. It was the urgency of Bellah's racist ideology that was his greatest flaw, overwhelming all that he created and, because it limited his humanity, it diminishes his achievement.

James Warner Bellah's Western novels are *Massacre* (1950) [short stories], *The Apache* (1951), *Sergeant Rutledge* (1959), *Ordeal at Blood River* (1959), *A Thunder of Drums* (1961), *Reveille* (1962) [short stories].

Bellah assisted on the screenplays of motion picture adaptations of his own works for *She Wore a Yellow Ribbon* (RKO, 1949), *Rio Grande* (Republic, 1950), and *Sergeant Rutledge* (Warner's, 1960), all directed by John Ford. One of his stories was used as the basis for *Fort Apache* (RKO, 1948) directed by John Ford and his *Saturday Evening Post* serial "The White Invaders" was used as the basis for *The Command*

(Warner's, 1954) directed by David Butler. Bellah wrote the novel and adapted it for the screen for *A Thunder of Drums* (M-G-M, 1961) directed by Joseph M. Newman and he worked on the screenplay for *The Man Who Shot Liberty Valance* (Paramount, 1962) directed by John Ford.

Bellah worked on several other screenplays and several television pilots and episodes, none of them Westerns. His final Western effort was the screenplay for *The Legend of Nigger Charlie* (Paramount, 1972) directed by Martin Goldman.

Bennett, Dwight. See Newton, Dwight Bennett.

Bennett, Emerson (1822–1905)

One of the founders of American frontier fiction in the Nineteenth century, born at Monson, Massachusetts. Bennett was educated at Monson Academy. At 17 he went to New York City intent on a literary career. Bennett contributed to the *Knickerbocker Magazine* and in 1843, while in Philadelphia, Pennsylvania, he wrote a short novel titled *The Unknown Countess* and entered it in a newspaper contest. Going West to Cincinnati, Ohio, in 1844, Bennett edited *Casket*, a weekly magazine, and contributed to several others. He traveled further West, venturing into Texas, and his first novel, *The Prairie Flower* (1849), proved to be a bestseller. This novel may actually have been based on a narrative written by an actual traveler on the Oregon Trail and a few of the scenes between the four trappers who figure in the story are surprisingly accurate in terms of dialogue. Some of the tall tales told in the book are from the tradition of Davy Crockett (see Historical Personalities), although some scholars have accused Bennett of textual plagiarism from George Frederick Ruxton's (q.v.) *Life in the Far West* (1849) which appeared in the same year. According to Henry Nash Smith in *Virgin Land: The American West As Symbol and Myth* (Cambridge: Harvard University Press, 1950), Bennett had nothing to contribute in *The Prairie Flower* to an interpretation of the mountain man's character and merely reshuffled "the standard themes—the trapper's love of freedom, his indifference to hardship and danger, his hatred of the dull life of settled communities." However, *The Prairie Flower* did include the first attempt to make a fictional character of Kit Carson, albeit only briefly, an effort which gave impetus to the subsequent utilization of Carson as a hero in countless dime novels (see Pulp and Slick Western Stories).

In 1847 Bennett returned to Philadelphia to live and remained there the rest of his life. He continued to write and both *Viola: or, Adventures in the Far Southwest* (1852) and *Clara Moreland* (1853) are considered to be Southwestern fiction, based on experiences Bennett had while in Texas.

Some discussion of Bennett's work is to be found in *The Early Novel of the Southwest* (Albuquerque: University of New Mexico Press, 1961) by Edwin W. Gaston, Jr.

Benteen, John. See Haas, Benjamin.

Berger, Thomas (1924 —) An author known for his satire of Western fiction,

Little Big Man (New York: Dial Press, 1964), born at Cincinnati, Ohio. Berger attended the University of Cincinnati where he received his Bachelor's degree in 1948. He worked as a librarian at the Rand School of Social Science in New York City from 1948–1951. In 1951–1952 he was on the staff of the *New York Times* index and in 1952–1953 he was the associate editor of *Popular Science Monthly* before he turned to writing fiction.

Little Big Man recounts the tragedy of the West, but it does so with a comedic eye; it reveals a natural, easy playfulness sparked by the impossibility of two such different cultures—that of the Native Americans and that of the whites—ever truly understanding one another. To an Indian, Berger believed a white man is very funny; to a white man an Indian is a clown. Neither wars nor treaties seem to change this basic conclusion and Berger had it both ways, trying to make his audience laugh at itself. After years of heroizing General Custer (see Historical Personalities), Berger reduced him to a madman; his white protagonist, when he is among the whites, is perpetually dissipated, but sober and circumspect when among the Indians. Whatever else might be said of it, however, *Little Big Man*, because of its preposterous contentions, is not pro-Indian, as it has often been called, but rather more simply anti-white.

D.W.

Little Big Man (National General, 1970) was directed by Arthur Penn.

Berry, Don (1932 —) An author with a reputation as a regional novelist of the Pacific Northwest, born at Redwood Falls, Minnesota. Berry's parents, who were musicians, moved often when he was a youth and Berry ended up leaving home when he was 15. He attended Reed College in Portland, Oregon (1949–1951) where he met Lloyd Reynolds, a teacher of calligraphy who proved a major influence on Berry's subsequent literary career. In the early 'Fifties Berry was interested in painting and lived for a time in Portland with poet Gary Snyder. In 1955, he decided to try his hand at writing. Berry wrote one short story a week while holding down a full-time job. During this apprenticeship period, he wrote science fiction stories, and after having received 144 rejection slips, his first story was accepted. Between 1956–1958, Berry published short stories and novelettes in various science fiction magazines.

Over the next three years, Berry wrote his trilogy which is considered the definitive fictional work about early pioneering in the Northwest coastal region. *Trask* (New York: Viking, 1960), set in 1848 on the Clatsop Plains in Oregon, is about Eldridge Trask, an actual early settler of the region, a former mountain man and a restless soul who decides to travel South to the Killamook Indian region where no white man lives in hope that he may begin a small white settlement with the cooperation of Kilchis, leader of the Killamooks. The journey, however, takes on new dimensions when Trask is forced to look inside himself for an answer to his restlessness and accepts the challenge of the "searching"—the rite of manhood practiced by both the Clatsop and Killamook Indians. Author Dorothy M. Johnson (q.v.) in her review of *Trask* wrote: "A very few writers can evoke truly a time and a way of life that they have experienced only in imagination. . . . This is the kind of

imagination Don Berry has. He has produced a book which I must call great. . . ."

In the second book of the trilogy, *Moontrap* (New York: Viking, 1962) which won the Spur Award from the Western Writers of America for the best historical Western novel of 1962, Berry shows how three mountain men view the progress of civilization in Oregon City, Oregon in 1850. The sympathetic protagonist, Webb, is a loner who feels only contempt for man's need for social order and his last journey to see his old trapping friends once more before he dies turns into a solitary flight back into the mountains. Berry returned to the Tillamook (Killamook) region of the Oregon coast in *To Build a Ship* (New York: Viking, 1963) set during the years 1852–1854.

Throughout his works Berry portrayed the Indian as an honorable man with a viable alternative culture who is exploited and manipulated over the years by the whites. His characters in *Trask* and *Moontrap* who reject the predominant view of Manifest Destiny and community spirit are admirable, particularly when they begin to view the world as the Indian does.

Glen A. Love in his chap-book *Don Berry* (Boise: Idaho State University Press, 1978) wrote that Berry "conveys to us a sacramental belief that transcendent power or energy awaits man's explorations within the natural world. Further Berry's work asserts that this participation, this ultimate reconciliation with the patterns of earth and sky, water and rock, must be undertaken in defiance of the conventional social order if one would reach his full potentiality for human freedom and awareness." In *To Build a Ship*, the first person narrator Ben Thaler does not seek a oneness with Nature nor does he respect Indian culture; rather, in seeking his own personal vision, he becomes part of the opportunistic white settlers who will stop at nothing to build their ship, so that they may get their supplies in from the outside world.

Although Berry questioned the ultimate reliability of recorded history, he wrote *A Majority of Scoundrels* (New York: Harper's, 1961) during this period, an "informal" history of the fur trade in the Rocky Mountains between 1822–1834.

For further information on Berry's work see *Don Berry* (Boise: Idaho State University Press, 1978) by Glen A. Love.

Bickham, Jack M(iles) (1930 —)

Author of formulary Western fiction, born at Columbus, Ohio. Bickham was graduated from Ohio State University in 1952 and then entered the U.S. Air Force. He was stationed in Oklahoma for his two years of service and, during that time, took some graduate courses at the University of Oklahoma. After his discharge, he worked as a newspaperman. He was a reporter for the *Norman Transcript* in Norman, Oklahoma, from 1956 to 1960 while completing his Master's degree, which he received in 1960 from the University of Oklahoma. He then went to work as an editorial writer for the Oklahoma Publishing Company in Oklaho-

ma City. After a full day at work, he customarily spent part of each evening on his self-imposed daily quota of 3,000 words of fiction or writing magazine articles.

Bickham's first novel, and the first of some thirty-seven Westerns, was *Gunman's Gamble*, published as half of an Ace Double Novel paperback in 1958. Five more Westerns for Ace appeared during the next three years before Bickham introduced one of his most successful literary experiments in *The Fighting Buckaroo* (New York: Berkley, 1961), a comic Western published under the pseudonym Jeff Clinton. The title refers to one Wildcat O'Shea and he is, in the most literal sense, a colorful character: He "had painted his saddle flaming orange, and his boots green and yellow. He wore a new blue hat, wide-brimmed, a red shirt, new deep-blue Levis, a black vest, and fancy Mexican spurs with purple rowels." The storyline is a straightforward Western/mystery, as O'Shea is blackmailed into serving temporarily as a deputy in order to investigate three unsolved murders in a neighboring town. O'Shea's capacity for drink and brawling is on a legendary scale; he is also susceptible to attractive women and a defender of underdogs. Such a character could not be abandoned after only one book. Indeed, the O'Shea series developed eventually into fourteen books published over a twelve-year period. The closest analogue in Western fiction is the series of Breckinridge Elkins burlesques which Robert E. Howard (q.v.) wrote for the pulp magazines in the 'Thirties, but the O'Shea books are less spontaneous and more sophisticated than Howard's stories. The series has been reprinted more than once, the last time with cover paintings by Jim Steranko which made O'Shea resemble actor Clint Eastwood in a red wig.

In 1967 Bickham's books began appearing as hard-covers in the Double D Western series from Doubleday. Bickham wrote two books about Charity Ross: *The War on Charity Ross* (New York: Doubleday, 1967), in which a young woman fights to keep her land after her husband is killed, and *Target: Charity Ross* (New York: Doubleday, 1968), a period murder mystery with an intriguing picture of Oklahoma City's underworld and its drug traffic in the 1890s. Another two-book "series," this one under the Jeff Clinton byline, consists of *Emerald Canyon* (New York: Doubleday, 1974) and *Shadow at Emerald Canyon* (New York: Doubleday, 1975) in which a group of farmers battle for survival against unscrupulous land agents. Bickham also did an entry in the Slocum porno-Western series, under the house name Jake Logan (see House Names), *Hanging Justice* (Chicago: Playboy Press, 1975).

Bickham then wrote *A Boat Named Death* (New York: Doubleday, 1975), after which he turned to other kinds of writing. Leaving aside the calculated farce of the Wildcat O'Shea novels, many of Bickham's books have ingredients not commonly found in the Western, such as the priest hero of *The Padre Must Die* (New York: Doubleday, 1967), or the humor of *The Apple Dumpling Gang* (New York: Doubleday, 1975) and certain of his other novels.

R.E.B.

Jack M. Bickham's Western novels are *Gunman's Gamble* (1958), *Feud Fury* (1959), *Killer's Paradise* (1959), *The Useless Gun* (1960), *Hangman's Territory* (1960), *Gunmen Can't Die* (1961), *Trip Home to Hell* (1965), *The Padre Must Die* (1967), *The War on Charity Ross* (1967), *Target: Charity Ross* (1968), *Decker's Campaign* (1970),

Jilly's Canal (1971) [alternate title: *Texas Challenge*], *Fletcher* (1971), *The Apple Dumpling Gang* (1971), *Dopey Dan* (1972), *Katie, Kelly, and Heck* (1973), *Baker's Hawk* (1974), *Dinah, Blow Your Horn* (1979).

Bickham's novels as Jeff Clinton are *The Fighting Buckaroo* (1961), *Wildcat's Rampage* (1962), *Range Killer* (1962), *Wildcat against the House* (1963), *Wildcat's Revenge* (1964), *Killer's Choice* (1965), *Wildcat Takes His Medicine* (1965), *Wanted: Wildcat O'Shea* (1966), *Wildcat on the Loose* (1967), *Watch Out for Wildcat* (1968), *Wildcat Meets Miss Melody* (1968), *Build a Box For Wildcat* (1969), *A Stranger Named O'Shea* (1970), *Wildcat's Claim to Fame* (1971), *Bounty on Wildcat* (1971), *Hang High, O'Shea* (1972), *Emerald Canyon* (1974), *Showdown at Emerald Canyon* (1975).

Bickham's novel under the Jake Logan house name is *Hanging Justice* (1975).

The Apple Dumpling Gang (Buena Vista, 1975) was directed by Norman Tokar and, a sequel, *The Apple Dumpling Gang Rides Again* (Buena Vista, 1979) was directed by Vincent McEveety. The only other film based on Bickham's Western fiction is *Baker's Hawk* (Doty-Dayton, 1976) directed by Lyman D. Dayton.

Binns, Archie (1899–1971) Author of fiction set in the Pacific Northwest, born at Port Ludlow, Washington. Binns' father was a pioneer in the state of Washington. At 18, Binns himself went to sea and the next year, in 1918, he enlisted in the U.S. Army. By 1923 he held the rank of Second Lieutenant in the Field Artillery Reserve. In 1922, Binns was graduated from Stanford University with a Bachelor's degree. Throughout the 'Twenties he worked as a journalist and in the 'Thirties he turned to writing short stories. His earliest fiction was sea stories but with *The Laurels Are Cut Down* (New York: Reynal & Hitchcock, 1937) he wrote a novel about two young men, bewildered and marked by fate, who wander from the Pacific Northwest to Siberia. *The Land is Bright* (New York: Scribner's, 1939) deals with the migration to Oregon in the 1850s. Much of Binns' subsequent fiction, emotionally vivid if structurally weak, utilizes the Pacific Northwest as its background. He was also the author of two excellent small scale histories, *Northwest Gateway: The Story of the Port of Seattle* (New York: Doubleday, 1941) and *Sea in the Forest* (New York: Doubleday, 1953), the latter being a definitive account of the history of Puget Sound.

Blacker, Irwin R(obert) (1919—)

An author known largely for his concern with the history of the Spanish conquests in the New World, born at Cleveland, Ohio. Blacker received a Bachelor's degree from Ohio University and a Master's degree from Western Reserve University. Entering the U.S. Army Engineers, he served during 1941–1945 and achieved the rank of Second Lieutenant and was awarded the Bronze Star. In 1949–1950 he was an English instructor at Purdue University and in 1950–1951 he worked with the Central Intelligence Agency in Washington, D.C. In the years 1956–1959 he was a staff writer for CBS-TV in New York.

Blacker's early fiction included *Irregulars, Partisans, Guerrillas* (New York: Simon & Schuster, 1954) and *Westering* (Cleveland: World, 1958), but his reputation as a novelist seems to hinge on his most ambitious book, *Taos* (Cleveland: World, 1959), centering on the historic conflict between the Spanish and the Indians in what now is known as New Mexico. Although much is contrived in the book and the stock characters often do improbable things, Mari Sandoz (q.v.) said of it that "these are incidental. Irwin Blacker not only can handle the melodramatic material but he manages real emotional impact by quieter scenes." Conversely, Oliver La Farge (q.v.) was less enthusiastic. "He works from the quite reasonable thesis that the conflict was primarily religious in motivation," he observed. "To exploit that thesis requires a good understanding of Spanish Catholicism of the period and the Pueblo religion, in both of which the author is deficient."

Blacker's strongest work appears to have been in his non-fiction historical works, such as *The Golden Conquistadores* (Indianapolis: Bobbs-Merrill, 1960) and *The Bold Conquistadores* (Indianapolis: Bobbs-Merrill, 1961). He was also concerned with the interplay between fiction and fact in treating the American West and edited two books of note on the subject, *The Old West in Fiction* (New York: Obolensky, 1961) and *The Old West in Fact* (New York: Obolensky, 1962).

Bolt, Lee. See Faust, Frederick.

Bonham, Frank (1914 —)

An author of formulary Western fiction, born at Los

Angeles, California. At the age of 12, Bonham's parents bought a small cabin in the mountains and, until he was grown, Bonham spent his summers at Big Bear Lake in Southern California. He tried writing his first short story when he was 10 and studied journalism and worked on the school paper in high school. He enrolled at Glendale Junior College from which he graduated in 1935. He could not continue his education because of the Depression and, by chance, met veteran Western pulp writer Ed Earl Repp. Bonham, who had been writing and trying to sell pulp mystery stories, was persuaded by Repp to ghost write Western stories to be published under Repp's name and from which they would split the royalties. This went on for three years, during which Bonham was averaging $125 a week, enough to get married on, when added to the $87.50 a week his fiancée was earning.

Bonham then began writing Western stories and serials for the pulps under his own name and finally published his first novel, *Lost Stage Valley* (New York: Simon & Schuster, 1948), a story which, in Bonham's words from his Foreward, "celebrates the courage and determination of the men who drove the stages, and the passengers who rode them." In the early 'Fifties, Bonham occasionally had his novels serialized in *The Saturday Evening Post* as well as published in hardbound editions. He wrote straight-forward, swift-paced action stories which tend to romanticize the white heroes but which are strictly formulary in structure and indifferent and stereotypical toward Native Americans. "I have tried to avoid," Bonham once remarked, "the conventional cowboy story, but I think it was probably a mistake. That is like trying to avoid crime in writing a mystery book. I just happened to be more interested in stagecoaching, mining, railroading, etc."

In 1960, Bonham turned to juveniles. However, in 1979, as part of an arrangement with Berkley Books, whereby all of his older Western novels were being systematically re-issued, Bonham agreed to write two new Western novels for them.

Frank Bonham's Western novels are *Lost Stage Valley* (1948), *Bold Passage* (1950), *The Outcasts of Crooked River* (1951) [alternate title: *Snake Track*], *Blood on the Land* (1952), *Night Raid* (1954), *The Feud at Spanish Ford* (1954), *Rawhide Guns* 1955), *Defiance Mountain* (1956), *Hard Rock* (1958), *Tough Country* (1958), *Last Stage West* (1959), *Sound of Gunfire* (1959), *One for Sleep* (1960), *Trago* (1962), *Cast a Long Shadow* (1964), *Logan's Choice* (1964), *Fort Hogan* (1980).

Stage to Tucson (Columbia, 1951) was directed by Ralph Murphy [based on *Lost Stage Valley*].

Bonner, Parker. See Ballard, Todhunter.

Bower, B[ertha] M[uzzy] (1871–1940)

Prolific author of formulary Western fiction, born Bertha Muzzy at Cleveland, Minnesota. Although she kept much of her personal life private, some facts about her are known. While Bertha was still a child, the Muzzy family moved to Montana where Bertha spent many hours roaming the ranges and visiting with cowboys—familiarizing herself with every aspect of ranch life. She was educated in public schools and by private tutors in Montana. Her father, who among many things was something of an architect, taught her music, how to draw house plans, and encouraged her to read a wide variety of books, including such authors as Dante, H. Rider Haggard, and John Milton, as well as the *Bible* and the Constitution.

Bertha's first job was as a schoolteacher. Subsequently, she married three times and had four children. Her first marriage was in 1890 to Clayton J. Bower, under whose name she wrote for her entire career. In 1906 she married Bertrand W. Sinclair, known as "Fiddleback" and, reputedly, something of a legendary character. Bower's third husband was Robert Ellsworth Cowan of Texas, a cowboy/bartender. Cowan himself later wrote a book of reminiscences titled *Range Rider* (New York: Doubleday, 1930) for which Bower provided an Introduction without mentioning the fact that they were married.

Bower spent many years in Montana's Chouteau County and then lived for brief periods of time in Idaho, Nevada, and Oregon. She lived in Los Angeles for the last twenty years of her life.

Bower began writing Western fiction in 1904 and her first novel, *Chip of the Flying-U* (New York: Dillingham, 1906), was pub-

B. M. Bower with Hoot Gibson who played Chip in Chip of the Flying U

lished two years before its book publication in Street & Smith's *Popular Magazine*. Bower derived the name for the Flying-U ranch from the old Flying-A brand of Montana. Heavily indebted to Owen Wister's (q.v.) *The Virginian* (New York: Macmillan, 1902), *Chip of the Flying-U* is a ranch romance, as are the bulk of Bower's subsequent books. However, unlike Wister, Bower considered the West the norm and throughout her fiction she poked fun at Easterners and Eastern values. In fact, quite often the major plot contrivance in a Bower novel is the arrival of an Easterner in the West, and he either adapts to the Western ways of doing things or returns to the East an acknowledged failure. Despite the fact that it contains very little action and no major conflicts, *Chip of the Flying-U* was an immediate success when it appeared in book form. Charles M. Russell (q.v.)—although he denied it—was Bower's prototype for Chip and he did provide the illustrations for the book edition, as he would for several later Bower novels. In the novel Chip is a ranch hand and a confirmed misogynist who likes to draw and who eventually falls in love with a woman with an Eastern medical education—she is dubbed the Little Doctor. Chip is no illiterate; he can quote long passages from the literary classics; but the most entertaining characters are the ranch hands, known collectively as the Happy Family. Chip and the Little Doctor marry at the end, but, in a sense, it is only a beginning, since Bower, as Clarence E. Mulford (q.v.) before her, decided to feature Chip or various members of the Happy Family in a whole series of books, of which the short story collection, *The Happy Family* (New York: Dillingham, 1910), is one of the best with its authentic portraits of everyday life on the range. In the early 'Thirties, Bower having become somewhat imprisoned by what she had done to all these characters in various previous books in the saga, started "back-dating" stories, telling about events in Chip's life *before* he met the Little Doctor.

The screenplay for *Chip of the Flying-U* (Selig, 1914) was written by Bower herself and, as a result, she became interested in the film industry and this interest carried over into her writing as early as *Jean of the Lazy A* (Boston: Little, Brown, 1915). In *The Quirt* (Boston: Little, Brown, 1920) the story tells of a film actress who comes to learn that there is a big difference between Western movies and the real West. In *The Phantom Herd* (Boston: Little, Brown, 1916) and its sequel *The Heritage of the Sioux* (Boston: Little, Brown, 1916) even the Happy Family becomes involved in movie-making.

There are Indians in *The Heritage of the Sioux*, but here, as elsewhere, they are not dealt with very realistically. In fact, this points up a major problem in Bower's fiction. She introduced all manner of "modernisms" from airplanes in *Skyrider* (Boston: Little, Brown, 1918) to German spies in *The Thunder Bird* (Boston: Little, Brown, 1919) to a science-fiction plot in *The Adam Chasers* (Boston: Little, Brown, 1927) just as, over the years, she broached any number of important social issues from divorce to the generation gap (when Chip's and the Little Doctor's son reaches college age): yet she invariably shied away from treating anything other than superficially. Nor was this all. By far the most serious disappointment is the role assigned to her heroines. They lack life and, although they might appear strong and independent in the early chapters, by the conclusion (and this includes the Little Doctor) they willingly, even cheerfully, accept a strictly domestic existence. Although Bower herself had been capable of making friends with cowboys, in her fiction a friendship between a man and a woman cannot occur without it leading to a romantic involvement.

Bower, it would seem in retrospect, was at her finest in the short story form and most of her short stories are superior in style, structure, and, above all, in genuine humor (as a result of character as many times as situation) to any of her novels. She received kindly reviews throughout her active career, although as a writer she neither matured nor improved. In the 'Fifties posthumous revisions and expansion of earlier stories began to appear in novel form under new titles, but it is uncertain if Bower herself had anything to do with them. Indeed, they diverge widely from all of her previous writing in both style and detail.

B. M. Bower's Western novels are *Chip of the Flying-U* (1906), *Her Prairie Knight* (1907), *The Lure of the Dim Trails* (1907), *The Range Dwellers* (1907), *The Lonesome Trail* (1909) [short stories], *The Long Shadow* (1909), *The Happy Family* (1910) [short stories], *Good Indian* (1912), *Lonesome Land* (1912), *The Gringos: A Story of the Old California Days* (1913), *The Uphill Climb* (1913), *Flying-U Ranch* (1914), *The Ranch of the Wolverine* (1914), *The Flying-U's Last Stand* (1915), *Jean of the Lazy A* (1915), *The Phantom Herd* (1916), *The Heritage of the Sioux* (1916), *The Lookout Man* (1917), *Starr of the Desert* (1917), *Cabin Fever* (1918), *Skyrider* (1918), *Rim O' the World* (1919), *The Thunder Bird* (1919), *The Quirt* (1920), *Casey Ryan* (1921), *Cow Country* (1921), *Laughing Water* (1922), *The Trail of the White Mule* (1922), *The Parowan Bonanza* (1923), *The Voice of Johnny-Water* (1923), *The Bellehelen Mine* (1924), *The Eagle's Wing* (1924), *Desert Brew* (1925), *Meadowlark Basin* (1925), *Black Thunder* (1926), *Van Patten* (1926), *The Adam Chasers* (1927), *White Wolves* (1927), *Hay-Wire* (1928), *Points West* (1928), *Rodeo* (1929), *The Swallowfork Bulls* (1929), *Fool's Gold* (1930), *Tiger Eye* (1930), *Dark Horse* (1931), *The Long Loop* (1931), *Rocking Arrow* (1932), *Open Land* (1933), *Trails Meet* (1933), *The Whoop-Up Trail* (1933), *The Haunted Hills* (1934), *The Dry Ridge Gang* (1935), *Trouble Rides the Wind* (1936), *Five Furies of Leaning Ladder* (1936), *Shadow Mountain* (1936), *The North Wind Do Blow* (1937), *Pirates of the Range* (1937), *The Wind Blows West* (1938), *The Singing Hill* (1939), *A Starry Night* (1939), *Man on Horseback* (1940), *Sweet Grass* (1940), *The Family Failing* (1941).

Films based on B. M. Bower's Western fiction are *Chip of the Flying-U* (Selig, 1914) directed by Colin Campbell, remade as *The Galloping Devil* (Canyon Pictures, 1920) directed by Nate Watt, remade as *Chip of the Flying-U* (Universal, 1926) directed by Lynn Reynolds, remade under this title (Universal, 1939) directed by Ralph Staub, *Shotgun Jones* (Selig, 1914) directed by Colin Campbell [source unknown], *Lonesome Trail* (Selig, 1914) directed by Colin Campbell [based on the short story "Lonesome Trail"], *The Reveler* (Selig, 1914) directed by Colin Campbell [based on the short story "The Reveler"], *The Up-Hill Climb* (Selig, 1914) directed by Colin Campbell, *When the Cook Fell Ill* (Selig, 1914) directed by Colin Campbell [based on the short story "When the Cook Fell Ill"], *How Weary Went Wooing* (Selig, 1915) directed by Tom Mix [source unknown], *North of 53* (Fox, 1917) directed by Richard Stanton [source unknown], *The Wolverine* (Associated, 1921) directed by William Bertram [based on *The Ranch of the Wolverine*], *Taming of the West* (Universal, 1925) directed by Arthur Rosson [based on *The Range Dwellers*], *Ridin' Thunder* (Universal, 1925) directed by Clifford S. Smith [based on *Jean of the Lazy A*], *Flying U Ranch* (Robertson-Cole, 1927) directed by Robert De Lacy, *Points West* (Universal, 1929) directed by Arthur Rosson, *King of the Rodeo* (Universal, 1929) directed by Henry MacRae [source unknown].

Bowie, Sam. See Ballard, Todhunter.

Brand, Max. See Faust, Frederick.

Braun, Matthew (1932 —) Author of Western fiction born and raised on a ranch in Oklahoma. In 1776 James Adair, a distant ancestor and author of *The History of the American Indians* (1775), married into the Cherokee tribe. Braun himself once noted this fact and the time spent during his youth among Cherokee and Osage Indians as contributing factors to his subsequent high regard for Indian culture and philosophy.

Braun fought in the middleweight division of the Golden Gloves 1949–1952 and in 1955 was graduated from college with a degree in journalism. He served in the U.S. Army and worked briefly for a small Oklahoma newspaper before entering upon a career in corporate journalism in 1956. In 1969 he quit the business world and retreated to a cabin in the mountains to write Western historical novels—which had long been his ambition. In 1972 within ten days of each other two novels were contracted for

by different publishers and both appeared later that year. In 1976 he received the Golden Spur Award from the Western Writers of America for his tenth novel, *The Kincaids* (New York: Putnam's, 1976), in the category Best Western Historical Novel. He lived at one time or another in Oklahoma, Texas, Arizona, California, Kansas, Colorado, and in New Hampshire.

Braun began making use of historical personalities through which to present his view of the American West already in his first novel, *Mattie Silks* (New York: Popular Library, 1972), which deals with the life and loves of a famous madam of the mining camps who became known as the queen of the red light district in Denver, Colorado. "Wild Bill" Hickock, Wyatt Earp, and "Buffalo Bill" Cody (see Historical Personalities) are also characters in this novel and Braun continued to people his fiction with scoundrels, misfits, outlaws, and lawmen who have become legends over the years. What distinguishes his treatment of these individuals is his reversal of popular trends, portraying Wyatt Earp, thinly disguised as Virge Hollister in *Cimarron Jordan* (New York: Fawcett, 1975) and including him in a subsequent novel by name, as a cold-blooded killer and thief, while romanticizing into heroes men such as Dallas Stoudenmire in *El Paso* (New York: Fawcett, 1973) and John Wesley Hardin in *Noble Outlaw* (New York: Popular Library, 1975).

His best work, unquestionably, is to be found in those novels where he addressed the sustaining social issues in American life, above all racial hostility. *Black Fox* (New York: Fawcett, 1972), for example, deals with the ways in which white men codified racism in the Nineteenth century and yet the novel approaches its portrayal of this dilemma with balance and sympathy for *all* the characters. A novel such as *Black Fox* takes its place alongside similar works by Benjamin Capps (q.v.) and Elmer Kelton (q.v.) as heralding a new direction in Western fiction which commands universal attention as historical fiction at its finest.

With *Jury of Six* (New York: Pocket Books, 1980)—a completely unreliable account of the last days of Billy the Kid—Braun launched a new series of novels featuring as a series character Luke Starbuck, a frontier detective. As the series developed in such entries as *Tombstone* (New York: Pocket Books, 1981) and *The Spoilers* (New York: Pocket Books, 1981), it would appear that it differed from similar series a generation before by authors such as W. C. Tuttle (q.v.) and William Colt MacDonald (q.v.) in that Starbuck becomes involved in actual historical situations and is pitted against real-life outlaws, gunmen, lawmen, politicians, and businessmen—the idea being to introduce at least the sense of history into what might seem at first glance to be only another formulary Western series.

Matthew Braun's Western novels are *Mattie Silks* (1972), *Black Fox* (1972), *The Savage Land* (1973), *El Paso* (1973), *Noble Outlaw* (1975), *Bloody Hand* (1975), *Cimarron Jordan* (1975), *Kinch* (1975), *Buck Colter* (1976), *The Kincaids* (1976), *The Second Coming of Lucas Brokaw* (1977), *Hangman's Creek* (1979), *Lords of the Land* (1979), *The Stuart Women* (1980), *Jury of Six* (1980), *Tombstone* (1981), *The Spoilers* (1981), *The Manhunter* (1981).

Bristow, Gwen (1903–1980) Author of historical Western fiction, born at Marion, South Carolina. Bristow received a Bachelor's degree from Judson College, a woman's college in Alabama, and studied journalism at Columbia University. During 1924–1935, Bristow worked as a reporter for the *Times-Picayune* in New Orleans. Her first book was a collaboration with her screenwriter husband, Bruce Manning, whom she married in 1929, *The Invisible Host* (New York: Mystery League, 1930), one of three mysteries that they wrote together which grew out of a scheme to murder their neighbors who had a "raucous radio."

Bristow soon branched off into writing historical novels. Her early work included a trilogy of Louisiana stories, beginning with pre-Revolutionary times and going up to World War I. Having moved to California, where her husband's work took them, Bristow realized how little she knew about that state's early history, having read only Helen Hunt Jackson's (q.v.) *Ramona* (1884). She began a period of self-education which determined the writing of her first novel set in the West, *Jubilee Trail* (New York: Thomas Y. Crowell, 1950), the traders' name for the Spanish trail which led from Sante Fe to Los Angeles in the 1840s. The book is about traveling on the Santa Fe trail and the early white American population in the Los Angeles area before the discovery of gold. Bristow worked on the novel for five years, traveling extensively and doing a vast amount of research in old records and books. *Calico Palace* (New York: Thomas Y. Crowell, 1970), which followed and also set in the 1840s, deals with San Francisco during the gold rush. The California gold rush is also the subject of her last novel, *Golden Dreams* (New York: Lippincott/Crowell, 1980).

Bristow, as many of her female contemporaries, wrote lengthy, romantic stories which feature strong, female characters. She was able to tell an exciting, suspenseful story, paying special attention to authentic backgrounds. Her first two novels set in the West were bestsellers and were translated into nine languages.

Jubilee Trail (Republic, 1955) was directed by Joseph Kane.

Brooker, Clark. See Fowler, Kenneth.

Brown, Dee (1908 —) Author of Western fiction and Western history, born at a Louisiana lumber camp where his father worked as a timberman. After his father's death, when Brown was five, he and his two sisters lived in various oil towns in the Southwest, where his mother was able to secure work as a store clerk. His first childhood friend was a young Indian boy with whom he attended cowboy and Indian movies and who cheered with the rest of the audience when the settlers or the cavalry were victorious. "I once asked him why he did that," Brown subsequently recalled, "and he said 'cause they're not real Indians.' To him they were just actors. All the books about Indians at that time were caricatures and after that I realized they weren't real Indians either."

Brown attended Arkansas State Teachers College and then went to George Washington University in Washington, D.C., where he graduated with a Bachelor's degree. It was during the Depression and a librarian's job with the Department of Agriculture was the best he could get. A born researcher, Brown began digging into original sources and references. He eventually moved on to the University of Illinois where he received a Master's degree and secured employment as a librarian. Following his retirement, Brown and his wife went to live in Little Rock, Arkansas.

Yellowhorse (Boston: Houghton Mifflin, 1956), Brown's first novel, deals sympathetically with the Native American and this humanism came to mark all of his later work, both fiction and non-fiction. *Bury My Heart At Wounded Knee* (New York: Holt, Rinehart, 1971), the book for which he is best known, was, according to Brown, "the product of twenty-five years of researching and writing other books. For a long while I collected Indian speeches without knowing exactly how I would use them. When I came to writing a history of the American West from the Indian point of view, the words of the Indians themselves gave the book much of its authority." Another of Brown's important non-fiction books was *The Gentle Tamers* (New York: Putnam's 1958) which deals with the life led by women on the frontier, one more aspect of the history of the American West completely distorted by Hollywood movies and a large segment of Western fiction (see Women on the Frontier).

Most of his fiction is informed by a solid historical content while losing nothing thereby in drama or characterization.

Dee Brown's Western novels are *Yellowhorse* (1956), *Cavalry Scout* (1958), *They Went Thataway* (1960), *Showdown at Little Big Horn* (1964), *The Girl from Fort Wicked* (1964), *Action at Beecher Island* (1967), *Tepee Tales* (1979) [short stories], *Creek Mary's Blood* (1980).

Brown, J(oseph) P(aul) S(ummers)

(1930 —) Author of Western fiction, born Joseph Paul Summers at Nogales, Arizona. Brown legally changed his name in 1945. Brown's father was an Arizona cattleman and Brown attended Notre Dame, graduating with a Bachelor's degree, in 1952. He began his career as a reporter for the *El Paso Herald Post* 1953–1954. From 1956–1958 he was a professional boxer, taking up cattle ranching as a career in 1958. "I have been a cattleman all my adult life," Brown once commented, "—born on a ranch of fifth-generation cattle people—also have been a pilot in the U.S. and Mexico. I have been a whiskey smuggler and have prospected for gold with diving gear in the rivers of Mexico's Sierra Madre. I wrote my first book to see if I could do it, the second because I had to do it, and the third because I loved doing it."

Brown's first novel was *Jim Kane* (New York: Dial, 1970), retitled *Pocket Money* for the paperback edition. *The Outfit* (New York: Dial, 1971) followed and *The Forests of the Night* (New York: Dial, 1974). Brown's stories of the West are characterized by rugged and realistic settings, con-

stant plot development, and an absence of most formulary elements. It is unfortunate he did not write more and that his work is not better known.

Pocket Money (National General, 1972) was directed by Stuart Rosenberg.

Burnett, W(illiam) R(iley)

(1899–1982) Hardboiled novelist who brought this fictional style to his Western novels and screenplays, born at Springfield, Ohio. Burnett attended Ohio State University and between 1921–1927 worked as a statistician for the state of Ohio. He wrote for eight years without acceptance and then published *Little Caesar* (New York: Dial, 1929) for which he is best remembered. *Saint Johnson* (New York: Dial, 1930) followed, a Western which fictionalized the Wyatt Earp legend (see Historical Personalities) in Tombstone, Arizona, closely following the fantasies about Earp set forth a few years previously by Walter Noble Burns (q.v.), although Burnett disguised his central characters by giving them different names.

After *Little Caesar* was bought by Warner Bros., Burnett went to Hollywood and became a screenwriter. During the next two decades he worked on a number of pictures, and wrote *Dark Command* (New York: Knopf, 1938), a novel about the renegade gangs during the Civil War. After this, Burnett did not return to the Western genre until *Adobe Walls* (New York: Knopf, 1953), a story about Walter Grein, Indian fighter. It is, however, more concerned with the politics and personalities in the conflicts than in portraying the historical ramifications of Indian fighting or the morality of the events themselves. *Pale Moon* (New York: Knopf, 1956), *Bitter Ground* (New York: Knopf, 1958), and *Mi Amigo* (New York: Knopf, 1959) followed. Of lesser note is Burnett's novelization of his screenplay for *Sergeants Three* (New York: Pocket, 1962), based on what is essentially a farcical remake of *Gunga Din* (RKO, 1939) transposed to the American West. *The Goldseekers* (New York: Knopf, 1962) is concerned with the Alaskan gold rush. *The Abilene Samson* (New York: Pocket, 1963) was Burnett's last Western and also perhaps his comic masterpiece.

Burnett appears to have been preoccupied above all with the end of the West and it was beyond him, and therefore beyond his characters, to imagine a synthesis of old and new or of white, Native American, and Mexican. Each group seems to be attempting to wipe the landscape clean, to begin anew, free from history or influence.

D.W.

Films based on W. R. Burnett's *Saint Johnson* are *Law and Order* (Universal, 1932) directed by Edward Cahn, *Wild West Days* (Universal, 1937) directed by Ford Beebe and Cliff Smith [a thirteen chapter serial], *Law and Order* (Universal, 1940) directed by Ray Taylor, remade under this title (Universal, 1953) directed by Nathan Jurand. *The Dark Command* (Republic, 1940) was directed by Raoul Walsh, and *Arrowhead* (Paramount, 1953) directed by Charles Marquis Warren [based on *Adobe Walls*].

Western films based on Burnett's original screen stories are *Belle Starr's Daughter* (20th-Fox, 1947) directed by Lesley Selander, *Yellow Sky* (20th-Fox, 1948) direct-

ed by William Wellman, *The Badlanders* (M-G-M, 1958) directed by Delmer Daves, *Sergeants Three* (United Artists, 1962) directed by John Sturges.

Burns, Walter Noble

(1872–1932) Historian whose biographies of frontier badmen were so romanticized as to read as fiction, born at Lebanon, Kentucky. Burns graduated from high school in Louisville, Kentucky, before commencing his career as a journalist with the *Louisville Evening Post* in 1890. Unlike Stephen Crane (q.v.), another journalist of the time, Burns did not become a correspondent during the Spanish-American War but instead volunteered for the First Kentucky Infantry and took part in the battle for Puerto Rico. After the war, Burns worked for several newspapers, eventually becoming Sunday editor for the *Chicago Inter-Ocean* in 1910, switching to the *Chicago Examiner* in 1915 and, finally, to the *Chicago Tribune* in 1918.

In his later years, Burns turned to writing popularized history as a sideline. His book *The Saga of Billy The Kid* (New York: Doubleday, 1926) very nearly turned the Kid into a hero and a sacrificial victim and, over the next four decades, exerted a tremendous impact on the popular image accorded the Kid in both fiction and films. Western author Eugene Manlove Rhodes (q.v.), who knew Pat Garrett personally, attacked Burns in an article titled "In Defense of Pat Garrett" (1927) contained in *The Rhodes Reader* (Norman: University of Oklahoma Press, 1957) and Kent Ladd Steckmesser in his book *The Western Hero in History and Legend* (Norman: University of Oklahoma Press, 1965) wrote of Burns' book that it "is neither an objective narrative of the Lincoln County War nor a reliable account of the Kid's career. It is rather a magnificent classic of American folklore and mythology."

Burns' next effort was *Tombstone* (New York: Doubleday, 1927) which attempted to achieve the same results with Wyatt Earp. As C. L. Sonnichsen (q.v.) wrote in *From Hopalong to Hud: Thoughts on Western Fiction* (College Station: Texas A&M University Press, 1978), "Burns was a newspaperman who saw his material with a feature writer's eye. . . . The Tombstone feud reminded him of a story from the Arthurian cycle. Wyatt was Sir Galahad, without fear and without reproach. His friends were knights of the Round Table (Burns actually uses the figure), and his enemies were the wicked earls who had to be laid low before there could be peace in the realm."

The same thing happened again when Burns came to write of Joaquín Murieta, a legendary character already worked over in the Nineteenth century in dime novels, in his book *The Robinhood of El Dorado* (New York: Coward, McCann, 1932). All in all, what Burns' "fictions" did accomplish was totally to distort the true nature and character of these Western personalities and yet his books were so well-received by the reading public that all the scholarship disproving his contentions has been by many largely ignored.

Films based on Walter Noble Burns' Western biographies are *Billy the Kid* (M-G-M, 1930) directed by King Vidor [based on *The Saga of Billy the Kid*], *Billy the Kid* (M-G-M, 1941) directed by David Miller [credited Burns' *The Saga of Billy the Kid* as its source], *The Robinhood of El Dorado* (M-G-M, 1934) directed by William Wellman.

Burroughs, Edgar Rice (1875–1950) Author of Western fiction, although better known as the creator of Tarzan, born at Chicago, Illinois. Burroughs, whose family was wealthy, attended a number of private schools before ending up at the Michigan Military Academy. He next enlisted in the U.S. Army and was stationed at Fort Grant, Arizona, with Troop B of the 7th Regiment of the U.S. Cavalry. Just ten years after Geronimo's surrender (see Native Americans), Burroughs visited many of the sites of the Apache wars before he was caught and discharged for being under age. Fifteen years followed during which he worked as a cattle drover in Idaho, an operator on an Oregon gold dredge, a railroad policeman at Salt Lake City, and failed at a number of business ventures. At 36 he found himself at a loss.

He possessed, however, a vivid imagination. He sold a serial about Martian life to the Munsey publications and his first Tarzan story appeared in 1912; his first novel appeared in 1914. Subsequently, his Tarzan novels alone sold 25 million copies in 56 languages. Burroughs eventually bought a ranch in Southern California and began dictating his books to secretaries. The area where he lived was shortly after named Tarzana in his honor.

The War Chief (Chicago: A.C. McClurg, 1927) was run first serially in *Argosy* in 1927. In it Burroughs tried to recreate the Apache way of life, using as his point of view character Shoz-Dijiji, the Black Bear, a white ostensibly adopted by Geronimo while still an infant. *Apache Devil* (Los Angeles: Edgar Rice Burroughs, Inc.,

1933) appeared as a sequel in *Argosy* in 1928. Nothing Burroughs wrote in the field of Western fiction before these two books—which was one novel, *The Bandit of Hell's Bend* (Chicago: A.C. McClurg, 1925)—and nothing he wrote afterwards—which also was only one novel, *The Deputy Sheriff of Comanche County* (Los Angeles: Edgar Rice Burroughs, Inc., 1940)—amounted to anything more than routinely formulary stories in which the Indians are portrayed as faceless, unmotivated savages. His contribution, therefore, to historical Western fiction must rest with this two-volume Apache saga. The main outline of the events surrounding the wars with the Apaches is substantially accurate in it and the historical personalities, besides Geronimo, include Cochise, Mangas Coloradas, Natchez (Naiche), Nanay, Juh (Whoa), General Crook, and General Miles. *Apache Devil* is a weaker novel then the *The War Chief* because Burroughs insisted on infusing into his narrative a formulary white villain and his gang and an imperiled rancher's daughter, plus the customary ranch romance between this girl and Shoz-Dijiji, made more acceptable to readers of that day by stressing that Shoz-Dijiji is actually white. Burroughs intended to write a third novel in this saga in which Shoz-Dijiji, having joined the ranks of the whites, would again be confronted by the typical villainy of a ranch romance. Fortunately he never wrote it and his two-book saga thus retains a certain consistency and integrity.

Busch, Niven (1903—) Author of some Western fiction and a screenwriter of Western films, born at Brooklyn, New York. At the age of 14 Busch was sent to the Hoosac Boarding School near Williamstown, Massachusetts. Following graduation, he enrolled at Princeton University but left in his sophomore year to become an associate editor of *Time*, a magazine which Busch's first cousin had helped to found.

Busch quit *Time* in 1931 to go to work in Hollywood as a screenwriter. His association with Western fiction began when he was called in to work on the story for William Wyler's *The Westerner* (United Artists, 1940). At the time Busch gave actor Gary Cooper credit for his assistance and later stated that Cooper "got me interested in the West."

Duel in the Sun (New York: Morrow, 1944) was Busch's first Western novel and it became a bestseller. "I thought," Busch once reflected, "the only way to succeed was to build a Western around a woman and use a sexual idea instead of an action idea." *The Furies* (New York: Dial, 1948) was Busch's second attempt at a Western, but it neither won the critical acclaim of its predecessor nor had its sales. Busch thenceforth turned to writing Western screenplays, the first and most successful of which was *Pursued* (Warner's, 1947), a mixture of sexuality, the Old West, and what film critics call *film noir*. "I wanted to treat Western characters like men and women," Busch once said about the roles of women in his Western fiction and his screenplays. "Women were scarce, so a woman exerted a fantastic charisma in that lonely country."

D.W.

Niven Busch's Western screenplays are *Pursued* (Warner's, 1947) directed by Raoul Walsh, *The Capture* (RKO, 1950) directed by John Sturges, *Distant Drums* (Warner's,

1951) directed by Raoul Walsh, *The Man From The Alamo* (Universal, 1953) directed by Budd Boetticher, *The Moonlighter* (Warner's, 1953) directed by Roy Rowland, *The Treasure of Pancho Villa* (RKO, 1955) directed by George Sherman.

Films based on Busch's Western novels are *Duel in the Sun* (Selznick, 1946) directed by King Vidor and *The Furies* (Paramount, 1950) directed by Anthony Mann.

Busch shared screen credit with Cameron Rogers for the story for *Belle Starr* (20th-Fox, 1941) directed by Irving Cummings.

Butler, Walter C. See Faust, Frederick.

C

Capps, Benjamin Franklin

(1922—) Author of Western fiction and non-fiction, the son of a cowboy, born at Dundee, Texas. Capps grew up on the land, riding horseback to a one-room school for his elementary education; when it came to high school he switched to taking a school bus into town. At 15, Capps began his university education at Texas Technological College in Lubbock, Texas in 1938–1939. He worked for a time as a surveyor and truck driver in Colorado and Texas. In 1942 he married and joined the U.S. Army Air Force. He remained in the service until 1945, attaining the rank of First Lieutenant, serving in the Pacific theatre. Following discharge, Capps completed his education, obtaining a Bachelor's degree from the University of Texas in 1948, and, in 1949, received his Master's degree from the same institution. As a result of this educational training, Capps was able to become an instructor in English and journalism for Northeastern State College, Tahlequah, Oklahoma from 1949 to 1951. At this point Capps' career took an interesting turn. He left teaching and for the next ten years worked as a tool and die maker for various companies.

In 1961, he decided to try his hand at

free-lance writing. His first Western novel, *Hanging at Comanche Wells* (New York: Ballantine, 1962), is Capps' most formulary Western. It features a triad hero—an old judge, a tired sheriff, and a young deputy—in the tradition of Clarence E. Mulford (q.v.) and William Colt MacDonald (q.v.). With even greater authenticity than Andy Adams' (q.v.) *Log of a Cowboy* (Boston: Houghton Mifflin, 1903), Capps' second Western, *The Trail to Ogallala* (New York: Duell, Sloan, 1964), deals with a cattle drive from Texas to Nebraska. The novel won the Spur Award from the Western Writers of America for 1964, the Golden Saddleman Award, as well as being selected by the National Association of Independent Schools as one of the ten best books of 1964 for pre-college readers. Capps also received a Spur Award for his next book, *Sam Chance* (New York: Duell, Sloan, 1965), which tells about the adventures of a Confederate veteran on the Western frontier. In this book, as in *The Brothers of Uterica* (New York: Meredith Press, 1967), Capps depicted the hardships encountered in the fight for survival in the Western wilderness.

Alan LeMay's (q.v.) *The Searchers* (New York: Harper's, 1954) may have influenced Capps in writing *A Woman of the People* (New York: Duell, Sloan, 1966), one of his finest novels. The story, told from the point of view of a white captive girl, deals with her dilemma over assimilation into a Comanche Indian tribe. The novel includes a vivid portrait of Comanche tribal life and reveals a deep understanding of this often savagely depicted people. In his sixth novel, *The White Man's Road* (New York: Harper's, 1969), which won both the Spur and Wrangler awards, Capps gave his readers an unusually grim view of reservation life among the Comanches.

The True Memoirs of Charley Blankenship (Philadelphia: Lippincott, 1972), a picaresque novel written for young people, is concerned with the episodic adventures of the title character who heads West at age 17 and works as a cattle drover, buffalo bone picker, and bronc-buster. This novel was followed by three works of non-fiction: *The Warren Wagontrain Raid* (New York: Dial, 1974) which won the Wrangler Award from the Western Heritage Society, and two Time-Life books, *The Indians* (Chicago: Time-Life, 1973) and *The Great Chiefs* (Chicago: Time-Life, 1975). Capps' next novel, *Woman Chief* (New York: Doubleday, 1979), is a fictional rendering of the life of an Atsina Indian who was taken captive by the Crow Indians. The book chronicles her life among the Crows where her exceptional accomplishments gained for her a place on the all-male war council.

Capps stated about his writing that "it is my ambition to write clearly and as simply and straightforwardly as the subject matter will permit." Capps' ability to combine enthralling plot-lines, interesting and well-developed characters, and authentic details about the West makes him one of the finest authors in the Western fiction genre.

D.K.-M.

Carder, Leigh. See Cunningham, Eugene.

Carson, Zeke. See Lutz, Giles A.

Carter, Forrest (1925—) An author known principally for his stories about Josey Wales born in the mountain country of Eastern Tennessee. Orphaned when he was

5, Carter, of mixed Cherokee and white parentage, went to live with his full-blood Cherokee grandmother and his mixed-blood grandfather. His only formal education was gained during a brief confinement in an orphanage. Homeless for a second time at 10 years of age, Carter worked as a cowboy and received broken bones and a steel pin in his knee to show for it.

Carter's first novel was *Gone to Texas* (New York: Delacorte/Eleanor Friede, 1975), an exciting adventure story about Josey Wales who, in revenge for wrongs done him by irregular troops during the Civil War, becomes the country's most wanted outlaw. It gained much prominence when it was made into a film starring Clint Eastwood. Carter wrote a sequel, *The Vengeance Trail of Josey Wales* (New York: Delacorte, 1976), which continues Wales' fictional adventures, and the same year published an autobiographical book, *The Education of Little Tree* (New York: Delacorte, 1976). While at work on these books, Carter found himself deeply interested in the Apaches of the Southwest, particularly in Geronimo, and eventually published a fictional treatment of Geronimo's career, *Watch for Me on the Mountain* (New York: Delacorte, 1978), which idealizes the Indian leader and pictures him as a mystic with supernatural powers.

Carter was a natural teller of tales, "a storyteller in council to the Cherokee nation," and he preferred the council storytelling method of the Native American as a means of passing on the history of his people. Critics have accused Carter of overuse of sex and violence, particularly in *Vengeance Trail*, but in his behalf it can be said that Carter painted masterly portraits of the country and the people he knew best, although he tended to be hardest, not without some justification, on white politicians and Christian missionaries.

C.L.S.

Carter's first Josey Wales novel, retitled to conform with the picture for paperback distribution, formed the basis for *Outlaw—Josey Wales* (Warner's, 1976) directed by Clint Eastwood.

Cassidy, Hopalong. See Mulford, Clarence E.

Cather, Willa Sibert (1873–1947) Pulitzer-Prize-winning author best known for her Southwestern classic, *Death Comes for the Archbishop* (New York: Knopf, 1927), and her Great Plains novels set in Nebraska, born Wilella which Cather herself shortened to Willa, near Winchester, Virginia. The Cather family moved to Nebraska in 1883. Curious about the strange environment of Nebraska, which was then pioneer territory, Cather spent many hours wandering over the prairie and visiting with foreign-born and second-generation American settlers many of whom she would use as models for characters in her pioneer stories. Cather was educated at home by family and friends, primarily in English and Greek classics and in Latin until the Cather family permanently settled in Red Cloud, Nebraska. Red Cloud was a small railroading town which Cather later used as the setting (although usually disguised) for some short stories and six of her thirteen novels.

Cather, who was very boyish in her youth, had plans to become a doctor; however, while attending the University of Nebraska in Lincoln, her ability to write was discovered and she decided upon a literary career. She began writing poems and short stories and contributed numerous columns and reviews to a local newspaper. Shortly after graduation Cather went to Pittsburgh where she worked as a professional journalist until 1901; she then began teaching. In 1906 she was invited to New York to join the staff of *McClure's* magazine and she lived there the rest of her life. She made a name for herself at *McClure's*, where she was managing editor until 1912, the year of the publication of her first novel and her third book, *Alexander's Bridge* (Boston: Houghton Mifflin, 1912), which had previously been serialized in *McClure's*.

The greatest influence on Cather's early stories was Henry James whom she greatly admired, but it was author Sarah Orne Jewett who provided the best advice to Cather when she wrote to her in a letter ". . . you must find your own quiet centre of life, and write from that to the world . . . in short, you must write to the human heart . . . ." Cather, who had had ambivalent feelings towards smalltown life and her years spent in Nebraska, finally found her own quiet spot when she went back to her past and wrote about her childhood experiences and the people she had met and come to love on the Nebraska prairies. This part of her life served as literary and spiritual inspiration for novels as *O Pioneers!* (Boston,

Houghton Mifflin, 1913) and *My Ántonia* (Boston: Houghton Mifflin, 1918).

After 1927 Cather's literary career began to decline, although her subsequent works were still widely read. While she never married, Cather did retain very close relationships with her family and friends. The deaths of her parents, two of her brothers, and an intimate friend from her days in Pittsburgh left her bereft. As the years went on, her health began to fail and a torn tendon in her wrist made it increasingly difficult to write. The advent of World War II convinced Cather that Twentieth-century American society, its materialism and technology, repudiated the spiritual values she had tried to set forth in her novels. She quit writing. She died from a cerebral hemorrhage in New York City.

Cather received many rewards and honors throughout her writing career. She was the first woman to receive an honorary degree from Princeton and was the first recipient of the *Prix Femina Americain* in 1933.

Cather's first important book, *O Pioneers!*, is a story set in pioneering days through 1900 dealing with the heroic deeds and qualities of first generation Bohemians and Swedes, written in a nostalgic and elegiac tone. This same technique was used in *My Ántonia* in which Cather again extolled the pioneering spirit and the achievements of the early Nebraska settlers. Both books were unique for their time in that they depicted unusually strong heroines who do not need male heroes to achieve their ends and live their lives. They represent the embodiment of the Western pioneer woman who accepts and overcomes the challenges of the harsh life-style of the plains.

Cather's pioneer stories qualify as regional novels, for the land is an integral part of the story, not merely a setting. In fact, in *O Pioneers!* the land is the true hero of the story. As Mari Sandoz (q.v.), who also came from Nebraska, Cather came to regard nature and the land as the heart of her stories.

Cather wrote in her prefatory notes to her essay collection, *Not Under Forty* (New York: Knopf, 1936), that for her "the world broke in two in 1922 or thereabouts." The tone of Cather's work became more and more bitter and a feeling of frustration and loss became the overall tone in such novels as *The Professor's House* (New York: Knopf, 1925) and *My Mortal Enemy* (New York: Knopf, 1926). In *One of Ours* (New York: Knopf, 1922)—a World War I story which partly takes place in Nebraska and for which Cather won the Pulitzer Prize despite the negative reception by critics—and *A Lost Lady* (New York: Knopf, 1923) Cather mourned nostalgically the passing of the pioneer era. *A Lost Lady* is a story about an aging beauty who, having survived the pioneer experience, dreams of the days when she entertained railroad workers. The book is often compared to Conrad Richter's (q.v.) *The Lady* (New York: Knopf, 1957) and is the only novel of Cather that was ever brought to the screen. She stipulated in her will that her stories were never again to be filmed nor were her letters to be reprinted.

When Cather no longer had stories to tell about Nebraska, it was perhaps inevitable she should turn to the Southwest, an area that had fascinated her for many years and to which she had traveled regularly since 1912. As early as 1909 in her short story "The Enchanted Bluff," she had been interested in the ancient cliff dwellers of pre-Columbian Arizona. The literary consequences of her visits to Arizona and New

Mexico were great: Part IV "The Ancient People" of *The Song of the Lark* (Boston: Houghton Mifflin, 1915), a story set for the most part in Colorado; "Tom Outland's Story," a story-within-a-story about the discovery of an ancient cliff dwelling city in *The Professor's House*; and *Death Comes for the Archbishop*.

Death Comes for the Archbishop is a narrative, as Cather herself preferred to call it, about the organization of the vast diocese in mid Nineteenth-century New Mexico by Archbishop Lamy and his vicar, Joseph P. Macheboeuf, renamed Jean Marie Latour and Joseph Vaillant for the book. The main events of the story were inspired by Cather's own experiences in New Mexico and by William Howlett's book, *The Life of the Right Reverend Joseph P. Macheboeuf*, which was printed privately in Pueblo, Colorado, in 1908. Although considered by some to be an historical novel, it is not so due to Cather's romanticized treatment of historical characters as Lamy and Kit Carson (see Historical Personalities). Western writer Harvey Fergusson (q.v.) felt Cather dealt with New Mexico as a tourist would and Mary Austin (q.v.), in whose home Cather finished the novel, was greatly angered over Cather's use of a French priest as a protagonist which Austin felt was a betrayal of New Mexico's Spanish heritage.

Death Comes for the Archbishop is written in an episodic and simple style from which it draws its true beauty. For Cather, the land of the Southwest and its inhabitants had been a tremendous spiritual experience and in writing *Death* she wanted to celebrate the early pioneering spirit, this time in another locality. *Death Comes for the Archbishop* is a lasting book, as Cather had told her publisher it would be.

Cather once wrote in an essay on short story writer Katherine Mansfield, of whom she thought highly: "The qualities of a second-rate writer can easily be defined, but a first-rate writer can only be experienced. It is just the thing in him which escapes analysis that makes him first-rate." So it is with Cather who through literary artistry transformed the efforts of early settlers on the Western frontier into abiding fictional narratives which are so important, not least of all because of the way they treasure the past and hold it dear.

For further information on Willa Cather and her works see *Willa Cather, Her Life and Art* (Lincoln: University of Nebraska Press, 1975) by James Woodress, *Willa Cather, Living* (New York: Knopf, 1953) by Edith Lewis, *The World of Willa Cather* (New York: Dodd, Mead, 1951) by Mildred Bennett, *Willa Cather* (New York: Knopf, 1953) by Edward K. Brown, *Willa Cather, A Critical Introduction* (Ithaca: Cornell University Press, 1951) by David Daiches.

Chaffin, James B. See Lutz, Giles A.

Challis, George. See Faust, Frederick.

Chin, Frank (Chew, Jr.) (1940 —)

A fifth-generation American author of the Chinese experience in the West whose ancestors worked on railroads and in the gold mines of the Pacific Coast area, born at Berkeley, California. During World War II, Chin's parents sent him back to his roots in the Motherlode country, the Sierra Nevadas, where, along with his growing-up experiences in the Chinatowns of Oakland and San Francisco, he acquired a deep understanding of the historical role that Chinese-Americans played in the development of the West. His writing is rich with this knowledge.

After attending the University of California at Berkeley, Chin won a fellowship in 1961 to the Writer's Workshop at the State University of Iowa. He then returned to California to complete his Bachelor's degree at the University of California at Santa Barbara in 1963. A brief period as the first Chinese-American brakeman on the Southern Pacific railroad was interrupted to apprentice as a television writer in Seattle, Washington. Chin worked for King Broadcasting Company in Seattle as a production writer and story editor before returning, once again, to California. There he became writer-in-residence at the University of California at Berkeley, also teaching at the University of California at Davis and San Francisco State College.

Chin won his first writing award in 1965, the Joseph Henry Jackson Award, for an unpublished novel, *A Chinese Lady Dies*. The following year he won the James T. Phelan Award for short fiction, much of which has been anthologized in *The Young American Writers* (New York: Funk & Wagnalls, 1967) edited by Richard Kostelanetz, *19 Necromancers from Now* (New York: Anchor Books, 1970) edited by Ishmael Reed, and *The Urban Reader* (New Jersey: Prentice-Hall, 1971) edited by Susan Cahill and Michele Cooper. But it is as a playwright and outspoken essayist that Chin is better known. *The Chickencoop Chinaman* was one of the first plays ever produced in the United States written by an Asian-American. *Chickencoop* won the East-West Players Playwriting Award in 1971 and opened at the American Place Theatre in New York in 1972. Critics praised Chin's creative skill and dramatic abilities, although several were uneasy about his polemics and the bitter realism of the Chinese-American experiences that he depicted. Act One of *Chickencoop* was published in *Aiiieeeee!: An Anthology of Asian-Americans* (Washington: Howard University, 1974) edited by Chin himself, Jeffrey Paul Chan, Lawson Fusao Inada, and Shawn Hsu Wong. Act Two was published in *Yardbird Reader, Volume III* (Washington: Howard University, 1974).

In 1974 he received both a Rockefeller Playwright's grant and a National Endowment for the Arts creative writing grant. Two of his plays also opened. *The Year of the Dragon* was produced by the American Place Theatre and televised for PBS' *Theatre in America* series. *Gee! Pop! . . .A Real Cartoon* previewed in San Francisco in December.

There are two key themes in Chin's work. The first deals with the subjugation of the Asian-American and the destruction of his/her cultural identity by racism and stereotyping. Alienation is a common theme for American writers today. Chin showed it in its most personal form, within the family, the Chinese family, whose usually strong ties disintegrate from the pressures of the outside white culture. The second theme is Chin's insistence upon the acceptance of Asian-Americans as Americans. In *The Chickencoop Chinaman* he emphasized the "Chinaman" as an American hybrid created especially out of the experiences of the West where he had been a pioneer. The Asian-American, Chin argued in all his work, is not just a sojourner or outsider, but an inside participant in the spoiled American dream.

P.O.

Chisholm, Matt. See Watts, Peter C.

Cisco Kid, The. See Porter, William Sydney.

Clark, Walter Van Tilburg

(1909–1971) Author and educator perhaps best known for his novel *The Ox-Bow Incident* (New York: Random House, 1940), born at East Orland, Maine. Clark moved West with his family in 1917, settling in Nevada which became the locale for nearly all of his subsequent fiction. Attending the University of Nevada, Clark received his Bachelor's degree in 1931 and went on for a Master's degree in English, writing a thesis on the Tristram legend. In 1932 he published a volume of poetry, filled with mythic concerns and literary allusions. Clark then assumed a teaching assistantship at the University of Vermont, this time concentrating in his studies on American literature and Greek philosophy. He was awarded a second Master's degree, writing a thesis on the poetry of Robinson Jeffers. Following marriage, Clark embarked on a career of high school teaching and coaching basketball at Cazenovia, New York.

Clark's first novel, *The Ox-Bow Incident*, won him an immediate place in American letters. Once it was sold for a motion picture version, Clark decided to concentrate exclusively on writing, publishing a number of short stories and working on his very long, and upon publication not very successful, novel, *The City of Trembling Leaves* (New York: Random House, 1945). In 1946 Clark went to live in Taos, New Mexico, returning to Nevada before the end of the decade. His third novel, *The Track of the Cat* (New York: Random House, 1949), came next, followed by his short story collection, *The Watchful Gods and Other Stories* (New York: Random House, 1950).

The critics tended to be extremely harsh on Clark, particularly with regard to his later books, and, reputedly, this was a factor in his ceasing to write. Whatever the case, he returned to teaching and wrote nothing more. In 1953 he resigned from the University of Nevada in protest over an autocratic administration and for the next decade held a number of university teaching positions and gave extensive guest lectures. In 1962 he returned to the University of Nevada as a writer-in-residence where he was joined on the faculty by his son, a doctoral candidate, in 1966.

According to Max Westbrook in his biographical and critical study, *Walter Van Tilburg Clark* (New York: Twayne Publishers, 1969), the two most significant influences on Clark's creative writing were Jeffer's poetry and the writings of psychologist C. G. Jung. Certainly few authors of Western fiction prior to Clark had approached their stories with his profound sense of erudition and mythic concerns. *The Ox-Bow Incident*, on the surface, deals with frontier justice and tells of three men encountered on the trail by a vigilante gang and mistakenly hanged for being cattle rustlers, only for them to be proven innocent. "The subject of *The Ox-Bow Incident*," Westbrook wrote in his book, ". . .is not a plea for legal procedure. The subject is man's mutilation of himself, man's sometimes trivial, sometimes large failures to get beyond the narrow images of his own ego. The tragedy of *The Ox-Bow Incident* is that most of us, including the man of sensitivity and the man of reason, are alienated from the saving grace of archetypal reality. Our lives, then, though not without possibility, are often stories of a cruel and irrevocable mistake."

The Track of the Cat is a novel which seeks to demonstrate how two hunters, killed pursuing a panther, symbolize the principle of evil in the world; they do not understand it. Whereas the two hunters who do understand evil are able to kill the panther.

With these two novels and his collection of short stories—many of which are of exceptionally high quality—Clark's reputation would appear secure as one of the most significant literary forces in Twentieth-century Western fiction.

The Ox-Bow Incident (20th-Fox, 1943) was directed by William Wellman as was *Track of the Cat* (Warner's, 1954).

For further information see Max Westbrook's *Walter Van Tilburg Clark* (New York: Twayne Publishers, 1969) and L. L. Lee's *Walter Van Tilburg Clark* (Boise: Idaho State University Press, 1973).

Clemens, Samuel Langhorne

(1835–1910) Perhaps the most important figure in Western American literature (and, maybe in American literature in general) in the Nineteenth century, born at

Florida, Missouri. When Clemens was 5, his family, which was always on the move, settled in Hannibal, Missouri, and there, in 1847, Clemens' father died. This put an end to the young Clemens' rather limited schooling and he was at once apprenticed to his brother Orion who ran a country paper, the *Missouri Courier*. In 1853 Clemens decided to head East as a journeyman printer but soon he was back with Orion who, by this time, was publishing a newspaper in Keokuk, Iowa.

In 1857 Clemens became an apprentice pilot on a Mississippi riverboat where he remained until the Civil War. He served about two weeks as a Second Lieutenant in the Confederate Army before, Orion having been appointed secretary to the governor of the Nevada Territory, he decided to go along. He prospected unsuccessfully in Nevada and finally became a reporter for a Carson City newspaper. By 1862 he was editing the *Enterprise* in Virginia City and it was here that he first adopted his pseudonym, Mark Twain, after a depth call used by Mississippi riverboat pilots. A ridiculous duel was the cause of his sudden departure from Nevada, landing him in San Francisco where he worked for a number of newspapers and met Bret Harte (q.v.) who very much impressed him. In 1865 he published his famed short story "The Celebrated Jumping Frog of Calaveras County" in a New York newspaper and was on his way to national fame as a humorist. He traveled to Hawaii as a reporter for the Sacramento *Union*, writing travel sketches, and, when he returned, the paper wanted him to do the same thing on a round the world tour. Instead, Clemens went to New York and joined a group traveling to the Mediterranean and Palestine. This tour and the resulting travel sketches, titled in book form *In-*

nocents Abroad (1869), established him as a writer and permitted him to meet and eventually to marry Olivia Langdon, daughter of a wealthy family. The marriage occurred in 1870; it was both an advantageous and a disastrous union, depending on how it is viewed. Olivia, according to many of Clemens' biographers, was a woman singularly without talent but surfeit with all the prejudices and conceits of her class. While she was alive, she encouraged Clemens to write—he was very lazy, as he made abundantly clear in *Roughing It* (1872), and without such prodding might not have written much at all; she also edited all that he wrote, making it consistent in values and outlook with the beliefs of her class. For this reason, the unexpurgated versions of many Mark Twain works had to wait for years after her death, and Clemens' death, to see the light of print; and this has brought about the situation that Mark Twain is as much loved and read today for what he did not publish when alive, as he was once admired for what he did publish.

In 1871 Clemens settled in Hartford, Connecticut, which would remain his home until 1891. In his off-hours he was perpetually at work on some get-rich-quick scheme, a common obsession among Americans at that time (as he would have been the first one to observe) and certainly since; in fact, he lost much of the money his books made in these schemes. A publishing firm with which he was involved—it brought out *The Adventures of Huckleberry Finn* (1884) and Ulysses S. Grant's memoirs and many less successful books—went bankrupt in 1894, leaving Clemens destitute. He decided that he must pay off his huge debts; and even if he might waver on this, Olivia would not. His solution was a triumphant world lecture tour, beginning in 1895.

Following the tour, Clemens lived abroad for several years in a villa in Florence. Olivia died in 1904 and Clemens returned to the States, building a home at Redding, Connecticut, which he called Stormfield. It was here that he lived with his daughter, Clara, and worked desultorily on his autobiography, alternating between bright moments and dismal despair. He died (of angina pectoris) as he believed he would, upon the reappearance of Halley's Comet which also had heralded his birth.

Van Wyck Brooks in *The Ordeal of Mark Twain* (New York: Dutton, 1920) saw Clemens as a victim of New England Puritanism embodied in Olivia and forcing him to repress all the inner rebellion he had had since youth. However, Edward Wagenknecht in the third edition of *Mark Twain: The Man and His Work* (Norman: University of Oklahoma Press, 1967) demonstrated that much of what Brooks claimed was based on erroneous information. Yet the fact remains that Clemens was profoundly frustrated, gloomy, and cynical, aside from his published writing, and hardly the symbol of the free-spirited frontiersman Bernard DeVoto saw in him in his book *Mark Twain's America* (Boston: Houghton Mifflin, 1932). Clemens was ambivalent about the frontier, about frontier freedom and frontier justice. In *Roughing It* he was appalled by the lack of justice and the chaos on the frontier; yet, living in Hartford during the Gilded Age, he would also become restless and, as Huckleberry Finn, pine to head out for the Territory, with its freedom from restriction and its carefree *savoir-faire*.

Lionel Trilling remarked in his book, *The Liberal Imagination* (New York: Viking, 1950), that Clemens, as Henry Adams, Walt Whitman, and William Dean Howells, "spoke of something that had gone out of American life after the Civil War, some simplicity, some innocence, some peace. None of them was under any illusion about the amount of ordinary human wickedness that existed in the old days, and Mark Twain certainly was not. The difference was in the public attitude, in the things that were now accepted and made respectable in the national ideal. It was, they all felt, connected with the new emotions about money." Clemens said it rather succinctly in *Mark Twain in Eruption* (New York: Harper's, 1940) edited by Bernard DeVoto: whereas before "the people had desired money," now they fell "down and worshipped it." The new American way of life was, "Get money. Get it quickly. Get it in abundance. Get it in prodigious abundance. Get it dishonestly if you can, honestly if you must."

It was this growing distrust of monopolistic business practices and the greed and obsession with money true of the Anglo-American on the frontier after the Civil War that was pilloried in Clemens' work and which also came, to an extent, to preoccupy Western fiction in general. Moreover, the spirit of independence represented by the way Clemens chose to end *The Adventures of Huckleberry Finn* when contrasted with Charles Dickens' conclusion of *Oliver Twist* (1837–1839) almost perfectly articulated the spiritual meaning of the American frontier—if not its physical, historical, and economic reality—in the last century and in this one.

Mark Twain left behind more than his humor; there was also his wisdom. "We all do no end of feeling," he once said, "and we mistake it for thinking. And out of it we get an aggregation which we consider a boon. Its name is Public Opinion. It is held in reverence. It settles everything. Some think it the Voice of God."

Films based on Samuel Clemens' work with a frontier setting are *Tom Sawyer* (Paramount, 1930) directed by John Cromwell, *Huckleberry Finn* (Paramount, 1931) directed by Norman Taurog, *The Adventures of Tom Sawyer* (United Artists, 1938) directed by Norman Taurog, *The Adventures of Huckleberry Finn* (M-G-M, 1939) directed by Richard Thorpe, *The Adventures of Mark Twain* (Warner's, 1944) directed by Irving Rapper, *The Adventures of Huckleberry Finn* (M-G-M, 1960) directed by Michael Curtiz, *Tom Sawyer* (United Artists, 1973) directed by Don Taylor.

Although the premises of the book are questionable, there is still much of interest in Van Wyck Brooks' *The Ordeal of Mark Twain* (New York: Dutton, 1920). Justin Kaplan's Pulitzer Prize winning *Mr. Clemens and Mark Twain* (New York: Simon & Schuster, 1966) has many virtues as biography and as a literary study and its premises are somewhat more sensible than were those of Van Wyck Brooks, but it begins *in media res* with Clemens coming to New York and neglects his early years on the river and in the West. The best overall book on Clemens perhaps remains Edward Wagenknecht's *Mark Twain: The Man and His Work* (Norman: University of Oklahoma Press, 1967) in its third edition while one of the most rewarding literary studies is Henry Nash Smith's *Mark Twain: The Development of a Writer* (Cambridge: Harvard University Press, 1962). For Clemens' relationship with Bret Harte, Margaret Duckett's *Mark Twain & Bret Harte* (Norman: University of Oklahoma Press, 1964) is highly recommended.

Clinton, Jeff. See Bickham, Jack M.

Coburn, Walt(er) (1889–1971) Prolific writer of pulp Western short novels—600,000 words during the 'Thirties and 'Forties—who was billed "The Cowboy Author" by his pulp publishers, born the son of a Montana cattleman at White Sulphur Springs, Montana. Coburn started out with every intention of becoming a cattleman as his father on whose ranch he worked, the Circle C in the Little Rockies of Northeastern Montana. In 1916, when the ranch was sold, Coburn went on to Globe, Arizona, where the Coburn Cattle Company had bought out the remnants of three large cow outfits on the San Carlos Apache Indian Reservation. In 1914 Coburn smashed his right ankle, but it did not prevent him enlisting as a cadet in the U.S. Signal Corps branch of the Air Corps during World War I, where he served for a year-and-a-half. In 1919 he went back to cowboying, only this time he injured his kneecap so badly that he was permanently disabled. He left Arizona and went to San Diego, California, where he had been stationed during the war and where now his widowed mother lived, and went to work first for the military as a civilian employee and then at various odd jobs. Reading a Western pulp story by Robert J. Horton in *Adventure Magazine*, a man he had known when Horton had been a newspaper reporter at Grand Falls, Montana, and recognizing in Horton's story the nucleus of a tale Coburn had once told him, Coburn wrote to Horton and asked how one went about becoming a writer. Horton was very enthusiastic about the idea and set down for Coburn the principles that would become Coburn's working philosophy all his years as a pulp writer: to read Roget's *Thesaurus*, O. Henry (q.v.), Jack London (q.v.), and Joseph Conrad, but not other Western stories; to write out a story and live it as it was written, with no plotting it out beforehand; and *never* to rewrite.

Coburn put Horton's suggestions into action and for the next two years wrote and wrote, earning endless rejection slips and becoming so depressed at times that, once, he even considered submitting to a glandular transplant by a quack doctor for a thousand dollars just to keep going. The persistence paid off. Jack B. Kelly of Fiction House Publications took a liking to Coburn's formulary stories and agreed to feature a Coburn story each month in *Action Stories*, one of Fiction House's pulps, paying Coburn three cents a word. It was Coburn's practice, all his writing life, to write 2,000 words every day, never rewriting, six days a week, with Sundays off, never working more than four or five hours a day but never taking a vacation longer than two or three days after finishing a story. Coburn started appearing in time in all the Fiction House publications and, after Jack Kelly's death in 1932, he branched out and appeared in all the pulp magazines he could, as many as three running one of his stories as a featured selection in a single month.

In 1937 Coburn moved to Tucson, Arizona, where he built a home and continued his writing schedule. When the pulps vanished—about 1950—he turned to writing Western paperback originals, but with marginal success. Most of his stories from the 'Thirties and 'Forties were issued and reissued in new formats, whether as part of *Walt Coburn's Western Magazine* which fluorished briefly during 1949–1950 or as Avon three-in-one reprints. Coburn was among the last people to talk to Tom Mix before Mix's fatal automobile accident on Arizona Highway 555 (as it is now known); but for all the unusual and unique personalities he came across in his lifetime, he could not somehow characterize any of them. Yet he could say of himself, in his last years, "...I have lived a full life and taken my share of hard knocks along with the good fortune that is my writing career. As the late lamented cowboy artist, Charlie Russell (q.v.), who was my good friend and neighbor in Great Falls, Montana, from the time I was six years old, once remarked: 'If I cash in my chips tonight, I'm ahead of the game.' I feel the same way."

Coburn's plots, as Nelson C. Nye's (q.v.), are frequently disappointing because of his insistence on not knowing beforehand where his story was going, but he compensated for this by including plenty of action and violence which were enough to keep the unsophisticated pulp audiences entertained. His inability to characterize anyone in his stories leaves his plots mechanical at best, with too much of the formulary skeleton showing, unlike Luke Short (q.v.) and the early Ernest Haycox (q.v.) who could so cleverly disguise a formulary plot that an intelligent and discerning reader, including Ernest Hemingway who liked Haycox, might be intrigued. Coburn could not and did not, which is perhaps why he remained in the pulps, whereas Short and Haycox soon graduated. While his fictional imagination had more substance than, say, Bradford Scott's (q.v.), his plots were as contrived as Scott's, and his heroes almost as colorless. Coburn accepted the racial stereotypes of the pulps and in a story as "Renegade Legions," appearing in *An Avon Triple Western* (New York: Avon, 1965), the only acceptable Mexicans are those who turn out to be actually white at the end. He did share one fine attribute with subsequent authors such as Gordon D. Shirreffs (q.v.) and Louis L'Amour (q.v.) in that his villains are not villainous for the sake of villainy, but basically economic exploiters, very similar to the land speculators and crooked bankers and politicians which populate the novels and stories of Eugene Manlove Rhodes (q.v.). Nor is this too surprising when it is recalled that Coburn became friends with Rhodes once Rhodes moved near La Jolla, California, in the late 'Twenties. Rhodes was one Western author Coburn *did* read.

Coburn wrote some 900 novelettes for 37 different pulp magazines in his lifetime, most of which are obscure and many of which have probably been lost. His Western novels are *The Ringtailed Rannyhans* (1927), *Mavericks* (1929), *Barb Wire* (1931), *Law Rides the Range* (1935), *Skypilot Cowboy* (1937), *Pardners of the Dim Trails* (1951), *The Way of a Texan* (1953), *Drift Fence* (1953), *The Burnt Ranch* (1954), *Gun Grudge* (1955), *Wet Cattle* (1956), *The Square Shooter* (1956), *Cayuse* (1956), *Beyond the Wide Missouri* (1956), *One Step Ahead of the Posse* (1956), *The Night Branders* (1956), *Violent Maverick* (1957), *Stirrup High* (1957), *Fear Branded* (1957), *Buffalo Run* (1959), *Free Rangers* (1959), *Border Jumper* (1959), *Invitation to a Hanging* (1959), *La Jornada* (1960), *Feud Valley* (1960), *Guns Blaze on Spiderweb Range* (1961).

Films based on Walt Coburn's Western fiction are *Fighting Fury* (Universal, 1924) directed by Clifford S. Smith [based on the pulp story "Triple Cross for Danger"], *Between Dangers* (Pathé, 1927) directed by Richard Thorpe [based on the pulp story "Ride 'Im Cowboy"], *The Desert of the Lost* (Pathé, 1927) directed by Richard Thorpe [based on the pulp story "The Sur-

vival of Slim"], *The Fightin' Comeback* (Pathé, 1927) directed by Tenny Wright [based on the pulp story "The Sun Dance Kid"], *Silent Men* (Columbia, 1933) directed by D. Ross Lederman [source unknown], *Rusty Rides Alone* (Columbia, 1933) directed by D. Ross Lederman [source unknown], *The Westerner* (Columbia, 1934) directed by David Selman [source unknown], *Return of Wild Bill* (Columbia, 1940) directed by Joseph H. Lewis [source unknown].

Cole, Jackson. See Scott, A. Leslie.

Colt, Clem. See Nye, Nelson.

Comfort, Will Levington (1878–1932) Principally known as an author of popular fiction and a journalist who achieved a remarkable novel in *Apache* (New York: Dutton, 1931) born at Kalamazoo, Michigan. Comfort grew up in Detroit and, reaching his maturity, went to work as a reporter for the *Detroit Journal*. In time he became a war correspondent and much of his fiction used as a background war and European colonialism as well as Oriental mysticism. Comfort finally moved to Los Angeles with his family and it was there that he wrote *Apache*, his last book. It is the fictionalized biography of Dasoda-hae, He That Is Just Sitting There, known to the white invaders as Mangas Coloradas. The novel depicts Dasoda-hae's education as a Membreño Apache warrior, his assumption of the leadership of his tribe, and his role in fighting for Indian survival in the Southwest. J. Frank Dobie (q.v.) in his *Guide to Life and Literature of the Southwest* (Dallas: South-

ern Methodist University Press, 1942) commented that "*Apache* remains for me the most moving and incisive piece of writing on Indians of the Southwest that I have found." His opinion is shared by Lawrence Clark Powell in *Southwest Classics* (Los Angeles: Ward Ritchie, 1974) and was also voiced by Oliver La Farge (q.v.) who commented on Comfort: "He has created for us the real Indian, his absurdity and his greatness, in a manner that few scientists and no other writers have achieved. Mr. Comfort knows his sources. The story is inherently a moving one, and tragic, as the history of the Indian must be. The story moves rapidly, with plenty of action and rich material. There are also passages of brilliant writing. The book is true and strong, an extraordinarily penetrating analysis of a real Indian."

D.K.-M.

Cook, Will (iam Everett) (1922–1964)
An author of formulary Western fiction, born at Richmond, Indiana. Cook ran away from home at 16 to join the Cavalry in Texas, falsifying his age. When he discovered that the Cavalry was becoming mechanized and horses being eliminated, he transferred into the Air Force. While serving in the South Pacific during World War II, Cook's leg was nearly shot off, but he was able to return to active duty in Alaska before the end of the war. He remained in Alaska for a time, working as a bush pilot. Upon his return to the continental United States, Cook pursued a number of occupations in the West, where he naturally gravitated, such as deep sea diver, salvage worker, judo instructor, and even deputy sheriff in Lake County in Northern California. When he decided to turn to writing, in 1951, instead of doing a definitive book on judo, which had been his ambition, his wife, Thea, convinced him to try Western fiction and he found the Western pulp magazines a ready market for his work.

In 1954 his first two novels were published, the vanguard of more than fifty under his own name and pseudonyms Wade Everett, James Keene, and Frank Peace. Some of his early novels appeared first in abbreviated form in the pulp magazines, one or two of them under the pseudonym Dan Riordan—the Riordan byline, however, seems to have been confined to magazine work; there is no record of a book under this name. Ten books were published first as hardcovers, five of them under the byline James Keene; the rest of Cook's novels appeared only as paperbacks in the United States and are, consequently, difficult to find. About a dozen titles were reprinted in hardcover form in England, but these editions are equally fugitive.

In 1964, while building a schooner in which Cook hoped with his wife to sail around the world, he succumbed to a fatal heart attack. The Everett byline had become sufficiently valuable by this time that Ballantine turned the name into a house name and Wade Everett novels began to appear written by others, such as *The Whiskey Traders* (New York: Ballantine, 1968) written by Giles A. Lutz (q.v.).

Along with his steady productivity, Cook maintained an enviable level of quality. His books range widely in time and place, from the Illinois frontier in 1811 to Southwest Texas in 1905, but each is peopled with credible and interesting characters whose interactions form the backbone of the narrative. Most of the books deal with more or less traditional Western themes—range wars, reformed outlaws, cattle rustling, Indian fighting—but there are also romantic novels such as *Sabrina Kane* (New York: Dodd, Mead, 1956) and exercises in historical realism such as *Elizabeth, By Name* (New York: Dodd, Mead, 1958).

Many of Cook's novels deal with the U.S. Cavalry and its encounters with various Indian tribes. These range from the sheer adventure and intrigue of *Trumpets to the West* (New York: Popular Library, 1956) to more thoughtful treatments such as *The Peacemakers* (New York: Bantam, 1961) and are among the best of their kind. Of particular interest are three related books: *Comanche Captives* (New York: Bantam, 1960) [alternate title: *Two Rode Together*], *The Peacemakers*, and *The Outcasts* (New York: Bantam, 1965). One of these deals, in order, with the rescue of captives from the Indians, one concerns attempts to establish peace with the Kiowa/Commanche coalition headed by Chief Quanah Parker, and the last deals with the dual problems of corrupt administration of Indian reservations and the reintegration of Indian captives into an often hostile white society. The books are tied together both thematically and by the presence of continuing characters such as Lieutenant (later Major) Jim Gary and Texas Ranger Guthrie McCabe. McCabe also appears in *The Tough Texan* (New York: Bantam, 1963), the story of a Ranger campaign against Mexican border bandits.

Other superior specimens of Cook's Western fiction are *The Wind River Kid* (New York: Fawcett, 1958) and *The Wranglers* (New York: Fawcett, 1960). *Kid* takes place in the Northwest logging country, in the small town of Rindo's Springs. In order to show his contempt for the current sheriff, the town's patriarch, Cadmus Rindo, picks a nameless drunk out of the jail and has him elected as the new sheriff. The drunk turns out to be a fugitive gunman named the Wind River Kid and everyone is in for a shock when he begins taking the sheriff's job seriously. In spite of the artificiality of the premise, the character of the Kid and of various townspeople are well drawn and believable. The title characters of *The Wranglers* are an almost-over-the-hill horse breaker and his brash young partner who decide to strike out on their own in the monument country of Southern Utah. Their struggles against weather, Indians, and rival horse-hunters go hand-in-hand with attempts to come to terms with their own insecurities and make a well-wrought tale, low-key but memorable.

A common feature of these two novels, and indeed of all of Cook's work, is his compassion for his characters. Although strong and competent, as they must be to survive in a wild and violent land, his heroes make mistakes, hurt people they care for, sometimes succumb to ignoble impulses. Cook did not overemphasize these frailties, but used them to add an extra dimension of believability to his work. Along with the books under his own name, Cook for some years produced at least one book each year under the pseudonym James Keene. In 1959 he adopted the pen-name Wade Everett for a series of novels for Ballantine Books. *First Command* (New York: Ballantine, 1959), *Temporary Duty* (New York: Ballantine, 1961), and others in this group are Cavalry stories with most of the same virtues as those under Cook's own name. The title character of *Last Scout* (New York: Ballantine, 1960) is an unregenerate hell-raiser named Wind-River Page who comes to Deadwood to live with his daughter's family. The old man resents being put out to pasture and rebels by helping his teen-aged grandson uncover the culprit in a series of gold robberies. Thanks to Ballantine's skilful promotion and their habit of periodically re-issuing books in matched sets, the Wade Everett books probably received a wider audience than those published under Cook's own name.

R.E.B.

Will Cook's Western novels under his own name are *Frontier Feud* (1954), *Prairie Guns* (1954), *Fury at Painted Rock* (1955), *Apache Ambush* (1955), *Bullet Range* (1955), *Sabrina Kane* (1956), *The Fighting Texan* (1956), *Trumpets to the West* (1956), *Lone Hand from Texas* (1957), *Badman's Holiday* (1958), *Elizabeth, By Name: Story of a Pioneer Woman* (1958), *Guns of North Texas* (1958), *The Wind River Kid* (1958), *Outcast of Cripple Creek* (1959), *We Burn Like Fire* (1959), *The Wranglers* (1960), *Comanche Captives* (1960) [alternate title: *Two Rode Together*], *Killer Behind a Badge* (1960), *The Peacemakers* (1961), *Ambush at Antlers Spring* (1962), *The Breakthrough* (1963), *The Tough Texan* (1963), *Last Command* (1964), *The Outcasts* (1965), *The Apache Fighter* (1967), *The Drifter* (1969), *Bandit's Trail* (1974).

Cook's novels as Wade Everett are *First Command* (1959), *Fort Starke* (1959), *Last Scout* (1960), *Big Man, Big Mountain* (1961), *Temporary Duty* (1961), *The Crossing* (1961), *The Big Drive* (1961), *Killer* (1962), *Shotgun Marshal* (1964), *Texas Ranger* (1964), *Top Hand* (1964), *Cavalry Recruit* (1964), *Bullets for the Doctor* (1964), *Vengeance* (1966), *Texas Yankee* (1966), *The Warrier* (1966).

Cook's novels as James Keene are the *The Texas Pistol* (1955), *The Brass and the Blue* (1956), *Justice, My Brother! A Novel of Oklahoma in the Early Nineteen Hundreds* (1957), *Seven for Vengeance* (1958), *McCracken in Command* (1959), *Iron Man, Iron Horse* (1960), *Sixgun Wild* (1960), *Gunnison's Empire* (1963), *Gunman's Harvest* (1963).

Cook's novels as Frank Peace are *Easy Money* (1955) and *The Brass Brigade* (1956).

The only film based on Will Cook's Western fiction is *Two Rode Together* (Columbia, 1961) directed by John Ford.

Coolidge, Dane (1873–1940) Author of Western fiction and non-fiction born at South Natick, Massachusetts. Coolidge spent his early life on his father's orange ranch at Riverside, California, or hunting and trapping in the mountains. He became a naturalist already in his youth. Entering Stanford University, Coolidge graduated in 1898 and went on to do graduate work at Harvard in 1898–1899. He worked in his summers as a field collector of animals for various institutions and in 1900 was a field collector in France and Italy for the U.S. National Museum. Returning to the American West, he became a wild-life photographer, specializing in desert animals. Thus he worked his way through mining towns, on Indian reservations, and ranches, collecting stories and everywhere making friends

among the Indians. For thirty-five years Coolidge was a director of the San Francisco's Boys' Club. He was married at Berkeley, California, in 1906 to Mary Elizabeth Burroughs Smith.

Coolidge's wife was a member of the California State Board of Education and was a professor of sociology at Mills College, working for years in social and economic research and in behalf of women's rights. Under her own name, Mary Coolidge wrote *Why Women Are So* (New York: Holt, 1912) and also produced a book on the social life, religion, arts, and crafts of the Southwest Indians in *Rain-Makers: Indians of Arizona and New Mexico* (Boston: Houghton Mifflin, 1912).

Dane Coolidge wrote his first Western novel in 1910, titled *Hidden Water* (Chicago: A.C. McClurg, 1910), and proceeded for the next thirty years to produce regularly Western novels of varying quality, vivid characterization, and strong plot values, based in many cases on stories he had heard during his travels. In his non-fiction books, the most notable of which were *Fighting Men of the West* (New York: Dutton, 1932), *Death Valley Prospectors* (New York: Dutton, 1937), and *Texas Cowboys* (New York: Dutton, 1937), Coolidge would frequently supply his own photo illustrations. Mary Coolidge co-wrote with him the non-fiction book *The Navaho Indian* (Boston: Houghton Mifflin, 1930).

Coolidge gave accurate descriptions of his Southwestern locales, ably and fairly characterized his strong and unconventional female characters, and in such novels as *War Paint* (New York: Dutton, 1929) provided a remarkable portrait of a horse to rival earlier efforts by Zane Grey (q.v.) and later ones by such authors as John Steinbeck (q.v.) and Lee Hoffman (q.v.). Unfortunately

Coolidge died before the paperback revolution and so only a few of his books appeared in paperback format, although in 1937 *The New York Times* declared "no man alive today writes better Westerns."

Dane Coolidge's Western novels are *Hidden Water* (1910), *The Texican* (1911), *Bat Wing Bowles* (1914), *The Desert Trail* (1915), *Rimrock Jones* (1917), *The Fighting Fool* (1918), *Shadow Mountain* (1919), *Silver and Gold* (1919), *Wunpost* (1920), *Lost Wagons* (1920), *The Scalp-Lock* (1924), *Under the Sun* (1926), *Gun-Smoke* (1928), *War Paint* (1929), *Horse-Ketchum* (1930), *Sheriff Killer* (1932), *Silver Hat* (1934), *The Fighting Danites* (1934), *Long Rope* (1935), *Wolf's Candle* (1935), *Snake Bit Jones* (1936), *Rawhide Johnny* (1936), *The Trail of Gold* (1937), *Ranger Two-Rifles* (1937), *Hell's Hip Pocket* (1938), *Comanche Chaser* (1938), *Wally Laughs-Easy* (1939), *Gringo Gold* [based on the life of Joaquín Murieta] (1939), *Yaqui Drums* (1940), *Bloody Head* (1940), *Bear Paw* (1941).

Cooper, James (Kent) Fenimore (1789–1851) Adding the Fenimore to his name in 1826 in an unsuccessful attempt to inherit some land, the founder of American frontier fiction was born at Burlington, New Jersey. Cooper's father was a

judge and later a member of the New York state legislature who moved, when his son was but a year old, to the wilderness region of Ostego Lake where he assumed large land holdings which in time came to be known as Cooperstown. From earliest childhood, therefore, Cooper was surrounded by the forests and even some representatives of the Indian nations which would later figure significantly in his fiction. Cooper was educated privately by a clergyman and, in 1802, he entered Yale, only to be expelled two years later because of a prank. After living for two years at Cooperstown, Cooper's father decided that he should go to sea and the youngster signed on as a seaman on a vessel sailing from Maine to England. A year later, upon his return, Cooper received a commission in the U.S. Navy. When, after two years, Cooper's assignment was to assist in establishing a fresh-water navy on the Great Lakes, he chaffed under the tedium, but had no choice in the matter, since he was otherwise without a means of making a living.

When Cooper's father died, Cooper joined with his brothers in dissipating the large estate. He also married a very proper woman who insisted he resign his commission. Together the couple settled down on a farm owned by Cooper's wife and Cooper, other than siring five daughters and two sons, busied himself as a country squire, his only other interest being a part ownership in a whaling vessel. In 1819, reading aloud to his wife from a recently published English romance, Cooper announced that he could write a better book himself. Since he was known to detest writing so much as a letter, Cooper's wife laughed, but Cooper remained obdurate and *Precaution* (1820), published anonymously, was the result.

It proved a turning point. Cooper found he could write with some facility by the standards of that day and he followed with *The Spy* (1821), a sea story, a variety of fiction where he was far more at home and informed than with life in the forests and where he was less prone to indulge his fantasies or to create what would in time become national myths. This was clearly shown when he produced *The Pioneers* (1823). Originally intended to tell the story of his father and Cooperstown, Cooper included among his characters his most memorable literary creation, Natty Bumppo, who would henceforth be variously known by the names given him by the people of the forest, Hawk-eye, Deerslayer, Pathfinder. In *The Pioneers* Bumppo is a man no longer young and is alone save for his friend, the Indian known as John Mohegan, who is a drunk.

Cooper, flushed by his literary success both in the United States and in Europe, left in 1826 to live abroad with his family—which he did for the next seven years. The year he departed he published his most famous novel, *The Last of the Mohicans* (1826), chronologically the second entry in the Leatherstocking saga. Cooper was living in Paris when he published *The Prairie* (1827) which tells of the death of Natty Bumppo. Therefore, chronologically, it is the last book in the saga, if not last in the order of composition.

Returning to the United States in 1833, Cooper found that everything had so changed that he was unable to bring himself at once to write additional historical romances. Although his books were earning him a fortune by the standards of that day— as much as $20,000 a year—he was also heavily in debt due to his penchant for living with the grand gesture. Settling in Cooperstown, he turned to writing history.

However, his *The History of the Navy of the United States of America* (1839) exposed him to so much criticism in the press, all of which he fought (some of it through litigation), that he turned again to frontier fiction, resuming the Leatherstocking saga with *The Pathfinder* (1840). In terms of chronology, this novel comes after the events recorded in *The Last of the Mohicans* but before those in *The Pioneers*. In *The Pathfinder* Natty Bumppo is middle-aged and has his one serious flirtation with love which ends with his rejecting it.

Feeling out of sorts even more than before with the United States of his day and its obsession with raping the wilderness and its overwhelming greed, Cooper moved farther back yet in his saga, concluding it with the book with which, chronologically, it begins, *The Deerslayer* (1841). It was this novel which was Cooper's own personal favorite. While Leatherstocking is as insistent in it as throughout the saga that he is totally without Indian blood, we are told of him that "he had caught the stoicism of the Indians, well knowing there was no more certain mode of securing their respect than by imitating their self-command." This is actually the first book in which Leatherstocking so much as addresses the question of the theft of Indian lands, yet he does this only to the extent of remarking that he is pleased that the white man has kept the Indian names for places " 'for it would be too hard to rob them of both land and name.' "

But Cooper remained ambivalent. In *The Oak Openings* (1848), one of his very last books, he not only decided to write a novel without a romance, but he chose as a hero a man who subdues the Indians and the wilderness, rising to a position of influence within his community and finally be-comes a state senator. Probably for this reason Henry Nash Smith concluded about Cooper in *Virgin Land: The American West as Myth and Symbol* (Cambridge: Harvard University Press, 1950) that he "was able to speak for his people on this theme because . . . he felt the problem more deeply than his contemporaries: he was at once more strongly devoted to the principle of social order and more vividly responsive to the ideas of Nature and freedom in the Western forest than they were. His conflict of allegiances was truly ironic, and if he had been able—as he was not—to explore to the end the contradictions in his ideas and emotions, the Leatherstocking series might have become a major work of art." This it did not; this it could not—as written and as filled as it is with contradictions. Cooper died at Cooperstown of sclerosis of the liver. But no matter his faults, he had founded American frontier fiction.

The Last of the Mohicans was in many ways a landmark. First, it established as a literary convention the division of Native Americans into two groups, those who, as Chingachgook and his son Uncas, are the allies of the Anglo-Americans and those who, as Magua, are savages to be identified with Satan. Chingachgook was the embodiment of what the French encyclopedists referred to as a "noble savage," but with a characteristic American twist. Land cannot be acceptably stolen from noble savages, so the savagery had to be emphasized more than the nobility and Cooper's Mohicans do not own any land! Cooper played upon the terror inspired by his forest savages and made it seem both by divine decree and by human justice inevitable that the white man should take the Indians' lands in exchange for giving them the "blessings" of Christianity with its white god, along with several things Cooper did not mention ever, such as venereal disease, enforced removal, and extermination.

The Last of the Mohicans is a romance, an American version of the kind of fiction Sir Walter Scott was writing in England about medieval times. There was no accuracy in it, nor any effort to be accurate. That was not Cooper's purpose, nor was it what his readers wanted. Mark Twain (q.v.) in his satirical essay "Fenimore Cooper's Literary Offences" cited *The Last of the Mohicans* and commented that when Hawk-eye, Chingachgook, Uncas, and company are searching for the Munro sisters the "trail is hopelessly lost." Calling Chingachgook by Chicago for short, Twain remarked "neither you nor I could ever have guessed out the way to find it. It was very different with Chicago. Chicago was not stumped for long. He turned a running stream out of its course, and there, in the slush in its old bed, were that person's moccasin tracks. The current did not wash them away, as it would have done in all other like cases—no, even the eternal laws of Nature have to vacate when Cooper wants to put up a delicate job of woodcraft on the reader." Nor is the aptness of this criticism lessened by the fact that in Cooper's novel it is Uncas, and not his father, Chingachgook, who diverts the water and is the first to see the footprints on the stream's bottom.

Cooper took numerous pains to fit his Indian savages into popular Christian mythology. When an Indian yells, "his cry was answered by a yell and a laugh from the woods, as tauntingly exulting as if fifty demons were uttering their blasphemies at the fall of some Christian soul." Even excusing his racial bias, Cooper personally knew nothing of Native American tribal history and he became hopelessly confused in *The Last of the Mohicans* and treated as interchangeable Maquas, Hurons, Iroquois, indeed the five nations of the Iroquois Confederacy; he could see none of their civilization nor the fact that the American form of government was derived from their articles of confederation. All he could say, at his most benevolent, was that "in a short time there will be no remains of these extraordinary people." And it was this book and the subsequent novels in the saga that white men were reading in Kentucky when all Native Americans in that state were banished to the Plains by President Andrew Jackson and given blankets infected with smallpox to accompany them on their journey; it was these books that were "in the air" when the pioneers pushed forth to those very Plains and set about duplicating in the West what had already been accomplished in the East: making the Native American *vanish*.

"It is hard—and a little discomforting—for critics," Leslie Fielder wrote in *Love and Death in the American Novel* (New York: Stein and Day, 1960), "to remember that the novel may function on the level of myth as well as that of literature." He went on to point out: "It no longer really matters whether one has actually read Cooper's books or not; he is possessed by them all the same, and just as [Alexandre] Dumas in Nineteenth-century France could call a work *Les Mohicans de Paris*, Bernard Malamud in Twentieth-century America can entitle a story 'The Last Mohican.' Neither has to doubt that he will be understood, for the title of Cooper's romance has become a part of the common symbolic language of the Western world."

The Munro daughters in *The Last of the Mohicans* established another venerable—or perhaps, in retrospect, not so venerable—stereotype. The one, the elder, Cora Munro, the dark hair, with her dusky complexion come of Negro blood in her heritage is passionate and vibrant; both Uncas, among the noble savages, and Magua, among the infernal savages, covets her; but neither can possess her because Cooper himself had a horror of miscegenation. For Uncas and Cora, it could only end one way, given this ingredient: they are united in death. It is the other, the younger, Alice Munro, the yellow hair, with her light complexion and trembling ways who is considered fit for life and a legitimate marriage to Major Duncan Heyward, the American Colonial in service to the Royal Army. The image of Alice Munro would persist in American literature, and by extension in Western fiction, for nearly a century and a half, "the girl" who needs saving and male protection in literally thousands of melodramas, adventure stories, and ranch romances.

D. H. Lawrence called Natty Bumppo "a saint with a gun," and so it was that at the very advent of American literature and frontier fiction the hero was cast in the mold of a man who resolves human predicaments through the violent use of firearms, as in *The Last of the Mohicans* when Hawk-eye shoots and kills Magua.

Certainly Natty Bumppo became a prototypical hero throughout the Nineteenth century in American fiction. Timothy Flint (q.v.) based his characterization of Daniel Boone on Bumppo in his largely fictional *The Life and Adventures of Daniel Boone, The First Settler of Kentucky, Interspersed with Incidents in the Early Annals of the Country* (1833). In *Virgin Land* Henry Nash Smith demonstrated how it was not until the subversive overtones of the Natty Bumppo frontiersman were smoothed over that a frontier figure could be made the hero of a

Western romance, as in the image of Kit Carson (see Historical Personalities) set forth in the anonymous account of Carson contained in James Madison Cutts' *The Conquest of California and New Mexico* (1847). Daryl Jones in *The Dime Western Novel* (Bowling Green: The Popular Press, 1978) traced the evolution of the Natty Bumppo character in the heroes of several Nineteenth-century dime novels.

Films based on James Fenimore Cooper's Leatherstocking Saga are *The Last of the Mohicans* (Associated Exhibitors, 1920) directed by Maurice Tourneur, remade under this title (Mascot, 1932) directed by B. Reeves Eason and Ford Beebe [a twelve chapter serial], (United Artists, 1936) directed by George B. Seitz, and under the title *Last of the Red Men* (Columbia, 1947) directed by George Sherman. *The Pioneers* (Monogram, 1941) was directed by Al Herman. *Deerslayer* (Republic, 1943) was directed by Lew Landers, remade under this title (20th-Fox, 1957) directed by Kurt Newman.

In addition to these films, the following films were influenced by Cooper's characters if not his stories. *Leatherstocking* (Biograph, 1909) was directed by D. W. Griffith, while in 1911 at least two one-reel films were produced under the title *The Last of the Mohicans*, one produced by Pat Powers, the other by Thanhouser. *Lederstrumpf* [*Leatherstocking*] (German, 1920) was directed by Arthur Wellin and released in two parts, *Der Wildtoter* [*The Deerslayer*] and *Der Letze Der Mohikaner* [*The Last of the Mohicans*]. This film was edited from twelve reels to five for its American release in 1921 under the title *The Deerslayer*. *Leatherstocking* (Pathé, 1924) was directed by George B. Seitz although it depended for most of its story on the plot to *The Deer-*

slayer [a ten chapter serial]. *Der Letze Mohikaner* (German-Italian-Spanish, 1965) directed by Harold Reinl had an American release under the title *The Last Tomahawk*. *The Deerslayer* (Vitagraph, 1913) bore at least a titular relationship to a Cooper novel if nothing else.

In 1956 a syndicated television series was aired in Canada titled *Hawkeye and the Last of the Mohicans*. In 1962 this series, directed by Sam Newfield, was edited into four features which were released to American television: *Along the Mohawk Trail*, *The Redmen and the Renegades*, *The Long Rifle and the Tomahawk* which was co-directed by Sidney Salkow, and *The Pathfinder and the Mohican*.

Among the better books on James Fenimore Cooper are *Pages and Pictures from the Writings of James Fenimore Cooper* (1861) by Susan Augusta Fenimore Cooper, Cooper's daughter who prepared this volume in lieu of an authorized biography which Cooper himself forbad, *James Fenimore Cooper* (New York: Sloane, 1949) by James Grossman later published in a new edition by Stanford University Press, and *James Fenimore Cooper* (New York: Twayne Publishers, 1962) by Donald A. Ringe.

Corle, Edwin (1906–1956) Biographer, short story writer, and author of fiction and non-fiction dealing with the Southwest born at Wildwood, New Jersey. Educated in public schools in Wildwood and, later, in Philadelphia, Pennsylvania, Corle (pronounced KORL) moved with his parents to

Southern California when he was 17 and completed high school in Hollywood. He attended the University of California at Los Angeles majoring in English and received his Bachelor's degree in 1928. Then he attended Yale University as a graduate student. While at Yale, he specialized in drama, studying playwriting. This assisted him, once he returned to California, to acquire jobs writing radio scripts and working in the writing departments of M-G-M and RKO. By 1932, with the publication of his first short story, "Amethyst," set in the Mojave desert, published in the *Atlantic Monthly*, Corle retired from other kinds of writing to devote himself exclusively to his literary career. Corle traveled to Europe and Mexico in the 'Thirties, his trips financed in part by a Guggenheim fellowship. In 1944 he married Jean Armstrong and they had one child, a daughter. They made their home in Santa Barbara.

Corle's collection of short stories, *Mojave* (New York: Liveright, 1934), was followed by his first novel, *Fig Tree John* (New York: Liveright, 1935). It is one of his best novels, telling of the White River Apache, Red Fire Bird or Fig Tree John, who travels from Arizona to see the Salton Sea and settles in California to raise his son. The novel exemplifies Corle's clear, terse writing style, his apt dialogue, his intimate knowledge of the country and the situation of the Native American people, and his ability to create interesting, vital characters, especially in the portrayal of Fig Tree John himself and Maria, the Chicano girl who marries Fig Tree John's son. Corle went on to write a variety of novels, *People of the Earth* (New York: Random House, 1937), *Burro Alley* (New York: Random House, 1938), and *Coarse Gold* (New York: Dutton 1942) among the better of them. His *Billy the Kid* (New York: Duell, Sloan, 1953) is certainly one of the most profoundly inaccurate accounts ever written of the Kid's life. Corle also wrote a number of historical books, perhaps the most outstanding being *Desert Country* (New York: Duell, Sloan, 1941) and *The Gila: River of the Southwest* (Lincoln: University of Nebraska Press, 1951).

D.K.-M.

Cox, William R(obert) (1901—)

An author known for formulary Western fiction, born at Peapack, New Jersey. Cox was educated in the Newark public school system and attended the Rutgers Extension. He also tutored English at Princeton and worked in the editorial department of the old *New York World* before turning to writing for the pulp magazines. It was not until 1940 that, at the instigation of his literary agent, Cox turned to trying his hand at Westerns. He was living at the time in Florida and he proceeded to read countless Western novels and watched as many Western films as he could see in theatres in Tampa and Bradenton. By switching around a crime novelette and giving it a Western setting, Cox sold his first Western story to *Dime Western*, the best pulp outlet of the day. However, he did not begin writing Western novels until the 'Fifties, and his first was *The Lusty Men* (New York: Pyramid, 1956). In time, Cox took over writing the Buchanan series by Jonas Ward (see House Names).

It is interesting to note that some of Cox's best Western novels have not sold as well as his potboilers. *The Outlawed* (New York: Signet, 1960) [retitled *Navaho Blood* in 1971] deals movingly with a full-blooded Navaho raised by white parents who falls in love with his foster sister and the non-fiction book, *Luke Short and His Era* (New York: Doubleday, 1958), is about the life of the historical gunman and card sharp whose name Frederick Glidden (q.v.) adopted as a pen-name; as biography it is particularly well-written. *Comanche Moon* (New York: McGraw-Hill, 1958) may well stand as the best Western novel Cox wrote.

William R. Cox's Western novels (with the exception of his Buchanan entries to be found under House Names) are *The Lusty Men* (1956), *Comanche Moon* (1958), *The Duke* (1959), *The Outlawed* (1960) [alternate title: *Navaho Blood*], *Bigger Than Texas* (1962), *Big Man from Brazos* (1962), *The Tall Texan* (1965), *The Gunsharp* (1965), *Black Silver* (1966), *Firecreek* (1967) [adapted from a screenplay by Calvin Clements released with that title by Warner's, 1967], *Law Comes to Razor Edge* (1967), *Day of the Gun* (1968), *Moon of Cobre* (1969), *The Sixth Horseman* (1971), *Jack O' Diamonds* (1972).

Crane, Stephen (1871–1900)

Novelist, journalist, and author of many Western sketches and stories, born at Newark, New

Jersey. Crane was the fourteenth child of a Methodist minister and, already as a youth, he shocked his family by rejecting their religion. Despite physical frailty, Crane liked swimming and baseball. He attended Lafayette College (1889–1890) and distinguished himself playing baseball for the varsity team at Syracuse University (1890–1891).

Crane was, however, an indifferent student. For the next five years, after leaving Syracuse, he made a precarious living as a free-lance writer for newspapers. Fascinated with New York's Bowery, while still at Syracuse, Crane began writing his first novel, *Maggie: A Girl of the Streets*, which he published at his own expense in 1893. *The Red Badge of Courage* (1895) was a Civil War novel based on Crane's reading of history and Leo Tolstoy as well as interviews with veterans, since Crane had never witnessed a war.

As early as August, 1892, Crane had proposed to the American Press Association that he submit sketches while taking a trip into the Far West. Once the Bacheller syndicate bought *The Red Badge* for newspaper syndication, Irving Bacheller agreed to finance such a trip, and early in 1895 Crane began a journey which took him through Nebraska, to the Southwest, and to Mexico.

"...What I contend for is the atmosphere of the West," Crane wrote back East in a letter, "which really is frank and honest and is bound to make eleven honest men for one pessimistic thief. More glory be with them." His first published Western story was "Horses—One Dash!" in 1895. Over the next three years, Crane continued to write Western stories, the best known among them as "The Five White Mice," set in Mexico City, and "The Bride Comes to Yellow Sky" being included in his collection *The Open Boat and Other Stories* (1898). One of Crane's finest short stories about an American cowboy ambushed and killed by a gang of Mexican bandits, "A Man and Some Others" (1897), elicited comments from Theodore Roosevelt (q.v.).

Because of the popularity of *The Red Badge*, Crane soon found himself in demand as a war correspondent. He was sent to Cuba to cover a rebellion and was shipwrecked off the coast of Florida in 1896. A stint covering the Spanish–American War aggravated his tuberculosis and, in May, 1900, Crane died in the Black Forest in Germany.

Frequently mistaken by critics of his time as a realist, Crane was actually an impressionist whose intention was "to write plainly and unmistakably . . .in the simplest and most concise way." He once remarked to an aspiring author, "Forget what you think about it and tell how you feel about it." Dreams, according to Crane, were the well-springs of his imagery and in his poetry he made ample use of them.

Crane's exceptional Western short novel, *The Blue Hotel*, was first included in his collection *The Monster and Other Stories* (1899). It introduced objective style into the Western story even more than Crane's previous stories of human confrontation with death and rivaled Bret Harte's (q.v.) stories in local color. It was vital to Crane's point of view that individual violence could often be, in the words of this story, "the apex of a human movement," a notion such later Western writers as Ernest Haycox (q.v.) in *Sundown Jim* (Boston: Little, Brown, 1937) would explore more fully. For this reason, Crane preferred surfaces to interiors in dealing with his characters. His long-term influence on Western writers as Walter Van Tilburg Clark (q.v.) and Jack Schaefer (q.v.)

was pronounced and they came to see him as one of the foremost literary experimentalists in the genre. It was only after Crane had reached Mexico City in his Western travels that his pessimism about life was condensed into the conviction that it was "the man who has not yet solved himself" who has not "discovered his own futility."

Fortunately the essential Western writings of Stephen Crane, along with sketches and letters, are collected in a single book, *The Western Writings of Stephen Crane* (New York: Signet Classics, 1979) edited by Frank Bergon. The best overall collection of Crane's fiction is *The Portable Stephen Crane* (New York: Viking, 1969) edited by Joseph Katz.

"The Bride Comes to Yellow Sky" was adapted for the screen as half of the two-part film, *Face to Face* (RKO, 1952) directed by Bretaigne Windust.

Crane biography is inadequate, the effort of Robert W. Stallman, *Stephen Crane* (New York: Braziller, 1968), being less than reliable. For critical studies of Crane's work, see *Stephen Crane* (New York: Twayne Publishers, 1962) by Edwin H. Cady and *Stephen Crane: From Parody to Realism* (Cambridge: Harvard University Press, 1966) by Eric Solomon.

Croy, Homer (1883–1965) An author known for his novels about American farm life, born on a farm at Maryville, Missouri, not far from the birthplace of Jesse and Frank James (see Historical Personalities).

Croy walked six miles to a country school. He paid his way through the University of Missouri by writing for local newspapers. According to Croy, he did not graduate because he failed English. However he was admitted to the University's school of journalism, the first student in one of the first journalism departments in the United States. He left school and found that Missouri managing editors were suspicious of a reporter with too much education. He could not get a job so he moved to New York where he began writing stories and articles for American novelist Theodore Dreiser who was editing three women's magazines. Once Croy published his first novel, *Boone Stop* (New York: Harper's, 1918), he found his situation vastly improved. Soon his books were noticed by Hollywood where *They Had to See Paris* (New York: Harper's, 1926) became Will Rogers' first talking picture, released by Fox in 1929.

Croy is credited with having written the first Western novel with powerful sexual overtones in *West of the Water Tower* (New York: Harper's, 1923). It was published anonymously and enjoyed a brisk trade sale. It was this fact which inspired the same publisher to issue Dorothy Scarborough's (q.v.) *The Wind* (New York: Harper's, 1925), which also deals with a controversial theme, in an anonymous edition. Croy's tales of country living and rural folks quickly established him as a popular author, in the vein of Ruth Suckow (q.v.) and others. Among his country novels are *Caught* (New York: Harper's, 1928), *Sixteen Hands* (New York: Harper's, 1938), *Family Honeymoon* (New York: Harper's, 1942), *Wonderful Neighbor* (New York: Harper's, 1945), *Corn Country* (New York: Duell, Sloan, 1947), and *What Grampa Laughed At* (New York: Duell, Sloan, 1948). *Country*

Cured (New York: Harper's, 1943) was Croy's autobiography.

In 1949 Croy began his series of Western biographies. *Jesse James Was My Neighbor* (New York: Duell, Sloan, 1949) did much to further the legend of the James gang, forgiving many of their crimes. Croy added a lengthy subtitle to the second of his Western biographies, *He Hanged Them High: A True Account of the Life and Deeds of Issac C. Parker, Sole Judge Over Western Arkansas and the Indian Territory in the Days of the Great Frontier* (New York: Duell, Sloan, 1952). Parker was a record setter. In 21 years, he sentenced 172 men to the gallows, 88 of whom were actually hanged in front of crowds up to 6,000 persons.

The last and, in many ways, most fascinating of Croy's biographies was *Last of the Great Outlaws* (New York: Duell, Sloan, 1958), a study of Cole Younger, one of the few outlaws who grew old enough to die in bed. Croy shrugged off Younger's misdeeds with an even more forgiving attitude than he had shown toward Jesse James. Younger was, according to Croy, "just the average man caught in a melon patch."

Croy was a straight-forward chronicler of the Western character and he preferred writing about legends or creating them, although *Our Will Rogers* (New York: Duell, Sloan, 1953) was something of an exception. *Wheels West: An Attempt to Simplify the Donner Story Told Through the Eyes of James Frazier Reed* (New York: Hastings House, 1955), *Trigger Marshal: The Story of Chris Madsen* (New York: Duell, Sloan, 1958), and *The Trial of Mrs. Abraham Lincoln* (New York: Duell, Sloan, 1962) are all written in the folksy mood of the earlier Western biographical triptych.

D.W.

Films based on Homer Croy's Western fiction are *West of the Water Tower* (Paramount, 1924) directed by Rollin Sturgeon and *I Shot Jesse James* (Lippert, 1949) directed by Sam Fuller [based on *Jesse James Was My Neighbor*].

Cullum, Ridgwell (1867–1943) A

British novelist, some of whose books are Western fiction, born at London, England. At 17, Cullum left England and embarked on twenty years of wandering to exotic places. He joined a gold rush in the Transvaal region of Africa and, after a few years, worked in the diamond mines of Kimberly in the Cape of Good Hope province. Furhunting and trading in the Far Northwest brought him to the Yukon, as, earlier, gold had lured Jack London (q.v.), and he nearly starved to death. Cullum then moved South, settling in Montana where he devoted himself to large-scale cattle ranching. He participated in the Sioux uprisings on the Pine Ridge and Rosebud reservations, although it is vague exactly what role he played. He may also have returned to Africa before settling finally in England in 1904. He had started writing; his second novel, *The Hound from the North* (London: Chapman, Hall, 1904), with a Northwestern setting, having had sufficient success that he decided to become a professional novelist. Cullum was almost alone in the field when he began writing his series of Canadian Northwestern novels and his knowledge of the terrain was heightened by his prospecting and cattle-raising experiences. Occasionally he would venture South in his fiction as he once had in his life, writing a Western as *Twins of Suffering Creek* (Philadelphia: Lippincott, 1912); and in the decade before World War I he readily held his own against the ascendant Zane Grey (q.v.) and another Englishman, William MacLeod Raine (q.v.). He continued writing, although not prolifically, through the middle decades, publishing his last book in 1938. His tales always moved and he had a gift for plotting although, in time, his work was widely imitated and somewhat obscured by James Oliver Curwood (q.v.) and James B. Hendryx (q.v.).

Ridgwell Cullum's Western and Northwestern novels are *The Story of the Foss River Ranch* (1903), *The Hound from the North* (1904), *In the Brooding Wild* (1905), *The Sheriff of Dyke Hole* (1909), *The Watchers of the Plains* (1909), *The Trail of the Axe* (1910), *The Night Riders* (1911),*The One Way Trail* (1911), *Twins of Suffering Creek* (1912), *The Golden Woman* (1913), *The Way of the Strong* (1914), *The Law-Breakers* (1914), *The Son of His Father* (1915), *The Men Who Wrought* (1916), *The Triumph of John Kars* (1917), *The Forfeit* (1917) [alternate title: *The Purchase Price*], *The Law of the Gun* (1918), *The Heart of Unaga* (1920), *The Man in the Twilight* (1922), *The Luck of the Kid* (1923), *The Riddle of Three-Way Creek* (1925), *The Child of the North* (1926), *The Candy Man* (1926), *Wolf Pack* (1927), *The Mystery of the Barren Lands* (1928), *The Tiger of Cloud River* (1929), *The Treasure of Big Waters* (1930), *Bull Moose* (1931), *The Flaming Wilderness* (1934), *The Vampire of N'Gobi* (1936), *One Who Kills* (1938).

Films based on Ridgwell Cullum's Western fiction are *The Yosemite Trail* (Fox, 1922) directed by Bernard J. Durning [based on *The One Way Trail*], *The Man Who Won* (Fox, 1923) directed by William Wellman [based on *The Twins of Suffering Creek*].

Culp, John H(ewett Jr.) (1907—)

Author of a remarkable group of books of frontier fiction, born at Meridian, Mississippi. Culp grew up in Fort Smith, on the Arkansas-Oklahoma border. In his youth he worked on ranches in Texas and Oklahoma, covering on horseback or on foot much of the territory that would later form the settings for his novels. He graduated from the University of Oklahoma in 1934 and spent the next seven years as a teacher in the Norman, Oklahoma, public schools. He served in the Army Air Corps during World War II and then, for more than twenty years, owned and operated a music store in Shawnee, Oklahoma. He began writing in the late 'Fifties.

His first novel was *Born of the Sun* (New York: Sloan, 1959), the tale of an epic trail drive from Texas to Abilene, Kansas, led by a young boy and a crew of wild Texas cowhands. The story was continued in a sequel, *The Restless Land* (New York: Sloan, 1962), again narrated by Martin Cameron, nicknamed the Kid, now 15 years old and the owner of Tail End Ranch. The two books recount the Kid's passage to maturity against the background of post-Civil War Texas.

In *The Bright Feathers* (New York: Holt, Rinehart, 1965) the Five Civilized Tribes and their struggle to adapt to the ways of white society are seen through the eyes of three young cowhands on a journey, comic and adventurous by turns, through the Oklahoma Territory. The history of the Five Civilized Tribes, though at an earlier point in time, also forms the background for *Timothy Baines* (New York: Holt, Rinehart, 1969). About the latter book, Vine Deloria, Jr., wrote in the Boston *Herald Traveler*: "The beauty of this book is that John Culp knows his subject well. He does not romanticize nor does he favor either white or Indian in his interpretation of his major theme. The book comes straight at the reader as a classic view of what life was like on the old Indian reserves of the Five Civilized Tribes."

All of Culp's novels are richly endowed with historical incident, with folk tales, tall stories, Indian legends, and with characters who are authentically part of the period and the locale in which they are set. Many of the incidents in his books derive from stories he heard from his grandfather who had been a member of the Frontier Battalion of the Texas Rangers.

A Whistle in the Wind (New York: Holt, Rinehart, 1968) is the story of a Comanchero camp in Texas from pre-Civil War days until the defeat of the Comanches and the coming of the homesteaders, told through episodes in the life of a remarkable and tragic heroine. *The Treasure of the Chisos* (New York: Holt, Rinehart, 1971) tells of young Colin O'Reiley's journey from St. Louis to the Chisos Mountains in Southwest Texas in search of his heritage. The background of *Oh, Valley Green!* (New York: Holt, Rinehart, 1972) concerns the U.S. Government's maneuverings leading to the annexation of Texas and California in the 1840s. As with all of Culp's novels, it is the human story in the foreground that holds the attention and engages the emotions. Culp wrote of characters who are real and natural enough to step right off the page, and of adventures which,

while seldom predictable, have the inevitable rightness which is the hallmark of the storyteller's art. His novels are mixtures of myth-making and history, informed by a scrupulous faithfulness to the nature of the people and the land about which he wrote.

R.E.B.

Cunningham, Eugene (1896–1957)

An author of Western fiction, born at Helena, Arkansas, Cunningham attended public schools in Dallas and Fort Worth, Texas, where he grew up, and in 1914–1919 he was enlisted in the U.S. Navy serving in the Mexican Campaign and then in World War I. He remained in the Naval Reserve until 1923. During World War II, Cunningham re-enlisted, serving in Naval Intelligence.

In 1921, Cunningham married and would later, upon occasion, dedicate his novels to one or another of his children. Cunningham toured Central America after his 1919 discharge, publishing local color articles in magazines and newspapers. His first Western novel was *The Trail to Apacaz* (New York: Dodd, Mead, 1924), a story about a soldier of fortune whose exploits have been largely in Mexico and Central America before he comes to the town of La Cruz on the Mexican-American border. Cunningham was living in San Francisco when he died.

The most prolific period for Cunningham was the decade of the 'Thirties and he seems to have been strongly influenced by Dashiell Hammett's novel, *Red Harvest* (New York: Knopf, 1929), in which there is so much killing that the characters become almost "blood simple." In *Riders of the Night* (Boston: Houghton Mifflin, 1932) Cunningham's plot involved the deaths of some seventy men. Beyond this, however, it was an innovative book in other ways. While Cunningham also employed the theme of two heroines between whom the protagonist must choose, he introduced the concept of a triad hero, although in support of his main hero; he called this trio of Sandrock Tom, Three Rivers, and Happy Jack the "Three Mesquiteers," an idea which obviously struck William Colt Mac-Donald (q.v.) who introduced his triad hero, the more familiar "Three Mesquiteers," Tucson Smith, Stony Brooke, and Lullaby Joslin, the next year in his book, the first in his series, *Law of the Forty-Fives* (New York: Covici, Friede, 1933). In *Riders of the Night* Cunningham also had a Mexican character named Chihuahua who speaks "border" English as did Eugene Manlove Rhodes' (q.v.) character Monte in *Pasó por Aquí* (Boston: Houghton Mifflin, 1927) and Clarence E. Mulford's (q.v.) imitative El Toro who appeared in *Corson of the JC* (New York: Doubleday, 1927).

Cunningham expanded the number of villains in need of killing for *Buckaroo* (Boston: Houghton Mifflin, 1933) to three hundred, battled against by three Texas Rangers. In *Buckaroo*, as in *Riders of the Night*, Cunningham's principal villain is both flamboyant and resourceful and in both novels the respective heroines are in love with him in preference to the main hero, until the end of the story. Cunningham steeped himself in the history and lore of the Southwest, as did Mulford, but, unlike Mulford, Cunningham had lived and grown up in the Southwest and his locations are more realistic and sundrenched. Also as

Mulford, Cunningham was fascinated with gunfighters and his vision of the Old West is heavily populated with them, thus furthering a trend which was taken over by William Colt MacDonald and others until the modern blood baths written by Terry Harknett (q.v.) in his popular Edge series. Cunningham's non-fiction work, *Triggernometry: A Gallery of Gunfighters* (New York: Press of the Pioneers, 1934), went through several editions before and after its 1941 re-issue as *Gunfighters All* and proved one of his most successful books.

As an author, Cunningham once commented, "I write right—out of ignorance. People and places can only be as I have seen and known them. . . . Frontier folk of my life have been forthright characters, explosive; they reacted to stimuli as naturally, automatically as aroused wolves. So I show them." His social views were distinctly Western and the fact that he had a crooked sheriff, a crooked deputy sheriff, and a crooked district attorney in *Buckaroo* had not changed by the time he came to write *Riding Gun* (Boston: Houghton Mifflin, 1956) where the principal villain is a lawyer. If Zane Grey's (q.v.) romantic fantasies about the West were popular with Easterners who liked to dream about an imaginary West, Cunningham's fictions had the virtue for Westerners of showing the social evils that came from the East fancifully defeated by Westerners.

Eugene Cunningham's Western novels are *The Trail to Apacaz* (1924), *Riders of the Night* (1932), *Buckaroo* (1933), *Diamond River Man* (1934), *Texas Sheriff* (1934), *Trail of the Macaw* (1935), *Redshirts of Destiny* (1935), *Quick Triggers* (1935), *Pistol Passport* (1936), *Whistling Lead* (1936), *Ranger Way* (1937), *Texas Triggers* (1938), *Gun Bulldoggers* (1939), *Red Range* (1939),

Spiderweb Trail (1940), *Buscadero Trail* (1951), *Gunsight Chance* (1951), *Riding Gun* (1956).

Cunningham's novels as Leigh Carder are *Outlaw Justice* (1935), *Border Guns* (1935), *Bravo Trail* (1938).

Eugene Cunningham wrote the Introduction to W. H. Hutchinson's biography of Eugene Manlove Rhodes *A Bar Cross Man* (Norman: University of Oklahoma Press, 1956) and the book contains several references to Cunningham and his work.

Curwood, James Oliver (1879–1927)

Author of fiction set in the Canadian Northwest and Alaska in a tradition begun by Jack London (q.v.), Rex Beach (q.v.), and Ridgwell Cullum (q.v.), born at Owosso, Michigan. Curwood was expelled from school in Owosso when he was 16. He then toured many of the Southern states by bicycle and, when he was 17, he travelled selling proprietary medicines. From 1898–1900 Curwood attended the University of Michigan. He commenced his writing career in 1900 as a reporter, later becoming managing editor, for the *Detroit News-Tribune*. Resigning from the latter position in 1907, he devoted himself for the next twenty years to writing, beginning with *The Courage of Captain Plum* (Indianapolis: Bobbs, Merrill, 1908). Employed for two years by the Canadian government as an explorer and a descriptive writer, he lived among the Eskimos and traveled thousands of miles by canoe, snow shoes, and pack train throughout the Hudson Bay country. His love for the wild North and his intimate knowledge

of its ways were reflected in the backgrounds and settings for his many novels. An avid conservationist, in 1926 Curwood was appointed to the Michigan State Conservation Commission, but he may well have best helped this cause through his romantic writings.

Curwood's Northland stories, as those of Ridgwell Cullum, are adeptly plotted, but unlike Cullum's, and more as Zane Grey's (q.v.), his stories tend to be almost overly exuberant in their descriptions of the land and mesmerizing with their romantic

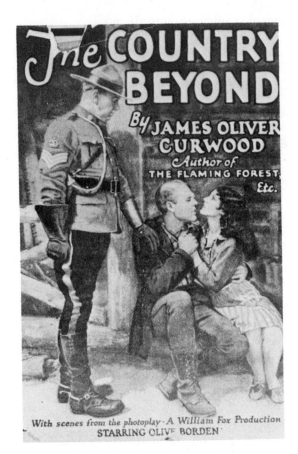

Dust jacket from James Oliver Curwood's The Country Beyond *(New York: Cosmopolitan Book Company, 1922) stressing the motion picture tie-in.*

and flamboyant characterizations. However, although Curwood's heroes are strong, handsome, and morally above reproach and his heroines beautiful, innocent, and intelligent, it would be wrong to dismiss them as flat or two-dimensional. In the Three Rivers trilogy, *The River's End* (New York: Cosmopolitan Book Corporation, 1919), *The Valley of Silent Men* (New York: Cosmopolitan Book Corporation, 1920), and *The Flaming Forest* (New York: Cosmopolitan Book Corporation, 1921), each hero is a member of the Royal Canadian Mounted Police faced with not getting his man and the consequent dilemma of adapting the law to fit each particular circumstance. Curwood showed an internal growth of character which, of itself, tends to sustain interest, rather than relying wholly on the thrill of the chase. Often the dramatic conflict centers on the untangling of mistaken identities, sometimes with variable results. In *The Alaskan* (New York: Cosmopolitan Book Corporation, 1923), the heroine's identity and purpose are unclear both to the hero and to the reader. *The Alaskan* is also a typical example of Curwood's treatment of the villain who is usually underdeveloped as a character, more the personification of evil than a human being. In *The Alaskan*— somewhat typical of Curwood's view—the villain symbolizes the onerous influence of the lower forty-eight states and their detrimental effect on the proper development of Alaska, a theme which Rex Beach shared. Curwood's popularity was certainly augmented through his creation of the dog Kazan in *Kazan* (New York: Cosmopolitan Book Corporation, 1914). The Kazan character became so well established through motion picture adaptations that in the late 'Forties the Whitman Publishing Company went so far as to have two additional adventures ghost-written. In fact, throughout the 'Thirties Curwood's name and literary reputation were so indelibly associated with the Canadian Northwest that frequently films would credit him with stories which had no more to do with him than that they were set in the Northwest and might have Royal Canadian policemen as characters. Ultimately, his romanticism and his sometimes extreme sentimentality mark him as too much the product of his generation and his novels have become dated.   J.N.

James Oliver Curwood's novels with a Canadian Northwestern or Alaskan setting are *The Courage of Captain Plum* (1908), *The Wolf Hunters* (1908), *The Great Lakes* (1909), *The Gold Hunters* (1909), *The Danger Trail* (1910), *The Honor of the Big Snows* (1911), *Philip Steele of the Royal Mounted* (1911), *Back to God's Country* (1911) [short stories], *Flower of the North* (1912), *Isobel* (1913), *Kazan* (1914), *God's Country and the Woman* (1915), *The Hunted Woman* (1916), *The Grizzly: A Companion Story to Kazan* (1916), *Baree, Son of Kazan* (1917), *The Courage of Marge O'Doone* (1918), *Nomads of the North* (1918), *The River's End* (1919), *The Valley of Silent Men* (1920), *The Flaming Forest* (1921), *The Golden Snare* (1921), *The Country Beyond* (1922), *The Alaskan* (1923), *God's Country—Trail to Happiness* (1923), *A Gentleman of Courage* (1924), *The Ancient Highway* (1925), *The Black Hunter* (1926), *Swift Lightning* (1926), *The Plains of Abraham* (1928), *The Glory of Living* (1928), *The Crippled Lady of Peribonka* (1929), *Green Timber* (1930).

Books based on Curwood's creation of the dog Kazan but not written by him are *Kazan in Revenge of the North* (1937) and *Kazan, King of the Pack* (1940).

Films based on Curwood's stories or

only his characters or settings are *The Wilderness Mail* (Selig, 1914) directed by Colin Campbell [source unknown], remade under this title (Ambassador, 1935) directed by Forrest Sheldon. *In Defiance of the Law* (Selig, 1914) was directed by Colin Campbell [based on *Isobel*]. *The White Mouse* (Selig, 1914) was directed by Colin Campbell [source unknown]. *The Fifth Man* (Selig, 1914) was directed by F.J. Grandon [source unknown]. *Four Minutes Late* (Selig, 1914) was directed by F.J. Grandon [source unknown]. *Getting a Start in Life* (Selig, 1915) was directed by Tom Mix [source unknown]. *The Battle of Frenchman's Run* (Vitagraph, 1915) was directed by Theodore Marston [source unknown]. *The Last Man* (Vitagraph, 1916) was direct-

ed by William Wolbert [source unknown]. *God's Country and the Woman* (Vitagraph, 1916) was directed by Rollin S. Sturgeon, remade as *God's Country and the Law* (Arrow, 1921) directed by Sidney Olcott, remade under the title *God's Country and the Woman* (Warner's, 1937). *The Hunted Woman* (Vitagraph, 1916) was directed by S. Rankin Drew, remade under this title (Fox, 1925) directed by Jack Conway. *The Danger Trail* (Selig, 1917) was directed by Frederick A. Thompson. *Baree, Son of Kazan* (Vitagraph, 1918) was directed by David Smith remade under this title (Vitagraph, 1925) directed by David Smith. *Back to God's Country* (First National, 1919) was directed by David M. Hartford, remade under this title (Universal, 1927) directed by Irvin Wil-

Kirby Grant and "Shinook" in Yukon Vengeance *(Allied Artists, 1954) which credited James Oliver Curwood for a story only to make use of his name.*

lat, (Universal, 1953) directed by Joseph Penney. *The Courage of Marge O'Doone* (Vitagraph, 1920) was directed by David Smith. *The River's End* (First National, 1920) was directed by Marshall Neillan, remade under this title (Warner's, 1930) directed by Michael Curtiz, (Warner's, 1940) directed by Ray Enright. *Nomads of the North* (First National, 1921) was directed by David M. Hartford. *Flower of the North* (Vitagraph, 1921) was directed by David Smith. *The Golden Snare* (First National, 1921) was directed by David M. Hartford. *Kazan* (Selig, 1921) was directed by Bertram Bracken, remade as *Ferocious Pal* (Principal, 1934) directed by Spencer Gordon Bennet. *The Broken Silence* (Arrow, 1922) was directed by Dell Henderson [source unknown]. *I Am the Law* (Affiliated, 1922) was directed by Edwin Carewe [based on the short story "The Poetic Justice of Uko San"]. *Jan of the Big Snows* (American, 1922) was directed by Charles M. Seay [based on *Honor of the Big Snows*]. *The Man from Hell's River* (Western, 1922) was directed by Irving Cummings [based on the short story "God of Her People"]. *The Valley of Silent Men* (Paramount, 1922) was directed by Frank Borzage. *Gold Madness* (Principal, 1923) was directed by Robert P. Thornby [based on the short story "The Man from Ten Strike"]. *Jacqueline, or Blazing Barriers* (Arrow, 1923) was directed by Dell Henderson [based on the short story "Jacqueline"]. *The Alaskan* (Paramount, 1924) was directed by Herbert Brenon. *The Ancient Highway* (Paramount, 1925) was directed by Irvin Willat. *The Gold Hunters* (Davis, 1925) was directed by Paul Hurst, remade as *Trail of the Yukon* (Monogram, 1949) directed by William X. Crowley. *My Neighbor's Wife* (Davis, 1925) was directed by Clarence Geldert [based on

the short story "The Other Man's Wife"]. *Steele of the Royal Mounted* (Vitagraph, 1925) was directed by David Smith [based on *Philip Steele of the Royal Mounted*]. *When the Door Opened* (Fox, 1925) was directed by Reginald Barker [based on the short story "When the Door Opened"]. *The Country Beyond* (Fox, 1926) was directed by Irving Cummings. *The Flaming Forest* (M-G-M, 1926) was directed by Reginald Barker. *Prisoners of the Storm* (Universal, 1926) was directed by Lynn Reynolds [based on the short story "The Quest of Joan"]. *Tentacles of the North* (Rayart, 1926) was directed by Louis Chaudet [based on the short story "In the Tentacles of the North"], remade as *Snow Dog* (Monogram, 1950) directed by Frank McDonald. *The Wolf Hunters* (Rayart, 1926) was directed by Stuart Paton, remade as *The Trail Beyond Lone Star* (Monogram, 1934) directed by Robert Bradbury, remade under the title *The Wolf Hunters* (Monogram, 1949) directed by Oscar "Budd" Boetticher. *Hearts of Men* (Anchor, 1928) was directed by James P. Hogan [source unknown]. *Thundergod* (Anchor, 1928) was directed by Charles J. Hunt [source unknown]. *Fighting Trooper* (Ambassador, 1934) was directed by Ray Taylor [based on the short story "Footprints"]. *Northern Frontier* (Ambassador, 1935) was directed by Sam Newfield [based on the short story "Four Minutes Late"]. *Code of the Mounted* (Ambassador, 1935) was directed by Sam Newfield [based on the short story "Wheels of Fate"]. *The Red Blood of Courage* (Ambassador, 1935) was directed by Jack English [source unknown]. *Trails of the Wild* (Ambassador, 1935) was directed by Sam Newfield [based on the short story "Caryl of the Mountains"]. *His Fighting Blood* (Ambassador, 1935) was directed by John English [source unknown]. *Vengeance of Rannah* (Reliable, 1936) was directed by Bernard B. Ray [source unknown]. *Valley of Terror* (Ambassador, 1937) was directed by Al Herman [source unknown]. *The Silver Trail* (Reliable, 1937) was directed by Raymond Samuels [source unknown]. *Whistling Bullets* (Ambassador, 1937) was directed by John English [source unknown]. *The Fighting Texan* (Ambassador, 1937) was directed by Charles Abbott [source unknown]. *Galloping Dynamite* (Ambassador, 1937) was directed by Harry Frazer [based on the short story "Dawn Rider"]. *Rough Riding Rhythm* (Ambassador, 1937) was directed by J.P. McGowan [based on the short story "Getting a Start in Life"]. *Roaring Six Guns* (Ambassador, 1937) was directed by J.P. McGowan [source unknown]. *Call of the Yukon* (Republic, 1938) was directed by B. Reeves Eason [based on *Swift Lightning*]. *God's Country* (Screen Guild, 1946) was directed by Robert Tansey [source unknown]. *'Neath Canadian Skies* (Screen Guild, 1946) was directed by B. Reeves Eason [source unknown]. *North of the Border* (Screen Guild, 1946) was directed by B. Reeves Eason [source unknown]. *Call of the Klondike* (Monogram, 1950) was directed by Frank McDonald [source unknown]. *Yukon Manhunt* (Monogram, 1951) was directed by Frank McDonald [source unknown]. *Northwest Territory* (Monogram, 1951) was directed by Frank McDonald [source unknown]. *Yukon Gold* (Monogram, 1952) was directed by Frank McDonald [source unknown]. *Fangs of the Arctic* (Monogram, 1953) was directed by Rex Bailey [source unknown]. *Northern Patrol* (Monogram, 1953) was directed by Rex Bailey [source unknown].

Curwood's autobiography, *Son of the Forests* (New York: Doubleday, 1930), was completed by Dorothea A. Bryan and published posthumously.

Cushman, Dan (1909 —) Author of Western fiction and historian born in Michigan. As an infant Cushman moved with his family to the Iron Range of Minnesota and soon again to Montana. Cushman grew up on what now is known as the Rocky Boy reservation. At the age of 15, he worked as a Linotype operator and reporter on the Big Sandy, Montana, weekly paper and while enrolled in the Big Sandy High School he was also a correspondent for the *Great Falls Tribune*, writing for fifteen cents per inch of copy. After graduating from the University of Montana, he worked as a miner, prospector, and geologist. He began writing for the pulp Western magazines as long as there was a market. In the 'Fifties, Cushman switched to books.

His novel, *Stay Away, Joe* (New York: Viking, 1953), became a bestseller, a Book-of-the-Month selection, and the Broadway musical *Whoop-Up* was based on it. Cushman's book *The Silver Mountain* (New York: Appleton-Century-Crofts, 1957) won him a Spur Award from the Western Writers of America. Cushman's novel *Brothers in Kickapoo* (New York: McGraw-Hill, 1962) was followed by an excellent history in McGraw-Hill's American Trails Series, *The Great North Trail* (New York: McGraw-Hill, 1966). Cushman also assembled a collection of pioneer recipes for a book he called *Dan Cushman's Cow Country Cook Book* (Great Falls: Stay Away, Joe Publishers, 1967), his own publishing company. Occasionally Cushman wrote a conventional Western, such as the paperback original, *The Long Riders* (New York: Fawcett, 1967), but his best work was in half humorous and half deeply serious novels as *Goodbye, Old Dry* (New York: Doubleday, 1959)

about the dry years in Montana, which, since Cushman re-issued the book himself, is now known as *The Muskrat Farm*. Perhaps the finest tribute paid to Cushman came from Vine Deloria, Jr., who wrote of *Stay Away, Joe*: "The favorite of the Indian people, gives a humorous but accurate idea of the problems caused by the intersection of two ways of life."

Cushman's original story was used as the basis for *Timberjack* (Republic, 1955) directed by Joseph Kane. *Stay Away, Joe* (M-G-M, 1968) was directed by Peter Tewksbury.

D

Daniels, John S. See Overholser, Wayne D.

Davis, H(arold) L(enoir) (1896–1960) Pulitzer Prize winning novelist and poet of the Northwest, born near Yoncalla, Douglas County, in Southwestern Oregon. Both of his parents' families had migrated from the Tennessee mountains in the Nineteenth century. Davis' father was a country schoolteacher and the family traveled about the state, allowing him to absorb a feeling for Western history that permeates his writing. As he grew up, Davis worked first as a printer's devil on a country newspaper, then as a sheepherder, and later as a cowboy, packer, deputy sheriff, and surveyor. He picked up smatterings of French, German, Spanish, Greek and Gaelic from local immigrants as well as Piute and Chinook.

He attended Stanford University in

1916–1917 but left college for the U.S. Army. He served with the United States Cavalry on the Mexican border, writing his first poems. In 1919, eleven of these poems, his first publication, won the Levinson Poetry Prize for that year in *Poetry Magazine*. After his military stint, Davis returned to the Northwest, settling down in the Puget Sound area of Washington. Teaming up with two other men, he wrote for a Seattle station a series of radio dramas about Paul Bunyon. Davis also appeared on the program, playing his guitar and singing several of the folk songs he had been collecting all his life. In several published manifestoes, one co-authored, Davis attacked Western regional literature for its stereotyped myths and romantic illusions and lack of the fresh sense of reality that comes from valid personal experience.

Davis' first prose works were three short stories published in the *American Mercury* in 1929. He continued to write for magazines, publishing in *Collier's* and *The*

Saturday Evening Post during the next two decades. After winning a Guggenheim Fellowship in 1932, Davis moved to Mexico City where he wrote his Pulitzer Prize winning novel, *Honey in the Horn* (New York: Harper's, 1935), a humorous but knifingly satiric novel about homesteading in Oregon during 1906–1908 which effectively illustrates Davis' theories about debunking the myths of the Western frontier. The hero, Clay Calvert, falls into one adventure after another in a landscape filled with rascals, scoundrels, romantic misfits, Indians, land exploiters, and a catalogue of homesteading types, all searching for the honey in the horn. Commentators have pointed out the symbolism of Clay's name and that of his woman Luz (light) in terms of his search for truth and knowledge; the hero, therefore, is as Davis, seeking to find reality in all the Western bunkum surrounding him.

Plagued by ill health, Davis moved to Oaxaca, Mexico, in 1953 where he continued to write. Following the amputation of a leg which confined him to a wheel chair, Davis' health worsened and he died of a heart attack while visiting in San Antonio, Texas, in 1960.

Davis was productive in the 'Forties, continuing to win awards for his work. *Proud Riders and Other Poems* (New York: Harper's, 1942) was followed by the novels *Harp of a Thousand Strings* (New York: Morrow, 1947), *Beulah Land* (New York: Morrow, 1949), and *Winds of Morning* (New York: Morrow, 1952), the latter a Book-of-the-Month selection. In these books he expounded on the theme of appearance versus reality on the American frontier with increasing emphasis on the growth of spiritual reality. *Winds of Morning*, set in Oregon as is *Beulah Land*, deals with Westering as a search for integrity and spiritual rebirth.

Many critics consider it and *Honey in the Horn* as Davis' two best books.

His last three books were a collection of short stories, *Team Bells Work Me and Other Stories* (New York: Morrow, 1953), a novel, *The Distant Music* (New York: Morrow, 1957), and a collection of essays in which he discussed at length the problems of a Western writer, *Kettle of Fire* (New York: Morrow, 1959).   P.O.

For further information see two critical biographies of H.L. Davis, Robert Bain's *H.L. Davis* (Boise: Idaho State University Press, 1974) and Paul T. Bryant's *H.L. Davis* (New York: Twayne Publishers, 1978).

Davis, Mollie Evelyn (1844–1909)

Author and poet, noted for Western local color in her prose, born Mary Eveline Moore at either Ladiga or White Plains, Alabama. The poverty-strickened Moore family relocated to Texas where Davis, whose gift for writing was recognized early, received a patchy education in rural schools. At 16, Davis' first poem was published in a local paper followed by more poems, stories, and orations. An association with Edward H. Cushing, editor of the *Houston Telegraph*, and his wife, who both took a personal interest in Davis, brought about the publication, by Cushing, of her first collection of poetry, *Minding the Gap* (1867). By the 1870s Davis' poetry was reaching a national audience.

In 1874 she married Thomas E. Davis, who served as editor-in-chief on the *Houston Telegram* and later the *New Orleans Picayune*. Davis contributed prose to both publications. Her earliest prose was a series of sketches, "Bits of Texas Life," which were published over the years 1884–1887 in the *New Orleans Picayune*. Her novels, *Under the Man Fig* (1895) and *The Wire Cutters* (1899), as well as many of her short stories, are excellent portraits of Nineteenth-century Texas in which Davis captured the speech, mannerisms, topography, and daily routines of the period. Davis is perhaps better known for her children's stories and for her novels set in Louisiana. However, her works on Texas were consistently praised for their accuracy, humor, compassion, and unique style.

Dawson, Peter. See Faust, Frederick and Glidden, Jonathan H.

Deming, Kirk. See Drago, Harry Sinclair.

Denver, Drake C. See Nye, Nelson.

Dexter, Martin. See Faust, Frederick.

Dobie, J(ames) Frank (1888–1964) Teacher, lecturer, student of Southwestern life and literature, a man who preferred to call himself a folklorist, born on a ranch South of San Antonio, Texas. Dobie grew up on the land. His earliest efforts as a

writer came as a result of working as a summer reporter for Texas newspapers. He attended Southwestern University from which he graduated with a Bachelor's degree in 1910 and went on to earn a Master's degree from Columbia University in 1914. In 1916, while employed as an instructor in English at the University of Texas at Austin, Dobie married Bertha McKee about whom he wrote in his preface to *Cow People* (Boston: Little, Brown, 1964) many years later: "The person to whom I owe most is a critic of style and a thinker named Bertha McKee Dobie. She has overlooked every line and influenced me to exercise the never sufficiently accomplished art of omission."

From 1917 to 1919 Dobie served in World War I with the U.S. Army Field Artillery, rising to the rank of First Lieutenant. Upon his return to the States, Dobie again resumed his duties at the University of Texas, but adamantly refused to go on for his Doctor's degree, claiming he had no interest in transferring the bones of scholarship from one graveyard to another. Instead he went to manage the million-acre Ralf ranch in 1919–1920. Returning once again to the University of Texas, he was an instructor in English 1921–1923 until he left for Oklahoma A&M College in Stillwater where he was head of the English department 1923–1925. In 1925 he came back to the University of Texas where he remained until 1947. When he proposed teaching a course on the life and literature of the Southwest, he was told that there was *no* literature. To this he countered: perhaps not, but there was plenty of life, and he would teach it. The course, over the years, grew in complexity and richness, and twice, once in 1942, and again in 1952, Dobie published his *Guide to Life and Literature of the Southwest* (Dallas: Southern Methodist University Press, 1952) which he did not copyright, suggesting that "anybody is welcome to help himself to any of it in any way." Among his students were Tom Lea (q.v.), the Western artist and author who came to illustrate some of Dobie's work, and even Western singer and motion picture cowboy, Tex Ritter.

Dobie was engaged by the Curtis publication, *Country Gentleman*, to run a series of articles on Texas and Southwestern folklore. He published *A Vaquero of the Brush Country* (Boston: Little, Brown, 1929) which he revised in 1943, but it was *Coronado's Children* (Dallas: Southwest Press, 1931), about lost gold mines, which won him national recognition when it was made a selection of the Literary Guild. A wide assortment of books dealing with Southwestern legends and life followed, of which *Tongues of the Monte* (New York: Doubleday, 1935) was his own personal favorite, but of which both *The Longhorns* (Boston: Little, Brown, 1941), illustrated by Tom Lea, and *The Mustangs* (Boston: Little, Brown, 1952) are also highly readable examples. "Human tracks and human blood will not wash out a soil," Dobie once wrote, reacting to a visit to Southern California and seeing the massive construction of shopping centers, "although cement may hide them." He looked for two things in folklore: for flavor and "for a revelation of the folk who nourished the lore." Toward the end of his life he commented: "I've been called a folklorist; I'm not one in a scientific way but have put hundreds of folk tales into books, writing them in my own style. I've been called a historian; I'm not one in the strict sense, but I suppose I can be called a historian of the longhorns, the mustangs, the coyote, and other characters of the West."

Although calling Dobie "no saint", Lawrence Clark Powell wrote of him in *Southwestern Classics* (Los Angeles: Ward Ritchie, 1974): "I have come to rank him with [William Butler] Yeats, the Irish laureate, in what each did to give his locale wider meaning. They reached heavenly heights paradoxically by looking earthward and listening to tales of their rural countrymen. The ruined towers of Yeats' Ireland have their Dobiean counterparts in the derelict haciendas of the Texan's borderlands."

For further information see *An American Original: The Life of J. Frank Dobie* (Boston: Little, Brown, 1978) by Ron Tinkle.

Douglas, Thorne. See Haas, Benjamin.

Drago, Harry Sinclair (1888–1980) One of the most polished and professional authors of formulary Western stories and novels, born at Toledo, Ohio. Educated in local schools, Drago enrolled at Toledo University only to quit and go to work as a reporter for the Toledo *Bee*. His journalism career was almost cut short when his editor declared that Drago was one of the worst reporters he had ever seen and that he was unable to write even the simplest story. Before getting fired, Drago persuaded the editor to give him a chance to do a feature story replete with pictures covering a stateline gambling establishment which was so well done the editor revised his opinion.

For the next two years Drago continued doing feature stories for the *Bee* and for the Toledo *Times*.

A few years later Drago took a job clerking in a book store, the Macauley Brothers. Drago did not remain long in retail sales but was soon transferred into the wholesale department. Drago liked traveling, proved capable, and his territory showed an increase. In his travels, meeting H.K. Fly who was affiliated with Bobbs-Merrill, the two went into a publishing venture specializing in theatrical and general trade books. Among the books published by their firm were the Boston Blackie stories of Jack Boyle, the Cappy Ricks stories of Peter B. Kyne (q.v.), and *West is West* (New York: H.K. Fly, 1917) by Eugene Manlove Rhodes (q.v.). It was during this period that Drago himself turned to writing, substantially editing several manuscripts. In 1923 he left the firm, having published two novels, *Suzanna: A Romance of Early California* (New York: Macauley, 1922) and, a collaboration with Joseph Noel, *Whispering Sage* (New York: Century, 1922). *Out of the Silent North* (New York: Macauley, 1923), a tale of the Northland in the tradition of Ridgwell Cullum (q.v.) and James Oliver Curwood (q.v.), was even more successful, being adapted to motion pictures as well as being serialized in a magazine.

By his later standards, Drago's productivity was modest but it was sufficient, by 1927, to get him a job in Hollywood working on screen stories for Tom Mix and Buck Jones. Drago then went on to work at M-G-M, although he resented the fact that frequently his work was confined to Western stories since most of his fiction had been in this vein. In 1932 Drago left Hollywood having worked on some 34 motion picture scripts and, after a year in Nevada, returned to the East, settling in White Plains, New York, where he lived until his death, concentrating on writing, producing at his zenith as many as four books a year, most of them under such pseudonyms as Bliss Lomax, Kirk Deming, Will Ermine, and even four entries in the Peter Field (see House Names) series published by William Morrow and Company.

"The better quality of today's Westerns," Drago once said, "is not thanks to any help from the big domes who ignore the Western or brush it off as trash. It is because there are better writers working in the field. The shabby plots, the cardboard characters which used to go, are not enough any more. Luke Short (q.v.), Norman Fox (q.v.), Frank Bonham (q.v.), and the others like them are real storytellers and craftsmen. The difficulty is to get booksellers to recognize this fact." And it is ranked with Luke Short and Norman A. Fox where Drago belongs. His best books, as *Stranger with a Gun* (New York: Dodd, Mead, 1957), are tightly plotted, engaging, and suspenseful formulary Westerns compared to his somewhat earlier and more pulp-oriented titles as *The Leatherburners* (New York: Doubleday, 1940). Drago's worst flaw perhaps was his tendency toward sentimentality, particularly when it comes to his endings, but this usually does not interfere with the pulse and dramatic pacing of his fiction. In his later years Drago concentrated on writing popular Western histories.

Harry Sinclair Drago's Western novels under his own name are *Suzanna: A Romance of Early California* (1922), *Whispering Sage* (1922) with Joseph Noel, *Out of the Silent North* (1923), *Smoke of the Forty-*

Five (1923), *Following the Grass* (1924), *The Snow Patrol* (1925), *The Desert Hawk* (1927), *Guardians of the Sage* (1932) [alternate title: *Top Hand with a Gun*], *Desert Water* (1933), *The Wild Bunch* (1934), *Trigger Gospel* (1935), *Montana Road* (1935), *Canyon of Golden Skulls* (1937), *Buckskin Empire* (1942), *Stagecoach Kingdom* (1943), *River of Gold* (1945), *Rustlers' Bend* (1949), *The Fight for the Sweetwater* (1950), *Pay-Off at Black Hawk* (1956), *The Loner* (1956), *Wild Grass* (1957), *Buckskin Frontier* (1959), *Fenced-Off* (1959), *Appointment on the Yellowstone* (1959), *Their Guns Were Fast* (1969) [short stories].

Drago's novels as Will Ermine are *Laramie Rides Alone* (1934), *Lobo Law* (1935), *Plundered Range* (1936), *Prairie Smoke* (1936), *Wind River Outlaw* (1936), *Barbed-wire Empire* (1937), *Lawless Legion* (1938), *Trail Trouble* (1938), *Cowboy, Say Your Prayers* (1939), *Rustlers' Moon* (1939), *Singing Lariat* (1939), *Boss of the Plains* (1940), *Rider of the Midnight Range* (1940), *My Gun is My Law* (1942), *Brave in the Saddle* (1943), *Busted Range* (1944), *The Iron Bronc* (1944), *Buckskin Marshal* (1945), *War on the Saddle Rock* (1945), *Outlaw on Horseback* (1946), *The Drifting Kid* (1947), *Last of the Longhorns* (1948), *Apache Crossing* (1950), *Watchdog of Thunder River* (1950), *The Silver Star* (1951), *Longhorn Empire* (1953).

Drago's novels as Bliss Lomax are *Closed Range* (1936), *The Law Bringers* (1937), *Mavericks of the Plains* (1938), *Colt Comrades* (1939), *The Leatherburners* (1940), *Secret of the Wasteland* (1940), *Gringo Gunfire* (1940), *Pardners of the Badlands* (1942), *Horsethief Creek* (1944), *Saddle Hawks* (1944), *Rusty Guns* (1944), *Outlaw River* (1945), *The Phantom Corral* (1946), *Trail Dust* (1947), *Shadow Mountain* (1948), *Sagebrush Bandit* (1949), *The Lost Buckaroo* (1949), *The Law Busters* (1950), *Guns Along the Yellowstone* (1952), *Riders of the Buffalo Grass* (1952), *Ambush at Coffin Canyon* (1954), *Stranger with a Gun* (1957), *Last Call for a Gunfighter* (1958).

Drago's novels as Kirk Deming are *Colt Lightnin'* (1938), *Grass Means Fight* (1938).

Drago's entries in the Peter Field series are *Canyon of Death* (1938), *The Tenderfoot Kid* (1939), *The Man from Thief River* (1940), *Law Badge* (1940).

Films based on Harry Sinclair Drago's Western fiction are *Out of the Silent North* (Universal, 1922) directed by William Worthington, *Whispering Sage* (Fox, 1927) directed by Scott R. Dunlap, *Secrets of the Wasteland* (Paramount, 1941) directed by Derwin Abrahams [based on the Bliss Lomax story but with Clarence E. Mulford's (q.v.) Hopalong Cassidy character], *Buckskin Frontier* (United Artists, 1943) directed by Lesley Selander [based on *Buckskin Empire*], *The Leatherburners* (United Artists, 1943) directed by Joseph E. Henabery [based on the Bliss Lomax story but with Mulford's Hopalong Cassidy character], *Colt Comrades* (United Artists, 1943) directed by Lesley Selander [based on the Bliss Lomax story but with Mulford's Hopalong Cassidy character].

Western films on which Drago received screen credit are *Silver Valley* (Fox, 1927) directed by Ben Stoloff, *The Cowboy Kid* (Fox, 1928) directed by Clyde Carruth, *Hello Cheyenne* (Fox, 1928) directed by Eugene Forde, *A Horseman of the Plains* (Fox, 1928) directed by Ben Stoloff, *Painted Post* (Fox, 1928) directed by Eugene Forde, *The Desert Rider* (M-G-M, 1929) directed by Nick Grindé [co-credit with Ted Shane], *The Overland Telegraph* (M-G-M, 1929) directed by John Waters [co-credit with Ward Wing], *Sioux Blood* (M-G-M, 1929) directed by John Waters, *Where East Is East* (M-G-M, 1929) directed by Tod Browning [co-credit with Browning].

Dufault, Joseph Ernest Nephtali

(1892–1942) A self-taught artist and writer of the American West who worked under the name Will James, born to a French-Canadian family in Eastern Canada. Dufault left home at fifteen years of age and thereafter repudiated his family name, calling himself instead Will James and claiming that he was an orphan. He wandered about the Western United States until 1914 when he was arrested for cattle rustling. In 1915 he was tried and sentenced to a prison term of twelve to fifteen months in the Nevada State Prison near Carson City. A series of odd jobs followed after his release, including a brief stint as a movie stunt man, until he was inducted into the service in May, 1918 and was sent to Camp Kearny, California, to break broncs. He was discharged in February, 1919, still a private.

It had long been James' ambition to be a Western artist/writer as Frederic Remington (q.v.) or Charles M. Russell (q.v.), and it was to this objective that he returned once he resumed civilian life. In 1920 he met Alice Conradt while staying at the Conradt home in Reno, Nevada, and they fell in love. The match was disapproved of by Alice's father who felt James should provide a better life for her than was then obviously within his means. For a brief time, in order to make good, James enrolled in the California School of Fine Arts in San Francisco,

but he soon dropped out. He had some success selling his sketches to small-circulation magazines or to be used in commercial advertising, but his big break came when he tried his hand at writing and *Scribner's Magazine* began accepting his work. James could not spell. His style was filled with grammatical errors. But he claimed that he wrote the way the people on the frontier spoke and no one in the East, who read him, either knew the difference or cared. His first book was *Cowboys: North and South* (New York: Scribner's, 1924).

James and Alice were married sometime before this book appeared and as he continued to write and draw, his work became increasingly popular. As he became more affluent, James turned more and more to alcohol. It became such a severe problem that Alice left him in 1934. She returned to help him when he ended up in a Tucson hospital suffering from the effects of a heart attack induced by a drinking spree. James was very anxious about his real family, it would seem—he kept their existence a secret even from his wife—and clandestinely paid a visit to them in Canada, asking them to destroy any letters or other materials which might disprove the legend he had made of himself. In the mid 'Thirties James and Alice parted again, in an effort to sort out their lives. James sought his answer increasingly in alcohol until the fatal heart attack which cost him his life while he was living in Hollywood, California.

James never wrote anything other than fiction, although several of his books purported to be nonfiction. *Smoky* (New York: Scribner's, 1926), one of his finest horse stories which won the Newberry Medal in 1934, is typical of James' charming penchant for writing a story in prose simple enough to be enjoyed by a child and yet engaging enough as not to be unappealing to an adult reader. *Lone Cowboy* (New York: Scribner's, 1930) purported to be James' official autobiography, but it was really his fantasy about himself. The true story had to await the appearance of Anthony Amaral's *Will James: The Gilt-Edged Cowboy* (Los Angeles: Westernlore Press, 1969).

Will James' Western novels are *The Drifting Cowboy* (1925), *Smoky* (1926), *The Cow Country* (1927), *Sand* (1929), *Sun Up* (1931) [short stories], *Big-Enough* (1931), *All in the Day's Riding* (1932) [short stories], *The Three Mustangeers* (1933), *Uncle Bill* (1934), *In the Saddle with Uncle Bill* (1935), *Home Ranch* (1935), *Scorpion: A Good Bad Horse* (1936), *Cowboy in the Making* (1937), *Look-See* (1938), *Dark Horse* (1939). James' non-fiction books might best be included among his fictions: *Cowboys: North and South* (1924), *Horses I've Known* (1940), *The American Cowboy* (1942).

Films based on Will James' Western fiction are *Smoky* (Fox, 1933) directed by Eugene Forde, *The Lone Cowboy* (Paramount, 1934) directed by Paul Sloane, remade under the title *Shoot Out* (Universal, 1971) directed by Henry Hathaway.

For further information see *Will James: The Gilt-Edged Cowboy* by Anthony Amaral revised and re-issued as *Will James: The Last Cowboy Legend* (Reno: University of Nevada Press, 1980).

Durham, Marilyn (1930 —) Author of two novels with Western settings, born at Evansville, Indiana. Durham received her formal education in Evansville. After she married, and had two children, she billed herself as a writing housewife.

Durham introduced a wide variety of interesting characters in her two refreshing Western novels, *The Man Who Loved Cat Dancing* (New York: Harcourt, Brace, 1972) and *Dutch Uncle* (New York: Harcourt, Brace, 1973). *The Man Who Loved Cat Dancing* in which the anti-hero is torn between his attraction to the unhappily married woman his band of train robbers kidnaps and the memories of his Indian wife, Cat Dancing, who is dead, was made into a film and the bestseller has been translated into twelve languages. The popularity of the book may have stemmed from the fact that the main female character, Catherine Crocker, is essentially a Twentieth-century heroine espousing contemporary views about women in a Nineteenth-century setting.

Set in New Mexico, *Dutch Uncle* focuses on Jake Hollander, an aging gunslinger turned professional gambler who is afraid to make commitments. Through a series of unusual circumstances he is saddled with the care of two Mexican children and the job of town marshal in a small mining community.

Durham's two novels are well-plotted stories with plenty of action and suspense as well as delightful characters. They are basically mainstream novels, concerned with the dynamics of human relationships, which only happen to be set in the West. Neither book evokes a feeling of the West of the period—both are set in the 1880s—nor is the Western landscape an integral part of the storyline.

The Man Who Loved Cat Dancing (M-G-M, 1973) was directed by Richard C. Sarafian.

E

Eastlake, William (1917 —) Author of Western fiction, born at Brooklyn, New York. Eastlake grew up in Caldwell, New Jersey. After high school, he hoboed Westward, ending up in Los Angeles working in a bookstore frequented by writers. During the Second World War, he was wounded during the Battle of the Bulge.

After the war, he returned to California and then went to a Cuba, New Mexico, ranch. His Western satiric novels, inspired by this period, *Go In Beauty* (New York: Harper's, 1956), *The Bronc People* (New York: Harcourt, Brace, 1958) a story set in the Southwest which includes a black cowboy, and *Portrait of an Artist with Twenty-Six Horses* (New York: Simon & Schuster, 1963), contrast Indian and white culture. *Castle Keep* (New York: Simon & Schuster, 1965) is a fantasy war novel as is his anti-Vietnam novel, *The Bamboo Bed* (New York: Simon & Schuster, 1969). *Dancers in the Scalp House* (New York: Viking, 1975), which was a return to a Western novel, attacks the industrial-technological society as does the revisionist-historical novel, *The Naked Descent Into Boston* (New York: Viking, 1978).

Walter Van Tilburg Clark once wrote of Eastlake: "William Eastlake has brought into sharpest focus all the questions about modern man and his values . . . with the most unimpeachable blend of sardonic realism and far-reaching myth." What this often comes to in practice is that Eastlake's novels employ Native American culture as a Greek chorus in critique of the Anglo-American culture which, historically, engulfed it but against which it has proved effective and ultimately indomitable. Each character in his Western fiction must find his own meaning, and he must find it alone. However universal might be his themes, his Western fiction is more than merely set in the Southwest; the land plays an integral part in each attempt at self-definition.

The most complete study of Eastlake's fiction is Gerald Haslam's *William Eastlake* (Austin: Steck-Vaughn, 1970).

Easton, Robert (1915 —) Author of Western fiction, born at San Francisco, California. Growing up on a California Spanish land grant cattle ranch and having traveled widely in the West as a child, Easton also worked as a ranch hand and day laborer before he attended Stanford University in 1933–1934. He then attended Harvard University, graduating with a Bachelor's degree in 1938 and returned to Stanford for postgraduate work in 1938–1939. In 1942–1946 Easton entered the U.S. Army attaining the rank of First Lieutenant and receiving the Combat Infantryman's Badge. Easton's initial impact on Western fiction came with the publication of *The Happy Man* (New York: Viking, 1943), a collection of short stories and sketches about life on a great California cattle ranch as seen through the eyes of Dynamite, a cowhand who had stepped, according to some critics, right out of the drawings of Frederic Remington (q.v.). The book was published while Easton was in the service. When he was discharged, he turned to other activities, including teaching English and acting as a writing consultant attached to the U.S. Naval Civil Engineering Laboratory at Port Hueneme, California. However, some of Easton's subsequent non-fiction has been of the first rank, including his *The Book of the American West* (New York: Messner, 1963) and his detailed and highly readable biography *Max Brand: The Big "Westerner"* (Norman: University of Oklahoma Press, 1970) devoted to the fabulous career of Easton's father-in-law, Frederick Faust (q.v.). Easton also edited a splendid collection of Max Brand's fiction in *Max Brand's Best Stories* (New York: Dodd, Mead, 1967).

Harry E. Maule, Western fiction editor at Random House when he assembled his anthology, *Great Tales of the American West* (New York: Random House, 1945), for the Modern Library, said of Easton's tales of contemporary ranch life in *The Happy Man* that "regardless of methods, most of the people, even on the headquarters ranch of the streamlined E1 Dorado Investment Company, have the stamp of the old West on them. Tradition dies hard."

Edson, J(ohn) T(homas) (1928—)

A British author of paperback formulary Westerns, born in a village in Derbyshire, England. Edson's father worked in the mines in Derbyshire and, nine months after Edson was born, he was killed in an underground accident. At 15 Edson himself left school to work as a haulage hand at a stone quarry. Two years later, in 1946, he was called up for military duty and served with a rifle brigade before transferring to service as a dog trainer with the Royal Army Veterinary Corps. He served in Germany, Austria, Singapore, Hong Kong, Benghazi, Kenya, and Cyprus. In 1963 he retired to civilian life.

Edson began writing while in school and then in the service and completed twelve novels during this period, all of which were later revised and published. He took two correspondence school courses in writing after returning to civilian life while he managed his fish and chips store and when he expressed his intention to write Westerns his teachers tried to discourage him. From one of them, however, he learned of a literary competition held by the British publishers, Brown Watson, Ltd. *Trail Boss* (London: Brown Watson, 1961), the first of Edson's "Floating Outfit" stories which came to number more than fifty volumes, won second place. While Edson continued to write Westerns for Brown Watson, he was also writing for boys' magazines as *Rover*, *Hotspur*, and *Victor* published by the D.C. Thompson Group. Edson was economical: many of these stories were later reworked into the "Floating Outfit" series. After a two-year stint at full-time writing, Edson tried a more conventional job, signing on as a postman. In 1967, after producing 42 books for Brown Watson at a rate of up to eight books a year, Transworld Publishers took over his contract. In 1973 he once again took to writing full-time.

Sometimes called "England's Zane Grey"—a tribute more to his productivity than to his style which can veer towards the clumsy in its haste—all but a handful of

Edson's 100-plus books are spun out of the lives and adventures of an interlocking set of attractive but derivative characters, both heroes and villains. Each of the "Floating Outfit" stories, where most of these characters are introduced, is made effective by its companions. As a jigsaw, it is a challenge to collect all the pieces. It is possible, however, to miss Edson's flair for characterization and action amid his scenes of carnage, which rival those of George G. Gilman (q.v.). His publishers claim that each book averages twelve major killings and, often, Edson's characters seem best defined by their individual means of dealing out death.

Edson also borrowed characters from other authors. Detective story writer Edgar Wallace's J.G. Reeder is in an Edson book with the permission of the Wallace estate. The Bunduki series features the great-grandson of a "Floating Outfit" member and the adopted son and great-granddaughter of Tarzan of the Apes. This series was published with the permission of the Edgar Rice Burroughs (q.v.) estate. According to Edson, one of his *bêtes noires* was critics. He claimed to have no interest in them or in their opinions of his work. The same attitude may be divined by his books. Either you like them or you do not.

D.W.

J.T. Edson's Western novels are *Trail Boss* (1961), *Sagebrush Sleuth* (1961), *The Ysabel Kid* (1962), *Rio Guns* (1962), *The Texan* (1962), *Waco's Debt* (1962), *The Hard Riders* (1962), *Arizona Ranger* (1962), *The Fastest Gun in Texas* (1963), *The Quiet Town* (1963), *The Half Breed* (1963), *The Rio Hondo Kid* (1693), *Gunsmoke Thunder* (1963), *The Drifter* (1963), *Wagons to Backsight* (1964), *Trigger Fast* (1964), *Gun Wizard* (1964), *Apache Rampage* (1964), *The Rio Hondo War* (1964), *Waco Rides In* (1964), *Troubled Range* (1965), *The Wildcats* (1965), *The Trouble Busters* (1965), *The Peacemakers* (1965), *The Fortune Hunters* (1965), *The Man from Texas* (1965), *The Bull Whip Breed* (1965), *Trouble Trail* (1965), *The Cow Thieves* (1965), *Slaughter's Way* (1965), *The Devil Gun* (1966), *A Town Called Yellowdog* (1966), *The Law of the Gun* (1966), *The Rushers* (1966), *Return to Backsight* (1966), *Guns in the Night* (1966), *Comanche* (1967), *Sidewinder* (1967), *The Fast Gun* (1967), *The Floating Outfit* (1967), *Terror Valley* (1967), *Hound Dog Man* (1967), *The Big Hunt* (1967), *The Colt and the Sabre* (1968), *The Rebel Spy* (1968), *The Hooded Riders* (1968), *Ranchland Hercules* (1968), *McGraw's Inheritance* (1968), *The Bad Bunch* (1968), *The Making of a Lawman* (1968), *Calamity Spells Trouble* (1968), *The Professional Killers* (1968), *The Bloody Border* (1969), *.44 Calibre Man* (1969), *Goodnight's Dream* (1969), *From Hide and Horn* (1969), *Cuchilo* (1969), *The Small Texan* (1969), *The Town Tamers* (1969), *Cold Deck, Hot Lead* (1969), *The 1/4 Draw* (1969), *The Deputies* (1969), *Under the Stars and Bars* (1970), *Back to the Bloody Border* (1970), *Kill Dusty Fog!* (1970), *White Stallion, Red Mare* (1970), *Point of Contact* (1970), *The Owlhoot* (1970), *A Horse Called Mogollon* (1971), *Bad Hombre* (1971), *Slip Gun* (1971), *To Arms! To Arms! In Dixie* (1972), *Go Back to Hell* (1972), *The South Will Rise Again* (1972), *Two Miles to the Border* (1972), *You're in Command Now, Mr. Fog* (1973), *The Big Gun* (1973), *Set Texas Back on Her Feet* (1973), *Blonde Genius* (1973), *Viridian's Trail* (1973), *The Hide and Tallow Men* (1974), *The Quest for Bowie's Blade* (1974),

The Sixteen Dollar Shooter (1974), *Young Ole Devil* (1975), *Get Urrea* (1975), *Bunduki* (1975), *Ole Devil and the Caplocks* (1976), *Ole Devil and the Mule Train* (1976), *Bunduki and Dawn* (1976), *Sacrifice for the Quagga God* (1976), *Ole Devil at San Jacinto* (1977), *Doc Leroy, M.D.* (1977), *"Cap" Fog, Texas Ranger, Meet Mr. Reeder* (1977), *Set A-Foot* (1978), *Beguinage* (1978), *Beguinage is Dead* (1978), *The Remittance Kid* (1978), *The Whip and the War Lance* (1979), *You're a Texas Ranger, Alvin Fog* (1979), *J.T.'s Hundredth* (1979), *The Gentle Giant* (1980), *J.T.'s Ladies* (1980).

Elliott, Ben. See Haas, Benjamin.

Elston, Allan Vaughan (1887–

1977) A somewhat prolific author of formulary Westerns born at Kansas City, Missouri. Educated at the University of Missouri, Elston graduated with a Bachelor's degree in civil engineering. He worked as a transitman for railroads in the West and Midwest 1909–1913 before going to work for the Chile Copper Company in Chuquicamata, Chile, as a resident engineer, 1913–1915. Returning to the States, Elston took up cattle ranching in Barela, Colorado, 1915–1917 and then joined with others in a consulting engineering firm.

In 1917–1918 Elston was in the U.S. Army, Corps of Engineers, where he attained the rank of Captain and in 1942–1945 he was deployed with the Tank Destroyers; he was finally discharged with the rank of Lieutenant Colonel. Elston had begun a career as a free-lance magazine writer al-

ready during the 'Twenties, but it was while enlisted during World War II that he started writing Western fiction. His first Western novel was *Guns on the Cimarron* (New York: Macrae Smith, 1943), followed later by *Hit the Saddle* (New York: Macrae Smith, 1947). Historical research into the American West soon became Elston's predominant interest and in writing a Western novel he would frequently do on-the-scene research as well as look up old newspapers and maps. Most of his novels, once he got going, were published first with the *New York Daily News* syndicate in a number of Eastern newspapers prior to book publication. Comparing Elston to others among his contemporaries, perhaps his slick, polished, well-controlled stories, always competently written, come nearest to the kind of Western fiction written by Clifton Adams (q.v.) and, at times, approach the precision of plotting characteristic of Luke Short (q.v.).

Allan Vaughan Elston's Western novels are *Guns of the Cimarron* (1943), *Hit the Saddle* (1947), *The Sheriff of San Miguel* (1949), *Ranch of the Roses* (1949), *Deadline at Durango* (1950), *Grass and Gold* (1951), *Roundup on the Picketwire* (1952), *Saddle Up for Sunlight* (1952), *Stage Road to Denver* (1953), *Wagon Wheel Gap* (1954), *Long Lope to Lander* (1954), *Forbidden Valley* (1955), *The Wyoming Bubble* (1955), *The Marked Men* (1956), *Last Stage to Aspen* (1956), *Grand Mesa* (1957), *Rio Grande Deadline* (1957), *Wyoming Manhunt* (1958), *Montana Masquerade* (1959), *Gun Law at Laramie* (1959), *Beyond the Bitterroots* (1960), *Sagebrush Serenade* (1960), *Timberline Bonanza* (1961), *Treasure Coach from Deadwood* (1962), *Roundup on the Yellowstone* (1962), *The Lawless Border* (1963), *Montana Passage* (1963), *The Seven Silver Mountains* (1964), *The Land Seekers* (1964).

Erdman, Loula Grace (1905?–
1976) Regional novelist and short story writer, born near Alma, Missouri. Edman's Missouri childhood was filled with tradition, stability, community spirit, and a strong sense of family which became dominant themes in her subsequent literary works. She received her Bachelor's degree from Central Missouri State College in 1931. She continued her studies at the University of Wisconsin in Madison after which she moved with her sister to Amarillo, Texas, where she taught English until 1945 at the elementary and junior high school level. Her first story was published in a small Kansas City-based magazine. Erdman had always aspired to become an author and, while teaching, she wrote whenever she had a chance. A few stories and sketches were published in magazines such as *Country Home*, *Christian Herald*, and *American Girl*. She also contributed several "confessions" to a confession magazine; one "confession" won a $500 prize. She received a Master's degree in 1941 from Columbia University. During her summer sessions at Columbia, Erdman studied creative writing under author Dorothy Brewster who encouraged her to write. Brewster convinced Erdman to enter a writing contest spon-

sored by a New York literary agency. She won second place.

At the suggestion of a librarian to write career books for young people, Erdman wrote her first book, *Separate Star* (New York: Longmans, Green, 1944). The book was about the teaching profession and was followed by a companion book about rural schools, *Fair Is the Morning* (New York: Longmans, Green, 1945). This latter book was written under great stress since Erdman's father, who was a strong patriarchal figure, was fatally ill. His death in November, 1944, determined the writing of her first regional novel, *The Years of the Locust* (New York: Dodd, Mead, 1946), which won the Dodd, Mead-*Redbook* prize novel award of $10,000. The story is about the effects the death of a strong patriarchal Missouri man has on the people around him, particularly the women in his life. The book, which became a bestseller, a book club selection, as well as being translated into Braille and several languages, marked a turning point in Erdman's literary career and had been written at West Texas State College in Canyon where she was a professor of English and creative writing in 1945, and later associate professor.

Her next regional novel, written for young people, *The Lonely Passage* (New York: Dodd, Mead, 1948), is similar in style to *The Years of the Locust* with its strong feeling of family solidarity in a Missouri setting. With *The Edge of Time* (New York: Dodd, Mead, 1950) Erdman attempted a more historical approach to fiction. The story, set in the Texas Panhandle, was extensively researched and revised before publication. In it she told the story, from the woman's point of view, about a young homesteading couple and the hardships they endure in the often harsh environment of Texas, although it is not as pessimistic as Dorothy Scarborough's (q.v.) *The Wind* (New York: Harper's, 1925). The Texas Panhandle is also the setting for her trilogy for young readers about the Pierce family—*The Wind Blows Free* (New York: Dodd, Mead, 1952), *Wide Horizon* (New York: Dodd, Mead, 1956), and *The Good Land* (New York: Dodd, Mead, 1960). In *The Far Journey* (New York: Dodd, Mead, 1955) the courageous actions of a young Missouri woman are told who travels with her son by covered wagon to be with her husband in Texas.

Erdman published a total of twenty-one books for both adult and juvenile audiences, many of which are set in the pioneering period of the West. *The Short Summer* (New York: Dodd, Mead, 1958), another regional novel set in Missouri, deals with the years of unawareness among people right before World War I. In *Many a Voyage* (New York: Dodd, Mead, 1958) Erdman told the story of Senator Edmund Ross of Kansas from the point of view of his wife. *Another Spring* (New York: Dodd, Mead, 1966) is considered by many her most important historical novel.

Erdman's novels were consistently praised for their "quiet" beauty and economy of words. Although her stories are often overly romantic, she depicted realistically various aspects of the pioneering era in Texas and Missouri. Having always been concerned with the needs of women, it is not surprising that Erdman drew sympathetic, vivid portraits of women. She once said that she could not write stories from the male point of view unless she was writing about an old man or an extremely sensitive young man. This is confirmed by the fact that her Texas cowboys are minor characters who in her novels serve as knights of the range.

For further information see *Loula Grace Erdman* (Austin: Steck Vaughn, 1970) by Ernestine P. Sewell and Erdman's autobiography *A Time To Write* (New York: Dodd, Mead, 1969).

Ermine, Will. See Drago, Harry Sinclair.

Evan, Evin. See Faust, Frederick.

Evans, Evan. See Faust, Frederick.

Evans, Max (1926—) Primarily a novelist of the Southwest and a writer of screenplays, born at Ropes, Texas. Evans came at age 11 to work on a cow ranch near Santa Fe, New Mexico. By the time he was 14, he was breaking horses, branding, fixing fence, and reading Honoré de Balzac in the bunkhouse.

Eventually Evans owned and operated his own ranch and also hunted and trapped professionally until his love for the coyote forced him to quit. He stated, subsequently, that a coyote appears in everything he wrote. After selling his ranch, which was near Clayton, New Mexico, Evans moved to Taos. He was already writing and painting by this time and for nine years he made a living from the sale of over 300 oil paintings.

Evans married Pat James of Taos just one year after his first fiction was published, a short story in the magazine section of the

Denver Post. His first book was a collection of stories, *Southwest Wind* (San Antonio: The Naylor Press, 1958). This was followed by a colorful biography of Long John Dunn of Taos, during which time Evans suffered a severe financial setback. Engaged in a mining venture while he was writing, he made a large sum of money but lost it overnight in addition to another $100,000. As Evans said later, "I had no paintings on hand, no money, no credit, and very little soap left." In desperation, he decided to write a novel. It was *The Rounders* (New York: Macmillan, 1960) and it was made into a successful motion picture starring Henry Fonda and Glenn Ford. Within five years Evans had paid off his huge debt.

Five books between 1964 and 1977 made a little money and Evans spent a great deal of time during this period in Hollywood, writing scripts. It is possible that the scriptwriting hurt his novelistic style, and yet he returned to Albuquerque to write fiction whenever he made enough money in Hollywood to support himself for a year or part of a year. While in Hollywood he worked with Sam Peckinpah, among others, and played the part of a stagecoach guard in the film which some critics feel to be Peckinpah's best, *The Ballad of Cable Hogue* (Warner's, 1970). From his experience on the set an entertaining and revealing book emerged, *Sam Peckinpah: Master of Violence* (Vermillion: Dakota Press, 1972).

The Rounders is a Western, but what makes it different from most other Westerns is that it is contemporary in terms of setting and its two cowboy protagonists cannot win at anything. They are eternal losers, getting our sympathy because they represent most of us. The victor in the conflict is society, not the traditional Western hero, the individual. In a sequel with some of the same characters, *The Hi Lo Country* (New York: Macmillan, 1961), it is the land rather than society which possesses the cowboys. Evans once said: "This has been the main point of my work—man's relationship to the earth and then what this relationship does to the way he relates to his fellow man."

In three short novels published in a single volume, *The One-Eyed Sky* (Boston: Houghton Mifflin, 1963), Evans divided his attention between the land and society. The title story features an old cow with her calf fighting off a coyote with hungry pups. The human element is very brief as a man enters the scene late in the story and decides, painfully but instinctively, which animal shall die. "The Great Wedding" sets up a confrontation between cowboys and society, between the primitive and the civilized, leading to many humorous situations.

J.R.M.

The Rounders (M-G-M, 1965) was directed by Burt Kennedy and inspired a short-lived television series in 1966.

A long and salty interview with Max Evans is to be found in *Three West* (Vermillion: Dakota Press, 1970) edited by John R. Milton.

Evarts, Hal G(eorge) (1887–1934)

Author of Western fiction, born at Topeka, Kansas. After attending only two years of high school in Topeka, Evarts worked as a surveyor in what was then still known as Indian Territory and found he liked the outdoor life. He went on to live in Wyoming and other Western states and worked as a rancher, trapper, licensed guide, and raiser of fur-bearing animals, in the process becoming an authority on hunting and trapping which led him to the position of outdoor editor for *The Saturday Evening Post*. He customarily contributed regular articles to the *Post* on these subjects. During World War I, he served for a time with the Officers Training Corps, receiving the commission of Second Lieutenant shortly before the Armistice.

In 1911 Evarts married Sylvia Abraham of Kansas City, Missouri, and his son, Hal, Jr., who was a student at Stanford University at the time of his death, has continued Evarts' literary tradition becoming a Western author himself. Evarts, Sr., after suffering several heart attacks and having moved to Southern California for the climate, went on a South American cruise in an effort to regain his health. He died aboard the steamship *Manolo* as the boat neared Rio de Janeiro, Brazil.

Evarts' first Western novel was *The Cross Pull* (New York: Knopf, 1920) and he followed it with several more novels exceptional for their reliance on actual historical events, relating him to Emerson Hough (q.v.) among his contemporaries, while at Evarts' best his characters could be compared with Eugene Manlove Rhodes' (q.v.) Westerners. Evarts enjoyed great popularity in France, as did James Oliver Curwood (q.v.), and, almost immediately, Evarts' best-known novel, *Tumbleweeds* (Boston: Little, Brown, 1923), was translated as *Herbes Volantes: Roman Du Far-West*. Dealing with the Cherokee land rush and the cowboys who worked on the ranches leasing grassland from the Indians under governmental sanction, the story so intrigued William S. Hart that he had it adapt-

ed for the screen, becoming both his last film appearance and his only epic Western. Evarts' last novel, *Wolf Dog* (New York: Doubleday, 1935), a dog story as is *The Cross Pull*, was published posthumously.

Hal G. Evarts' Western novels are *The Cross Pull* (1920), *The Bald Face* (1921), *Passing of the Old West* (1921), *The Yellow Horde* (1921), *The Settling of the Sage* (1922), *Fur Sign* (1922), *Tumbleweeds* (1923), *Spanish Acres* (1925), *The Painted Stallion* (1926), *The Moccasin Telegraph* (1927), *Fur Brigade* (1928), *Tomahawk Rights (1929)*, *The Shaggy Legion* (1930), *Short Grass* (1932), *Wolf Dog* (1935).

Films based on Hal G. Evarts' Western fiction are *The Silent Call* (First National, 1921) directed by Lawrence Trimble starred Strongheart, the dog, in the lead [based on *The Cross Pull*], *Tumbleweeds* (United Artists, 1925) was co-directed by King Baggot and William S. Hart, *The Santa Fe Trail* (Paramount, 1930) was co-directed by Otto Brower and Edwin H. Knopf [based on *Spanish Acres*], *The Big Trail* (Fox, 1930) directed by Raoul Walsh [source unknown] credited Evarts for the original story.

Evarts, Hal G(eorge) (Jr.) (1915—)

Author of Western fiction and son of Western novelist Hal G. Evarts (q.v.), born at Hutchinson, Kansas. Evarts attended Stanford University, where he was enrolled at the time of his father's sudden death. Upon graduation, Evarts set out for Europe and continued to travel around the world back-packing in 1936–1937. When he returned to Southern California, he worked briefly as a Hollywood screenwriter and became a reporter for trade journals and newspapers. In 1939 he returned to Europe to write for the Paris edition of the *New York Herald-Tribune* until the fall of France. Enlisted in the U.S. Army 1943–1945, he served in the 89th Infantry Division in Europe.

After his discharge, Evarts turned to commercial fiction writing, primarily for slick magazines such as *The Saturday Evening Post* and *Collier's*. In the late 'Fifties, he turned to writing Western novels, along with a series of non-Western juveniles, many of them for Scribner's, while most of his subsequent Westerns were paperback originals. Evarts, as Frank Bonham (q.v.), perhaps ranked his juveniles above his Westerns, but his Western fiction betrays the same trend toward simplicity and straight adventure. "I was born in a small Midwestern town in the heart of the Kansas wheat belt. . . . My father was a natural-born storyteller, and from childhood I wanted to be a writer too. I often accompanied my father on his wide travels to gather material for stories and articles on camping and hunting trips over much of the West, to Mexico, Alaska, the Florida Keys, New Guinea, and the South Pacific. My primary function as a writer is to entertain." In a sense this is correct; Evarts' novels do seek only to entertain. They depend largely on stereotypes and are extremely formulary. In *The Blazing Land* (New York: Dell, 1960) Evarts' Apaches start out giving off "a potent smell of sweat and grease and smoke and bird lime and the Lord knows what all," and they do not get any better!

Hal G. Evarts' Western novels are *Ambush Rider* (1957), *Jedediah Smith, Trail Blazer of the West* (1959), *The Blazing Land* (1960), *Branded Man* (1965), *Sundown Kid* (1969), *Man without a Gun* (1972), *The Night Riders* (1972), *The Settling of the Sage* (1972) [revised from *The Settling of the Sage* (1922) by Hal G. Evarts, Sr.], *The Long Rope* (1972), *The Man from Yuma* (1972), *Fugitive's Canyon* (1972).

Everett, Wade. See Lutz, Giles A. and Cook, Will.

Farrell, Cliff (1899 —) Author of formulary Western fiction, born at the same place as Zane Grey (q.v.): Zanesville, Ohio. After attending public schools in Zanesville, Farrell went to Los Angeles where he got a job as telegraph editor with the *Los Angeles Examiner*. He worked up to night news editor and then to sports news editor in a career that spanned 1925–1956. Farrell published his first Western novel, *Follow the New Grass* (New York: Random House, 1954), and followed it with *West with the Missouri* (New York: Random House, 1955) before retiring from newspaper work altogether to concentrate on writing Western fiction. He became a regular author of Doubleday Double D Westerns, the best among them perhaps being *Return of The Long Riders* (New York: Doubleday, 1964) and *The Renegade* (New York: Doubleday, 1970), the latter winning a Golden Spur Award from the Western Writers of America. Farrell falls easiest into that category of highly competent writers of traditional formulary Westerns along with Clifton Adams (q.v.), Giles A. Lutz (q.v.), and Lewis B. Patten (q.v.), although he never quite attained the vivid intensity and the polished, precise plotting of Luke Short (q.v.).

Cliff Farrell's Western novels are *Follow the New Grass* (1954), *West with the Missouri* (1955), *Santa Fe Wagon Boss* (1958), *Ride the Wild Trail* (1959), *The Lean Rider* (1960), *Fort Deception* (1960), *Trail of the Tattered Star: A Historical Novel of the West* (1961), *The Walking Hills* (1962), *Ride the Wild Country* (1963), *Return of the Long Riders* (1964), *Cross-Fire* (1965), *Bucko* (1965), *Comanch'* (1966), *The Guns of Judgment Day* (1967), *Death Trap on the Platte* (1968), *Treachery Trail* (1969), *The Renegade* (1970), *Owlhoot Trail* (1971), *Patchsaddle Drive* (1972), *Shoot-Out at Sioux Wells* (1973), *Terror in Eagle Basin* (1976), *The Devil's Playground* (1976).

Fast, Howard (1914 —) Author of one important Western novel, *The Last Frontier* (New York: Duell, Sloan, 1941), born at New York City. Fast left high school in the late 'Twenties and was rejected by the U.S. Navy because of his youth. He spent the next three or four years traveling around the country working at odd jobs such as shipping clerk in a factory, laborer in a lumber camp, and a page boy in the New York Public Library. For a time he studied at the National Academy of Design. Fast sold his first story in 1932 and his first novel, *Two Valleys* (New York: Dial, 1933), was published the next year.

The Last Frontier is about the fated 1878 trek of three hundred Cheyenne Indi-

ans from their Oklahoma reservation back to their homelands in the Black Hills. While the theme was handled less adequately by Alan LeMay (q.v.) and far more poignantly by Mari Sandoz (q.v.), Fast's account does reflect his socialistic convictions and his view of the whites is that they want to be in on the finish of the Cheyenne nation—a fact well known to the Cheyennes—and that the trek represents nothing so much as the last time it will ever be so easy legally to kill a man in the United States as it was to shoot a Cheyenne. Fast, however, did confine himself to characterizing *only* the white men.

D.W.

Faust, Frederick (1892–1944) Author of over 300 Western novels, born at Seattle, Washington. Of his nineteen pseudonyms, George Owen Baxter, Evan Evans, and Max Brand were primarily associated with Faust's Western fiction. At a very early age Faust moved with his parents to the San Joaquin Valley of California. His parents were poor and, apparently to compensate for living a life in which there was sometimes not enough to eat, Faust turned to medieval romantic literature and his own vivid imagination. It was the extraordinary amount of work Faust did as a youth which strained and enlarged his heart. When orphaned, he went to live with a distant relative, Thomas Downey, a high school principal. Faust was 16 and Downey introduced him to a classical education, Faust becoming intensely interested in Greek and Roman literature and mythology. He matriculated at the University of California at Berkeley and showed significant promise already then as a writer. His natural inclination was toward poetry and one of the most moving experiences of his undergraduate years was hearing British poet Rupert Brooke read aloud from his works. Due to his arrogance and his attitude toward the administration, however, after four years Faust was denied the right to graduate.

Faust became convinced that to die in battle was the best, most heroic kind of death, a rather romantic notion which presumably prompted him to try to get into World War I by emigrating to Canada. All of his efforts, however, came to nothing, and in 1917, in New York City, unable to get shipped overseas even in the ambulance corps, Faust turned to what from then on would be his principal aim in life, to be a great poet. At this he was also unsuccessful. Working at manual labor, in his outrage, Faust wrote a letter of protest over the social injustice of it all to *The New York Times* and, amazingly, he was given assistance by Mark Twain's (q.v.) sister who arranged for Faust to see Robert H. Davis, an editor with the Munsey publications. Although the story is probably apocryphal, Davis is reputed to have given Faust a brief plot idea, told him to go down the hall to a room where there was a typewriter, only to have Faust return some six hours later with a completed 7,800 word story that Davis thought suitable for publication. However it happened, Faust became a regular contributor to the Munsey publications and, presently,

felt his career sufficiently secure that he returned to California intent on marrying his college sweetheart, Dorothy Schilling. Returning to New York, Faust continued his writing career.

It was Davis' idea, having lost Zane Grey (q.v.) to the slick magazine markets, that Faust should try to duplicate his success and write Western stories and novels. At a party one night, Faust and a group of people came up with the pseudonym Max Brand, "the Jewish cowboy" as it was put humorously, and it was under this byline that Faust published *The Untamed* in *All-Story Weekly* in 1918. It is among Faust's many books perhaps the closest he came to serious fiction because it symbolized Faust's own inner conflicts, the war waged in his soul between his desire to live the unfettered life of a great poet and the necessity of family obligations which kept him chained to a typewriter filling up reams of paper with pulp stories which, while popular with readers, Faust himself regarded with contempt. *The Untamed* concerns the life of Whistling Dan Barry and his two constant companions, Black Bart, a wolf dog, and Satan, his stallion. Faust continued Dan Barry's saga through two more books, *The Night Horseman* (New York: Putnam's, 1920) and *The Seventh Man* (New York: Putnam's, 1921), before Barry was dead and Black Bart and Satan returned to a life in the wilderness. Barry, however, did leave behind him a daughter, and it is her story which is told in the final volume, *Dan Barry's Daughter* (New York: Putnam's, 1924).

In the early 'Twenties, Faust took his family to live in Katonah, New York, and it was here that he raised white bull terriers which he would permit to run loose over the estate. He must have studied their habits carefully because one of his most notable, although least appreciated, books has a white bull terrier as its principal character, *The White Wolf* (New York: Putnam's, 1926). As Jack London (q.v.) in *White Fang* (New York: Macmillan, 1906) who felt constrained to repudiate the message of freedom with which he had ended *Call of the Wild* (New York: Macmillan, 1903) and had White Fang seek domestic life with humans, Faust rejected the wilderness into which he had earlier abandoned Black Bart and Satan and had White Wolf come to live a happy, domestic life with his former master.

When Davis was released from the Munsey publications, Faust changed his affiliation to Frank Blackwell, editor of *Western Story Magazine*. Blackwell, for whom Faust might have as many as three serials running simultaneously in a single issue under three different pseudonyms, believed in one basic plot: pursuit and capture; he would admit only one variation to this plot: delayed revelation. Hence nearly all of Faust's Western fiction which was run serially in *Western Story Magazine* followed this convention.

In 1921 Faust made the painful and, for him, tragic discovery that he had a chronic and incurable heart condition from which he might die at any moment. Different parts of his heart would beat at different rates and, sometimes, would seem not to beat at all. This may have been due in part to physical strain as a youth but also to emotional origins in Faust's erratic, contradictory, and, in truth, tormented life. After consulting any number of heart specialists, Faust became concerned over his mental condition and sought analysis with H.G. Baynes in England, a Jungian analyst, and finally went to Zurich where he consulted C.G. Jung. Jung refused to take him as a patient, but he did advise Faust that his best hope was to live a simple life. This advice Faust rejected completely. He went to Italy where he rented a large villa, lived extravagantly and was perpetually in debt. Faust believed that to be able to write the pulp fiction he wrote he had to dream. Part of that dream was the way he lived in his Florentine villa. What Faust would not accept as a dream was his intention to write great poetry, even though on one occasion he had to publish his poetry himself. Faust came to love the grand gesture—pretending that time, money, and courtesy were endless, while privately he was besieged and overburdened by his many debts. The bills did compel him to do one thing: to write and publish between one million and one million and a half words each and every year.

Faust's speed in writing and his reliance on pulp magazines resulted in many of his Western stories suffering from cardboard characterizations and casual plotting, more dependent on superficial action than on reasoned development. When he sought to overcome these deficiencies in the early 'Thirties, his American literary agent and his editors warned him that he was writing too well—what was needed was less characterization, more story! Faust was too financially pressed to do anything but acquiesce. Hence a plot as that of *Riders of the Plains* (New York: Dodd, Mead, 1940) wherein the hero evolves from country hick to star college athlete to helpless cripple to mysterious gunfighter to bandit to loyal son and lover.

Under pressures from his agent and editors, Faust found himself coming more and more to the United States, usually leaving his family in Italy. For periods of time he was literally a captive of his agent, working many long hours in the agent's office revising a story or writing a new one to specification. By 1932, the president of Harper's told Faust that Zane Grey's sales had dropped off to 30,000 copies a year. Dodd, Mead had been publishing the Max Brand Westerns for years, having taken over from Putnam's. Harper's wanted their own line of Westerns and so the Evan Evans pseudonym was born. Faust could readily do this. He was writing the equivalent of six to seven novels a year for the pulps, so many in fact that up to 25 years after his death pulp serials were still being issued for the first time in book form.

Both Faust and his agent wanted him to move into the slick magazines, which paid better than the pulps. Faust, studying the market, found that conditions with the slicks were somewhat more awesome than with the pulps. Writing for Blackwell, he had had to worry only about a pursuit and capture plot frame; the slicks sought to dominate their contributors' minds. Writing for the slicks, Faust learned, was a matter of attitudes and ideas—good writing had nothing to do with it. Beyond entertainment, which pulp and slick fiction alike provided, slick fiction had to deliver an ideological message to its readers which agreed with the editorial policy of the magazine's editors. Perhaps it is for this reason that so much of the slick fiction of the 'Thirties and 'Forties has become quickly dated, Faust's from the 'Thirties included, while Faust's pulp serials from the 'Twenties are still bought at the rate of a million copies a year. Ideology is time-bound.

Hollywood beckoned. Faust had been selling stories to motion picture companies since Fox Film Corporation bought *The Untamed* as a vehicle for Tom Mix, and before that. But even as recently as *Destry Rides Again* (New York: Dodd, Mead, 1930) which Universal wanted as the basis for a film with Walter Huston but which ended up starring Tom Mix, Faust had been paid only $1,500. The appeal from Hollywood now meant that Faust would be paid $1,500 *a week* to work on screenplays.

Faust brought his family to Hollywood and, seemingly, turned his back on Europe, which was about to plunge into another war. While at M-G-M, he breathed new life into his Dr. Kildaire property—Columbia Pictures had earlier made a film based on Faust's first Kildaire story—and an entire series was launched starring Lew Ayres and Lionel Barrymore.

Switching from studio to studio, never very happy, and drinking heavily upon occasion as he had been accustomed to do periodically despite his heart condition, Faust talked more and more about great writers who had started writing their most noteworthy fiction in middle age, because he was middle-aged and he feared with his motion picture commitments, his slick magazine writing, his steady out-pouring of Western stories and novels, he would never achieve his goal. Those who worked with him in Hollywood were amazed at the fecundity of his mind, his ability to plot stories. Faust himself had some simple advice on the process: read a story half way through and then imagine how it will come out. Then put on a new beginning and you have a different story, one all your own.

He had missed the Great War as it had been called. He refused to miss World War II. He pulled sufficient strings to become a war correspondent and he sailed to the Italian front where he lived with men in foxholes, in mud, green troops in some of the bloodiest conflict of the entire war, men who had grown up reading his stories with their superhuman heroes and their grand deeds, and that is where he died, on a dark night in 1944, from a shrapnel wound.

Faust has been condemned by those who admire realistic detail in Western fiction for ignoring historical accuracy and for failing to provide even minimal descriptions from his frontier settings. In point of fact, Faust detested the Western states and only under duress would he so much as travel through them. Invariably he resorted in his fiction to his two basic themes: the son in search of the illustrious father and the warrior who has an Achilles heel. As the West in the Western fiction of Louis L'Amour (q.v.), Faust's West has nothing to do with the real physical West; it has to do with mythical, superhuman entities—and, again, as with L'Amour, this seems to be precisely what attracts readers to him.

Although during his lifetime Faust published Western fiction in novel form under the pseudonyms Max Brand, Evan Evans, and several others as well, in re-issue all of his titles have been altered to Max Brand or Max Brand writing as Evan Evans. Therefore, in this bibliographical listing no distinction is made between the many pseudonyms, although the year of original publication is given. Frederick Faust's Western novels are *The Untamed* (1919), *Trailin'* (1920), *Riders of the Silences* (1920), *The Night Horseman* (1920), *Free Range Lanning* (1921), *The Seventh Man* (1921), *Donnegan* (1923), *Alcatraz* (1923), *The Long, Long Trail* (1923), *Dan Barry's Daughter* (1924), *The Range-Land Avenger* (1924), *Bull Hunter* (1924), *Bull Hunter's Romance* (1924), *The Bronze Collar* (1925), *Jerry Peyton's Notched Inheritance* (1925), *Jim Curry's Test* (1925), *King Charlie's Riders* (1925), *The Shadow of Silver Tip* (1925), *Beyond the Outpost* (1925), *The Black Sig-*

nal (1925), *Wooden Guns* (1925), *Blackie and Red* (1926), *Fire Brain* (1926), *The Splendid Rascal* (1926), *The Brute* (1926), *Train's Trust* (1926), *Ronicky Doone* (1926), *The White Wolf* (1926), *Monsieur* (1926), *Ronicky Doone's Treasure* (1926), *The Whispering Outlaw* (1926), *On the Trail of Four* (1927), *The Mountain Fugitive* (1927), *The Blue Jay* (1927), *The Trail to San Triste* (1927), *Western Tommy* (1927), *Bandit's Honor* (1927), *The Outlaw Tamer* (1927), *The Mustang Herder* (1927), *Pleasant Jim* (1928), *The Trap at Comanche Bend* (1928), *Gun Gentlemen* (1928), *Señor Jingle Bells* (1928), *Lost Wolf* (1928), *Pillar Mountain* (1928), *Children of Night* (1928), *The Gun Tamer* (1929), *Tiger Man* (1929), *Mistral* (1929), *Mystery Ranch* (1930), *Destry Rides Again* (1930), *Smiling Charlie* (1931), *The Killers* (1931), *The Happy Valley* (1931), *Valley Vultures* (1932), *Twenty Notches* (1932), *The Jackson Trail* (1932), *Slow Joe* (1933), *Montana Rides* (1933), *The Longhorn Feud* (1933), *The Return of the Rancher* (1933), *The Outlaw* (1933), *The Thunderer* (1933), *Timbal Gulch Trail* (1934), *Call of the Blood* (1934), *The Sheriff Rides* (1934), *The Rancher's Revenge* (1934), *Montana Rides Again* (1934), *Red Devil of the Range* (1934), *Brothers on the Trail* (1934), *The Seven of Diamonds* (1935), *King of the Range* (1935), *Hunted Riders* (1935), *Brother of the Cheyennes* (1935), *Rustlers of Beacon Creek* (1935), *Happy Jack* (1936), *The Song of the Whip* (1936), *The King Bird Rides* (1936), *South of Rio Grande* (1936), *Trouble Trail* (1937), *The Streak* (1937), *The Golden Knight* (1937), *Six Golden Angels* (1937), *The Iron Trail* (1938), *The Naked Blade* (1938), *Singing Guns* (1938), *Dead or Alive* (1938), *Marble Face* (1939), *Fightin' Fool* (1939), *Gunman's Gold* (1939), *The Dude* (1940), *Danger Trail*

(1940), *Riders of the Plains* (1940), *The Border Kid* (1941), *The Long Chance* (1941), *Vengeance Trail* (1941), *Silvertip* (1942), *The Man from Mustang* (1942), *Silvertip's Strike* (1942), *Silvertip's Round-Up* (1943), *Silvertip's Trap* (1943), *Silvertip's Chase* (1944), *The Fighting Four* (1944), *Silvertip's Search* (1945), *The Stolen Stallion* (1945), *Valley Thieves* (1946), *Mountain Riders* (1946), *The Border Bandit* (1947), *Valley of Vanishing Men* (1947), *The False Rider* (1947), *The Rescue of Broken Arrow* (1948), *Flaming Irons* (1948), *Hired Guns* (1948), *Gunman's Legacy* (1949), *The Bandit of the Black Hills* (1949), *Seven Trails* (1949), *Smuggler's Trail* (1950), *Single Jack* (1950), *The Firebrand* (1950), *Sawdust and Six Guns* (1950), *The Galloping Broncos* (1950), *The Bait and the Trap* (1951), *The Hair-Trigger Kid* (1951), *Tragedy Trail* (1951), *Border Guns* (1952), *Strange Courage* (1952), *Outlaw Valley* (1953), *Smiling Desperado* (1953), *The Tenderfoot* (1953), *Outlaw's Code* (1954), *The Gambler* (1954), *The Visible Outlaw* (1954), *Speedy* (1955), *Outlaw Breed* (1955), *The Big Trail* (1956), *Trail Partners* (1956), *Lucky Larribee* (1957), *Blood on the Trail* (1957), *The White Cheyenne* (1960), *The Long Chase* (1960), *Tamer of the Wild* (1962), *Mighty Lobo* (1962), *The Stranger* (1963), *The Garden of Eden* (1963), *Golden Lightning* (1964), *The Gentle Gunman* (1964), *Torture Trail* (1965), *The Guns of Dorking Hollow* (1965), *Ride the Wild Trail* (1966), *Larramee's Ranch* (1966), *Rippon Rides Double* (1968), *The Stingaree* (1968), *Thunder Moon* (1969), *Clung* (1970), *Black Jack* (1970), *Trouble Kid* (1970), *Harrigan* (1971), *Timbral Gulch* (1971), *The Luck of the Spindrift* (1972), *Drifter's Vengeance* (1972), *Cheyenne Gold* (1972).

Frederick Faust's nineteen pseud-

onyms were Frank Austin, George Owen Baxter, Lee Bolt, Max Brand, Walter C. Butler, George Challis, Peter Dawson (not to be confused with the same pseudonym later used by Jonathan Glidden (q.v.)), Martin Dexter, Evin Evan, Evan Evans, John Frederick, Frederick Frost, Dennis Lawton, David Manning, M.B., Peter Henry Morland, Hugh Owen, Nicholas Silver, Henry Uriel.

Films based on Frederick Faust's Western fiction are *The Adopted Son* (Metro, 1917) directed by Charles Brabin [based on the serial of that title in *All-Story Weekly,* 1917], *Lawless Love* (Fox, 1918) directed by R. Thornby [source unknown], *The Un-*

A Max Brand Story in All-Story Weekly *from 1927 stressing a motion picture tie-in.*

tamed (Fox, 1920) directed by Emmett J. Flynn remade as *Fair Warning* (Fox, 1930) directed by Alfred Werker, *The Night Horseman* (Fox, 1921) directed by Lynn F. Reynolds, *Trailin'* (Fox, 1921) directed by Lynn F. Reynolds, *Just Tony* (Fox, 1922) directed by Lynn F. Reynolds [based on *Alcatraz*], *Three Who Paid* (Fox, 1923) directed by Colin Campbell [based on the short story "Three Who Paid"], *Mile-A-Minute Romeo* (Fox, 1923) directed by Lambert Hillyer [based on the short story "Gun Gentlemen"], *The Gun Fighter* (Fox, 1923) directed by Lynn F. Reynolds [based on the short story "Hired Guns"], *Against All Odds* (Fox, 1924) directed by Edmund Mortimer [based on the short story "Cuttle's Hired Man"], *The Best Bad Man* (Fox, 1925) directed by J.G. Blystone [based on *Señor Jingle Bells*], *The Flying Horseman* (Fox, 1926) directed by Orville O. Dull [based on the short story "Dark Rosaleen"], *The Cavalier* (Tiffany, 1928) directed by Irvin Willat [based on the short story "The Black Rider"], *A Holy Terror* (Fox, 1931) directed by Irving Cummings [based on *Trailin'*], *Destry Rides Again* (Universal, 1932) directed by Ben Stoloff, remade under this title (Universal, 1939) directed by George Marshall, *The Valley of Vanishing Men* (Columbia, 1942) directed by Spencer Gordon Bennet [a fifteen chapter serial], *The Desperadoes* (Columbia, 1943) directed by Charles Vidor [based on an original story], *Rainbow Over Texas* (Republic, 1946) directed by Frank McDonald [source unknown], *Singing Guns* (Republic, 1950) directed by R.G. Springsteen, *Branded* (Paramount, 1951) directed by Rudolph Maté, *My Outlaw Brother* (United Artists, 1951) directed by Elliott Nugent [based on *South of Rio Grande*], *Destry* (Universal, 1954) directed by George Marshall, *The Hired Gun* (M-G-M, 1957) directed by Ray Nazarro [source unknown].

The Fighting Streak (Fox, 1922) directed by Arthur Rosson [based on *Free Range Lanning* written under Faust's byline George Owen Baxter].

Faust also worked on the screenplay for *The Deerslayer* (Republic, 1943) directed by Lew Landers.

Destry (ABC, 1964) was a television series for a single season.

Radio adaptations were done of *Destry Rides Again* (CBS, 1945) and of the film version of *Singing Guns* (CBS, 1947).

The best book which exists on Faust is still *Max Brand: The Big "Westerner"* (Norman: University of Oklahoma Press, 1970) by Robert Easton.

Ferber, Edna (1885–1968) Pulitzer Prize winning author of Western historical novels, short stories, and plays (most of the plays written in collaboration with George S. Kaufman), born at Kalamazoo, Michigan. Ferber was educated in public schools in Appleton, Wisconsin, where the nomadic Ferber family finally settled. To help support her family, at 17 Ferber became the first full-time female reporter for the *Appleton Daily Crescent* and later she worked for the *Milwaukee Journal* and contributed pieces to the *Chicago Tribune*. While working as a reporter Ferber, who had dreams of studying drama, began writing short stories and was finally published in a national magazine in 1909. Her first novel appeared in 1911. However, her real success came with the Emma McChesney stories, about a traveling saleswoman, which were published in *American Magazine*, and, later, in *Cosmopolitan* before they were brought out in hardcover form. She won the Pulitzer Prize in 1924 for *So Big* (New York: Doubleday, 1924), a novel about farming in the Midwest.

Ferber settled in the East and became known for being outspoken. Her strong female heroines exemplified her personal feelings about men and women: women are doers, men are dreamers. She never married. Little is remembered about her often sentimental stories and novels which are basically escapist, but in the four novels she devoted to the building of communities on the frontier she earned for herself a rightful reputation for having eloquently depicted a passing way of American life.

Ferber's *Cimarron* (New York: Doubleday, 1930) is one of the few novels along with Courtney Riley Cooper's *Oklahoma* (Boston: Little, Brown, 1926) that describes vividly the land rush of 1889 when yet another section of what was once called Indian Territory was opened up to settlers. Upon publication, *Cimarron* became a bestseller and critics considered it a romantic Western. Ferber herself, however, had intended it to be ". . . a malevolent picture of what is known as American womanhood and American sentimentality." Ferber showed the triumph of greed and materialism over the pioneering spirit; she showed it even among the Indians—which was accurate, but in only a few cases.

Great Son (New York: Doubleday, 1945) is set in Seattle while *Giant* (New York: Doubleday, 1952) concerns the making of modern Texas. These books became somewhat controversial in that the people living in these localities often resented Ferber's portrayal of their home states. However, she did become nationally recognized as a contributing force in Alaska's becoming the forty-ninth state due to the popularity of *Ice Palace* (N.Y.: Doubleday, 1958) which was published four months before Alaska's acceptance into the Union. Ferber showed the many good qualities of Alaskans and their vast land. Throughout *Ice Palace* Ferber contrasted the characters who want

Publicity for Cimarron *(RKO, 1931) based on the Edna Ferber novel.*

Alaska to be accepted as a state with those greedy characters who only want to exploit the land for its resources.

The films based on Edna Ferber's Western novels are *Cimarron* (RKO, 1931) directed by Wesley Ruggles, remade under this title (M-G-M, 1961) directed by Anthony Mann, *Giant* (Warner's, 1956) directed by George Stevens, *Ice Palace* (Warner's, 1960) directed by Vincent Sherman.

For further information see Ferber's two autobiographies, *A Peculiar Treasure* (New York: Doubleday, 1939), *A Kind of Magic* (New York: Doubleday, 1963), and Julie Goldsmith Gilbert's *Ferber, A Biography of Edna Ferber and Her Circle* (New York: Doubleday, 1978).

Fergusson, Harvey (1890–1971)

Primarily a novelist of the old Southwest, born at Albuquerque, New Mexico. Fergusson's maternal grandfather, Franz Huning, arrived in Santa Fe in 1850 and became a successful merchant in Albuquerque during the years following 1857 and Fergusson, who loved the wilderness and was insatiably curious about the history and people of New Mexico, seemed closer to his grandfather than to his own father, Harvey Butler Fergusson, who was a territorial delegate to Washington, then a Representative from the new State of New Mexico, and who was a friend of novelist Emerson Hough (q.v.). It was Fergusson's father who sent him to Washington and Lee University in Virginia and who urged him to take a newspaper job in Washington, D.C., a year after graduation. A few years after striking up a friendship with H.L. Mencken (who introduced him to the Knopf publishing firm), Fergusson began writing his first novel and in 1923 he moved to New York City and established himself as a free-lance writer. It would be two decades and ten books before his association with Knopf terminated.

In 1931 Fergusson left New York for good, accepting part-time jobs as a writer with several motion picture companies. Seven of his books (half of his total production) had been written and published while he lived in the East. Three more appeared during his residence in Hollywood; and the last four were written in Berkeley where he lived for almost thirty years before his death. It would seem that at least part of Fergusson's sensibility in his best novels— all of which are set in New Mexico—came from his many years away from his native state. Yet Fergusson maintained that he was "highly indigenous and very deeply rooted in [his] home environment," by which he meant the West as well as his home state. He had little time for writers who only seemed to be Western but who did not know from intimate experience the facts of the West, one of the more prominent being Willa Cather (q.v.).

Of Fergusson's five major novels, three constitute a trilogy of sorts, covering a period of almost 100 years in the Nineteenth century Southwest, from the mountain men to the struggle between Anglos and Spanish during settlement and, finally, the uneasy union of the two cultures. *Wolf Song* (New York: Knopf, 1927), *In Those Days* (New York: Knopf, 1929), and *Blood of the Conquerors* (New York: Knopf, 1921) were reprinted in a single volume called *Followers of the Sun: A Trilogy of the Santa Fe Trail* (New York: Knopf, 1936). In his Introduction to this volume, Fergusson insisted that "what ails the huge and infantile body of our conventional Western romance, from Beadle's dime novels on down, is not that its stories are melodramatic but that its heroes and heroines are lifeless." His own novels are a blend of the romantic and the realistic, but their focus is always on character in relation to the land and its past.

Fergusson's interest in, and portrayal of, women in the West is somewhat unusual and may stem from his tragic second marriage. In 1927, the year *Wolf Song* was published, he left New York for a year, returned to the West and married Rebecca McCann, to whom *Wolf Song* is dedicated. She died of pneumonia before the year ended and Fergusson went back to New York, never to marry again. The sensitively drawn female characters in his later novels may well be a tribute to Rebecca.

Wolf Song, which could be the finest novel of the mountain man despite the popularity of A.B. Guthrie's (q.v.) *The Big Sky* (New York: Sloane, 1947), is poetic and evocative. Although Fergusson said that it did not lend itself to a motion picture treatment, it was filmed with Gary Cooper and Lupe Velez in the title roles. The film did not please Fergusson because of its emphasis on sex. Late in life he spoke disparagingly of the female star's "pneumatic bosom" bouncing through the picture.

It is generally agreed that in addition to *Wolf Song* Fergusson's best novels are his last two: *Grant of Kingdom* (New York:

Morrow, 1950) and *The Conquest of Don Pedro* (New York: Morrow, 1954). One is panoramic and the other concentrates on a Jewish peddler, but both recreate the Nineteenth-century Southwest with an authority and stylistic felicity possessed by few Western writers.

Fergusson's work was never given the attention it deserved during his lifetime, but he is being re-discovered, a trend which began in the 'Seventies.

J.R.M.

Wolf Song (Paramount, 1929) was directed by Victor Fleming.

Two useful introductions to Harvey Fergusson's life and work are *Harvey Fergusson* (Austin: Steck-Vaughn, 1969) by James K. Folsom and *Harvey Fergusson* (New York: Twayne Publishers, 1975) by William T. Pilkington. Also worth mentioning is the chapter devoted to Fergusson in *Southwest Classics* (Los Angeles: Ward Ritchie, 1974) by Lawrence Clark Powell and the chapter on him in *The Novel of the American West* (Lincoln: University of Nebraska Press, 1980) by John R. Milton.

Fisher, Clay. See Allen, Henry Wilson.

Fisher, Vardis (1895–1968) Scholar, essayist, journalist, and author of Western historical fiction and of a wide variety of non-fiction works born at Annis, Idaho. Fisher's parents were Mormons whose ancestors were Mormon converts who had traveled West with Joseph Smith. At 6, Fisher moved with his family to the Antelope Hills region on the South Fork of the Snake River, where the Fisher family lived off the land and civilization was thirty miles from their mountain-surrounded home. For five years Fisher did not leave the remote basin area and he came to have mixed feelings about this lonely period of his youth. He and his brother and sister received their early education from their mother, Temperance, until Fisher was about 12, at which time he attended a frontier school and went on to graduate from Rigby High School in Rigby, Idaho. His education at the University of Utah in Salt Lake where he received his Bachelor's degree in 1920 was disrupted by World War I. Fisher first served as an enlisted officer candidate in the Air Force from which he retired and as a draft volunteer in the U.S. Army where he attained the rank of Corporal. He went on to obtain his Master's degree in 1922 and Doctor's degree *magnum cum laude* in 1925 from the University of Chicago. In 1924, his first wife, whom he had married in 1917 and with whom he had had two children, committed suicide. This marked a crisis in his life and, according to several scholars, provided Fisher with the unquenchable need for introspection which informed his subsequent literary output.

While working as an assistant professor in English at the University of Utah between the years 1925–1928, Fisher published his first book, *Sonnets to an Imaginary Madonna* (New York: Harold Vinal, 1927), a collection of poems. Fisher, who had repudiated Mormonism at age 18, left the University of Utah where he was considered an unorthodox and liberal educator and became assistant professor in English at Washington Square College in New York City 1928–1931. His first published novel, *Toilers of the Hills* (Boston: Houghton Mifflin, 1928), set in the Antelope Hills of Fisher's childhood, marked the birth of a new regional literature since it was the first significant fiction to come out of the Rocky Mountains region. Upon publication of *Toilers of the Hills*, which was actually the sixth novel Fisher had written, Fisher was immediately linked with Hamlin Garland (q.v.) and Willa Cather (q.v.). Fisher, however, personally felt Cather was a totally unrealistic writer since she had failed to deal with the brutalities of pioneer life. In *Toilers* and other regional novels by Fisher as *Dark Bridwell* (Boston: Houghton Mifflin, 1931) and *April: A Fable of Love* (Idaho: Caxton, 1937), the latter a rather comic story which is the only novel in which Fisher used a female protagonist, he depicted his own ambivalence about the beauties and harshnesses of the land.

In 1931, Fisher, wanting to devote all his time to writing, returned to Idaho. He taught several terms at Montana State University, however, before formally terminating his teaching career in 1933. From 1935–1939 he served as the director of the WPA Writer's Project in Idaho which marked an important period in his artistic development because he had to learn the discipline which goes with extensive research. Almost single-handedly Fisher completed *Idaho: A Guide in Word and Picture* (Idaho: Caxton, 1937), *The Idaho Encyclopedia* (Idaho: Caxton, 1938), and *Idaho Lore* (Idaho: Caxton, 1939), a composite of regional information much of which remains of permanent value.

Divorcing his second wife in 1939, the

next year Fisher married Opal Laurel Holmes who was his spiritual and intellectual companion for the rest of his life and with whom he co-authored his last book, *Gold Rushes and Mining Camps of the Early American West* (Idaho: Caxton, 1968). Fisher spent his final years at Thousand Springs on the Snake River where he built his own home.

Fisher, as his father, never believed in an eight-hour work day. During the four-year period when he was devoting ten hours a day to the WPA project, he was devoting six hours a day to his own research for his first historical novel, *Children of God: An American Epic* (New York: Harper's, 1939), which won the Harper Prize of $10,000 in 1939 and is Fisher's best-known work. For many years he had been contemplating writing a novel on Mormonism and had spent years reading books and documents both in favor and against the Church of the Latter-Day Saints. In his essay "Creative Historical Research in Fiction" (1940), Fisher stated that he had wanted "to be impartial, to see the whole matter in reasonably clear perspective, and to avoid all editorializing and moral implications." The general consensus upon publication was that *Children of God* was historically objective and the best book on the subject. In it, Fisher described the Mormon's beginnings in the 1820s as well as their persecution, heroism, and their migration across the Western frontier to establish their church and depicted in the final section the failure of the church to defend itself following the death of Brigham Young. As is true of all of his historical novels, although Fisher himself considered them only "extra" books and was more concerned with his other literary efforts, *Children of God* is panoramic and is a faithful and vivid representation of this period in the settling of the frontier.

His second historical novel, *City of Illusion* (New York: Harper's, 1941), deals with the rise and fall of Virginia City, Nevada where silver was discovered in 1859 and examines the illusions of wealth and power and how it changes the lives of a wide variety of people. Fisher told a story of the city through use of the legendary characters, Eilley and Sandy Bowers, by paralleling their accumulation of money and subsequent poverty with the history of Virginia City which ultimately became a ghost town after having enjoyed international notoriety.

The Mothers: An American Saga of Courage (New York: Vanguard, 1943) is the story of the ill-fated Donner expedition across the Sierra Nevadas in 1846–1847. Fisher told this tragic episode of the Westering movement from the point of view of the mothers in the group who in order to survive became cannibals. He did manage to underplay the sensationalism of the story and thus restored the proper perspective surrounding the naiveté of a group of Midwestern farmers on their trek to California. That same year Fisher published his first book in the "Testament of Man" series, a twelve-volume undertaking in which he wanted to come to terms with the spiritual and psychological evolution of man. For the next thirteen years Fisher devoted himself to this series which was financially unsuccessful and ultimately left without a publisher when the Vanguard Press dropped the series. In 1956 Alan Swallow offered to take up publishing the series and in order to circulate his name among the public again, Fisher wrote *Pemmican* (New York: Doubleday, 1956), a love story set during the Pemmican War 1815–1821 between the Hudson Bay Company and the Northwest

Company for control of the Western fur trade. It marked the first time Fisher used fictional events and characters within an historical framework, whereas in his prior historical novels he had always used real characters and historical events. The events surrounding the Pemmican War are historically reliable, however, and the book, which has been compared to A.B. Guthrie's (q.v.) *The Big Sky* (New York: Sloane, 1947), is unique for Fisher since the love story between a mountain man and a white girl, who has been raised by Blackfoot Indians, ends happily.

With his next historical novel, *Tale of Valor* (New York: Doubleday, 1958), Fisher dealt with the epic story of the Lewis and Clark expedition. The novel, which is considered by most to be the best novelization of the excursion, differs from such novels as Emerson Hough's (q.v.) *The Magnificent Adventure* (New York: Appleton, 1916) in that Fisher penetrated into the characters' minds and dramatized Lewis' and Clark's extraordinary qualities of leadership. *Tale of Valor* is perhaps the most action-packed historical novel Fisher ever wrote. His interest in the subject continued with his nonfictional book *Suicide or Murder? The Strange Death of Governor Meriwether Lewis* (Denver: Alan Swallow, 1962) in which he examined all the available evidence about the mysterious death of Meriwether Lewis in 1809 after he became governor of the Louisiana Territory.

Fisher was most capable as a fictional author in the medium of the novel and consequently only one volume of his short stories was ever collected. *Love and Death* (New York: Doubleday, 1959) includes thirteen short stories and fragments from six of his novels; seven of the short stories are set in the Antelope Hills region and all were written in the 'Thirties. "The Scarecrow" (1934), narrated by Vridar Hunter, the main protagonist of Fisher's tetralogy, and a prototype of Fisher himself, is perhaps his most famous short story, since it has been included in numerous anthologies. In the story, Fisher dealt with the kinship between man and animals in their fight for survival.

Mountain Man: A Novel of Male and Female in the Early American West (New York: Morrow, 1965) was Fisher's last novel and won the Wrangler Award from the National Cowboy Hall of Fame for the Best Western Historical Novel for 1965. The story focuses on the legend surrounding "Liver Eating" Johnson, called Sam Minard in the book, who supposedly killed over 200 Crow Indians in a bloody vendetta after the murder of his Flathead Indian wife, and the legend surrounding Jane Morgan. The book, which contains some of Fisher's most lyrical prose, also includes some graphically brutal scenes, as does *Pemmican*. Both books, however, show the barbarous actions of whites and Indians alike in their most primitive form in their fight for survival. The novel enjoyed a large readership when it was reprinted after the success of the film adaptation, *Jeremiah Johnson* (Warner's, 1972).

Fisher turned out thirty-five books in his lifetime including twenty-six novels, along with literary criticism, controversial journalism, and, as Mary Austin (q.v.), several provocative essays attacking the Eastern Establishment for its failure to recognize the importance of Western authors and Western literature. Because he was so prolific, Fisher's work is often uneven. However, he does deserve more serious attention than he has received in the past. He was an iconoclast who never stopped pursuing his insatiable need to understand man and his behavior. Since all of Fisher's novels are novels of ideas and philosophic concerns, his historical and regional novels transcend the ordinary adventure story. As many critics, historians, and scholars have already realized, Fisher is a reliable historian who chronicled the vision and courage, along with the brutalities, of the early settlers of the West in both his historical and regional fiction.

Jeremiah Johnson (Warner's, 1972) was directed by Sydney Pollack [based on *Mountain Man*].

For further information see *Vardis Fisher* (New York: Twayne Publishers, 1965) by Joseph M. Flora, *Three West* (Vermillion: Dakota Press, 1970) edited by John R. Milton, *Vardis Fisher: The Frontier and Regional Works* (Boise: Idaho State University Press, 1972) by Wayne Chatterton.

Fleischman, A(lbert) S(idney)

(1920 —) Author of Western fiction and juvenile fiction with a Western setting, born at Brooklyn, New York. Fleischman's initial intention was to become a magician and in 1936, together with a high school classmate, he put together a two-hour magic show and went on tour. Upon his return to New York, he began writing short stories. He was 17 when he published his first book, a manual for magicians. During World War II Fleischman served as a yeoman aboard a destroyer escort in the Pacific. Upon his discharge, he attended San Diego State College from which he received his Bachelor's degree in 1949. While still attending college, he was writing mystery novels and worked briefly for a San Diego newspaper. In 1955, film director William Wellman hired him to help adapt his novel *Blood Alley* (New York: Fawcett, 1954) for the screen and a longterm collaboration resulted.

Yellowleg (New York: Fawcett, 1960) was the last of a series of paperback original novels Fleischman wrote for Gold Medal Books published by Fawcett, and the only Western. It is a revenge story with a particularly gruesome premise, that of a former Union soldier searching for a scarred man who scalped him. "Every writer wants to try a Western," Fleischman commented at the time, and his impetus came when he learned that scalping had first been introduced to the Indians by the white man.

As the 'Sixties began, Fleischman had apparently reached an impasse in his career. His resolution came with publication of *Mr. Mysterious & Company* (Boston: Little, Brown, 1962), the first of his subsequently long list of juveniles. As an author of adult fiction, Fleischman had received few letters from readers; as an author of juveniles, he suddenly found himself receiving thousands of letters. Often in these juveniles Fleischman turned to the West for his settings; indeed, Mr. Mysterious is a frontier magician who outwits both Indians and outlaws. *By the Great Horn Spoon* (Boston: Little, Brown, 1963) is the story of a scion of a once prosperous Boston family and his butler who join in the California gold rush. Through clever and whimsical schemes, they save two fortunes, reform outlaws, and find and lose gold. Although the book is filled with solid information and history about early California and gold mining, the form is nevertheless that of an allegorical fairy tale. *Chancy and the Grand Rascal* (Boston: Little, Brown, 1966) is also set in the West, involving riverboats and spiced by much telling of tall tales. *Me and the Man on the Moon-Eyed Horse* (Boston: Little, Brown, 1977) is the story of a boy who foils a train wrecker and saves a circus. Fleischman received a National Book Award nomination for *Humbug Mountain* (Boston: Little, Brown, 1978), a story inspired by the career of fabulist Frederick Faust (q.v.), and *Jim Bridger's Alarm Clock and Other Tall Tales* (New York: Dutton, 1978) is an even more explicit attempt at frontier hyperbole. Eric Von Schmidt, himself an author, painter, and folksinger, has illustrated Fleischman's children's books for Little, Brown, and apparently it has been a profitable collaboration for both men.

D.W.

Films based on A.S. Fleischman's Western novels are *The Deadly Companions* (Pathé-American, 1961) directed by Sam Peckinpah [based on *Yellowleg*], *The Adventures of Bullwhip Griffin* (Buena Vista, 1967) directed by James Neilson [based on *By the Great Horn Spoon*].

Flint, Timothy (1780–1840)

Author of *Francis Berrian* (1826) which can be cited as the first novel of the Southwest written in English, born near North Reading, Massachusetts, Flint was educated at Phillips Andover Academy and at Harvard University, from which he was graduated in 1800. He then taught school at Cohasset, Massachusetts, and became a minister at Marblehead. From 1802–1814 Flint served as a minister of the Congregational church at Luenburg, Massachusetts. He had a keen interest in natural science and chemical experiments that resulted in charges of counterfeiting—probably unjustified—and prompted his forced resignation. After a year of missionary work in New Hampshire, he set out for the West to continue his missionary activities. From 1815–1825 Flint traveled throughout the Mississippi Valley, spending 1819 in Arkansas, and he was the first Protestant minister to administer communion in St. Louis. He went on to lecture and preach in New Orleans. A long illness ensued, from which he never fully recovered, and he went East where his sole activity became writing and editing.

Flint's first novel tells of Francis Berrian who leaves his theological studies at Harvard to search for adventure in the West. He ends up falling in love with a Spanish girl and subsequently rescues her from a hostile Indian named Menko with the help of an Indian maiden named The Red Heifer. Berrian also manages to join a Mexican revolutionary, eventually saving his fiancée's parents and their priest from death. The novel is important because, however tritely written, it established popular stereotypes which would remain predominant in Southwestern literature for the next one hundred years: the manly Anglo-American, the beautiful Spanish señorita, the treacherously vindictive Spanish-American lover, the menacing Indian, the sweet, self-sacrificing Indian maiden, and the scheming Roman Catholic priest.

The same year as *Francis Berrian* Flint published a non-fiction work he titled *Recollections of the Last Ten Years*. His work enjoyed some success and he was motivated to write three more adventure novels, all in the same vein: *The Life and Adventures of*

Arthur Clenning (1828), *George Mason, The Young Backwoodsman* (1829), and *The Shoshone Valley* (1830). None of these later novels, however, was set in the Southwest.

In addition to assuming certain editorial jobs for magazine publications, Flint also edited *The Personal Narrative of James Ohio Pattie of Kentucky* (1830), a rather colorful account of an early Western trapper.

Besides Flint's own book of *Recollections*, he was the subject of a biography, *Timothy Flint* (Cleveland: Arthur H. Clark, 1911) by J.E. Kirkpatrick, and much about his work can be found in *The Early Novel of the Southwest* (Albuquerque: University of New Mexico Press, 1961) by Edwin W. Gaston, Jr.

Flynn, Robert (Lopez) (1932 —)

Author known chiefly for his first novel, *North to Yesterday* (New York: Knopf, 1967), born at Chillicothe, Texas. The son of a farmer, Flynn served in the U.S. Marine Corps 1950–1952 and his stage play, *Journey to Jefferson*, won the Special Jury Award, Theatre of Nations. *North to Yesterday* won the Texas Institute of Letters Award and the Western Heritage Award. Author Brian Garfield (q.v.) said of it that it is "a thoughtful, tragicomic parable of all America . . . an ungentle satire on the foolishness of those who live in the past, as well as the blindness of those who turn their backs on it." In this story of a cattle drive from Texas to Kansas, unlike similar books by Harry Sinclair Drago (q.v.) and Benjamin Capps (q.v.), Flynn tried to give massive historical details to attain an air of verisimilitude; and if his descriptions often slowed up his narrative, they helped usher in a new spirit of historical realism in the writing of Western fiction.

Foote, Mary Anna Hallock

(1847–1938) Illustrator and author of novels set in the West, born Mary Hallock at Milton, New York. Her father, a farmer, believed in the value of books and she read widely from his library when she was young. She was educated at Poughkeepsie Female College Seminary where her artistic talents were discovered. She took a three-year course in the women's art school at the Cooper Institute in New York City. She began her career as an artist contributing illustrations to Fields, Osgood & Company, a publishing firm, and to numerous periodicals as *Harper's Weekly*, *Scribner's Monthly*, and later to *Century* magazine. She was soon considered one of the top Eastern illustrators. Upon her marriage in 1876 to Arthur DeWint Foote, her career took a new direction and she was henceforth associated with the West.

Foote and her husband, a civil engineer whose work took him to various Western mining regions, spent the next half-century in the West. Foote, who believed in becoming totally involved in her work, found herself frustrated living in the West as a "protected" Eastern gentlewoman and she found it increasingly difficult to draw. Some of her best art work, however, depicted Western mining scenes. In her frustration she wrote to her editors about her problems and pieces of her letters were spliced together and published in *Scribner's Monthly*. A new career was launched when Foote was encouraged by both Helen Hunt Jackson (q.v.) and her editors to take up writing as a career. Her first book, *The Led-Horse Claim* (1883), a romance of the silver boom, appeared after being serialized in *Century* magazine, for which she also provided illustrations. Leadville, Colorado, where the Footes were stationed from 1878 to 1880, served as the background for this novel and her next two, *John Bodewin's Testimony* (1886), considered by many to be her best work, and *The Last Assembly Ball* (1889). The cold, harsh winters of Colorado determined a move to the silver mines of Mexico after the birth of the first of the Footes' three children. The stagecoach ride to Michoacan, Mexico, in 1881 provided Foote with material for a series of articles for *Century* which she also illustrated. Her husband's work next took them to Boise, Idaho, where they remained for ten years before finally settling in California where they lived for thirty years. A number of books with an Idaho setting resulted, among them *The Chosen Valley* (1892) and *Coeur D'Alene* (1894).

Foote continued to write articles and stories for a number of years. She spent her last days near Boston and saw her literary reputation fall into obscurity. She died of arteriosclerosis at the age 90.

Foote's biggest mistake was in pandering to her editors who felt that her books must have happy endings. Her use of realistic and authentic settings in her mining stories evoked comparisons with works by Mark Twain (q.v.) and Bret Harte (q.v.); however, the formulary love stories make them ultimately flat and incapable of sustaining interest.

Mary Hallock Foote's novels with a Western setting are *The Led-Horse Claim, A Romance of a Mining Camp* (1883), *John Bodewin's Testimony* (1886), *The Last Assembly Ball, and the Fate of a Voice* (1889), *The Chosen Valley* (1892), *Coeur D'Alene* (1894), *In Exile and Other Stories* (1894) [short stories], *The Cup of Trembling and Other Stories* (1895) [short stories], *The Little Fig-Tree Stories* (1899) [short stories], *The Prodigal* (1900), *The Desert and the Sown* (1902), *A Touch of Sun and Other Stories* (1903) [short stories], *The Royal Americans* (1910), *A Picked Company* (1912), *The Valley Road* (1915), *Edith Bonham* (1917).

For further information see *Mary Hallock Foote* (Boise: Idaho State University Press, 1972) by James H. Maguire and *A Victorian Gentlewoman in the Far West: The Reminiscences of Mary Hallock Foote* (San Marino: The Huntington Library, 1972) edited with an Introduction by Rodman W. Paul.

Ford, Lewis. See Patten, Lewis, B.

Foreman, L(eonard) L(ondon)

(1901 —) Author of formulary Western fiction, born at London, England. After serving in the British Army during World War I, Foreman immigrated to the United States and, working at various odd jobs, began contributing to the Western pulp magazines during the 'Thirties. His first Western novel to be published in book form was *Don Desperado* (New York: Dutton, 1941). Foreman's finest fiction is characterized by a short, almost clipped, laconic style with all the emphasis on action. However, unlike other writers who began in the pulps, notably Nelson C. Nye (q.v.) and Walt Coburn (q.v.), Foreman seems to have thought out his plots ahead of sitting down to write, although he did not rival Luke Short (q.v.) whose specialty was structuring well-made Westerns. In addition, Foreman was upon occasion resourcefully innovative, within the confines of formulary Western fiction. His series of books about the adventures of Rogue Bishop are filled with unusual variations, such as *Rogue's Legacy* (New York: Doubleday, 1968) in which Bishop takes as a ward a 14-year-old girl who has been orphaned and leaves her with a former prostitute to be raised. Foreman's books are sometimes remarkable for their realistic atmosphere and his creative use of bizarre characters, somewhat reminiscent of John Reese's (q.v.) technique.

L.L. Foreman's Western novels are *Don Desperado* (1941), *The Renegade* (1942), *The Road to San Jacinto* (1943), *Gunning for Trouble* (1953), *Arrow in the Dust* (1954), *Woman of the Avalon* (1955), *Lone Hand* (1956), *Return of the Texan* (1958), *Desperation Trail* (1959), *Long-Rider* (1961), *Spanish Grant* (1962), *Lobo Gray* (1963), *Farewell to Texas* (1964), *The Mustang Trail* (1965), *The Silver Flame* (1966), *Rogue's Legacy* (1968), *Triple Cross at Trinadad* (1971).

Films based on L.L. Foreman's Western fiction are *The Savage* (Paramount, 1952) directed by George Marshall [based on *The Renegade*], *Arrow in the Dust* (Allied Artists, 1954) directed by Lesley Selander, *The Lone Gun* (United Artists, 1954) directed by Ray Nazarro [source unknown], *The Storm Rider* (20th-Fox, 1957) directed by Edward Bernds [source unknown].

Fowler, Kenneth A(brams)

(1900 —) Author and editor of Western fiction, born at New York City. Following graduation from New York University in 1922, Fowler joined the editorial staff of *The Yonkers New York Herald-Statesman* where between 1925 and 1937 he was city hall reporter and editorial page columnist. In 1937 he joined Smith and Street Publications and became affiliated with *Western Story Magazine*. During World War II Fowler served in the Army Air Force Intelligence and, following his honorable discharge, became an executive with the Todd Shipyards Corporation in New York City in the public relations department. After two years with Todd, he returned to editorial work with Popular Publications, where he edited two of the firm's magazines, *Dime Western* and *Star Western*. In 1949 he began to free-lance and in 1972 he moved to Florida where he was appointed editor of *The Roundup*, the monthly magazine of the Western Writers of America. He served in that capacity until 1978 when he returned to writing. His novel *Jackals' Gold* (New York: Doubleday, 1980) bears an inscription to Fowler's wife: "For Martha—because of that unforgettable day on McDonald River when we shared with Grace and August Lenniger the terrifying adventure that inspired this book." August Lenniger was Fowler's literary agent. The adventure referred to occurred in Montana when the Fowlers and Lennigers were returning from a Western Writers of America convention in Helena and the small boat in which they were fishing was unexpectedly caught up in a rapids and capsized, flinging all of them into a raging torrent. On the whole Fowler's Western fiction has been essentially in the formulary mode.

Kenneth Fowler's Western novels are *Outcast of Murder Mesa* (1954), *The Range Bum* (1955), *Summons to Silverhorn* (1957), *Ride with a Dark Moon* (1962), *Juggernaut of Horns* (1962), *Dead Reckoning* (1968), *Jackals' Gold* (1980).

Fowler's novels as Clark Brooker are *Lone Gun* (1955), *Fight at Sun Mountain* (1957).

Fox, Brian. See Ballard, Todhunter.

Fox, Norman A(rnold) (1911–1960) Author of formulary Western fiction, born at Sault Ste. Marie, Michigan. Fox grew up in Montana and it was his deep knowledge of his adopted state which prompted him to make it the setting for most of his Western novels. His first two Westerns were published in 1941 by the Phoenix Press, a bottom-of-the-line house that produced small editions (usually no more than 2,000 copies) for lending libraries, and then went on to write at least thirty more Westerns, plus some four hundred stories for the pulps and other magazines. The $200 per book which was Phoenix's standard payment could not have been much of an incentive for a struggling writer, so it should be no surprise that after five books Fox moved on to Dodd, Mead which remained his hardbound publisher for the rest of his career. Fox was one of the founding members of the Western Writers of America and drafted that organization's constitution. He died of cancer.

All but two of Fox's novels were written for hardbound publication. The first exception was *Winchester Cut* (New York: Fawcett, 1951) published in Gold Medal's line of original paperbacks under the pseudonym Mark Sabin, the name of the leading character in Fox' *Stormy in the West* (New York: Dodd, Mead, 1950) from the previous year. This novel was later reworked (and improved) and published in hardcover as *Stranger From Arizona* (New York: Dodd, Mead, 1956) under Fox's own name. The other paperback original was *Broken Wagon* (New York: Ballantine, 1954).

In Fox's novels specific details of Western history are seldom in the foreground, although in *Stormy in the West* the great Montana blizzard of 1886 is an important element in the story. Montana's valleys, mountains, and badlands and their changing seasons form a vivid continuing backdrop throughout his fiction. Many of Fox's heroes are caught up in a conscious or unconscious quest for self-knowledge; driven by a desire for vengeance, as Larry Madden in *Tall Man Riding* (New York: Dodd, Mead, 1951) or Terry Mullane in *Rope the Wind* (New York: Dodd, Mead, 1958); or by a need to discover the truth about the past, as the orphaned Will Yeoman in *The Rawhide Years* (New York: Dodd, Mead, 1953); or simply by the longing to find something solid around which to build a life, as gunfighter Reb Kittredge in *Roughshod* (New York: Dodd, Mead, 1951).

Sometimes a character has already reached the security of knowing himself and it is the people around him who must grow out of their prejudice and enmity. Ross Kingman in *Reckoning at Rimbow* (New York: Dodd, Mead, 1958) returns with his wife and teenaged children to the town he had left in anger seventeen years before. His struggle to overcome the antagonism of townsmen and ranchers alike, and to make a secure home for his family without being pushed into violence, make a satisfying and unusual story.

Fox's short stories, such as those collected in *The Valiant Ones* (New York: Dodd, Mead, 1957), are often built around historical personages or events. As Fox said in his Foreword to the book, "[T]he background of each [story] is as authentic as research and my personal knowledge of the West could make it; and in several of the selections the fiction is interwoven with actual historical happenings so that men of history walk side by side with men and women of my invention." Alexander Majors, Kid Curry, General Jack Casement, and other figures from the annals of the West play significant roles in these well wrought tales. In the posthumously published novel, *The Trembling Hills* (New York: Dodd, Mead, 1960), Fox blended reality and fiction in an unusual way. The Montana earthquake of August, 1959 was moved fifty years into the past to provide the climax for a story of incipient range war.

To quote again from Fox's Foreword to *The Valiant Ones*: "Detractors of the Western story as a fiction medium claim that the cowboy has been shaped into a myth-symbol and that the other frontier types have been glorified beyond reality as well. Yet for every dramatic scene the fictioneer has provided, history has provided an even more dramatic one, and the most colorful characters of Western fiction had their living counterparts." In his fiction, Fox dealt with the standard ingredients of the formulary Western, but he handled these ingredients with skill and respect, and peopled his stories with characters whose thoughts and problems were of as much interest to the reader as the details of the action. Novels such as *Tall Man Riding, Badlands Beyond* (New York: Dodd, Mead, 1957), *Reckoning at Rimbow*, and *The Hard Pursued* (New York: Dodd, Mead, 1960) are worthy of a place in any permanent library of Western fiction.   R.E.B.

Norman A. Fox's Western novels are *Gun-Handy* (1941), *The Gunsight Kid* (1941), *The Six-Gun Syndicate* (1942), *The Stampede Kid* (1942), *Lord Six-Gun* (1943), *The Thundering Trail* (1944), *Thorson of Thunder Gulch* (1945), *Silent in the Saddle* (1945), *The Valley of Vanishing Riders* (1946) [alternate title: *Riders in the Rain*], *Dead End Trail* (1946), *Cactus Cavalier* (1947), *The Rider from Yonder* (1947), *The Devil's Saddle* (1948), *The Feathered Sombrero* (1948), *Shadow on the Range* (1949), *The Thirsty Land* (1949), *Stormy in the West* (1950), *The Phantom Spur* (1950), *Roughshod* (1951), *Tall Man Riding* (1951), *Ghostly Hoofbeats* (1952), *Long Lightning* (1952), *The Rawhide Years* (1953), *Broken Wagon* (1954), *Night Passage* (1956), *Stranger from Arizona* (1956) [alternate title: *Arizona Stranger*], *Badlands Beyond* (1957), *The Valiant Ones* (1957), *Rope the Wind* (1958), *Reckoning at Rimbow* (1959), *The Hard Pursued* (1960) [alternate title: *Showdown at Signal*], *The Trembling Hills* (1960), *They Rode the Shining Hills* (1968).

Fox's novel as Mark Sabin is *Winchester Cut* (1951), which was reworked into *Stranger from Arizona* (see above).

Films based on Norman A. Fox's Western fiction are *Gunsmoke* (Universal, 1953) directed by Nathan Juran [based on *Roughshod*], *Tall Man Riding* (Warner's, 1955) directed by Lesley Selander, *The Rawhide Years* (Universal, 1956) directed by Rudolph Maté, *Night Passage* (Universal, 1957) directed by James Neilson.

Frazee, Steve (1909 —) Author of formulary Western fiction, born at Salida, Colorado. Frazee attended Western State College of Colorado and was graduated with a Bachelor's degree. He had worked at heavy construction and mining for ten years, 1926–1936, before entering Western State College to earn his degree and continued to work at various jobs while there. Following graduation, he became a high school instructor in journalism while trying his hand at free-lance writing. From 1950–1963 he was a building inspector for the City of Salida as well as a director of the Salida Building and Loan Association. Frazee at-

tempted to give all of his Westerns a strong historical flavor, but his weakest area was in his highly romanticized and questionable treatment of Native Americans.

Steve Frazee's Western novels are *Shining Mountains* (1950), *Pistolman* (1952), *Lawman's Feud* (1953), *Sharp the Bugle Calls* (1953), *Spur to the Smoke* (1954), *The Sky Block* (1954), *Cry Coyote* (1955), *Many Rivers To Cross* (1955), *Tumbling Range Woman* (1956), *He Rode Alone* (1956), *High Cage* (1957), *Running Target* (1957), *Desert Guns* (1957), *Gold at Kansas Gulch* (1958), *Rendezvous* (1958), *Smoke In The Valley* (1959), *The Alamo* (1960), *Hellsgrin* (1960).

Films based on Steve Frazee's Western fiction are *Many Rivers to Cross* (M-G-M, 1955) directed by Roy Rowland [based on a Frazee short story which he later expanded to a novel], *Running Target* (United Artists, 1956) directed by Marvin R. Weinstein [source unknown], *Wild Heritage* (Universal, 1958) directed by Charles Haas [source unknown], *Gold of the Seven Saints* (Warner's, 1961) directed by Gordon Douglas [source unknown].

G

Garfield, Brian (1939 —) A prolific author of formulary Westerns, born at New York City. Despite his birthplace, Garfield was proud of having early moved to Arizona with his family and it was from the University of Arizona that he received his Bachelor's degree at the age of 20. While still an undergraduate, he served briefly in the U.S. Army and Army Reserve. An accomplished musician, he played in a dance band called "The Casuals" in Tucson and, after graduation, he toured with another dance band, "The Palisades." He returned to the University of Arizona for graduate study in English and was an instructor at the University while he completed work on his Master's degree which he received in 1963. By this time his writing career was well under way. He moved back to the East coast to write full-time.

Although known equally for his novels of suspense, Garfield began his career as a Western writer and maintained a strong interest in the West and in Western fiction as a literary form. He started writing fiction in his early teens. At the age of 15 he was trying to sell Western short stories to the last remaining pulp magazines. He persuaded Western writer Luke Short (q.v.) to look at some of his manuscripts. Short not only took this apprentice work seriously, but, in Garfield's words, "took me in hand and kept me working until he turned me into a writer. I owe much of my life to him."

From the start of his career Garfield was a partisan and a hard-working member of writers' organizations such as the Western Writers of America and, later, the Mystery Writers of America. He served as President of the Western Writers of America and was later elected a Director of that organization, contributing many articles and columns to its official journal, *The Roundup*. In 1968 he edited a WWA anthology, *War Whoop and Battle Cry* (New York: Scholastic, 1968), and many of Garfield's contributions to *The Roundup* deal with the necessity of extending the boundaries of the Western to recognize the work of such writers as Larry McMurtry (q.v.), Charles Portis (q.v.), and Edward Abbey (q.v.) who dealt with Western Americana in sophisticated and non-formulaic terms.

Garfield's first novel, *Range Justice* (New York: Avalon, 1960), was followed by two more Western novels for the same lending-library market in 1961, one of them under the pseudonym Frank Wynne. 1962 saw publication of two novels by Brian Wynne Garfield, two by Frank Wynne, and one each by Bennett Garland and Frank O'Brian, which were additional pseudonyms. With *Mister Sixgun* (New York: Ace, 1964) under the pseudonym Brian Wynne, Garfield began his successful series featuring the continuing character of Marshal Jeremy Six. The town of Spanish Flat and some of its inhabitants were borrowed from Garfield's first novel to serve as background for the series. The Jeremy Six stories, all published in paperback by Ace, proved so popular that when Garfield abandoned the series after eight books, Ace tried, unsuccessfully, to continue it still using the Brian Wynne pseudonym. The steady production of Westerns persisted until the late 'Sixties when Garfield began branching out into contemporary novels and suspense stories.

Garfield called his early books "on-the-job training" and added "the mistakes unfortunately are there for everybody to see." This judgment is appropriate for much of the lending-library material, but is unfairly harsh when applied to his other early works. From the beginning Garfield refused to stay within the bounds of the formulary Western. *The Lawbringers* (New York: Macmillan, 1962) is an historical novel based on the career of Burt Mossman, founder of the Arizona Rangers. *Seven Brave Men* (New York: Monarch, 1962), originally published as by Bennett Garland, is also based on an historical incident, being the story of the Cook's Canyon Massacre and of the "seven deadly men who for four days, on a waterless mountaintop, held off three hundred picked Apache warriors." Told with gritty realism and relentless pace, it makes compelling reading. Equally compelling is *Bugle and Spur* (New York: Ballantine, 1966) as by Frank O'Brian, a grim story of Cavalry/Apache warfare. The name of the unyielding Cavalry Colonel, Drew Mallory, was later used as the pseudonym for one of Garfield's suspense novels.

Even after he moved away from the period Western, Garfield continued to use Western settings for some of his novels. The spy novel *Deep Cover* (New York: Delacorte, 1971) takes place in and around Tucson, Arizona. Two crime novels, *Relentless* (New York: World, 1972) and *The Threepersons Hunt* (New York: M. Evans, 1974), feature Sam Watchman, a Navaho Indian member of the Arizona State Police.

In *Wild Times* (New York: Simon & Schuster, 1979), Garfield described the book as the result of "the slow-growing audacity to write a novel that would distill an accumulation of everything I knew and felt about the Old West." Subtitled "The True Life of Col. Hugh Cardiff," it is a picaresque and episodic tale of the life of the "king of crack shots" from his adolescence during the Civil War into old age. Historical events and characters thread through the narrative and there is plentiful commentary on life in the West as it really was, but the ultimate vision is romantic and larger-than-life. It is an exhilarating contribution to the literature of the American West.

R.E.B.

Brian Garfield's Western novels under his own name are *Range Justice* (1960) [alternate title: *Justice at Spanish Flat*], *The Arizonans* (1961), *The Lawbringers* (1962),

Trail Drive (1962), *Vultures in the Sun* (1963), *Apache Canyon* (1963), *The Vanquished* (1964), *Valley of the Shadow* (1970), *Sliphammer* (1970), *Sweeny's Honor* (1971), *Gun Down* (1971) [alternate title: *The Last Hard Men*].

Garfield's novels as Bennett Garland are *Seven Brave Men* (1962), *High Storm* (1963) [in collaboration with T.V. Olson (q.v.) but without credit], *The Last Outlaw* (1964), *Rio Chama* (1967).

Garfield's novels as Frank O'Brian are *The Rimfire Murders* (1962), *Bugle and Spur* (1966), *Arizona* (1969), *Act of Piracy* (1975).

Garfield's novels as Brian Wynne are *Mister Sixgun* (1964), *The Night It Rained Bullets* (1965), *The Bravos* (1966), *The Proud Riders* (1967), *A Badge for a Badman* (1967), *Brand of the Gun* (1968), *Gundown* (1969), *Big Country, Big Men* (1969).

Garfield's novels as Frank Wynne are *Massacre Basin* (1961), *The Big Snow* (1962), *Arizona Rider* (1962), *Dragoon Pass* (1963), *Rails West* (1964), *Rio Concho* (1964), *Lynch Law Canyon* (1965), *Call Me Hazard* (1966), *The Lusty Breed* (1966), *The Wolf Pack* (1966).

Garfield also contributed two entries to series written under house names (see House Names) which are *Savage Guns* (1968) by Alex Hawk and *Buchanan's Gun* (1968) by Jonas Ward.

The Last Hard Men (20th-Fox, 1976) was directed by Andrew McLaglen [based on *Gundown*].

Garland, Bennett. See Garfield, Brian.

Garland, Hamlin (1860–1940) Essayist, poet, short story writer, and novelist of the Midwest and the Far West, born at West Salem, Wisconsin. Garland moved with his family to the Iowa prairie at the age of 8, where he encountered the difficult rural life that he later wrote about. In 1881 he graduated from the Cedar Valley Seminary in Osage, Iowa, and taught school for a year in Illinois. Soon, however, he sought the greater cultural influence of Boston where he spent much of one winter reading in the Boston Public Library and where he became familiar with the writings of Henry George and Herbert Spencer who had an effect on his world-view. While in Boston he also attended the Boston School of Oratory and met William Dean Howells and other prominent authors.

After a trip to his father's Dakota farm, Garland began writing his stories about life on the plains of the Midwest. His first short fiction appeared in *Century*, *Harper's Weekly*, and *Arena*. Garland moved to Chicago, Illinois, in 1893, where he remained until 1916. While there, in 1899, he married Zulime Taft and, in time, they had two daughters. In 1916, Garland moved his family to New York where they remained until 1929. In that year the Garlands finally "went West," moving to California, where Garland died in 1940 in Hollywood.

Interspersed in Garland's life were numerous trips to the West which certainly influenced his Far West writings. In 1892 he journeyed to visit his uncle, David Garland, in Santa Barbara, California; in 1895 he went with two artist friends to visit the Isleta, Laguna, Zuñi, and Acoma Pueblos of the Southwest; Garland also took an extensive jaunt through the Dakotas, Montana, and the Lame Deer reservation in 1896–1897 followed by a journey to the Northwest and Canada in 1898. His honeymoon trip with Zulime encompassed Arizona, New Mexico, and Colorado in 1899. A trip to visit the Southern Cheyennes and Arapahoes in Darlington, Oklahoma, helped provide him with material for his Indian fiction.

Garland's Western writings seem to fall into three recognizable phases. In Garland's earliest works, such as *Main-Travelled Roads* (1891), he sought to dispel the myth of the West as a land of plenty and the home of the "good life" by portraying the hard work and grim realities of actual Western living. These stories are populated with men on the edge of despair and women grown old before their time. "Under the Lion's Paw" is perhaps the best known story from the above cited collection, depicting what happens to the small farmer in the clutches of a land speculator.

In Garland's middle phase, work done primarily during the years 1895–1917, he appeared to try to perpetuate the myth of the glorious West, especially in his Rocky Mountain romances. These books usually involved Easterners transplanted in the West or Westerners journeying East for a comparison of life-styles, and a period of self-learning. Of his Far Western writings, Garland reflected "for forty years an infinite drama has been going on in those wide spaces of the West—a drama that is as thrilling, as full of heart and hope and battle, as any that ever surrounded any man—a life that was unlike any ever seen on earth, and which should have produced its characteristic literature, its native art chronicle." And, indeed, Garland peopled his fiction with characters of the West: miners, outlaws, grubstakers, cattlemen, marshals, farmers, and Indians, and tried to portray accurately the regional dialects. *The Eagle's Heart* (New York: Harper's, 1900) perhaps typifies Garland's writing from this period.

In Garland's final phase, which was mostly autobiographical, he again attempted to demythologize the West. In books such as *A Son of the Middle Border* (New York: Macmillan, 1917), *A Daughter of the Middle Border* (New York: Macmillan, 1921), and *Back-Trailers from the Middle Border* (New York: Macmillan, 1928), Garland told of the moving West of his family and himself from Wisconsin to Iowa to Dakota, and the hardships encountered. Although Garland's approach to the West fluctuates from the realistic to the romantic, it does seem justified to comment, as does Robert Gish in *Hamlin Garland: The Far West* (Boise: Idaho State University, 1976), that "Garland's writings deal with the constantly shifting location of the West as place and idea and with the need for each of us to find it for himself and to proclaim it dead or alive."

D.M.-K

For further information on Hamlin Garland, see *Hamlin Garland: A Biography* (Austin: University of Texas Press, 1960) by Jean Holloway, *Hamlin Garland and the Critics* (Troy: Whitson, 1973) by Jackson Bryer, *Hamlin Garland: The Far West* (Boise: Idaho State University, 1976) by Robert Gish.

Gerstäcker, Friedrich (1816–1872) Prolific author of travel books and novels about the American frontier and the Far West, born at Hamburg, Germany. In-

spired in part by James Fenimore Cooper's (q.v.) novels, he left home in 1837 intent on experiencing the American wilderness, as very shortly thereafter would George Frederick Ruxton (q.v.) and shortly before had Charles Sealsfield (q.v.), each one in turn adding to a growing literature about the frontier. After working in New York City, Gerstäcker visited Niagara and Toronto and then set out on a walking tour of the frontier carrying only a rifle, a few belongings in a handkerchief, and fifteen dollars. Working at odd jobs—hunting buffalo, stoking and cooking on a Mississippi riverboat, managing a hotel in Louisiana—he wandered for several years through Ohio, Illinois, Missouri, Arkansas, and Texas keeping an intimate journal of his experiences. His first book was compiled from this chronicle and published after his return to Germany in 1843, titled *Streif-Und Jagdzüge Durch Die Vereinigten Staaten Nord Amerikas* (translated as *Wild Sports in the Far West*) (1844). Whereas Charles Sealsfield's account of the American frontier was that of a politically conscious, educated gentlemen traveling by gig and steamboat within the settled West, Gerstäcker's naive memoir offered an unpolished, firsthand view of the trackless hinterland, as did Ruxton's *Adventures in Mexico and the Rocky Mountains* (1847). Gerstäcker knew the West better than any other German writer of the Nineteenth century and his *Wild Sports in the Far West* was to become a classic of travel literature.

Over the next six years Gerstäcker lived in Germany and produced nine novels and travel books based upon his American experiences. The most popular of these were *Die Regulatoren in Arkansas* (*The Regulators of Arkansas*) (1845) and *Die Flusspiraten des Mississippi* (*The River Pirates of the Mississippi*) (1848). These fast-paced, sequential novels combined realistic portrayals of frontier conditions, tender love stories, gripping adventure, and can still be read with enjoyment. Gerstäcker's treatment of the Indian Assowaum, the companion to the trapper Brown in *The Regulators of Arkansas*, is similar to Sealsfield's Tokeah and Cooper's Chingachgook as well as Karl May's (q.v.) Winnetou.

Between 1849 and 1852 Gerstäcker made a world tour, stopping *en route* in California during the height of the gold rush. After his return to Germany, he began a second stretch of furious literary activity, writing twenty-two books in eight years. *Kalifornische Skizzen (California Sketches)* (1856) and *Gold!* (1858) were based on his experiences in the gold fields, but his masterpiece of this period was *Nach Amerika (To America!)* (1855). The only novel of the German immigration that can compare with O.E. Rölvaag's (q.v.) novel of the Norwegian immigration, *Giants in the Earth* (New York: Harper's, 1927), it traces the destinies of a shipload of credulous, optimistic German immigrants who land at New Orleans and progress through disillusionment, suffering, and eventual prosperity in a harsh and lonely land.

In 1860–1861 Gerstäcker was again in the United States. In 1862 he accompanied Prince Ernst von Coburg-Gotha to Egypt and Abyssinia and, in 1867–1868, he returned for a final visit to the United States.

Gerstäcker never considered himself a literary figure, but rather a man of action and the practical life who had become a writer nearly by accident. His books were dashed off in a rough and vigorous style intended to appeal to the audience he cared most about: the dissatisfied working people who were likely to respond to the lure of America. His heroes were usually simple farmers and men of the backwoods, upright and hardworking, while his villains often led dual lives as arrogant, murdering thieves by night and respectable physicians, judges, or army officers by day. Along with Sealsfield's novels, Gerstäcker's writings helped inspire the great German immigration of the mid-Nineteenth century and, although below Sealsfield in literary quality and social insight, Gerstäcker's novels were a more realistic introduction to the dangers and hardships of American pioneer life. His works have become an important source for historians studying life on the American frontier.

J.D.F.

Giles, Janice Holt (1909 —) Author of Western historical fiction, born at Altus, Arkansas. Giles was taken as a child to Eastern Oklahoma where her parents worked as teachers. In 1917 the family returned to Arkansas where Giles was educated. She attended courses at Little Rock Junior College, the University of Arkansas, and at Transylvania College in Lexington, Kentucky, while working at various jobs. While serving as the assistant to the dean at Presbyterian Seminary in Louisville, Kentucky, she began work on her first novel, *The Enduring Hills* (Philadelphia: Westminster Press, 1950), the first in her Piney Ridge trilogy about mountain life in Kentucky which sold over 110,000 copies in its first year of publication. She became a permanent Kentuckian upon her second marriage in 1949 to Henry Giles, who was also a writer. In 1950 she began a fulltime career as a free-lance writer and novelist.

In a series of novels begun in 1953, Giles traced the settlement of the American frontier through four generations of a Kentucky family who eventually move West. In the first three books in the Fowler family saga, *The Kentuckians* (Boston: Houghton Mifflin, 1953), *Hannah Fowler* (Boston: Houghton Mifflin, 1956), and *The Believers* (Boston: Houghton Mifflin, 1957), Giles dealt with the early settlement of Kentucky. The subsequent books set in the West depict various aspects of the pioneers' achievements for which Giles did in-depth research. *Johnny Osage* (Boston: Houghton Mifflin, 1960) is the story about Johnny Fowler and his friendship with the Osage Indians. Her treatment of Indians is sympathetic as it was in *The Plum Thicket* (Boston: Houghton Mifflin, 1954), a story set in Arizona about a mixed-blood who recounts his early memories of the Indian Territory before the invasion of the white man. The character, customs, ceremonies, and dress of the Osage Indians as well as their troubles with other Indian tribes, the encroaching white settlers, and the fanatic missionaries is handled well. *Voyage to Santa Fe* (Boston: Houghton Mifflin, 1962) is also about Johnny Fowler, but it is more a woman's story since it is told through the eyes of Johnny's wife. Among the many reference books that Giles used for *The Great Adventure* (Boston: Houghton Mifflin, 1967), a story about Joe Fowler, a mountain man, were books by Mari Sandoz (q.v.) and Paul Horgan (q.v.). *Six Horse Hitch* (Boston: Houghton Mifflin, 1969) traces the development of the stagecoach lines.

Giles continuously received excellent reviews for her saga of the Western frontier in which she adeptly wove history with fiction. Although her heavy use of romance sometimes bogs down the story-line, her stories told from the feminine viewpoint of the pioneers are interesting. Author Jessamyn West (q.v.) said of Giles that "Mrs. Giles is a writer we should cherish . . . a writer who makes our past available to us. . . ."

For further information see Giles' autobiography, *Forty Acres and No Mule* (Philadelphia: Westminster Press, 1952).

Gilman, George G. See Harknett, Terry.

Gipson, Fred (1908–1973) Short story writer and novelist of the American Southwest, born at Mason, Texas. Gipson, of German-Irish descent, spent his childhood as one of seven children working hard on the family farm. However, the difficulty of farm life developed in the young Gipson an intensive knowledge of the natural world and a real appreciation of family relationships which recur throughout his written works.

Gipson graduated from Mason High School in 1926 and took a number of jobs such as soda jerk, ranch hand, bookkeeper, and reporter to get through the Depression. During the years 1934–1937, Gipson attended the University of Texas at Austin, majoring in journalism. Although he never received a degree, presumably the course work proved of some assistance. In January, 1936, Gipson published his first short story, "Hard-Pressed Sam," in *Southwest Review*. It was the first of many Gipson would publish in *Southwest Review* over the years and, as he later acknowledged, this factor helped establish him as an important literary figure of the Southwest.

Gipson became a reporter for the Corpus Christi *Caller-Times* in 1937 and then worked for newspapers in San Angelo, Texas, and Denver, Colorado. Although he claimed not to be a very good reporter, Gipson did use his reporting experiences to learn more about the people and the regions where he worked. Fired from a newspaper job in 1940, he finally began his free-lance writing career. "I just bowed my neck," Gipson remarked, "and started writing."

By 1944 Gipson's writing career had begun to take hold. That year he had stories published in *Collier's* and one reprinted in *Reader's Digest*. In fact, three of Gipson's stories which had first appeared in the *Southwest Review* were reprinted by *Reader's Digest*. Gipson's straightforward short story style appealed to Donald Day who hired him to write the life story of Colonel Zack Miller, the well known Western rancher and principal of the Miller 101 Ranch Wild West Show. The Colonel and Gipson spent a month together on a Texas ranch after which Gipson returned to Mason with a bundle of notes which resulted in *Fabulous Empire: Colonel Zack Miller's Story* (Boston: Houghton Mifflin, 1946). In this biography, Gipson showed his real talent for story-line, character development, and dialogue, plus his understanding of the land and the people on it. Gipson followed his success by trying his hand at novels, the first, and one of the most popular, being *Hound-Dog Man* (New York: Harper's, 1949). As the subsequent, and even more successful, *Old Yeller* (New York: Harper's, 1956), *Hound-Dog Man* was an initiation story telling of a young boy's entrance into the wonders and hardships of the Western frontier. Gipson's accuracy of detail about frontier life and his realistic dialogue earned him the comment that "he . . . raised

the tone and embellished the reputation of Southwestern letters."

D.M.-K

Fred Gipson's Western novels are *Hound-Dog Man* (1949), *The Home Place* (1950), *Big Bend* (1952), *Cowhand* (1953), *Recollecton Creek* (1955), *The Trail-Driving Rooster* (1955), *Old Yeller* (1956), *The Cow Killers* (1956), *Savage Sam* (1962).

Films based on Fred Gipson's Western fiction are *Return of the Texan* (20th-Fox, 1952) directed by Delmer Daves [based on *Hound-Dog Man*], *Old Yeller* (Buena Vista, 1958) directed by Robert Stevenson, *Savage Sam* (Buena Vista, 1963) directed by Norman Tokar.

For further information see *Fred Gipson* (Austin: Steck-Vaughn, 1967) by Sam H. Henderson and *Fred Gipson: Texas Storyteller* (Austin: Shoal Creek Publisher, 1980) by Mike Cox.

Glidden, Frederick Dilley

(1908–1975) Known as "the dean of living Western writers" for much of his forty-year career writing under the pseudonym Luke Short, born at Kewanee, Illinois. Glidden, early determined on a career as a newspaperman, enrolled in the School of Journalism at the University of Missouri from which he received a Bachelor's degree in 1930. While still an undergraduate, he wrote a play called *Retraction* which won a prize from the University's Dramatic Arts Club and was published by the University in its series of Dramatic Prize Plays. After graduation, Glidden worked for a number of newspapers, but no job lasted for long. The Depression years were not auspicious ones for starting a career. With typical deprecation, he later described his newspaper experience in the following terms: "I've read or heard that all newspapermen are disappointed writers, but in me you behold a writer who is a disappointed newspaperman. I've been fired from more newspapers than I like to remember, even if I could. . . . [T]here was an allergy about me that affected city editors in strange ways, causing them to point to the doorway, request me to pass through it, and tell me never to darken it again. Subsequently, I discovered that the allergy did not affect magazine and book editors, and that if I stayed 2,000 miles away from them I was safe—which might explain my living in the West."

Abandoning his hopes of a life in journalism, Glidden became a wanderer throughout the American and Canadian West. He worked as a logger and an archaeologist's assistant, and spent two years in Northern Canada as a trapper. All of these experiences were later put to good use in his books. In 1934 Glidden married Florence Elder of Grand Junction, Colorado. Within a year he was well launched on his career as a Western writer. In 1941 Glidden's older brother, Jonathan Glidden (q.v.), would also become a Western writer, using the name Peter Dawson. Glidden's pseudonym, Luke Short, was chosen by his agent after a publisher had complained that his real name sounded "too phony." It was only after the pseudonym had become established that Glidden discovered that

Luke Short had been the name of an actual Western gunman.

The Gliddens became the parents of two sons and a daughter. They lived for a time in Pojoaque Valley, just North of Santa Fe, New Mexico. In 1947 they moved to Aspen, Colorado. Glidden rented an office above the U.S. Post Office and, in that sparsely furnished room, at least half his novels were written. In later years he dictated his work to a secretary while pacing from one end of the office to the other. The time not spent on his writing or with his family was devoted to his third major interest, a passion for fishing.

On two occasions tragedy touched the Gliddens. In 1957 Frederick's brother, Jonathan, died suddenly. Three years later a son, James, was killed in an accident while at Princeton University.

Through good times and bad, Glidden maintained his involvement with his adopted community and worked at his writing, averaging slightly more than one book per year. Finally, in 1975, after a nine-month battle against cancer, he died at the age of 67.

Luke Short's first novel, *The Feud at Single Shot*, was serialized in *Adventure* in 1935 and published in book form by Farrar & Rinehart a year later. From the beginning, Short's fiction appeared in top-of-the-line pulp magazines such as *Adventure*, *Argosy*, and *Blue Book*, as well as in Street and Smith's *Western Story Magazine*, the biweekly magazine made famous as the principal showcase for the writing of Max Brand (q.v.). Within three years Short was selling stories to *Collier's* and he placed his first *Saturday Evening Post* serial in 1941. Through the years, ten of Short's novels appeared as *Post* serials and three appeared in *Collier's*. The two magazines even shared a serial: when *Collier's* ceased publication in January, 1957, partway through the serialization of *Doom Cliff* [alternate title: *The Whip* (New York: Bantam, 1957)], the reader outcry was so great that the *Post* picked up the conclusion of the novel. Early in his career Short had also tapped another market for serials: newspapers such as the *New York Daily Herald* and the *Chicago Tribune*. This "newspaper connection" would serve him well in later years. For nearly ten years after the collapse of most of the markets for magazine fiction in the late 'Fifties, Short's novels continued to be serialized in the *Herald*.

Any attempt to assess Short's early development as a writer runs head-on into the complexity of his publishing history. His books may be arranged according to the order of original magazine serialization or of first British book publication or of first U.S. book appearance, and three entirely different lists will result. An illustration is provided by G.W. Harris' review of *Dead Freight For Piute* (New York: Doubleday, 1940) in his *New York Times Book Review* column of 9 February 1941 (the same column, incidentally, in which Harris reviewed the prize-winning first novel of Short's brother, Peter Dawson). Harris referred to *Dead Freight* as "the best of the four Luke Short novels so far." The book was actually Short's fifteenth novel: nine of the previous fourteen had seen book publication only in England and two others had not yet appeared in book form. Many of Short's magazine serials from 1937–1940 did not have U.S. book editions until the 'Fifties.

Short's early writings show the unmistakable influence of Ernest Haycox (q.v.). Short himself acknowledged some of the elements of Haycox's style which he admired: the handling of mood and dialogue,

and the "self-reliant, laconic" heroes. In one or two early novels, such as *The Branded Man* (London: Collins, 1939), Short's second novel in order of composition, the Haycox influence was carried to an extreme and the story's lack of conviction makes it clear that Short was not comfortable with the stately, Homeric mode which Haycox often adopted.

But Luke Short soon found his own voice. At his best (which was most of the time) he wrote a lean, uncluttered, vigorous prose. Although his plots were often complex, they were unfolded with such naturalness that they never seemed confusing or over-elaborate. He could create a mood or set a scene with a minimum of effort. And his dialogue, without awkward attempts at dialect, reads as if it might actually have been spoken by real people. He also had a healthy share of sheer storytelling know-how, of the kind that can grab a reader by the scruff of the neck and drag him bodily into the story. Witness the opening pages of *Sunset Graze* (New York: Doubleday, 1942), so skilfully provoking the reader's curiosity that it is impossible not to continue with the rest of the story, or the climax of *Bold Rider* (London: Collins, 1939), an exercise in pure edge-of-the-chair suspense.

Short dealt with most of the settings and themes of the formulary Western, handling them with a skill and attention to detail that raised them to a new level of quality. A Western feud carried to the point of all-out war is the framework of *Marauders' Moon* (New York: Dell, 1955). The old tale of greedy cattlemen preying on weaker neighbors received two widely different treatments in *Ride The Man Down* and *Ramrod* (New York: Macmillan, 1943). The quest of vengeance for the death of a loved one is the subject of *Coroner Creek* (New

York: Macmillan, 1946). Hard-rock mining forms the background for *Hard Money* (New York: Doubleday, 1940) and *High Vermillion* (Boston: Houghton Mifflin, 1948). Short also created a gallery of outlaws ripe for reformation. The title character of *Bold Rider* is the supremely arrogant Poco St. Vrain, with a hair-trigger temper and an unshakeable code of honor. *Hardcase* (New York: Doubleday, 1942) features Dave Coyle, a daredevil whom no jail is strong enough to hold. And in *Bought with a Gun* (London: Collins, 1943) we meet irreverent, cynical Sam Teacher—"There's a stockmen's bounty of ten dollars for wolves, twenty-five dollars for mountain lion, and five thousand for Sam Teacher."

While remaining within the framework of the outdoor adventure story, Short also wrote novels with modern settings. *Barren-Land Murders* (New York: Fawcett, 1951) is a contemporary spy story set in the Canadian Northwest. *Last Hunt* (New York: Bantam, 1962) is a tale of murder and detection in the Western mountain country. *Silver Rock* (Boston: Houghton Mifflin, 1953) is the story of an ex-Marine's battle to put a Colorado silver mine on a functioning basis against opposition from local politicians and unscrupulous mining operators while *Rimrock* (New York: Random House, 1955) tells of uranium mining and a conflict with big business against the small mine owner.

Short's most ambitious novel, and his own favorite among his books, was *And the Wind Blows Free* (New York: Macmillan, 1945). Framed as the story of an epic struggle to establish a cattle empire in Indian Territory, the novel is also a rich character study and an affecting love story.

The early 'Fifties appeared to mark a period of increased activity in Short's writing, with three or four new titles in some years. This appearance was deceptive, since most of the "new" books were reprints of magazine serials from the 'Thirties. All of the reprints were in paperback form, and all but one were published by Dell Publishing Company. They were so succesful that Dell decided to launch a new magazine named after the author. *Luke Short's Western Magazine* made its debut with an issue dated April–June, 1954. Edited by Don Ward, it was a well-designed digest-sized magazine, modeled on the earlier *Zane Grey's Western Magazine*. It was intended for quarterly publication, with each issue to feature a reprint of a Luke Short novelette. Despite its quality, it lasted less than a year, becoming one more victim of the distribution troubles which killed off most newsstand fiction magazines by the mid 'Fifties.

Some thirty million copies of his fifty novels of the West were published and read all over the world during his lifetime, and the number increases yearly. For a generation of readers, Luke Short's books established a standard of excellence against which the work of other Western writers was measured. His influence on other writers, both personally and through his writing, was notable. Brian Garfield (q.v.) and T.V. Olsen (q.v.) are among those who have particularly acknowledged his influence. In 1969 he received the Levi Strauss Golden Saddleman Award from the Western Writers of America for his contributions to Western fiction. He also received the Western Heritage Award from the National Cowboy Hall of Fame and the Western Heritage Center.

R.E.B.

Luke Short's Western novels, with the titles of first book publication whether American or British given first, are *The Feud at Single Shot* (1936), *Guns of the*

Double Diamond (1937) [alternate title: *The Man on the Blue*], *Misery Lode* (1938) [alternate title: *King Colt*], *Bull-Foot Ambush* (1938) [alternate title: *Marauders' Moon*], *Six Guns of San Jon* (1939) [alternate title: *Savage Range*], *The Gold Rustlers* (1939) [alternate title: *Bold Rider*], *Flood Water* (1939) [alternate title: *The Branded Men*], *Raiders of the Rimrock* (1939), *Brand of Empire* (1940), *Bounty Guns* (1940), *War on the Cimarron* (1940) [alternate title: *Hurricane Range*], *Dead Freight for Piute* (1940) [alternate titles: *Western Freight* and *Bull-Whip*], *Gunman's Chance* (1941) [alternate title: *Blood on the Moon*], *Hardcase* (1942), *Sunset Graze* (1942) [alternate title: *The Rustlers*], *Ride the Man Down* (1942), *Bought with a Gun* (1943), *Ramrod* (1943), *And the Wind Blows Free* (1945), *Coroner Creek* (1946), *Station West* (1947), *High Vermillion* (1948) [alternate title: *Hands Off!*], *Fiddlefoot* (1949), *Ambush* (1950), *Vengeance Valley* (1950), *Barren Land Murders* (1951) [alternate title: *Barren Land Showdown*], *Trumpets West* (1951) [short novel], *Play a Lone Hand* (1951), *Raw Land* (1952), *Saddle by Starlight* (1952), *Silver Rock* (1953), *Rimrock* (1955) *The Whip* (1957), *Summer of the Smoke* (1958), *First Claim* (1960), *Desert Crossing* (1961), *The Some-Day Country* (1964) [alternate title: *Trigger Country*], *First Campaign* (1965), *Paper Sheriff* (1966), *The Primrose Try* (1967), *Debt of Honor* (1967), *The Guns of Hanging Lake* (1968), *Donovan's Gun* (1968), *The Deserters* (1969), *Three for the Money* (1970), *Man from the Desert* (1971), *The Outrider* (1972), *The Stalkers* (1973), *The Man from Two Rivers* (1974), *Trouble Country* (1976).

Luke Short also edited the following Western anthologies of short stories: *Cattle, Guns and Men* (1955), *Frontier: 150 Years of the West* (1955), *Colt's Law* (1957), *Rawhide and Bob-Wire* (1958).

Films based on Luke Short's Western fiction are *Ramrod* (United Artists, 1947) directed by Andre de Toth, *Coroner Creek* (Columbia, 1948) directed by Ray Enright, *Albuquerque* (Paramount, 1948) directed by Ray Enright [based on *Dead Freight for Piute*], *Station West* (RKO, 1948) directed by Sidney Lanfield, *Blood on the Moon* (RKO, 1948) directed by Robert Wise, *Ambush* (M-G-M, 1949) directed by Sam Wood, *Vengeance Valley* (M-G-M, 1951) directed by Richard Thorpe, *Silver City* (Paramount, 1951) directed by Byron Haskin [based on *High Vermillion*], *Ride the Man Down* (Republic, 1953) directed by Joseph Kane, *Hell's Outpost* (Republic, 1954) directed by Joseph Kane.

For further information see *Luke Short* (New York: Twayne Publishers, 1981) by Robert L. Gale.

Glidden, Jonathan H(urff)

(1907–1957) Author of formulary Western fiction and older brother of Frederick D. Glidden (q.v.) born at Kewanee, Illinois. Although Jonathan's career started later than that of his brother, he quickly established an enviable reputation for fine writing which owed nothing to the fame already attached to Luke Short since, for years, it was not generally known that the two authors were even remotely related. Glidden graduated from the University of Illinois and during the 'Thirties worked as a salesman. In 1940 he saw an announcement of a $2,000 contest for Western manuscripts sponsored by Dodd, Mead. He wrote a novel called *The Crimson Horseshoe* (New York: Dodd, Mead, 1941) and submitted it under the name Peter Dawson. The novel won the prize and it was published the next year. The pseudonym did not completely succeed in hiding the author's identity since his real name was mentioned in *Publisher's Weekly*'s announcement of the contest results. G.W. Harris in the *New York Times Book Review* wrote that the book was "noteworthy for its organization and handling as well as the quality of its writing." The title refers not to an actual horseshoe but to the horseshoe bend of a railroad which is important to the action of the story. A second Peter Dawson book, *The Stagline Feud* (New York: Dodd, Mead, 1941), appeared later that year and Harris declared it "better organized and better written than his first." Possibly the best of Dawson's early books was the third, *Gunsmoke Graze* (New York: Dodd, Mead, 1942), a rich and complex story which combines half a dozen standard Western plots and does justice to all of them: the returned prodigal and his unyielding father, an unjust accusation of murder, a clever land-grabbing scheme, a little rustling, romance, and headlong action.

During World War II Glidden served as an officer in Air Force Intelligence and did no writing for four years. He resumed with *High Country* (New York: Dodd, Mead, 1947) and proved that he had lost none of his skill. Two years later he moved into the slick magazines. He died at the age of 50.

Renegade Canyon (New York: Dodd, Mead, 1949), the first Dawson novel to be serialized in the *Saturday Evening Post*, is set in a Cavalry outpost in the Arizona Territory and concerns a court-martialed officer's attempt to clear his name by tracking down the white renegade whose dealings with the Apaches have resulted in dozens of deaths. In *The Outlaw of Longbow* (New York: Dodd, Mead, 1951), another *Post* serial, Dawson momentarily lost his touch. He boxed his hero into an impossible situation—escaped from unjust imprisonment in the Territorial Prison at Yuma, but unable to prove his innocence because all the witnesses were dead—and then just brushed all the difficulties away with a hasty clinch and into-the-sunset fade-out. With *Ruler of the Range* (New York: Dodd, Mead, 1952) the lapse had passed and we have a satisfying mixture of cattlemen vs. sheepmen and conniving over hidden gold. *Man on the Buckskin* (New York: Dodd, Mead, 1957), another tale of a man framed into Yuma Prison for a murder he did not commit, was the last Peter Dawson book to be published by his long-time hardcover publishers, Dodd, Mead. Dawson's last *Post* serial, *Treachery At Rock Point* (New York: Dell, 1957), an uneven novel, was published in hardcover only in England.

R.E.B.

Peter Dawson's Western novels are *The Crimson Horseshoe* (1941), *The Stagline Feud* (1941), *Gunsmoke Graze* (1942), *Long Ride* (1942), *Trail Boss* (1943), *High Country* (1947), *Royal Gorge* (1948), *The Stirrup Boss* (1949), *Renegade Canyon* (1949), *Canyon Hell* (1949), *The Outlaw of Longbow* (1951), *Ruler of the Range* (1952), *The Wild Bunch* (1953), *Dead Man Pass* (1954), *The Big Outfit* (1955), *Leashed Guns* (1955), *Man on the Buckskin* (1957), *Treachery at Rock Point* (1957), *The Savages* (1959), *The Texas Slicks* (1961), *The Half Breed* (1962), *Bloody Gold* (1963), *Yancy* (1963), *The Showdown* (1964), *The Blizzard* (1968).

Peter Dawson also edited the Western anthology *The Killers* (1955).

The only film based on Peter Dawson's Western fiction is *Face of a Fugitive* (Columbia, 1959) directed by Paul Wendkos [based on the short story "Long Gone"].

Green, Ben K(?). (1912–1974) Es-

sayist, Western fiction and nonfiction writer, expert on horses and horse trading, born at Cumby, Texas. Green came from a long line of ranchers and farmers in the area. Green left home to roam at an early age and spent his youth and manhood in the horse and cattle country of the West, especially all over Texas. Green, this notwithstanding, was accepted by Texas A&M University and then he went to Cornell University in New York to study veterinary medicine, doing post-graduate work abroad at the Royal College of Veterinary Medicine in England. Green, upon occasion, denied all this extensive education. In any case, what there is no denying is that he worked as a veterinarian throughout the Southwest and that his knowledge of horses was extensive. In fact, during his lifetime he was called by many "the greatest living expert on horses." During his early years Green also worked as a cowboy, rancher, horse trader, in addition to a horse doctor in Texas, Mississippi, Oklahoma, and other states. In his later years he settled down as a veterinarian in Fort Stockton, Texas, and then near Fort Worth and San Angelo, finally ending up on his own ranch near Cumby where he could watch his horses and write.

Green chose to be buried in a 100 feet × 100 feet area in a four-acre pasture adjoining his ranch. As he explained before he died, "I roamed free and always had plenty of elbow room during my span on this earth. And I don't aim to be crowded in after I'm gone."

Green's contributions to the West, both fiction and non-fiction, are valuable, enthralling, and contain real knowledge and humor about the Western experience shared by men, horses, and cattle. His nonfiction works deal exclusively with horses. He wrote such notable books as *Horse Conformation* (Flagstaff: Northland, 1963) and *The Color of Horses* (Flagstaff: Northland, 1974). However, his strongest impact remains his semi-fictionalized tales of his own experiences as a cowboy, horse trader, and veterinary, in such collections as *Horse Tradin'* (New York: Knopf, 1967), *Wild Cow Tales* (New York: Knopf, 1969), and *The Village Horse Doctor: West of the Pecos* (New York: Knopf, 1971). *The Last Trail Drive through Downtown Dallas* (Flagstaff: Northland, 1971) is concerned with Green's boyhood experience when he moved one hundred head of horses from the Paint Rock country to East Texas. It was followed by *A Thousand Miles of Mustangin'* (Flagstaff: Northland, 1972), *Some More Horse Tradin'* (New York: Knopf, 1972), and *Ben Green Tales* (Flagstaff: Northland, 1974).

There are few writers of the West who can surpass Green in his ability to tell a story that captures place, the people, and the moment. A.C. Green, another noted Texas writer, said of him that he "had the most native ability for writing about his own experiences of any Texas author. And I think he represented the last real voice of old-time Texas in literature."

D.M.-K.

No biography exists on Green, but there is *Ben K. Green: A Descriptive Bibli-*

ography of *Writings by and about Him* (Flagstaff: Northland, 1977) by Robert A. Wilson.

Gregory, Jackson (1882–1943) An author known principally for his Western fiction, born at Salinas, California. Gregory attended the University of California receiving a Bachelor's degree in Letters before he pursued a career in teaching and finally in administration in several California high schools. In the first decade of the Twentieth century, Gregory deserted education to work as a newspaper reporter for several newspapers both in the United States and Canada. He died at his brother's home in Auburn, California, shortly after completing a novel.

He published his first Western, *Under Handicap* (New York: Harper's, 1914), which was re-issued again in 1936, and followed it with five more Western novels before the end of World War I. Among them was *Wolf Breed* (New York: Dodd, Mead, 1917) which is a Northwestern, set in Canada. Gregory tried to vary his locations and settings as much as possible and, accordingly, *Redwood and Gold* (New York: Dodd, Mead, 1928) has a California background while *Sentinel of the Desert* (New York: Dodd, Mead, 1929) is set along the American-Mexican border in the Southwest. In terms of this variety of locations, as well as in terms of style and structure, Gregory was closest to Dane Coolidge (q.v.), Hal G. Evarts, Sr., (q.v.), and the early novels of Harry Sinclair Drago (q.v.). *Lords of the Coast* (New York: Dodd, Mead, 1935) is a notable effort at a more ambitious historical novel.

His more traditional Western novels are, to be sure, inferior to those of Eugene Manlove Rhodes (q.v.), but Gregory did remain Rhodes' superior at plot development. Yet all of this notwithstanding, even Gregory's best Westerns are flawed by his heavy sentimentality.

Jackson Gregory's Western novels are *Under Handicap* (1914), *The Outlaw* (1916), *The Short Cut* (1916), *Wolf Breed* (1917), *The Joyous Trouble Maker* (1918), *Six Feet Four* (1918), *Judith of Blue Lake Ranch* (1919), *The Bells of San Juan* (1919), *Man to Man* (1920), *Desert Valley* (1921), *The Everlasting Whisper* (1922), *Timber-Wolf* (1923), *The Maid of the Mountain* (1925), *The Desert Thoroughbred* (1926), *Redwood and Gold* (1928), *Sentinel of the Desert* (1929), *Mystery at Spanish Hacienda* (1929), *The Trail to Paradise* (1930), *The Silver Star* (1931), *Splendid Outlaw* (1932), *The Shadow on the Mesa* (1933), *Red Rivals* (1933), *Riders across the Border* (1933), *High Courage* (1934), *Into the Sunset* (1936), *Mountain Men* (1936), *Sudden Bill Dorn* (1937), *Powdersmoke on Wandering River* (1938), *Far Call* (1940), *Ace in the Hole* (1941), *Red Law* (1941), *Border Line* (1942), *Two in the Wilderness* (1942), *Man from Texas* (1942), *Man from Painted Rock* (1943), *Aces Wild at Golden Eagle* (1944), *Hermit of Thunder King* (1945).

Films based on Jackson Gregory's Western fiction are *Bells of San Juan* (Fox, 1922) directed by Scott Dunlap, *Man to Man* (Universal, 1922) directed by Stuart Paton, *Two Kinds of Women* (Robertson-Cole, 1922) directed by Colin Campbell [based on *Judith of Blue Lake Ranch*], *Hearts and Spurs* (Fox, 1925) directed by W.S. Van Dyke [based on *The Outlaw*], *The Everlasting Whisper* (Fox, 1925) directed by J.G. Blystone, *Timber Wolf* (Fox, 1925) directed by W.S. Van Dyke, *Desert Valley* (Fox, 1926) directed by Scott Dunlap, *Sudden Bill Dorn* (Universal, 1937) directed by Ray Taylor, *The Laramie Trail* (Republic, 1944) directed by John English [based on *Mystery at Spanish Hacienda*].

Grey, Zane (1872–1939) Prolific author of Western fiction, born Pearl Zane Gray (he later changed the spelling of Gray to Grey and dropped the Pearl) at Zanesville, Ohio. The city was named for Colonel Ebenezer Zane, a Quaker exiled from Denmark and who shipped to America with William Penn in 1682, a relative on Grey's mother's side. The Colonel was charged with defending Fort William Henry during the Revolutionary War and was awarded, for his services, ten thousand acres of land in the Ohio Valley by George Washington and the Continental Congress. Unfortunately Grey's father was an itinerant at best and the family had little money, although the stories of past greatness bemused the young Grey. He had a natural aptitude for baseball and it was sufficient to pave the way for his admission into the University of Pennsylvania. Although basically an indifferent student, he somehow managed to graduate with a degree in dentistry in 1896. He opened a practice in New York City and

from 1898 to 1904 he worked at it conscientiously. He rented a room in a hall in the shadow of the Elevated Railroad and with a tomcat for company strove to become a writer. His first novel, *Betty Zane* (New York: Charles Francis Press, 1903), a story which featured Ebenezer Zane and his sister, the Betty of the title, was stoutly rejected by publishers and, try as he might, all Grey could succeed at placing were a few articles on fishing with magazines. Grey had met Lina Elise Roth in 1900 and they courted for five years before they were married. With her financial help, he published *Betty Zane* himself. Grey followed the book with two more book-length manuscripts, *The Spirit of the Border* (New York: A.L. Burt, 1906) and *The Last Trail* (New York: Outing, 1909), which concluded his saga of the Zanes, but these novels also initially met with rejection. As a trilogy about pioneer life, the three bear a resemblance to James Fenimore Cooper's (q.v.) Leatherstocking saga, but Grey's backwoodsman, Lewis Wetzel, kills far more readily than ever had Cooper's Hawk-eye and he lacks Hawk-eye's humanity; in fact, Grey's fictions never rise above being rather weak imitations.

Upon his marriage, primarily because of his wife's faith in him, Grey closed his dental office and moved into a cottage on the Delaware River, near Lackawaxen, Pennsylvania, provided for him, his wife, and his mother by his brother, a professional baseball player. In point of fact, Grey could not have found a better wife. She assisted him in every way he desired and yet left him alone when he demanded solitude; trained in English at Hunter College, she proof-read every manuscript he wrote and polished his prose; she managed all financial affairs and permitted Grey to indulge himself, at will, in his favorite recreations, hunting and fishing. All during 1906, Grey pursued writing but managed only to publish one four-page article. In early 1907, having placed *The Spirit of the Border* with a reprint house for no advance but with a royalty arrangement, Grey had the good fortune to meet Colonel C.J. "Buffalo" Jones, a retired buffalo hunter in the East trying to raise money to support a scheme he had for crossing buffalo and cattle which was met with ridicule. Grey suggested that he should accompany Jones back to the West and publicize his efforts. It required most of Lina Grey's savings for Grey to make the trip and, despite his reluctance, she insisted he do it. Arriving in Flagstaff, Arizona, Jones led Grey across the desert on horseback to the Grand Canyon. In Grey's memoir of the journey, *The Last of the Plainsmen* (New York: Outing, 1908), Grey narrated how he chased buffalo, explored ancient Indian ruins, captured wild horses, tracked and roped mountain lions, all the time acquiring a deep love for the West as he saw it, a land of romance and enchantment which he described in prose as purple as the sage which so overwhelmed him.

Returning to the East and Lackawaxen, Grey decided to try his hand at a Western romance rather after the fashion of Owen Wister's (q.v.) immensely popular *The Virginian* (New York: Macmillan, 1902), but first, in order to support himself and his family—now that a son had been born—he tried a juvenile, *The Short Stop* (Chicago: A.C. McClurg, 1909), which he placed readily and began on two more which were accepted by Harper's in New York City. Completing *The Heritage of the Desert* (New York: Harper's, 1910), he took it to Harper's literary editor, Ripley Hitchcock. Hitchcock had rejected *The Last of the*

Zane Grey standing at the foot of Nonnezoshe. The natural wonder figured prominently in Grey's novel The Rainbow Trail *(New York: Harper's, 1915)*

Plainsmen with the comment, delivered to Grey in person: "I don't see anything in this to convince me you can write either narrative or fiction." The rejection had had such an impact on Grey that he actually had found himself clinging to a lamp post in the street to retain his balance. But he kept trying. And this time with success. Hitchcock agreed to publish *The Heritage of the Desert.*

It remains, to be sure, one of Grey's finest Western novels and the profound effect the desert had had on him is vibrantly captured so that, after all these years, it still comes alive for the reader. In many ways, too, the novel is a prototype for all of Grey's subsequent fiction. The heroine, Mescal, is akin to numerous other Grey heroines—Jane Withersteen in *Riders of the Purple Sage* (New York: Harper's, 1912), Madeline Hammond in *The Light of Western Stars* (New York: Harper's, 1914), Joan Randle in *The Border Legion* (New York: Harper's, 1916), and even as late as Majesty Stewart in the posthumously published *Majesty's Rancho* (New York: Harper's, 1942)—and it takes her a considerable time to realize that she really loves the hero. The principal villain in *The Heritage of the Desert*—a type not too frequently encountered in Grey's fiction, with the possible exception of *Desert Gold* (New York: Harper's, 1913)—is the embodiment of the Yankee business spirit that will stop at nothing to exploit the land and the people for his own profit. He is killed by the hero, but, then too, the hero is also capable, as so many of Max Brand's (q.v.) heroes and so many other heroes in the formulary Western, of letting badmen off if there is a chance of rehabilitation.

Grey's next novel, *Riders of the Purple Sage*, met with rejection from Hitchcock because Hitchcock feared that its anti-Mormon sentiment would have severe repercussions. Grey asked a vice president of Harper's to read the novel and, once he did and his wife did, the book was accepted for publication. It became Grey's all-time bestseller, with sales of over two million copies during Grey's lifetime and probably again as many since his death. The novel is also generally cited as Grey's masterpiece, although an equally strong argument could be made for its sequel, *The Rainbow Trail* (New York: Harper's, 1915). *Riders of the Purple Sage* is dominated by dream imagery and nearly all of the characters, at one time or another, are preoccupied with their dreams. In its hero, the gunman Lassiter, Grey also added another of his truly unforgettable prototypes, the experienced Westerner to be contrasted with the neophyte Easterner, Lassiter with his "leanness, the red burn of the sun, and the set changelessness that came from years of silence and solitude . . . the intensity of his gaze, a strained weariness, a piercing wistfulness of keen, gray sight, as if the man was forever looking for that which he never found." In this, too, Lassiter is the prototype of all those searchers and wanderers which are to be found in Grey's fiction, John Shefford in *The Rainbow Trail*, Adam Larey in *Wanderer of the Wasteland* (New York: Harper's, 1923) and its sequel, published posthumously, *Stairs of Sand* (New York: Harper's, 1943), and, to an extent, Buck Duane in *The Lone Star Ranger* (New York: Harper's, 1915) and Rich Ames in *Arizona Ames* (New York: Harper's, 1932). In *Riders of the Purple Sage*, it is the heroine, Jane Withersteen, because of her mental domination by Mormonism, who is the innocent who must be educated into the ways—in Grey's romantic idiom, the call—of the West. Also in this novel for the first time Grey made tremendously effective use of sound to supplement his visual sense when Lassiter rolls a giant stone that causes a landslide and forever seals him, Jane, and little Fay in Surprise Valley, heard but not seen, as the hangings are heard but not seen in *The Border Legion* or the buffalo stampede is heard and not seen in *The Thundering Herd* (New York: Harper's, 1925).

Through the 'Teens, Grey's popularity grew with each successive novel, many of them attaining the bestseller lists and staying there. In the spring of 1913, Grey returned to the canyons of Arizona and Utah for inspiration and, henceforth, he took repeated trips into the far reaches of the Western states searching for settings for his stories, often writing long descriptions in his notebooks before he even had a plot. He early became interested in the potential of motion picture versions of his works, especially after he sold his early novels to William Fox of the Fox Film Corporation, and, for a time, he tried producing films based on his works himself, surrendering finally to Jesse L. Lasky's offer to produce between two and three Zane Grey films a year for Paramount release, guaranteeing Grey $25,000 per film as a royalty. In 1925, Grey's best year, he had an income of $575,000. He built an Indian Navaho home on Catalina, acquired a cabin on the Rogue River in Oregon, purchased a hunting lodge on the rim of the Grand Canyon in the Tonto, occupied a permanent residence in Altadena, California, and drastically expanded the dwelling at Lackawaxen. Grey continued to travel and soon acquired a large, sea-going yacht, undertaking deep sea fishing and, in time, held several world records for his catches. In addition to his Western fiction, Grey also wrote numerous books about his hunting and fishing experiences as well as scores of articles. Each of his novels was sold to various slick magazines for prepublication serialization and he commanded as much as $50,000 for serial rights.

It was in 1922 that Grey wrote *The Vanishing American* (New York: Harper's, 1925) and that it appeared in the *Ladies Home Journal*, a Curtis publication as were *The Saturday Evening Post* and *The Country Gentleman*. The story tells of Nophaie, a full-blood Navaho brave, kidnapped when a child and educated by the whites, returning to his reservation only to find it dominated by an unscrupulous Indian agent and, even worse, a vicious missionary who uses his dogmatic beliefs as earlier had Grey's Mormons: to get his way. If Grey had a philosophy at all, he was a social Darwinist, a man who believed that human existence and the survival of the races are guided by the ineluctable laws of an evolutionary scheme which endorses industrial progress and endows white civilization with a natural superiority, provided, however, the "heritage of the desert" is always kept in mind. In one of Grey's Indian stories, "Blue Feather," unpublished until long after his death, when it appeared in *Blue Feather and Other Stories* (New York: Harper's, 1961), Grey gave his vision of evolutionary social history, highest to lowest: "Human being, man, Indian, savage, primitive beast."

In *The Vanishing American*, Grey stripped Nophaie of his Nopah religion, but made him reject the missionary's Christianity as well, arriving at some nebulous pantheism which somehow still retains the white Christ as a manifestation of God along with Nature, His most intimate manifestation. Grey sums up his formulation about the Native American this way: "Indians were merely closer to the original animal progenitor of human beings." Nophaie falls in love with the blonde-haired, blue-eyed school teacher and so inspired by this love is he that it prompts him to bring Grey's doctrine of virginity to his people. Morgan, the missionary, likes to seduce young Indian maidens at his mission school. One of them, Gekin Yasha, is taught by Nophaie that "when a white woman loves she holds herself sacred for the man who has won her." It does not do Gekin Yasha much good. She is seduced by Morgan, becomes pregnant, returns to the reservation and marries an Indian, only to pay the price

Building a set on the Navaho Reservation on the border between Utah and Arizona for use in the first film version of Zane Grey's The Vanishing American *(Paramount, 1925).*

frequently paid in Zane Grey's West for sexual intercourse outside a monogamous relationship: she dies.

In the magazine version, Nophaie, in his dramatic betrayal of himself and his people, comments: "Let the Indians marry white women and Indian girls marry white men. It would make for a more virile race . . . absorbed by the race that has destroyed him. Red blood into white! It means the white race will gain and the Indian vanish. . . ." And so was born an even more questionable view of the Native American who, to Cooper, had been either a villain or a noble savage. Nophaie is a "romantic" savage who wants to vanish for the betterment of the white race. He says: " 'Example of the white man's better ways would inev-

itably follow association.' " The story ends—or the magazine version ended—with Nophaie and the yellow hair in each other's arms, about to achieve Grey's synthesis of "red blood into white." But this ending, to say nothing of Grey's treatment of Christian missionaries, caused such a furor for the *Ladies Home Journal,* with thousands upon thousands of letters of protest, that Harper's refused to publish the book until Grey changed the ending. This he did. In the novel version, he had Nophaie fatally shot and, dying, he had him murmur: "vanishing . . . vanishing . . . vanishing." This proved more acceptable to Grey's readers.

Since Paramount frequently filmed Grey's books when they were still in serial form—Grey had stepped up his production to get more money from the magazines and, hence, Harper's was building up a backlog of novels, willing to publish only two a year whereas Grey was writing three and sometimes four a year—for the motion picture version of *The Vanishing American*, Lucien Hubbard, who did the adaptation, borrowed a portion from the first chapter of *The Thundering Herd* and some of "Blue Feather" so the film would have a Prologue in which it could be shown visually how the Indians had preyed on each other, one tribe wiping out another, weaker tribe, until at last, the culmination so far of evolution, the white man arrived in the New World and signalled to all Native Americans who had survived evolution thus far that the time had come for them to vanish.

Ann Ronald in *Zane Grey* (Boise: Idaho State University, 1975) may conclude, as she did, that ultimately we read Grey's books "not because he tells us about life, but because he does not." However, that was not the case in the 'Twenties, when Grey was at the height of his fame. Grey took umbrage at the way his *Vanishing American* was treated by hostile readers and defended it on the basis that it was "pro-Indian" and for this reason incited riotous comment. As recently as the paperback collection, *Zane Grey's Greatest Indian Stories* (New York: Belmont Tower, 1975), the back cover reads in part: "Half a century before Wounded Knee, America's greatest action writer, Zane Grey, was writing swiftly-paced stories about the Indians, and he was the first modern author to treat the 'noble savage' with sympathy and understanding."

As for *Ladies Home Journal* and all other Curtis publications, especially *The Saturday Evening Post*, what the problem with Grey's serial meant was that for the life of these magazines it was no longer permissible to the editorial departments for Native Americans to be characterized in any way except as warriors and renegades, which they felt was the way in which the American people wanted them characterized, and in which belief they may well have been right.

In an article "My Own Life" for *The American Magazine* which was reprinted in *Zane Grey* (New York: Harper's 1928), a tribute to the author, Grey noted, in writing of Lina, "Let no man ever doubt the faith and spirit and love of a woman!" It was as if in all his romances Grey and his wife were the hero and heroine. Because he was inclined to such extravagance, he took to dividing his income with Lina, in the end a very prudent thing, since by the mid 'Thirties there was virtually no demand for Zane Grey serials—his stories had become so repetitious, the writing so lacking in vitality or even the old romantic veneer—and Harper's had so many novels in their vaults that there was no income to be derived from writing another one. The motion picture productions of his works became largely remakes, using footage lifted *en masse* from the silent versions and intercut with new scenes, and all of them definitely low-budget affairs. The romance between the public and Zane Grey was on the wane and, increasingly, he appealed only to a juvenile audience. Indeed, this was probably the audience for which he had always written. In early books as *The Light of Western Stars* he had set his story in the contemporary West of that day, 1912, and both *Call of the Canyon* (New York: Harper's, 1924) and *The Vanishing American* were set in the period immediately after what then was known as the Great War; but as the United States went through the shocks of the Depression, Grey found it more difficult than ever to set one of his novels during the time in which he was living. He did make one effort to do so in *Majesty's Rancho*, featuring now as parents the young couple he had first brought together in *The Light of Western Stars*, and told the story of their daughter and her eventual marriage to Lance Sidway who saves her from the hands of a ruthless modern gangster. When an older Gene Stewart tells an older Madeline Hammond Stewart that the Depression and lack of markets for his cattle have brought back all the old despondency—Grey himself was always subject to excessively dark and brooding moods, especially about money—Madeline (much as Lina Elise Grey, whom Grey called Dolly, counseled Grey) counsels Stewart, " 'Who could foresee what would happen to the cattle business?' " and goes on to reassure him that " 'for fifteen years there had been too much money to spend . . . for ten years we ran behind, a little more every year. Then came the crash. . . .' "

All of which, somehow, did not visibly cheer Grey. He became bitter and found it more difficult to write. He and his family, consisting of Dolly, two sons and a daughter, lived on what Dolly had saved. In 1929 he quarreled with the Arizona Game and Fish Commission because they had refused to grant him a license to hunt bear out of season and he had sworn never to return to the state, and he did not. He tried a transoceanic voyage to find new inspiration for his writing, perhaps the Pacific islands, and, ultimately, Australia, where he was widely fêted as a literary lion and out of which came a novel with Grey's Western plot moved to the Australian plains, *The Wilderness Trek* (New York: Harper's, 1944) which he could sell nowhere and which had to wait until five years after his death for Harper's to be in a position to release it.

Grey, as his older brother Romer, to whom he was always very close, believed in the strenuous life. Romer had known no serious illnesses but one day in 1934 his heart simply stopped beating, as seems often to be the case among the advocates of prolonged and intense physical activity. It should have served as a foreshadowing for Grey himself, but it did not. During the summer of 1937, fishing the North Umpqua River in Oregon, Grey collapsed from a heart attack. He thought nothing of it and, against medical advice to the contrary, was convinced that the way to strengthen his heart muscle was vigorously to exercise it. As Frank Gruber (q.v.) recorded in *Zane Grey: A Biography* (New York: World, 1970), "Dolly, who knew that the greatest fear of his life had always been that of growing old—and admitting it—stilled her remonstrances." Early the morning of 22 October 1939 Dolly was awakened by a call from Grey. Rushing to his room, she found him clutching his chest. "Don't ever leave me, Dolly!" he pleaded. He lived until the next morning when, after rising and dressing, he sat down again on his bed, cried out suddenly, and fell over dead.

In his final years, his son Romer had taken over managing his father's work and he had even arranged to involve Zane Grey's name with a comic strip series about King of the Royal Mounted in an effort to make money. He did manage to sell two of Grey's more recent and as yet unpublished manuscripts to the *New York Sunday Times* to be run as serials, although the sum received was $15,000, down considerably from what it had once been. With Grey's death, Romer took over completely, aided by Grey's wife, and many of the books

A *cover from the* Zane Grey Western Magazine.

published subsequently were obviously subjected to considerable editorial elaboration in order to make them publishable—many of them had existed in no more than outline form—and, for this reason, virtually every Zane Grey novel or story not published at least in serial form during his lifetime is probably of somewhat dubious origin. Not that this was necessarily a bad thing. Grey once made the mistake himself of submitting a manuscript—*The Thundering Herd*—to *The Ladies Home Journal* without his wife's editorial polishing and, even though it was his best market, it was returned with numerous suggestions on how it should be rewritten. In a sense, other than his very first books, Zane Grey's works were very much a corporate and collective enterprise, more so with each passing year, especially during the late 'Twenties and early 'Thirties, and it is likely that by the late 'Thirties he could not write very much at all.

Lawrence Clark Powell in *Southwestern Classics* (Los Angeles: Ward Ritchie, 1974) wrote that Grey's "work steadily worsened," but he also said of it and of Grey: "He had the gift of narrative. He was a born storyteller, a simplifier. Life to him was black or white, never gray. His characters were heroic figures with primitive emotions. While they lived out their melodramas, the story-line never weakened." Which, in a way, only echoes what T.K. Whipple wrote of Grey already in the 'Twenties, reprinted in Whipple's *Study Out the Land* (Berkeley: University of California Press, 1943): "Of course he has an amazing, an incredible simplicity and unsophistication of mind, a childlike naiveté—but that is what makes him what he is, a fashioner of the heroic myths." It is possible to grant Grey this and still to agree with Ann Ronald that particularly in Grey's historical novels there is a substantial "conflict between plot and theme." Grey might lament the passing of the buffalo, as he did in *The Thundering Herd*, or the effects of the coming of the railroad as he did in *The U.P. Trail* (New York: Harper's, 1918), or the "vanishing" of his romantic Indians, but his plots contradict these feelings, the pleasure he made tactilely real when showing how buffalo can be shot in huge numbers from a blind, the glib assurances that the removal of the buffalo and the Indian and the coming of the railroad will make the West safe for the settlers the way, during Grey's halcyon days, Americans were taught to believe that they were making the world safe for democracy. *Man of the Forest* (New York: Harper's, 1920) is a failure as a mountain man story if compared to comparable works by Harvey Fergusson (q.v.), A.B. Guthrie, Jr. (q.v.), or Vardis Fisher (q.v.), but it has its place in Grey's romantic world, while the implied sexuality in novels as *The Lone Star Ranger* and *Wildfire* (New York: Harper's, 1917) is far more stimulating than had he been more explicit. There is little in Western fiction generally that can equal the terrific and dramatic races of horses and men in *Riders of the Purple Sage* or Mescal's race in *The Heritage of the Desert*, and few gunmen in the more formulary literature are as attractive as Nevada as he appears in *Forlorn River* (New York: Harper's, 1927) and *Nevada* (New York: Harper's, 1928), although in *Wild Horse Mesa* (New York: Harper's, 1928) Grey as much betrayed wild horses as he did the buffalo in *The Thundering Herd*, due to his Darwinist philosophy.

It could be Gary Topping put it best in his essay "Zane Grey's West" in *The Popular Western* (Bowling Green: The Popular Press, 1974): Grey "saw the West the way he did, one might say, because he saw the East the way he did. Secondly, however, Grey has never received due credit for the comparatively high degree of realism in his books. His cowboys, for example, actually raise cattle, get tired, dirty, and drunk, and curse, albeit mildly, when angry. Finally, Grey was philosophically a child of his times. In an age that extolled moral incorruptibility, the manly virtues and 'the strenuous life,' Grey's novels revealed a world in which those values reigned supreme."

Zane Grey's novels with a pioneer or Western setting are *Betty Zane* (1903), *The Spirit of the Border* (1906), *The Last of the Plainsmen* (1908), *The Last Trail* (1909), *The Heritage of the Desert* (1910), *Riders of the Purple Sage* (1912), *Desert Gold* (1913), *The Light of Western Stars* (1914), *The Lone Star Ranger* (1915), *The Rainbow Trail* (1915), *The Border Legion* (1916), *Wildfire* (1917), *The U.P. Trail* (1918), *The Desert of Wheat* (1920), *Man of the Forest* (1920), *The Mysterious Rider* (1921), *To the Last Man* (1922), *Wanderer of the Wasteland* (1923), *Tappan's Burro* (1923) [short stories], *Call of the Canyon* (1924), *The Thundering Herd* (1925), *The Vanishing American* (1925), *Under the Tonto Rim* (1926), *Forlorn River* (1927), *Nevada* (1928), *Fighting Caravans* (1929), *The Wolf Tracker* (1930), *The Shepherd of Guadaloupe* (1930), *Sunset Pass* (1931), *Arizona Ames* (1932), *Robber's Roost* (1932), *The Drift Fence* (1933), *The Hash Knife Outfit* (1933), *Code of the West* (1934), *Thunder Mountain* (1935), *The Trail Driver* (1936), *The Lost Wagon Train* (1936), *West of the Pecos* (1937), *Raiders of Spanish Peaks* (1938), *Western Union* (1939), *Knights of the Range* (1939), *Thirty Thousand on the Hoof* (1940), *Twin Sombreros* (1941), *Majesty's Rancho* (1942), *Stairs of Sand* (1943), *The Wilderness Trek* (1944), *Shadow on the Trail* (1946), *Valley of Wild Horses* (1947), *Rogue River Feud* (1948), *The Deer Stalker* (1949), *The Maverick Queen* (1950), *The Dude Ranger* (1951), *Captives of the Desert* (1952), *Wyoming* (1953), *Lost Pueblo* (1954), *Black Mesa* (1955), *Stranger from the Tonto* (1956), *The Fugitive Trail* (1957), *Arizona Clan* (1958), *Horse Heaven Hill* (1959), *The Ranger and Other Stories* (1960) [contains the title story and "Avalanche," "Canyon Walls," and "From Missouri"], *Blue Feather and Other Stories* (1961) [contains the title story and "The Outlaws of Palouse" under the title "The Horse Thief" and "Quaking' Asp Cabin"], *Boulder Dam* (1963).

In addition to the above, Grey also was credited with writing the copy for the comic strip *King of the Royal Mounted* and, therefore, with the authorship of *King of the Royal Mounted* (Racine: Whitman Publishing, 1936), *King of The Royal Mounted and the Northern Treasure* (Racine: Whitman Publishing, 1937), *King of the Royal Mounted in the Far North* (Racine: Whitman Publishing, 1938), *King of the Royal Mounted Gets His Man* (Racine: Whitman Publishing, 1938), *King of the Royal Mounted Policing the Far North* (Racine: Whitman Publishing, 1938), *King of the Royal Mounted and the Great Jewel Mystery* (Racine: Whitman Publishing, 1938). Grey also collaborated with Mrs. Helen Cody Westmore on a revision of *Buffalo Bill: Last of the Great Scouts* (New York: Grosset & Dunlap, 1918) which purported to be factual but which is so fanciful that it must be classed as fiction.

Upon the death of Zane Grey's eldest son, Romer Grey, his younger son, Loren Grey, began editing a series of books for Belmont Tower in which many of Grey's hitherto unpublished short stories, or short stories which have not appeared since their original magazine publication, or the condensed magazine versions of longer novels, or first versions of subsequently expanded novels were included. Among those which have so far appeared are *Zane Grey's Greatest Animal Stories* (1975), *Zane Grey's Greatest Western Stories* (1975), *Zane Grey's Savage Kingdom* (1975), *Zane Grey's Greatest Indian Stories* (1975) [note: this volume contains the original ending to *The Vanishing American*], *Zane Grey's Yaqui* (1976), *Zane Grey's Tenderfoot* (1977), *The Buffalo Hunter* (1978).

Films based on Zane Grey's Western fiction, many of the titles made and remade as noted, are *The Last Trail* (Fox, 1918) directed by Frank Lloyd, remade under this title (Fox, 1921) directed by Emmett J. Flynn, (Fox, 1927) directed by Lewis Seiler, (Fox, 1933) directed by James Tinling. *Riders of the Purple Sage* (Fox, 1918) directed by Frank Lloyd, remade under this title (Fox, 1925) directed by Lynn Reynolds, (Fox, 1931) directed by Hamilton MacFadden, (Fox, 1941) directed by James Tinling. *The Light of Western Stars* (Sherman-United, 1918) directed by Charles Swickard, remade under this title (Paramount, 1925) directed by William K. Howard, (Paramount, 1930) directed by Otto Brower and Edwin H. Knopf, (Paramount, 1940) directed by Lesley Selander. *The Border Legion* (Goldwyn, 1918) directed by T. Hayes Hunter, remade under this title (Paramount, 1924) directed by William K. Howard, (Paramount, 1930) directed by Otto Brower and Edwin H. Knopf, (Republic, 1940) directed by Joseph Kane. *The Rainbow Trail* (Fox, 1918) directed Frank Lloyd, remade under this title (Fox, 1925) directed by Lynn Reynolds, (Fox, 1932) directed by David Howard. *Desert Gold* (KayBee, 1914) directed by Scott Sidney, remade under this title (Paramount, 1921) directed by T. Hayes Hunter, (Paramount, 1926) directed by George B. Seitz, (Paramount, 1936) directed by James Hogan. *The Lone Star Ranger* (Fox, 1923) directed by Lambert Hillyer, remade under this title (Fox, 1930) directed by A.F. Erickson, (20th-Fox, 1942) directed by James Tinling, and remade under the title *The Last of the Duanes* (Fox, 1919) directed by J. Gordon Edwards and further remade under this second title [based on the magazine serial title for *The Lone Star Ranger*] (Fox, 1924) directed by Lynn Reynolds, (Fox, 1930) directed by Alfred L. Worker, (20th-Fox, 1941) directed by James Tinling. *The U.P. Trail* (Hodkinson, 1919) was directed by Jack Conway. *Riders of the Dawn* (Hodkinson, 1920) was directed by Hugh Ryan Conway [based on *The Desert of Wheat*]. *Man of the Forest* (Paramount, 1921) directed by Benjamin B. Hampton, remade under this title (Paramount, 1926) directed by John Waters, (Paramount, 1933) directed by Henry Hathaway. *The Mysterious Rider* (Paramount, 1921) directed by Benjamin B. Hampton, remade under this title (Paramount, 1927) directed by John Waters, (Paramount, 1933) directed by Fred Allen, (Paramount, 1938) directed by Lesley Selander. *Golden Dreams* (Goldwyn, 1922) directed by Benjamin B. Hampton [based on an original screen story] was remade under the title *Rocky Mountain Mystery* (Paramount, 1935) directed by Charles Barton. *When Romance Rides* (Goldwyn, 1922) directed by Eliot Howe, Charles O. Rush, and Jean Hersholt [based on *Wildfire*] was remade as *Red Canyon* (Universal, 1949) directed by George Sherman. *To the Last Man* (Paramount, 1923) directed by Victor Fleming, remade under this title (Paramount, 1933) directed by Henry Hathaway. *The Heritage of the Desert* (Paramount, 1924) directed by Irvin Willat, remade under this title (Paramount, 1932) directed by Henry Hathaway, (Paramount, 1939) directed by Lesley Selander. *Wanderer of the Wasteland* (Paramount, 1924) directed by Irvin Willat, remade under this title (Paramount, 1935) directed by Otto Lovering, (RKO, 1945) directed by Edward Killy and Wallace Grissell. *Call of the Canyon* (Paramount, 1925) directed by Victor Fleming was remade under this title (Republic, 1942) directed by Joseph Santley. *Code of the West* (Paramount, 1925) directed by William K. Howard, remade under the title *Home on the Range* (Paramount, 1935) directed by Arthur Jacobson and remade as *Code of the West* (RKO, 1947) directed by William Berke. *The Thundering Herd* (Paramount, 1925) directed by William K. Howard was remade under this title (Paramount, 1933) directed by Henry Hathaway. *The Vanishing American* (Paramount, 1925) directed by George B. Seitz, remade under this title (Republic, 1955) directed by Joseph Kane. *Wild Horse Mesa* (Paramount, 1925) directed by George B. Seitz, remade under this title (Paramount, 1932) directed by Henry Hathaway, (RKO, 1947) directed by Wallace Grissell. *Forlorn River* (Paramount, 1926) directed by John Waters was remade under this title (Paramount, 1937) directed by Charles Barton. *Born to the West* (Paramount, 1926) directed by John Waters [source unknown] was remade under this title (Paramount, 1937) directed by Charles Barton. *Lightning* (Tiffany, 1927) was directed by James C. McKay [based on the short story "Lightning"]. *Nevada* (Paramount, 1927) directed by John Waters, remade under this title (Paramount, 1935) directed by Charles Barton, (RKO, 1944) directed by Edward Killy. *Drums of the Desert* (Paramount, 1927) was directed by John Waters [based on *Captives of the Desert*]. *Avalanche* (Paramount, 1928) was directed by Otto Brower [based on the short story "Avalanche"]. *The Water Hole* (Paramount, 1928) was directed by F. Richard Jones [based on *Lost Pueblo*]. *Under the Tonto Rim* (Paramount, 1928) directed by Herman C. Raymaker, remade under this title (Paramount, 1933) directed by Henry Hathaway (RKO, 1947) directed by Lew Landers. *The Vanishing Pioneer* (Paramount, 1928) was directed by John Waters [source unknown]. *Stairs of Sand* (Paramount, 1929) was directed by Otto Brower and remade under the title *Arizona Ma-*

honey (Paramount, 1936) directed by James Hogan. *Sunset Pass* (Paramount, 1929) directed by Otto Brower, remade under this title (Paramount, 1933) directed by Henry Hathaway, (RKO, 1946) directed by William Berke. *Fighting Caravans* (Paramount, 1931) directed by Otto Brower and David Burton, remade under the title *Wagon Wheels* (Paramount, 1934) directed by Charles Barton. *Golden West* (Fox, 1932) was directed by David Howard [source unknown]. *Robber's Roost* (Fox, 1933) directed by David Howard, remade under this title (United Artists, 1955) directed by Sidney Salkow. *Smoke Lightning* (Fox, 1933) was directed by David Howard [based on the short story "Canyon Walls"]. *Life in the Raw* (Fox, 1933) was directed by Louis King [source unknown]. *The Dude Ranger* (Fox, 1934) was directed by Edward F. Cline. *West of the Pecos* (RKO, 1934) directed by Phil Rosen, remade under this title (RKO, 1945) directed by Edward Killy. *Thunder Mountain* (Fox, 1935) directed by David Howard, remade under this title (RKO, 1947) directed by Lew Landers. *Drift Fence* (Paramount, 1936) was directed by Otto Lovering. *The End of the Trail* (Columbia, 1936) was directed by Erle C. Kenton [based on the short story "Outlaws of Palouse"]. *The Arizona Raiders* (Paramount, 1936) was directed by James Hogan [based on *Raiders of Spanish Peaks*]. *Roll Along Cowboy* (20th-Fox, 1937) was directed by Gus Meins [source unknown]. *Thunder Trail* (Paramount, 1937) was directed by Charles Barton [based on *Arizona Ames*]. *Knights of the Range* (Paramount, 1940) was directed by Lesley Selander. *Western Union* (20th-Fox, 1941) was directed by Fritz Lang. *Gunfighters* (Columbia, 1947) was directed by George Waggoner [based on *Twin Sombreros*]. *The Maverick Queen* (Republic, 1956) was directed by Joseph Kane.

Films were also based on Zane Grey's comic strip *King of the Royal Mounted* and they are *King of the Royal Mounted* (20th-Fox, 1936) directed by Howard Bretherton, *King of the Royal Mounted* (Republic, 1940) directed by William Witney and John English [a twelve chapter serial], *Yukon Patrol* (Republic, 1942) directed by William Witney and John English [a feature version of the 1940 serial], and *King of the Mounties* (Republic, 1942) directed by William Witney [a twelve chapter serial].

In all, 108 theatrical feature films were made based on Zane Grey's fiction, which is something of a record. In addition, two feature films were made which featured Zane Grey playing himself, *South Sea Adventurers* (Principal, 1932) and *White Death* (Australian made, released in 1936 in Sydney, Australia). Grey also appeared in a few short subjects showing his skill at fishing.

Dick Powell's Zane Grey Theatre (CBS, 1956–1962) produced and hosted by Powell made use of Grey's name although the stories that were dramatized had nothing to do with Grey's fiction.

A radio series, short-lived, was syndicated in 1937 called *Riders of the Purple Sage*.

Frank Gruber's *Zane Grey: A Biography* (New York: World, 1970), although done with the co-operation of Zane Grey, Inc., is a slap-dash effort, totally unreliable, and Gruber seems not even to have read *Riders Of The Purple Sage* which he singled out for praise based on its sales figures in that he got the plot wrong when he retold it. Carlton Jackson's *Zane Grey* (New York: Twayne Publishers, 1973) is too much a series of dull plot resumés to qualify as valid literary criticism and, here again although not so often, the plot summaries prove to be unreliable. Jane Karr's *Zane Grey: Man of the West* (New York: Greenberg, 1949) is more a resumé of Grey's hunting and fishing trips than it is either a biography or a literary critique of his fiction. Somewhat better is *Zane Grey* (Boise: Idaho State University Press, 1975) by Ann Ronald. All of which means that, despite Grey's popularity and his tremendous impact on Western fiction, no one has yet accorded him even an adequate literary biography.

Gruber, Frank (1904–1969) Author

of formulary Western fiction, born at Elmer, Minnesota. As a young boy, Gruber read the works of Horatio Alger and by the age of 10 he had decided to be a writer himself—and had even completed a book written in pencil on cutdown pieces of wrapping paper. When he was 12, the family spent six months on a farm in Michigan. It was here that Gruber first encountered the works of Zane Grey (q.v.) in the form of a magazine reprint of *The Light of Western Stars* (New York: Harper's, 1914). Within two weeks after the family's return to Chicago, young Frank had read all of the Grey books published up to that time. He completed high school in Chicago and got a job, using his spare time in renewed attempts at writing. He accumulated rejection slips from the full spectrum of the magazine world and even tried what seemed to him to be "the lowest form of writing": short, inspirational stories for the Sunday school papers. It was in this area that he made his first sale, a short-short story called "The Two Dollar Raise" in 1927.

Using his new status as a "published writer," although the story had yet to appear in print, Gruber obtained a job as editor of a small farm paper called *The Turkey World*. For the next seven years he worked on a variety of farm and business papers throughout the Midwest. He sold a few stories to the pulp magazines and, finally, in 1934 he moved to New York City to make an all-out effort to break into the pulp magazine market. After a lean six months of making the rounds of editorial offices and bombarding them with stories, he began selling regularly. He quickly established himself as a prolific and successful contributor to pulps. Over the next twenty years his stories and serials appeared in more than fifty magazines, from *Adventure* to *Weird Tales*, from *Black Mask* to *Western Trails*. He wrote a few sports stories and a handful of fantasy tales, but the bulk of his writing was for the mystery/detective and Western markets. Most of his pulp writing appeared under his own name, although a few of his Western short stories appeared under house names (see House Names) such as Jackson Cole, Tom Gunn, and Sam Brant.

While he had no trouble selling his Western stories, Gruber was dissatisfied with their artificiality. He wrote to Ernest Haycox (q.v.) for advice and as a result of the correspondence which developed he began to read non-fiction works about the West—to study it, rather than merely write about it. In 1938 Gruber decided it was time to try his luck with a novel. He wrote *Peace Marshal* (New York: Morrow, 1939) in three weeks and it was serialized in *Adventure* magazine. The novel eventually amassed sales of over a million copies in English language reprint editions and was translated into eighteen languages. Gruber's second novel was a detective story. Indeed, from the appearance of *Peace Marshal* to the end of 1942, Gruber published fifteen books, twelve of them detective stories, three of them Westerns. His second Western, *Outlaw* (New York: Farrar and Rinehart, 1941), did not meet with the success of its predecessor; it is a grim and downbeat story of the aftermath of the Civil War on the Missouri frontier. In spite of flowing comments from reviewers, the book sold fewer than 2,000 copies in its original edition and has never received the attention from readers that its quality merits. It was followed by *Gunsight* (New York: Dodd, Mead, 1942), a fast-moving story of the attempt to bring law and order to a bloody Arizona boomtown. A fourth Western novel was serialized in *Adventure* in 1940 under the title "Quantrill's Flag," but it had to wait until 1954 for a book edition when it was published as a paperback original titled *Quantrill's Raiders* (New York: Ace, 1954).

In 1942 film rights to *Peace Marshal* were purchased by Harry Sherman and it was filmed under the title *The Kansan* (United Artists, 1943) starring Richard Dix. Along with the movie sale came the offer of a screenwriting job and the Grubers moved to Hollywood. Although the original assignment was for only six weeks, it led to further work and the transfer to California eventually proved permanent. Among Gruber's early screen credits were the screenplays for an Errol Flynn adventure, *Northern Pursuit* (Warner's, 1943), and the film version of Eric Ambler's *The Mask of Dimitrios* (Warner's, 1944). Gruber's screenwriting career lasted into the 'Sixties and ranged from "B" programmers to Technicolor first-run features as *Silver City* (Paramount, 1951) based on a novel by Luke Short (q.v.) and

Gruber's own adaptation of his novel *Town Tamer* (New York: Rinehart, 1957) as *Town Tamer* (Paramount, 1965).

In 1945 Gruber resumed writing detective novels and in 1948–1949 he wrote three Westerns. His most concentrated period of Western writing was in the 'Fifties when he published thirteen Western novels and only two detective novels. During this same period he was writing Westerns for television. He created three highly successful series for television, *Tales of Wells Fargo* (NBC, 1957–1962), of which he was co-owner, *The Texan* (CBS, 1958–1959), and *Shotgun Slade* (Syndicated, 1959–1960). Gruber wrote many of the scripts for these shows himself and was instrumental in bringing in many of his fellow members of the Western Writers of America as scriptwriters.

As the popularity of television Westerns dwindled in the early 'Sixties, Gruber turned to writing suspense novels, many of them with foreign locales or based on facets of archaeology which was one of his hobbies. Gruber's *The Pulp Jungle* (Los Angeles: Sherbourne Press, 1967) was a collection of his reminiscences as a pulp writer and contains anecdotes on the major pulp writers and editors with a full chapter on Frederick Faust (q.v.) whom Gruber knew in Hollywood. Gruber's last two books were published posthumously, *Zane Grey: A Biography* (New York: World, 1970), a largely adulatory work commissioned by Zane Grey, Inc., in which sales volume is equated with quality, and *Wanted!* (New York: Bantam, 1971), a novel about the Benders, a notorious Kansas family of murderers and worse.

Gruber's fictional Westerns of the 'Fifties are the work of an accomplished professional, skilled at satisfying the expectations of his audience, but not interested in going beyond those boundaries. The stories are entertaining and fast-moving, but for the most part not distinguishable from the formulary Westerns being written by a dozen others during that same period. Many of the protagonists are former Quantrill raiders trying to escape their pasts, although Gruber had said all that needed saying on this theme, and said it well, in *Outlaw* back in 1941. These books also frequently feature "cameo" appearances by historical figures such as Billy the Kid, Bat Masterson, and Sam Bass. In 1955 Gruber perfected what he called "The Basic Western Plots." *Buffalo Grass* (New York: Rinehart, 1956) is probably the best of Gruber's Westerns from the 'Fifties. More ambitious than the others, it is the story of the founding and growth of a Kansas trail town in the late 1860s and of the feud that develops between the town's two founders.

R.E.B.

Frank Gruber's Western novels are *Peace Marshal* (1939), *Outlaw* (1941) [alternate title: *Rebel Road*], *Gunsight* (1942), *Fighting Man* (1948), *Broken Lance* (1949), *Smoky Road* (1949) [alternate title: *The Lone Gunhawk*], *Fort Starvation* (1953), *Quantrill's Raiders* (1954), *Bitter Sage* (1954), *Johnny Vengeance* (1954), *Bugles West* (1954), *The Highwayman* (1955) [alternate title: *Ride to Hell*], *The Man from Missouri* (1956) [two short novels], *Buffalo Grass* (1956) [alternate title: *The Big Land*], *Lonesome River* (1957), *Town Tamer* (1957), *Tales of Wells Fargo* (1958) [short stories], *The Marshal* (1958), *The Bushwhackers* (1959), *This Gun Is Still* (1967), *The Dawn Riders* (1968), *The Curly Wolf* (1969), *Wanted!* (1971).

Films based on Frank Gruber's Western fiction are *The Kansan* (United Artists,

1943) directed by George Archainbaud [based on *Peace Marshal*], *Tension at Table Rock* (RKO, 1956) directed by Charles Marquis Warren [based on *Bitter Sage*], *The Big Land* (Warner's, 1957) directed by Gordon Douglas [based on *Buffalo Grass*], *Town Tamer* (Paramount, 1965) directed by Lesley Selander.

Western screenplays for which Gruber received credit are *Fighting Man of the Plains* (20th-Fox, 1949) directed by Edwin L. Marin, *Dakota Lil* (20th-Fox, 1950) directed by Lesley Selander, *The Cariboo Trail* (20th-Fox, 1950) directed by Edwin L. Marin, *The Texas Rangers* (Columbia, 1951) directed by Phil Karlson, *Warpath* (Paramount, 1951) directed by Byron Haskin, *Silver City* (Paramount, 1951) directed by Byron Haskin, *Denver & Rio Grande* (Paramount, 1952) directed by Byron Haskin [Gruber was also credited with the original screen story], *Pony Express* (Paramount, 1953) directed by Jerry Hopper, *Rage at Dawn* (RKO, 1955) directed by Tim Whelan, *Arizona Raiders* (Columbia, 1965) directed by William Witney.

Gulick, Grover C(leveland) "Bill"

(1916 —) Author of Western fiction, born at Kansas City, Missouri. Gulick first became interested in writing while attending the University of Oklahoma in 1940. His first efforts were sports stories and some of these were compiled into his first book, *Cowboy, Fisherman, Hunter* (Kansas City: Brown-White-Lowell Press, 1942), written in collaboration with Larry Mersfelder. Gulick then went to Greenwich Village for nine months during 1943–1944 and, in his words, "did a bachelor stint." He turned to writing juvenile novels with a Western setting, collaborating with Thomas Rothrock, *Abilene or Bust* (New York: Cupples & Leon, 1944) and *Desolation Trail* (New York: Cupples & Leon, 1945).

This experience convinced Gulick that his true *mètier* was writing Western fiction, and he began writing short stories, first for pulp magazines, until he finally became a regular contributor to *The Saturday Evening Post*. A *Post* editor once told him, "What I like about your stories is that they're not Westerns," whereas two of those *Post* stories won Spur Awards from the Western Writers of America as Best Western Short Story of the Year, "Thief in Camp" from 1958 and "The Shaming of Broken Horn" which was published in the *Post* in 1960. Although, in the beginning, Gulick tended to write conventionalized and formulary action stories, they did not appeal to him and he set to looking for humorous angles and also delved into historical research on the West.

The first novel Gulick wrote which achieved wide commercial success was *Bend of the Snake* (Boston: Houghton Mifflin, 1950), which was filmed as *Bend of the River* (Universal, 1952). For a short period, following his marriage, Gulick lived in the Berkshires of Western Massachusetts, and then went to Southern California for a six-month stay. Sojourns followed in Arizona, Oklahoma, and Mexico before he came to stay in the Pacific Northwest, buying a small ranch in the country near Walla Walla in Washington.

Gulick's wife Jeanne was long interested in little theatre and at her urging Gulick turned, occasionally, to write outdoor dramas, the most significant of which was perhaps *Trails West*, an outdoor musical drama which ran for 55 performances in 1976 and 54 performances in 1977. It deals with the period between the coming of the Lewis and Clark party in 1805 through the mountain man era, the missionary period, and the Oregon Trail days in 1855. For production in the amphitheatre in Fort Walla Walla Park, Gulick was additionally made project coordinator for a grant from the Washington Commission for the Humanities to assure that Indian advisors and historians were hired, to make certain that the Indian side of treaty negotiations was accurately portrayed, that Indian actors appeared in tribal roles, and for public seminars to be held to stress the effects of the Stevens Treaties of 1855 on Indian rights to land, fish, water, and sovereignty today. Gulick's most successful non-fiction book has been *Snake River Country* (Idaho: Caxton, 1971), focusing on that country, in words and photographs, with which Gulick is most familiar.

Probably Gulick's most important contribution to Western fiction is his insistence on retaining a sense of humor and hyperbole, so typical of earlier writers in the field as Owen Wister (q.v.) and Alfred Henry Lewis (q.v.) and somehow lost almost altogether beneath the heavy romanticism made popular by Zane Grey (q.v.) or the sober fiction typical of Ernest Haycox (q.v.) and Luke Short (q.v.). Perhaps best known of his humorous Western novels, because it was filmed under the same title, was *The Halle-*

lujah Trail (New York: Doubleday, 1963), which told of the misadventures befalling a shipment of liquor to Denver sought, for various reasons, by the Indians and women's temperance league and involving the U.S. Cavalry.

Bill Gulick's Western novels are *Bend of the Snake* (1950), *A Drum Calls West* (1952), *A Thousand for the Cariboo* (1954), *White Men, Red Men, and Mountain Men* (1955), *The Land Beyond* (1958), *Showdown in the Sun* (1958), *The Shaming of Broken Horn* (1961), *The Moon-Eyed Appaloosa* (1962), *The Hallelujah Trail* (1963), *They Came to a Valley* (1966), *Liveliest Town in the West* (1969), *The Country Club Caper* (1970), *Treasure in Hell's Canyon* (1979).

His outdoor dramas include *The Magic Musket* (1953), *Pe-wa-oo-yit: The First Treaty Council* (1955), *Trails West* (1976).

Films based on Bill Gulick's Western fiction are *Bend of the River* (Universal, 1952) directed by Anthony Mann, *The Road to Denver* (Republic, 1954) directed by Joseph Kane, *The Hallelujah Trail* (United Artists, 1965) directed by John Sturges.

Guthrie, A(lfred) B(ertram), Jr. (1901 —) Pulitzer Prize-winning short story writer, novelist, essayist, and poet whose historical fiction deals with the settlement and development of the Northwest, born at Bedford, Indiana. Guthrie was raised in Choteau, Montana, where his family moved when he was 6 months old. Guthrie's father, a bookish man who became the first principal of the Teton County Free High School, fell in love with the "big sky" of Montana which helped to develop in the young Guthrie a love for the West and its history. "It was a fine country to grow up in. To find riches, a boy had only to go outside," wrote Guthrie in his casual, yet sensitive, autobiography, *The Blue Hen's Chick* (New York: McGraw-Hill, 1965). While attending public high school, Guthrie began doing odd jobs at the local newspaper, the *Choteau Acantha,* which his father had owned and unwisely sold. Having never felt comfortable in cities, after attending the University of Washington at Seattle in 1919, Guthrie transferred to the University of Montana at Missoula. In 1923 he received his degree in journalism. Between 1923–1926, Guthrie worked on a vegetable ranch in Mexico, for an electric company and a grocery store chain in California, for the Montana census bureau, and finally for his uncle's feed mill in New York before he landed a job as cub reporter for the *Lexington Leader* in Kentucky. Guthrie stayed with the *Leader* from 1926 to 1947, holding various positions including executive editor.

Guthrie had always wanted to write fiction, but he had assumed it would be an avocation. He began reading Westerns and detective stories. Guthrie felt he could write as well as any of the authors he had read and began writing his first book in 1936, *Murders at Moon Dance* (New York: Dutton, 1943), a detective story with a Western setting. The story with its formulary characters and plotline was set in the mythical town of Moon Dance which was the setting for five of the short stories later collected in *The Big It and Other Stories* (Boston: Houghton Mifflin, 1960). Guthrie stated that although it was not the worst book ever written, it was definitely a contender; however, "... a writer must write a first book. ..."

Guthrie was stricken with encephalitis—sleeping sickness—in 1943 and he returned to Montana to recuperate at which time he became determined to write a novel about the rise and fall of the mountain man between 1830–1843. After several unsuccessful attempts at the book, which became *The Big Sky* (New York: Sloane, 1947), the first in his famous frontier trilogy, Guthrie applied for and won the Nieman Fellowship at Harvard where he met Theodore Morrison, a professor of English, who was extremely instrumental in the writing of the book. The story's protagonist, Boone Caudill, leaves his home in Kentucky at the age of 17 to find adventure on the frontier and eventually becomes a mountain man. "Each man kills the thing he loves" was the basic theme of *The Big Sky* according to Guthrie, who adeptly depicted the self-wrought destruction of the mountain man. As the wind in Dorothy Scarborough's *The Wind* (New York: Harper's, 1925), the Mississippi River in Mark Twain's *The Adventures of Huckleberry Finn* (1884), or the desert in Ann Ahlswede's *The Savage Land* (New York: Ballantine, 1962), the land—the open spaces and the big sky—serves as the unifying motif in the novel as it does in all of Guthrie's fiction. In a talk at a history conference in Montana in 1954 which was published under the title "The Historical Novel," Guthrie said, "What we need to remember, in the reconstruction of heroes, is just that no one ever was perfect. I wanted to show the mountain man—in this first book of mine—for what he was, or what he seemed honestly to me to have been—not the romantic character, the virtuous if unlettered Leatherstocking, but the engaging, uncouth, admirable, odious, thoughtless, resourceful, loyal, sinful, smart, stupid, courageous character that he was and had to be." *The Big Sky* ranks as one of the best books on the life of the mountain man along with Harvey Fergusson's (q.v.) *Wolf Song* (New York: Knopf, 1927), Forrester Blake's *Johnny Christmas* (New York: Morrow, 1948), and Vardis Fisher's (q.v.) *Mountain Man* (New York: Morrow, 1965).

Encouraged by the kind reception to *The Big Sky*, Guthrie quit newspaper work when his publishers urged him to write another novel. *The Way West* (New York: Sloane, 1949), written in six months, became a Book-of-the-Month Club selection and won the Pultizer Prize in 1950, as well as earning Guthrie an honorary Doctor of Literature degree from his alma mater and numerous assignments from periodicals as *Holiday*. In it Guthrie dealt with a single wagon train on its trek from Independence, Missouri, to Oregon in 1845. Dick Summers, the experienced mountain man from *The Big Sky*, is hired as a scout and guide for the wagon train and serves as the bridge between the two books. Through an interesting cast of characters, each of whom has a different reason for moving to Oregon, Guthrie chronicled the physical and psychological hardships along the trail, particularly for the women, as well as the tediousness of the slow journey which took months. Without ever becoming melodramatic, Guthrie, who saw too many funerals at a young age—six of the nine Guthrie children died early—showed how tragedy often struck the family unit. Many critics and historians feel *The Way West* is the best novel about the Oregon Trail. However, James K. Folsom in *The American Western Novel* (New Haven: Yale University Press, 1966) felt the actions of Lije Evans, the main character, are all too predictable at the expense of suspense to the story. The infallibility of Evans appears to represent the triumph of the individual and the pioneering spirit. Guthrie did, however, do a remarkable job contrasting the two ways of life—mountain man and farmer—through use of his characters Lije Evans and Dick Summers and one feels that ultimately the individual's life is more important than community spirit. Guthrie himself seemed to opt for the untamed, perhaps freer life of the mountain man.

Howard Hawks, who directed the film version of *The Big Sky*, recommended Guthrie for the job of screenwriter on the adaptation of Jack Schaefer's (q.v.) novel *Shane* (Boston: Houghton Mifflin, 1949); Guthrie was hired at a salary of $1,500 per week in 1951. Although Guthrie enjoyed the work, he knew he could not stay permanently in Hollywood. However, after leaving, he did return several times to work on the scripts for *The Kentuckian* (United Artists, 1955) and *These Thousand Hills* (20th-Fox, 1958), this last based on the third novel in his trilogy and the least successful of the three. Guthrie felt the book was not as successful as the earlier novels because it "dealt with the cowpuncher and had to avoid, if it could, the stylized Western myth." As *The Way West*, Guthrie used a multiple point of view in *These Thousand Hills* (Boston: Houghton Mifflin, 1956) and focused on the life of Lat Evans, Lije Evans' grandson, who leaves Oregon in the 1880s to become a cattle rancher in Montana. Lat eventually gets his ranch and becomes a pillar of the community after a career of wolf hunting and bronc busting. However, the discovery of his earlier relationship with a prostitute, Callie, almost brings about the ruin of his marriage to a "respectable" woman and threatens his potential career as a politician. In this and Guthrie's subsequent novels he dealt with the psycho-sexual workings of his characters. Lat is somewhat of a moral hypocrite as is Benton Collingsworth in *Arfive* (Boston: Hougton Mifflin, 1970) which won the Western Heritage Wrangler Award. Guthrie was highly criticized for being deficient in his goal to portray cattle ranching in Montana. However, Walter Van Tilburg Clark (q.v.) in his essay "When Settlers Began to Take Over" (1956) felt Guthrie did not miss the mark, but rather was dealing with a more complex age than he had in his earlier novels. Lat Evans is best described as a transitional character in a less unwavering and more complicated period.

In 1953, Guthrie returned permanently to live in Montana.

His subsequent work intensified and deepened certain of his themes. The title story in *The Big It and Other Stories* appeared in a somewhat altered form in *These Thousand Hills* as a comical yarn spun by one of Evans' wolfing partners. All but two of the stories contained in this collection were published in magazines from slick to literary, as *Collier's, Esquire, The Saturday Evening Post, Liberty, Southwest Review,* and *Gunsmoke.* All of the stories are set in the West and range from comic to ironic to morbid tragedy as "Ebbie" (1951), a brutal story about the blinding of a dog which was based on an actual experience from Guthrie's youth. "First Principal" (1953), published under the title "Newcomer" in *Gun-*

smoke, anticipated *Arfive* and the main character, a male school principal in both, is no doubt based on Guthrie's father. Guthrie used Choteau, Montana, as the model for Arfive, Montana, where the novel is set. In the story Guthrie depicted the building of a small community with a cast of interesting but ordinary people. Guthrie's portrayal of women—both prostitutes and struggling wives and mothers—is realistic and insightful for this period of frontier life. *The Last Valley* (Boston: Houghton Mifflin, 1975) continues the story of Arfive, Montana, as a prospering community, although it contains more political overtones.

Guthrie returned to the Western-detective genre with his novel *Wild Pitch* (Boston: Houghton Mifflin, 1973), a mystery story set in Montana featuring a Sherlock Holmes and Doctor Watson association reincarnated as a small-town sheriff, Chick Charleston, and his 17-year-old helper, Jason Beard. *A Genuine Article* (Boston: Houghton Mifflin, 1977) continues the adventures of Charleston and Beard although a romantic interest is incorporated into the storyline for Beard. Both novels were well-received and Guthrie was praised for his skill in weaving the two genres and for his ability to create tension in a pastoral atmosphere. *A Genuine Article* was followed by *No Second Wind* (Houghton Mifflin, 1980).

Guthrie tried his hand at poetry although his output was minimal. He also wrote articles on such varied topics as history, personal reminiscences, travel, and anecdotal pieces. His greatest achievement as an historical novelist was his ability to recreate a past period accurately and believably through use of his vast first-hand knowledge and extensive research on the Western experience. He portrayed the West with both its beauties and flaws and his characters, although ordinary people, are interesting and credible at the same time. Guthrie once said: "It has to be more than history faintly inhabited by figures. It has to be people, it has to be personalities, set in a time and place subordinate to them. Perhaps the hardest lesson for us historical novelists, as it is also the hardest lesson for any writer of fiction, is that it isn't event that is important; it is human and individual involvement in and response to event."

Along with Fergusson and Fisher, Guthrie was certainly one of the finest authors of Western fiction writing in this century. Very few authors have been able to bring American history to life so powerfully with so much understanding and wisdom as Guthrie.

Films based on A.B. Guthrie's Western fiction are *The Big Sky* (RKO, 1952) directed by Howard Hawks, *These Thousand Hills* (20th-Fox, 1958) directed by Richard Fleischer, *The Way West* (United Artists, 1967) directed by Andrew McLaglen.

Guthrie worked on the screenplays for *Shane* (Paramount, 1953) directed by George Stevens, *The Kentuckian* (United Artists, 1955) directed by and starring Burt Lancaster.

For further information see Guthrie's autobiography *The Blue Hen's Chick* (New York: McGraw-Hill, 1965) and *A.B. Guthrie, Jr.* (Austin: Steck-Vaughn, 1968) by Thomas W. Ford.

H

Haas, Benjamin Leopold (1926–1977) Author of the Fargo series of Western novels as well as other Western fiction under the pseudonyms Richard Meade, Ben Elliott, Thorne Douglas, John Benteen (the name he used for the Fargo series as well as other books), and his own name, born at Charlotte, North Carolina. Haas earned his diploma from Central High School in Charlotte in 1943. His English teacher urged him to write and he was also later encouraged to do so by Douglas Henderson, a maternal uncle. When he was 18, Haas sold his first Western story, "Who Would Die for Poverty Range?," which appeared in the August, 1944 issue of the old pulp, *.44 Western*.

From 1944 to 1946 Haas served in the U.S. Army, part of the time in the Philippines. After his discharge he tried again to write, spending several hours a day at the typewriter, but without success. In 1949 he moved to Raleigh and shortly thereafter he sold his first novel. From then on he made his living as a writer.

Haas was tremendously prolific, never writing less than 5,000 words a day and generally much more, although not all of it Western fiction. For years prior to 1959 he had actually worked at two full-time jobs. His success began when he decided to send his manuscripts to small paperback houses instead of trying for acceptance in the major leagues. Almost immediately he was in demand. While grinding out potboilers, he also made an effort at more serious fiction, and wrote *The Foragers* (New York: Simon & Schuster, 1962) and *Look Away, Look Away* (New York: Simon & Schuster, 1964), neither one a Western.

Returning to Raleigh, he began to work on his popular "series" Westerns—Fargo, Sundance, and Rancho Bravo. Between 1966 and his death ten years later, he wrote at least forty-six Westerns and three more major novels. In 1968, in spite of his first heart attack, he wrote fifteen books. As productive as he was, he would not settle for anything less than his best and insisted that even his minor work must be authentic. With his friend, newspaper editor Jim Henderson, he made numerous trips to the West gathering material. He suffered his second heart attack and thereafter wrote only five or six more novels, all Westerns. His heart failed him for the last time in the course of a business trip to New York City.

As a writer, Haas was self-taught and a meticulous craftsman. He would often tell aspiring writers, "*You* must be your own harshest critic." He was quite willing, when he believed his manuscript was imperfect, to dump years of work in a trash can and start over. His major books went through five to nine rewrites before he considered them finished. His son Joel, with whom he collaborated on *The Border Jumpers* (New York: Belmont Tower, 1976) and *Death Valley Gold* (New York: Belmont Tower, 1976), both in the Fargo series, reported that he turned out over sixty-four identifiable novels and perhaps as many as twenty more. Writing under the pseudonym John Benteen, he turned out nineteen titles in the Fargo series between 1968 and 1977. The Sundance series contained fourteen titles.

The Rancho Bravo group, written under the name Thorne Douglas, contained five titles. He also wrote *A Helluva Way to Die* (New York: Belmont Tower, 1967) under the name Jack Slade (see House Names). He specialized in rugged male characters and fast action. When formulary Westerns began increasingly to supply their readers with extra quantities of violence, Haas went with the tide.

C.L.S.

Under the name Richard Mead, Benjamin Haas wrote two novelizations of Western films, *Rough Night in Jericho* (1967) and *Cimarron Strip* (1967). Also under this name he wrote three original Western novels: *Big Bend* (1968), *Cartridge Creed* (1973), *Gaylord's Badge* (1975).

Haas' novels as Ben Elliott are *Contract in Cartridges* (1964), *Brother with a Gun* (1964).

Haas' novels as Thorne Douglas are *Calhoon* (1972), *The Big Drive* (1973), *Kilraine* (1975), *Night Riders* (1976), *The Mustang Men* (1977).

Between 1969 and his death in 1977, Haas wrote his Fargo, Sundance and Cutler series for Belmont Tower under the name John Benteen. The first two proved so popular that novels pirating his name and his characters soon began to appear without his consent. Only those which Haas himself wrote follow. For the Fargo series, he wrote *Fargo* (1969), *Panama Gold* (1970), *Alaska Gold* (1970), *Massacre River* (1970), *The Sharpshooter* (1970), *Wolf's Head* (1970), *Valley of Skulls* (1970), *Apache Raiders* (1970), *The Wildcatters* (1970), *The Black Bulls* (1971), *Killing Spree* (1971), *Phantom Gunman* (1971), *Shotgun Man* (1973), *Killer's Moon* (1976), *Hell on Wheels* (1976),

The Border Jumpers (1976), *Death Valley Gold* (1976), *Dakota Badlands* (1977), *Fargo and the Texas Rangers* (1977). For the Sundance series he wrote *Overkill* (1970), *Dead Man's Canyon* (1970), *Death in the Lava* (1971), *The Pistoleros* (1972), *The Bronc Trail* (1972), *The Wild Stallions* (1973), *Taps at Little Big Horn* (1973), *The Ghost Dancers* (1973), *Run for Cover* (1976), *Manhunt* (1976), *Silent Enemy* (1977), *Riding Shotgun* (1977). For the Cutler series he wrote *Wolf Pack* (1972), *The Gunhawks* (1972).

Hall, Oakley (Maxwell) (1920—)

An author at his best in writing Western fiction, born at San Diego, California. From 1939–1943 he served in the U.S. Marine Corps. In 1947 he received his Bachelor's degree from the University of California at Berkeley and in 1950 he received his Master's degree from the Iowa State University where, until 1952, he worked as a member of the University's Writers' Workship. As O.M. Hall he published his first novel, *Murder City* (New York: Farrar, Straus, 1949), and launched on a career of writing mystery/suspense fiction.

Hall's first Western novel was *Warlock* (New York: Viking, 1958), and it was nominated for a Pulitzer Prize. In it, Hall took a traditional story and peopled it with enough well-drawn characters to make a book unusual in its historical romance. While the novel is about specifics—about gunfighters and provisional governments—it is also about frontier populations and their myths. Hall was insistent that *Warlock* not be seen as a simple action Western. The death of its chief protagonist, a pivotal moment of the plot, is concluded offstage; the man is shot in the back. "By combining what did happen with what might have happened," Hall wrote in his Introduction, "I have tried to show what should have happened. . . . The pursuit of truth, not of facts, is the business of fiction."

Hall returned to the Western genre with *The Adelita* (New York: Doubleday, 1978), a story in which the rhetoric was simpler but the tone still epic, and *The Badlands* (New York: Atheneum, 1978). The latter is set during a rare, brief moment in which a Twentieth-century man could still move West and enter the Nineteenth century. As a novel, it stands as an effective, if romantic, evocation of the end of the West and a reassuring sign of strength in the continuation of a mythic tradition.

D.W.

Warlock (20th-Fox, 1959) was directed by Edward Dmytryk.

Hamilton, Donald (Bengtsson)

(1916 —) Author of some Western fiction, born at Uppsala, Sweden. Hamilton came to the United States at 8. He studied chemistry at the University of Chicago from which he received his Bachelor's degree in 1938. He spent four years in the Naval Reserve during World War II working as a chemist and attaining the rank of Lieutenant. In 1941 Hamilton married and later, with their two sons and two daughters, the Hamiltons settled in Santa Fe, New Mexico.

From 1946 on Hamilton worked as a freelance writer and photographer (the same "cover" occupation often used by Matt Helm). His first novel was *Date with Darkness* (New York: Rinehart, 1947), a superior story of counter-espionage. *Smoke Valley* (New York: Dell, 1954) was Hamilton's first Western novel, expanded from a *Collier's* serial. The novel's hero, John Parrish, is the quintessential Hamilton protagonist: the quiet, self-contained man, with a clear-sighted awareness of both his capabilities and his faults, avoiding violence until pushed into it but, when the push comes, willing to take whatever action is necessary and accept responsibility for the consequences.

The hero of *Mad River* (New York: Dell, 1956) is younger and not quite so self-assured. As John Parrish, however, he suffers the consequences of misplaced chivalry towards an unscrupulous woman. James McKay in *The Big Country* (New York: Dell, 1958) is a Maryland sea captain who comes to Texas in 1886 to claim as his bride the daughter of a local cattleman only to find himself in the midst of a relentless feud. *The Man from Santa Clara* (New York: Dell, 1960) [alternate title: *The Two-Shoot*] is possibly the best of Hamilton's five Westerns, a tale of tangled emotions and bitter vengeance, and of the deceptively quiet stranger who supposedly came to New Mexico Territory in search of peace but whom an antagonist describes as "a walking shot-gun, looking for a target." *Texas Fever* (New York: Fawcett, 1960) is the story of a trail drive from Texas to Missouri in the years following the Civil War, a well done if familiar combination of formulary ingredients.

The same year *Texas Fever* appeared

also marked the publication of the first Matt Helm book, to which series Hamilton then devoted himself. He did, however, edit an anthology for the Western Writers of America, *Iron Men and Silver Stars* (New York: Fawcett, 1967), in which was included his own short story, "The Guns of William Longley," an interesting although pedestrian initiation narrative which, nonetheless, won the WWA Spur Award that year as the best Western short story.

R.E.B.

Films based on Donald Hamilton's Western fiction are *The Violent Men* (Columbia, 1955) directed by Rudolph Maté [based on *Smoke Valley*] and *The Big Country* (United Artists, 1958) directed by William Wyler.

Hardin, Clement. See Newton, Dwight Bennett.

Hardin, Dave. See Holmes, L.P.

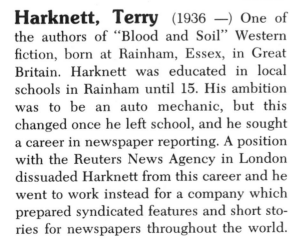

Harknett, Terry (1936 —) One of the authors of "Blood and Soil" Western fiction, born at Rainham, Essex, in Great Britain. Harknett was educated in local schools in Rainham until 15. His ambition was to be an auto mechanic, but this changed once he left school, and he sought a career in newspaper reporting. A position with the Reuters News Agency in London dissuaded Harknett from this career and he went to work instead for a company which prepared syndicated features and short stories for newspapers throughout the world.

After serving two years with the Royal Air Force, Harknett thought he would try his hand at a novel, was not successful, and, following a few months again at Reuters, he went to work for the publicity department at Twentieth Century-Fox's London office. Eight years more of editing a trade weekly elapsed before Harknett was able to concentrate all his time on writing fiction.

The New English Library came to Harknett with the idea for the Edge series. Harknett wrote four synopses for as many books, which were accepted, and the novels followed. The series was designed to concentrate on blood, gore, castration, torture, rape, and murder, all done for the sake of pure sensationalism and vicarious pleasure. Originally The New English Library did not think the Edge series would get past the fourth book, so Harknett packed every imaginable violent activity he could into those books; but by the sixth entry in the series, it proved a solid success and went on to sell over four million copies in the English language and in translation.

Harknett contracted to write a screenplay for a motion picture that was never produced and it was this script which he adapted for the initial offering in the Jubal Cade series. Edgar Rice Burroughs (q.v.) had a serious artistic purpose behind his two Apache books concerning Shoz Dijiji; in Harknett's Apache series the terrorist elements were emphasized with no attempt, as Burroughs made, to humanize and explain; again it was a question of pure sensationalism.

While Harknett continued to live as a recluse in England, his popularity became such that a fan club was started by his readers which gained an international membership.

After the first three entries in the Jubal Cade series were published under the penname Charles R. Pike, Harknett quit and Charles R. Pike became a house name in 1975 (see House Names). The Apache series was co-authored with Laurence James under the pseudonym William M. James, but Harknett withdrew from this series in 1979. These withdrawals allowed him to concentrate his efforts on the Edge series. If anything, the violence in the Edge series intensified, while the only thing "Western" about these novels is the setting and manner of dress.

C.L.S.

Terry Harknett's two series under the name George G. Gilman (the Edge series and the Steele series) are: (novels about Edge) *The Loner* (1972), *Ten Thousand Dollars American* (1972), *Apache Death* (1972), *Killer Breed* (1972), *Blood on Silver* (1972), *The Blue, the Grey, and the Red* (1973), *California Killing* (1973), *Seven out of Hell* (1973), *Bloody Summer* (1973), *Vengeance is Black* (1973), *Sioux Uprising* (1974), *The Biggest Bounty* (1974), *A Town Called Hate* (1974), *The Big Gold* (1974), *Blood Run* (1975), *The Final Shot* (1975), *Vengeance Valley* (1975), *Ten Tombstones to Texas* (1976), *Ashes and Dust* (1976), *Sullivan's Law* (1976), *Rhapsody in Red* (1976), *Slaughter Road* (1977), *Echoes of War* (1977), *The Day Democracy Died* (1977), *Violence Trail* (1978), *Savage Dawn* (1978), *Death Drive* (1978), *Eve of Evil* (1978), *The Living, the Dying, and the Dead* (1978), *Waiting for a Train* (1979), *The Guilty Ones* (1979), *The Frightened Gun* (1979), *The Hated* (1979), *Towering Nightmare* (1979), *Death Deal* (1980), *Red Fury* (1980), *A Ride in the Sun* (1980), *Town on Trial* (1981), *Vengeance at Ventura* (1981), *Massacre Mission* (1982); (novels about Steele) *The Violent Peace* (1974), *The Bounty Hunter* (1974), *Hell's Junction* (1974), *Valley of Blood* (1975), *Gun Run* (1975), *The Killing Art* (1975), *Cross Fire* (1975), *Comanche Carnage* (1976), *Badge in the Dust* (1976), *The Losers* (1976), *Lynch Town* (1976), *Death Trail* (1977), *Bloody Border* (1977), *Delta Duel* (1977), *River of Death* (1977), *Nightmare at Noon* (1978), *Satan's Daughters* (1978), *The Hard Way* (1978), *The Tarnished Star* (1979), *Wanted for Murder* (1979), *The Big Game* (1979), *Bloody Border* (1979), *The Hard Way* (1979), *River of Death* (1980).

The Apache series (co-authored with Laurence James) with titles crediting William M. James with authorship are *The First Death* (1974), *Knife in the Night* (1974), *Duel to the Death* (1975), *Death Train* (1975), *Fort Treachery* (1976), *Sonora Slaughter* (1976), *Blood Line* (1977), *Blood on the Tracks* (1977), *The Naked and the Savage* (1978), *All Blood is Red* (1978), *The Cruel Trail* (1978), *Fool's Gold* (1978), *The Best Man* (1979).

The Jubal Cade series titles written by Harknett under the name Charles R. Pike are *The Killing Trail* (1974), *Double Cross* (1974), *The Hungry Gun* (1975).

What began Harknett on his career apparently was his fictionalization of *A Fistful of Dollars* (United Artists, 1967) directed by Sergio Leone. Harknett ghosted his fictionalization under the name Frank Chandler and it was published in London by Tandem Books in 1972.

Harte, (Francis) Bret(t) (1836–1902)

Hailed during his lifetime as the *doyen* of American writers and lauded for his local color Western stories, born at Albany, New York. Harte suffered from ill health and was confined from the time he was 6 until he was 10. It was during this period that he read widely from his father's library. Harte's father, who was a schoolteacher, constantly encouraged his son's literary interests and when he was 11 Harte had his first poem published in the *New York Sunday Atlas*. During his early teens, he worked both in a lawyer's office and in the accounting room of a merchant. In 1854 he deserted the East to go to California where he worked variously as a printer, a schoolteacher, and in a mint. He also began publishing short sketches and poems in magazines. In 1857, when he became a typesetter for the *Golden Era* in San Francisco, he contributed several sketches to this publication and an earlier version of his short novel, *M'liss: An Idyll of Red Mountain* (1863), based on his experiences as a schoolteacher in a mining district, appeared during this time. The latter was, and remains, Harte's longest, most sustained inspiration and vividly captures the people who had come West in pursuit of gold. By 1868, Harte had achieved local fame as a literary

artist and was made editor of a new magazine, the *Overland Monthly*. It was in the pages of this periodical that Harte's most famous stories first saw publication, "The Outcasts of Poker Flat" and "The Luck of Roaring Camp." Because of the national circulation of the *Overland Monthly*, Harte's tales, so filled with new characters, new experiences, and new ways of looking at things, caused a sensation in the East and his reputation soon blossomed throughout the country. Harte's poem "The Heathen Chinee" (1870) was on everybody's lips and it was a national bestseller in its hardbound book edition.

In Margaret Duckett's *Mark Twain & Bret Harte* (Norman: University of Oklahoma Press, 1964), Duckett noted the fascination which writing about and for children exercised on Harte. Indeed, British novelist Charles Dickens was among Harte's favorite writers and when news of Dickens' death reached him at the *Overland Monthly*, Harte wrote of Dickens: "No one before him wrote so tenderly of childhood, for no one before him carried into the wisdom of maturity an enthusiasm so youthful—a faith so boylike." Since in *M'liss* children are central characters—M'liss, the orphan of Smith's Pocket, and the young boy, Risty—Duckett's hypothesis in *Mark Twain & Bret Harte* may well be justified, namely, "that the shabby little M'liss with her friend Risty stood, recognized or unrecognized, in the shadowy backgrounds of Mark Twain's mind when he was writing [*The Adventures of*] *Tom Sawyer* [1876] and [*The Adventures of*] *Huckleberry Finn* [1884] [and this] is altogether compatible with Bernard De Voto's conclusion in *Mark Twain's America* [Boston: Little, Brown, 1935] that with Tom Sawyer, Mark Twain found the theme best suited to his interest, his experience, and his talents. And it does not dim in any way any appreciation of Mark Twain's artistic achievements in writing his two most famous books." And it was while editing the *Overland Monthly* that Harte helped Mark Twain's early literary career.

In 1871, at the behest of several Eastern editors, Harte went to New York City, as it turned out never to return to the West. His great fame had preceded him and even spread to Europe. For a time he lived extravagantly and relished his position of being a literary idol. Soon he fell into financial difficulties, tried lecture tours, found himself unable to perform on publishers' contracts, and so with relief accepted a position as a U.S. consular agent in Crefeld, Germany, in 1878, leaving behind his wife, with whom he definitely did not get along, and his four children. Two years later he was transferred to Glasgow, eventually settling in London where he continued to write short stories and was a welcome guest in literary circles. It was in London, when Mark Twain was also there, that Hamlin Garland (q.v.) interviewed them both separately. Twain had collaborated with Harte in 1877 on a play titled *Ah Sin*, based on Harte's poem "The Heathen Chinee," an experience which tended to make Twain bitterly denunciatory about Harte thenceforth. Garland, recording his memories in *Roadside Meetings* (New York: Macmillan, 1930), was surprised to find that an old, white-haired figure wearing striped trousers, a cutaway coat over a fancy vest, spats, and, somewhat incredibly, a monocle was the author of "The Luck of Roaring Camp." Harte tended to be aloof and reticent. Twain was more outspoken, whenever the occasion presented itself, and in *Mark Twain in Eruption* (New York: Harper's, 1940), published posthumously and edited by Bernard DeVoto, Twain commented: "Bret Harte was one of the pleasantest men I have ever known. He was also one of the unpleasantest men I have ever known."

In the last years of his life, Twain was a literary giant and Harte, who died in 1902 and who had been such a bright star on the literary horizon, had fallen somewhat into obscurity. Yet in his short fiction Harte introduced a number of original characters and often wrote several stories featuring them in various roles. Among the most memorable, certainly, are his stage driver, Yuba Bill, the gambler, John Oakhurst, the garrulous Spanish-American, Enrique Saltello, the lawyer and gentleman, Colonel Culpepper Starbottle, the intelligent backwoods practitioner, Dr. Duchesne (better known in most localities as "Dr. Doochesny"), another roaming gambler and sardonic wit, Jack Hamlin (who appeared in some nineteen short stories and Harte's novel of 1876, *Gabriel Conroy*), along with memorable one-time appearances by Salomy Jane who saves an outlaw and makes a new life for herself, Cherokee Sal, the prostitute in "The Luck of Roaring Camp" (1868), and several memorable Chinese, among them See Yup and Wan Lee. Harte could and did also write sympathetically of animals, especially of dogs and horses, and he was ever a champion for the oppressed. Not only did he object to the fashion in which Chinese and Blacks were made the victims of racial intolerance, but when the citizens of a town where he was the editor of the local paper massacred a village of nearby Indians, the diatribe he printed forced him to depart for San Francisco.

Harte's literary West was not the black and white stereotype of good versus evil true of so many later writers. It was instead an image of a harsh, hostile world where, quite literally, luck or even a change in the weather could mean the difference between life and death. His bad men were occasionally softhearted and his good men were often unjust and tyrannical. "It *was* a very special world, that gold-rush world," Walter Van Tilburg Clark (q.v.) wrote of him in his Foreword to *Bret Harte: Stories of the Early West* (New York: Platt & Munk, 1964), "with ways of living, thinking, feeling, and acting so particularly its own that there has never been anything quite like it anywhere, before or since. Which is what the literary histories mean when they call Bret Harte a local-color writer."

The Writings of Bret Harte were published in twenty volumes (eighteen of fiction and two of poetry) in a Standard Library Edition by Houghton Mifflin in Boston, 1896–1904. Paperback collections of his short stories are frequently published, although the hardbound collection introduced by Walter Van Tilburg Clark, *Bret Harte: Stories of the Early West*, is perhaps the best selection to be found in a single volume.

Films based on Bret Harte's Western fiction are *In the Aisles of the Wild* (Biograph, 1912) directed by D.W. Griffith [source unknown.], *Salomy Jane* (Alco Films, 1914) directed by Paul Armstrong remade under this title (Paramount, 1923) directed by George Melford, *The Half-Breed* (Triangle, 1916) directed by Allan Dwan [based on the short story "In the Carquinez Woods"], *M'liss* (Paramount, 1918) directed by Marshall Neilan [based on *M'liss: An Idyll of Red Mountain*], remade as *The Girl Who Ran Wild* (Universal, 1922) directed by Rupert Julian remade as *The Man from Red Gulch* (PDC, 1925) directed by Edmund Mortimer, *The Outcasts of Poker Flat* (Universal, 1919) direct-

Publicity for an early film based on a Bret Harte story.

ed by John Ford remade under this title (RKO, 1937) directed by Christy Cabanne and (20th-Fox, 1952) directed by Joseph M. Newman, *Fighting Cressy* (Pathé, 1919) director unknown [based on the short novel *Cressy*], *The Flaming Forties* (PDC, 1924) directed by Tom Forman [based on the short story "Tennessee's Partner"] remade as *Tennessee's Partner* (RKO, 1955) directed by Allan Dwan, *The Golden Princess* (Paramount, 1925) directed by Clarence Badger [based on the short story "The Golden Princess"], *Taking a Chance* (Fox, 1928) directed by Norman Z. McLeod [based on the short story "The Saint of Calamity Gulch"], *The Luck of Roaring Camp*

(Monogram, 1937) directed by Joseph M. Newman.

For further information see *Bret Harte: Argonaut and Exile* (Boston: Houghton Mifflin, 1931) by George R. Stewart, *Bret Harte: A Biography* (Boston: Little, Brown, 1966) by Richard O'Connor, and the most valuable critical study of Harte's fiction *Mark Twain & Bret Harte* (Norman: University of Oklahoma Press, 1964) by Margaret Duckett.

Haycox, Ernest (1899–1950) During his lifetime the dean of writers of Western pulp fiction, magazine serials, and short stories, born at Portland, Oregon. Haycox spent his boyhood in logging camps, shingle mills, on ranches and in small towns. He served with his National Guard regiment on the Mexican border in 1916 and, later, for fourteen months, was sent to France with the American Expeditionary Force during World War I. In 1919–1920 Haycox attended Reed College, outside Portland, and went on to the University of Oregon at Eugene from which he graduated with a Bachelor's degree in 1923 and where his papers and personal library are now located. While still an undergraduate, Haycox started writing fiction, living in an abandoned

chicken coop where he literally papered three walls with rejection slips before his stories began to sell. In fact "Corporal's Story" (1921), his first published fiction, appeared in the *Overland Monthly* which, at one time, Bret Harte (q.v.) had edited. Haycox's early fiction from 1922–1923 was mostly sea stories—subsequently Haycox' style would be compared to that of Joseph Conrad who also worked in this genre—but by 1924, increasingly, Haycox was writing Western fiction and, except for some short stories set during the American Revolution, it was as a Western writer that he made his literary reputation.

What certainly made a difference in Haycox's life was his leaving Oregon after graduation and a short stint as a reporter for *The Oregonian* and going to New York. There he met Jill Marie Chord, an artist from Oregon. They were married and moved back to Oregon where Haycox lived for the rest of his life, raising a family—a son and a daughter—and renting an office in downtown Portland where he would go every day to write just as if it were a regular job. "It seemed reasonable," Haycox once told his son, "... that a fellow who writes about the West ought to be able to live in it." For Haycox, the West symbolized not only a way of life but a spiritual freedom, an antidote to disillusionment, no matter how fraught with hardship it might be. His relationship with Jill deepened and matured his innate romanticism and, although he would scarcely have thought it possible for a woman to function *without* need of a man, he also did not think it was possible for a man to function adequately without a woman.

In the late 'Twenties, Haycox was appearing regularly in *Short Stories* and in *West*, both of which were published by Doubleday, Doran, and his first hardbound novel, *Free Grass* (New York: Doubleday, 1929), ran serially in *West* prior to book publication. This turned out to be the marketing procedure Haycox followed with all his fiction during the 'Thirties and 'Forties, simply because the pay from magazines was so much more lucrative than book sales. Of Haycox' early pulp fiction, Ron Goulart wrote in *Cheap Thrills: An Informal History of the Pulp Magazines* (New Rochelle: Arlington House, 1972) that many of Haycox' heroes, "despite their pulp Western names, are complex, patient, introspective men. Haycox wrote of violence in a quirky, sometimes sensual way, and his pulp stories must be among the few to show a man becoming really attracted to, and often aroused by, a woman."

Free Grass resurrected an old convention in romantic fiction: instead of there being one heroine, there are two, and part of the hero's dilemma is to find out which one is right for him. Haycox subsequently became fascinated with this aspect of plotting and resorted to it frequently in novel after novel, in *Whispering Range* (New York: Doubleday, 1931), *Saddle and Ride* (Boston: Little, Brown, 1940), *Canyon Passage* (Boston: Little, Brown, 1945), and as late as his last magazine serial, *Long Storm* (Boston: Little, Brown, 1946) and his major effort as a novelist, *The Earthbreakers* (Boston: Little, Brown, 1952), as well as in others. Throughout the 'Thirties Haycox also worked to provide added dimensions to all of his characters. His heroes became more and more introspective, although never abandoning the commitment to action indigenous to the magazine serial; his villains became complicated and morally aware. *Man in the Saddle* (Boston: Little, Brown, 1938), in addition to two heroines, has one of the heroines marry the villain, who is

scarcely what traditionally had been meant by a villain, a man who, instead of being evil, is just flawed, given over to the disease of possession, envy, and the will to power. Sometimes, as in *Whispering Range* or in *Deep West* (Boston: Little, Brown, 1937), one of the men in with the rustlers turns out to be a close friend of the hero's; and again the agony which the Virginian did not feel for an errant friend in the Owen Wister (q.v.) novel but which he perhaps should have felt is probed, only now with greater insight and compassion. More than any other writer, Haycox sought to lay bare the moral issues which, it seemed to him, were a vital part of Western fiction and, in this way, prepared the way for those who were to push forward in this direction, such writers as Walter Van Tilburg Clark (q.v.), Will Henry (q.v.), and Edward Abbey (q.v.). Much of the discovery in Haycox' best plots is self-discovery and much of the tension is psychological, not physical, tension.

His influence on other writers was considerable. Some of it may be questionable, such as Luke Short's (q.v.) proclivity for a time to imitate the plot of the two heroines which flaws Short's otherwise fine novels *Hard Money* (New York: Doubleday, 1938) and *Ramrod* (New York: Macmillan, 1943), to name only two, or Will Henry's *Who Rides with Wyatt* (New York: Random House, 1954). Haycox' *Sundown Jim* (Boston: Little, Brown, 1938), one of his very best formulary Westerns, is also one of the very few stories that he wrote in which the protagonist is silhouetted in isolation against the hostile background of a Western community.

Perhaps even more notable are Haycox' women. In *Rim of the Desert* (Boston: Little, Brown, 1941), the heroine, Aurora Brant, overshadows the male protagonist,

Jim Keene, through her rich and exuberant characterization. It is also in *Rim of the Desert* that Haycox recreated a blizzard of such power and unforgettable savagery that it conjures up images that stay with a reader, just as, on a smaller scale, he could produce an almost equally powerful effect in a short story as "Blizzard" (1939), collected in *Prairie Guns* (Boston: Little, Brown, 1954).

Haycox' Western novels, and his short stories, embodied his philosophy of life. He believed that frequently men and women fall victim to basic compromises in life which make them forever prisoners to their own emotions. He saw accumulated wealth as the basic source of evil and, frequently, his villains, or, after 1935, characters who were morally questionable, were that way precisely because of a moral inferiority brought about through unethical compromises. In dealing with the relationships between men and women, Haycox was intensely monogamous.

There were also faults and shortcomings in his fiction. It should, however, be said in Haycox' behalf that more than a few of these were as a result of the markets for which he wrote. In the middle 'Thirties, his stories and serials ran regularly in *Collier's* and in the 'Forties he was the leading Western writer appearing in *The Saturday Evening Post*. Because of the dispute that had once arisen over Zane Grey's (q.v.) *The Vanishing American* when it ran serially in the *Ladies Home Journal* in 1922, it was not the policy of "slick" magazines, as these were, sensitively or compassionately to portray Native Americans, and in this Haycox adhered to editorial policy; hence in *The Border Trumpet* (Boston: Little, Brown, 1939) and *Bugles in the Afternoon* (Boston: Little, Brown, 1944) the emphasis is on the U.S. Cavalry and the Indians are not characterized. The same is true for the many Cavalry short stories Haycox wrote, which in quality rival those of James Warner Bellah (q.v.). But in some areas, Haycox would not compromise. He might not characterize Native Americans—which made them, at best, ambiguous and of dramatic interest only—but he would not make a hero of General Custer (see Historical Personalities). In a letter to his editor at Little, Brown, Haycox wrote in 1943 concerning *Bugles in the Afternoon*: "This whole Custer thing is not in the hands of scholars. It is in the hands of partisans who started with a conviction and thereafter spent years hunting for facts to justify their view." In *The Border Trumpet*, which is set in Arizona—where Haycox went to research the book—there is a character, a scout, who undermines what was the philosophy of the big circulation magazines, that the American middle-class way of life was the best man would or could ever have on this planet, when he remarks to the protagonist about Indian smoke signals: " 'Someday those things won't show against the sky. Then it will be a different country. I don't take much to your kind of civilization, Tom. Put a man in a town, in a house, give him a steady job and let him worry about his pay check—and he ain't a natural man any more. The Lord never meant us to live that way.' "

"Restraint is habitual with me," Haycox once wrote to W.F.G. Thacher, his teacher of creative writing at the University of Oregon with whom he maintained a lifelong correspondence. "I boil inside but am fairly placid outside." Haycox was constantly striving to break away from formulary Westerns. He would say at times: "I could not write some of the stories I wrote five years ago. I wish I could, since I enjoyed them so much. But my fingers will not trace the same patterns—and it would be foolish of me to try to force them into the old patterns." He wanted to write historical fiction, which with such books as *Alder Gulch* (Boston: Little, Brown, 1941), dealing with Henry Plummer's reign of terror, came to set the tone for most of his work in the 'Forties. But integrating his fictional characters with historical personalities was not enough. He wanted to write novels which, while historically accurate, went farther yet, which probed into the spiritual and moral forces within the Westward expansion, the greed and the idealism, of how the land itself shaped men and women and men and women changed the land. *The Earthbreakers* was his initial published attempt in this new direction, coming a full two years after he had written anything for magazine consumption. It was a mixed success, but the direction was all there, and the promise.

The publication of *The Earthbreakers* came when it did because it was issued posthumously. Haycox had been ill with cancer for several months before he underwent surgery in August, 1950; two months later he was dead. "He was a gentle writer," Brian Garfield (q.v.) wrote about him, "seldom brutal but always masculine. There isn't much blood-and-thunder in Haycox, but then you have the pleasure of believing in the real conflicts he portrays—a belief often hard to come by in the more popular fiction of pure action. . . . His stories are superbly readable, today as yesterday; you can still read a Haycox story you've read eight times before, and get something new and enjoyable out of it."

A whole new generation became familiar with Ernest Haycox thanks to the assiduous efforts of his wife, Jill Marie, who oversaw the paperback re-issue not only of his magazine serials but the many book collections of his short stories which, in turn, were issued in paperback, as well as paperback re-issue of most of his pulp fiction. Of course, not all of his fiction is of uniform quality, but enough of it is to make it remarkable. D.B. Newton (q.v.) once summarized Haycox' most important legacy this way: "[H]e proved once and for all that even the lowly Western can be lifted, with enough skill and care and imagination, from the level of pulp fiction to something approaching very near to Art."

Ernest Haycox' Western novels, which for the most part were run serially in magazines before hardbound publication, include: *Free Grass* (1929), *Chaffee of Roaring Horse* (1930), *Whispering Range* (1931), *Starlight Rider* (1933), *Riders West* (1934), *Rough Air* (1934) [basically a Hollywood novel], *The Silver Desert* (1935), *Trail Smoke* (1936), *Trouble Shooter* (1937), *Deep West* (1937), *Sundown Jim* (1938), *Man in the Saddle* (1938), *The Border Trumpet* (1939), *Saddle and Ride* (1940), *Rim of the Desert* (1941), *Trail Town* (1941), *Alder Gulch* (1942), *Action by Night* (1943), *The Wild Bunch* (1943), *Bugles In the Afternoon* (1944), *Canyon Passage* (1945), *Long Storm* (1946), *The Earthbreakers* (1952), *The Adventurers* (1954).

Anthologies of Haycox' pulp novels (referred to for purposes of distinction as *serials* as opposed to his hardbound novels which however, as noted, were also almost all serialized), short novels, and short stories fall into two categories: those which were published in hardbound format initially with subsequent paperback reprints and those which, after prior pulp or magazine publication, were collected in original paperback editions. With the exception of *Son of the West* (1930) which for a time was given the paperback title *Clint* but which now is known as *Dead Man's Range* all paperback dates are as of original soft-cover publication.

The hardbound anthologies include: *Rough Justice* (1950), *By Rope and Lead* (1951), *Pioneer Loves* (1952), *Murder on the Frontier* (1953), *Outlaw* (1953), *Prairie Guns* (1954), *The Last Rodeo* (1955), *Winds of Rebellion* (1964) [this last consisting of stories with a Revolutionary War background and, uniquely, was never re-issued in softbound format].

The softbound anthologies include: *Head of the Mountain* (1950) [a serial first published in 1950], *Rawhide Range* (1952) [short stories], *The Grim Canyon* (1953) [short novel, consisting of the title short novel (1928), *Discovery Gulch* (1929), and *Blizzard Camp* (1932)], *Guns Up* (1954) [short novels, consisting of the title short novel (1928) and *The Trail of the Barefoot Pony* (1929)], *Gun Talk* (1956) [short stories], *On the Prod* (1957) [a serial originally titled *Fighting Man* (1930)], *Lone Rider* (1959) [short novels, consisting of the title short novel originally titled *The Black Clan* (1931) and *Lin of Pistol Gap* (1930)], *Guns of the Tom Dee* (1959) [short novels, consisting of the title short novel (1930) and *The Valley of the Rogue* (1925)], *Brand Fires on the Ridge* (1959) [short novels, consisting of the title short novel (1929) and *Night Raid* (1929)], *The Feudists* (1960) [a serial first published in 1932], *A Rider of the High Mesa* (1960) [a serial first published in 1927], *Vengeance Trail* (1960) [short novels, consisting of the title short novel originally titled *No Speak Pass* (1931) and *Invitation by Bullet* (1929)], *The Man from Montana* (1964) [short stories], *Outlaw Guns* (1964) [short novels, consisting of *Renegade Law* (1929), *Ambushed* (1927),

and *Rimrock and Rattlesnakes* (1926)], *Six-Gun Duo* (1965) [short novels, consisting of *The Killers* (1930) and *The Gun Singer* (1931)], *Trigger Trio* (1966) [short novels, consisting of *The Octopus of Pilgrim Valley* (1928), *Ride Out* (1931), and *The Fighting Call* (1932)], *Powdersmoke and Other Stories* (1966) [short stories], *Guns of Fury* (1967) [short novels, consisting of *The Hour of Fury* (1933) included above in *Guns Up* (1954) and *Night Raid* (1929) included above in *Brand Fires on the Ridge* (1959)], *Wipe Out the Brierlys* (1967) [a serial first published in 1929], *Starlight and Gunflame* (1973) [short novels, consisting of the title short novel (1928), *Red Romain* (1930), and *Crossfire* (1931)], *Frontier Blood* (1974) [short novels, consisting of the title short novel (1926), *Manhunt* (1931), *The Roaring Hour* (1932), and *The Kid from River Red* (1932)], *Dead Man Range* (1975) [a serial formerly titled *Clint* first published as *Son of the West* (1930)].

Films based on Ernest Haycox' Western fiction are *Union Pacific* (Paramount, 1939) directed by Cecil B. DeMille [based on the novel *Trouble Shooter*], *Stagecoach* (United Artists, 1939) directed by John Ford remade under this title (20th-Fox, 1966) directed by Gordon Douglas [based on the short story "Stage to Lordsburg"], *Apache Trail* (M-G-M, 1942) directed by Richard Thorpe and remade as *Apache War Smoke* (M-G-M, 1952) directed by Harold Kress [based on the short story "Stage Station"], *Sundown Jim* (20th-Fox, 1942) directed by James Tinling, *Abilene Town* (United Artists, 1946) directed by Edwin L. Marin [based on *Trail Town*], *Canyon Passage* (Universal, 1946) directed by Jacques Tourneur, *Montana* (Warner's, 1950) directed by Ray Enright [based on an original screenplay by Haycox], *Man in the Saddle* (Columbia, 1951) directed by Andre DeToth, *Bugles in the Afternoon* (Warner's, 1952) directed by Ray Rowland, *The Far Country* (M-G-M, 1954) directed by Anthony Mann [based peripherally on the novel *Alder Gulch*].

Several of Haycox' Western stories were adapted for television: "A Day in Town" (*Medallion Theatre*, CBS, 1953), "The Windmill" (*General Electric Theatre*, 1954), "Outlaw's Reckoning" (*American Theatre*, ABC, 1954), "The Inscrutable Man" (*Tales of Wells Fargo*, 1954), "Toll Road" (*Tales of Wells Fargo*, 1958), "Tavern At Powell's Ferry" (*Cimarron City*, 1958), "The New Schoolmarm" (*Cimarron City*, 1958), "The Last Rodeo" (*General Electric Theatre*, 1958), "The Castaway" (*General Electric Theatre*, 1958), "Fourth Son" (*General Electric Theatre*, 1958), "Deadline" (*Alfred Hitchcock Presents*, 1958).

Many of Haycox' Western stories, and one novel, were narrated or dramatized for radio: "Salute to Time" (NBC,, 1940), "At Anselm's (George Jessel, narrator, 1944), "Canyon Passage (Camay Program, 1946), "Hard Passage" (ABC, 1948), "Cry Deep, Cry Still" (ABC, 1948), "No Time for Dreams" (ABC, 1948), "Wild Jack Rhett" (CBS, 1948), "Call This Land Home" (NBC, 1947), "Fourth Son" (NBC, 1957), "Custom of the Country" (NBC, 1957), "High Wind" (NBC, 1957), "Deep Horizons" (NBC, 1957).

Hecklemann, Charles N(ewman) (1913 —) Author of formulary Western fiction, born at New York City. Hecklemann attended the University of No-

tre Dame and received a Bachelor's degree in 1934 and for a time in the 'Thirties wrote for the *Brooklyn Daily Eagle* before publishing his first Western novel, *Vengeance Trail* (New York: Arcadia House, 1944). In 1941–1958 he served as vice president and editor-in-chief of Popular Library and subsequently became associated with Hawthorn Books Inc. Under the pseudonym Charles Lawton, Hecklemann wrote a number of sports and adventure books for the juvenile market. Hecklemann's Western fiction, unfortunately, tended to be merely a humdrum reworking of formulary materials while his vision of the West was populated by aggressive gunfighters and there was, invariably, a lot of gun action, putting his fiction in the category of an updated version of William Colt MacDonald's (q.v.) gunfighter stories of an earlier period and an anticipation of Terry Harknett's (q.v.) Edge series which even further intensified the violence and killing.

Charles N. Hecklemann's Western novels are *Vengeance Trail* (1944), *Lawless Range* (1945), *Six-Gun Outcast* (1946), *Deputy Marshal* (1947), *Guns of Arizona* (1949), *Outlaw Valley* (1950), *Danger Rides the Range* (1950), *Two-Bit Rancher* (1950), *Let the Guns Roar* (1950), *Fighting Ramrod* (1951), *Hell in His Holsters* (1952), *The Rawhider* (1952), *Hard Man with a Gun* (1954), *Bullet Law* (1955), *Trumpets in the Dawn* (1958), *The Big Valley* (1966), *The Glory Riders* (1967), *Stranger from Durango* (1971). *The Big Valley* above was a novelization of the television series of the same title (ABC, 1965–1969).

Films based on Charles N. Hecklemann's Western fiction are *Frontier Feud* (Monogram, 1945) directed by Lambert Hillyer [source unknown], *Stranger from Santa Fe* (Monogram, 1945) directed by Lambert Hillyer [source unknown], *Deputy Marshal* (Lippert, 1949) directed by William Berke.

Hendryx, James B(eardsley) (1880–1963) Creator of Corporal Downey of the Royal Mounted and Connie Morgan, protagonist in a series of juvenile adventure novels, born at Sauk Center, Minnesota. Hendryx was enrolled for two years at the University of Minnesota before he quit to become a traveling salesman. He worked for a time as a cowhand and then became a special writer for the *Cincinnati Enquirer*. The most formative experience of his life was his departure for the gold fields in the Klondike. It was here that he first absorbed his material about life in the North and met the real-life prototype of Corporal Downey. Hendryx published his first Western novel, *The Promise: A Tale of the Great Northwest* (New York: Putnam's, 1915), and followed it the next year with the first entry in his juvenile series, *Connie Morgan in Alaska* (New York: Putnam's, 1916). Later on in his career, Hendryx, who soon became a prolific author, added his saga about the doings in a frontier town he called Halfaday Creek.

In later life Hendryx divided his time between Lee's Point at Sutton's Bay, Michigan, and Thessalon in Ontario.

In view of the number of books with a Northwestern setting that Hendryx wrote, he invites comparison with James Oliver Curwood (q.v.) and Rex Beach (q.v.), but his stories are somewhat lacking in Curwood's sentimentality—which is a definite virtue—and Hendryx was often somewhat more adept at interesting settings than was Beach. In his use of weather and sensitivity to the environment as an integral part of a story, Hendryx often approached Jack London (q.v.) and it is these images and the atmosphere which a reader tends to remember after reading one of his novels.

James B. Hendryx' novels with a Western or Northwestern setting are *The Promise: A Tale of the Great Northwest* (1915), *Connie Morgan in Alaska* (1916), *The Gun-Brand* (1917), *Connie Morgan of the Mounted* (1918), *The Texan: A Story of the Cattle Country* (1918), *Connie Morgan in the Lumber Camps* (1919), *The Gold Girl* (1920), *Prairie Flowers* (1920), *Connie Morgan in the Fur Country* (1921), *Snowdrift: A Story of the Land of Strong Cold* (1922), *Connie Morgan in the Cattle Country* (1923), *North* (1923), *Without Gloves* (1924), *Marquand the Silent* (1924), *At the Foot of the Rainbow* (1924), *The Challenge of the North* (1925), *Connie Morgan with the Forest Rangers* (1925), *Oak and Iron, of These Be the Breed of the North* (1925), *Downey of the Mounted* (1926), *Frozen Inlet Post* (1927), *Gold—and the Mounted* (1928), *Man of the North* (1929), *Connie Morgan Hits the Trail* (1929), *Blood on the Yukon Trail* (1930), *In the Days of Gold* (1930), *Corporal Downey Takes the Trail* (1931), *Raw Gold* (1933), *The Yukon Kid* (1934), *Outlaws of Halfaday Creek* (1935), *Connie Morgan in the Arctic* (1936), *Grubstake Gold* (1936), *Blood of the North* (1938), *Black John of Halfaday Creek* (1939), *Edge of Beyond* (1939), *The Czar of Halfaday Creek* (1940), *Hard Rock Man* (1940), *Gambler's Chance* (1941), *Law and Order on Halfaday Creek* (1941), *Gold and Guns on Halfaday Creek* (1942), *New Rivers Calling* (1943), *Strange Doings on Halfaday Creek* (1943), *It Happened on Halfa-*

day Creek (1944), The Way of the North (1945), Skullduggery on Halfaday Creek (1946), Courage of the North (1946), The Saga of Halfaday Creek (1947), On the Rim of the Arctic (1948), Murder in the Outlands (1949), Justice on Halfaday Creek (1949), Badmen of Halfaday Creek (1950), The Stampeders (1951), Murder on Halfaday Creek (1951), Sourdough Gold (1952), Intrigue on Halfaday Creek (1953), Gold is Where You Find It (1953), Good Men and Bad (1954).

Films based on James B. Hendryx' Western fiction are *Prairie Trails* (Fox, 1920) directed by George Marshall [source unknown], and *Snowdrift* (Fox, 1923) directed by Scott Dunlap [based on *Snowdrift: A Story of the Land of Strong Cold*].

Henry, O. See Porter, William Sydney.

Henry, Will. See Allen, Henry Wilson.

Herbert, Arthur. See Shappiro, Herbert Arthur.

Hillerman, (Anthony G.) "Tony"

(1925 —) Essayist, journalist, and novelist of the American Indian Southwest, born at Sacred Heart, Oklahoma. Hillerman's early life was spent in a farming atmosphere, but Hillerman was also influenced by and absorbed in the lives of the Indians with whom he grew up. This exposure to Native American culture in Oklahoma provided him with his appreciation of Indian ways and rituals which he utilized in his later novels about the Southwestern tribes in New Mexico and Arizona.

Hillerman began his college education at Oklahoma State University in 1943 and received his Bachelor's degree from the University of Oklahoma in 1946. During the years 1943–1945, he also served in the U.S. Army and was awarded the Bronze Star, the Silver Star, and a Purple Heart. In 1948 Hillerman began an illustrious career in journalism. He started as a reporter for the *Borger News Herald* in Borger, Texas; then he served as city editor for the *Morning-Press Constitution* in Lawton, Oklahoma, from 1948–1950. Also in 1948 Hillerman was married and six children were the eventual result, three boys and three girls. In 1950 Hillerman began work for the United Press International as the political reporter for Oklahoma City. 1952 saw Hillerman moving to New Mexico where he became Bureau Manager for the United Press International in Santa Fe. In 1954 he transferred to the *New Mexican*, a Santa Fe paper, where he served first as political reporter and, later, as editor until 1963. That year Hillerman re-entered academic life when he became assistant to the president of the University of New Mexico in Albuquerque and chairman of the department of journalism in 1966, the same year he acquired his Master's degree in journalism from the University of New Mexico.

Although still somewhat involved in academic affairs, Hillerman was able, after 1970, to produce first rate suspense novels set in the Navaho, Hopi, and Zuni cultures of the Southwest. Even though he once stated that his ethnological material "is not intended to meet scholarly and scientific standards," it is evident that Hillerman was extremely well informed about the customs, rituals, and daily lives of the contemporary

Southwest Indians. His first novel, *The Blessing Way* (New York: Harper's, 1970), introduced Joe Leaphorn, a Navaho policeman who serves as the central character in Hillerman's novel and who constantly must make the transition between the more modern mechanized world of law enforcement which he represents and the older, ritualized world of the Indian cultures. *The Blessing Way* involves a search for a Navaho Wolf-Witch, an intriguing scheme to steal information about a guided missile system, and an interesting, detailed depiction of the Navaho "Enemy Way" ceremony, all combined in a novel about magic and murder.

Two later novels, *The Fly on the Wall* (New York: Harper's, 1971) and *Dance Hall of the Dead* (New York: Harper's, 1973), deal with a clash of cultures between the Zunis and the Navahos. *Dance Hall of the Dead* received the Edgar Award from the Mystery Writers of America as the best detective novel of 1973. Hillerman's subsequent novel, *Listening Woman* (New York: Harper's, 1978), was selected as a Book-of-the-Month Club alternate.

Hillerman's work very successfully brings the contemporary cultures of the Southwest before the eyes of his readers and, in each instance, produces "a mystery with literary value." The desert high country is portrayed with realism and believability, its peoples, its cultures, and its problems.

D.K.-M.

Historical Personalities
Already early in the Nineteenth century, it was customary for Americans to mytholo-
gize, distort, enhance, and make believe concerning their history as a sovereign nation. However, this mythologization process, if universal, has never been standardized; it has, instead, been subject to widely divergent interpretations. What remains characteristic of it as a whole, though, is the tendency to present American historical personalities as inevitably larger-than-life and staunchly to adopt a cavalier attitude toward factual accuracy or literal truthfulness. Nor has this process shown any tendency over the years of diminishing; it is, in fact, as strong a current in American thought today as it was at any time in the Nineteenth century.

Certainly the keystone of the American mythologizing process is the history of the frontier and the American West. Most Americans, to say nothing of people all over the world whose exposure to the United States is often limited to the products of American popular culture, may actually believe that walk-downs along deserted town streets between opposing gunmen were commonplace on the frontier, that Indians were mindless savages bent only on mutilation, murder, and rape of white women as well as obstacles to civilization, that law and order were possible only through heroic, self-sacrificing men who for neither personal gain nor enrichment of any kind devoted themselves to the cause of justice and social harmony.

John G. Cawelti in both *The Six-Gun Mystique* (Bowling Green: The Popular Press, 1971) and *Adventure, Mystery and Romance: Formula Stories as Art and Popular Culture* (Chicago: University of Chicago Press, 1976) made an effort to generalize about basic patterns and principles in formulary Westerns, both fiction and film, but his findings are suspect primarily because his grasp of the source materials—which would have required more extensive reading of Western fiction and viewing of Western films than he did—was insufficient.

On the other hand, C.L. Sonnichsen was far less critical of the Western mythology in *From Hopalong to Hud: Thoughts on Western Fiction* (College Station: Texas A&M University Press, 1978). "I suggest," he wrote, that ". . . we want to have roots in ancient times like other peoples, but we don't stay in one place long enough to grow them. We move about freely, and some of us live on wheels. Many of us know nothing about our own grandfathers. Pride of family is denied to all but a few of us. Pride of race has to be built. Any group with a thousand year history has these things provided, but the American is a newcomer and not yet completely at home in his vast country. All he has is the mythical West, and he needs it desperately."

Although scarcely intended to be complete, any representative list of those historical personalities of the American frontier who have been singularly subjected to varying interpretations and have risen to the status of folk heroes and heroines would have to include Daniel Boone, Davy Crockett, Kit Carson, George Armstrong Custer, Jesse James, Belle Starr, Billy the Kid, "Wild Bill" Hickok, Calamity Jane, Wyatt Earp, and Buffalo Bill Cody.

DANIEL BOONE (1734–1820) was born at Berks County, Pennsylvania. Due to squabbles with fellow Quakers, the Boone family relocated to the Yadkin Valley of North Carolina. Daniel had only the most rudimentary education and was at best half-literate. Interested in the forests and life in the wilderness, Boone became an expert marksman and a capable pathfinder. Engaging in long hunts, Boone joined an expedition to the St. Johns River of Florida and in 1767 went hunting in the Eastern Appalachian region of Kentucky. Again in 1769, accompanied by several others, Boone led an exploration party into Kentucky and for at least two years wandered by himself throughout central Kentucky. In 1773 Boone led his own family—he had married in 1756 to Rebecca Bryan; it is not known how she reacted to his frequent and prolonged absences—and several others to settle in Kentucky. He founded Fort Boonesborough in 1775 and managed to defend successfully this outpost during the Revolutionary War period. It was also during this same period that Boone became involved in a conflict with the Indians for possession of Kentucky and his supervision of the Treaty of Sycamore Shoals excluded most of the Indian claims to the territory. All that remained for the Kentucky tribes was their eventual removal from the state once Andrew Jackson became President. Nor did Boone himself fare very well. He was court-martialed for being captured by the Shawnees on the Licking River and most of the lands he claimed as his own were confiscated on the grounds of improper registry. He then relocated to the state of Virginia where he served briefly in the Virginia general assembly but in 1799 he moved with his family by dugout canoe to Missouri where he was happy to trap, hunt, and dream of venturing even farther West until his death in 1820.

While he was still alive, Boone's life was transformed by contemporary mythologists. John Filson was the first architect of the Boone legend, publishing his account of Boone in *The Discovery, Settlement, and Present State of Kentucke* (1784). True to form, Filson got around the theft of Boone's lands in Kentucky by portraying him as a man selflessly concerned only with the development of Kentucky to become a powerful state in the Union and whose only desire in life was that his fellow countrymen should benefit from all his effort and sufferings, wanting nothing for himself. *The Adventures of Daniel Boone* (1813) by Daniel Bryan, one of Boone's nephews, was an epic poem which emphasized Boone's total devotion to social progress, replete with councils in Heaven and Hell similar to the poetry of John Milton, that is, similar in aspiration if not execution. The *Niles' Register* in 1816 even described an interview with Boone and concluded that "this singular man could not live in Kentucky when it became settled . . . he might have accumulated riches as readily as any man in Kentucky, but he *prefers the woods*, where you see him in the dress of the roughest, poorest hunter."

Frontier author Timothy Flint (q.v.) wrote a biography about Boone shortly after Boone's death, *The Life and Adventures of Daniel Boone, The First Settler of Kentucky, Interspersed with Incidents in the Early Annals of the Country* (1833), which became the most widely read book published about a frontier personality in the first half of the Nineteenth century. Flint made Boone a symbol for the cult of pastoral simplicity, although he was constantly vacillating between picturing Boone as an advance scout for civilization and a man who utterly rejected the values of civilization in order to pursue life in the wilderness. As Henry Nash Smith put it in *Virgin Land: The American West as Symbol and Myth* (Cambridge: Harvard University Press, 1950), "if Daniel Bryan's epic represents the limit of the possible absurdity in making Boone the harbinger of civilization and re-finement, this [Flint's book] may stand as the opposite limit of absurdity in making him a cultural primitivist. The image of the Western hero could serve either purpose."

Julie Roy Jeffrey in *Frontier Women: The Trans-Mississippi West 1840–1880* (New York: Hill and Wang, 1979) broke down further the significance of the various Nineteenth-century views of Boone in terms of the regional relevance of each. The Eastern interpretation of Boone's life stressed that he represented a negative force and that fascination with Boone or men as him would incline young men to leave home and, once in the wilderness, abandon or be forced to abandon all the values considered fundamental to civilized society. The Southern interpretation cast Boone more or less as a character out of the historical romances of Sir Walter Scott. William Gilmore Simms (q.v.), a novelist of the 1830s, wrote of him that "in an age of chivalry—during the Crusades . . . [Boone] could have been a knight-errant, equally fearless and gentle. That he would have been a Squire of Dames is very uncertain— but he loved his wife, and risked his scalp more than once to rescue beauty from the clutches of the savage." The Western interpretation had it that Boone was primarily a man of action, a wilderness hero. James Fenimore Cooper (q.v.) in basing his hero Natty Bumppo of the Leatherstocking saga on Boone made use of all three interpretations and it was as a result of Cooper's popularity that both Daniel Boone and Davy Crockett became common heroes in dime novels in the third quarter of the Nineteenth century as Daryl Jones pointed out in *The Dime Novel Western* (Bowling Green: The Popular Press, 1978). By the middle of the Twentieth century all such distinctions, however, had become sufficiently blurred that Bill Elliott, a movie cowboy, could appear in *The Great Adventures of Wild Bill Hickok* (Columbia, 1938), *Overland with Kit Carson* (Columbia, 1939), *The Return of Daniel Boone* (Columbia, 1941), and *The Son of Davy Crockett* (Columbia, 1941) and be identically attired with Dub "Cannonball" Taylor as his perpetual sidekick, no matter who he was, without arousing any dubiety in audiences.

DAVY CROCKETT (1786–1836), born on the Nolichucky River in Greene County, Tennessee, far more than Daniel Boone had a direct hand in creating a legend around himself. As Boone, he was poorly educated, but in his case more from inclination than lack of opportunity. He tried his hand at working with cattle, freight hauling, and farm labor, finding none of them especially profitable. In 1805 he married the first of his three wives—on the rebound, as it were, after his original fiancée jilted him on their wedding day—and, in 1811, moved his family to Middle Tennessee. When Indian fighting broke out, Crockett was quick to join the local militia and he did take part in some minor skirmishes in the Creek campaign in Alabama, but by the time of the battle of Horseshoe Bend he was safely at home, having resigned his commission. He next joined Major Russell's battalion and marched off to Alabama and Florida, but saw even less action and, after a stint of patrol duty around Mobile, returned to Tennessee. When his first wife died, he married a widow and, following a futile land-hunting journey to Alabama, moved his family deeper into West Tennessee where he became a justice of the peace in Lawrence County, then a court referee, and finally was *elected* a colonel of the militia. This convinced him of his viability as a political candidate and in 1820 he was elected to the Tennessee legislature. In 1823, as a result of a practical joke, he was renominated for the legislature and was again elected. In 1825 he was defeated in his bid for election to the United States Congress, but he was elected to that office in 1827, re-elected in 1829, defeated in 1831, and re-elected in 1833. Crockett's Whig supporters had long been manufacturing and fabricating tall tales about him to encourage voters to believe him to be a hero and a valiant protector of human rights and, in 1834, he collaborated with Thomas Chilton in producing a highly romanticized autobiography. It did not particularly help him next time at the polls and he was defeated. Arriving in San Antonio in February, 1836, he joined the opposition to Mexico and on 6 March lost his life when Santa Anna's Mexican regulars stormed the Alamo.

Somehow this was but the finishing touch needed to make Crockett a true national hero and, before long, everything that was corrupt and disagreeable about the man was sedulously removed and only the legend remained. The tall tale itself became indelibly associated with the Davy Crockett tradition and novelist Emerson Bennett (q.v.) relied on it for his novel *The Prairie Flower: or, Adventures in the Far West* (1849), as did others, dime novelists in the 1860s in particular. It was not until Vernon L. Parrington's *Main Currents of American Thought* (New York: Harcourt, Brace, 1930) that the Crockett mythos was seriously and analytically dissected. As Stanley Edgar Hyman put it in *The Armed Vision* (New York: Knopf, 1948), Parrington "strips the legendary hero down to the real Crockett: a rather pathetic figure, ignorant, boastful, and ambitious; built up as an American symbol by skilled Whig publicists who wanted a coonskin hero to oppose to [Andrew] Jackson; used by the Whigs as long as he was usable; and then when his backwoods constituents repudiated his voting record of uninterrupted support for Eastern banking interests, tossed aside by his Whig friends. Parrington shows how the legend was built step by step, conjectures shrewdly as to who ghosted each of the books, shows the constant anti-Jackson propaganda smuggled into their comedy, and at the end shows Crockett, like so many mythologized real heroes, coming to believe the legends himself." A comment Julie Roy Jeffrey made in *Frontier Women* about *A Narrative of the Life of Col. David Crockett*, the book which Crockett wrote with Chilton, is perhaps also worth noting, namely that his wives were "insignificant in the story of his life and certainly far less important than the other symbols of his vaunted achievements, pelts, votes, and fame." Already at the beginning of fantasizing about the frontier, women were given no greater role than that of "the girl" which they would occupy in Western fiction, to such a large extent, and in Western films later, far into the Twentieth century.

KIT CARSON (1809–1868), was born Christopher Houston Carson near Richmond, Kentucky, and soon thereafter moved with his family to Missouri where his father acquired a farm. At the age of 14, Carson was apprenticed to a saddle-maker but fled from his employment in 1826, joining a caravan bound for New Mexico. After briefly visiting Santa Fe, Carson ventured to Taos which was a meeting place for mountain men. From 1828 to 1831 Carson accompanied Ewing Young, a noted trapper, through Southern Arizona to California and back, learning the beaver trade. For several years

after that, Carson wandered up and down the Rocky Mountains and throughout the Far West trapping and gained thereby an intimate knowledge of frontier trails. Carson attended the fur trading rendezvous with Jim Bridger, the famed frontiersman, in 1835 on the Green River and engaged successfully in a duel. He took an Arapaho wife and, when she died, co-habited with a Cheyenne woman who apparently, after a time, chucked him out. However, the fact remains that he lived on and off with various Indian tribes for months without seeing another white man. In 1842, on a visit to Missouri to see relatives, Carson met John C. Frémont who was preparing the first of his Western expeditions. Frémont engaged Carson as a guide and over the next several years was repeatedly grateful that he did. Frémont publicized Carson's skill as a scout and guide in his reports and this was duly noted by James Madison Cutts in his *The Conquest of California and New Mexico* (1847) and Charles E. Averill, a fabulist of the period, fictionalized an account titled *Kit Carson, The Prince of the Gold Hunters: Or, The Adventures of the Sacramento* (1849) which was widely read. Between Frémont's first and second expeditions, in 1843, Carson married 15-year-old Josefa Jaramillo of Taos and soon became involved with the war against Mexico. Following the hostilities, Carson returned to Taos and in 1849 took up ranching at nearby Rayado. DeWitt C. Peters, an Army surgeon stationed near Carson's home, thought Carson an ideal frontier hero, perhaps as a result of having read about him first in Emerson Bennett's *The Prairie Flower*, and began work on his own laudatory, even outlandish biography, *The Life and Adventures of Kit Carson, The Nestor of the Rocky Mountains, From Facts Narrated by Himself*

(1858), which was published during Carson's lifetime and which further served to establish Carson as a hero for dime novelists.

In 1853 Carson drove a herd of sheep to California with his business partner, Lucien Maxwell, and that same year was appointed Indian agent for the tribes of Northern New Mexico. According to most accounts, Carson conducted himself creditably at this post, although it must also be stated that all of those accounts were written by white men. General James F. Rusling in his book *Across America* (1874) recalled his interview with Carson in 1867 and wrote that Carson "declared that all our Indian troubles were caused originally by bad white men. . . . He pleaded for the Indians as 'pore ignorant creatures,' whom we were daily despoiling of their hunting grounds and homes." Although Native Americans might question Carson's opinion of them as "pore ignorant creatures," it should also be said in his behalf that as an Indian agent he never was known to cheat them, which cannot be said of many agents charged with similar duties.

In 1861 Carson resigned as agent to serve in the Union Army, commissioned a Colonel in the First New Mexico Volunteer Infantry Regiment. His main job during the Civil War was fighting Indians. The Mescalero Apaches surrendered to him and to defeat the Navahos he pursued a scorch the earth policy, burning and destroying all their food supplies to force their capitulation. General Carleton, Carson's commanding officer, was dissatisfied with what he interpreted as Carson's reluctance to carry out this policy with all due haste and in September, 1863, Carleton wrote out for Carson what the official policy toward the Navahos was to be: "Say to them—'Go to the Bosque Redondo, or we will pursue and destroy you. We will not make peace with you on any other terms. . . . This war shall be pursued against you if it takes years, now that we have begun, until you cease to exist or move. There can be no other talk on the subject." By the summer of 1864, some 8,000 Navahos surrendered to him. Carson next was deployed against the Kiowas, and defeated them. As Harvey Fergusson (q.v.) wrote in *Rio Grande* (New York: Knopf, 1933), "it was Carson who conquered the Navahos after three governments had tried and failed. Moreover, when they had been put on a reservation in a hot country that threatened to kill them all it was Carson who insisted that they be restored to their native range. Patience and a dogged will were his winning qualities in action. He was excessively honest and wholly without greed. In his later years he showed the fine sense of justice and the selfless devotion to social purposes which are certainly elements of greatness."

After serving briefly as commander of Fort Garland in Southern Colorado, Carson and his family settled at Boggsville, near Las Animas, Colorado. It was there that his wife died and the same year Carson died at nearby Fort Lyon from a hemorrhage, calling for a dish of his favorite food and having an old friend sit by him swapping yarns about the old days until his breath failed him.

In *The Western Hero in History and Legend* (Norman: University of Oklahoma Press, 1965), Kent Lad Steckmesser wrote of Carson that for him "less of a gap exists between history and the legend than is the case with other Western characters, particularly the outlaws and gunfighters. He did perform some notable exploits, although he had no great historical significance. He was virtuous, although somewhat less so than the legend claims. He spoke of his exploits with becoming modesty, and he was respected by most of his contemporaries. Thus he could become a model for his group, and he did. The prominence of the mountain man as a type in the literature and legend of the West is linked with the popular representations of Kit Carson." Henry Nash Smith in *Virgin Land* voiced a similar sentiment, although somewhat more harshly, when he wrote that the "portrait of Kit Carson" in the popular fiction of the Nineteenth century "establishes the lines along which the Wild Western story was to develop for the next half century, until it should reach the seemingly indestructible state of petrifaction which it exhibits in our own day and is apparently destined to maintain through successive geological epochs while subtler and more ambitious literary forms come and go."

GEORGE ARMSTRONG CUSTER (1839–1876) has been deleted from many elementary and secondary school textbooks used in American schools and replaced, if at all, by Sitting Bull, but for nearly a century he was one of the most endurable frontier heroes. Born at New Rumley, Ohio, he entered West Point and distinguished himself by being a disciplinary problem with the number of demerits he acquired—ninety-seven, whereas one hundred would have resulted in expulsion. Assigned to the Fifth Cavalry in the Army of the Potomac during the Civil War, Custer attracted attention to himself by his daring recklessness in battle and his spectacular showmanship in manner of dress and personal conduct. In 1864 Custer married Elizabeth Bacon who subsequently wrote three books about her frontier experiences (see Women on the Frontier). When the war ended, Custer held the rank of

Elizabeth Custer (r.), General Custer (center), and a friend.

Major General, but this reverted to the rank of Captain in 1866 following the cessation of hostilities. By this time, however, the U.S. Army was committed by the federal government to a policy of genocide against the remaining Indian nations and Custer saw this as a personal opportunity to win new acclaim. He was appointed Lieutenant Colonel and attached to the newly formed Seventh Cavalry. In 1867 this regiment played a significant part in the Hancock campaign the objective of which was to remove the Sioux and Cheyenne from the path of the transcontinental railroad. Due to a number of military excesses, such as cruel treatment of deserters and forced marches with his troops, Custer was court-martialed, convicted, and suspended from rank for one year. General Sheridan commuted this sentence before it expired because he needed, he said, Custer to fight Indians, and it was Custer's victory at the Battle of the Washita where he surrounded the Cheyenne village of Chief Black Kettle and wiped out most of them which earned the glorious reputation for his command. Despite controversy in the press inspired by the wholesale slaughter of a tribe that was at peace with the U.S. government, Custer continued his operations against non-reservation tribes in Oklahoma.

The summer of 1869 Custer spent at Fort Hays, Kansas, where he began his autobiography, *My Life on the Plains* (1874), which was published first as a series of magazine articles. The principal purpose of the book was to consolidate in the public's mind Custer's own estimation of himself as a national hero. However, Kent Ladd Steckmesser in *The Western Hero in History and Legend*, while supposedly attempting to explicate the Custer myth, curiously praised the book as striking "a realistic note" in one respect, that being Custer's "views of the Indians." What was that realistic note? Custer wrote: "It is to be regretted that the character of the Indian as described in [James Fenimore] Cooper's interesting novels is not a true one. . . . Stripped of the beautiful romance with which we have been so long willing to envelope him, transferred from the inviting pages of the novelist to the localities where we are compelled to meet with him, in his native village, on the war path, and when raiding upon our frontier settlements and lines of travel, the Indian forfeits his claim to the appellation of the '*noble* red man.' We see him as he is, and, so far as all knowledge goes, as he ever has been, a *savage* in every sense of the word; not worse, perhaps, than his white brother would be similarly born and bred, but one whose cruel and ferocious nature far exceeds that of any wild beast of the desert. . . . In him we will find the representative of a race . . . between which and civilization there seems to have existed from time immemorial a determined and unceasing warfare. . . ." By writing persuasively in this fashion, Custer was in the advance guard of propagandists who were intent on replacing the equally false notion of the Native American as a noble child of Nature with the image of a born warrior incapable of any other behavior. Only three years after Custer's *My Life on the Plains* was published, Sitting Bull remarked to his own people about white/red relations: "We cannot dwell side by side. Only seven years ago we made a treaty by which we were assured that the buffalo country should be left to us forever. Now they threaten to take that away from us. My brothers, shall we submit or shall we say to them: 'First kill me before you take possession of my Fatherland. . . .'" Following the discovery of gold in the Black Hills in 1875 the U.S. government ordered the Sioux to leave their Powder River hunting grounds which had been guaranteed to them forever in the treaty of 1868—a treaty which in the late 1970s became the subject of much heated litigation in federal court—and it was as a result of participating in this removal order that Custer and his command lost their lives in the battle of Little Big Horn in 1876.

Black Elk, a Sioux medicine man, told John G. Neihardt (q.v.) in *Black Elk Speaks* (New York: Morrow, 1932), referring to Custer by his Lakotah name, Pahuska [Yellowhair], that on the Little Big Horn battlefield "there were not many of our own dead there, because they had been picked up already; but many of our men were killed and wounded. They shot each other in the dust. I did not see Pahuska, and I think nobody knew which one he was." A national memorial shrine now marks the battlefield, located in Southeastern Montana, but the tributes are only to Custer and his men; there are no memorials to the Native Americans who lost their lives in the encounter. Custer's defeat, while it was only a momentary victory for the Indian nations, made of Custer a hero in nearly everyone's eyes and the extermination of the Indians a national *cause célèbre*. Elizabeth Custer, because her pension was inadequate, began the trend to glorify her husband's memory, although even she found herself indebted to Frederick Whittaker's *Popular Life of General George A. Custer* (1876) which portrayed Custer as a misunderstood hero and victim to Indian cunning and political corruption. It was not until the mid Twentieth century, with the publication of novels as Ernest Haycox' (q.v.) *Bugles in the Afternoon* (Boston: Little, Brown, 1944), that the Custer myth began being questioned in Western fiction, but even at that Haycox made no effort to characterize the Native American point of view in his account and his novel had been preceded only three years before by Raoul Walsh's *They Died with Their Boots On* (Warner's, 1941) which totally romanticized Custer. Mari Sandoz (q.v.) in her historical account, *Battle of the Little Big Horn* (Philadelphia: Lippincott, 1966), stressed Custer's political ambitions for the presidency as one of his prime motives whereas in Western fiction, against a counterpoint of many novels about the battle still partial to Custer, Thomas Berger (q.v.) in *Little Big Man* (New York: Dial, 1964) tried to reduce the conflict to parody and picture Custer as a frantic, almost comic lunatic. Obviously, whether as a diminished hero or as a nearly Satanic villain, the Custer of legend has still a long literary and cinematic life before him.

But if the contemporary trend has been to make villains out of traditional heroes, it is only a modern counterpart to a much older trend to make heroes out of men who were in fact villains. One of the earliest examples of a frontier murderer and thief

transformed into a popular hero by the press while he was still alive and actively engaged in brigandage was JESSE JAMES (1847–1882). Three years after Jesse was born at Clay County, Missouri, Jesse's father left home to go to California where he died. James' mother remarried in 1855. When the Civil War started, Jesse's older brother, Frank James, joined William Clarke Quantrill's raiders, Jesse soon following suit, serving under "Bloody Bill" Anderson, and the two pursued a career of plunder and murder. After the war, they launched their careers in bank robbery and murder. Many innocent bystanders were killed during the string of audacious bank robberies in which Jesse participated. The public tended to romanticize this pillaging and Jesse was often compared to a modern Robin Hood, a popular ballad telling of how "he took from the rich and he gave to the poor," which was certainly not among his primary objectives. When the James gang expanded their activities to include train holdups, there were apologists who hastened to point out that this was part of a concerted plan to seek redress for dishonest dealings and high tariffs charged by the railroads. When the railroads responded by hiring Pinkerton detectives to hunt down the James gang and a fire bomb, flung into a window of the James home, killed Jesse's young half-brother and blew off his mother's arm, public sympathy immediately went to the James gang as victims of economic exploitation. So great did public support for the James brothers become that the Missouri legislature nearly voted amnesty for the entire gang. This was just before Jesse's blunder in 1876 of attempting to rob the bank at Northfield, Minnesota, with the Younger brothers—Cole Younger was popularly known as "Little John" to Jesse's

Jesse James

"Robin Hood." Three men were killed, the Youngers captured, Jesse and Frank barely escaping with their lives. For three years the James brothers lived under assumed names in Nashville, Tennessee. They renewed their robbery activities in 1879 and in 1881, after the murder of two men during a holdup, the state of Missouri offered a reward of $5,000 each for Frank and Jesse. Robert Ford shot Jesse to death on 3 April 1882. Ford had made a deal with Governor Thomas Crittenden of Missouri to execute Jesse. Ford later went on tour with Wild West shows, re-enacting the shooting. Frank James surrendered a few months after Jesse's murder and was tried three times unsuccessfully before being released. Frank then retired from outlawry and himself, upon occasion, took to making personal appearances with Wild West shows, perfectly willing to reaffirm the legendary character of the James gang's exploits. At one time, in fact, when Theodore Roosevelt (q.v.) organized the Bull Moose party in a bid for the Presidency, he hired Frank to be his personal body guard.

Already by the end of the 1870s a series of dime novels appeared celebrating the heroic deeds of the James brothers. The Postmaster General in 1883 threatened Frank Tousey, one of the most active publishers of these lurid and sensational books, with cancelling his second-class postal privileges if he did not withdraw some of the more inflammatory titles, yet by 1901 both Tousey and Street and Smith, another pulp publisher, had both inaugurated separate series of books devoted to the adventures of the James gang. Over the next two years a total of 277 novels appeared in Tousey's *James Boys Weekly* and Street and Smith's *Jesse James Stories*. Public clamor became such by 1903 that the U.S. government brought pressure to bear on these publishers and both firms discontinued publication. When silent screen cowboy Fred Thomson appeared in *Jesse James* (Paramount, 1927) which attempted to whitewash Jesse, public furor was such that Thomson's film career was finished. But the need to mythologize the James brothers proved too great. Little over a decade later Roy Rogers and Gabby Hayes could appear in a film titled *Days of Jesse James* (Republic, 1939) in which Don Barry, playing Jesse as an innocent victim of big business, offered to put Roy through medical school, and other than the film being banned in the state of Missouri there was no noticeable reaction. The same year Henry King furthered this trend with his own highly romanticized version of the James legend which completely blamed the railroad for the James' criminal indiscretions, in *Jesse James* (20th-Fox, 1939). Another decade and Republic was in full swing casting the James brothers as serial heroes in *Adventures of Frank and Jesse James* (Republic, 1948) and *The James Brothers of Missouri* (Republic, 1950). Another decade yet and Hollywood in its inimitable fashion could treat Jesse as a member of its pantheon of superheroes in *Jesse James Meets Franken-stein's Daughter* (Embassy, 1966).

The image of Jesse in Western fiction began to change when Will Henry (q.v.) published *Death of a Legend* (New York: Random House, 1954) in which he set out to record "a true bill of indictment returned against the persistently misrepresented life of a cold-blooded murderer." No matter, the legend persists and as recently as *The Day Jesse James Was Killed* (New York: Signet, 1961) by Carl W. Breihan, re-issued in 1979, Jesse is portrayed romantically as a misfit, the author writing: "Death. When the moment arrived for this young man named Jesse Woodson James, he seemed to accept it as inevitable, and he went without a struggle."

If the dime novelists made Jesse James the king of the bandits, they made BELLE STARR (1848–1889) the queen, a role she herself would have approved and endorsed. Born on a farm near Carthage, Missouri, in 1866 she met Cole Younger, who was then a member of the James gang, and he probably fathered her first child, Pearl. Younger at any rate disappeared and Belle within a year joined forces with Jim Reed, a notorious bank robber and outlaw. Belle bore him a son, Edward, and, dressing in velvet skirts and plumed hats, riding her mare, Venus, engaged in all manner of outlawry with Reed's gang. When Reed was shot by one of his own men, Belle left her children and went into hiding in that portion of Indian Territory then occupied by the Five Civilized Tribes, organizing her own band of horse and cattle thieves. Staying for a while with an Indian called Blue Duck, she eventually settled down with a Cherokee named Sam Starr in a common law marriage. In 1883 she and Sam were indicted on a charge

Belle Starr and Blue Duck

of horse theft and were sentenced to five months in the federal prison at Detroit. Once out of prison, the two resumed their outlaw activities until Sam was killed in a gunfight in 1886. Next Belle chose Jim July, a young Creek Indian, as her companion. When he was summoned to Fort Smith to face larceny charges, Belle accompanied him part of the way but turned back before reaching the fort. The next day she was shot from behind and killed; it is not known by whom. Belle's daughter Pearl had the following poem inscribed on her mother's gravestone:

> Shed not for her the bitter tear,
> Nor give the heart to vain regret;
>
> 'Tis but the casket that lies here,
> The gem that filled it sparkles yet.

At the same time that Twentieth Century-Fox was romanticizing the James gang in *Jesse James* and *The Return of Frank James* (20th-Fox, 1940), Belle Starr could not be left out. Gene Tierney, who had appeared in *The Return of Frank James*, was cast as the lead in *Belle Starr* (20th-Fox, 1941), which in turn was based on an original screen story by Niven Busch (q.v.). And even when Belle Starr was not used as a character, she proved prototypical, as, for example, in *Hellfire* (Republic, 1949) in which Marie Windsor was cast as a female outlaw leader called "Doll Brown," accompanied by Bill Elliott, a self-appointed preacher intent on saving her soul, a film which ends with the heroine assassinated by vicious and evil men, fading to a shining, golden crucifix. A realistic fictional treatment of her career had to wait for *Belle Starr: A Novel* (Boston: Atlantic-Little, Brown, 1979) by Speer Morgan which, while insightful, never resorts to glamourizing her life or her actions.

BILLY THE KID (1859–1881) was born Henry McCarty at (according to what he told a census taker in 1880) some place in Missouri. He had to wait until Walter Noble Burns' (q.v.) *The Saga of Billy the Kid* (New York: Doubleday, 1926) before he was elevated to the position of a hero and a martyr. The dime novels, with one exception, portrayed the Kid as "a fiend incarnate" in Don Jenardo's *The True Life of Billy the Kid* (1881), "a common cut-throat" in J.C. Cowdrick's *Silver-Mask, The Man of Mystery: Or, The Cross of the Golden Keys* (1884), or "the bloodthirstiest little cowpuncher what ever straddled a horse" in Francis W. Doughty's *Old King Brady and "Billy the Kid": Or, The Great Detective's Chase* (1890). The exception was Edmund Fable's *Billy the Kid, The New Mexico Outlaw: Or, The Bold Bandit of the West* (1881) which sought to justify the Kid's behavior as revenge for relentless and unwarranted persecution.

Perhaps the reason that the Kid's transformation into a hero had so long to wait was that Pat Garrett (1850–1908), the man who shot and killed the Kid in the dark in Pete Maxwell's bedroom without the Kid being armed or even knowing who it was, published his own account in *The Authentic Life of Billy the Kid* (1882). For many New Mexicans, including author Eugene Manlove Rhodes (q.v.), Garrett was a hero and, obviously, if Garrett was a hero, the Kid had to be a villain. The Lincoln County War, in which the Kid was a participant, was for a long time filled with obscurities and confusions. The best book so far to appear on Garrett is *Pat Garrett: The Story of a Western Lawman* (Norman: University of Oklahoma Press, 1974) by Leon C. Metz and it makes a number of interesting points. First, while popular legend has it that the Kid killed twenty-one men during his brief life, a more accurate figure is four, and these under life-and-death desperation circumstances. Second, while legend also claims that Garrett and the Kid supposedly rode together and even stole cattle together prior to Garrett's election to the office of sheriff of Lincoln County, there is absolutely no documentation to support this. Third, and last, it would seem that from what evidence there is it was Wayne Brazel who shot Garrett in the back of the head while Garrett was urinating, the man who indeed confessed to the crime, was actually tried for it, and who was acquitted! As Metz put it: "The two men had argued bitterly, and when Garrett turned his back, Brazel took the safe way out and shot him. . . . There were no conspiracies, no large amounts of money changing hands, no top guns taking up positions in the sandhills. It was simply a case of hate and fear erupting into murder along a lonely New Mexico back road."

Once Burns' book was published, in order for the Kid to be made a hero and yet to keep Garrett himself a hero, the screenplay for King Vidor's *Billy the Kid* (M-G-M, 1930) depicts the Kid, played by Johnny Mack Brown, as a victim of injustice and a sympathetic Garrett, played by Wallace Beery, lets the Kid and his girl escape into Mexico and pretends for all the world that he shot and killed him. It was this film which opened the way for the Kid to join the pantheon of "B" Western heroes, first in *Billy the Kid Returns* (Republic, 1938) with Roy Rogers followed by an entire series of low-budget Westerns in which the Kid was played first by Bob Steele and then by Buster Crabbe. *Billy the Kid* (M-G-M, 1941) with Robert Taylor as the Kid finds him shot at the end, but the tone of the film suggests that the Kid is a victim of circumstances. In *The Outlaw* (United Artists, 1943), Howard Hughes' version of a sexualized Billy the Kid story, the Kid, played by Jack Buetel, is permitted to slip across the border with sensuous Jane Russell while a phony grave is set up. *The Left-Handed Gun* (Warner's, 1958) carried on the tradition that the Kid was left-handed—which he was not—and Paul Newman played him as a neurotic with a Christ complex. The height of absurdity was probably reached with *Billy the Kid vs. Dracula* (Embassy, 1966). *Dirty Little Billy* (Columbia, 1972), as Edwin Corle's (q.v.) novel *Billy the Kid* (New York: Duell, Sloan, and Pearce, 1953), went in the opposite direction, trying to make the Kid a vicious criminal. Sam Peckinpah provided his own version of the legend in *Pat Garrett and Billy the Kid* (M-G-M, 1973) in which Garrett, played by James Coburn, is depicted as a man who has sold out to the Santa Fe ring (in history, the ring was opposed to Garrett almost as much as it was to the Kid);

he must kill the Kid, played by Kris Kristofferson, who is almost Christ-like, for his own advantage, the Kid being a man fated for death because he wants to be free in a land dominated by Eastern money.

JAMES BUTLER "WILD BILL" HICKOK (1837–1876) was born at Homer, La Salle County, Illinois. Joseph G. Rosa in what is probably the finest biography about Hickok, *They Called Him Wild Bill: The Life and Adventures of James Butler Hickok* (Norman: University of Oklahoma Press, 1964, newly revised edition, 1974), drew a portrait of a man who was frequently cruel, who invariably shot to kill, who in his dealings with men and women was often callous and indifferent. But he did not—perhaps rightly—moralize. Eugene Cunningham (q.v.) in *Triggernometry* (New York: Press of the Pioneers, 1934) recorded one old cowboy named Pascal Brown who remembered seeing Hickok in 1871 when he was city marshal at Abilene; eschewing holsters, in later life Hickok carried his guns in his belt or in a silk sash, wearing them butts-forward for a "twist" or "Cavalry" draw. "When I came along the street," Brown recalled, "he was standing there with his back to the wall and his thumbs hooked in his red sash. He stood there and rolled his head from side to side looking at everything and everybody from under his eyebrows—just like a mad old bull. I decided then and there I didn't want any part of him."

Although in 1867 Hickok had scouted for Custer and was, for a time, a deputy United States marshal and lawman in various communities, he apparently had a weakness for gambling, which kept him usually in the company of a town's criminal element; he was also a heavy drinker and more than once was arrested for brawling and vagrancy when he was out of work. He was not a peace officer in Deadwood, Dakota Territory, when he was assassinated by Jack McCall, nor does it seem, in retrospect, that he was likely to have become one. He was playing poker when he died and his poker hand, aces and eights, became known subsequently as a dead man's hand.

During his lifetime, Hickok was proud of his reputation with his guns and, for a time, even toured with Buffalo Bill, although he proved on the whole not to like show business and tended to be obnoxious to everyone around him. Dime novelists did much to create a legend around him, as in Prentiss Ingraham's *Wild Bill, the Pistol Dead Shot: Or, Dagger Don's Double* (1882). Hickok did not particularly like Martha "Calamity Jane" Cannary (1850?–1903) while he was alive and perhaps it was frontier hyperbole that rendered Jane's last words as "Bury me next to Bill" and even more, frontier malice or frontier humor, which prompted her body to be buried some twenty feet from "Wild Bill" in the Mount Moriah cemetery.

William S. Hart sentimentalized the portrayal of Hickok when he filmed *Wild Bill Hickok* (Paramount, 1923) and stressed Hickok's faltering eye-sight without any reference to its probable cause (venereal disease), thus surrounding his life with unnecessary pathos. By the time Cecil B. DeMille came to direct *The Plainsman* (Paramount, 1936), in which Gary Cooper was cast as Hickok, the Hickok/Calamity Jane legend was in full flower. Jean Arthur, charming, beautiful, passionate, playing Jane was her virtual antithesis. Yet it is Cooper's sad, brooding, troubled depiction of Hickok which saves the film from being a total debacle, with James Ellison cast as an

heroic Buffalo Bill, DeMille's son-in-law Anthony Quinn playing an Indian, and John Miljan portraying Custer as a hero and martyr. The film inspired Columbia Pictures to star Bill Elliott in a serial about Hickok's supposed adventures and, indeed, this portrayal established Elliott as a matinee idol, going on to play Hickok in several features and retaining throughout his career the spurious appellation "Wild Bill." Guy Madison went on to portray Hickok on radio in *Wild Bill Hickok* (Mutual, 1952) and for years on television in *Wild Bill Hickok* (Syndicated, 1952–1954, CBS, 1954–1957, ABC, 1957–1958), further perpetuating the fantasies about Hickok. Perhaps Rosa said it best in his Hickok biography when he remarked: "Make no mistake: Wild Bill had not changed—society had. In an age of rough, tough humanity, Hickok, [William] Tilghman, [Bat] Masterson, and to some lesser extent the Earps, were the exceptions—which is why they are remembered. But it's hardly likely that they would appreciate their promotion to sainthood on modern television—probably they would be more interested in the profits being made in their names."

Western fiction is little better. J.T. Edson (q.v.) included Calamity Jane as a character in several of his novels—to cite but one author—and, ignoring historical accuracy, described her as almost a vamp with lips "made for laughter or kissing" and wearing a Cavalry shirt "its neck opened far enough to give a tantalizing glimpse of the opening of the valley between her breasts." In itself this might not be so bad, but it is compounded and worsened by the claim Edson's publishers made for him, that he provided "the most exciting and realistic portrait of the West in literature."

WYATT EARP (1848–1929) unlike Hickok, owes much of his modern reputation for heroics to Stuart N. Lake's highly romanticized and factually untrue account in *Wyatt Earp: Frontier Marshal* (Boston: Houghton Mifflin, 1931). C.L. Sonnichsen spent two chapters of his book, *From Hopalong to Hud: Thoughts on Western Fiction,* tracing both the historical/biographical accounts of Earp's supposed exploits and surveying the entire range of Wyatt Earp fantasies in Western fiction. Certainly the most reliable account of Earp's entire life is to be found in *I Married Wyatt Earp: The Recollections of Josephine Marcus Earp* (Tucson: University of Arizona Press, 1976), edited by Glenn G. Boyer. The most charitable thing that can be said about the fiction inspired by the Earp mythos, from W.R. Burnett's (q.v.) *Saint Johnson* (New York: Dial, 1930) through Will Henry's *Who Rides with Wyatt* (New York: Random House, 1955), perhaps Henry's most disappointing and unreliable historical Western, to Philip Ketchum's (q.v.) *Wyatt Earp* (Racine: Whitman Publishing, 1956), is that it is heavily indebted to Lake's original account and perpetuates the image of Earp which has long been a staple of Western films. Burnett's *Saint Johnson* was filmed three times under the title *Law and Order,* beginning in 1932, and Lake's book has been filmed three times, the third make by John Ford titled *My Darling Clementine* (20th-Fox, 1946). *Doc* (United Artists, 1971) was an attempt to deal realistically with Earp, showing him to be a cold-blooded killer and even somewhat of a coward, while both John Sturges' films, *Gunfight at the O.K. Corral* (Paramount, 1957) and *Hour of the Gun* (United Artists, 1967), are the sheerest fiction. Nor did the long-running and very successful television series *The Life and Legend of Wyatt Earp* (ABC, 1955–1961) with Hugh O'Brien as Wyatt help matters, at least with the popular mind. Just by weight alone, the myth-making media have perhaps obscured forever the true personality and somewhat limited achievements of Wyatt Earp as either a peacemaker or as a human being. Earp spent his later years in Los Angeles, willing to reminisce and tell tall tales about himself with anybody who had the price of a drink. His eventual fame as a folk hero did nothing for him personally.

It was not so with WILLIAM FREDERICK "BUFFALO BILL" CODY (1846–1917). Although he had scouted with Custer and had both "Wild Bill" Hickok and Sitting Bull appear with his Wild West show at various times, Cody owed his initial bid for international notoriety to Edward Z.C. Judson, a dime novelist who wrote under the pseudonym Ned Buntline. On a trip West in 1869, Judson contacted Major Frank North with the intention of turning him into a dime novel hero. North declined but suggested Cody be used instead. Cody was quite willing and, when Judson returned to New York, he apotheosized Cody into the hero of a *New York Weekly* serial titled *Buffalo Bill, the King of the Border Men.* This serial was brought out in book form, printed and reprinted, and as late as 1928 was being offered in the Sears, Roebuck catalogue, listed at twenty-two cents. The serial, to say the least, began a Buffalo Bill fad in the East. James Gordon Bennett, editor of the *New York Herald,* had once been on a hunting trip along with General Phil Sheridan for which Cody served as guide and he had written Cody up as "the beau ideal of the plains." Both Bennett and Sheridan encouraged Cody to come to New York, which also suited Judson whose serial had been adapted for the stage by Fred G. Maeder. Upon seeing the stage play, the theatre manager offered Cody $500 a week to play himself, but Cody, too timid perhaps, demurred. But all was not lost. Judson convinced Cody to come to Chicago with Cody's friend, Texas Jack Omohundro, and twenty Indians and they opened in a show, written by Judson, which lasted for four hours and consisted primarily of "killing" Indians. After a three-year association with Judson, Cody and Omohundro organized their own show. By 1878 Prentiss Ingraham had virtually become Cody's staff writer and had composed Cody's stage sketches; he went on to write Cody's autobiography, *The Life of Hon. William F. Cody, Known as Buffalo Bill, the Famous Hunter, Scout, and Guide* (1879), and, before his death in 1904, Ingraham had to his credit more than two hundred pulp stories about Buffalo Bill as well as the probable authorship of a great many of the dime novels about his exploits signed by Cody himself.

Cody might tell later movie cowboy Tim McCoy when they met that he had read so many of the books written about him that he himself did not know what was fact or fiction, but, fortunately, much of the truth has been uncovered in Don Russell's *The Lives and Legends of Buffalo Bill* (Norman: University of Oklahoma Press, 1960). The year after Cody died, Zane Grey (q.v.) collaborated with Helen Cody Westmore to produce *Last of the Great Scouts* (New York: Grosset & Dunlap, 1918), an ostensible biography of Cody which was as fanciful as any of the dime novel adventures.

With a total of 557 original dime novels about him, it might seem that many of Cody's contemporaries would have object-ed to him and to his show, but that was not quite the case. Mark Twain (q.v.), after attending performances two days in a row of the Buffalo Bill Wild West show, wrote Cody a note in which he claimed that it "brought vividly back the breezy, wild life of the Great Plains and Rocky Mountains, and stirred me like a war song. Down to its smallest details, the show was genuine. . . ." Frederic Remington (q.v.) saw in it a protest against "those horrible badges of the slavery of our modern social system, when men are physically figures, and mental and moral cogwheels and wastes of uniformity— where the greatest crime is to be an individual, and the unpardonable sin is to be out of fashion."

In the early 1940s, Hollywood screenwriter Gene Fowler contacted film director William Wellman and claimed that he had spent years researching the life of Buffalo Bill and had a screenplay that would finally debunk him. Wellman became enthusiastic about the project, but, before they could go into production, Fowler regretted himself, saying that he did not want to destroy a national hero and, together with Wellman, after a lot of drinking, burned his screenplay. What was filmed instead was the romanticized and ridiculous *Buffalo Bill* (20th-Fox, 1944) with Joel McCrea playing Cody. Prior to this time, Buffalo Bill as a screen character had led sort of a saturnine existence, mostly in such chapter plays as *In the Days of Buffalo Bill* (Universal, 1922), *Fighting with Buffalo Bill* (Universal, 1926), *Battling with Buffalo Bill* (Universal, 1931), played by Art Acord in the first, Wallace MacDonald in the second, and by Tom Tyler in the third, all three serials citing as their source the sixty page book attributed to Cody, *The Great West that*

Was (New York: Palmer & Oliver, 1916), and the low-budget silent feature *Buffalo Bill on the U.P. Trail* (Sunset, 1926). The Wellman film gave the character a new lease on life, at least among such low-budget productions as *Buffalo Bill Rides Again* (Screen Guild, 1947) with Richard Arlen as Bill and *Buffalo Bill in Tomahawk Territory* (United Artists, 1952) with Clayton Moore, this last one of the worst Western films ever made. By the time Robert Altman came to direct what is reputedly a more factually and historically accurate account of Cody's life in *Buffalo Bill and the Indians, or Sitting Bull's History Lesson* (United Artists, 1976), there was perhaps no longer any memory of Buffalo Bill to tarnish, much less question, and the public seemed disinterested in the subject even with Paul Newman cast as Buffalo Bill.

All of which may mean in the end that Kent Ladd Steckmesser was right when in *The Western Hero in History and Legend* he wrote: ". . . The basic appeal of the legendary heroes is that they served good causes. They were servants of justice and truth, defenders of the meek and the oppressed. They became actors in the great allegory of Good versus Evil, an allegory whose roots are deep in American history. That service in such causes may be historically unfounded is of little relevance in the legend. Because Americans have generally cast themselves in idealistic roles, they have been able to identify with these heroic representatives of the national character." It will remain for a future generation of Americans to determine whether such legends, and the national identification with them, is a sign of spiritual vigor or a denial of the actual reality of what historically happened on the frontier, a sort of communal agreement to reject a true understanding of what happened so as to preserve an adolescent and ill-deserved sense of artificial innocence.

Hoffman, Lee (1932 —) Author of formulary and historical Western fiction, born at Chicago, Illinois. Hoffman, who is a woman, once wrote: "When I run up against that 'How can you, a mere woman, write Westerns?' attitude, I mention that in my youth I owned a number of horses, did some trail riding in Colorado and Wyoming, and once worked as a shill to a horse trader in Kansas. I don't go into details about the trail riding being connected with a stay at a dude ranch, or the job with the horse trader only lasting a couple of weeks. (He got arrested.)" Hoffman's family moved to Savannah, Georgia, where Hoffman spent her teens. She started writing as a hobby in the sixth grade, graduating from pencil on tablet paper quickly to pen on note-book paper. ("I produced a great number of 500 to 1,000 word novels, mostly Westerns, which I passed around among friends to read.") She attended Armstrong Junior College in Atlanta from 1949 to 1951. During her first year of college she discovered science fiction fandom and made many friends in the "sf" world, founding her own monthly magazine, *Quandry*, which readily attracted an enthusiastic audience. After graduation she continued her activities in amateur journalism and was elected president of one of the science fiction amateur press associations in 1952. After moving to New York City in 1956, Hoffman married science fiction editor, Larry Shaw. She worked as assistant editor of two magazines, *Infinity* and *Science Fiction Adventures*, from 1956 until they ceased publication in 1958. She later said that the experience taught her "a lot about how *not* to write, but not much about how to do it."

After her marriage ended in divorce, Hoffman lived in Greenwich Village and worked at several jobs in the editorial and printing fields. In addition to her interest in science fiction, she continued to be an avid Western fan. Finally, in 1965, she completed a book-length Western of her own and submitted it to Donald Wollheim, editor at Ace Books. After some cutting at Wollheim's suggestion, the book was accepted and published as *Gunfight at Laramie* (New York: Ace, 1966). Shortly after acceptance of her first book, Hoffman was commissioned by Ace to write a comic Western, and this became her second book, *The Legend of Blackjack Sam*, all about "the notorious showdown at the O'Shea corral." The years of writing for the amateur press and for her own amusement now paid off. Hoffman settled into a career as a free-lance writer of Westerns and science fiction. She left New York City in 1971 to live in Florida.

In a review of Hoffman's third Western, *Bred To Kill* (New York: Ballantine, 1967), R.S. Coulson described the hero as "more typical of the period than most fictional cowboys: uneducated, not too bright, and bewildered by conflicting demands of law and loyalty." Hoffman made the character believable, sympathetic, and totally engaging.

Believable and unstereotyped characters are also a feature of *The Valdez Horses* (New York: Doubleday, 1967), and other books such as *The Yarborough Brand* (New York: Avon, 1968) and *West of Cheyenne* (New York: Doubleday, 1969); character and motivation are as important as the details of the plot. Not that Hoffman skimped on action: there are fist-fights, gunfights, and chases, but they serve the story rather than being the story's reason for existence. Hoffman refused to be predictable. Even in such a standard situation as the rancher/nester conflict in *Loco* (New York: Doubleday, 1969), the nature of the opposing groups and the battle between them do not follow any of the usual patterns. Hoffman also wrote several comic Westerns, such as *Wiley's Move* (New York: Dell, 1973) and *The Truth about the Cannonball Kid* (New York: Dell, 1975), the latter a farce about a naive hero and his con-man associates.

R.E.B.

Lee Hoffman's Western novels are *Gunfight at Laramie* (1966), *The Legend of Blackjack Sam* (1966), *Bred to Kill* (1967), *The Valdez Horses* (1967), *Dead Man's Gold* (1968), *The Yarborough Brand* (1968), *West of Cheyenne* (1969), *Wild Riders* (1969), *Return to Broken Crossing* (1969), *Loco* (1969), *Wiley's Move* (1973), *The Truth about the Cannonball Kid* (1975), *Trouble Valley* (1976), *Fox* (1976), *Nothing but a Drifter* (1976), *Sheriff of Jack Hollow* (1977), *The Land Killer* (1978).

Chino (Intercontinental Releasing Corp., 1976) was directed by John Sturges [based on *The Valdez Horses*],

Hogan, (Robert) Ray (1908 —)

Prolific author of more than 110 Western novels, under his own name and the pseudonym Clay Ringold, born at Willow Springs, Missouri. Hogan's father was the town marshal at Willow Springs. Later the family moved to Albuquerque, New Mexico, when Hogan was 5, and his father joined the Albuquerque police force and, for a few years, the family owned the Overland Hotel. According to Hogan, tales told by his father and the men who stayed at the hotel, as well as those told by old timers whom he interviewed, served as the basic plots for many of his Western novels.

Hogan attended high school in Albuquerque and took a correspondence course from the Hoosier Institute of Journalism and special courses in English and literature from the University of New Mexico. He worked at a variety of jobs including managing a retail tire store for twelve years. Although he had been writing since he was a boy, Hogan was in his forties when his first novel, *Ex-Marshal* (New York: Signet, 1956), was published.

At his best it would take Hogan about two months to write a book. His writing averaged about 2,000 words a day. This rapid output as well as public demand for sharply drawn characters may account for the uncomplicated two dimensional charac-

ters which people Hogan's books. An example of this in the books from the 'Seventies is the series hero, Shawn Starbuck. In more than twenty novels, Starbuck, whose inheritance from his father cannot be claimed until he finds his brother, Ben, searches throughout the West, riding from one adventure to another. The serial nature of this series insures that Starbuck will escape the romantic entanglements common in many Western novels. Another of Hogan's novels, such as *Showdown on Texas Flat* (New York: Ace, 1972), reflect this same lack of feminine influence on the hero.

Hogan wrote two non-fiction books, *The Life and Death of Clay Allison* (New York: Signet, 1961), a New Mexico outlaw, and *The Life and Death of Johnny Ringo* (New York: Signet, 1963), Hogan's favorite historical character. Two of his books were used as the basis for episodes in the television series, *Cheyenne* (ABC, 1957–1963).

J.N.

Ray Hogan's Western novels under his own name or his occasional pseudonym, Clay Ringold, are *Ex-Marshal* (1956), *Friendless* (1956), *Walk a Lonely Trail* (1957), *Longhorn Law* (1957), *Land of the Strangers* (1957), *Outlaw Marshal* (1958), *Hangman's Valley* (1958), *Wanted: Alive* (1958), *Marshal without a Badge* (1959), *The Shotgunner* (1960), *The Hasty Hangman* (1960), *Guns Against the Sun* (1960), *Lead Reckoning* (1960), *Ride to the Gun* (1960), *Ambush at Riflestock* (1960), *Marshal for Lawless* (1961), *Track the Man Down* (1961), *The Ridgerunner* (1961), *New Gun for Kingdom City* (1962), *The Shotgunners* (1962), *Stranger in Apache Basin* (1963), *The Outside Gun* (1963), *Trail of the Fresno Kid* (1963), *Last Gun at Cabresto*

(1963), *The Trackers* (1964), *Hoodoo Guns* (1964), *Man from Abranco Negra* (1964), *Dead Man on Black Horse* (1966), *Panhandle Pistolero* (1966), *Border Bandit* (1966), *Killer's Gun* (1966), *The Hellsfire Lawman* (1966), *Texas Lawman* (1967), *The Wolver* (1967), *Outlaw's Mountain* (1967), *Legacy of the Slash M* (1967), *Devil's Butte* (1967), *Trouble at Tenkiller* (1967), *The Gunmaster* (1968), *Return to Rio Fuego* (1968), *Killer on the Warbucket* (1968), *The Hell Road* (1968), *The Moonlighters* (1968), *Man Who Kills a Marshal* (1969), *Reckoning in Fire Valley* (1969), *Trail to Tucson* (1969), *Bloodrock Valley War* (1969), *Texas Guns* (1969), *The Hooded Gun* (1969), *The Rimrocker* (1970), *Searching Guns* (1970), *Guns Along the Jicarilla* (1970), *Jackman's Wolf* (1970), *The Outlawed* (1970), *Duel in Labrima Valley* (1971), *Three Cross* (1971), *Deputy of Violence* (1971), *A Bullet for Mr. Texas* (1971), *The Marshal of Babylon* (1971), *Brandon's Posse* (1971), *A Man Called Ryker* (1971), *Showdown on Texas Flat* (1972), *The Hangmen of San Sabal* (1972), *The Hell Merchant* (1972), *Lawman for Slaughter Valley* (1972), *The Night Hell's Corners Died* (1972), *Conger's Woman* (1973), *Passage to Dodge City* (1972), *Day of Reckoning* (1973), *The Devil's Gunhand* (1973), *The Vengeance Gun* (1973), *The Guns of Stingaree* (1973), *Skull Gold* (1973), *Highroller's Man* (1973), *The Jenner Guns* (1974), *Wolf Lawman* (1974), *The Scorpion Killers* (1974), *Man without a Gun* (1974), *The Tombstone Trail* (1974), *Betrayal at Tombstone* (1975), *Roxie Raker* (1975), *The Texas Brigade* (1975), *Honeymaker's Son* (1975), *The Last Comanchero* (1975), *The Doomsday Marshal* (1975), *Day of the Hangman* (1975), *The Vigilante* (1975), *The Proving Gun* (1975), *High Green Gun*

(1976), *The Yesterday Rider* (1976), *The Regulator: Bill Thompson* (1976), *The Shotgun Rider* (1976), *The Iron Jehu* (1976), *Omaha Crossing* (1977), *Bounty Hunter's Moon* (1977), *The Doomsday Posse* (1977), *Tall Man Riding* (1977), *A Gun for Silver Rose* (1977), *The Peace Keeper* (1977), *Gun Trap at Arabella* (1978), *Adam Gann, Outlaw* (1978), *The Glory Trail* (1978), *The Raptors* (1979), *The Doomsday Trail* (1979), *Overkill at Saddlerock* (1979), *The Hellborn* (1979), *Dead Gun* (1980), *Lawman's Choice* (1980), *Ragan's Law* (1980), *Pilgrim* (1980), *The Hell Raiser* (1980), *Town Tamer* (1981), *Outlaw's Pledge* (1981), *Decision at Doubtful Canyon* (1981), *The Doomsday Bullet* (1981).

Holmes, L(lewellyn) P(erry)

(1895 —) Author of a vast number of Western novels and stories under his own name and pseudonyms Matt Stuart, Dave Hardin, and Perry Westwood, born in a snowed-in log cabin at Breckenridge, Colorado, atop the Rocky Mountains. According to Holmes, he was literally born with an urge to write. After graduating from high school, Holmes took to writing for the pulps and was a major contributor for Leo Margulies' line of pulp publications (see Pulp and

Slick Western Stories). His first hardbound novel was *Roaring Range* (New York: Greenberg, 1935) and he followed it with an occasional Western, but it was not until the 'Fifties that Holmes turned his major attention away from the pulp markets and concentrated on book fiction. Holmes' chief reason for writing Western fiction was that it was the country he knew best, having been born there and having lived there all his life. He liked the Western setting, the action of the formulary plots, the romance and color of the land, and the lack of moral ambiguity permitted in the standard pulp story. As Nelson C. Nye (q.v.) and Walt Coburn (q.v.), Holmes never attempted to let a well-made plot supersede the constant demand for action and a story that moves. His novel *Somewhere They Die* (Boston: Little, Brown, 1955), one of his best and with fewer typical pulp ingredients, was purchased for the screen by actor/producer Dick Powell and was intended as a John Wayne vehicle, a project curtailed at the time by Powell's unexpected death.

L.P. Holmes' Western novels under his own name are *Roaring Range* (1935), *Gunman's Greed* (1936) [alternate title: *Bloody Saddles*], *The Law of Kyger Gorge* (1936), *Destiny Range* (1936), *Outlaws of Boardman's Flat* (1941), *Flame of Sunset* (1947), *Apache Desert* (1948), *Dead Man's Saddle* (1948), *Water, Grass, and Gunsmoke* (1948) [alternate title: *Range Pirate*], *Desert Rails* (1949), *Black Sage* (1950), *Summer Range* (1951), *High Starlight* (1952), *Delta Deputy* (1953), *The Plunderers* (1955), *Somewhere They Die* (1955), *Modoc, The Last Sundown* (1957), *Catch and Saddle* (1959), *Hill Smoke* (1959), *Night Marshal* (1961), *Smoky Pass* (1962), *Wolf Brand* (1962), *The Buzzards of Rocky Pass* (1963),

The Shackled Gun (1963), *Side Me at Sundown* (1963), *Edge of Sundown* (1964), *The Hardest Man in the Sierras* (1965), *The Savage Hours* (1966), *The Maverick Star* (1969), *Showdown on the Jubilee* (1970), *Rustler's Moon* (1971), *Rawhide Creek* (1975).

Holmes' novels as Matt Stuart are *Dusty Wagons* (1946) [alternate title: *Savage Guns*], *Gun Law at Vermillion* (1947), *Smoky Trail* (1947), *Gunsmoke Showdown* (1948) [alternate title: *Saddle-Man*], *Bonanza Gulch* (1949) [alternate title: *Bloody Bonanza*], *Wire in the Wind* (1950) [alternate title: *Nevada Rampage*], *Sunset Rider* (1951) [alternate title: *The Fugitive Gun*], *Deep Hills* (1954) [alternate title: *Rider into Gunsmoke*], *The Lonely Law* (1957), *Wild Summit* (1958), *Tough Saddle* (1959), *Warrior Creek* (1960), *The Hackamore Feud* (1964), *Edge of the Desert* (1966) [alternate titles: *Lady of Battle Mountain* and *Shadow of the Rim*].

Holmes' novel as Dave Hardin is *Brandon's Empire* (1953) and as Perry Westwood is *Six-Gun Code* (1953).

Horgan, Paul (1903 —) Author of historical Western fiction, born at Buffalo, New York. Horgan moved with his family at the age of 11 to Albuquerque, New Mexico, a locale which would inspire nearly all of his later Western fiction and historical books. His formal schooling ended after three years as a cadet at the New Mexico Military Institute. When his father died in 1922, the family moved back East, Horgan going on to Rochester, New York, where for three years he worked on the production staff at the Eastman Theatre. At 26, Horgan returned to Albuquerque, this time to be a librarian at the New Mexico Military Institute. In his spare time, Horgan began writing novels, achieving his first true success with *The Fault of Angels* (New York: Harper's, 1933) which won Horgan the Harper Prize. It was a novel dealing with professional musicians, a world he encountered while living in Rochester.

Horgan seemed to come into his own when he began setting his fictional works in the Southwest, with *Main Line West* (New York: Harper's, 1936) and *Lamp on the Plains* (New York: Harper's, 1937) centering on a boy's worldly education, *Far from Cibola* (New York: Harper's, 1938) dealing with New Mexicans in search of government aid, and *The Habit of Empire* (New York: Rydal, 1938) focusing on Sixteenth-century New Mexico.

Horgan left his library post to join the U.S. Army Information Branch (1942–1946) during World War II, rising to the rank of Lieutenant Colonel and receiving the Legion of Merit. Following the war, Horgan returned to the New Mexico Military Institute and from 1947–1949 he was assistant to the president. Thence followed a series of directorships, chairmanships, fellowships, university appointments, and well over fifteen honorary degrees as his work became widely recognized and critically acclaimed.

Perhaps Horgan's *magnum opus* was his non-fiction account in two volumes titled *Great River: The Rio Grande in North American History* (New York: Rinehart, 1954) which earned him a Pulitzer Prize. Horgan later edited his own abridgement of this work, making it accessible to the majority of readers, titled *The Heroic Triad* (New York: Holt, Rinehart, 1970). In fiction, Horgan's *A Distant Trumpet* (New York: Farrar, Straus, 1960) was perhaps his most popular success. It tells the story of Matthew and Laura Hazard, a young U.S. Army couple who begin their married life at a remote Cavalry outpost in the Arizona Territory during the final years of the Apache campaigns. It was in the tradition of books and stories then currently in vogue by Ernest Haycox (q.v.) and James Warner Bellah (q.v.), but in its somewhat sympathetic portrait of the Apaches went beyond them all, even anticipating the change in the way the Indian wars would henceforth be treated in the more impartial historical fiction of subsequent decades.

A devout Roman Catholic, Horgan also dealt with the missionary theme in a short novel titled *The Devil in the Desert: A Legend of Life and Death in the Rio Grande* (New York: Longmans, 1952), a story certainly to be compared with Willa Cather's (q.v.) *Death Comes for the Archbishop* (New York: Knopf, 1927) and Owen Wister's (q.v.) *Padre Ignazio* which was also issued separately from its inclusion in Wister's *The Jimmyjohn Boss and Other Stories* (New York: Harper's, 1900). However, Horgan's religious commitment was not so significant in assessing the stature of his fiction as was his importance as a regional author of rare clarity, depth, and consistency. While some of his books have tended to be overly long, less experimental, and shunning completely any of the realities of modern life, they are generally accurate historically as fiction, thorough and incisive when non-fiction.

A Distant Trumpet (Warner's, 1964) directed by Raoul Walsh was a rather pedestrian rendering of Horgan's novel, with a Cavalry vs. Indian plot.

Hough, Emerson (1857–1923)

Journalist and sportsman who wrote many novels, short stories, and articles about the American West, born at Newton, Iowa. Hough was educated at Iowa State University and received a law degree. In 1889 he passed the bar examination and set up practice in White Oaks, New Mexico, gaining some firsthand experiences and a sense of setting which he would later use in his Western fiction. He also became Western representative for George Bird Grinnell's magazine *Forest and Stream* published in Chicago, Illinois. His first book, *The Story of a Cowboy* (New York: Appleton, 1897), was one in a series edited by Ripley Hitchcock who would later become Zane Grey's (q.v.) editor, and the book was praised by both Hitchcock and Theodore Roosevelt (q.v.). Hough's first novel, *The Girl at the Halfway House* (New York: Appleton, 1900), was followed by a bestseller, *The Mississippi Bubble* (Indianapolis: Bobbs-Merrill, 1902). In all, Hough went on to write eighteen novels, a series of juveniles, and several popular historical works. He also wrote a regular column for *The Saturday Evening Post* titled "Out of Doors." As a conservationist, he was credited with saving the buffalo herd in Yellowstone National Park.

Of his most artistically successful novel, Eugene Manlove Rhodes (q.v.) said, "once he made a great magic with 9/10 of *Heart's Desire* [New York: Macmillan, 1905]." But the novel proved a financial failure and Hough turned to writing highly fanciful historical fiction. His most successful novel with a Western setting came late in his career, *The Covered Wagon* (New York: Appleton, 1922). In this novel two pitched battles are fought with Indians, the first against 2,000 Sioux warriors, the second against half as many Crow and Bannock warriors, with the sharpshooting white men finishing off at least a hundred Indians. Four prominent mountain men are woven into the plot: Bill Jackson, Jim Bridger, Kit Carson, and Caleb Greenwood. Bridger, in fact, even leads part of the wagon train to Oregon without thought of compensation! The part that goes to California focuses attention on gold-mining and the hero, at long last, wins the comely heroine. This novel was followed by another woven from the same cloth, *North of 36* (New York: Appleton, 1923). Both were filmed, *The Covered Wagon* (Paramount, 1923) having a longer New York run than D.W. Griffith's *Birth of a Nation* (Epoch, 1915) and establishing itself as the first cinematic epic Western—"epic" does not mean, however, that it did not retain the essential plot of the novel because this it certainly did.

Emerson Hough's novels with a Western setting are *The Girl at the Halfway House* (1900), *The Mississippi Bubble* (1902), *Heart's Desire* (1905), *54-40 or Fight* (1909), *The Magnificent Adventure* (1916), *The Man Next Door* (1917), *The Broken Gate* (1917), *The Sagebrusher* (1919), *The Covered Wagon* (1922), *North of 36* (1923), *Mother of Gold* (1924), *The Ship of Souls* (1925).

Films based on Emerson Hough's Western fiction are *The Sagebrusher* (Hodkinson, 1920) directed by Edward Sloman, *The Covered Wagon* (Paramount, 1923) directed by James Cruze, *The Man Next Door* (Vitagraph, 1923) directed by Victor Schert-

Jack Holt in North of 36 *(Paramount, 1924) directed by Irvin Willat.*

zinger, *Way of a Man* (Pathé, 1924) directed by George B. Seitz [a ten chapter serial also released in a feature version] [source unknown], *North of 36* (Paramount, 1924) directed by Irvin Willat, remade as *The Conquering Horde* (Paramount, 1931) directed by Edward Sloman and as *The Texans* (Paramount, 1938) directed by James Hogan, *Ship of Souls* (Associated Exhibitors, 1925) directed by Charles Miller, *One Hour of Love* (Tiffany, 1927) directed by Robert Florey [based on *The Broken Gate*].

Delbert E. Wylder who wrote the chapbook *Emerson Hough* (Austin: Steck-Vaughn, 1969) is currently at work on a full scale study of Hough to be published by Twayne Publishers.

House Names This was a tradition which began in the Nineteenth century when publishers of dime novels created a house name for a series of novels written by any number of different people. The pulp Western magazines (see Pulp and Slick Western Stories) were an outgrowth of the dime novels and were often published by the same companies which had carried (or were still carrying) a line of dime novels. The tradition of the house name was simply retained.

In the early 'Thirties, when Francis

Thayer Hobson became editorial director of William Morrow and Company, he decided to start a line of hardbound Western novels to be published under the house name Peter Field. The series, written by many different authors, proved to be one of the most successful, running to 78 entries in all and lasting from 1933 until 1965.

The entries were also, in most cases, reissued in the 'Forties and 'Fifties in hardbound format under the Morrow Jefferson House imprint, a separate corporation set up by Hobson to protect the copyrighted introductions written for the re-issues by Morrow's most successful author, Erle Stanley Gardner, a close personal friend of Hobson. Among the anonymous contributors were E.B. Mann (q.v.), Harry Sinclair Drago (q.v.), and Davis Dresser who under the pseudonym Brett Halliday created the Michael Shayne series of detective novels. According to veteran Western writer Nelson C. Nye (q.v.) payment for a book-length manuscript in this series was a flat $500 without royalties. The titles, with the actual author's name in brackets following the title and year, were *Outlaws Three* (1933) [Francis Thayer Hobson], *Dry-Gulch Adams* (1934) [Francis Thayer Hobson], *Gringo Guns* (1935) [Francis Thayer Hobson], *The Boss of the Lazy 9* (1936) [E.B. Mann], *Coyote Gulch* (1936) [Samuel Mines], *Mustang Mesa* (1937) [Ed Earl Repp], *Canyon of Death* (1938) [Harry Sinclair Drago], *The Outlaw of Eagle's Nest* (1938) [S. Lancer Cheney], *The Tenderfoot Kid* (1939) [Harry Sinclair Drago], *Doctor Two-Guns* (1939) [Harry Sinclair Drago], *The Man from Thief River* (1940) [Harry Sinclair Drago], *Law Badge* (1940) [Harry Sinclair Drago], *Guns from Powder Valley* (1941) [Davis Dresser], *Powder Valley Pay-Off* (1941) [Davis Dress-

er], *Trail South from Powder Valley* (1942) [Davis Dresser], *Law Man of Powder Valley* (1942) [Davis Dresser], *Fight for Powder Valley* (1942) [Davis Dresser], *Powder Valley Vengeance* (1943) [Davis Dresser], *Sheriff on the Spot* (1943) [Davis Dresser], *The Smoking Iron* (1944) [Davis Dresser], *Maverick's Return* (1944) [Tom West], *Midnight Round-Up* (1944) [Davis Dresser], *Death Rides the Night* (1944) [Davis Dresser], *The End of the Trail* (1945) [Davis Dresser], *The Road to Laramie* (1945) [Davis Dresser], *Gambler's Gold* (1946) [Fred East], *Powder Valley Showdown* (1946) [Davis Dresser], *Ravaged Range* (1946) [Fred East], *Trail from Needle Rock* (1947) [Fred East], *Return to Powder Valley* (1948) [Robert J. Hogan], *Outlaw Valley* (1949) [Robert J. Hogan], *Sheriff Wanted!* (1949) [Robert J. Hogan], *Blacksmoke Trail* (1950) [Robert J. Hogan]. From this point on all the entries were written by Lucien W. Emerson. They were *Powder Valley Ambush* (1950), *Back Trail to Danger* (1951), *Canyon Hide-Out* (1951), *Marauders of the Lazy Mare* (1951), *Guns in the Saddle* (1952), *Powder Valley Holdup* (1952), *Riders of the Outlaw Trail* (1952), *Three Guns from Colorado* (1952), *Dig the Spurs Deep* (1953), *Guns Roaring West* (1953), *Montana Maverick* (1953), *Powder Valley Deadlock* (1954), *Powder Valley Stampede* (1954), *Ride for Trinidad* (1954), *War in the Painted Buttes* (1954), *Breakneck Pass* (1955), *Outlaw of Castle Canyon* (1955), *Rawhide Rider* (1955), *Saddles to Santa Fe* (1955), *Powder Valley Renegade* (1956), *Strike for Tomahawk* (1956), *Wild Horse Lightning* (1956), *Guns for Grizzly Flat* (1957), *Man from Robber's Roost* (1957), *Powder Valley Manhunt* (1957), *Raiders at Medicine Bow* (1957), *Hangman's Trail* (1958), *Rustler's*

Rock (1958), *Sagebrush Swindle* (1958), *Drive for Devil's River* (1959), *Outlaw Express* (1959), *Trail to Troublesome* (1959), *Double-Cross Canyon* (1960), *Powder Valley Plunder* (1960), *Rattlesnake Range* (1961), *Rimrock Riders* (1961), *Wolf-Pack Trail* (1961), *Cougar Canyon* (1962), *The Outlaw Herd* (1962), *Powder Valley Ransom* (1962), *Outlaw Deputy* (1963), *Powder Valley Getaway* (1963), *Trail Through Tascosa* (1963), *Rustler's Empire* (1964), *Feud at Silvermine* (1965).

These novels are all set in the fictional Powder Valley and feature a triad hero similar to notions developed by Eugene Cunningham (q.v.) and William Colt MacDonald (q.v.) both of whom had come up with the idea of the "Three Mesquiteers." In the case of the Peter Field books, the trio was Pat Stevens, owner of the Lazy Mare ranch and sometimes sheriff of Powder Valley, Sam Sloan and Ezra, partners in the ES ranch and friends of Pat who help him out of the scrapes he finds himself in. There is, however, at least one exception to this, and that is *The Tenderfoot Kid* ghosted by Harry Sinclair Drago which does not feature this trio.

One of the most sensationally popular, albeit wholly formulary, Western series was the Buchanan books published under the house name Jonas Ward. One of the novels, *The Name's Buchanan*, was even filmed under the title *Buchanan Rides Alone* (Columbia, 1958) directed by Budd Boetticher. Although Boetticher treated the character comically, in the novels he is actually a loner, a sophisticated and hardboiled soldier of fortune riding through the West and into various adventures. The first six entries in this series were written by William Ard (1922–1960) who, as Davis Dresser when he

was writing Peter Field entries, also wrote detective fiction. Ard's Buchanan entries are *The Name's Buchanan* (1956), *Buchanan Says No* (1957), *One Man Massacre* (1958), *Buchanan Gets Mad* (1958), *Buchanan's Revenge* (1960), *Buchanan on the Prod* (1960). Following Ard's death, the series was dropped for eight years until Fawcett, the publisher, decided to give it a major promotion and continue it and it became one of the bestselling of all paperback Western series. Brian Garfield (q.v.) wrote *Buchanan's Gun* (1968) and was succeeded by William R. Cox (q.v.) who wrote all the subsequent entries to date which are *Buchanan's Gamble* (1972), *Buchanan's Siege* (1972), *Buchanan on the Run* (1973), *Get Buchanan* (1973), *Buchanan Takes Over* (1974), *Buchanan Calls the Shots* (1975), *Buchanan's Big Showdown* (1975), *Buchanan's Texas Treasure* (1976), *Buchanan's Stolen Railway* (1977), *Buchanan's Manhunt* (1978).

Other paperback publishers also began their own series under house names. The Paperback Library used the house name Alex Hawk with contributions from such noted writers as Elmer Kelton (q.v.) and Brian Garfield. Belmont/Tower Books' Jack Slade series, Western novels characterized by violence and bloodshed, were written by such veterans as Todhunter Ballard (q.v.) and Ben Haas (q.v.) along with several others.

The same practice was also pursued with the 1980's rash of pornographic Westerns. There is virtually nothing "Western" about these novels to distinguish them from hard-core pornography save the costuming and the period in which they are set. Playboy's series by Jake Logan recounting the sexual escapades of John Slocum were written by a wide variety of authors, Howard Pehrson (q.v.) among them. Warner Books' Renegade series about the erotic Captain Gringo were written by Lou Cameron under the house name Ramsay Thorne and the Longarm series published by Jove Books under the house name Tabor Evans were actually written by three authors, Will C. Knott (q.v.), Lou Cameron, and Mel Marshall. Taken as a whole the pornographic Westerns cannot be judged as Western fiction but rather as pornography; their contribution as fiction is wholly negligible.

Howard, Robert E(rvin) (1906–1936)

An author who occasionally wrote Western fiction, born at Peaster, Texas. Howard spent most of his life in various small towns in Western and Central Texas. During his teens his family settled in Cross Plains and Howard completed high school there and in Brownwood where he also attended Howard Payne College. He had decided at an early age that he wanted to be a writer. At the age of 15 he made his first serious attempts at fiction writing and achieved his first professional sales three years later: three short fantasy stories for *Weird Tales* magazine. Although he subsequently wrote a wide variety of fiction for many other pulp magazines, *Weird Tales* remained his most reliable market and during the 'Thirties he was one of that magazine's most popular contributors. In 1936, just as Howard was breaking into the more prestigious magazine fiction markets, his career came to an abrupt end. When he was told that his mother was near death and would not recover from a long-standing illness, he left her bedside, went out to his car, and shot himself.

Howard is best remembered for his fantasy stories. He was the first successful practitioner of that branch of adventure-fantasy known as "sword-and-sorcery" fiction. His tales of barbarian swordsmen and Celtic adventurers have been reprinted in numerous hardcover and paperback editions and have met with a degree of success that Howard himself could never have anticipated.

In spite of this concentration on fantastic fiction, Howard's first book—published in England the year after his death—was a collection of his Western tall tales from *Action Stories Magazine. A Gent from Bear Creek* (London: Herbert Jenkins, 1937; reprinted West Kingston: Donald M. Grant, 1965) recounts, in an outrageous backwoods vernacular, the exploits of a Pecos Bill-like character named Breckinridge Elkins, "six and a half feet tall, possessing the strength of an ox and the modesty of a Munchausen." For nearly thirty years *Gent* remained a rare book, much sought after by a growing band of Howard enthusiasts. The first U.S. edition was finally published in 1965, followed a year later by a second collection, *The Pride of Bear Creek* (West Kingston: Donald M. Grant, 1965), consisting of seven stories, and followed by a third volume of seven stories, *Mayhem on Bear Creek* (West Kingston: Donald M. Grant, 1979). Although the humor is sometimes heavy-handed and the situations repetitious (not unusual for a series of pulp magazine stories about a continuing character), the tales are nonetheless enjoyable when taken in measured doses.

The Howard revival of the 'Sixties and

'Seventies led to the disinterment of his traditional Western stories in addition to the tall tales. These were collected in two paperback volumes, *The Vultures of Whapeton* (New York: Zebra Books, 1975), consisting of four stories, and *The Last Ride* (New York: Berkley, 1978), consisting of seven stories. With the exception of the title story in the former volume, a short novel based loosely on the career of gunfighter Henry Brown, the stories are without literary interest.

R.E.B.

Hunter, John. See Ballard, Todhunter.

I

Ingram, Hunter. See Lutz, Giles A.

Irving, Washington (1783–1859) Essayist, biographer, historian, and author of frontier fiction, born at New York City. The youngest of eleven children, Irving was little impressed by his father's stern Presbyterianism and was even secretly confirmed in the Episcopal church with his mother's connivance. He attended a half dozen private schools, none of them very good, but he compensated for this by being a voracious reader and it was only delicate health which prevented him from following his brothers to college at Columbia. In 1798 he began to read law but he was more interested in literary pursuits and in 1803 he accompanied an expedition to Montreal through upper state New York.

Ill health, after his return, forced him abroad. He remained in Rome for two years. When, in 1806, he returned to the United States, he was admitted to the bar, largely because of his winning manner, and he desultorily practiced the law until 1810. In the interim, he was engaged in literary pursuits, principally humorous sketches. During the War of 1812 he was *aide-de-camp* to Governor Daniel Tompkins. In 1813–1814 he edited the *Analectic Magazine* in Philadelphia and the next year his brothers sent him to Liverpool to manage the branch there of their mercantile firm in which Irving was a silent partner. His first full-length book, the comic *Knickerbocker's History of New York* (1809), had preceded him to Great Britain and earned him the friendship of Sir Walter Scott, Thomas Moore, and Lord Byron. Scott interested Irving in German literature and romantic history and this prompted his natural leaning toward the picturesque in *The Sketch Book* (1819–1820) which contained Irving's minor classics, the immortal tales of "Rip Van Winkle" and "The Legend of Sleepy Hollow."

After a period of relative idleness, in 1826 Irving went to Madrid, under semi-official status, to write his *History of the Life and Voyages of Christopher Columbus* (1828), a work which lay the corner stone for American historical and biographical writing and one which probably deserves its reputation as his finest effort. Irving was recalled to London in 1829 to serve as secretary of the United States Legation and, in 1832, he returned to America in triumph, hailed as the father of American literature. Wearying of the adulation, Irving embarked in 1832 on an expedition that was to visit the Osage and Pawnee Indian nations. From this grew Irving's body of remarkable writings about the American West, *A Tour on the Prairies* (1835) which was a book of memorable travel sketches, *Astoria* (1836) which was an account of John Jacob Astor's fur-trading enterprises in the Rocky Mountains and the Pacific slope, and *The Adventures of Captain Bonneville, U.S.A.* (1837) which was a novel about a French soldier-of-fortune's trapping expeditions across the Great Plains and among the foothills of the Rockies. John Francis McDermott, in his introductory essay to the re-issue of *A Tour on the Prairies* (Norman: University of Oklahoma Press, 1956), remarked of this book that "its perennial popularity owes much to the suavity, the urbanity, the geniality, the grace of expression which his critics have commonly allowed Irving, for the man could write as few of his contemporaries could. But the book is more than a literary exercise. Its true worth and its enduring fascination lie in the brilliantly drawn pictures of frontier life that flow from the pencil of a great genre artist."

Upon his return to the East, in 1842, after declining various offers, Irving accepted an appointment as minister to Spain. After four years in this capacity, he resumed the life of a country gentleman on his estate near Tarrytown, New York, putting all of his remaining energy into writing his *Life of Washington* (1855–1859). This left him exhausted and he died of a heart attack soon after its completion.

While he was touring the prairies, Irving had written to his brother, Peter, about the trip and about his "opportunity of seeing the remnants of those great Indian tribes, which are now about to disappear as independent nations, or to be amalgamated under some new form of government. I should see those fine countries of the 'Far West,' while still in a state of pristine wildness, and behold herds of buffaloes scouring their native prairies, before they are driven beyond the reach of a civilized tourist." The important word here is "civilized." It did not occur to Irving that the Indian nations might have any rights whatsoever to their lands; that they were, in fact, civilized people rather than suited, at best, only to be wards of the invaders' government. Pierre Beatte, the half-breed hunter who had joined the expedition, inspired Irving to observe that he "had altogether more of the red than the white man in his composition; and as I had been taught to look upon all half-breeds with distrust, as an uncertain and faithless race, I would gladly have dispensed with the services of Pierre Beatte." But as the journey progressed—and this must be pointed out in Irving's favor—his opinion of Beatte was modified and he found himself musing that "an Indian hunter on a prairie is like a cruiser on the ocean, perfectly independent of the world, and competent to self-protection and self-maintenance. He can cast himself loose from everyone, shape his own course, and take care of his own fortunes. I thought Beatte seemed to feel his independence, and to consider himself superior to us all, now that we were launching into the wilderness." Although Irving himself subscribed to what historian Henry Nash Smith termed the "cult of refinement," as in the fiction of James Fenimore Cooper (q.v.), emerging in his prose was a figure new to world literature, the American backwoodsman, the pathfinder, the man with wilderness skills who was, in his environment, a more perfectly adapted human being than sophisticated Easterners with their European snobbishness. Moreover, it is an enduring image, recurring again and again, in literature from Cooper to Vardis Fisher's (q.v.) *Mountain Man* (New York: Morrow, 1965), in films from Anthony Mann's remarkable *The Last Frontier* (Columbia, 1955) to Sydney Pollack's *Jeremiah Johnson* (Warner's, 1972); and so powerful still is this image that French film historian Jean-Louis Leutrat in *Le Western* (Paris: Armand Colin, 1973) could see reflected in films as *Jeremiah Johnson* and *Man in the Wilderness* (Warner's, 1971) "subjects that used to be potentially very rich" (*sujets [que] etaient potentiellement d'une grande richesse*).

"On the one hand," G. Edward White observed about Irving in *The Eastern Establishment and the Western Experience* (New Haven: Yale University Press, 1968), "he turns up his Eastern nose at the lack of manners and social grace on the frontier, and on the other he describes a 'wild wood life' as free from the chains that bind one, such as manners and grace."

The best book on Washington Irving's life and work remains Stanley T. Williams' *The Life of Washington Irving* (New York: Oxford University Press, 1935), although a good sense of Irving, his times, and his contemporaries can be found in *Sojourners* (New York: Atheneum, 1979) by Philip McFarland.

J

Jackson, Helen Hunt (1830–1885) Author best known for her novel *Ramona* (1884) and supporter of Indian rights, born Helen Fiske at Amherst, Massachusetts. She was educated in private schools in Massachusetts, where she met poet Emily Dickinson who remained a life-long friend, and in New York. Upon the untimely deaths of her first husband, Lieutenant Edward Hunt, and their two children, Helen turned to writing. Her early poetry, written under the pen-name Marah, was published in *The Nation* and the New York *Evening Post*. Her poems were later collected and Helen became one of Ralph Waldo Emerson's favorite female poets. Her literary apprenticeship was guided by essayist Thomas Wentworth Higginson and she soon began writing prose. She disliked the alliteration of Helen Hunt so she adopted a variety of

pseudonyms—H.H., Rip Van Winkle, Saxe Holm, and No Name.

Helen loved to travel and, in 1873, due to health problems, she went to Colorado where she met William Sharpless Jackson, whom she married in 1875. Not having to worry about supporting herself any more, Jackson could devote full time to her literary career and her first novel was *Mercy Philbrick's Choice* (1876), followed by *Hetty's Strange History* (1877), and *Nelly's Silver Mine* (1878).

While in Boston in 1879, Jackson heard Standing Bear, Chief of the Ponca Indians, and Bright Eyes, a mixed-blood spokesperson for Indian rights, talk on tribal wrongs. She became concerned over the white man's treatment of the Indians. After extensive research, she published and sent to government officials and Congressmen, at her own expense, *A Century of Dishonor* (1881), her bitter arraignment of the federal government for its handling of Indian affairs. The following year she was commissioned, along with Abbot Kinney, to review the living conditions of the mission Indians of California. No action was taken by the government upon the submission of their report so Jackson decided to use the information she had collected in novel form to aid the Indian cause: *Ramona* was the result. Jackson had felt *Ramona* could do for the Indians what her friend Harriet Beecher Stowe's *Uncle Tom's Cabin* (1852) had done for the blacks; however, readers of *Ramona* were more impressed by the romantic images of the Southern California missions and the Spanish Dons than with the Indians' problems.

In *Ramona* the missions represent a means of preservation for the Indians, as well as salvation. However, J. Frank Dobie (q.v.) pointed out in his Introduction to the 1959 Limited Editions Club reprint that, in fact, "the Spanish word for a mission Indian was *Indio reducido*—a reduced Indian. He was reduced from freedom." Writers Mary Hunter Austin (q.v.) and Marah Ellis Ryan (q.v.) would handle the Church's often harmful influence on the Indian more realistically. The romantic happy ending in *Ramona* served only to weaken Jackson's intention for it to be a novel of protest. Many aspects, however, were authentic, particularly the victimization of the Indians by the white land usurpers, and, while most of her works have been forgotten, *Ramona*, her greatest contribution, has been in print for almost a century.

Ramona was brought to the screen four times under this title (Biograph, 1910) directed by D.W. Griffith, (Clune, 1916) directed by Donald Crisp, (United Artists, 1928) directed by Edwin Carewe, (20th-Fox, 1936) directed by Henry King.

For further information see *Helen Hunt Jackson* (New York: Appleton, 1939) by Ruth Odell.

James, Cy. See Watts, Peter C.

James, Will. See Dufault, Joseph Ernest Nephtali.

James, William M. See Harknett, Terry.

Johnson, Dorothy M(arie)

(1905 —) Author of Western fiction and non-fiction books best known for his two short story collections, *Indian Country* (New York: Ballantine, 1953) and *The Hanging Tree* (New York: Ballantine, 1957), born at McGregor, Iowa. Johnson grew up in Whitefish, Montana, where she graduated from high school. She received her Bachelor's degree from the University of Montana at Missoula and was a contributor to the campus literary magazine, *Frontier*. She worked as a stenographer in Okanogan, Washington, and Menasha, Wisconsin, before moving to New York City where she worked as magazine editor for Gregg Publishing Company and the Farrell Publishing

Corporation from 1935–1950. During this fifteen year period, Johnson began writing short stories and magazine articles in her spare time. She also became interested in the Plains Indians and began studying their culture after having believed all Indians were bad despite the fact that she grew up in the West. (She later became an adopted member of the Crow Indian tribe with the name Kills Both Places.) In 1950, she moved back to Montana and settled in Whitefish where she worked as news editor for the weekly newspaper the *Whitefish Pilot*. In 1952, Johnson became secretary-manager of the Montana State Press Association in Missoula where she made her home. She taught magazine article writing and editing in the School of Journalism at the University of Montana.

Her first book, *Beulah Bunny Tells All* (New York: Morrow, 1942), was a collection of short stories previously published in *The Saturday Evening Post* about a fictional schoolteacher. Her second book, *Indian Country*, which was re-issued as *A Man Called Horse* due to the great success of the film based on a short story included in the collection with the same title, was originally published simultaneously in hardback and paperback form and has stood the test of time going through fifteen printings as of 1979. The book contains eleven previously published Western stories which had appeared in magazines such as *Collier's*, *Argosy*, *Cosmopolitan*, *The Saturday Evening Post*, and *Better Living*. *Indian Country* was followed by *The Hanging Tree*, a collection of ten stories including "Lost Sister" which won the Spur Award from the Western Writers of America for Best Western Story for 1956 and which was also made into a chamber opera by James Eversole entitled "Bessie." Both collections have been praised for their verbal economy, authenticity, style, and characterization. Johnson, as A.B. Guthrie, Jr. (q.v.), broke away from Western stereotypes and instead wrote about ordinary people, some of whom are not particularly admirable, whose actions sometimes take on heroic dimensions in the face of frontier adversity. Her vast knowledge of frontier life make her situations and characters credible, particularly her stories told from a child's or a woman's point of view. The stories with female protagonists are highly original with unusual plot elements which make them an important addition to the Western genre which is generally considered a masculine-dominated world. In stories in which Johnson focused on Native Americans, she showed the Indian life-style as a viable alternative culture although more often than not her whites, who live for a time among the Indians, return to the white culture. Author Jack Schaefer (q.v.) in his Introduction to *Indian Country* wrote: "Here is no glamorizing, no romantic gilding, of settlers or of Indians. Here is something finer and more gripping, the honest portrayal of good and bad, of strength and frailty, of the admirable and the contemptible, in both white settlements and Indian villages."

Johnson's subsequent output was largely juvenile-oriented non-fiction and fiction books—*Some Went West* (New York: Dodd, Mead, 1965), *Flame on the Frontier* (New York: Dodd, Mead, 1967), and *Witch Princess* (Boston: Houghton Mifflin, 1967). Her books *Famous Lawmen of the Old West* (New York: Dodd, Mead, 1963) and *Western Badmen* (New York: Dodd, Mead, 1970), written for young readers, are not altogether reliable general introductions to their subjects. Noteworthy are her books *Sitting Bull: Warrior for a Lost Nation* (Philadelphia: Westminster, 1969), a fictionalized biography of Sitting Bull, chief and holy man of the Teton Sioux, and *The Bloody Bozeman* (New York: McGraw-Hill, 1971), a history dealing with the trail to the gold fields in Montana between the years 1862–1868. Her two later works of fiction, *Buffalo Woman* (Dodd, Mead, 1977), which won the Western Wrangler Award from the National Cowboy Hall of Fame, and its sequel, *All the Buffalo Returning* (New York: Dodd, Mead, 1979), give a fine portrait of the everyday life of the Oglala Sioux beginning in 1820 and are very sympathetic in their treatment of the Indian.

Johnson also wrote several non-Western books on Greece for young readers and *The Bedside Book of Bastards* (New York: Dodd, Mead, 1973) which she co-authored with R.T. Turner and which consists of biographical sketches of villains from the Fourth century B.C. to 1900. Three films and several radio and television scripts have been produced based on Johnson's stories. As S. Omar Barker (q.v.) and Ernest Haycox (q.v.), Johnson was a master of the short story medium. Her non-fiction books include a wealth of historical facts, although there are some errors. In 1976, she was the recipient of the Levi Strauss Golden Saddleman Award "for bringing dignity and honor to the legends and history of the West."

Films based on Dorothy M. Johnson's Western fiction are *The Hanging Tree* directed by Delmer Daves [based on the short novel "The Hanging Tree"], *The Man Who Shot Liberty Valance* (Paramount, 1962) directed by John Ford [based on the short story "The Man Who Shot Liberty Valance"], *A Man Called Horse* (National General, 1970) directed by Elliott Silverstein [based on the short story "A Man Called Horse"], *Return of a Man Called Horse* directed by Irvin Kershner [based on the short story "A Man Called Horse"].

Kantor, MacKinlay (1904–1977)

An author of quite a number of short stories dealing with frontier life such as those collected in the anthology *Frontier: Tales of the American Adventure* (New York: New American Library, 1959) and one bona-fide historical novel with a Midwestern frontier setting, *Spirit Lake* (New York: World, 1961), born at Webster City, Iowa. Kantor began his career working for the Webster City *Daily News* where his father was editor. In the 'Thirties, as a result of the success of his short stories in various magazines and novels as *The Jaybird* (New York: Coward, McCann, 1932), he found himself in Hollywood where he worked for various studios as a screenwriter, principally for Paramount, M-G-M, Samuel Goldwyn, and Twentieth Century-Fox. He functioned as a war correspondent during World War II and, briefly, in 1948–1950, even went to work for the New York Police Department as a uniformed officer in order to research his novel, *Signal Thirty-Two* (New York: Random House, 1950), just as he had previously taken hobo trips through the Midwest searching for material for stories. Surely one of his best Midwestern novels to emerge from these earlier experiences was *Happy Land* (New York: Coward, McCann, 1943).

Many of Kantor's stories are about simple people, some of them ingenuous first person narratives, and in his elemental naturalism and concern for family and domestic scenes he might best be compared with Ruth Suckow (q.v.) and even more so with Conrad Richter (q.v.). Indeed, *Happy Land*, which ran serially in *The Saturday Evening Post*, was issued with Richter's *Tacey Cromwell* (New York: Coward, McCann, 1943) in a combined volume. Kantor's *The Gun-Toter and Other Stories of the Missouri Hills* (New York: New American Library, 1963) might also be classed among the better examples of his homespun Western fiction.

Although *Spirit Lake* was published after Kantor's halcyon days as a *Post* writer, it retained his *Post*-engendered attitudes toward portraying Native Americans as brutish savages, as well as a gratuitous effort supposedly to penetrate into their "barbaric" motivations. In this novel, set in Iowa in 1857 and otherwise meticulously, even exhaustively researched, Kantor drew his pioneers as wholly sympathetic and innocent victims of the Indians' vengeance and the scene of the pioneers' slaughter is particularly horrifying.

"My stories," Kantor once remarked, "have appeared in an appalling number of magazines, sublime, ridiculous, and penny-dreadful. I used to write a great deal of stuff for the pulp detective-and-crime story magazines, in the years when I had to make my living that way, and I don't think that my rather complicated talents were harmed in the least. The severe routine of such endeavor stimulated my sense of plot and construction, which needed such stimulation very badly indeed. I was well aware that the stuff I wrote had little value, except

that in most cases it made entertaining narrative."

Films based on MacKinlay Kantor's Western fiction are *The Man from Dakota* (M-G-M, 1940) directed by Leslie Fenton [source unknown], *Gentle Annie* (M-G-M, 1944) directed by Andrew Martin [based on the short novel of the same title published in *Happy Land and Gentle Annie* (New York: Sun Dial Press, 1944)], *Outlaw Territory* [alternate title: *Hannah Lee*] (Broder/Realart, 1953) directed by John Ireland and Lee Garmes [source unknown].

Keene, James. See Cook, Will.

Kelton, Elmer (1926 —) Newspaperman and novelist of the Southwest born on a ranch at Andrews County, Texas. Kelton spent his youth and early manhood associating with cowboys and Western old-timers around the Midland-Odessa ranching country of West Texas. There he picked up the knowledge of the ways of the working cowboy and rancher that served him so well in his Western novels. He came from a long line of the type of people that he so often wrote about, and had a genuine appreciation for their way of life and their special brand of values. His great-grandfather "came out into West Texas about 1875 with a wagon and a string of horses, started a big family and died young, leaving four boys to break broncs, punch cattle and make a living the best way they could, supporting their mother and two baby sisters. I never was much of a cowboy myself, but the heritage stayed with me."

After his graduation from high school, Kelton enlisted in the U.S. Army and served in the European theatre. He received his Bachelor's degree from the University of Texas in Austin in 1948, and proceeded to carve out for himself a very promising career in journalism in San Angelo, Texas, where he made his home. From 1948–1963, he served as the farm and ranch editor for the *San Angelo Standard Times*; from 1963–1968, he was editor for *Ranch Magazine* based in San Angelo; and in 1968 he became associate editor of the *West Texas Livestock Weekly*, a newspaper for farmers and ranchers in the area.

"Economics," Kelton stated, "have dictated that my fiction writing through the years be a sideline." After serving his stint in the U.S. Army, Kelton, who had written some Western stories in high school, began making his living somewhat precariously by writing. Because he could not sell any of his early stories, Kelton came very near giving up writing Western fiction several times. However, in 1947, Fanny Ellsworth, the editor of *Ranch Romances* magazine, bought his appropriately titled story "There's Always Another Chance" for $50. The story appeared in the April, 1948 issue and Kelton's "sideline" career was launched. He enjoyed a moderate success publishing Western stories in *Ranch Ro-*

mances and other pulp magazines until the popularity of the pulps began to wane in the 'Fifties. It was Kelton's New York agent who suggested that he try his hand at a book-length Western and his first novel, *Hot Iron* (New York: Ballantine, 1955), was a fair success. The story is set in Texas and deals with the cattle business, a subject with which Kelton was intimately familiar and which he later wrote about in other Western novels as *Barbed Wire* (New York: Ballantine, 1957) and *Llano River* (New York: Ballantine, 1966). His second novel, *Buffalo Wagons* (New York: Ballantine, 1956), a story about hide hunters in Comanche Territory in the early 1870s, won for Kelton his first of three Spur awards from the Western Writers of America.

Not one to be nostalgic or sentimental about the old West, Kelton portrayed the Southwest—with his main focus being Texas—truthfully and objectively. In an address to the Texas Folklore Society, Kelton said: "As a fiction writer I have always tried to use fiction to illuminate history, to illuminate truth, at least as I see the history and truth. A fiction writer can often fire a reader's interest enough to make him want to dig into the true story and make him search out the real history to find out for himself what happened." Folklore and history play an important part in Kelton's fiction, particularly in his more historically oriented novels as his Texas tetralogy about the fictional Buckalews which began with *Massacre at Goliad* (New York: Ballantine, 1965), a novel for which Kelton felt an especial fondness. The tetralogy also included *After the Bugles* (New York: Ballantine, 1967), *Bowie's Mine* (New York: Ballantine, 1971), and *Long Way to Texas* (New York: Doubleday, 1976), this last written under the pseudonym Lee

McElroy. Kelton wrote two other books under the pen-name McElroy: *Joe Pepper* (New York: Doubleday, 1975), a unique first person narrative dealing with a man caught between the ideas of the old West and the new West, and *Eyes of the Hawk* (New York: Doubleday, 1981). The idea of a man having out-lived his time was a recurring theme in Kelton's fiction.

Kelton, as Dorothy M. Johnson (q.v.) and A.B. Guthrie, Jr. (q.v.), broke away from Western stereotypes in his fiction and instead wrote about simple people—the working cowboy, the working rancher, and the working lawman. The working cowboy is best depicted in *The Day the Cowboys Quit* (New York: Doubleday, 1971) which won a Spur Award and also was chosen as the best regional novel by the Border Regional Library Association of Texas, New Mexico, and Mexico. The story deals with a cowboy strike in the Texas Panhandle in 1883 and features a rather unique conflict between ranch owners and their cowboys, with one man, Hugh Hitchcock, in the middle between the employer he respects and the cowboys who look to him for leadership. The conflict quite often in Kelton's Westerns is not supplied by the formulary hero vs. villain convention, but rather by confrontations between opposing beliefs or viewpoints.

Kelton received another Spur Award from the Western Writers of America and the Western Heritage Award from the National Cowboy Hall of Fame for *The Time it Never Rained* (New York: Doubleday, 1973) which is considered, almost unanimously, Kelton's best book. Set in contemporary West Texas during a seven year drought, *The Time it Never Rained* is an excellent example of Kelton's adeptness at characterization. Charlie Flagg, the protagonist of the story, possesses the qualities Kelton most admired—determination, integrity, and endurance. He is one of the most memorable characters in contemporary Western literature. As Harvey Fergusson (q.v.) and Mary Austin (q.v.), the portrayal in Kelton's fiction of Mexicans, their culture and their relationships with whites, is both insightful and human.

"As a livestock reporter," Kelton once wrote, "I am in everyday contact with the kinds of people I write my stories about, the spiritual sons and grandsons of the characters in my historical works and, in many cases, the actual characters in my more contemporary stories." Perhaps what makes Kelton one of the most important contemporary Western authors is the tremendous respect he had for the people he wrote about. His men and women are sensitively drawn people of integrity who suffer great hardships in building their homes and working the land.

D.M.-K. with V.P.

Elmer Kelton's Western novels under his own name are *Hot Iron* (1955), *Buffalo Wagons* (1956), *Barbed Wire* (1957), *Shadow of a Star* (1959), *The Texas Rifles* (1960), *Donovan* (1961), *Bitter Trail* (1962), *Horsehead Crossing* (1963), *Massacre at Goliad* (1965), *Llano River* (1966), *After the Bugles* (1967), *Captain's Rangers* (1968), *Hanging Judge* (1969), *Bowie's Mine* (1971), *The Day the Cowboys Quit* (1971), *Wagontongue* (1972), *The Time it Never Rained* (1973), *Manhunters* (1974), *The Good Old Boys* (1978), *The Wolf and the Buffalo* (1980).

Kelton's novels as Lee McElroy are *Joe Pepper* (1975), *Long Way to Texas* (1976), *Eyes of the Hawk* (1981).

Kelton's novel as Alex Hawk is *Shot Gun Settlement* (1969).

Kesey, Ken

Kesey, Ken (1935 —) An author who during the 'Sixties was acclaimed for his use of Western imagery in two novels, born at La Junta, Colorado. At a very early age Kesey moved to Oregon with his family where he learned to swim, shoot, and hunt. He attended the University of Oregon, receiving his Bachelor's degree in 1957. While there, he acted in college dramatic productions; following graduation, he made a brief attempt at acting in Hollywood. He received a writing fellowship for graduate work at Stanford University in Palo Alto, California.

When at Stanford, Kesey became a paid volunteer—$75 a day—for researchers who were studying psychotropic drugs, including LSD. He also began work as a ward attendant in a mental hospital. It was a quiet place where he could work on *Zoo*, a novel about North Beach in San Francisco. Presently Kesey abandoned *Zoo* and began *One Flew Over the Cuckoo's Nest* (New York: Viking, 1962), an allegorical tale set inside a mental hospital. Kesey's narrator is Chief Bromden, a huge, archetypal Indian, the son of a chief: ". . . your Vanishing American, six-foot sweeping machine, scared of its own shadow." The chief feigns the silence of a deaf mute; his narration goes from the naturalistic to the visionary. The fact that this book is considered a Western novel is more than a little a tribute to literary critics, particularly Leslie A. Fiedler who in *The Return of the Vanishing American* (New York: Stein and Day, 1969) made the somewhat expansive claim that any story featuring a Native American was, by definition, a Western.

Kesey's second novel, *Sometimes a Great Notion* (New York: Viking, 1964), is a book as powerful and complex as it is lengthy. It is about the end of the old urge to move West, about families that have left a trail of generations as they moved towards the Pacific Ocean. They move North to Oregon, to the last of the Western frontiers. Kesey's loggers still believe in omens but his Indians are whores; they stay indoors and cast spells, spending their allotments on booze and television sets.

Tom Wolfe's garrulous journal, *The Electric Kool-Aid Acid Test* (New York: Farrar, Straus, 1968), made Kesey almost better known as a character than as an author. It followed the years after Kesey's successes, telling of Rabelaisian, drugged revels with Kesey and the Merry Pranksters, a band of friends who included Stewart Brand, publisher of the "Whole Earth Catalogue," Neal Cassady, the model for Dean Moriarty in Jack Kerouac's *On the Road* (New York: Viking, 1957), and Larry McMurtry (q.v.).

Kesey became an ally of the Hell's Angels and an evangelistic hero for the drug culture before he was twice arrested for possession of marijuana in 1965 and 1966. Instead of facing the possibility of a five-year prison sentence, he jumped bail and fled to Mexico. He was captured by the F.B.I. when he returned to California. Disillusioned with the movement he championed, Kesey spent five months on a county work-farm, then left for Springfield, Oregon, going to work as a farmer and claiming that he would not write another novel until his family had grown to maturity.

Kesey may have been a two-book author, but any assessment of him must take into account the vision contained in *One Flew Over the Cuckoo's Nest*. The Anglo-

American has created a mechanical, hermetic, delusional world for himself; he is incapable of understanding either the natural order—which he would bend to his will—or the essential beauty in life. *One Flew Over the Cuckoo's Nest* is not merely a Western because it has a Native American in it; more importantly, it embodies within it the spiritual experience engendered by the West itself, an experience usually distorted or repressed in the Anglo-American view which perceives the land only for its use-value.   D.W.

Films based on Kesey's two novels are *Sometimes a Great Notion* (Universal, 1971) directed by Paul Newman and *One Flew Over the Cuckoo's Nest* (United Artists, 1975) directed by Milos Foreman.

Ketchum, Philip

(1902 —) A prolific author of formulary Western fiction, born at Trinidad, Colorado. Ketchum graduated from the University of Denver and also studied at Long Beach State College and New York University. He spent some years as a social worker in Nebraska, Colorado, and Arizona, and was at one time executive director of the Omaha Welfare Federation and Community Chest. During World War II he served as Pacific Coast director of the United Seamen's Service.

Already in the 'Thirties Ketchum had become a heavy contributor to the pulp magazines and over a twenty-year period he produced nearly a thousand stories for adventure, detective, and Western pulps. His first novel was a detective story, *Death in the Library* (New York: Thomas Y. Crowell, 1937). When Dell began publishing its line of paperbacks in 1943, this was the first novel to be issued.

Ketchum's main thrust, however, was in Western fiction, although several of his early paperbacks were expanded from stories he originally wrote for *Ranch Romances* and other pulps. These are strictly formulary Westerns, built out of standard ingredients: stolen herds, Apache attacks, greedy land barons, unjustly accused loners. But as familiar as these plot elements might be, they are handled with smooth skill; the characters are frequently offbeat and always interesting; and the action is well paced. Typical of these novels are *Desperation Valley* (New York: Popular Library, 1955), *The Elkhorn Feud* (New York: Popular Library, 1956), and *Dead Man's Trail* (New York: Popular Library, 1957). In *The Great Axe Bretwalda* (Boston: Little, Brown, 1955) Ketchum also tried his hand, with mixed results, at historical fiction.

In the books published in the late 'Fifties, Ketchum moved away from the easy plot resolutions of the formulary Western and introduced a note of cynicism and grimness not present in even the most violent of the earlier books. Two titles published in the same year mark the extremes of this transition. *Gun Code* (New York: Signet, 1959) and *The Hard Man* (New York: Avon, 1959) begin with the same situation, a young man returning after an absence of years to the town where his father had been killed and searching for the truth behind events that the town had thought safely buried. In *Gun Code* the young man finds friends on all sides, even among those he had thought guilty of the old crime, and wins through to safety and fortune with surprisingly little pain. In *The Hard Man*, on the other hand, the searcher finds that virtually the entire town had been guilty of his father's murder: those who did not take active part had, through venality or cowardice, allowed the crime to take place, and profited from it, had conspired to conceal it, and are now driven to new violence to keep the secret hidden. They ultimately fail, but the hero's victory is not without its emotional cost.

In the mid 'Sixties Ketchum created a series character for Lancer Books. Elijah Cabot Pickering, scion of a wealthy New England shipping family, goes West to make his fortune after a bitter quarrel with his father. Using only the name Cabot, he becomes known as *The Man Who Tamed Dodge* (New York: Lancer Books, 1967), *The Man Who Turned Outlaw* (New York: Lancer Books, 1967), and *The Man Who Sold Leadville* (New York: Lancer Books, 1968). Cabot is obsessed with the need to make money and this singlemindedness insulates him from any lasting relationships with the people he meets. Although the stories are smoothly told, the character cannot engage the reader's sympathies.

For a genre that has sometimes been accused of being a bastion of male chauvinism, the Western has produced a surprising number of strong, self-reliant female characters. Some of the most interesting appear in Ketchum's novels, such as Cora Dawes and the half-Cheyenne, Neh-anna, in *Wyoming* (New York: Ballantine, 1967) and Clara Rostig in *Buzzard Ridge* (New York: Ballantine, 1970). These and other novels written for Ballantine Books in the 'Sixties bear little resemblance to the formulary Westerns of Ketchum's early career. The settings are out

of the ordinary, the characters fully rounded, and the plot developments grow out of internal necessity rather than the external constraints of a traditional mold. It is for these books that Ketchum should be recognized.

R.E.B.

Philip Ketchum's Western novels are *Texan on the Prod* (1952), *Guns of the Barricade Bunch* (1953), *The Saddle Bum* (1953), *The Texas Gun* (1954), *Gun Law* (1954), *Desperation Valley* (1955), *Rider from Texas* (1955), *The Night of the Coyotes* (1956), *Longhorn Stampede* (1956), *The Elkhorn Feud* (1956), *The Big Gun* (1956), *Six-Gun Maverick* (1957), *Dead Man's Trail* (1957), *Feud at Forked River* (1958), *Decision at Piute Wells* (1959), *Gun Code* (1959), *The Deadshot Kid* (1959), *Gunfire Man* (1959), *The Hard Man* (1959), *Gunsmoke Territory* (1960), *Apache Dawn* (1960), *The Stalkers* (1961), *Traitor Guns* (1962), *Harsh Reckoning* (1962), *The Night Riders* (1966), *The Man from Granite* (1967), *Wyoming* (1967), *The Man Who Tamed Dodge* (1967), *The Man Who Turned Outlaw* (1967), *The Man Who Sold Leadville* (1968), *The Men of Moncada* (1968), *Cabot* (1969), *Mad Morgan's Hoard* (1969), *Support Your Local Sheriff* (1969), *Halfbreed* (1969), *Gila Crossing* (1969) *The Cougar Basin War* (1970), *Rattlesnake* (1970), *Buzzard Ridge* (1970), *Judgment Trail* (1971).

Support Your Local Sheriff (New York: Popular Library, 1969) was a novelization of *Support Your Local Sheriff* (United Artists, 1969) directed by Burt Kennedy.

King, Charles (1844–1933) Author
of historical romances set in the West, born
at Albany, New York. King was descended
from a distinguished line of American
statesmen, including having been the great-
grandson of Rufus King, one of the framers
of the Constitution. He grew up in the state
of Wisconsin where his father was editor of
the *Milwaukee Sentinel*. He was 16 at the
outbreak of the Civil War. King's father, a
West Point graduate, assumed command of
the famous Iron Brigade and rose to the rank
of Major General; his son served in the
Brigade as mounted orderly until his appointment to West Point by Abraham Lincoln. At the Academy King achieved the
highest possible cadet office, that of Cadet
Adjutant, before a scandal concerning theft
occurred in which King was mistakenly im-
plicated. He was suspended during the inquiry, impeached by circumstantial evidence, and was only cleared for
reinstatement when another cadet finally
confessed. For the rest of his life King
exhibited a nearly paranoid distrust of circumstantial evidence and the way it could
be misread; this concern became a major
theme in many of his novels and indeed
almost the whole plot of such books as *An
Apache Princess* (New York: Hobart, 1903).

King received his Army commission in
1866 and was sent to New Orleans to take
command of a Gatling gun platoon involved in putting down several Reconstruction riots. While stationed in Louisiana, he
met Adelaide Yorke whom he married in
1872. After briefly serving as an instructor at
West Point in 1870 he was shipped West to
join the Fifth Cavalry in Nebraska, General
Crook's regiment. He served in the field in
several Plains campaigns and was then—
two years after his wedding in New Orleans—transferred to the Arizona Territory
to participate, again under Crook, in the
campaigns against the Chiricahua and Mim-
breño Apaches. He fought at Diamond
Butte and Black Mesa and at Sunset Pass his
right shoulder was shattered by a bullet, an
injury which caused him to be invalided out
of active service for a year. By 1876 he was
back in battle, serving as Regimental Adjutant of the Fifth Cavalry against the Sioux in
Nebraska, Montana, and Dakota; he was in
the field with Crook when Custer was killed
at the Little Big Horn. A year later King was
transferred West to serve in the campaign
against the Nez Perce who were presumed
to be under the leadership of the heroic
Chief Joseph, after which, troubled again by
his shoulder wound, he retired in 1879 with
the rank of Captain and returned to his
native Wisconsin.

This notwithstanding, King found it impossible to stay out of uniform. Within
months he joined the Wisconsin Militia,
later to become the National Guard, and
soon was serving as a Colonel, training
week-end soldiers and administering the
state organization. King assumed a short-
lived job in Honolulu as the first U.S.
General of the Military Department of Hawaii. He organized that department swiftly
and then took command of an infantry brigade deployed in the Philippine Insurrec-

tion where he saw considerable action battling Moro rebels. Finally he returned to Wisconsin holding the rank of Brigadier General, promoted to Major General in 1929, and held his commission in the Wisconsin National Guard until 1932.

Throughout his active military and administrative career, King managed to write some fifty-seven novels, several hundred short stories and essays, as well as various collaborations on more than ten other books besides his novels. Not all of what he wrote was set in the West; in fact, much of it was not. King's first work was a limited edition pamphlet entitled *Campaigning with Crook* (1880) containing a series of newspaper sketches he had written and published for his father's newspaper, the *Milwaukee Sentinel*. King followed this with a novel, a romance set against the Indian campaigns in the West titled *The Colonel's Daughter: Or, Winning His Spurs* (1882). It established the formulas King would tend to use in his Western fictions: romantic intrigues, a carefully concealed secret, and a gossip-obsessed frontier fort amid an Indian campaign.

Five years later he continued the story with a sequel titled *Marion's Faith* (1887). King's novel *The Deserter* (1887) was a bestseller in its time and he quickly followed it with *Laramie; Or, The Queen of Bedlam* (1889). Convinced that he could make more money by writing more quickly, King invested in an Ediphone dictating machine in 1890 and used both it and a secretary to "manufacture" his books. He did produce novels at a faster rate, to be sure, but in style they underwent a very marked deterioration and their plots lacked either freshness or ingenuity. *Captain Blake* (1891), *Foes in Ambush* (1893), *An Army Wife* (1896), and *A Daughter of the Sioux*

(New York: Hobart, 1902), among others, simply cannot compare with his earlier books.

The strong points of King's fiction, however, the verisimilitude to the actual conditions of frontier Army life, remained essentially unchanged. All later writers of fiction concerned with the Cavalry/Indian battles owed him a debt. But whereas King might be reliable and accurate about fort life, he was unfortunately lacking in any sympathy whatsoever for Native Americans and he regarded all Indians as hopeless savages. While he often depicted Indian agents as blundering and self-serving, he was too aloof from his Indian characters ever to make them human for his readers. Indeed, in *An Apache Princess*, an Apache maiden is attracted to Neil Blakely, a Lieutenant of the Cavalry, and commits several vicious and violent acts in her romantic pursuit of him before he finally succeeds in convincing her that, he being white, and she being "red," she will be better off marrying one of her own people.

Charles King's novels with a frontier setting are *The Colonel's Daughter; Or, Winning His Spurs* (1883), *Kitty's Conquest* (1884), *Marion's Faith* (1886), *The Deserter* (1887), *From the Ranks* (1887), *Two Soldiers* (1888), *Laramie; Or, The Queen of Bedlam* (1889), *Dunraven Ranch* (1890), *Campaigning with Crook and Stories of Army Life* (1890) [short stories], *Starlight Ranch, and other Stories of Army Life on the Frontier* (1890) [short stories], *Captain Blake* (1891), *A Soldier's Secret; A Story of the Sioux War of 1890* (1892), *An Army Portia* (1893), *Foes in Ambush* (1893), *Sergeant Croesus* (1893), *The Story of Fort Frayne* (1895), *An Army Wife* (1896), *Trumpeter Fred; A Story of the Plains* (1896), *Trooper Ross and Signal Butte* (1896), *A*

Garrison Triangle (1896), *Warrior Gap: A Story of the Sioux Outbreak of 1868* (1897), *A Wounded Name* (1898), *Sunset Pass; Or, Running the Gauntlet Through Apache Land* (1900), *The Way of the West* (1902), *A Daughter of the Sioux* (1903), *An Apache Princess* (1903), *Captured; The Story of Sandy Ray* (1906), *The Further Story of Lieutenant Sandy Ray* (1906), *Tonio, Son of the Sierras; A Story of the Apache War* (1906), *Lanier of the Cavalry; Or A Week's Arrest* (1909).

Kinkaid, Matt. See Adams, Clifton.

Kirkland, Caroline Matilda

(1801–1864) Author credited with being the first writer exemplifying frontier realism in her fiction, born Caroline Stansbury at New York City. She was educated in New York in schools run by her aunt which Kirkland probably taught in after completing her own education. Her marriage in 1828 to William Kirkland, founder of the magazine *Christian Inquirer* and a land speculator, took her to Michigan in 1836 for six years. Her experiences living in a log cabin and enduring the hardships of frontier life, both mental and physical, were useful to her in her fictional works.

Upon the death of her husband, Kirkland took over as editor on the *Christian Inquirer,* served as editor on the *Union Magazine of Literature and Art,* and edited a series of gift annuals for numerous publishing houses. In her later years Kirkland was concerned with the less fortunate and devoted some of her writing to this issue. She died in her sleep. The family's literary tradition was carried on by her son, Joseph Kirkland, a writer of Midwestern stories, who was instrumental in encouraging the young Hamlin Garland (q.v.) to write.

A New Home—Who'll Follow? Or, Glimpses of Western Life (1839), written under the pseudonym Mrs. Mary Clavers, a fictional narrative cast in the form of letters to cultivated Eastern friends, was largely autobiographical. *Forest Life* (1842) and *Western Clearings* (1845), the latter a collection of short stories, followed, although *Western Clearings* is of less literary merit. Kirkland's gift for observation made her characters and descriptions of frontier life uniquely realistic in contrast to many of her contemporaries who romanticized the frontier. Kirkland was one of the first novelists to state clearly the role of women in the pioneering movement, although the idea of Eastern refinement obstinately informed all of her works.

Knibbs, H(enry) H(erbert)

(1874–1945) An author of Western fiction who, although born at Niagra Falls, Ontario, because of American parentage and living in the United States when he reached his majority, automatically became an American citizen. Known to his friends as Harry Knibbs, he attended Woodstock College at Woodstock, Ontario, at the age of 14. At 15, he went to Ridley College at St. Catherine's, Ontario, spending three years there. It was then that he migrated to Buffalo, New York, and found employment as a wholesale coal salesman with a Michigan/Ontario territory. He quit this to clerk in the Lehigh Valley Railroad office and then hoboed for two years in the Middle West. Returning to Buffalo, he married and went to work as a stenographer in the Division Freight Office of the B.R.P. Railway. When he was summoned to the Rochester office to become private secretary to the traffic manager, he built a house, but did not really settle. At 34 he rented out the house and enrolled at Harvard to study English, which he did for three years. In 1910, he migrated to California and wrote his first Western novel, *Lost Farm Camp* (Boston: Houghton Mifflin, 1912).

Knibbs then proceeded to travel extensively in California, New Mexico, and Arizona, hoping to duplicate in his books the accuracy of locale which he so admired in Eugene Manlove Rhodes' (q.v.) fiction. Rhodes had first met Knibbs while Knibbs was still working in the East for the railroad. Knibbs based his outlaw leader, "The Spider," in *The Ridin' Kid from Powder River* (Boston: Houghton Mifflin, 1919) on Rhodes and it almost disrupted their friendship because Rhodes felt Knibbs had taken unnecessary fictional liberties with the truth—in the novel Knibbs has "The Spider" give his young hero, Pete Annersley, a start on the owlhoot trail. Knibbs more than made up for his characterization, however, in *Partners of Chance* (Boston: Houghton Mifflin, 1921) in which he based his hero, Cheyenne Hastings, completely on Rhodes, making him a cheerful wanderer of the plains and deserts, a man always with a song on his breath, and a man who dislikes violence, a man who befriends John Bartley, a writer from the East, and for a while they become saddle pards. What Rhodes remembered of the West was its kindness and its generosity and so it is not surprising to find Knibbs commenting in this novel: "In direct and effectual kindliness, without obvi-

ously expressed sympathy, the Westerner is peculiarly supreme." Yet, whatever truth there was in this, and there was much, Knibbs himself as a novelist was purely epigonal. The notion of an author from the East coming to the West and writing, in effect a story within a story, was an old device by 1921. B.M. Bower (q.v.) had used it previously in *The Lure of the Dim Trails* (New York: Dillingham, 1907), as had Charles Alden Seltzer (q.v.) in *The Two Gun Man* (London: Outing, 1911), and, for that matter, as had Owen Wister (q.v.) in *The Virginian* (New York: Macmillan, 1902). Too often Knibbs' plots tend to be unduly flimsy, totally lacking in substance, and he did not have Rhodes' force of per-

Dust cover from H. H. Knibbs' Temescal *(Boston: Houghton Mifflin, 1925).*

sonality nor his charismatic dialogue to carry him. Beyond this, and even more disastrous, Knibbs too early became slavishly dependent on the ranch romance superstructure and so his books, most of which were run serially in Street and Smith pulp publications before hardbound appearance, always tend to disappoint in the end due to the need for a romantic contrivance, a flaw which was shared by many of Knibbs' contemporaries, some of them finer writers than he was.

Where Knibbs did shine was in his ability to characterize true Western types and particularly pioneer family life. In his final years, Knibbs began publishing stories in *The Saturday Evening Post*, which had been Rhodes' primary magazine market, and to flesh out *The Proud Sheriff* (Boston: Houghton Mifflin, 1934) by Rhodes, published posthumously, Knibbs wrote a lengthy and highly anecdotal introduction.

H.H. Knibbs' Western novels are *Lost Farm Camp* (1912), *Stephen March's Way* (1913), *Overland Red* (1914), *Sundown Slim* (1915), *Riders of the Stars* (1916), *Tang of Life* (1917), *Jim Waring of Sonora-Town* (1918), *The Ridin' Kid from Powder River* (1919), *Partners of Chance* (1921), *Wild Horses* (1924), *Temescal* (1925), *Sungazers* (1926), *Sunny Mateel* (1927), *The Tonto Kid* (1936).

Films based on H.H. Knibbs' Western fiction are *Overland Red* (Universal, 1920) directed by Val Paul remade as *The Sunset Trail* (Universal, 1924) directed by Ernst Laemmle, *Sundown Slim* (Universal, 1920) directed by Val Paul remade as *The Burning Trail* (Universal, 1925) directed by Arthur Rosson, *The Ridin' Kid from Powder River* (Universal, 1924) directed by Edward Sedgwick remade as *The Mounted Stranger* (Universal, 1930) directed by Arthur Rosson.

Knibbs contributed the original story for the film *Tony Runs Wild* (Fox, 1926) directed by Thomas Buckingham.

Knott, Will C(arol) (1927 —) Author of formulary Western fiction, born at Boston, Massachusetts. Knott attended elementary and secondary schools in Boston. He served in the U.S. Air Corps, stationed at Lowry Field in Denver, Colorado, until his discharge in 1947. In 1951, he graduated from Boston University and taught school in West Virginia, Connecticut, New Jersey, and New York. Knott's affection for the West began while he was stationed in Denver, and, whenever possible, he spent his summer months in the Western states. He began his literary career writing more than thirty juvenile novels—sports, mystery, and science fiction—under his own name and two pseudonyms, Bill J. Carol and Bill Knott. Having always enjoyed reading Westerns and believing native Westerners to be a friendly, genial people, Knott turned to writing Western fiction. He viewed the Western as a classic story form of good versus evil. *The Vengeance Seeker #1* (New York: Ace, 1975) was his first Western and also the first in a series of four books about the adventures of one-eyed Wolf Caulder, who in the first book is left to die after five saddle tramps have killed his parents. Perhaps the most interesting aspect of Knott's Western fiction is his ability to create interesting characters as in *Stampede* (New York: Berkley, 1978), a pursuit story in which two friends are placed at odds with each other.

"I believe in heroes and in a place and a land that makes them," Knott once said. "The West was that place because that is what we want it to be—that is what we need it to be. For me, writing fiction is a way of recreating a myth that many of us could do worse than to live by."

Will C. Knott's Western novels are *Vengeance Seeker #1* (1975), *Vengeance Seeker #2* (1975), *Vengeance Seeker #3* (1976), *Caulder's Badge* (1977), *Killer's Canyon* (1977), *Kiowa Blood* (1977), *Stampede* (1978), *Red Skies Over Wyoming* (1980), *The Golden Mountain* (1980), *Lyncher's Moon* (1980), *The Return of Zach Stewart* (1980).

Kyne, Peter B(ernard) (1880–1957)

An author born at San Francisco, California, whose association with Western fiction was peripheral at best, but whose influence, especially in terms of his contributions of stories for Western films, was significant. Educated in public schools, Kyne went to work at 16 in a general store. He particularly enjoyed sales work. He enlisted in the U.S. Army and saw action during the Spanish-American War. In 1910, he turned to writing and one of his short stories, "Broncho Billy and the Baby" (1910), appeared in *The Saturday Evening Post*. Screen rights were purchased by G.M. Anderson who went on to play the Broncho Billy character for years in hundreds of films. Kyne revised this story and published it as a novel, *Three Godfathers* (New York: Doran, 1913), which was to be subsequently filmed a total of six times, two of the film versions directed by John Ford. Basically a variation of the "divine child" archetype which Bret Harte (q.v.) employed in his short story, "The Luck of Roaring Camp" (1869), it tells of how three outlaws are "reformed" by happening on an infant baby in the desert wilderness. Kyne's fiction was so charged with sentimentality that it can no longer be read with pleasure, but during the middle decades of the Twentieth century he was one of the most popular American authors.

Peter B. Kyne's Western novels are *Three Godfathers* (1913), *The Valley of the Giants* (1918), *The Pride of Palomar* (1921), *Dude Woman* (1940).

Some of Kyne's short stories, usually from *The Saturday Evening Post*, inspired Western films, but he also wrote a number of original screen stories. Most of those listed as [source unknown] are of this latter variety. *Broncho Billy and the Baby* (Essany, 1908) was directed by G.M. Anderson. *Judge Not, or the Woman of Mona Diggins* (Universal, 1915) was directed by Robert Leonard and Harvey Gates [based on the short story "Renunciation"]. *What the River Foretold* (Universal, 1915) was directed by William Franey and Joseph Franz [source unknown]. *The Parson of Panamint* (Paramount, 1916) was directed by William Desmond Taylor [based on the short story of the same title] and remade under this title (Paramount, 1941) directed by William McGann. *The Three Godfathers* (Universal,

1916) was directed by Edward J. LeSaint and was remade as *Marked Men* (Universal, 1919) directed by John Ford, *Hell's Heroes* (Universal, 1929) directed by William Wyler, and then again as *The Three Godfathers* (M-G-M, 1936) directed by Richard Boleslawski, (M-G-M, 1948) directed by John Ford, and (ABC-TV, 1974) directed by John Badham. *A Motion to Adjourn* (Arrow, 1921) directed by Roy Clements [source unknown] was based on a Kyne story as were *The Innocent Cheat* (Arrow, 1921) directed by Ben Wilson [source unknown], *Red Courage* (Universal, 1921) directed by Reeves Eason [based on the short story "The Sheriff of Cinnabar"], *While Satan Sleeps* (Paramount, 1922) directed by Joseph Henabery [source unknown], *Back to Yellow Jacket* (Arrow, 1922) directed by Ben Wilson [source unknown], *One-Eighth Apache* (Arrow, 1922) directed by Ben Wilson [source unknown], *The Buckaroo Kid* (Universal, 1926) directed by Lynn Reynolds [based on the short story "Oh, Promise Me"], *War Paint* (M-G-M, 1926) directed by W. S. Van Dyke [source unknown], *California* (M-G-M, 1927) directed by W.S. Van Dyke [source unknown], *Galloping Fury* (Universal, 1927) directed by Reeves Eason [based on the short story "Tidy Toreador"],

A Hero on Horseback (Universal, 1927) directed by Del Andrews [based on the short story "Bread Upon the Waters"], *The Rawhide Kid* (Universal, 1928) directed by Richard Thorpe [source unknown], *Tide of Empire* (M-G-M, 1929) directed by Allan Dwan [source unknown], *Wild Horse* (Allied, 1931) directed by Richard Thorpe and Sidney Algier [source unknown], *The Local Bad Man* (Allied, 1932) directed by Otto Brower [source unknown], *Heroes of the West* (Universal, 1932) directed by Ray Taylor [a twelve chapter serial] [source unknown], *Flaming Guns* (Universal, 1932) directed by Arthur Rosson [source unknown], *Gallant Defender* (Columbia, 1935) directed by David Selman [source unknown], *Valley of Wanted Men* (Conn, 1935) directed by Alan James [source unknown], *The Mysterious Avenger* (Columbia, 1936) directed by David Selman [source unknown], *Secret Patrol* (Columbia, 1936) directed by David Selman [source unknown], *Code of the Range* (Columbia, 1936) directed by C.C. Coleman, Jr., [source unknown], *Stampede* (Columbia, 1936) directed by Ford Beebe [source unknown], *Belle Le Grande* (Republic, 1951) directed by Allan Dwan [source unknown].

L

La Farge, Oliver (Hazard Perry) (1901–1963)

Novelist, anthropologist, longtime president of the Association on American Indian Affairs and author of numerous short stories on the Southwest which deal primarily with the Indian, born at New York City to a highly respected Eastern family. La Farge included in his ancestry Benjamin Franklin and Oliver Hazard Perry. At a young age he was nicknamed "Indian Man" by his parents because of his dark hair and eyes. Educated at Groton, La Farge won letters in football, rowing, and track; then, in 1920, he entered Harvard where he rowed two years on the Harvard Varsity crew. In the summer of

Oliver La Farge

1921 he went on the Harvard expedition to Tsegi Canyon on the Navaho reservation in Arizona. There his interest in Indians as subject matter for fiction began. As early as 1922 La Farge had two stories appear in the *Harvard Advocate* which employed Navaho themes. During the summers of 1923 and 1924 he returned to the Navaho reservation where he increased his knowledge of and friendship with the Navaho nation. In 1924 he was awarded his Bachelor's degree *cum laude* in anthropology.

After graduation La Farge moved to New Orleans and accepted an appointment in the Department of Middle American Research as an ethnologist at Tulane University. This experience permitted him to become assistant director of the First Tulane Expedition to Central America. It was followed by another expedition to Guatemala which resulted in the publication of his first anthropological work, collaborating with Frans Blom, *Tribes and Temples* (New Orleans: Tulane University Press, 1927). Meanwhile La Farge was also concentrating on his literary career. His first commercial short story appeared in *Dial Magazine* in 1927. *Laughing Boy* (Boston: Houghton Mifflin, 1929), which deals with the Navaho Indian, Laughing Boy, and his love for Slim

Girl, a Navaho woman trapped between the Indian and white worlds, was his first novel and it won the Pulitzer Prize. "To choose Navaho Indians as your material," Owen Wister (q.v.) commented on *Laughing Boy*, "to exclude the white man, save as the merest accidental accessory, to depend wholly on a young Navaho lover and his mate—and to bring it off—is a most uncommon feat . . . a daring experiment, triumphantly successful." The novel was revolutionary in that it actually laid the ground work for the many realistic Indian novels to come and it was obviously written by a man who was sympathetic to the customs, traditions, philosophy, art, and religion of the Navahos about whom he wrote even though he was still very much an outsider. He once lamented, "I've always found it difficult to get people to believe that Indians are like what they really are. James Fenimore Cooper's (q.v.) devastating work is too well done."

In 1930 La Farge received the O. Henry Prize for his short story, "Haunted Ground," and that same year he received his Master's degree from Harvard and was elected a director of the Eastern Association of Indian Affairs. He became a research associate at Columbia University. The 'Thirties saw a tremendous increase in La Farge's literary output. *Sparks Fly Upward* (Boston: Houghton Mifflin, 1931) described one of the Indian leaders of the people's revolution in Central America; *All the Young Men* (Boston: Houghton Mifflin, 1935) was a collection of short stories, most notable for the story "Higher Education" which presented the excruciating problems of a young Indian girl educated at the white Indian school and then returned to the reservation. *The Enemy Gods* (Boston: Houghton Mifflin, 1937) was the crowning achievement of the decade and perhaps the best book he ever wrote, a perceptive and moving portrait of the difficulty, maybe the impossibility, of the Native American adapting to white culture. It was also during this time that La Farge became president of the Association on American Indian Affairs, a position which he held for the most part of the next thirty years.

Moving to Santa Fe, New Mexico, in 1940, La Farge continued to work closely with Native Americans, especially the Navahos and Apaches. From these endeavors came such anthropological works as *As Long as the Grass Shall Grow* (New York: Longmans, Green, 1940), *The Changing Indian* (Norman: University of Oklahoma Press, 1941), and eventually the juvenile book, *The American Indian* (New York: The Golden Press, 1960). He also published an introspective and interesting autobiography entitled *Raw Material* (Boston: Houghton Mifflin, 1945) which expressed many of his ideas on Native Americans and the misconceptions about them, as did his series of essays which appeared in *The Man with the Calabash Pipe* (Boston: Houghton Mifflin, 1966). *A Pause in the Desert* (Boston: Houghton Mifflin, 1957) and *Door in the Wall* (Boston: Houghton Mifflin, 1965) completed La Farge's collections of short stories, both of which reflect his anthropological and literary interest in the peoples of the Southwest and Central America.

He was lauded by the critics of his time for his treatment of Native Americans in his novels and stories, and he deserves recognition for having broken what was once new ground. He brought to the genre of Western fiction a tremendous understanding of, a feeling for, and a belief in Native Americans as human beings and his works contain the language rhythms and expressions of Native Americans, accurate, detailed descriptions of Indian life, and a genuine comprehension of the Indian thoughts and feelings of those nations which he studied.

D.K.-M.

Among the better studies devoted to Oliver La Farge are Lawrence Clark Powell's essay in *Southwest Classics* (Los Angeles: Ward Ritchie, 1974), Everett A. Gillis' *Oliver La Farge* (Austin: Steck-Vaughn, 1967), T.M. Pearce's *Oliver La Farge* (New York: Twayne Publishers, 1973), and, above all, D'Arcy McNickle's *Indian Man* (Bloomington: Indiana University Press, 1971).

L'Amour, Louis (1908 —) A particularly popular author of formulary Western fiction, born at Jamestown, North Dakota. When L'Amour's family lost their holdings during the agricultural depression of the early 1920s, L'Amour left home, traveling and working at a number of odd jobs. Toward the end of the 'Thirties, L'Amour tried his hand at writing, beginning with book reviews. He also wrote poetry. *Smoke from this Altar* (London: Lusk Publishers, 1939) contains thirty-nine of his poems.

During World War II, L'Amour served with the U.S. Tank Destroyer Corps and also with the Transportation Corps. It was not until sometime after the war that he seriously launched himself as a Western writer, contributing stories and serials to various pulp publications, such as *West Magazine* and *Giant Western*. His first Western novel was *Westward the Tide* (London: Worlds Work, 1950) which incorporated in embryonic form an ecological theme—concern for the conservation and preservation of natural resources and wild life forms—which would also preoccupy subsequent novels. Under the house name Tex Burns L'Amour wrote four Hopalong Cassidy novels for Doubleday & Company because the original creator of the character, Clarence E. Mulford (q.v.), no longer wanted to write about him and the publisher was anxious to cash in on the popularity that the old films and new television series which featured actor William Boyd in the role of Cassidy were having on television. L'Amour was required to draw the Cassidy character after Boyd's portrayal rather than the original red-headed, heavy-drinking, smoking, cursing, fighting gunslinger in the Mulford stories. Also during this same period, L'Amour wrote a number of stories and two novels under the pen-name Jim Mayo. When *Hondo* (New York: Fawcett, 1953), published under his own name, and *Utah Blaine* (New York: Ace, 1954), published under the Jim Mayo pseudonym, were made into motion pictures, L'Amour decided to write strictly under his own name, producing a minimum of three new novels every year. He settled in Los Angeles, married, and began to raise a family. Adept at the art of self-promotion, L'Amour merchandised both himself and his fiction, driving around the country in a motor home, appearing on radio talk shows as an expert on Western lore, and dressing himself in cowboy garb.

L'Amour's early Western fiction constitutes his best work, albeit limited by the formulary conventions which he adopted at the very beginning and never abandoned. *Hondo* is most often cited by critics as perhaps L'Amour's most noteworthy effort and it is entertaining reading, with its self-sufficient, taciturn, capable protagonist, its evocation of the desert lands of Arizona, and its dramatic, if unsympathetic, use of Apaches. *Last Stand at Papago Wells* (New York: Fawcett, 1957) provides an equally powerful evocation of the desert, but already this early L'Amour's prolificacy and his refusal to revise his first draft led to one of the characters counting six dead after an Indian attack when there were only five characters killed. Over the years this tendency worsened so that in *The Iron Marshal* (New York: Bantam, 1979), L'Amour called a character Bert on one page and Hank a few pages later; another character is introduced as a "lean, wiry old man" only to have him turn out to be 29; and still another character breaks into a Swedish accent for one bit of dialogue.

With the publication of *The Daybreakers* (New York: Bantam, 1960), L'Amour began the first of three family sagas, series in which he dealt with a number of different generations, featuring in each book various members of these sprawling families. The Sacketts were first, followed by the Chantrys, and then the Talons. The basis, presumably, for these family sagas derived from an experience L'Amour had when he was 16 and in New Mexico, involved in a street fight. "When it looked like I was winning," he once recalled, "the other guy's two friends started to jump me. There were two fellows in the crowd who pulled those guys off, and one took a club and suggested they let us alone to fight it out. Afterwards, we got to be good friends—

the men were cousins.... They told me they never got in fights because one had thirteen brothers and one had sixteen."

In L'Amour's *Guns of the Timberlands* (Jason Press, 1955) a distinction is made between two kinds of men, "them that come to build, and them that come to get rich quick and get out." L'Amour's villains are usually hybrids of this latter variety. In the same novel the reader is informed that one of the sympathetic characters "was a disciple of the belief that evil always gets what it deserves, and he enjoyed seeing his philosophy borne out." In L'Amour's West the builders are the winners. This is the historical fantasy which informs nearly all of his fiction. "They were tough, strong people, people with a vision and nerve," Scott R. McMillan wrote concerning L'Amour's Westerners in his Introduction to the reissue of L'Amour's *Showdown at Yellow Butte* (Boston: Gregg Press, 1980). "They did what they had to do when they had to do it, without compunction. They survived and they built. L'Amour knows this, loves this about them, and tells us this in all his stories." L'Amour's many Westerns celebrate the middle-class values of one-settlement culture in the United States and the stories with their super-heroes are so written that it would almost seem that Nature itself endorses this view.

While it is true that L'Amour's novels are structured so that a new action sequence or story element is introduced every eight hundred words or so, the technique does make for fast-pacing, and, for some readers, this is more than enough justification to overlook inconsistencies in characters or plotting.

Louis L'Amour's Western novels are *Westward the Tide* (1950), *Hondo* (1953), *Showdown at Yellow Butte* (1953), *Crossfire Trail* (1954), *Utah Blaine* (1954), *Kilkenny* (1954), *Heller with a Gun* (1955), *To Tame a Land* (1955), *Guns of the Timberland* (1955), *The Burning Hills* (1956), *Silver Canyon* (1956), *Last Stand at Papago Wells* (1957), *Sitka* (1957), *The Tall Stranger* (1957), *Radigan* (1958), *The First Fast Draw* (1959), *Taggart* (1959), *The Daybreakers* (1960), *Flint* (1960), *Sackett* (1961), *Shalako* (1962), *Killoe* (1962), *High Lonesome* (1962), *Lando* (1962), *Fallon* (1963), *Catlow* (1963), *Dark Canyon* (1963), *How the West Was Won* (1963), *Mojave Crossing* (1964), *Hanging Woman Creek* (1964), *Kiowa Trail* (1964), *The Highgraders* (1965), *The Sackett Brand* (1965), *The Key-Lock Man* (1965), *The Broken Gun* (1966), *Kid Rodelo* (1966), *Kilrone* (1966), *Mustang Man* (1966), *The Sky-Liners* (1967), *Matagorda* (1967), *Down the Long Hills* (1968), *Chancy* (1968), *Brionne* (1968), *The Empty Land* (1969), *The Lonely Men* (1969), *Conagher* (1969), *Galloway* (1970), *The Man Called Noon* (1970), *Reilly's Luck* (1970), *North to the Rails* (1971), *Under the Sweetwater Rim* (1971), *Tucker* (1971), *Callaghen* (1972), *Treasure Mountain* (1972), *Ride the Dark Trail* (1972), *The Quick and the Dead* (1973), *The Ferguson Rifle* (1973), *The Man from Skibbereen* (1973), *Sackett's Land* (1974), *The Californios* (1974), *The Man from the Broken Hills* (1975), *War Party* (1975) [short stories], *Rivers West* (1975), *Over the Dry Side* (1975), *To the Far Blue Mountains* (1976), *Where the Long Grass Blows* (1976), *The Rider of Lost Creek* (1976), *Borden Chantry* (1977), *The Mountain Valley War* (1978), *Fair Blows the Wind* (1978), *The Iron Marshal* (1979), *The Proving Trail* (1979), *Bendigo Shafter* (1979), *Yondering* (1980), *Comstock Lode* (1981).

L'Amour's Western novels as Tex Burns are *Rustlers of West Fork* (1951), *Trail to Seven Pines* (1951), *Riders of High Rock* (1951), *Trouble Shooter* (1951).

Films based on Louis L'Amour's Western fiction are *Hondo* (Warner's, 1953) directed by John Farrow, *Four Guns to the Border* (Universal, 1954) directed by Richard Carlson [source unknown], *Treasure of Ruby Hills* (Allied Artists, 1955) directed by Frank McDonald [based on the short story "Rider of the Ruby Hills"], *Stranger on Horseback* (United Artists, 1955) directed by Jacques Tourneur [source unknown], *Blackjack Ketchum, Desperado* (Columbia, 1956) directed by Earl Bellamy [based on *Kilkenny*], *The Burning Hills* (Warner's, 1956) directed by Stuart Heisler, *Utah Blaine* (Columbia, 1957) directed by Fred F. Sears, *The Tall Stranger* (Allied Artists, 1957) directed by Thomas Carr [based on the short story "Showdown Trail"], *Apache Territory* (Columbia, 1958) directed by Ray Nazarro [based on *Last Stand at Papago Wells*], *Guns of the Timberland* (Warner's, 1960) directed by Robert D. Webb, *Heller in Pink Tights* (Paramount, 1960) directed by George Cukor [based on *Heller with A Gun*], *Taggart* (Universal, 1965) directed by R.G. Springsteen, *Kid Rodelo* (Spanish, 1966) directed by Richard Carlson, *Hondo and the Apaches* (M-G-M, 1967) directed by Lee H. Katzin [based on the short story "The Gift of Cochise"], *Shalako* (Cinerama, 1968) directed by Edward Dmytryk, *Catlow* (M-G-M, 1971) directed by Sam Wannamaker.

A television series was made based on the Hondo character, *Hondo* (ABC, 1967–1968), and the Sackett saga was made the basis for a mini-series, *The Sacketts* (NBC, 1979).

Lane, Rose Wilder (1887–1968)

An author who wrote a number of stories dealing with the pioneer experience, born in a "claim shanty" near De Smet, Dakota Territory. The daughter of Almanzo Wilder and Laura Ingalls Wilder (q.v.), the author of the "Little House" books, Lane's birth and childhood experiences living on a homestead were related in Wilder's posthumous book, *The First Four Years* (New York: Harper's, 1971). The Wilder family was unable to get by on their homestead and when Lane was still a child they moved to the Ozark Mountain region of Missouri. After graduating from high school in Crowley, Louisiana, where the Wilder family had settled for a time, Lane moved to San Francisco where she worked as a reporter and feature writer for a local newspaper. She was also employed as an office clerk, a telegrapher, and she sold farm land before marrying Gilette Lane in 1909 whom she divorced in 1918. In 1920, she made her first of several trips to Albania where she lived in medieval surroundings in the mountains. Her best known work, *Peaks of Shala* (New York: Harper's, 1923), a nonfiction book, resulted from this trip as well as several short stories and articles.

Lane spent most of her life in New York producing short stories and articles for various popular periodicals besides writing her books. She authored the "official" biographies on Henry Ford and Herbert Hoover. She also claimed at one time to have been the ghost writer of Frederick O'Brien's *White Shadows in the South Seas* (New York: Century, 1919) although she later stated she acted only as his secretary and the book was his own. She remained active all of her life and in 1966, at the age of 78, she was sent to Vietnam as a war correspondent. At the time of her death from a heart attack she was planning a world tour.

In the mid 'Twenties, Lane began writing stories set in the Ozark Mountains region of Arkansas and Missouri and was considered the region's official spokesperson. Although competently written, Lane's pioneer stories lack depth of character and appear to be weak imitations of her mother's stories. In *Let the Hurricane Roar* (London: Longmans, Green, 1933), her best pioneer story re-issued in paperback as *Young Pioneers* (New York: Bantam, 1976), she made use of a strong female character who is forced to spend the winter alone with her baby in an isolated homestead dugout. The struggles and hardships her characters are forced to endure are told with little feeling as was also true in *Free Land* (London: Longmans, Green, 1938). This story, set in the Dakota Territory during the 1880s, describes a young couple's first five years in the West.

Young Pioneers (ABC, 1975) was based on *Let the Hurricane Roar*.

Lanham, Edwin Moultrie (1904—)

An author of Southwestern fiction, born at Weatherford, Texas. Lanham attended Williams College in 1923–1926 and studied art in Paris 1926–1930. Upon returning to the States, he became a reporter for the *New York Evening Post* in 1930 and remained in newspaper work until 1944 when he quit to become a fulltime free-lance writer. *The Wind Blew West* (New York: Longmans Green, 1935) was his first novel, telling the story of people lured by railroad speculators to a town in West Texas where one of the principal characters is a Prohibition lawyer. This was followed by *Banner at Daybreak* (New York: Longmans, Green, 1937), a sort of sequel in which the career of the lawyer's expatriate son is traced from his life in France through his return to the Southwest. *The Stricklands* (Boston: Little, Brown, 1939) was concerned with tenant farmers in Oklahoma, published the same year that John Steinbeck (q.v.) published his novel of the Oklahoma exodus, *The Grapes of Wrath* (New York: Covici, Friede, 1939). Lanham's fourth novel was titled *Thunder in the Earth* (New York: Harcourt, Brace, 1941) and dealt with sudden oil wealth in Texas. In 1942 it received an award as the best Texas novel of the previous year from the Texas Institute of Letters. Lanham then turned to writing detective and mystery fiction.

Lawrence, D(avid) H(erbert)

(1885–1930) English novelist, poet, essayist, and playwright born at Eastwood, Nottinghamshire, England. Although best known for his controversial erotic fiction, Lawrence spent much of his time during 1922–1925 in the Southwestern United States. It was his last great creative period and he produced a wealth of regional essays and poems, in addition to several short stories, a short novel, and a novel set in this region.

Son of a coalminer and a teacher, Lawrence broke the barriers of his class through self-education, scholarships, and teaching posts. His unhappy childhood in a mining town made him hate industrialism and served as a background to much of his early fiction. His first novel, *The White Peacock* (London: Heinemann, 1911), appeared the same year his teaching career ended due to an illness diagnosed as tuberculosis and it was this illness which would eventually cause his death. He went to Germany in 1912 with Frieda Weekley née von Richthoven, the wife of a professor, whom he married in 1914 once she secured a divorce. During the First World War, Lawrence resided in England, living precariously by his writing, until 1919 when he moved abroad. In 1922 he visited Ceylon and Australia prior to his arrival in the United States on 22 September. Mabel Dodge Luhan, the art patroness, was instrumental in getting Lawrence to go to Taos, New Mexico, which was fast becoming an important artists' colony frequented by such writers as Mary Austin (q.v.) and Willa Cather (q.v.). "The moment I saw the brilliant, proud morning shine high up over the deserts of Santa Fe," Lawrence later wrote, "something stood still in my soul, and I started to attend."

Lawrence's Southwestern writings were given their first impetus through his contact with the Indians; almost immediately after his arrival he attended the annual fiesta on the Jicarilla Apache reserve. The ceremonials accompanied by the mesmerizing drumming had an overwhelming effect on him. Although Lawrence intended originally to write a novel set in New Mexico, a trip to Mexico City in early 1923 altered his plans and his novel, *The Plumed Serpent* (New York: Knopf, 1926), with its emphasis on landscape and archaic rituals, was set in old Mexico. By June, 1923 Lawrence had written the first draft of the novel. However,

before completing his final draft, which he did in late 1925, he wrote two short stories and the short novel, *St. Mawr* (New York: Knopf, 1925) in 1924. "The Woman Who Rode Away" was a short story about a bored, frustrated wife who escapes to her freedom only to be used as a sacrificial victim by an isolated tribe of Indians. The short story "The Princess" was written after Lawrence's horseback tour of the Sangre de Cristo mountains. Lawrence Clark Powell in *Southwest Classics* (Los Angeles: Ward Ritchie, 1974) wrote about "The Princess": "Here is the essence of his genius for the description of nature and sexual conflict between a primitive man and a sophisticated woman, between the native and the foreign, instinct and intellect. It is a touchstone for all Southwestern writing." Lawrence carried over his abhorrence of the parasites of industrial society in England to his short novel, *St. Mawr*, although the closing chapters were set in Texas and on his ranch, known as Kiowa Ranch, which was twenty miles from Taos.

Although Lawrence had wanted to title his novel *Quetzalcoatl* after the ancient deity of the Aztec Indians, his publisher, Alfred A. Knopf, preferred to use the translation, *The Plumed Serpent*. The story deals with a European woman who, having severed her ties with her past, travels to Mexico in search of some kind of fulfillment. She becomes involved with two men who are attempting to revive the primitive religion of the ancient Aztecs. The opening chapters are largely autobiographical and include a bullfight which was based on Lawrence's own experience in Mexico City when he had been a spectator at a bullfight which he found extremely brutal. Lawrence had an uncanny ability to assimilate a culture in a very short period of time and was always able to capture a sense of place in his novels. Katherine Anne Porter (q.v.) in her essay on Lawrence's novel, titled "Quetzalcoatl" (1926) and contained in *The Days Before* (New York: Harcourt, Brace, 1952), wrote that "all of Mexico that can be *seen* is here, evoked clearly with the fervor of things remembered out of impressions that filled the mind to bursting. There is no laborious building up of local color, but an immense and prodigal feeling for background, for every minute detail seen with the eyes of a poet." The book, however, was considered a failure upon publication due quixotically to the fact that critics wanted to know why Lawrence did not do what his heroine had done, to wit, stay in Mexico and follow the religion of Quetzalcoatl.

Lawrence's essays on everyday life in the Southwest and on Indian rituals were collected in one of his many classic travel books, *Mornings in Mexico* (New York: Knopf, 1927), while his *Studies in Classic American Literature* (New York: Thomas Seltzer, 1923) includes essays on the work of James Fenimore Cooper (q.v.) and was praised by many.

For further information on D.H. Lawrence see *Lorenzo in Taos* (New York: Knopf, 1932) by Mabel Dodge Luhan and *D.H. Lawrence in Taos* (Albuquerque: University of New Mexico Press, 1971) by Joseph Foster.

Lawton, Dennis. See Faust, Frederick.

Lea, Tom, Jr. (1907 —) Western novelist, historian, and artist-illustrator, born at El Paso, Texas. Lea's father, who had come to El Paso as a lawyer, became a judge, and finally was elected the city's mayor. Among his friends was J. Frank Dobie (q.v.), a prominent student of Texas lore whose books Tom, Jr., was to illustrate profusely and well.

Lea grew up on horseback, riding out over the open desert and into the mountains, areas that dominate his paintings and his writing. Although he wrote some poetry, it was to art that Lea turned first. After graduating from high school, he went to the Art Institute in Chicago and became a muralist of note with commissions from the U.S. Post Office in Washington, D.C., the U.S. Courthouse in El Paso, and the El Paso Public Library. During World War II, Lea turned equally to writing when he became an artist-correspondent for *Life* magazine and traveled with the American Armed Forces. His first published pieces were from this period. After the war, Lea became a book and magazine illustrator until a *Life* assignment to paint different kinds of cattle involved him in his first self-illustrated novel, *The Brave Bulls* (Boston: Little, Brown, 1949), a realistic yet glamorous story about bullfighting in Mexico that won several critical literary awards.

In *The Wonderful Country* (Boston: Little, Brown, 1952) Lea returned to the Southwest of his childhood experiences and recreated El Paso in the 1880s as El Puerto (The Door), the border city between Mexico and Texas. The hero, Martin Brady, can redeem himself by joining the Texas Rangers, or continue his wild life as a hired gun bound in loyalty to the Casas family who raised him. Lea manages to have this American think as a Mexican as he crosses the border into what is now unfamiliar territory to him. *The Wonderful Country,* well-illustrated by Lea, was even more popular than his first novel.

Lea's next artistic and literary venture was a two-volume history of *The King Ranch* (Boston: Little, Brown, 1957) which won the Summerfield Roberts Prize as the best book of Texas history of that year as well as the 1957 Book Design Award from the Dallas Museum of Fine Arts. History is sometimes stranger than fiction, and this double book is dramatically written with all the urgency of an adventure story.

The Hands of Cantu (Boston: Little, Brown, 1964) again focuses on men and animals. Here the story is about the importance of raising the best Spanish horses in the New World and the hands that must train them properly, that must bring civilization to the land. It is this combination of the old and the new in juxtaposition to each other that fascinated Lea the most and brought out the best dramatic qualities of his writing and his art.

P.O.

The Brave Bulls (Columbia, 1951) was directed by Robert Rossen and *The Wonderful Country* (United Artists, 1959) was directed by Robert Parrish.

For further information see *Tom Lea, Artist in Two Mediums* (Austin: Steck-Vaughan, 1967) by John O. West.

Lee, Ranger. See Snow, Charles H.

Leighton, Lee. See Overholser, Wayne D.

LeMay, Alan (1899–1964) Author of Western fiction, screenwriter, and occasionally a film producer, born at Indianapolis, Indiana. LeMay attended Stetson University in Deland, Florida, and graduated in 1922 from the University of Chicago. He served as a Second Lieutenant in the U.S. Infantry in 1918 and was a First Lieutenant with the Illinois National Guard 1923–1924. LeMay sold his first short story when 16 years old and, upon graduation, turned to writing as a career. His first published novel, *Painted Ponies* (New York: Doran, 1927), was a Western and in some ways the most balanced Western novel he was ever to write. It contained several themes that would be elaborated in his later fiction, telling the story of Slide Morgan who is relentlessly pursued by Abner Cade because Slide has killed Cade's brother and, in the course of his flight, Slide joins up with the Cheyenne Indians on their long trek back to their homeland from their U.S. Government captivity on a reservation in the Southwest. While the trek itself would be better treated in greater depth by subsequent authors as Mari Sandoz (q.v.), LeMay's sympathies were clearly with the Indians and he devoted a moving chapter to their eventual slaughter by the U.S. Cavalry. Insofar as he attempted to show both the Native American and white points of view in *Painted Ponies*, the novel might almost serve as a prototype for more recent novels written by Will Henry (q.v.).

In the next decade, LeMay produced several novels, a number of them rather routine Westerns until he entered the motion picture industry as a screenwriter. In the late 'Thirties and throughout the 'Forties, LeMay scripted several films, a few of which are worthy of mention. His novel *Useless Cowboy* (New York: Farrar and Rinehart, 1943) was adapted by him for Gary Cooper's first independent production, *Along Came Jones* (RKO, 1945), and he adapted Zane Grey's (q.v.) *Twin Sombreros* (New York: Harper's, 1940) for the first Ranown production, *Gunfighters* (Columbia, 1947) starring Randolph Scott.

Following *Useless Cowboy*, LeMay wrote only three more novels before his death, and it is on these that his reputation seems to rest. *The Searchers* (New York: Harper's, 1954)—the novel ran serially in *The Saturday Evening Post* which had a longstanding anti-Indian editorial policy—tells of Amos Edwards' six year search, together with young Mart Pauley, for Edwards' niece, Debbie, captured by the Comanches when she was 11. It is a theme perhaps better treated by Benjamin Capps (q.v.) in *A Woman of the People* (New York: Duell, Sloan, 1966), but it excited both critical and popular acceptance at the time of its publication. John Ford chose to film it, although he had to romanticize the Amos Edwards character to fit John Wayne who portrayed him; hence, Edwards could not die at the end, as he did in the novel, and in the film he even came out a hero.

The Unforgiven (New York: Harper's, 1957) also ran in *The Saturday Evening Post* and, predictably, the Kiowas are depicted as even more brutal savages than the Comanches are in *The Searchers*. LeMay was able to accomplish this because, unlike *Painted Ponies*, he made no effort to ever characterize the Indians or their way of life, much less their point of view. Yet, in *The Unforgiven*, LeMay did deal dramatically with cultural differences between "red" and white as he saw them according to his own anti-Indian bias, placing all the blame on tradition; and he made a contrast between a white raised among the Kiowas and Rachel Zachery, a girl suspected of having Indian blood, raised among white settlers. Race

and savagery were, in LeMay's view, as culture, wholly relative.

In his last novel, *By Dim and Flaring Lamps* (New York: Harper's, 1962), as in *The Searchers* and *The Unforgiven*, LeMay demonstrated again his solid virtues as a novelist, his ideological intent to one side: his graphic sense of place, a fastidious reconstruction of what pioneer life was from the white point of view, and his adept talent for building and sustaining suspense and conflict.

Alan LeMay's Western novels are *Painted Ponies* (1927), *Gunsight Trail* (1931), *Bug Eye* (1931), *Winter Range* (1932), *Cattle Kingdom* (1933), *Thunder in the Dust* (1934), *The Smoky Years* (1935), *Useless Cowboy* (1943), *The Searchers* (1954), *The Unforgiven* (1957), *By Dim and Flaring Lamps* (1962).

LeMay adapted his novel *Useless Cowboy* and wrote the screenplay for *Along Came Jones* (RKO, 1945) directed by Stuart Heisler. He provided original stories and screenplays for *The Walking Hills* (Columbia, 1949) directed by John Sturges and *Rocky Mountain* (Warner's, 1950) directed by William Keighley. He provided the screenplays for *San Antonio* (Warner's, 1945) directed by David Butler, *Cheyenne* (Warner's 1947) directed by Raoul Walsh, and *Gunfighters* (Columbia, 1947) directed by George Waggner. He worked as writer/producer on the twenty minute short subject *Trailin' West* (Warner's, 1949) directed by George Templeton and on the features *The Sundowners* (Eagle-Lion, 1950) directed by George Templeton and *High Lonesome* (Eagle-Lion, 1950) which LeMay himself directed.

The Searchers (Warner's, 1956) was directed by John Ford and *The Unforgiven*

(United Artists, 1960) was directed by John Huston.

Leonard, Elmore (1925 —) An author of Western fiction, born at New Orleans, Louisiana. In 1936 Leonard's family moved to Detroit, Michigan, and Leonard remained in the Detroit area. He graduated from the University of Detroit in 1950 with a Bachelor's degree. He began writing in 1951 and could not decide whether to specialize in crime fiction or Westerns, but finally determined to write Western fiction, researching Arizona, Apaches, and the U.S. Cavalry. He subscribed to *Arizona Highways* to give him a visual feel for the terrain he intended to describe. His first published work was a short novel with an Apache/Cavalry background which appeared in *Argosy*. For the next eight years, Leonard continued to write in his spare time, producing five Western novels and some thirty short stories. The short story "3:10 to Yuma," which first appeared in *Dime Western* in 1953 and was subsequently anthologized by Peter Dawson (q.v.) in *The Killers* (New York: Bantam, 1955), was made into a successful and controversial motion picture. "The Hostages" (1956) which appeared in *Argosy* became the basis for *The Tall T* (Columbia, 1957) directed by Budd Boetticher.

Leonard's first Western novel was *The Bounty Hunters* (Boston: Houghton Mifflin, 1954) and was followed by *The Law at Randado* (Boston: Houghton Mifflin, 1955), *Escape from Five Shadows* (Boston: Houghton Mifflin, 1956), *Last Stand at Saber River* (New York: Dell, 1957), and *Hombre* (New York: Ballantine, 1961). This last was again used as the basis for a very successful film of the same title, *Hombre* (20th-Fox, 1967) directed by Martin Ritt and featuring Paul Newman.

"My objective has always been to write lean prose," Leonard once said, "authentic-sounding dialogue, and a plot, a story that comes out of the characters—because of who they are—rather than simply throwing characters into a tight situation." It is perhaps due to this objective that virtually all of Leonard's Western fiction escaped the formulary molds so common to the genre. His protagonists occasionally die at the end of a story; his characters, especially the men, are never black and white, invariably human, flawed, and subject to passion. Beyond this, Leonard remained committed to action and his stories are usually told through action. In the late 1970s, after extraordinary success as a mystery/suspense writer, Leonard returned once more to the Western and published *Gunsights* (New York: Bantam, 1979).

Films based on Elmore Leonard's Western fiction are *The Tall T* (Columbia, 1957) directed by Budd Boetticher [based on the short story "The Hostage"], *3:10 to Yuma* (Columbia, 1957) directed by Delmer Daves [based on the short story of the same title], *Hombre* (20th-Fox, 1967) directed by Martin Ritt, *Valdez is Coming* (United Artists, 1971) directed by Edwin Sherin [based on the original novel of the same title published by Fawcett Gold Medal (1970)].

Lewis, Alfred Henry (1858–1914) Author known for local color in his Wolf-

ville stories written under the pseudonym "Dan Quin," born at Cleveland, Ohio. Lewis began his career in journalism working as a Washington correspondent for *The Chicago Times*. His interest in the West and his travels there prompted him to create the character of the "Old Cattleman" who narrates the Wolfville stories, the first of which appeared in the *Kansas City Star* in 1890. They were eventually collected into a series of volumes published under Lewis' real name, the first of which was *Wolfville: Episodes of Cowboy Life* (New York: Stokes, 1897), followed by *Sandburrs* (New York: Stokes, 1898), *Wolfville Days* (New York: Stokes, 1902), *Wolfville Nights* (New York: Stokes, 1902), *Wolfville Folks* (New York: D. Appleton, 1908), and finally, *Faro Nell and Her Friends* (New York: Dillingham, 1913). As Bret Harte (q.v.) and Owen Wister (q.v.), Lewis stressed local color, but unlike Harte he did so at the expense of a well-made plot and unlike either Harte or Wister he was hampered by his narrator who has a penchant, as have many of Mayne Reid's (q.v.) characters, to talk in the vernacular making Lewis' stories less than enjoyable for a modern reader.

Lewis did produce one somewhat influential novel with a Western setting. This was *The Sunset Trail* (New Jersey: A.S. Barnes, 1905) and is a novelized biography of Bat Masterson whom Lewis knew and to whom he dedicated the book. It initiated the trend of flattering portraits of frontier lawmen which culminated in the 'Thirties in popular biographies by Stuart N. Lake and William Noble Burns (q.v.) that were similarly idealizing about Wyatt Earp (see Historical Personalities).

Films based on Alfred Henry Lewis' Western fiction are *Dead Shot Baker* (Vitagraph, 1917) directed by William Duncan

[based on *Wolfville Stories*], *The Tenderfoot* (Vitagraph, 1917) directed by William Duncan [source unknown], *Faro Nell, or in Old Californy* (Paramount, 1929) directed by William Watson [based on *Faro Nell and Her Friends*].

Logan, Ford. See Newton, Dwight Bennett.

Lomax, Bliss. See Drago, Harry Sinclair.

London, Jack (1876–1916) An author noted for his Northland fiction, born John Chaney at San Francisco, California, the illegitimate son of W.H. Chaney and Flora Wellman. Eight months after Jack's birth, his mother married John London of Pennsylvania and the couple led a precarious life running a grocery store and then a chicken ranch and finally a boarding house. London claimed later that he had had no childhood and perhaps in a sense he had not. Once he learned of his origin, he made every effort to cover it up and fabricated numerous stories about his descent from frontier scouts and trappers. What perhaps alone saved him was his discovery of the world of books at the Oakland Public Library and from the age of 10 on he became an avid reader. Odd jobs on paper routes, in canneries, in bowling alleys, in jute mills, on ice wagons, at ten cents an hour for a ten-hour day, or longer hours yet, gave him a permanent distaste for the drudgery and tragedy of the working class. It early made him a socialist.

At 15 to escape work for poverty wages, he went on the road as a tramp, which earned him the nickname of "Sailor Kid" by riding the blinds over the Sierra Nevadas. At 16 he tried being an oyster pirate and his wanderlust finally took him to sea aboard the eighty ton sealing vessel, the *Sophie Sutherland*, bound for Japan and Siberia. It was while on this voyage that he began the bouts of heavy drinking which he later would record vividly in his semiautobiographical novel, *John Barleycorn* (New York: Century, 1913).

Deciding to live by his brain rather than his brawn, once London returned to San Francisco, at 19, he entered as a freshman at Oakland High School. He was jailed for an attack on capitalism at City Hall Park and the newspapers labeled him "The Boy Socialist." Cramming nineteen hours a day, he managed to enter the University of California, but had to leave before this first year was completed in order to support his mother and step-father by working in a laundry. When gold was discovered in the Klondike in 1896, London thought this might be the answer and, borrowing enough money to get there, he set out. Of the human horde heading to the Klondike, only 50,000 ever reached the interior and only 1,000 returned richer than when they started. London was not one of the latter group. In fact, he apparently worked but little at actual mining, spending most of his time in saloons talking to old-timers about the gold rushes they had been in. London was prudent enough, however, to perceive that of the $60,000,000 spent on outfits and transport only $10,000,000 was ever mined from the ground and that most of this went to the giant corporations which followed after the prospectors and relieved them of their claims as soon as they were profitable. London learned, in the words of Andrew Sinclair in *Jack: A Biography of Jack London* (New York: Harper's, 1977), "it is the old story, that in America riches are gained not by stooping to till the earth, but by ripping out the treasures that lie beneath."

Returning again to San Francisco, Jack found that his step-father had died. He went back to day-laboring, but also intent on becoming a writer, working with the fresh material he had gained from his experiences in the Northland.

In 1899 the *Atlantic Monthly* bought his story "An Odyssey of the North" which, as a breath of fresh air, introduced readers to the Northland as London had experienced it. It was the first of a series of truly remarkable short stories which showed men and animals pitted against Nature, or men against animals, or men against men, such as "To Build a Fire," which was collected in *Lost Face* (New York: Macmillan, 1910) and showed the difficulty of survival in the cold wastelands; "In a Far Country," which was collected in *The Son of the Wolf* (Boston: Houghton Mifflin, 1900), and showed the devastating effects on two men of cabin fever during the long winter; "The Law of Life," which was collected in *Children of the Frost* (New York: Macmillan, 1902), and told of an old Indian left by his tribe to starve because of their poverty and hunger. The spirit of these stories culminated in what may well remain London's most lasting contribution to world literature, *Call of the Wild* (New York: Macmillan, 1903), which on the surface is a dog story, but which, beneath that surface, becomes an allegory for modern man's struggle to dominate Nature in which Nature and wilderness triumph when Buck, a wolf-dog, follows the wolf pack into the wastelands and becomes their leader. London was in such desperate financial need that he sold the book to the publisher for a flat $2,000 only to see it sell well over a million and a half copies. London sought to reverse Buck's story when he wrote *White Fang* (New York: Macmillan, 1906) where he attempted to tell a story of a dog which becomes domesticated in the end. It was almost as if he was transfixed all his life and vacillated between the endings of Mark Twain's (q.v.) *The Adventures of Huckleberry Finn* (1884) and Charles Dickens' *Oliver Twist* (1837–1839). In the short story "Bâtard," collected in *The Faith of Men and Other Stories* (New York: Macmillan, 1904), he varied all these themes and told of a dog and a man held together by hate until, at last, the dog, whipped and tormented by the man, is able to kill him. In perhaps his finest evocation of man's relationship to the land, "All Gold Canyon," collected in *Moon-Face and Other Stories* (New York: Macmillan, 1906), London showed the horrible waste and rape of the earth perpetrated by man.

London went on to write stories with many different settings, the most notable probably being those he set in the South Seas, but his Northern adventures, which were so often so much more than that, inspired an entire school of fiction which was often not more than adventure stories, many of the early novels of Rex Beach (q.v.), much of the fiction James Oliver Curwood (q.v.), James B. Hendryx (q.v.) and even Max Brand's (q.v.) early fiction.

As Earle Labor, one of London's best critics, wrote in his Introduction to *The Great Short Works of Jack London* (New York: Harper's, 1965): ". . . when London writes that 'Like giants they toiled, days flashing on the heels of days like dreams as they heaped the treasure up,' he is obviously modulating his imagery in terms of a farther and deeper music than that of the ordinary, phenomenal world. Buck's is a world of the *unconscious* (Jung called it the 'collective unconscious'), the primordial world against which modern man has erected inhibiting barriers of rationality and the social ethic but a nonetheless real world to which he would return, in dreams, to find his soul." London's Northland fiction and stories as "All-Gold Canyon" capture the frontier spirit of the Westward expansion just after the American frontier had closed; and the savagery with which men hacked and tore and left the land in ruins was a phenomenon that would persist. It is to London's credit as a writer that he found no romance in this.

Films based on Jack London's Northland fiction are *Two Men of the Desert* (Biograph, 1913) directed by D.W. Griffith [source unknown], *The Mohican's Daughter* (American Releasing Corp., 1922) directed by S.E.V. Taylor [based on the short story "The Story of Jees Uck"], *The Son of the Wolf* (Robertson-Cole, 1922) directed by Norman Dawn [based on the short story "The Son of the Wolf"], *Stormy Waters* (Tiffany, 1928) directed by Edgar Louis [based on the short story "Yellow Handkerchief"], *Smoke Bellew* (First Division, 1929) directed by Scott Dunlap [based on the book *Smoke Bellew* (New York: Macmillan, 1912)], *Wolf Call* (Monogram, 1939) directed by George Waggoner [source unknown], *Queen of the Yukon* (Monogram, 1940) directed by Phil Rosen [source unknown—this and the prior film probably just used London's name as a box-office draw], *North to the Klondike* (Universal, 1942) directed by Erle C. Kenton [based on the short story "Gold Hunters of the North"], *Alaska* (Monogram, 1944) directed by George Archinbaud [based on the short story "Flush of Gold"].

Call of the Wild was brought to the screen a total of three times under this title, (Biograph, 1908) directed by D.W. Griffith, (Pathé, 1923) directed by Fred Jackman, and (United Artists, 1935) directed by William Wellman. *White Fang* was also filmed three times under this title, (F.B.O., 1925) directed by Larry Trimble, (20th-Fox, 1936) directed by David Butler, and (American Cinema, 1975) directed by Peter Collinson.

Irving Stone's *Jack London, Sailor on Horseback* (Boston: Houghton Mifflin, 1938; New York: Doubleday, 1978) cannot be recommended by itself because of its flagrant errors, but it does have a rare vividness and he did bring Jack London alive as a personality. Therefore, it is best to temper this book with Andrew Sinclair's *Jack: The Biography of Jack London* (New York: Harper's, 1977) and Earle Labor's biographical *and* critical study, *Jack London* (New York: Twayne Publishers, 1974).

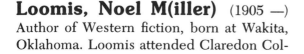

Loomis, Noel M(iller) (1905 —)
Author of Western fiction, born at Wakita, Oklahoma. Loomis attended Claredon Col-

lege in 1921 and the University of Oklahoma in 1930. Between these years he worked as a printer, editor, and free-lance journalist all over the West. In the early 'Fifties, with the publication of *Rim of the Caprock* (New York: Macmillan, 1952), he launched his career as an author of Western fiction. Perhaps his best-known Western novel is *Johnny Concho* (New York: Fawcett, 1956), but he won a Silver Spur Award from the Western Writers of America for *Short Cut to Red River* (New York: Macmillan, 1958). In another direction he published in fictional form stories involving characters from such popular television Western series as *Have Gun, Will Travel* (New York: Dell, 1960) and *Bonanza* (New York: Popular Library, 1960). He also published a notable history, *The Texas–Santa Fe Pioneers* (Norman: University of Oklahoma Press, 1958). Although Loomis' Western fiction exhibits a general historical accuracy, he also tended to stress violence and the ruthless savagery of frontier life and too often he resorted to formulary conventions.

Noel M. Loomis' Western novels are *Rim of the Caprock* (1952), *Trouble on Crazyman* (1953), *The Buscadero* (1953), *Tejas Country* (1953), *West to the Sun* (1955), *North to Texas* (1955), *Johnny Concho* (1956), *Wild Country* (1956), *Hang the Men High* (1957), *The Maricopa Trail* (1957), *Wells Fargo, Danger Station* (1958) [based on the television series *Tales of Wells Fargo* (NBC, 1957–1962)], *Short Cut to Red River* (1958), *Above the Palo Duro* (1959), *Cheyenne War Cry* (1959), *Have Gun, Will Travel* (1960) [based on the television series (CBS, 1957–1963)], *Bonanza* (1960) [based on the television series (NBC, 1959–1973)], *Ferguson's Ferry* (1962).

Johnny Concho (United Artists, 1956) was directed by Don McGuire.

Lutz, Giles A(lfred) (1910 —) Prolific author of formulary Western novels written under his own name and the pseudonyms Reese Sullivan, Wade Everett, Gene Thompson, James B. Chaffin, Hunter Ingram, Alex Hawk, Sebastian Morales, and Zeke Carson, born at Kansas City, Missouri. For a ten year period Lutz raised pedigree Black Angus cattle and in 1954 he published his first Western novel, *Fight or Run* (New York: Popular Libarary, 1954). He won the Spur Award from the Western Writers of America for his book *The Honyocker* (New York: Doubleday, 1961) which was voted the best Western novel for that year. A big rancher versus homesteader story, in this novel Lutz presented a sympathetic portrait of homesteaders although by the fade, beaten by the land, they relinquish their homesteads. The theme of the weak brother was used in *The Honyocker*—in this case two weak brothers—which Lutz used again in the subsequent *Lure of the Outlaw Trail* (New York: Doubleday, 1979). In this latter story the protagonist's lazy, greedy twin brothers join Butch Cassidy's Hole-in-the-Wall gang fearing that if they do not get rich quick they will end up as their broken-down father.

Lutz' knowledge of historical events and people were often incorporated into the framework of his fictional story-lines as is the case in *The Magnificent Failure* (New York: Doubleday, 1967) in which he included as a character Louis Riel, leader of the Western Canadian *metis* (people of mixed French-Canadian and Indian ancestry). His novels, however, cannot be considered historical novels since he often created ridiculous situations for these historical persons, as in *The Outsider* (New York: Fawcett, 1973) in which the protagonist teaches Mangas Coloradas, the great war chief of the Apaches, jujitsu. Lutz, as Lewis B. Patten (q.v.) and Clifton Adams (q.v.), can be ranked as a competent storyteller who included plenty of action in his well-plotted stories. Romance plays an important part in his books, and, upon occasion he drew interesting female characters who do not slow down the story. Also he was able to draw very admirable old people of integrity and conviction. In the 'Sixties, Lutz authored a number of "modern sex novels" under the pen-names Curt Conovan and Brad Curtis, anticipating (although he never joined it) the later trend toward porno-Westerns.

Giles A. Lutz' Western novels under his own name are *Fight or Run* (1954), *To Hell and Texas* (1956), *The Golden Bawd* (1956), *Fury Trail* (1957), *Gun the Man Down* (1957), *Outcast Gun* (1958), *Relentless Gun* (1958), *The Challenger* (1960), *The Homing Bullet* (1960), *The Wild Quarry* (1961), *The Honyocker* (1961), *The Long Cold Wind* (1962), *Gun Rich* (1962), *The Golden Land* (1963), *Halfway to Hell* (1963), *Killer's Trail* (1963), *The Blind Trail* (1964), *The Bleeding Land* (1965), *The Hardy Breed* (1966), *The Magnificent Failure* (1967), *Wild Runs the River* (1968), *The Lonely Ride* (1971), *The Unbeaten* (1972), *The Outsider* (1973), *The Grudge* (1974), *The Offenders* (1974), *The Black Day* (1974), *Blood Feud* (1974), *The*

Stubborn Breed (1975), *Stagecoach to Hell* (1975), *My Brother's Keeper* (1975), *Night of the Cattlemen* (1976), *A Drifting Man* (1976), *The Way Homeward* (1977), *A Time for Vengeance* (1977), *The Turnaround* (1978), *The Ragged Edge* (1978), *The Shootout* (1978), *Lure of the Outlaw Trail* (1979), *The Echo* (1979), *Killer's Trail* (1980), *The Great Railroad War* (1981), *Thieve's Brand* (1981).

Lutz' novels as Reese Sullivan are *The Blind Trail* (1960), *Nemesis of Circle A* (1965), *Dead Like a .45* (1966), *The Demanding Land* (1966), *The Trouble Borrower* (1968), *The Deadly Deputy* (1969), *Man on the Run* (1971), *The Stranger* (1972).

Lutz' novels as Gene Thompson are *Six Guns Wild* (1957), *Range Law* (1962), *The Branded One* (1964), *Ambush in Abilene* (1967), *Massacre* (1974), *The Deserter* (1974).

Lutz' novels as Alex Hawk are *Tough Town* (1969), *Drifter's Luck* (1970), *Mexican Standoff* (1970), *Half Breed* (1971).

Lutz' novels as Sebastian Morales are *The Cicano Kid* (1973), *Trail of Blood* (1975).

Lutz' novels as Hunter Ingram are *The Trespassers* (1965), *Man Hunt* (1967), *Contested Valley* (1968), *The Long Search* (1969), *Forked Tongue* (1970), *Border War* (1972), *Fort Apache* (1975), *The Forbidden Land* (1975).

Lutz' novels as James B. Chaffin are *Guns of Abilene* (1959), *The Wolfer* (1968).

Lutz' novel as Wade Everett is *The Whiskey Trailers* (1968) and his novel as Zeke Carson is *Buffalo Soldier* (1975).

McCaig, Robert Jesse (1907 —)

Author of formulary Western fiction born at Seattle, Washington. Very early in his life McCaig moved with his family to Great Falls, Montana, where he attended local public schools. In 1925 he went to work for the Montana Power Company of Great Falls, in the accounting division, and remained with the utility until his retirement as division chief accountant in 1972.

McCaig turned to writing Western fiction as an avocation with *Toll Mountain* (New York: Dodd, Mead, 1953), and the next year became a member of the Western Writers of America. Most of McCaig's Western novels are highly entertaining and some employ an unusual hero and plot. In *The Shadow Maker* (New York: Ace, 1970), for example, a frontier photographer who captures in pictures the commission of a train robbery is forced by circumstances to become a member of the outlaw band while actually working undercover for a vigilante group. McCaig was not above employing heroes who resort to means other than gunplay to solve social crises, and occasionally his protagonists demonstrate deep Roman Catholic sentiments.

Robert McCaig's Western novels include *Toll Mountain* (1953), *Haywire Town* (1954), *Danger West* (1954), *Bronc Stomper* (1956), *Snow on the Prairie* (1958), *The Rangemaster* (1958), *Wild Justice* (1958), *Drowned Man's Lode* (1959), *The Burntwood Men* (1961), *That Nester Kid* (1962), *Crimson Creek* (1962), *The Gotherson Spread* (1966), *The Shadow Maker* (1970), *The Danger Trail* (1975), *The Stone-*

man's Gap (1976), *Marcy Tarrant* [with Edith McCaig] (1978), *The Devil's Band* (1981).

Pass (1981), *Mustang Fever* (1981), *Silver Slot* (1981), *The Legend of the Lone Ranger: A Novelization* (1981).

McCarthy, Gary (1923 —) Author of

Western fiction in a formulary mode, born at South Gate, California. "I spent my childhood in Los Angeles riding horses and watching the skies go from blue to gray and the pungent dairies and citrus groves being replaced with tract houses and freeways," McCarthy once commented. "I joined the Navy at 17 in search of adventure. There was no adventure. I never left the great naval hospital of San Diego. But I tended the sick and I heard the old ones tell their last stories. Sometimes, I wrote about them." McCarthy attended the University of California at Pomona and the University of Nevada at Reno. He made his appearance on the Western scene with the publication of *The Derby Man* (New York: Doubleday, 1976).

The Derby Man is about Darby Buckingham, a portly New Yorker who writes dime novels and decides to go West to find story material. He finds it in a town where Sheriff Zeb Cather, an aging lawman, is up against desperate odds. Together, Darby and Cather stand side by side confronting the deadly guns of the Ratons. The book was successful enough for McCarthy to launch Darby as a series character.

Gary McCarthy's Western novels are *The Derby Man* (1976), *The First Sheriff* (1979), *The Showdown at Snakegrass Junction* (1979), *The Pony Express War* (1980), *Winds of Gold* (1980), *Explosion at Donner*

McCrackin, Josephine (1838–

1920) Author of short stories set in the Southwest and a noted conservationist, born Josephine Woempner at Petershagen, Germany. In 1846 the Woempner family immigrated to the United States, settling in St. Louis, Missouri, where McCrackin was educated. After traveling extensively in the Southwest with her husband, Jackson McCrackin, (whom she married in 1864 and who suffered from paranoia), McCrackin finally left him because of his repeated threats on her life. In 1869, in order to support herself, Josephine submitted a sketch about her experiences in wartime Washington, D.C., to Bret Harte's (q.v.) magazine, *The Overland Monthly*. Harte encouraged her to write about her adventures in the Southwest and his influence can be seen in her stories which combine melodramatic events with a realistic Western setting.

Many of McCrackin's stories are autobiographical in that they deal with heroines fleeing their mates and their subsequent difficulties in earning a living in a society that distrusts an independent woman. McCrackin had limited literary talent but her description of desert scenery and military life were written with love and enthusiasm and American writers as Ambrose Bierce found both McCrackin and her stories "most interesting." Her short stories, which were first published in various magazines, were collected in three volumes—*Overland Tales* (1877), *Another Juanita* (1893), and *The Woman Who Lost Him* (Pasadena: G.W. James, 1913).

McCulley, Johnston (1883–1958)

Author of Western fiction known chiefly as the creator of that Robin Hood facsimile of Old California, Zorro, born at Ottawa, Illinois. McCulley got his start writing for the pulp magazines, particularly *All-Story Magazine* and *Adventure*. It was in this format that many of his serialized novels were purchased by motion picture companies and then, subsequent to the release of the film versions, the novels were issued in book form. *The Curse of Capistrano* is a case in point. It was filmed as *Mark of Zorro* (United Artists, 1920) directed by Fred Niblo and starring Douglas Fairbanks, Sr., as Zorro. In book form it was published as *The Mark of Zorro* (New York: Grosset & Dunlap, 1924). Having purchased rights to the character, Fairbanks then, using an entirely different story and one not written by McCulley, made *Don Q, Son of Zorro* (United Artists, 1925).

Throughout the 'Twenties several other magazine serials McCulley published under his own name and, in one instance, under the pseudonym Harrington Strong, were used as the basis for films. Finally, in the mid 'Thirties, moving to Hollywood, McCulley became active as a screenwriter, either producing original stories and screenplays, such as that of *The Outlaw Deputy* (Puritan, 1935), or simply suggesting story ideas, such as that for *The Bold Caballero* (Republic, 1937), yet another entry in the Zorro series. McCulley continued working in the film industry throughout the 'Forties and it was only near the end of his life that he returned again to writing Western fiction with such novels as *Iron Horse Town* (New York: Arcadia House, 1952) and *Texas Showdown* (New York: Arcadia House, 1953).

Films based on the Zorro character created by Johnston McCulley are *Mark of Zorro* (United Artists, 1920) directed by Fred Niblo, *Don Q, Son of Zorro* (United Artists, 1925) directed by Donald Crisp, *The Bold Caballero* (Republic, 1936) directed by Wells Root, *Zorro Rides Again* (Republic, 1937) directed by William Witney and John English [a twelve chapter serial], *Zorro's Fighting Legion* (Republic, 1939) directed by William Witney and John English [a twelve chapter serial], *Mark of Zorro* (20th-Fox, 1940) directed by Rouben Mamoulian, *Zorro's Black Whip* (Republic, 1944) directed by Spencer Gordon Bennet and Wallace Grissell [a twelve chapter serial], *Son of Zorro* (Republic, 1947) directed by Spencer Gordon Bennet and Fred C. Brannon [a thirteen chapter serial], *Ghost of Zorro* (Republic, 1949) directed by Fred C. Bannon [a twelve chapter serial].

In 1959 Walt Disney produced an ABC-TV series called *Zorro* that lasted one season of 39 episodes. In 1960–1961 Disney ran four one-hour segments of *Zorro* on his weekly television program. In the interim, parts of this series were spliced together to form the theatrical motion picture *The Sign of Zorro* (Buena Vista, 1960) directed by Norman Foster and Lewis R. Foster and *Zorro the Avenger* (Buena Vista, 1961) directed by Charles Barton. The character then carried on sort of a half-life in several

European productions the first of which was *Il Segno di Zorro* (Italian, 1952) directed by Mario Soldati retitled for its American release *Zorro's Dream,* followed by *Zorro the Avenger* (Spanish, 1961) directed by Joequin Luis Romero Marchent, *Zorro E I Tre Moschettiere* (Italian, 1961) directed by Luigi Capuano retitled for its American release *Zorro and the Three Musketeers,* *Zorro Contro Maciste* (Italian, 1961) directed by Umberto Lenzi retitled for its American release *Zorro Vs. Maciste. Zorro and the Three Musketeers* changed its title again for American television release to *Mark of the Musketeers* and *Zorro Vs. Maciste* became on American television *Samson and the Slave Queen.* Next came *Il Segno di Zorro* (Italian, 1963) directed by Mario Caiano retitled for its American release *Mark of Zorro, Three Swords of Zorro* (Italian, 1964) directed by Richard Blasco, *Oath of Zorro* (Spanish-Italian, 1963) directed by Richard Blasco, *Shade of Zorro* (Italian-Spanish, 1963) directed by Francesco De Masi, *Behind the Mask of Zorro* (Italian, 1964) directed by Richard Blasco, *Adventures of the Brothers X* (Mexican, 1964) directed by Frederic Curiel, *The Masked Avengers* (Mexican, 1964) directed by Frederic Curiel, *The Lone Rider* (Mexican, 1964) directed by Ralph Baledon, *The Valley of the Disappearing* (Mexican, 1964) directed by Ralph Baledon, *Zorro, the Rebel* (Italian, 1966) directed by Piero Pierotti, *Grandsons of Zorro* (Italian, 1968) directed by Franco Franchi and Ciccia Ingrassia, *Zorro, the Navarra Marquis* (Italian, 1969) directed by Francois Monty, *El Zorro* (Italian, 1969) directed by Georgi Ardisson, *Zorro at English Court* (Italian, 1969) directed by Franco Montemorro, *Zorro, the Knight of the Vengeance* (Spanish, 1970) directed by Jose Louis Merion, *Zorro the Domineer* (Span-

ish, 1970), *Erotic Adventures of Zorro* (Entertainment Ventures, 1972) directed by Colonel Robert Freeman [an X-rated version of the Zorro story], *El Hijo Del Zorro* (Italian-Spanish, 1973) directed by Gian Franco Baldanelle, *Mark of Zorro* (ABC-TV, 1974) directed by Don McDougall [a made-for-television motion picture], *Zorro* (United Artists, 1975) directed by Duccio Tessari, *Zorro, The Gay Blade,* (20th-Fox, 1981) directed by Peter Medak.

Other films based on McCulley's stories are *The Kiss* (Universal, 1921) directed by Jack Conway [based on the short story "Little Erolinda"], *Captain Fly-By-Night* (Robertson-Cole, 1922) directed by William K. Howard [based on the novel *Captain Fly-By-Night* (New York: G.H. Watt, 1926)], *Ride for Your Life* (Universal, 1924) directed by Edward Sedgwick [source unknown], *The Ice Flood* (Universal, 1926) directed by George B. Seitz [based on the short story "The Brute Breaker"], *Black Jack* (Fox, 1927) directed by Orville E. Dull [based on the short story "The Broken Dollar"], *Saddle Mates* (Pathé, 1928) directed by Richard Thorpe [based on the magazine serial of the same title (1924) published under the pseudonym Harrington Strong], *The Trusted Outlaw* (Republic, 1937) directed by R.N. Bradbury [source unknown].

Of the more than fifty screenplays and screen stories on which McCulley worked, he is credited with the following original Western film stories: *The Outlaw Deputy* (Puritan, 1935) directed by Otto Brower, *Rootin' Tootin' Rhythm* (Republic, 1937) directed by Mack Wright, *Rose of the Rio Grande* (Monogram, 1938) directed by William Nigh, *Overland Mail* (Universal, 1942) directed by Ford Beebe and John Rawlins [a fifteen chapter serial], *Outlaws of Stampede Pass* (Monogram, 1943) directed by

Wallace Fox, *South of the Rio Grande* (Monogram, 1945) directed by Lambert Hillyer [this was a Cisco Kid film], *Mark of the Renegade* (Universal, 1951) directed by Hugo Fregonese.

MacDonald, William Colt

(1891–1968) Author of formulary Western fiction born at Detroit, Michigan. MacDonald completed grammar school and three months of high school before he quit and turned to writing for trade magazines and doing publicity work in the Detroit area. This was not, however, serious writing and it was not until 1929 that MacDonald decided that he had best forego all other employment and concentrate on Western fiction, publishing his first novel, *Restless Guns* (New York: Chelsea House, 1929). "I quit my job cold," MacDonald later recalled. "I said if I was going to be a writer, why wasn't I writing fiction. I had a lot of luck. My wife was pregnant. She said, go ahead and write. Lots of help, severest critic, and all that. I sold *Restless Guns* first as a magazine serial and then as a book."

MacDonald's early success at having his Western fiction published led him to Hollywood. In 1932 MacDonald worked in the story department at Columbia Pictures doing screenplays for that studio's series Westerns with Tim McCoy in many of which MacDonald combined a mystery plot along with the usual Western ingredients. The best of these, surely, was *Man of Action* (Columbia, 1933). It was also while at Columbia that MacDonald developed the concept of a sagebrush trio of frontier do-gooders based on Alexandre Dumas' idea of *les trois mousquetaires*. The first book appearance of MacDonald's "Three Mesquiteers" was *Law of the Forty-Fives* (New York: Covici, Friede, 1933) and it was brought to the screen in 1935. By 1936 Republic Pictures began filming Mesquiteer pictures on a regular annual schedule while MacDonald continued writing Western novels, some with the Mesquiteers, many without them.

His basic plot in most of his novels in the 'Thirties and 'Forties, no matter who his hero or heroes, is that of an invincible gunman or a trio of gunmen riding into a troubled area controlled by a master outlaw with a large gang and cutting down the odds until the master outlaw is dispatched in the last chapter. This notion was far from original with MacDonald. It was a plot already adumbrated by Eugene Cunningham (q.v.) and Cunningham, in his novel *Riders of the Night* (Boston: Houghton Mifflin, 1932), even anticipated the idea of the "Three Mesquiteers," referring by this appellation to three of his characters.

With *Gunsight Range* (New York: Doubleday, 1949) MacDonald introduced another character who would soon inspire his own series, Gregory Quist, railroad detective. This idea was no more original. It could be traced back to Frank H. Spearman's (q.v.) Whispering Smith or even some of the detective Western novels of W.C. Tuttle (q.v.). But, for all that, the Quist books are sometimes entertaining in their own right.

MacDonald himself claimed, and not without justification, that *The Mad Marshal* (New York: Pyramid, 1958) was his best novel. It is the story of a disreputable town marshal who forms a very profitable liaison with the madam of a brothel and proceeds thoroughly to swindle the town until, of course, he is caught in the end. But the characterizations are among MacDonald's best and Arvila Priest, the madam, is by far his best female creation.

William Colt MacDonald's Western novels are *Restless Guns* (1929), *Gun Country* (1929), *Don Gringo* (1930), *Rustlers' Paradise* (1932), *Law of the Forty-Fives* (1933), *Six-Gun Melody* (1933), *Powdersmoke Range* (1934), *Riders of the Whistling Skull* (1934), *The Singing Scorpion* (1934), *King of the Crazy River* (1934), *Ghost Town Gold* (1935), *Roarin' Lead* (1935), *The Red Rider of Smoky Range* (1935), *Bullets for Buckaroos* (1936) [reissued as *Bullet Trail*], *California Caballero* (1936), *Trigger Trail* (1936), *The Deputy of Carabina* (1937), *Spanish Pesos* (1937), *Sleepy Horse Range* (1938), *Six-Shooter Showdown* (1939), *Black Sombrero* (1940), *The Phantom Pass* (1940), *Renegade Roundup* (1940), *The Battle at Three-Cross* (1941), *Boomtown Buccaneers* (1942), *The Crimson Quirt* (1942), *The Riddle of Ramrod Range* (1942), *The Shadow Rider* (1942), *Rebel Ranger* (1943), *The Vanishing Gunslinger* (1943), *The Three Mesquiteers* (1944), *Cartridge Carnival* (1945), *Thunderbird Trail* (1946), *Wheels in the Dust* (1946), *Bad Man's Return* (1947), *Master of the Mesa* (1947), *Dead Man's Gold* (1948), *Gunsight Range* (1949), *Powdersmoke Justice* (1949), *The Killer Brand* (1950), *Mesquiteer Mavericks* (1950), *Stir up the Dust* (1950), *Blind Cartridges* (1951), *Ranger Man* (1951), *The Galloping Ghost* (1952), *Three-Notch Cameron* (1952), *Law and Order Unlimited* (1953), *Lightning Swift* (1953), *Mascarada Pass* (1954), *The Range Kid* (1955), *The Comanche Scalp* (1955), *Destination Danger* (1955), *The Devil's Drum* (1956), *Flaming Lead* (1956), *Ridin' Through* (1957), *Action at Arcanum* (1958), *Blackguard* (1958), *The Mad Marshal* (1958), *Guns Between Sons* (1959), *Tombstone for a Troubleshooter* (1960), *The Gun Branders* (1960), *Wildcat Range* (1961), *West of Yesterday* (1964), *The Osage Bow* (1964), *The Gloved Saski* (1964), *Fugitive from Fear* (1966), *Marked Deck at Topango Wells* (1968), *Alias Dix Ryder* (1969).

Western films based either on books by MacDonald or characters created by him are *Law of the 45's* (First Division, 1935) directed by J.P. McCarthy, *Powdersmoke Range* (RKO, 1935) directed by Wallace Fox, *Too Much Beef* (Colony, 1936) directed by Robert Hill, *The Three Mesquiteers* (Republic, 1936) directed by Ray Taylor, *Ghost Town Gold* (Republic, 1936) directed by Joseph Kane, *Roarin' Lead* (Republic, 1936) directed by Mack V. Wright and Sam Newfield, *Riders of the Whistling Skull* (Republic, 1937) directed by Mack V. Wright, *Hit the Saddle* (Republic, 1937) directed by Mack V. Wright, *Gunsmoke Ranch* (Republic, 1937) directed by Joseph Kane, *Come on Cowboys* (Republic, 1937) directed by Joseph Kane, *Range Defenders* (Republic, 1937) directed by Mack V. Wright, *Heart of the Rockies* (Republic, 1937) directed by Joseph Kane, *The Trigger Trio* (Republic, 1937) directed by William Witney, *Wild Horse Rodeo* (Republic, 1937) directed by George Sherman, *The Purple Vigilantes* (Republic, 1938) directed by George Sherman, *Call the Mesquiteers* (Republic, 1938)

Julian Rivero (l.) and Tim McCoy (r.) in a scene from Man of Action *(Columbia, 1933) directed by George Melford with an original screenplay by William Colt MacDonald.*

directed by John English, *Outlaws of Sonora* (Republic, 1938) directed by John English, *Riders of the Black Hills* (Republic, 1938) directed by George Sherman, *Heroes of the Hills* (Republic, 1938) directed by George Sherman, *Pals of the Saddle* (Republic, 1938) directed by George Sherman, *Overland Stage Raiders* (Republic, 1938) directed by George Sherman, *Santa Fe Stampede* (Republic, 1938) directed by George Sherman, *Red River Range* (Republic, 1938) directed by George Sherman, *The Night Raiders* (Republic, 1939) directed by George Sherman, *Three Texas Steers* (Republic, 1939) directed by George Sherman, *Wyoming Outlaw* (Republic, 1939) directed by George Sherman, *New Frontier* (Republic, 1939) directed by George Sherman, *The Kansas Terrors* (Republic, 1939) directed by George Sherman, *Cowboys from Texas*

(Republic, 1939) directed by George Sherman, *Heroes of the Saddle* (Republic, 1940) directed by William Witney, *Pioneers of the West* (Republic, 1940) directed by Lester Orlebeck, *Covered Wagon Days* (Republic, 1940) directed by George Sherman, *Rocky Mountain Rangers* (Republic, 1940) directed by George Sherman, *Oklahoma Renegades* (Republic, 1940) directed by Nate Watt, *Under Texas Skies* (Republic, 1940) directed by George Sherman, *The Trail Blazers* (Republic, 1940) directed by George Sherman, *Lone Star Raiders* (Republic, 1940) directed by George Sherman, *Prairie Pioneers* (Republic, 1941) directed by Lester Orlebeck, *Pals of the Pecos* (Republic, 1941) directed by Lester Orlebeck,

A one-sheet from Powdersmoke Range *(RKO, 1935) based on the novel by William Colt MacDonald. Pictured on top are Guinn "Big Boy" Williams (l.), Hoot Gibson, Tom Tyler, and Harry Carey with "Boots" Mallory and Bob Steele pictured below.*

Saddlemates (Republic, 1941) directed by Lester Orlebeck, *Gangs of Sonora* (Republic, 1941) directed by John English, *Outlaws of the Cherokee Trail* (Republic, 1941) directed by Lester Orlebeck, *Gauchos of El Dorado* (Republic, 1941) directed by Lester Orlebeck, *West of Cimarron* (Republic, 1941) directed by Lester Orlebeck, *Code of the Outlaw* (Republic, 1942) directed by John English, *Raiders of the Range* (Republic, 1942) directed by John English, *Westward, Ho* (Republic, 1942) directed by John English, *The Phantom Plainsmen* (Republic, 1942) directed by John English, *Shadows on the Sage* (Republic, 1942) directed by John English, *Valley of Hunted Men* (Republic, 1942) directed by John English, *Thundering Trails* (Republic, 1943) directed by John English, *The Blocked Trail* (Republic, 1943) directed by Elmer Clifton, *Santa Fe Scouts* (Republic, 1943) directed by Howard Bretherton, *Riders of the Rio Grande* (Republic, 1943) directed by Albert De Mond.

During MacDonald's tenure as a screenwriter at Columbia Pictures, he wrote the stories for the following Western films in Columbia's Tim McCoy series: *Texas Cyclone* (Columbia, 1932) directed by D. Ross Lederman, *The Riding Tornado* (Columbia, 1932) directed by D. Ross Lederman, *Two-Fisted Law* (Columbia, 1932) directed by D. Ross Lederman, *Daring Danger* (Columbia, 1932) directed by D. Ross Lederman, *The Western Code* (Columbia, 1932) directed by J.P. McCarthy, *Man of Action* (Columbia, 1933) directed by George Melford.

McElroy, Lee. See Kelton, Elmer

MacLeod, Austin. See Raine, William MacLeod.

McMurtry, Larry (Jeff) (1936 —)
Magazine writer and book reviewer whose early novels were set in contemporary Texas, born at Wichita Falls, Texas. McMurtry grew up in the environs of Archer City, Texas, which became Thalia in his subsequent novels. Receiving his Bachelor's degree from North Texas State College in 1958, McMurtry was already at work on his first novel, *Horseman, Pass By* (New York: Harper's, 1961). Upon publication, it had a very poor trade sale—about fifteen hundred copies—but it was sold to motion pictures and filmed under the title *Hud* (Paramount, 1963) starring Paul Newman. The novel also earned McMurtry the Jesse Jones Award of the Texas Institute of Letters in 1961, a Wallace Stegner Fellowship at Stanford University, a Guggenheim Fellowship, and an instructorship in English at Rice University. In 1959, McMurtry married and in 1960 he received a Master's degree from Rice University.

Horseman, Pass By is concerned with an adolescent boy coming of age in rural Texas in the present day. It established both the structure and the themes of much of McMurtry's later fiction. The structure seems to be a projection of Edgar Allan Poe's "The Fall of the House of Usher" (1839) into the modern West. The family we meet at the beginning is devastated at the end. McMurtry's principal theme is an obsession, almost adolescent in its urgency, with sexuality, including sexual intercourse with animals.

Leaving Cheyenne (New York: Harper's, 1963) was McMurtry's second novel. It deals with a relationship so improbable and grotesque that even McMurtry himself, in his collection of autobiographical literary essays, *In a Narrow Grave* (Austin: Encino Press, 1968), admitted it is a "male journalist's fantasy." The plot, simply put, is about a woman who prefers for forty years sleeping with two men who are best friends, as if this were the most natural and ordinary thing she could do. No effort is made to probe into the obvious psychological complexity such a *ménage à trois* would need to survive much less remain stable.

The Last Picture Show (New York: Dial, 1966) found McMurtry concerned again with adolescent sexuality and the boredom come of living in a small rural town. There is, however, in this novel, beyond the sexuality, which is true of all of McMurtry's fiction, a definite sense of nostalgia. Raymond L. Neinstein suggested in *The Ghost Country: A Study of the Novels of Larry McMurtry* (Berkeley: Creative Arts Book Company, 1976) that the "bitterness" in much of the tone of the novel "is only a mask for nostalgia." The opposite seems to be more the case and the nostalgia merely masks the bitterness. Neinstein went on to quote Patsy Carpenter from McMurtry's next novel, *Moving On* (New York: Simon & Schuster, 1970), whose abortive affair with a graduate student was told in 800 pages, ". . . she was not meat for a good case history, much less a novel. It had all been trivial . . . ." and concluded: "Alas, her judgment is very close to the truth."

The subject of sexuality among dull and uninteresting people is not made less so just because it is sexuality. *All My Friends Are Going to be Strangers* (New York: Simon & Schuster, 1972) goes even further in this direction. It is a semi-autobiographical novel about a Texas writer whose first novel is sold to motion pictures and who proceeds, through the course of the story, to have sexual intercourse with every female he meets, until, since many of them are married and others simply neurotic, they become "strangers" to him. *Terms of Endearment* (New York: Simon & Schuster, 1975) is but a variation on this theme, only instead of a promiscuous male who is left on the brink of suicide at the end, it is a promiscuous female, sort of a larger-than-life throwback to the promiscuous Molly of *Leaving Cheyenne*. McMurtry's next novel, *Somebody's Darling* (New York: Simon & Schuster, 1978), employs a similiar theme, although it is set in Hollywood and not Texas, with a heroine who does not want to be seduced in order to be in motion pictures but who, nonetheless, is, and repeatedly.

Films based on Larry McMurtry's Western fiction are *Hud* (Paramount, 1963) directed by Martin Ritt [based on *Horseman, Pass By*], *The Last Picture Show* (Columbia, 1971) directed by Peter Bogdanovich, *Lovin' Molly* (Columbia, 1974) directed by Sidney Lumet [based on *Leaving Cheyenne*].

McNickle, D'Arcy (1904–1977) Western novelist, historian, and essayist born at St. Ignatius, Montana, on the Flathead reservation. McNickle was the son of a Pennsylvanian father and a Chippewa-Cree-French mother. His father had originally escaped from Canada during a rebellion and was adopted into the Flathead nation.

McNickle attended a Jesuit reservation school and then went to the Chemawa Indian School in Oregon. After graduating from high school in Missoula, Montana, he then attended the University of Montana, Oxford University, and the University of Grenoble in France. Writing and service to the Indian nations formed the double focus of McNickle's life. His first novel, *The Surrounded* (New York: Dodd, Mead, 1936), is the tragic story of a mixed-blood youth whose mother is Indian and whose father is white.

While working on the Federal Writers Project in Washington, McNickle was called to the attention of John Collier, then Commissioner of Indian Affairs, and he was appointed to the U.S. Indian Bureau where he served for sixteen years. His second book, an historical and anthropological survey of American Indian life, *They Came Here First* (Philadelphia: Lippincott, 1949), brought him an invitation to write about the Indians of North America for the *Encyclopedia Britannica*. *Indians and Other Americans* (New York: Harper's, 1959), written with Harold E. Fey, followed, as, in 1962, did *Indian Tribes of the United States, Ethnic and Cultural Survival*, later revised and re-issued as *Native American Tribalism: Indian Survivals and Renewals* published by the Oxford University Press for the Institute of Race Relations in London. Short and to the point, it is one of the best overviews of Indian/white relations.

McNickle's remaining two novels appeared at widely spaced intervals. *Runner in the Sun: The Story of Indian Maize* (New York: Holt, 1954) is a story about the Mesa Verde Indians. *Wind from an Enemy Sky* (New York: Harper's, 1978), his finest fictional work written shortly before he died, is a vigorous and gripping drama about the Little Elk Indians seen entirely from the Indian point of view. The heroic story of the old leader, Bull, his grandson, Antoine, returning from school to accept his Indian heritage, the "good" white men and the "bad" white men, as well as the "good" and "bad" Indians, is told with rare impartiality and insight.

McNickle also wrote a notable biography, *Indian Man: A Life of Oliver La Farge* (Bloomington: Indiana University Press, 1971).

P.O.

Manfred, Frederick (1912 —) Author noted for historical Western fiction, born on a farm near Doon, Iowa. Manfred was baptized Frederick Feikema, and, accordingly, his first seven novels were published under the name Feike Feikema, only partly a pen-name since in Frisian usage the names Frederick and Feike are considered interchangeable. In 1952 a legal name change was made, with Frederick retaining Feikema as a middle name and adding a new surname (Manfred from Fred-Man).

His Frisian and Dutch Reformed Church background led Manfred to Calvin College in Grand Rapids, Michigan, where he rebelled against the restrictions of the Church as well as against many of the formalities and Latinate grammar of the English language. As a free spirit, eager to explore and to find his own style and language based on American speech, he was restless and stubborn, characteristics which got him into trouble at college. Yet, he disciplined himself in those subjects he cared for and in sports, playing baseball and becoming much publicized as a basketball star.

After graduation—during the Depression—Manfred hitchhiked around the country, working at a variety of temporary jobs and finally playing semi-professional basketball. In the late 'Thirties one newspaper referred to him as the tallest basketball player in the United States, at six feet nine inches. A foray across the dust bowl of South Dakota provided him with his first novel, *The Golden Bowl* (St. Paul: Webb, 1944), often considered to be his best. Just prior to its publication, Manfred came down with tuberculosis as the result of hard work and malnutrition. During his stay at Glen Lake Sanitorium (outside Minneapolis), he met Maryanna Shorba, whom he married in 1942.

A prolific writer (eighteen novels and several other books), Manfred remained true to his vision, accepting advice and editorial suggestions from no one. He was constantly drawn back to his early life in Iowa for material—his "novels of experience." Yet, a loosely-related series of five novels under the collective title of *The Buckskin Man* gave him a deserved reputation as a major Western novelist. The five tales are historical in nature although not to an equal degree. *Conquering Horse* (New York: Mc-Dowell-Obolensky, 1959) sensitively portrays the vision quest of a young Indian in prewhite times—around 1800 on the Great Plains—and has been hailed as one of the best of its kind. *Lord Grizzly* (New York: McGraw-Hill, 1954) is based on the exploits of mountain man Hugh Glass whose crawl for survival in South Dakota in 1823 is legendary [and was also used by Vardis Fisher (q.v.) in his novel, *Mountain Man* (New York: Morrow, 1965)]. With *Scarlet*

Plume (New York: Trident, 1964) Manfred introduced a white/Indian love story into the aftermath of a Sioux uprising in Minnesota in 1862. An Oedipal theme in the Black Hills of 1876 provides the basis for *King of Spades* (New York: Trident, 1966). The final tale of the series, *Riders of Judgment* (New York: Random House, 1957), makes use of the Johnson County cattle war in Wyoming in 1892 to bring cattlemen into Manfred's broad portrait of Western American life in the previous century.

Avowedly regional in place, subject matter, and language, Manfred's Western fiction grew out of his belief that "it is still the intuitive, the instinctive part of man that is the real artist." As an artist of the West, Manfred wrote in a rhythmic style that frequently approaches poetry, paid careful attention to the smallest of details, and colorfully evoked a land and its spirit that is often interpreted superficially, if not mistakenly, by less knowledgeable writers. For Manfred, the study of the American West was a search for identity.

J.R.M.

Frederick Manfred's Midwestern and Western novels are *The Golden Bowl* (1944), *Boy Almighty* (1945), *This Is the Year* (1947), *The Chokecherry Tree* (1948), *The Primitive* (1949), *The Brother* (1950), *The Giant* (1951), *Lord Grizzly* (1954), *Morning Red* (1956), *Riders of Judgment* (1957), *Conquering Horse* (1959), *Arrow of Love* (1961) [short stories], *Wanderlust* (1962) [a one-volume revision and abridgement of *The Primitive*, *The Brother*, and *The Giant*], *The Man Who Looked Like the Prince of Wales* (1965), *King of Spades* (1966), *Apples of Paradise* (1968) [short stories], *Eden Prairie* (1968), *The Manly-*

Hearted Woman (1975), *Milk of Wolves* (1976), *Green Earth* (1977).

Mann, E(dward) B(everly) (1902—)

Prolific author of Western fiction in the 1930s before he returned to other pursuits, born at Hollis, Kansas. Mann's first novel, *The Man from Texas* (New York: Morrow, 1931), impressed Thayer Hobson, an editor at Morrow and the head of the firm. Hobson wanted to begin a Western line and so, in addition to the regular Mann titles, he wrote three Western novels himself under the house name (see House Names) Peter Field and persuaded Mann to write the fourth in the series. Mann also wrote extensively for the pulp Western magazines and, although his last Western novel, *Gunsmoke Trail* (New York: Morrow, 1942), was published in 1942, a collection of three short novels, featuring Mann's range detective "The Whistler"—not to be confused with the popular radio and movie mystery/suspense series from the 'Forties—were re-issued in book form more than a decade later, *The Whistler* (New York: Greenberg, 1953). Mann subsequently, with Fred E. Harvey, paid tribute to the state where he long lived in their book *New Mexico: Land of Enchantment* (East Lansing: Michigan State University Press, 1955), a work of non-fiction.

E.B. Mann's Western novels are *The Man from Texas* (1931), *The Blue-Eyed Kid* (1932), *The Valley of Wanted Men* (1932), *Killer's Range* (1933), *Stampede* (1934), *Gamblin' Man* (1934), *Rustlers' Roundup* (1935), *Thirsty Range* (1935), *Elsombra* (1936), *The Boss of the Lazy 9* (1936) [published under the house name Peter Field], *With Spurs* (1937), *Comanche Kid* (1937), *Shootin' Melody* (1938), *Gun Feud* (1939), *Troubled Range* (1940), *Gunsmoke Trail* (1942), *The Whistler* (1953).

Films based on E.B. Mann's Western fiction are *Guns for Hire* (Kent, 1932) directed by Lew Collins [source unknown], *Desert Phantom* (Supreme, 1936) directed by S. Roy Luby [source unknown], *Boss Rider of Gun Creek* (Universal, 1936) directed by Lesley Selander [based on *The Boss of the Lazy 9*], *Stormy Trails* (Colony, 1936) directed by Sam Newfield [based on *Stampede*], *Lightnin' Crandall* (Republic, 1937) directed by Sam Newfield [source unknown], *Trail of Vengeance* (Republic, 1937) directed by Sam Newfield [source unknown], *Guns in the Dark* (Republic, 1937) directed by Sam Newfield [source unknown], *Ridin' the Lone Trail* (Republic, 1937) directed by Sam Newfield [source unknown].

Manning, David. See Faust, Frederick.

Marshall, Gary. See Snow, Charles H.

Mathews, John Joseph (1895–1979)

Western novelist, biographer, essayist, and historian, born on the Osage reservation in Oklahoma. Although Mathews was only one-eighth Indian descent, he was listed on the tribal roles and served on the Osage Tribal Council in later life. Mathews' mother was of Norman-French descent. "Joe" Mathews spent his youth riding and roaming the countryside before attending the University of Oklahoma and serving as a

Second Lieutenant in the Air Force. Interested in the natural sciences, he continued his studies at Oxford University and the University of Geneva, Switzerland, traveling in Europe and Africa before returning to the United States.

Retiring to a sandstone house he helped build himself a few miles outside Pawhuska, Oklahoma, Mathews began to write. His first book, *Wah'kon-tah: The Osage and the White Man's Road* (Norman: University of Oklahoma Press, 1932), became a bestseller when it was selected by the Book-of-the-Month Club. Two years later, Mathews gave his fictional account of Indian/white relationships in *Sundown* (Norman: University of Oklahoma Press, 1934), a story of Challenge Windzer, son of a mixed-blood father and a full-blood Osage mother; the author described Chal's life of assimilation and alienation from birth to his mid thirties. Chal's mother and father symbolize in themselves the conflicting red and white traditions with which Chal has to deal. The mother refuses to change from her old Osage ways. The father believes that Washington will help the Osages, becoming quickly rich from the discovery of oil on their lands. Betrayed and disillusioned, he commits suicide, leaving his son with enough money after he graduates from the University of Oklahoma to drink and drift.

Mathews' novel was well received but he did not write again for some time. His next book, *Talking to the Moon* (Chicago: University of Chicago Press, 1945), was an autobiographical account of his own attempts to find his part in the balance of Nature by living alone in his small stone house for ten years and reflecting, as had Henry David Thoreau, on himself and his relationship to Nature. His only biography, *The Life and Death of an Oilman: The Career of E.W. Marland* (Norman: University of Oklahoma Press, 1951), and a large history of his people, *The Osages: Children of the Middle Waters* (Norman: University of Oklahoma Press, 1961), followed.

P.O.

May, Karl (1842–1912) Phenomenally popular author of travel and adventure novels, many of which were set in the American West, born at Hohenstein-Ernstthal, Saxony in Germany. May's vision was impaired as a child because of malnutrition. He spent his youth in the shadow of the great famine that swept Central Europe in the mid 1840s and the economic dislocations which led to the tragic weavers' rebellion of 1844. But he was a gifted youth. The sacrifices of May's family and the largesse of the Church enabled him to finish school and enter a teachers' training college in 1857. Soon after graduation in 1861, however, he was arrested for stealing a watch and sentenced to a prison term which ended all possibility of a teaching career. May claimed throughout his life to have been innocent of this theft. After several months' imprisonment, the depressed and bitter May swore vengeance on bourgeois society and began a life of fraud, swindle, and larceny which lasted twelve years and sent him back to jail for stretches from 1865–1868 and 1870–1874. While incarcerated, he read voraciously in the prison library, devouring travel memoirs and adventure stories of distant lands, particularly those about the Arab world and the American frontier.

In 1875 the chastened May began his literary career writing village tales and cheap adventure stories for an unscrupulous publisher of family magazines and trashy short novels. Although he had never traveled outside Germany, in 1879 he produced two books on the American "wild" West, *Jenseits der Felsengebirge (Beyond the Rocky Mountains)* and *Im Fernen Westen (In the Far West.)* Over the next thirty years, drawing mainly from atlases, ethnological studies, and travelers' journals, May published a spate of similar books, the best and most popular of which was the trilogy *Winnetou* (1893–1910). Set in the plains and mountains of the West and Southwest at about the time of the Civil War, it chronicles the deeds of a knightly band of heroic "men of the West" surrounding a young German adventurer, "Old Shatterhand," and his blood brother, Winnetou, the noble chief of the Mescalero Apaches. In this band were "Old Firehand," "Old Surehand," "Sharpeye," "Old Wabble," and Sam Hawkens. Themselves men of untarnished integrity and valor, they are nevertheless constantly being vilified, double-crossed, and ambushed by an assortment of white scoundrels and misled Indians such as the gold-hungry, malevolent Santer, the cowardly murderer Rattler, or the elusive white renegade chief of the Poncas, Tim Finnetey, alias Parronoh. These are evil men, creatures of hybris who recognize no law above their selfish impulses. It is the diabolical Santer, for example, who murders Winnetou's father and sister; Rattler who kills the saintly white teacher of the Apaches, Klekih-petra; and Parronoh who slays Ribanna, "Old Firehand's" Indian wife. The Indians hate the white men who are spreading across the plains as a pestilence, but, as in Charles Sealsfield's (q.v.) *Tokeah* (1829), there are no truly bad Indians in *Winnetou*, only angry and naive victims of the whites' cruelty and greed. As "Old Shatterhand" is the apotheosis of Christian manhood, Winnetou is the pagan ideal, the noble savage. This symbol of Nature's innocent perfection first appeared to May during his imprisonment and was, for years, "like a light shining behind me day and night." May compared Winnetou to a "deer that has not only retrained its scent but sees and hears with its soul," and contrasted him with white men who are as "docile domestic animals." Whatever Winnetou's qualitites, there is never any doubt that May considered the perfect Christian morally superior to the model heathen: upon his death, Winnetou acknowledges Christ and requests that an "Ave Maria" be sung for him. Despite the gross lack of realism and moralizing sentimentality, it is still an exciting series of stories abounding in hair-raising surprises, outrageous comedy, and unforgettable characters.

May's five years of anonymous toil as a hack writer were followed by two decades of success, especially after the publication of the first volume in the *Winnetou* series in 1893 and his equally popular novel of the exotic Near East, *Durch die Wüste (In the Desert)* (1892), which made him a bestselling writer in Germany, particularly among the youth. Responding in part to demands from his growing public, May gradually began to pretend that he was, in fact, characters from his books. He had photographs taken of himself in Western garb and Oriental costume which he signed and sent to his fans. But wealth and fame had the disadvantage of making his life a matter of public curiosity and malice which led in 1904 to the scandalous revelation of his early years of crime and imprisonment and to the even more damaging discovery that he had never been to the United States at all, much less had experienced the adventures narrated in his Westerns. The pose had been a relatively harmless fraud, but in light of his criminal record it appeared to be but another episode in a long history of swindle and moral hypocrisy. Humiliated by these disclosures and his own attempts at denial, May made a three-month tour of America in 1908 but traveled no farther West than Buffalo, New York, and Toronto, Canada. In his last years he wrote two justifications of his life which some critics consider his finest literary works, *Ardistan und Djinnistan (Ardistan and Djinnistan)* (1908–1909), a symbolic novel set in the Orient, and his autobiography, *Mein Leben Und Streben (My Life and Strivings)* (Freiburg: Fehsenfeld, 1912). Abused in the press and defeated in court in his suits for defamation of character, May died a broken man.

Until recently Karl May has been considered beneath contempt by most literary critics and historians. At best he was recognized as a master of juvenile adventure stories and a popular writer of escapist fiction for the common man. His novels were, for the most part, hastily written, uneven, and inconsistent; his characters lacking in psychological complexity and unrealistic; his stories tangles of unlikely coincidence and improbable action. This was largely as a result of May's method of working which resembled automatic writing without revision; "The truth is," he wrote, "that I never think about my style. I write down what comes out of my soul, and I write it as I hear it. I change nothing and I polish nothing. My style is my soul. It is not my style, but my soul that speaks to the reader." This technique accounts for much of the breathless excitement and rapid pace of his novels as well as for their unconscious symbolism and archetypal characterizations; indeed, the renewed interest in May's work is principally an outgrowth of contemporary interest in these symbolic and archetypal elements.

He was praised by men as diverse as Adolph Hitler, Albert Einstein, Albert Schweitzer, and Hermann Hesse. Einstein, who preferred May's tales of the Orient, once commented: "My whole adolescence stood under his sign. Indeed, even today he has been dear to me in many a desperate hour."

J.D.F.

Karl May's Western novels are *Jenseits der Felsengebirge (Beyond the Rocky Mountains)* (1879) [short stories], *Im Fernen Westen (In the Far West)* (1879) [short stories], *Waldröschen (Rose of the Woods)* (1882), *Der Sohn des Bärenjägers (The Bear-Hunter's Son)* (1890) [short stories], *Das Goldlager (The Gold Camp)* (1890) [short stories], *Der Hauptmann der Deutschen Ansiedler (The Captain of the German Settlers* (1890) [short stories], *An den Ufern des Ohio, Oder der Erste Ansiedler in Kentucky (On the Banks of the Ohio, Or the First Settler in Kentucky* (1890) [short stories], *Tekumshe, Der Grosse Häuptling der Cherokees (Tekumseh, The Great Chief of the Cherokees)* (1892), *Winnetou* (1893),

Der Schatz im Silbersee (The Treasure of Silver Lake) (1894), *Der Alte Sicherhand (Old Surehand)* (1894–1896), *Weinacht (Christmas)* (1897) [short stories], *Der Schwarze Mustang (The Black Mustang)* (1899) [short stories], *Winnetous Erben (Winnetou's Heritage)* (1910).

Winnetou has been filmed twice in Germany, in 1963 and 1965, and a documentary of three hours in length was done on Karl May's life for German television in 1975. *The Treasure of Silver Lake* (Columbia, 1965) directed by Radenko Ostojic and *Frontier Hellcat* (Columbia, 1966) directed by Stipe Delic [based on *Old Surehand*] were both released under these titles and dubbed into English in the United States. *Old Shatterhand* (Spain, 1966) was directed by Hugo Fregonese [based on the May character].

The Seabury Press of New York announced in 1977 publication of the first comprehensive English translations of Karl May's works beginning with *Winnetou*. For a critical and biographical study of May, A. Schmidt's *Sitara und der Weg Dorthim, Studie über Wesen, Werk, und Wirkung Karl Mays* (Berlin and Weimar: Fisher Verlag, 1963), untranslated but the title of which would be rendered *Sitara and the Path to the Interior, A Study on the Nature, Work, and Effect of Karl May*, is to be recommended as well as the various volumes of the *Jahrbuch der Karl May-Gesellschaft (Yearbook of the Karl May Society)*, old series, Volumes 1–16, 1918–1933, and new series, Volumes 1–9, 1970–1979.

Mayo, Jim. See L'Amour, Louis.

Meade, Richard. See Haas, Benjamin.

Miles, John. See Bickham, Jack M.

Milton, John R(onald) (1924 —) Author and critic of Western fiction, born at Anoka, Minnesota. Milton was in the U.S. Army 1943–1946, assigned to the Pacific theatre of World War II. After the war, he received his Bachelor's and Master's degree from the University of Minnesota and his Doctor's degree in American literature and creative writing from the University of Denver. He taught at the University of South Dakota and in 1963 he founded the *South Dakota Review*. He was also one of the founders of the Western Literature Association.

Milton's literary impact was manifold. He was a poet, *The Loving Hawk* (Fargo: North Dakota Institute for Regional Studies, 1962) having been his first book of poems, followed by *The Tree of Bones* (Denver: Verb Publications, 1965), *This Lonely House* (Minneapolis: James D. Thueson, Publisher, 1968), *The Tree of Bones and Other Poems* (Vermillion: Dakota Press, 1973), and *The Blue Belly of the World* (Vermillion: Spirit Mound Press, 1974). As editor of the *South Dakota Review*, Milton was a constant unswerving force, championing Western writing as the equal to that of any other region. He also sought out authors in whom he took a great personal interest and published as a consequence, some very insightful and valuable books, *Conversa-*

tions with *Frank Waters* (Chicago: Swallow Press, 1971) and *Conversations with Frederick Manfred* (Salt Lake City: University of Utah Press, 1974). Frank Waters (q.v.) and Frederick Manfred (q.v.) along with Max Evans (q.v.), Walter Van Tilburg Clark (q.v.), and Harvey Fergusson (q.v.) comprise what Milton, in his writings of a critical nature, termed the "higher echelon" of Western writers. Milton's sympathetic interest in the Native American prompted him to write two full-scale and eminently readable biographies, *Oscar Howe: The Story of an American Indian* (Minneapolis: Dillon Press, 1972) and *Crazy Horse: The Story of an American Indian* (Minneapolis: Dillon Press, 1974). He edited *The American Indian Speaks* (Vermillion: Dakota Press, 1969) and *American Indian II* (Vermillion: Dakota Press, 1971). His book *Three West* (Vermillion: Dakota Press, 1970) contains an interesting conversation with Max Evans.

Milton wrote a novel, *Notes to a Bald Buffalo* (Vermillion: Spirit Mound Press, 1976), along with two important contributions to literary criticism, *The Literature of South Dakota* (Vermillion: Dakota Press, 1976) and *The Novel of the American West* (Lincoln: University of Nebraska Press, 1980). Milton's *South Dakota: A History* (New York: Norton, 1976) can be said to be definitive.

"That Eastern readers and critics have dismissed the conventional Western novel is not nearly as important, or tragic," Milton once commented, "as the fact that they have lumped together *all* Western novels until they think no more of Harvey Fergusson, Frank Waters, and Walter Van Tilburg Clark than they do of Max Brand (q.v.), Zane Grey (q.v.), Owen Wister (q.v.), *et al*. They have not understood that the West has just as good writing as the East, and that there is a tremendous difference between [Grey's] *Riders of the Purple Sage* [New York: Harper's, 1912] and [Clark's] *The Ox-Bow Incident* [New York: Random House, 1940]. Even some Westerners do not understand this. And this misconception is precisely what I am trying to correct. I may fail. But it is about time someone tried." Milton might conceivably be criticized for having drawn too tight a circle around those whom he permitted into his "higher echelon," but unquestionably he had an impact among literary scholars.

Momaday, N(avarre) Scott

(1934 —) Essayist, lecturer, professor of English, and Native American author, born near Lawton, Oklahoma. When he was 1, Momaday moved with his parents to Northern New Mexico where he grew up on reservations that contained Navahos, Apaches, and Jemez Pueblo Indians. He spent his youth at Jemez Springs, New Mexico. Momaday received a good formal education at home since both of his parents had taught in Indian schools besides his attendance in parochial and public schools. He received his high school diploma from the Augusta Military Academy in Virginia in 1952. He then attended the University of New Mexico, took a year off to study law in 1956–1957 at the University of Virginia, and received his Bachelor's degree in political science from New Mexico in 1958. He afterwards went directly to a teaching job at Dulce, New Mexico, on the Jicarilla Apache Indian Reservation. In 1959 he married Gaye Mangold, and they had three daughters.

In that same year, Momaday returned to academic life when Stanford awarded him a Creative Writing Fellowship. He remained at that institution to obtain both his Master's degree in 1960 and his Doctor's degree in 1963. Momaday then became a faculty member at the University of California at Santa Barbara. Winning a Guggenheim Fellowship for 1966–1967, he journeyed to Amherst, Massachusetts, to do a critical study of the poet Emily Dickinson.

The year 1969 marked two important events for Momaday: he was initiated into the Taimpe Society, an ancient and respected Kiowa organization, and he joined the faculty of the University of California at Berkeley as an associate professor of English and comparative literature. In 1972 Momaday returned to Stanford as a professor of English and comparative literature except for a year spent at New Mexico State University as a visiting professor in 1972–1973. Momaday also worked as a columnist for the Santa Fe *New Mexican* supplement *Viva*, where his columns covered a variety of subjects from elephant jokes to comments on Billy the Kid.

Although Momaday made valuable contributions in other fields of American literature, he was principally noted as a writer of the American West. His concern was with the Native American and his place in contemporary society. Momaday once said, "I don't know what an Indian is. The 'American Indian'—that term is meaningless; to me it means very little" What this expressed was Momaday's unhappiness with the idea that Indians are totally different from other men or that Indians must fit into some preconceived, stereotyped image. The Indian as a human being, trying to cope with two cultures, was Momaday's subject matter. He added, 'None but an Indian, I think, knows so much what it is to have existence in two worlds and security in neither." His goal became assimilation into a single society for both the white man and the Indian, each learning from the other. Momaday's first literary attempts were in the field of poetry. He appeared in print in 1959 in the *New Mexico Quarterly* with a poem entitled, "Earth and I Give You Turquoise." Other poems followed in that magazine as well as in *The Southern Review*. As a result of these publications, Momaday was asked to submit some poetry to Harper & Row, but, instead, he sent the manuscript of *House Made of Dawn* (New York: Harper's, 1968) for the Harper Prize Novel Contest; in 1969 the book won the Pulitzer Prize for fiction. The story deals with Abel, a Twentieth-century Indian, who desires to retreat to the mysticism of Indian culture and who is plagued by the problems of urban, relocated Indians in Los Angeles, and Abel's final deculturation and self-acceptance.

Momaday's second major work, *The Way to Rainy Mountain* (Albuquerque: University of New Mexico Press, 1969), might be described as at once an autobiography, an epic account of the Kiowa's golden age, and a creation hymn. The book is steeped in Kiowa mythology and legend, such as the Kiowa creation myth in which the Kiowas came into the world one at a time through a hollow log. A pregnant woman got stuck in the log and few people could get out. Thus there are not many Kiowa people. Each section of the book divides into three parts: Kiowa legend, lore collected by white historians or anthropologists, and Momaday's own memories. The work is an attempt to teach non-Indians just how much they can learn and share in the Indian experience.

D.K.-M.

For further information see *N. Scott Momaday* (Boise: Idaho State University, 1973) by Martha Scott Trimble.

Morales, Sebastian. See Lutz, Giles A.

Morgan, Mark. See Overholser, Wayne D.

Morland, Peter Henry. See Faust, Frederick.

Morrow, Honoré Willsie (1880–1940)

An author whose early novels are set in the Southwest, born Honoré McCue at Ottomwa, Iowa. After graduating from the University of Wisconsin at Madison, Honoré married Henry Elmer Willsie, a construction engineer, whom she divorced in 1922. The following year she married William Morrow who was then treasurer of the Frederick A. Stokes' publishing firm and later became head of his own publishing company.

In the first decade of the Nineteenth century, unable to interest any New York editors in her early efforts at fiction, Morrow went to Arizona to visit with friends. She soon became fascinated with the West and began gathering material for regional stories. Her writing career was established when she began publishing articles in *Collier's* and *Harper's Weekly* on a wide variety of subjects, including Western life, immigration, divorce, and the U.S. Reclamation Act. In 1914 Morrow became editor of *De-lineator*, a woman's magazine, proving herself a capable executive. In 1919, after the publication of a half dozen novels, Morrow decided to devote all her time to writing fiction and she resigned from her editorship.

In her books *The Heart of the Desert* (New York: Stokes, 1913) and *The Enchanted Canyon* (New York: Stokes, 1921), as well as in other early novels, Morrow advocated desert and forest reclamation. Morrow also strongly believed in the need to return to the spirit and faith of the early pioneers which became a recurrent theme in her Western fiction. Although not a native Westerner, she was praised by many for her facility to capture regional landscape and customs. Notwithstanding, author Eugene Manlove Rhodes (q.v.) in his article "The West That Was" (1922) included in *The Rhodes Reader* (Norman: University of Oklahoma Press, 1957) wrote about Morrow's novel *Slim Jim* (New York: Stokes, 1915), ". . . a masterpiece save for its blindness as to all meaning of the West." Morrow branched out from the Southwest in books as *On to Oregon* (New York: Morrow, 1926) and *We Must March: A Novel of the Winning of Oregon* (New York: Stokes, 1925), and was one of the early authors to write historical novels before they became popular in the 'Thirties.

Honoré Willsie Morrow's Western novels are *The Heart of the Desert* (1913), *Slim Jim* (1915), *Lydia of the Pines* (1917), *The Forbidden Trail* (1919), *The Enchanted Canyon* (1921), *Judith of the Godless Valley* (1922), *The Exile of the Lariat* (1923), *We Must March* (1925), *On to Oregon* (1926), *Beyond the Blue Sierra* (1932).

Seven Alone (Doty-Dayton, 1974) was directed by Earl Bellamy [based on *On to Oregon*].

Mulford, Clarence E(dward)

(1883–1956) Author of Western fiction noted chiefly for his creation of Hopalong Cassidy and the Bar 20 saga, born at Streator, Illinois. Mulford's family moved to Brooklyn, New York, in 1889. After completing high school, Mulford pursued a career in civil service. Already as a youth Mulford proved quiet and reclusive. He fell much under the spell of Owen Wister's (q.v.) novel, *The Virginian* (New York: Macmillan, 1902), and began assembling a vast library on the development of the American frontier, in his enthusiasm constructing wooden models of famous forts. Although he had yet to leave the East, Mulford set out to write about the West and entered a short story contest sponsored by *Metropolitan Magazine* in 1906 and shared in the first prize. He followed this success with a series of connected Western stories featured in Casper Whitney's *Outing Magazine*. These stories were published as a picaresque novel titled *Bar 20* (London: Outing, 1907). Mulford next wrote *The Orphan* (London: Outing, 1908), a novel very much an imitation in style and spirit of *The Virginian*.

Over the next two years, Mulford conceived of his notion of a saga to be told through an extended series of novels and stories with Western locales and developed a group of basic characters to play against the background of major historical events in the settling of the Southwest: the great cattle ranches, the long trail drives, the coming of the railroad and barbed wire, the war with Mexico, the mining camps, and the shift of national attention from the Southwest to the Northwest once gold was discovered in Montana. One of the central characters of this saga was red-haired, cursing, smoking, hard-drinking, rough but grimly ethical Bill Cassidy who had first appeared in *Bar 20*. In *The Coming of Cassidy and the Others* (Chicago: A.C. McClurg, 1913), Mulford narrated how Cassidy was wounded in his thigh by a bullet and subsequently had a limp. "And from this on," Mulford wrote, "up to the time he died, and after, we will forsake 'Bill' and speak of him as Hopalong Cassidy, a cowpuncher who lived and worked in the days when the West was wild and rough and lawless; and who, like others, through the medium of the only court at hand, Judge Colt, enforced justice as he believed it should be enforced."

With the publication of *Hopalong Cassidy* (Chicago: A.C. McClurg, 1910) Mulford switched his publishing affiliation from Outing to McClurg and, once Fox Film Corporation purchased screen rights to *The Orphan*, which was retitled *The Deadwood Coach* (Fox, 1924) and starred Tom Mix, Mulford switched publishers again, this time to the New York house of Doubleday.

There were authors before Mulford, such as James Fenimore Cooper (q.v.) and even Owen Wister, and authors contemporaneous with him as B.M. Bower (q.v.), who relied heavily on series characters to people a saga, but no one, perhaps, until Louis L'Amour (q.v.) in his saga of the Sacketts did so quite to the extent that Mulford did. *Hopalong Cassidy* tells of Hoppy's marriage

Maynard Dixon's conception of Hopalong Cassidy (on horseback) from the original edition of Clarence E. Mulford's Hopalong Cassidy *(Chicago: A. C. McClurg, 1910).*

Three (Chicago: A.C. McClurg, 1921) finds Hoppy and Red Connors helping Johnny out of some difficulties in a strange cattle town and *Tex* (Chicago; A.C. McClurg, 1922) describes how Tex Ewalt marries and settles down. At this point Mulford had written ten books and only three of them had dealt in any way with romance. He refused to compromise and include more romance. *Bring Me His Ears* (Chicago: A.C. McClurg, 1923), *Black Buttes* (New York: Doubleday, 1923), and *Rustlers' Valley* (New York: Doubleday, 1924) are books written about different characters not included in the Bar 20 saga, set against divergent locales and dealing with desperate

to Mary Meeker. *Bar 20 Days* (Chicago: A.C. McClurg, 1911) is another picaresque collection of related stories set in a different time and narrating various adventures of the Bar 20 punchers working for ranch foreman Buck Peters: Hoppy, Red Connors, and youthful Johnny Nelson. It also features Tex Ewalt, a fast gunman and cardsharp, who had first been introduced in *Bar 20*. The next book, *Buck Peters, Ranchman* (Chicago: A.C. McClurg, 1912), finds Peters leaving the Bar 20 to found his own spread in the Montana Territory.

Johnny Nelson is featured as the main character in *The Man from Bar 20* (Chicago: A.C. McClurg, 1918) and the next book, *Johnny Nelson* (Chicago: A.C. McClurg, 1920), tells of Johnny's marriage. *The Bar 20*

Dust jacket from the original edition of Johnny Nelson *(Chicago: A. C. McClurg, 1920).*

events. *Hopalong Cassidy Returns* (New York: Doubleday, 1925) begins after the deaths of Hoppy's wife and child and tells of his encounter, accompanied by his longtime friend, Red Connors, with a hard, lean, wild youngster named Mesquite Jenkins. *Cottonwood Gulch* (New York: Doubleday, 1925) was Mulford's version of the story of Henry Plummer and the vigilante movement at Alder Gulch, although it would be better handled by Ernest Haycox (q.v.) in *Alder Gulch* (Boston: Little, Brown, 1942) and Will Henry (q.v.) in *Reckoning at Yankee Flat* (New York: Random House, 1958), and, surprisingly, had been better handled even in Zane Grey's *The Border Legion* (New York: Harper's, 1916).

Hopalong Cassidy's Protégé (New York: Doubleday, 1926) carries forward the relationship between Hoppy and Mesquite. With *Corson of the JC* (New York: Doubleday, 1927) Mulford initiated a wholly new saga, but, in many ways, it was derivative of what was being done by other authors of Western fiction. The Corson books are primarily detective stories after the fashion made popular by W.C. Tuttle (q.v.) and even Mulford's comic duo of Nueces and Shorty bear a certain resemblance to Tuttle's range detectives Hashknife Hartley and Sleepy Stevens. The good bad man in the Corson books, and an ally of Corson, is the Mexican cattle thief El Toro who talks the same kind of border English Monte does in Eugene Manlove Rhodes' (q.v.) *Pasó Por Aquí* (Boston: Houghton Mifflin, 1927) which had run the previous year in *The Saturday Evening Post*. *Mesquite Jenkins* (New York: Doubleday, 1928) narrates Mesquite's adventures alone on the trail without Cassidy. Finally, with *Hopalong Cassidy and the Eagle's Brood* (New York: Doubleday, 1931), Mulford achieved his *magnum opus* bringing together *all* his principal characters in a single novel: Hoppy, Johnny Nelson, and Tex Ewalt joined by Matt Skinner from *Rustlers' Valley*, Dave Saunders from *Cottonwood Gulch*, Wyatt Duncan from *Black Buttes*, and Corson from the Corson saga.

Mulford was writing prolifically and had just published two more novels when, early in 1935, he received a letter from Hollywood producer Harry Sherman proposing a series of motion pictures to be based on his Bar 20 saga. Reputedly Sherman met Mulford in New York City and, quite inebriated, the two signed an agreement on a piece of toilet paper. The films, starring William Boyd, the complete antithesis to the Hopalong Cassidy of the novels, proved very popular and Mulford, pleased with his film royalties of five percent, tired of writing. He published his last book, *Hopalong Cassidy Serves a Writ* (New York: Doubleday, 1941), just prior to World War II. Wanting more novels, Doubleday, once the Hopalong Cassidy films began being shown on television, commissioned Louis L'Amour to write four new novels, under the name Tex Burns, with the added provision that the new novels were to picture Hopalong Cassidy as he was portrayed by William Boyd, including the black clothes and the white hair.

Long after Mulford's death, the city of Fryeburg, Maine, undertook to have all of Mulford's novels, and those by Tex Burns, reprinted by the Aeonian Press in an arrangement with Doubleday & Company. However, since no one had bothered to renew the motion picture copyrights on the fifty-four Hopalong Cassidy films produced by Harry Sherman, those pictures fell into the Public Domain, a situation which inspired a number of lawsuits among litigants claiming exclusive rights to distribute the films.

Clarence E. Mulfords's Western novels are *Bar 20* (1907), *The Orphan* (1908), *Hopalong Cassidy* (1910), *Bar 20 Days* (1911), *Buck Peters, Ranchman* (1912), *The Coming of Cassidy and the Others* (1913), *The Man from Bar 20* (1918), *Johnny Nelson* (1920), *The Bar 20 Three* (1921), *Bring Me His Ears* (1922), *Tex* (1922), *Black Buttes* (1923), *Rustlers' Valley* (1924), *Hopalong Cassidy Returns* (1924), *Cottonwood Gulch* (1925), *The Bar 20 Rides Again* (1926), *Hopalong Cassidy's Protégé* (1926), *Corson of the JC* (1927), *Mesquite Jenkins* (1928), *Me an Shorty* (1929), *The Deputy Sheriff* (1930), *Hopalong Cassidy and the Eagle's Brood* (1931), *Mesquite Jenkins, Tumbleweed* (1932), *The Round-up* (1933), *Trail Dust* (1934), *On the Trail of the Tumbling T* (1935), *Hopalong Cassidy Takes Cards* (1937), *Hopalong Cassidy Serves a Writ* (1941).

The four Hopalong Cassidy novels written by Louis L'Amour under the name Tex Burns are *Rustlers of West Fork* (1951), *Trail to Seven Pines* (1951), *Riders of High Rock* (1951), *Trouble Shooter* (1951).

Films based on Clarence E. Mulford's Western fiction are *The Deadwood Coach* (Fox, 1924) directed by Lynn Reynolds [based on *The Orphan*] and *Hopalong Cassidy* (Paramount, 1935) directed by Howard Bretherton [based on *Hopalong Cassidy*]. Films based on Clarence E. Mulford's characters are *The Eagle's Brood* (Paramount, 1935) directed by Howard Bretherton, *The Bar 20 Rides Again* (Paramount, 1935) directed by Howard Bretherton, *Call of the Prairie* (Paramount, 1936) directed by Howard Bretherton, *Three on the Trail* (Paramount, 1936) directed by Howard Bretherton, *Heart of the West* (Paramount, 1936) directed by Howard Bretherton, *Hopalong Cassidy Returns* (Paramount, 1936) directed by Nate Watt, *Trail Dust* (Paramount, 1936) directed by Nate Watt, *Borderland* (Paramount, 1937) directed by Nate Watt, *Hills of Old Wyoming* (Paramount, 1937) directed by Nate Watt, *North of the Rio Grande* (Paramount, 1937) directed by Nate Watt, *Rustlers' Valley* (Paramount, 1937) directed by Natt Watt, *Hopalong Rides Again* (Paramount, 1937) directed by Lesley Selander, *Texas Trail* (Paramount, 1937) directed by David Selman, *Heart of Arizona* (Paramount, 1938) directed by Lesley Selander, *Bar 20 Justice* (Paramount, 1938) directed by Lesley Selander, *Pride of the West* (Paramount, 1938) directed by Lesley Selander, *In Old Mexico* (Paramount, 1938) directed by Edward D. Venturini, *Sunset Trail* (Paramount, 1938) directed by Lesley Selander, *The Frontiersman* (Paramount, 1938) directed by Lesley Selander, *Partners of the Plains* (Paramount, 1938) directed by Lesley Selander, *Cassidy of Bar 20* (Paramount, 1938) directed by Lesley Selander, *Range War* (Paramount, 1939) directed by Lesley Selander, *Law of the Pampas* (Paramount, 1939) directed by Nate Watt, *Silver on the Sage* (Paramount, 1939) directed by Lesley Selander, *The Renegade Trail* (Paramount, 1939) directed by Lesley Selander, *Sante Fe Marshal* (Paramount, 1940) directed by Lesley Selander, *The Showdown* (Paramount, 1940) directed by Howard Bretherton, *Hidden Gold* (Paramount, 1940) directed by Lesley Selander, *Stagecoach War* (Paramount, 1940) directed by Lesley Selander, *Three Men from Texas* (Paramount, 1940) directed by Lesley Selander, *Doomed Caravan* (Paramount, 1941) directed by Lesley Selander, *In Old Colorado* (Paramount, 1941) directed by Howard Bretherton, *Border Vigilantes* (Paramount,

A *scene from* Hopalong Rides Again *(Paramount, 1937) with George "Gabby" Hayes (l.), William Boyd as Hopalong Cassidy, Billy King, William Duncan as Buck Peters, Russell Hayden, and Lois Wilde in the foreground.*

1941) directed by Derwin Abrahams, *Pirates on Horseback* (Paramount, 1941) directed by Lesley Selander, *Wide Open Town* (Paramount, 1941) directed by Lesley Selander, *Outlaw of the Desert* (Paramount, 1941) directed by Howard Bretherton, *Riders of the Timberline* (Paramount, 1941) directed by Lesley Selander, *Secret of the Wastelands* (Paramount, 1941) directed by Derwin Abrahams [based on Bliss Lomax' (q.v.) novel by this title], *Stick to Your Guns* (Paramount, 1941) directed by Lesley Selander, *Twilight on the Trail* (Paramount, 1941) directed by Howard Bretherton, *Undercover Man* (United Artists, 1942) directed by Lesley Selander, *Lost Canyon* (United Artists, 1942) directed by Lesley Selander, *Colt Comrades* (United Artists, 1943) directed by Lesley Selander, [based on Bliss Lomax' *Colt Comrades*], *Bar 20* (United Artists, 1943) directed by Lesley Selander, *Hoppy Serves a Writ* (United Artists, 1943) directed by George Archainbaud, *Border Patrol* (United Artists, 1943) directed by Lesley Selander, *The Leatherburners* (United Artists, 1943) directed by Joseph Henabery [based on Bliss Lomax' *Leatherburners*], *False Colors* (United Artists, 1943) directed by George Archainbaud, *Riders of the Deadline* (United Artists, 1943) directed by Lesley Selander, *Mystery Man* (United Artists, 1944) directed by George Archainbaud, *Forty Thieves* (United Artists, 1944) directed by Lesley Selander, *Texas Masquerade* (United Artists, 1944) directed by George Archainbaud, *Lumberjack* (United Artists, 1944) directed by Lesley Selander, *The Devil's Playground* (United Artists, 1946), directed by George Archainbaud, *Fool's Gold* (United Artists, 1947) directed by George Archainbaud, *Unexpected Guest* (United Artists, 1947) directed by George Archainbaud, *Dangerous Venture* (United Artists, 1947) directed by George Archainbaud, *The Marauders* (United Artists, 1947) directed by George Archainbaud, *Silent Conflict* (United Artists, 1948) directed by George Archainbaud, *The Dead Don't Dream* (United Artists, 1948) directed by George Archainbaud, *Sinister Journey* (United Artists, 1948) directed by George Archainbaud, *Borrowed Trouble* (United Artists, 1948) directed by George Archainbaud, *False Paradise* (United Artists, 1948) directed by George Archainbaud, *Strange Gamble* (United Artists, 1948) directed by George Archainbaud.

Hopalong Cassidy (NBC, 1948–1952) appeared as a half hour television series, the first group teaming William Boyd with Andy Clyde, the second group teaming Boyd with Edgar Buchanan.

Hopalong Cassidy was broadcast on the Mutual radio network in 1949 with William Boyd and Andy Clyde.

Native Americans

While a great many books have been published about Native Americans, their history and culture, and even more fictional works have used them in varying contexts, it is unfortunate that so few of these images are wholly reliable and that so much of what has been written has been influenced by white men's stereotypes.

GENERAL HISTORIES

Perhaps the best place to begin is in terms of a general historic overview of Native American history from prehistoric times through the present. The single finest book of a general nature to appear so far is Arrell Morgan Gibson's *The American Indian: Prehistory to the Present* (Massachusetts: D.C. Heath, 1980). It is an extremely well-researched, well-documented survey characterized by a balanced perspective. Gibson's study is also perhaps to be supplemented by two additional general histories, Ruth M. Underhill's revised edition of *Red Man's America* (Chicago: University of Chicago Press, 1971) and Angie Debo's revised edition of *A History of the Indians of the United States* (Norman: University of Oklahoma Press, 1979).

Although still by way of general books, but with a somewhat narrower focus, are Edward H. Spicer's *A Short History of the Indians of the United States* (New York: D. Van Nostrand, 1969) and the revised edition of D'Arcy McNickle's (q.v.) *They Came Here First: The Epic of the American Indian* (New York: Harper's, 1975). McNickle questioned the division into ten culture areas usually used by anthropologists in classifying the multitude of Indian nations, and it should therefore be noted that Ruth

M. Underhill did manage to introduce a greater degree of clarity in her methods of classification in *Red Man's America*. Spicer's book, however, is especially notable for the number of original documents which are reproduced and McNickle's history focuses particularly on Indian treaties.

Following such general histories, it would be advisable to become familiar with the volumes in The Civilization of the American Indian Series published by the University of Oklahoma Press and, as of 1980, numbering some 146 titles, each on a specific tribe or aspect of Native American history or culture. On the whole, the entries in this series tend to be factually reliable and do not argue on behalf of special interest groups. For example, Donald E. Worcester's *The Apaches: Eagles of the Southwest* (Norman: University of Oklahoma Press, 1979) is a much more objective account of this much-maligned people than, in contrast, James L. Haley's *Apaches: A History and Culture Portrait* (New York: Doubleday, 1980) which already in the preface finds the author stating his belief that the Apaches today have no right to claim any land within the continental United States—land, as plunder, belonging to the spoils of the victor—and the history and culture portrait more or less proving the old adage that "world history is the judgment of history" and that the "right" people were the victors.

INDIAN WARS

The most popular book on this subject has been Dee Brown's (q.v.) *Bury My Heart at Wounded Knee: An Indian History of the American West* (New York: Holt, Rinehart, 1971), but, if viewed somewhat objectively, it is very much a reversal of traditional white men's histories, i.e., faceless, motiveless white savages making war on long-suffering, saintly, downtrodden Indians. In its way it continued a trend begun by Paul I. Wellman (q.v.) in *Death on Horseback* (Philadelphia: Lippincott, 1947), although in Brown's defense it must be noted that factually he was far more reliable than Wellman. All of which means that a general history on this specific subject that is at once factually reliable and balanced in perspective has yet to be written, although many books on various aspects of the subject, e.g., Mari Sandoz' (q.v.) *Cheyenne Autumn* (New York: McGraw-Hill, 1953), have appeared.

Somewhat related to the Indian wars is the reservation system which was the Anglo-American alternative to extermination, and both interesting factual studies, such as Clark Wissler's re-issued *Red Man Reservations* (New York: Macmillan, 1971), and stirring fictional treatments, such as D'Arcy McNickle's *The Surrounded* (New York: Dodd, Mead, 1936) and Benjamin Capps' (q.v.) *The White Man's Road* (New York: Harper's, 1969), have been published.

RELIGION

Ruth M. Underhill's companion volume to *Red Man's America, Red Man's Religion: Beliefs and Practices of the Indians North of Mexico* (Chicago: University of Chicago Press, 1965), is a good book with which to begin studying a very complex subject. Underhill described Indian religious behavior, belief, and ceremonies in understandable, non-technical terms. Frank Waters' (q.v.) two studies on aspects of this subject are also to be recommended, *Masked Gods: Navaho and Pueblo Ceremonialism* (Albuquerque: University of New Mexico Press, 1950) and *Book of the Hopi* (New York: Viking, 1969).

Members of the many Christian sects generally do not appreciate having Biblical stories reduced to myths and legends, and perhaps the same courtesy should have been long ago extended to Native American peoples. However such was not the case and in view of the titles of most of these books, nothing can be done to correct this situation here. Therefore, collections of Indian myths, legends, and tales are most easily subsumed under the heading of literature.

INDIAN LITERATURE

There are two general collections worthy of mention as valuable introductions, Frederick W. Turner's *The Viking Portable North American Indian Reader* (New York: Viking, 1974), a fine sampling of myths, tales, poetry, oratory, and autobiography, and Alan R. Velie's *American Indian Literature: An Anthology* (Norman: University of Oklahoma Press, 1979) which has a much wider selection of Indian poetry and—something Turner's collection does not have—a selection of Native American songs accompanied by piano scores. Both collections have parts of the Winnebago trickster cycle, Velie's more of it than Turner's, and a good complement to reading this cycle is Paul Radin's *The Trickster: A Study in American Indian Mythology* (New York: Philosophical Library, 1956) with additional commentaries by C.G. Jung and Karl Kerényi.

Theodora Kroeber rewrote nine California Indian stories for *The Inland Whale* (Bloomington: Indiana University Press, 1959), but for all of its virtues it does not have, of course, the cultural depth—nor was this the author's intention—of George Bird Grinnell's studies, *Pawnee Hero Stories and Folk-Tales* (1889; reissued by the University of Nebraska Press, 1961) with its notes on the origins, customs, and character of the Pawnee people, *Blackfoot Lodge Tales: The Story of a Prairie People* (1892; reissued by the University of Nebraska Press, 1962), and *By Cheyenne Campfires* (New Haven: Yale University Press, 1926). Of almost equal interest are Ruth Warner Giddings' *Yaqui Myths and Legends* (Tucson: University of Arizona Press, 1959), Ella A. Clark's *Indian Legends from the Northern Rockies* (Norman: University of Oklahoma Press, 1966), and Eugene Lee Silliman's collection of Blackfoot tales by James Willard Schultz (Apikuni), *Why Gone Those Times?* (Norman: University of Oklahoma Press, 1974).

Not since the height of the Roman Republic has the art of oratory been the consummate art it was among the American Indians. *Indian Oratory: Famous Speeches by Noted Indian Chieftains* (Norman: University of Oklahoma Press, 1971) edited by W.C. Vanderwerth is perhaps the best overall collection. Vine Deloria's *Custer Died for Your Sins* (New York: Macmillan, 1969) is a more modern example of a contemporary Sioux' view of the dominant Anglo-American culture.

AUTOBIOGRAPHIES AND BIOGRAPHIES

A good place to begin is by reading Lynne Woods O'Brien's *Plains Indian Autobiographies* (Boise: Idaho State University, 1973) which surveys the principal works written by Plains Indians with or without the assistance of a collaborator from an alien culture. One of the most interesting of the "as told to" autobiographies is *Plenty-Coups, Chief of the Crows* (Lincoln: University of Nebraska Press, 1962) by Frank B. Linderman, originally published as *American: The Life Story of a Great Indian, Plenty-Coups, Chief of the Crows* (New York: John Day, 1930).

It was a practice among the Plains Indians for every young brave to go out into the wilderness and through fasting wait for a vision to come to him. The vision was to give shape to his entire life in the future and might be equally relevant to the life of his nation. Certainly the best known of these visions is that narrated in *Black Elk Speaks* (New York: Morrow, 1932) "as told to" poet John G. Neihardt (q.v.). Black Elk was a Sioux medicine man and a book more concerned with the metaphysics and rituals of the Sioux is *The Sacred Pipe: Black Elk's Account of the Seven Rites of the Oglala Sioux* (Norman: University of Oklahoma Press, 1953) edited and recorded by Joseph Epes Brown.

Because there was not until recently any tradition of women's autobiography and because white men were little interested in Native American women, only a few Native American women's autobiographies have appeared, one of the most important being *Pretty-Shield, Medicine Woman of the Crows* (New York: John Day, 1932) "as told to" Frank B. Linderman.

In those cases where Native Americans were removed from reservations and educated in white schools, those who chose to write autobiographies did so with the intention of comparing Indian and white cultures. Almost invariably, Native American authors came to perceive that the honesty and truthfulness, the concern for others and the instinctive generosity of Native Americans were qualities all too distinctly Indian whereas it was the lack of these very qualities—however much they might be praised by white men—which characterize successful white men in the white culture. Charles A. Eastman, a Sioux who became a physician, wrote *From the Deep Woods to Civilization, Chapters in the Autobiography of an Indian* (Boston: Little, Brown, 1931) in which he recorded his greatest shock as being the discovery, when he became a lobbyist for Indian treaty rights in Washington, D.C., that buying legislators' votes was part of the accepted white man's civilization. Luther Standing Bear's three part autobiography is of enduring quality also, *My People the Sioux* (Boston: Houghton Mifflin, 1928), *My Indian Boyhood* (Boston: Houghton Mifflin, 1931), and *Land of the Spotted Eagle* (Boston: Houghton Mifflin, 1933).

Among Southwestern Native American autobiographies, one of the very best is *Sun Chief: The Autobiography of a Hopi Indian* (New Haven: Yale University Press, 1942) by Don C. Talayesva, an articulate account of the conflict between cultures. To this should be added *Geronimo: His Own Story* (New York: Ballantine, 1971), originally edited by S.M. Barrett but in this edition newly edited with an Introduction by Frederick W. Turner.

Without a doubt one of the finest Indian biographies is *Crazy Horse: The Strange Man of the Oglalas* (New York: Hastings House, 1942) by Mari Sandoz who many have said was more Indian than Anglo-American, although it was culture by adoption. Also highly to be recommended are Stanley Vestal's *Sitting Bull, Champion of the Sioux: A Biography* (Norman: University of Oklahoma Press, 1957) and Angie Debo's *Geronimo: The Man, His Time, His Place* (Norman: University of Oklahoma Press, 1976).

CULTURAL RESOURCES

Native Americans have nowhere been more misrepresented than in Hollywood films. This subject has been addressed in the five-part series *Images of Indians* (PBS, 1980).

For further recommended readings and sources of interest throughout this entire field, it is suggested that the following book, with a fully annotated bibliography, be consulted: *The Frontier Experience: A Reader's Guide to the Life and Literature of the American West* (work in progress) co-edited by Jon Tuska and Vicki Piekarski.

Neihardt, John G(neise-nau) (1881–1973) Western poet and author of Western fiction, born near Sharpsburg, Illinois. In 1886 Neihardt went to live with his family in his pioneer grandparents' sod-house on the upper Solomon River in Kansas. In 1891 the family moved to Wayne, Nebraska, having also lived briefly in Kansas City, and it was in Wayne that Neihardt graduated from the Nebraska Normal College with a Bachelor's degree at the age of 16. Until 1901, Neihardt worked at various odd jobs and published his first book of poetry, *The Divine Enchantment* (New

York: James T. White, 1900), which was heavily influenced by Vendanta philosophy; in 1901 he became an assistant to a trader working among the Omaha Indians on their reservation. For a time he edited a country weekly, the *Bancroft Blade*.

In 1908 he married Mona Martinsen, a sculptress and a former student of French sculptor, Auguste Rodin. Although Mona came from a family of comfortable wealth, she willingly committed herself to sharing Neihardt's frugal life of a poet while Neihardt worked on what he felt to be his masterpiece, the five American epics contained in his *A Cycle of the West* (New York: Macmillan, 1949). The first of these was *The Song of Hugh Glass* (New York: Macmillan, 1915). It attempted to wed the epical tone of Homer and Virgil to telling the anecdotal history of an American mountain man. *The Song of Three Friends* (New York: Macmillan, 1917) followed, a poem devoted to the lives of three men engaged in the early fur trade. Neihardt also took as his models the conventions of the Victorians and, for this reason, some critics have found his poetry too self-consciously literary while his themes have been declared less heroic than those in *The Iliad* or *The Aeneid*. The tone as well as the content began to change somewhat with the third in the cycle, *The Song of the Indian Wars* (New York: Macmillan, 1925). It combined the discoveries Neihardt had made concerning Native American metaphysics with the psychology of C.G. Jung. This stance was furthered, while the sense of tragedy became intensified, in *The Song of the Messiah* (New York: Macmillan, 1935). *The Song of Jed Smith* (New York: Macmillan, 1941) completed the cycle, a spiritual journey remarkable for the hardships Neihardt endured to finish it and, taken as a whole, whatever its weaknesses as epic, a personal achievement of the first order. In his old age, no longer able to read print, bus-loads of students would still regularly visit Neihardt and sit around his wheel-chair as he would recite his poetry from memory.

Yet, perhaps, Neihardt's ultimate importance as an American author, and his contribution to American literature, may rest with his short story collections, *The Lonesome Trail* (New York: John Lane, 1907) and *Indian Tales and Others* (New York: Macmillan, 1926). Equally worthy of consideration is his work as an amanuensis for the aged Sioux medicine man, Black Elk. Neihardt himself recognized that the fulfillment of American ideals, both cultural and spiritual, could not be separated from the vision of man's role as part of Nature true for Native Americans, that indeed only with the Native Americans as full participants could the great sorrows of nearly four hundred years be overcome through a newly discovered fraternity. He believed that not until all subsequent Americans came to love and respect the land as much as Native Americans always have would there be a truly spiritual and epical period.

This may have been undue idealism. But it was believed in by the Sioux themselves who, at Neihardt's funeral service in 1973, held their own sacred ceremony. It remains a tribute to Neihardt that in *Black Elk Speaks* (New York: Morrow, 1932) he came as close as any white man has ever come to perceiving the world and life as it is perceived by the Native American and the strange characteristic about the book is that of an uncanny permanence, a delicate and ineffable sensibility, the power and inner spiritual grandeur of a vision which, in the last analysis, exceeds words and the conceptualizations of language, an immersion into pure imagery, myth, and mystical understanding.

For further information see *John G. Neihardt* (Boise: Idaho State University Press, 1976) by Lucile F. Aly and the Afterword in *Black Elk Speaks* (New York: Pocket Books, 1972).

Newton, D(wight) B(ennett)

(1916—) Author of formulary Western fiction, born at Kansas City, Missouri. Newton wrote under his own name, and also under the pseudonyms Dwight Bennett, Clement Hardin, Ford Logan, and Dan Temple. He was educated in Kansas City schools and attended the University of Kansas City where he received a Master's degree in history. Although he apparently always knew he wanted to write, he came across a Max Brand (q.v.) story in a magazine at the age of 12 and that convinced him he should try his hand at Westerns.

Newton entered the U.S. Army during World War II and found himself stationed for a time in Oregon. He liked the state so much that he eventually came to live permanently in Bend, Oregon. Newton's first Western novel was *Guns of the Rimrock* (New York: Phoenix, 1946). His novel *Range Boss* (New York: Pocket, 1949) was the first Western novel bought and published as a paperback original, initiating a practice which is now fairly common but was once unthought of among paperback houses.

Almost from the beginning Newton felt the Nineteenth-century West a special subject, ranking with the Homeric and Arthurian sagas; in his words, "a story of men and women, often larger-than-life, working out their destinies by the most direct and dramatic of means, in a simpler time of epic proportions and against a magnificent setting." Max Brand's "larger-than-life" quality can be detected in Newton's books, as well as in his stated intentions, but what makes Newton's books different, and superior, to Brand's potboilers is his scrupulous attention to natural terrain—his sense of *real* places in the West.

D.B. Newton's Western novels under his own name are *Guns of the Rimrock* (1946), *The Gunmaster of Saddleback* (1948), *Range Boss* (1949), *Shotgun Guard* (1950), *Six-Gun Gamble* (1951), *Guns Along the Wickiup* (1954), *Rainbow Rider* (1954), *The Outlaw Breed* (1955), *Maverick Brand* (1962), *On the Dodge* (1962), *Guns of Warbonnet* (1963), *The Savage Hills* (1964), *Bullets on the Wind* (1964), *Fury at Three Forks* (1964), *The Manhunters* (1966), *Hideout Valley* (1967), *The Tabbart Brand* (1967), *Shotgun Freighter* (1968), *The Wolf Pack* (1968), *The Judas Horse* (1969), *Syndicate Gun* (1972), *Massacre Valley* (1973), *Range Tramp* (1973), *Trail of the Bear* (1975), *The Land Grabbers* (1975), *Bounty on Bannister* (1975), *Broken Spur* (1977), *Triple Trouble* (1978) [an anthology containing *Rainbow Rider* and two short novels], *The Texans* (1979), *Disaster Creek* (1981).

Newton's novels as Clement Hardin are *Hellbent for a Hangrope* (1954), *Cross Me in Gunsmoke* (1958), *The Lurking Gun* (1961), *The Badge Shooters* (1962), *Outcast of Ute Bend* (1965), *The Ruthless Breed* (1966), *The Paxman Feud* (1967), *The Oxbow Deed* (1967), *Ambush Reckoning* (1968), *Sheriff of Sentinel* (1969), *Colt Wages* (1970), *Stage Line to Rincon* (1971).

As Ford Logan, Newton has written *Fire in the Desert* (1954) and as Dan Temple *Outlaw River* (1955), *The Man from Idaho* (1956), *Bullet Lease* (1957), *Gun and Star* (1964).

Nye, Nelson C(oral) (1907 —) Author of formulary Western fiction, born at Chicago, Illinois. Nye early turned to writing pulp Westerns and published his first Western novel while still in his twenties, *Two-Fisted Cowpoke* (New York: Greenberg, 1936). He was prolific, producing as many as six novels a year under his own name or pseudonyms as Clem Colt and Drake C. Denver. Nye also worked for over forty years as a book reviewer on such newspapers as the *Cincinnati Times-Star*, *Buffalo Evening News*, *Tombstone Epigraph*, among others, and was for four years the frontier fiction columnist for *The New York Times Book Review*. Nye once summed up his philosphy for writing Western fiction this way: "The reader of Westerns don't want no part of 'history' that isn't history—he never was crazy about history in the first place. All he's hunting is a good, absorbing story of he-man adventure. . . . He don't want to be preached to, harangued at, nagged at, taught, or anything that adds up to discomfort. He wants to be entertained, period." Apparently these sentiments paid off for Nye, since, during his career, he produced over a hundred novels in addition to several books on his own personal hobby, the raising of quarter horses. His books sold over 30,000,000 copies and were translated into more than fifteen foreign languages. He retired from writing in 1971.

As Walt Coburn (q.v.), Nye stressed action and adventure at the expense of a coherent plot; his novels are filled with loose ends, characters who are introduced elaborately only to do nothing and never be seen again, situations and events that seem about to happen but which are left hanging or ignored altogether once the story takes a new turn, almost as if he wrote a book with a come-what-may attitude and refused ever to go back and rework that story when it got out of hand, and too many times it does.

C.L. Sonnichsen reported in his book *From Hopalong to Hud: Thoughts on Western Fiction* (College Station: Texas A&M University Press, 1978) that, according to Nye, Homer Croy (q.v.) was the first to produce a "sexy" Western in *West of the Water Tower* (New York: Harper's, 1923), and that Nye was the second with *Riders by Night* (New York: Dodd, Mead, 1950). Croy's novel deals with a seduction. Nye's novel is about an extremely attractive woman who is a "hoofer" and a virgin and who, wanting a husband, runs an advertisement in a newspaper to which the head of a gang of horse thieves responds. Of course, the girl immediately falls in love with the horse thief and by the end of the story the thief has helped round up his gang, made restitu-

tion, and can now settle down to married life with the "hoofer," no doubt breaking her into the delights of sexuality. Owen Wister (q.v.) had his Virginian wear down the schoolmarm's resistance to him when he was wounded by Indians and Nye resorted to a similar device in *Riders by Night*—which points up another failing of his books: they are riddled with clichés. The way women are portrayed never brings them to life and Indians, if they appear at all, are mindless savages. Having been written hurriedly, Nye's books suffer from errors of haste as do those of Louis L'Amour (q.v.). Nye broke off *Rider on the Roan* (New York: Ace, 1967) with half the plot still hanging and *Long Run* (New York: Macmillan, 1959), for which Nye was given the Spur Award by the Western Writers of America, is a formulary story which has been better written by others.

Nye's anti-historical attitude in his books was further augmented by his penchant to make heroes of unusual types, the horse thief in *Riders by Night*, a con man in *Wild Horse Shorty* (New York: Macmillan, 1944) and its sequel *Blood of Kings* (New York: Macmillan, 1946), or a man on the dodge in *Rider on the Roan*. This was not original with Nye, but it is more or less *typical*, and, as such, does constitute a departure from the moral purity usually ascribed to Western heroes by authors working in the Owen Wister tradition. Nye, also to his credit, read widely in Western fiction, promoting it continuously through his newspaper review work and his long-time association with the Western Writers of America.

Nelson C. Nye's Western novels under his own name are *Two-Fisted Cowpoke* (1936), *The Killer of Cibecue* (1936), *The Leather Slapper* (1937), *Quick-Fire Hombre*

(1937), *The Star-Packers* (1937), *G Stands for Gun* (1938), *The Bandit of Bloody Run* (1939), *Pistols for Hire* (1941), *Salt River Ranny* (1941), *Gunfighter Breed* (1942), *Cartridge-Case Law* (1944), *Wild Horse Shorty* (1944), *Blood of Kings* (1946), *The Barber of Tubac* (1947), *Gunman Gunman* (1949), *Riders by Night* (1950), *Caliban's Colt* (1950), *Thief River* (1951), *Born to Trouble* (1951), *Desert of the Damned* (1952), *Wide Loop* (1952), *Come A-Smokin* (1953), *Hired Hand* (1954), *The Red Sombrero* (1954), *Quick-Trigger Country* (1955), *The Lonely Grass* (1955), *The Parson of Gunbarrel Basin* (1955), *Bandido* (1957), *Maverick Marshal* (1958), *The Overlanders* (1958), *Long Run* (1959), *Horses, Women & Guns* (1959), *The Wolf That Rode* (1960), *The Last Bullet* (1960), *Gunfight at the OK Corral* (1960), *Not Grass Alone* (1961), *Hideout Mountain* (1962), *Rafe* (1962), *Death Valley Slim* (1963), *The Kid from Lincoln County* (1963), *Bancroft's Banco* (1963), *The Seven Six-Gunners* (1963), *Treasure Trail from Tucson* (1964), *Rogue's Rendevous* (1965), *Gunfeud at Tiedown* (1965), *Ambush at Yuma's Chimney* (1965), *The Marshal of Pioche* (1966), *Iron Hand* (1966), *Single Action* (1967), *Trail of Lost Skulls* (1967), *Rider on the Roan* (1967), *A Lost Mine Named Salvation* (1968), *Wolf Trap* (1969), *The Trouble at Pena Blanca* (1969), *Gringo* (1969), *The Texas Gun* (1970), *Kelly* (1971), *Trouble at Quinn's Crossing* (1971), *Hellbound for Ballarat* (1971), *The Clifton Contract* (1972).

The Waddy From Roarin' Fork (1944) was a Nelson Nye title published only in the United Kingdom.

Nye's books as Clem Colt are *Gunsmoke* (1938), *The Shootin' Sheriff* (1939), *The Bar Nothing Brand* (1939), *Center-Fire Smith* (1939), *Trigger Finger Law* (1940), *Hair Trigger Realm* (1940), *The Five Diamond Brand* (1941), *The Sure-Fire Kid* (1942), *The Desert Desperadoes* (1942), *Triggers for Six* (1942), *Trigger Talk* (1942), *Rustler's Roost* (1943), *Smoke-Wagon Kid* (1943), *Guns of Horse Prairie* (1943), *Fiddleback Ranch* (1944), *Maverick Canyon* (1944), *Renegade Cowboy* (1944), *Gunslick Mountain* (1945), *Once in the Saddle* (1946), *Coyote Song* (1947), *Saddle-Bow Slim* (1948), *Tough Company* (1952), *Strawberry Roan* (1953), *Smoke Talk* (1954).

Nye's books as Drake C. Denver are *The Feud at Sleepy Cat* (1940), *Tinbadge* (1941), *Wildcats of Tonto Basin* (1941), *Gun Quick* (1942), *Breed of the Chaparral* (1946).

O

O'Brian, Frank. See Garfield, Brian.

Ogden, George Washington (1871–1966) An author of Western

fiction in a formulary mode, born at Lawrence, Kansas. The son of a farmer, Ogden left home at 17 and worked as a railroad section hand. His education, which had been in Kansas public schools, ended in a formal sense at this time, but Ogden himself had an insatiable curiosity about people and, from early on apparently, an interest in becoming a writer. He started writing poetry and submitting it to the *Kansas City Star*. When one of his poems was accepted for publication, he was invited by the paper's literary editor to pay a visit. It marked for him the beginning of his career as a reporter, later journalist, and finally an editor. He went on to become city editor for the *Kansas City Times* before it was purchased by the *Star*, and he went on to work in an editorial capacity for the *Chicago Tribune* and Munsey magazine syndicate.

Ogden tried writing longer fiction, while still publishing poems, short stories, and articles in magazines and newspapers, and *Tennessee Todd* (New York: A.S. Barnes, 1903) was his first novel. It deals with Middle Western farm life. It was not until *The Well Shooters* (Chicago: A.C. McClurg, 1914) that Ogden turned to Westerns, and henceforth most of his production was in Western fiction. He was very much in the vein of such contemporaries as Hal G. Evarts, Sr. (q.v.) and Dane Coolidge (q.v.), trying to inject as much humor into his books as did W.C. Tuttle (q.v.), and yet trying to base most of his fictions on actual historical incidents. *Claim Number One* (Chicago: A.C. McClurg, 1922), for example, deals with a man's struggle to establish his ownership of a rich former Indian reservation that he had won in a drawing. Prior to book publication, it had been featured as a serial in the *Kansas City Star*. If Ogden's fiction is marred by anything, it would be his penchant for plots of the poor-boy-makes-good variety. From time to time, he would revert and write an agrarian romance, as he did in *The Bond Boy* (Chicago: A.C. McClurg, 1922). His best Western novel may well be *The Guard of Timberline* (New York: Dodd, Mead, 1934) with its dramatic setting during a forest fire.

George Washington Ogden's Western novels are *The Well Shooters* (1914), *The Long Fight* (1915), *Rustler of Wind River* (1917), *Land of Last Chance* (1919), *The Duke of Chimney Butte* (1920), *The Flockmaster of Poison Creek* (1921), *Trail's End* (1921), *Claim Number One* (1922), *The Baron of Diamond Trail* (1923), *Trail Rider* (1924), *Cow Jerry* (1925), *Road to Monterey* (1925), *Valley of Adventure* (1926), *West of Dodge* (1926), *Short Grass* (1927), *Sheep Limit* (1928), *Cherokee Trails* (1928), *Sooner Land* (1929), *Wasted Salt* (1930), *Steamboat Gold* (1931), *Fenced Water* (1931), *Men of the Mesquite* (1932), *White Roads* (1932), *A Man of the Badlands* (1933), *The Guard of Timberline* (1934), *Ranger of Blackwater* (1934), *Deputy Sheriff* (1935), *Whiskey Trail* (1936), *The Ghost Road* (1936), *Stockyards Cowboy* (1937), *Windy Range* (1938), *West of the Rainbow* (1942), *Custodian of Ghosts* (1951).

Films based on Ogden's Western fiction are *The Duke of Chimney Butte* (Robertson-Cole, 1921) directed by Frank Borzage, *The Trail Rider* (Fox, 1925) directed by W.S. Van Dyke.

Olsen, T(heodore) V(ictor)

(1932 —) Author of Western fiction born at Rhinelander, Wisconsin. Olsen was a fourth generation resident of the Rhinelander community, founded during the once-booming logging industry in Northern Wisconsin. He was educated in the Rhinelander public school system and, according to him, his childhood was unremarkable except for his inordinate preoccupation with reading novels by Zane Grey (q.v.) and Edgar Rice Burroughs (q.v.).

It was Olsen's intention, upon entering high school, to become a professional cartoonist, but that soon changed to creative writing. He enrolled in the University of Wisconsin at Stevens Point and in his junior year commenced work on a novel, *Haven of the Haunted* (New York: Ace, 1956), which he sold to a paperback house three months after he graduated with a Bachelor's degree. The next four years proved hard ones for Olsen, with the virtual disappearance of the pulp markets, and his only successes were several short stories for *Ranch Romances*, last of the pulp markets which also soon vanished (see Pulp and Slick Western stories), and a second Western novel, *The Man from Nowhere* (New York: Ace, 1959). His first published short story was bought and adapted for the television series *Dick Powell's Zane Grey Theatre* in 1957.

With the sale of *McGivern* (New York: Fawcett, 1960) to Gold Medal Books as an original, along with three more novels in quick succession, Olsen's career took a turn for the better and he continued to write formulary Western novels along with an occasional historical or contemporary novel in hardcover. His *magnum opus* was *Arrow in the Sun* (New York: Doubleday, 1969) which served as the basis for the controversial film *Soldier Blue* (Avco-Embassy, 1970) —based on the Sand Creek massacre of 1864.

T.V. Olsen's Western novels are *Haven of the Haunted* (1956), *The Man from Nowhere* (1959), *McGivern* (1960), *High Lawless* (1960), *Gunswift* (1960), *Ramrod Rider* (1961), *Brand of the Star* (1961), *Savage Sierra* (1962), *Break the Young Land* (1963) [written under the pseudonym Joshua Stark], *A Man Called Brazos* (1964), *Canyon of the Gun* (1965), *The Stalking Moon* (1965), *The Hard Men* (1965), *Bitter Grass* (1967), *The Lockhart Breed* (1967) [written under the pseudonym Joshua Stark], *Blizzard Pass* (1968), *Arrow in the Sun* (1969), *Keno* (1970) [written under the pseudonym Joshua Stark], *A Man Named Yuma* (1971), *Eye of the Wolf* (1971), *Summer of the Drums* (1972), *Starbuck's Brand* (1973), *Mission to the West* (1973), *Run to the Mountain* (1974), *Track the Man Down* (1972), *Day of the Buzzard* (1976), *Westward They Rode* (1976), *Bonner's Stallion* (1977), *Roots of the North* (1979), *Rattlesnake* (1979).

Films based on T.V. Olsen's Western fiction are *The Stalking Moon* (National General, 1969) directed by Robert Mulligan, *Soldier Blue* (Avco-Embassy, 1970) directed by Ralph Nelson [based on *Arrow in the Sun*].

Overholser, Wayne D(aniel) (1906 —) Prolific author of formulary Western fiction, born at Pomeroy, Washington. Overholser wrote Western fiction under his own name and six pseudonyms, Lee Leighton, Joseph Wayne, John S. Daniels, Mark Morgan, Wayne Roberts, and Dan J. Stevens. He grew up in Washington and Oregon and once worked for a short time in a sawmill on the Oregon coast. After finishing high school in 1924, he spent a year at Albany College and another at Oregon Normal School. From 1926 to 1942 he taught school in Tillamook, Oregon, except for 1928–1929 during which he was principal of a school in Mohler, Oregon. In 1934 he married Evaleth Miller. He studied at the University of Montana in 1934 and at the University of Southern California in 1939 and, ultimately, received his Bachelor's degree from the University of Oregon. In 1942 the Overholsers moved inland to Bend, Oregon, where he taught for three more years before turning to full-time writing. In 1948 the family moved to Boulder, Colorado. The Overholsers had three sons, John, Stephen, and Daniel whose names provided the ingredients for two of their father's pseudonyms: John S. Daniels, and Dan J. Stevens.

Overholser's desire to write developed early, but for some time he was not certain what he wanted to write. An interest in Western history, fostered by Oregon's rich pioneer tradition, led to a natural choice. By the mid 'Thirties he was selling short stories and novelettes to the Western pulp magazines. Ten years later his output included longer stories, from which some of his early books were drawn. His first novel, *Buckaroo's Code* (New York: Macmillan, 1947), had first appeared in *Western Action Magazine* for October, 1945. A 1946 magazine novel, *Gun Crazy*, was published as a paperback book in 1950. His third hardcover novel, *Draw or Drag* (New York: Macmillan, 1950), had appeared in shortened form in a magazine under the title "Showdown Valley."

The Colorado Authors' League presented an award to Overholser for the best adult fiction of 1950; he won the same award again ten years later. He was one of the six founders of the Western Writers of America in 1952. He served on that organization's board of directors in 1953 and again in 1957–1958.

For most of the 'Fifties and 'Sixties Overholser produced three or four new novels each year. On two occasions the annual tally climbed as high as seven. The use of pen-names was therefore inevitable. Publishers and writers seldom want to risk flooding the market with too many new titles under a single byline. The books published under Overholser's own name, principally by Macmillan, follow most closely the patterns of the formulary Western. As all of the author's work they are written with skill and an uncommon sensitivity to both people and places. *Steel to the South* (New York: Macmillan, 1951) tells of an attempt to build a railroad in central Oregon against the opposition of a self-styled king of the desert. In *Tough Hand* (New York: Macmillan, 1954) a young woman returns with a trail herd and a crew of hardcases to regain the ranch from which she had been driven years earlier. *Cast a Long Shadow* (New York: Macmillan, 1955) is a story of conflict arising out of the tangled claims to ownership of a Spanish land grant.

Many of the books written under the Joseph Wayne pen-name are concerned with the evolving character of a locale. For example, *By Gun and Spur* (New York: Dutton, 1952) is a story of the founding of an Oregon town very much as Bend, where the Overholsers were living during the 'Forties.

The first Joseph Wayne novel, *The Sweet and Bitter Land* (New York: Dutton, 1950), tells of the settling of an Oregon valley and of the larger-than-life cattleman, Matt Strang, whose vision shaped its early history. *The Long Wind* (New York: Dutton, 1953) is a story of homesteaders in the valley of the Frenchman Creek in Western Nebraska.

The books by Lee Leighton, written for Ballantine's line of Western paperbacks, are often built around interesting central characters whose growth and interaction with their surroundings are the main focus of attention. The title character of *Big Ugly* (New York: Ballantine, 1966) is Bill Shell who returns to his Nebraska home after several years as a gunfighter and attempts to build a useful life for himself and the woman he loves. *Bitter Journey* (New York: Ballantine, 1969) chronicles twenty years in the life of Bill Lang as he changes from gunman to Army scout to deputy sheriff and respectable citizen.

When it is well done, one of the most satisfying types of Western novel is the story of the coming to maturity of a young man (or a young woman) against a frontier background. Wayne Overholser made several notable contributions using this plot, such as Joseph Wayne's *The Sweet and Bitter Land*, Lee Leighton's *Killer Guns* (New York: Ballantine, 1969), and *The Violent Land* (New York: Macmillan, 1954) under his own name.

When veteran Western writer William MacLeod Raine (q.v.) died in 1954, he left a final novel unfinished. The manuscript of *High Grass Valley* was completed by Overholser and published in 1955. Overholser collaborated on one book with Robert G. Athearn, *Silent River* (New York: Avalon, 1956), published under the pseudonym

Wayne Roberts and *Colorado Gold* (New York: Ballantine, 1958) with Chad Merriman published under the pseudonym Gifford P. Chesire. Two Joseph Wayne books and one Lee Leighton book were written in collaboration with Lewis B. Patten (q.v.) as well as one juvenile, *The Meeker Massacre* (New York: Cowles Book Company, 1969), based on the Ute wars of 1879, under their own names. This last book won the Western Writers of America Spur Award for the best Western juvenile novel of the year.

Overholser's son, Stephen, wrote *A Hanging in Sweetwater* (New York: Doubleday, 1974), which won a Spur award for best Western novel. This first novel was followed by others just as good. It was clear that Wayne Overholser's tradition of award-quality Western fiction was ably being carried on by a second generation.

R.E.B.

Wayne D. Overholser's Western novels under his own name are *Buckaroo's Code* (1947), *West of the Rimrock* (1949), *Gun Crazy* (1950), *Draw or Drag* (1950), *Steel to the South* (1951), *Fabulous Gunman* (1952), *Valley of Guns* (1953), *The Violent Land* (1954), *Tough Hand* (1954), *Cast a Long Shadow* (1955), *Gunlock* (1956), *Desperate Man* (1957), *The Lone Deputy* (1957), *Hearn's Valley* (1958), *War in Sandoval County* (1960), *Standoff at the River* (1960), *The Judas Gun* (1960), *The Killer Marshal* (1961), *The Bitter Night* (1961), *The Trial of Billy Peale* (1962), *A Gun for Johnny Deere* (1963), *To the Far Mountains* (1963), *Death of a Cattle King* (1964), *Day of Judgment* (1965), [alternate title: *Colorado Incident*], *Ride into Danger* (1967), *Summer of the Sioux* (1967), *North to Deadwood* (1968), *Wheel of Fortune* (1968), *Buckskin Man* (1969), *The Noose* (1971), *The Long Trail*

North (1972), *Brand 99* (1972), *Sun on the Wall* (1973), *Red Snow* (1976), *The Mason County War* (1976), *The Dry Gulcher* (1977), *The Trouble Kid* (1978), *The Cattle Queen Feud* (1979), *Nightmare in Broken Bow* (1980).

Overholser has collaborated under his own name to finish *High Grass Valley* (1955) by William MacLeod Raine and with Lewis B. Patten wrote *The Meeker Massacre* (1969).

Overholser's novels as John S. Daniels are *Gunflame* (1952), *The Nester* (1953), *The Land Grabbers* (1955), *The Man from Yesterday* (1957), *Smoke of the Gun* (1958), *The Crossing* (1958), *Ute Country* (1959), *The Gunfighters* (1960), *The Hunted* (1964), *Deadline* (1965), *War Party* (1966), *Trail's End* (1966), *The Day the Killers Came* (1968), *The Three Sons of Adam Jones* (1969).

Overholser's novels as Lee Leighton are *Law Man* (1953), *Beyond the Pass* (1956), *Tomahawk*, (1958) [with Lewis B. Patten], *Colorado Gold* (1958) [with Chad Merriman], *Fight for the Valley* (1960), *Gut Shot* (1961), *Big Ugly* (1966), *Hanging at Pulpit Rock* (1967), *Bitter Journey* (1969), *Killer Guns* (1969), *You'll Never Hang Me* (1971), *Cassidy* (1973), *Greenhorn Marshal* (1974), *The Diablo Ghost* (1978).

Overholser's novel as Mark Morgan is *Fighting Man* (1953).

Overholser's novel as Wayne Roberts is *Silent River* (1956) [with Robert Athearn].

Overholser's novels as Dan J. Stevens are *Oregon Trunk* (1950), *Wild Horse Range* (1951), *Blood Money* (1956), *Hangman's Mesa* (1959), *Robbery at Bright Water* (1962), [alternate title: *Gun Trap at Bright Water*], *The Land Beyond* (1964), *West to Durango* (1966), *Killer from Owl Creek* (1967), *Stranger in Rampart* (1968), *Landgrabbers* (1969), *The Dry Fork Incident* (1969), *Hunter's Moon* (1973).

Overholser's novels as Joseph Wayne are *The Sweet and Bitter Land* (1950) [alternate title: *Gunplay Valley*], *The Snake Stomper* (1951), *By Gun and Spur* (1952) [alternate title: *Gun and Spur*], *The Long Wind* (1953), *Bunch Grass* (1954), *The Return of the Kid* (1955), *Showdown at Stony Crest* (1957) [with Lewis B. Patten], *Pistol Johnny* (1960), *The Gun and the Law* (1960) [with Lewis B. Patten], *The Bad Man* (1962), *Land of Promises* (1962), *Deadman Junction* (1963), *Proud Journey* (1963), *Red Is the Valley* (1967).

Films based on Wayne D. Overholser's Western fiction are *Star in the Dust* (Universal, 1956) directed by Charles Haas [based on *Law Man*], *Cast a Long Shadow* (United Artists, 1959) directed by Thomas Carr.

Owen, Hugh. See Faust, Frederick.

P

Parkman, Francis (1823–1893) An historian of the American frontier whose works, in particular *The Oregon Trail* (1849), came to influence the writing of Western fiction by others, born at Boston,

Massachusetts. An inheritance from his paternal grandfather who was a merchant permitted Parkman to devote his life to literature. As a child he was frail and in ill health, probably due to the same neurotic condition which plagued him all his adult life. He prepared for admission to Harvard University at Chauncy-Hall School but once he began his University career it was interrupted by illness. He went to Europe to recover and, following his return, received his Bachelor's degree in 1844 and his Bachelor's degree at law in 1846 although he had never intended to practice law and was never admitted to the bar. He was extremely interested in Native Americans and already at this youthful age sketched out his plan to write a history of the American forest. In 1846 he embarked on his famous overland journey which he recorded in *The Oregon Trail*. This was Parkman's reaction to the Native Americans whom he met: "For the most part, a civilized white man can discover very few points of sympathy between his own nature and that of an Indian. With every disposition to do justice to their good qualities, he must conclude that an impassable gulf lies between him and his red brethren. Nay, so alien to himself do they appear, that after breathing the air of the prairie for a few months or weeks, he begins to look upon them as a troublesome and dangerous species of wild beast."

Perhaps A.B. Guthrie, Jr., (q.v.) said it best in his Introduction to a re-issue of *The Oregon Trail* (New York: Mentor Books, 1950) when he wrote: "Parkman showed the confident ignorance of youth in attempting to assess Indian character, as manifested through behavior, by the measures of his own culture. I think it can be said, however, that few men had a quicker eye than he and none his purpose and ability to commit observations to paper. In these fresh-old pages we see the Sioux if we do not understand them."

When Parkman returned to the East, his psychological condition had visibly worsened. He was unable to bear light and invented a machine whereby he could write without seeing, although he dictated much of his work, satisfied if he could compose six sentences a day. His next important book was *Conspiracy of Pontiac and the Indian War of Conquest in Canada* (1851). He followed this with an indifferent novel, *Vassall Morton* (1856), and then resumed his efforts at recording the history of the European battle for domination of the New World, an area which found him more at home.

His last book, *A Half Century of Conflict* (1892), was no more charitable toward Native Americans than had been his first book, and, in terms of his influence, it was regrettable, since he surely was one of the founders of American history written by American historians and the way Western writers conceived of the West, and he set the tone and embodied the viewpoints which have long survived him. Of special interest are the two volumes published concerning Parkman's Western journey, The Journals of Francis Parkman (New York: Harper's, 1947).

Patten, Lewis B(yford) (1915–1981) Prolific author of formulary Western novels, born at Denver, Colorado. Patten attended the University of Denver. He owned and ran a cattle ranch in Western Colorado for six years before deciding that there had to be an easier way to earn a living. Having always liked reading Western fiction, Patten decided to try his hand at writing it and *Massacre at White River* (New York: Ace, 1952) was his first published book. The following year, "Guns of the Vengeful" appeared in *Giant Western Magazine*. Included in his early works are several Westerns written under the pseudonym Lewis Ford, two books under the name Gene Autry, and under the name Jim Bowie an entry in the Bowie novel series. In the late 'Fifties, Patten collaborated on three books with Wayne D. Overholser (q.v.): *Showdown at Stony Crest* (New York: Dell, 1957) and *The Gun and the Law* (New York: Dell, 1960) which were published under Overholser's pen-name Joseph Wayne and *Tomahawk* (New York: Ballantine, 1957) published under Overholser's pen-name Lee Leighton. In 1969, they collaborated on *The Meeker Massacre* (New York: Cowles Book Company, 1969), about the 1879 Ute Indian wars, published under Patten's and Overholser's own names, which won the Western Writers of America Golden Spur Award. Patten was the recipient of the Spur Award on two other occasions — in 1968 for *The Red Sabbath* (New York: Doubleday, 1968) and in 1972 for *A Killing in Kiowa* (New York: Signet, 1972).

From 1954 Patten turned out at least one book per year, more often three, and some years as many as six. A compelling storyteller, his treatment of the formulary plot conventions incorporated some unusual characters and storyline twists. On several occasions he made use of a teen-age protagonist as in *Top Man with a Gun* (New York: Fawcett, 1959) in which a 16-year-old

seeks revenge for the deaths of his father and sister or in *The Ordeal of Jason Ord* (New York: Doubleday, 1973) in which a 16-year-old is falsely accused of murder. Patten was perhaps best known for his book *Death of a Gunfighter* (New York: Doubleday, 1968), a marshal story which was made into a successful film. Quite often Patten's villains do not fall into the stereotyped mustache-twirling outlaw category, but, rather, are ordinary citizens. In *Death of a Gunfighter*, the people of the town turn against their marshal for the very reason they hired him — his expertise with a gun. A major conflict in many of Patten's stories is the alienation of the lawman by his peers and the townspeople. In *The Gallows of Graneros* (New York: Doubleday, 1975) a dim-witted Apache is a convenient suspect for an alleged rape and is hanged by a vigilante group. The marshal is forced to face alone the confrontation with the Apaches who wish to avenge the death of one of their tribal members.

Lewis B. Patten's Western novels are *Massacre at White River* (1952), *Gene Autry and the Ghost Riders* (1955) [published under Gene Autry's name], *Gunsmoke Empire* (1955), *Rope Law* (1956), *Gun Proud* (1957), *Pursuit* (1957), *Gene Autry and the Arapaho War Drums* (1957) [published under Gene Autry's name], *Showdown at Stony Crest* (1957) [with Wayne D. Overholser, published under the pen-name Joseph Wayne], *Valley of Violent Men* (1957), *Tomahawk* (1957) [with Wayne D. Overholser, published under the pen-name Lee Leighton], *Massacre at San Pablo* (1957), *White Warrior* (1958), *Five Rode West* (1958), *Sunblade* (1958), *Home Is the Outlaw* (1958), *The Adventures of Jim Bowie* (1958) [published under the name Jim Bowie], *Showdown at War Cloud* (1958), *The*

Man Who Rode Alone (1959), The Ruthless Men (1959), Top Man with a Gun (1959), Savage Star (1959), The Gun and the Law (1960) [with Wayne D. Overholser, published under the pen-name Joseph Wayne], Hangman's Country (1960), The Angry Horsemen (1960), Savage Town (1960), Renegade Gun (1961), Law of the Gun (1961), Outlaw Canyon (1961), The Gold Magnet (1962), The Scaffold at Hangman's Creek (1962), Flame in the West (1962), Vengeance Rider (1962), The Tarnished Star (1963), Guns at Gray Butte (1963), The Ruthless Range (1963), The Guilty Guns (1963), Ride for Vengeance (1964), Killer from Yuma (1964), Giant on Horseback (1964), Wagons East (1964), Proudly They Die (1964), The Arrogant Guns (1965), Cheyenne Drums (1965), Deputy from Furnace Creek (1966), Prodigal Gunfighter (1966), No God in Saguard (1966), Odds Against the Circle L (1966), Death Waited at Rialto Creek (1966), Bones of the Buffalo (1967), The Star and the Gun (1967), Ambush Creek (1967), Death of a Gunfighter (1968), The Red Sabbath (1968), The Meeker Massacre (1969) [with Wayne D. Overholser], The Youngerman Guns (1969), Posse from Poison Creek (1969), Apache Hostage (1970), Six Ways of Dying (1970), Red Runs the River (1970), A Death in Indian Wells (1970), Guilt of a Killer Town (1971), Hands of Geronimo (1971), Showdown at Mesilla (1971), Massacre Ridge (1971), Ride the Hot Wind (1971), Track of the Hunter (1971), The Homesteader (1972), Trial of Judas Wiley (1972), Feud at Chimney Rock (1972), A Killing in Kiowa (1972), The Cheyenne Pool (1972), The Gun of Jesse Hand (1973), Redskin (1973), The Tired Gun (1973), The Hide Hunters (1973), The Ordeal of Jason Ord (1973), Two for Vengeance (1974), Bounty Man (1974), Death Stalks Yellow-Horse (1974), Lynching at Broken Butte (1974), The Angry Town of Pawnee Bluffs (1974), The Orphans of Coyote Creek (1975), Vow of Vengeance (1975), The Gallows of Graneros (1975), The Lawless Breed (1976), Ambush at Soda Creek (1976), Man Out-Gunned (1976), Ride a Crooked Trail (1976), Trial at Apache Junction (1977), The Killings at Coyote Springs (1977), Hunt the Man Down (1977), Villa's Rifles (1977), Cheyenne Captives (1978), Death Rides a Black Horse (1978), The Law in Cottonwood (1978), The Trail of the Apache Kid (1979), Ride a Tall Horse (1980).

Patten's novels under the name Lewis Ford are Gunmen's Grass (1954), Gunfighter from Montana (1955), Maverick Empire (1964).

Films based on Patten's Western fiction are Red Sundown (Universal, 1956) directed by Jack Arnold [based on Gun Proud], Death of a Gunfighter (Universal, 1969) directed by Allen Smithee, Don't Turn the Other Cheek (Italian-Spanish, 1974) directed by Duccio Tessari [based on Killer From Yuma].

Pattullo, George (1879–1967) Noted short story writer for magazines who in the first decade of the Twentieth century concentrated on local color tales with a Western setting, born at Woodstock, Ontario. Pattullo attended the Woodstock Collegiate Institute before pursuing a career in journalism working for newspapers in Montreal, London, and Boston, until 1908, when he inherited wealth and could afford to retire to devote himself full-time to magazine writing. He was a prolific short story

writer first for *McClure's* and, later, *The Saturday Evening Post*. Pattullo became a special correspondent for *The Saturday Evening Post*, accompanying the American Expeditionary Force into France in 1917-1918 and in 1919 he went to Germany. Returning to the States, he spent the remainder of his life as a resident of New York City, writing society stories. Pattullo published several of his Western short stories in a collection titled *The Untamed* (New York: Fitzgerald, 1911) and followed it with a novel, *The Sheriff of Badger: A Tale of the Southwest Border* (New York: Appleton, 1912).

W.H. Hutchinson, who in his Introduction to *The Rhodes Reader* (Norman: University of Oklahoma Press, 1957) compared Pattullo's initial impact on Western fiction to a "skyrocket," claimed that Pattullo's story "Corazón," in *The Untamed*, "may well be the finest story about a horse ever written." On the other hand, Edwin W. Gaston, Jr., in his book *The Early Novel of the Southwest* (Albuquerque: University of New Mexico Press, 1961), addressing himself to Pattullo's novel *The Sheriff of Badger*, written as a result of experiences Pattullo had while on a trip into the Southwest that culminated in his marrying Lucile Wilson of Dallas, Texas, in 1913, was far more negative. Contrasting Zane Grey (q.v.) and George Pattullo with Andy Adams (q.v.) and Eugene Manlove Rhodes (q.v.), Gaston preferred the realism of Adams and Rhodes to the romanticism of Grey and Pattullo. "As a result of Grey's and Pattullo's work," Gaston wrote, "as well as that of many who followed them, a superficial concept of the cowboy developed which has plagued range fiction ever since. This concept reveals a figure at utter variance with the true cowboy. . . . The cumulative effect of such cowboy literature has been to mold and stiffen a human being into a cardboard figure, armed with blazing six-shooters and roaming the West in search of high adventure." Depending on a reader's taste, however, such romanticism may indeed be a virtue rather than a vice.

Peace, Frank. See Cook, Will.

Pehrson, Howard (1914 —) Author of Western fiction, born at Marshall, Minnesota. Pehrson was educated at the University of Minnesota and spent many years as an advertising executive before devoting himself to writing Western fiction in 1966. His first Western novel was *Outlaw Doc* (New York: Warner Books, 1969), published under the pseudonym David King. Pehrson wrote subsequently under a total of three pseudonyms. As David King, he went on to write *There Was a Crooked Man* (New York: Warner Books, 1970), *Butch Cassidy, the Sundance Kid, and the Wild Bunch* (New York: Warner Books, 1970), *Rage on the Range* (New York: Doubleday, 1977), and *The Fiddler* (New York: Doubleday, 1978). As Matt Weston, he wrote two books in the Morgan series with *Morgan* (New York: Warner Books, 1970) and *Morgan's Revenge* (New York: Warner Books, 1971). As Jake Logan (see House Names) he wrote two entries in the Slocum series, *Ride Slocum, Ride* (Chicago: Playboy Press, 1975) and *Slocum's Gold* (Chicago: Playboy Press, 1976). Pehrson's Westerns tend to stress savage conflict. In *Rage on the Range*, his protagonist is scalped by marauding Indians and mauled by a wolf before, more dead than alive, he reaches Green River, Wyoming, and finds himself in the middle of a war between cattlemen and sheepmen. His books also enjoyed popularity abroad.

Perry, George Sessions (1910–1956) Novelist and short story writer, contributing chiefly to *The Saturday Evening Post* and known for his regional interest in the Southwest, born at Rockdale, Texas. Perry attended three different universities, including Purdue, but never got beyond his freshman year. After knocking around the world a bit, he began writing short stories which regularly appeared in the *Post*. During World War II Perry was a war correspondent for the *Post* and for *The New Yorker*.

Perry received a co-script writing credit for the film *Arkansas Traveler* (Paramount, 1938) and, as an avocation, raised Hereford cattle on his ranch in Milam County, Texas. His novel *Walls Rise Up* (New York: Doubleday, 1939) is set in the Brazos River bottoms near his boyhood home at Rockdale. It served as a forerunner for *Hold Autumn in Your Hand* (New York: Viking, 1941), a romantic story about poor farmers which won both the National Book Award and the 1941 award for the best Texas book of the year from the Texas Institute of Letters. It was later filmed as *The Southerner* (United Artists, 1945). Critics of the novel called it an optimist's version of John Steinbeck's (q.v.) novel of two years previously, *The Grapes of Wrath* (New York: Covici, Friede, 1939). Perry's *Hackberry Cavalier* (New York: Viking, 1944) consists of a series of stories about backwoods types in Texas,

held together by its central character, Edgar Selfridge, whose great adventure is becoming a war correspondent. The stories are nearly all of the tall tale variety and invariably have happy endings. The year before Perry had edited a notable anthology, embodying the same principles, titled *Roundup Time: A Collection of Southwestern Writing* (New York: McGraw-Hill, 1943). Perry's play *My Granny Van* (New York: McGraw-Hill, 1949) was produced in-the-round in Dallas, and has a Rockdale, Texas, setting and he persisted in this optative vein with the novel, *Tale of a Foolish Farmer* (New York: McGraw-Hill, 1951).

The Southerner (United Artists, 1945) was directed by Jean Renoir.

Pike, Charles R. See Harknett, Terry.

Porter, Katherine Anne (1890–1980) Pulitzer Prize-winning short story writer, novelist, and essayist, some of whose stories have a Western setting, born at Indian Creek, Texas. A great-great-great-granddaughter of Daniel Boone, Porter was raised in Texas and Louisiana in a household filled with relatives and servants, many of "ripening age," which gave her a unique understanding of family tradition that became an important aspect of her subsequent fictional

works. She was educated at home until age 8, and then attended small Southern convent schools where she received an excellent classical education. At a very early age she began to write and before publishing her first story, "Maria Concepcíon," in *Century* magazine in 1923, she had destroyed hundreds of stories. Her early career as a writer included book reviewing, political writing, editing, ghostwriting, and hack writing of all kinds for various publications and newspapers including the Fort Worth *Critic* and Denver's *Rocky Mountain News*. Porter lived in a number of places including Denver, Chicago, Mexico City, New York City, Paris, France, Louisiana, upper state New York, Washington, D.C., and Maryland, this last where she finally made her home. In 1918, while in Denver, she barely survived the influenza epidemic. Shortly thereafter, a chest problem was diagnosed as tuberculosis and she spent eighteen months in a sanitarium in West Texas. Although the diagnosis was erroneous, Porter continued to be plagued by illness.

"Maria Concepcíon" was the first of many rich explorations of the inner workings of her heroines. The story, set in Mexico as were her next two published stories "Virgin Violeta" and "The Martyr" which also appeared in *Century* magazine, was collected in her first book, *Flowering Judas* (New York: Harcourt, Brace, 1930), a collection of psychologically penetrating stories set in Mexico and the United States which was re-issued in 1935 with four additional stories. Her next two collections, *Pale Horse, Pale Rider* (New York: Harcourt, Brace, 1938) and *The Leaning Tower and Other Stories* (New York: Harcourt, Brace, 1944), both included stories featuring her well-known creation, Miranda. The Miranda stories, which are primarily set in Texas, include "Old Mortality" and "Pale Horse, Pale Rider," two short novels in *Pale Horse, Pale Rider*, and "The Old Order," a series of short vignettes in *The Leaning Tower*, and are about the childhood and early womanhood of Miranda, her family, and her environment. Although many critics believe Miranda to be an autobiographical character, Porter called her an "observer." "Noon Wine," in *Pale Horse, Pale Rider*, is perhaps one of Porter's best stories about life on a rural farm in Texas.

A collection of essays and occasional pieces was published under the title *The Days Before* (New York: Harcourt, Brace, 1952) and her only novel was *Ship of Fools* (Boston: Little, Brown, 1962). She was the recipient of many awards including a Guggenheim Fellowship in 1931, the Gold Medal from the Society of Libraries of New York in 1940, the O. Henry Award in 1962, and the National Book Award in 1966, the same year she received the Pulitzer Prize for *The Collected Stories of Katherine Anne Porter* (New York: Harcourt, Brace, 1965). *The Collected Essays and Occasional Writings of Katherine Anne Porter* (New York: Delacorte, 1970) was published in 1970. Although she never received a college degree, she served as a guest lecturer at a number of colleges from 1949 through 1962 and was Writer-in-Residence at the University of Virginia in Charlottesville in 1958. She received honorary degrees from a number of colleges such as North Carolina Women's College, Smith College, the University of Michigan, and the University of Maryland.

Porter's short stories and short novels, although lacking in plot, are well-written, well thought out character studies which often have a dream-like quality about them. She was perhaps at her best when she recalled her own past and wrote about children or old people who believe in building a home for their family. Solidarity and tradition within the family is a recurring theme in her stories, along with sudden unexpected acts of violence that often occur in life, and the inevitability of death. If one accepts Mary Austin's (q.v.) definition of a regional author that the region, as a character, must be an integral part of the story and that the story must be of the region, not about it, then Porter was not really a regional writer. The region, the land, in her stories serves only as a background and many times the reader is not even certain where the story is set unless it is clearly stated. Unlike the unceasing wind and the dry open spaces of Dorothy Scarborough's (q.v.) Texas novel, *The Wind* (New York: Harper's, 1925), which comes to mind, with Porter one remembers Mr. Thompson and Mr. Hatch of "Noon Wine" or the strength and strong will of Maria Concepcíon. This is not meant as a slight to Porter for she was able to create unforgettable characters. J. Frank Dobie wrote about her that "her stories penetrate psychology, especially the psychology of a Mexican hacienda, with rare finesse. Her small canvases sublimate the inner realities of men and women. She appeals only to cultivated taste, and to some tastes no other fiction writer in America today is her peer in subtlety."

The teleplay *Noon Wine* (ABC, 1966) was directed by Sam Peckinpah.

For further information see *Katherine Anne Porter* (New York: Twayne Publishers, 1965) by George Hendrick, *Katherine Anne Porter: The Regional Stories* (Austin: Steck-Vaughn, 1967) by Winifred S. Emmons, and *Katherine Anne Porter* (New Jersey: Prentice-Hall, 1979) edited by Robert Penn Warren.

Porter, William Sydney (1862–1910)

Creator of the Cisco Kid, author of numerous short stories with a Western setting published under the name O. Henry, born at Greensboro, North Carolina. Porter's mother died when he was 3 and he attended a school taught by an aunt which he left when he was 15. He then worked for five years in his uncle's drugstore before, in 1882, departing for Texas for reasons of health; he suffered from lung disease. He spent two years on a ranch owned by friends from Greensboro and it was here that he picked up smatterings of French and German and a good bit of Spanish which he would later incorporate into his stories. Going to Austin, Texas, in 1884 he spent ten years, first as a clerk and bookkeeper, then as a draftsman in a state land office, and finally as a bank teller. It was this last job which got him into trouble. He eloped with his first wife in 1887. He began on a career of writing short sketches, some of which appeared in the *Detroit Free Press* and in 1894 he bought a newspaper titled *Iconoclast* for $250, retitling it *The Rolling Stone*. A year later he gave up this paper and tried a year in Houston where the *Daily Post* carried his "Tales of the Town" and "Some Postscripts," columns which were later collected in book form. It was at this point that Porter was summoned to Austin to stand charges for embezzlement of funds from the

First National Bank. Porter, it would seem was only nominally guilty, but he did not help matters much by catching a train in the opposite direction, landing in New Orleans, Louisiana. Here he unloaded bananas before heading for British Honduras. Once there he made the acquaintance of Al Jennings, the train robber who later became a motion picture actor, and his brother Henry who were hiding out with $30,000 from a successful robbery. Porter joined them and together they traveled throughout South America and Mexico until news of his wife's serious illness brought him back to Austin in 1897. That was it for Porter. In March of the next year he was sentenced to five years in the Ohio State Penitentiary, lessened to three years and three months for good behavior. It was not a total ordeal since Porter got to work in the prison pharmacy, was permitted to sleep in the prison hospital, and, occasionally, could even roam the streets at night. Porter probably took his pen-name from Orrin Henry, a prison guard.

Once he was released, in July 1901, Porter went first to Pittsburgh, Pennsylvania, and finally to New York City, the latter place as the result of Gilman Hall, an editor of *Ainslee's Magazine*. He found writing easy to put off and only wrote if prodded and hassled by editors; the two quarts of whiskey he drank a day seemed not to interfere with his creative faculties in the least. He died of tuberculosis shortly after establishing a literary career and marrying a second time.

Heart of the West (New York: Doubleday, 1904) was Porter's collection of Western short stories and it contains "The Caballero's Way" which features a character named the Cisco Kid. His stories, by modern standards, are dull, repetitive, mechanical, filled with forgotten slang and flat char-

acters, with an opacity of personality to make the surprise twists at the end effective. But they served the public well at the time he wrote them.

Films based on O. Henry's story "The Caballero's Way" are *The Caballero's Way* (Societe Française, 1914) with no director credited, *The Border Terror* (Universal, 1919) directed by Harry Harvey, and *In Old Arizona* (Fox, 1929) directed by Raoul Walsh and Irving Cummings [this last was the first all-talking Western feature film]. Films based on the Cisco Kid character are *The Cisco Kid* (Fox, 1931) directed by Irving Cummings, *The Return of the Cisco Kid* (20th-Fox, 1939) directed by Herbert I.

Warner Baxter as the Cisco Kid in In Old Arizona *(Fox, 1929) directed by Raoul Walsh and Irving Cummings.*

Leeds, *The Cisco Kid and the Lady* (20th-Fox, 1939) directed by Herbert I. Leeds, *Viva Cisco Kid* (20th-Fox, 1940) directed by Norman Foster, *Lucky Cisco Kid* (20th-Fox, 1940) directed by H. Bruce Humberstone, *The Gay Caballero* (20th-Fox, 1940) directed by Otto Brower, *Romance of the Rio Grande* (20th-Fox, 1941) directed by Herbert I. Leeds, *Ride On, Vaquero* (20th-Fox, 1941) directed by Herbert I. Leeds, *The Cisco Kid Returns* (Monogram, 1945) directed by John P. McCarthy, *(The Cisco Kid) In Old New Mexico* (Monogram, 1945) directed by Phil Rosen, *South of the Rio Grande* (Monogram, 1945) directed by Lambert Hillyer, *The Gay Cavalier* (Monogram, 1946) directed by William Nigh, *South of Monterey* (Monogram, 1946) directed by William Nigh, *Beauty and the Bandit* (Monogram, 1946) directed by William Nigh, *Riding the California Trail* (Monogram, 1947) directed by William Nigh, *Robin Hood of Monterey* (Monogram, 1947) directed by Christy Cabanne, *King of the Bandits* (Monogram, 1947) directed by Christy Cabanne, *The Valiant Hombre* (United Artists, 1949) directed by Wallace Fox, *The Gay Amigo* (United Artists, 1949) directed by Wallace Fox, *The Daring Caballero* (United Artists, 1949) directed by Wallace Fox, *Satan's Cradle* (United Artists, 1949) directed by Ford Beebe, *The Girl from San Lorenzo* (United Artists, 1950) directed by Derwin Abrahams.

Other Western films, not based on the character of the Cisco Kid, are *The Texan* (Paramount, 1930) directed by John Cromwell [based on the short story "The Double-Dyed Deceiver"] remade as *The Llano Kid* (Paramount, 1939) directed by Edward Venturini; and *Black Eagle* (Columbia, 1948) directed by Robert Gordon [based on the short story "The Passing of the Black Eagle"]. *O. Henry's Full House* (20th-Fox, 1952), a compendium film, contained an episode titled "The Ransom of Red Chief" based on the short story of that title directed by Howard Hawks.

The Cisco Kid (Syndicated, 1951–1955) was seen on television, 156 half-hour episodes in all, many of them in color, with Duncan Renaldo in the title role.

The Cisco Kid (Mutual, 1943) was heard on radio for one year with Jackson Beck as the Kid.

Portis, Charles (McColl) (1933—)

Reporter and Western novelist born at El Dorado, Arkansas. Portis was the son of Samuel Palmer Portis, a school superintendent, and he was educated in Arkansas public schools. He joined the U.S. Marines 1952–1955, attaining the rank of Sergeant. After discharge, he entered the University of Arkansas from which he received a Bachelor's degree with a major in journalism in 1958. Following graduation, Portis worked as a reporter for the *Commercial Appeal* in Memphis, Tennessee, in 1958, as a reporter for the *Arkansas Gazette* in Little Rock from 1959–1960, and a New York reporter and London correspondent for the *New York Herald-Tribune* from 1960–1964.

In 1964 Portis turned to writing fiction, publishing first *Norwood* (New York: Simon & Schuster, 1966), a mainstream novel which soon became a motion picture. His next book, *True Grit* (New York: Simon & Schuster, 1968), proved a literary blockbuster, selling over a million copies. The novel was also serialized in *The Saturday Evening Post*. Paramount Pictures and Batjac,

John Wayne's production company, vied for screen rights, and they finally went to Paramount for $300,000, although Wayne was signed to star as the indomitable lawman, Rooster Cogburn, a role for which Wayne won his only Oscar.

True Grit, as a novel, has been called "an epic and a legend" and "a book that speaks to every American who can read." Perhaps this praise is somewhat excessive, but there is no denying that Portis did write an excellent tale of Western fiction filled with memorable characters as Cogburn who sets out to find the murderer of the father of Mattie Ross, a hard-headed enterprising teenage girl.

D.K.-M.

True Grit (Paramount, 1969) was directed by Henry Hathaway.

Postl, Karl Anton (1793–1864)

Popular author who wrote travel sketches and novels of American life in both English and German under the pen-name Charles Sealsfield, born at Poppitz, Moravia, then under Austrian rule. After completing Gymnasium, the equivalent to the American high school, in Znaim, Postl attended Charles University at Prague, initially as a student of philosophy but, later, after being pressured by his family, as a candidate for the priesthood. Postl entered the monastic *Kreuzherrenorden* of Prague in 1814 and, in 1816, was ordained and appointed secretary to the order's grand master. Never an enthusiastic priest, Postl preferred mixing in the worldly circles of Austria's aristocracy and higher bureaucracy where he was welcome by virtue of his position and as a well-mannered young man who was fluent in French, played the piano, a connoisseur of wines, and an excellent hand at whist. He also kept a horse, a cellar of choice vintages, and cultivated friendships with Freemasons and other men of liberal opinion. In 1822 Postl was reprimanded for allowing his social obligations to interfere with his religious duties and was threatened with reassignment to a small and distant rural parish. In the shadow of this frightful prospect, he abandoned the priesthood and, with the help of the Freemasons, fled Austria in the spring of 1823 to seek his fortune in the New World.

It was during this first sojourn in the United States, from 1823 to 1826, that Postl assumed the identity of Charles Sealsfield, "clergyman, native of Pennsylvania." Residing for a time in New Orleans and then in Kittanning, Pennsylvania, he made two trips along the Western frontier gathering material for his first book, *The United States of North America As They Are in Their Political, Religious, and Social Relations* (1827). In it he sketched a vast and chaotic land, rich in opportunity and danger, teeming with every conceivable human type relentlessly pursuing but one object: money. For Postl, as for most educated Europeans, America seemed the personification of avarice and bad manners. Yet it was precisely, he believed, the bold, violent, and greedy men—even murderers and thieves—who were best fit to tame the wilderness and who were in turn civilized by the frontier with its institutions of democracy and private property. This was a theme that would be developed more fully in his later novels. General Andrew Jackson, recently defeated for the presidency, was idolized by Postl as the embodiment of backwoods republicanism just as he savagely ridiculed John Quincy Adams as a reactionary aristocrat behind whose fashionably cool facade strutted a would-be king, a callous, cynical manipulator of the masses. Henry Clay was derided as a brazen, unflappable liar and political climber whose amazing career was only understandable in terms of the morose stupidity of the average Kentuckian — that "half horse, half-alligator" subhuman which Postl delighted in lampooning. He was not blind to the contradictions in American life, where humanitarian idealism existed alongside Indian wars and slavery and where free "democratic" elections often became drunken brawls over crude slogans selfishly understood. Nevertheless, he judged it a glorious country where a strong, intrepid man could make his fortune unencumbered by classes, kings, armies, spies, and taxes.

Returning to Europe in 1826, Postl first offered himself as a spy to the Austrian government, claiming to have knowledge of secret British plans to sow revolution on the continent. Rejected as a mere adventurer, Postl penned a witty and bitter account of conditions within the Hapsburg dynasty and then went again to the United States. He lived for a time at Kittanning before traveling to Mexico and arriving in New Orleans in March, 1829 with considerable wealth with which he bought a 1,500 acre cotton plantation on the Red River. Abandoning this venture after several months, he moved to New York City to become editor of the Bonapartist journal *Courier des États Unis* and published his first novel, *The Indian Chief, or Tokeah and the White Rose* (1829). In 1831, he moved to Switzerland where he remained until his death.

In *The Indian Chief*, a noble savage, Tokeah, warrior chief of the Oconees, although an implacable enemy of the intruding settlers, saves the life of an infant white girl, White Rose, and raises her as a sister to his only daughter, Canondah. When, some years later, the pirate Lafitte attacks Tokeah's village and kills Canondah, the chief takes White Rose to New Orleans and gives her as wife to the man she loves, a handsome, courageous English aristocrat whose life she had saved in the swamps. With the remnants of his ever-diminishing tribe, childless Tokeah retreats Westward only to be killed by hostile Plains Indians for whom he was an intruder. Whereas Indians were mentioned only as the cunning enemies of General Jackson in *The United States of North America*, in *The Indian Chief* they are uniformly honest, taciturn, brave, and have a decided moral edge on the uncouth, grasping backwoodsmen, many of whom are escaped criminals from the East. For the knightly Tokeah to be driven from his home by such men as these seems tragic, but the injustice is resolved in the far grander spectacle of a superior, universal civilization rightly triumphing over barbarism. Although sentimental and below the standard of his later novels as literature, *The Indian Chief* presents a relatively graphic picture of frontier life and Indian culture. When revised and published in Zürich, Switzerland, as *Der Legitime und die Republikaner (The Legitimate and the Republican)* in 1833, it was to establish its author as a leading representative of the ethnographic school of writing.

Between 1833 and 1843 Postl produced a spate of anonymously published novels whose popularity on both sides of the Atlantic earned him the title once held by Sir Walter Scott, "The Great Unknown." His best and most popular novels are *Nathan Der Squatter-Regulator (Nathan the Squatter-Regulator, or the First American in Texas)* (1838) and *Das Cajütenbuch (The Cabin Book, or National Characteristics)* (1841). As in *The Indian Chief* Postl sought to create the "higher" *Volksroman*, a novel in which the hero is not an individual but an entire people whose characteristics are manifested in a series of dramatic events or realized in a representative figure. In Nathan Strong, loosely based on the cattleman-adventurer Philip Nolan, Postl portrayed the exemplary pioneer: huge, fierce, and indomitable, a man who had studied philosophy in Germany before coming to Texas, driven by a burning hunger for freedom and property. In *The Cabin Book*, the heroes are the settlers of the Texas prairie, hardened, wily farmers and ranchers who win the struggle for independence in 1836. By contrast, the demoralized Mexicans are obviously victims of an oppressive and unjust social order.

Postl's earliest works were strongly influenced by James Fenimore Cooper (q.v.) whose novels began appearing in Germany in the 1820s. Highly critical of Cooper's characters, he thought them unrealistic and exaggerated: his Indians talked too much, his civilized ladies were lifeless, and his trappers unbelievable. He liked least *Notions of the Americans: Picked Up by a Travelling Bachelor* (1828) whose treatment of slavery he found "barren, exclusive, unloveable, even inhuman." Whereas Cooper's novels tended to be historical romances set in decorative locales with characters lacking in sociological dimensions, Postl treated contemporary realities wherein people were shaped by and struggled with social conditions. During the 1840s there was a veritable Sealsfield "mania" when pirated translations began appearing in *Blackwood's Magazine* and from the Winchester publishing house in New York. Many considered him a great American novelist. Henry Wadsworth Longfellow acknowledged his influence and referred to him as "our favorite Sealsfield," whereas, on the contrary, Edgar Allan Poe thought the enthusiasm for his books "utterly ridiculous."

J.D.F.

Pulp and Slick Western Stories

The distinctions "pulp" and "slick" are derived from the kinds of paper on which the various periodicals were printed. Dime novels were pulp publications the way *The Saturday Evening Post* was a slick publication.

The pulp Western in fact had its beginnings in the dime novels of the Nineteenth century. The opening of the West had been heralded first in two epic poems, *The Mountain Muse* (1813) by Daniel Bryan and *The Backwoodsman* (1818) by James Kirk Paulding, after which came the first three novels in James Fenimore Cooper's (q.v.) Leatherstocking saga, *The Pioneers* (1823), *The Last of the Mohicans* (1826), and *The Prairie* (1827) as well as Timothy Flint's (q.v.) Southwestern novel, *Francis Berrian* (1826). Emerson Bennett's (q.v.) novel *The Prairie Flower* (1849) sold over a hundred thousand copies and was the first attempt to make a fictional hero of Kit Carson (see Historical Personalities). Coupled with the sensationalism of Mayne Reid's (q.v.) novels, the market was ripe for a popular and inexpensive series of Western adventure stories. In 1858 Erastus and Irwin Beadle, after success with *The Dime Song Book*, engaged Robert Adams as a partner, moved their place of business from Buffalo to New York City, calling their firm the House of Beadle and Adams. The first complete novel under one cover offered for a dime — hence the appellation "dime novel" — was Ann S. Stephens' (q.v.) *Malaeska: The Indian Wife of the White Hunter* (1860). It sold 65,000 copies within the first few months. Edward S. Ellis' *Seth Jones: Or, the Captives of the Frontier* (1860) soon followed and it sold 60,000 copies almost immediately, was translated into half a dozen languages, and, in time, sold 600,000 copies.

Orville J. Victor, formerly a journalist from Sandusky, Ohio, became Beadle and Adams' editor-in-chief, a position he retained for thirty years. Once rival publishers began to spring up, Victor had a ready solution: he advised Beadle writers to "kill more Indians." Although the formats might vary the stories were nearly all the same. They ran generally between 30,000 and 50,000 words with the main emphasis on continuous action and inflated descriptions. Not all dime novels were Westerns, but a good many of them were. Unlike Cooper who at least attempted to face the tragic consequences of America's total commitment to material progress, the dime novelists avoided the darker issues and instead celebrated the doctrine of Manifest Destiny. Percy St. John, as one example among all too many, wrote in *Queen of the Woods: or, The Shawnee Captive* (1868) of the pioneers: "Never weary, never conquered, they advanced still onward toward the setting sun, laying first the foundations of home and then of empire." This same spirit passed into Western films in the Twentieth century and almost word for word a similar sentiment was expressed on a title card from *Overland with Kit Carson* (Columbia, 1939), a fifteen chapter serial.

The earliest dime novels, heavily indebted to Cooper's Leatherstocking, employed backwoodsmen as their heroes, although in the very beginning they fell into two types: the violent ugly white man who is invariably an Indian-hater and the saintly forest guide in the wilderness. Lew Wetzel, a well-known Kentucky scout, was the model for the violent ugly white man in adventures as Emerson Radman's *Lew Wetzel, the Scout: or, The Captives of the Frontier* (1866). After 1870, however, this type was increasingly relegated to a secondary role, usually in support of the virtuous backwoodsman hero. Daniel Bryan's *The Mountain Muse* had used Daniel Boone as its central character, and Daniel Boone initially, followed quickly by Davy Crockett, became fictionalized dime novel heroes in the Leatherstocking tradition. Before long, the violent ugly white man vanished completely and was replaced by a comic sidekick, an innovation which was also later transposed to films.

With the growing idealization of Western heroes in the 1870s, it became a standard theme that redemption could be had only through the sacrifice of the wilderness to "progress" and in *Boone, the Hunter: or, The Backwoods Belle* (1873) even Boone himself is characterized as a martyr to the advance of "civilization" (note: for progress and civilization read materialism, greed, and destruction of the wilderness). Moreover, the dime novel hero sought to embody the notion that all class distinctions are false and that, ultimately, a man must be judged instead on his innate worth as a human being. All such heroes, predictably, are guided by an infallible sense of right and wrong, devoting themselves to putting down self-seekers.

Once the dime novelists got hold of Kit Carson, there was a transition in heroes, the backwoodsman being replaced by the plainsman. After his brief appearance in *The Prairie Flower*, Carson became the central character in Charles A. Averill's *Kit Carson, The Prince of Gold Hunters* (1849) and from the 1860s through the 1890s Carson appeared in more than seventy original tales and reprints. As late as Willa Cather's (q.v.) *Death Comes for the Archbishop* (New York: Knopf, 1927) he was still being idealized, a trend which carried over to the movies where, among others, John Mack Brown, Bill Elliott, and, for television, Bill Williams impersonated Carson. Yet, historically, Carson was somewhat more of a mountain man than a plainsman. The prototype *par excellence* of the plainsman had to wait for Edward Z.C. Judson, who wrote under the pseudonym Ned Buntline, to glamorize an obscure frontier scout he had met at Fort McPherson, Nebraska, William F. Cody (see Historical Personalities), who first appeared in *Buffalo Bill, The King of the Border Men* (1869). This novel was made into a successful stage play and, before long, Cody began his own show business career. When Prentiss Ingraham, Cody's publicity director, took over the Buffalo Bill stories, writing some 121 of the total 557 Buffalo Bill entries, he exaggerated Cody's exploits to an even more incredible degree. Because of Cody's theatricalism, he is dressed as garishly in the novels as he was in person and thus began the tradition

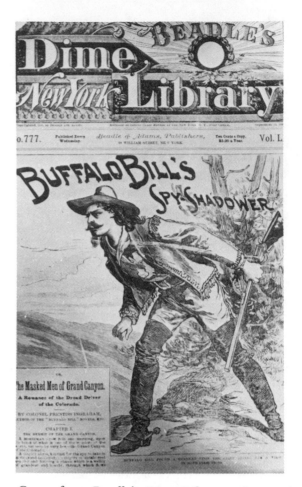

Cover from Beadle's Dime Library edition of Buffalo Bill's Spy-Shadower.

of the gaudily dressed Western hero later most memorably personified in films by Gene Autry and Roy Rogers.

Two less prominent types of heroes in dime novels were outlaws and, chronologically *last* of all, cowboys. Edward L. Wheeler produced *Deadwood Dick, The Prince of the Road: or, The Black Rider of the Black Hills* (1877) for Beadle and Adams, and it inaugurated an entire series of Deadwood Dick adventures. Other firms, seeking to compete, did not bother with fictional outlaws (although seven different road agents insisted they had been the model for Deadwood Dick), but chose actual criminals by name to idealize as heroes, men such as Jesse and Frank James, the Younger brothers, the Daltons, Butch Cassidy, and the Sundance Kid. Already in the Nineteenth century Americans were concerned about widespread political corruption, monopolistic power, and legal banditry, so it was inevitable they would respond somewhat sympathetically to anti-Establishment outsiders, even when they were highly fanciful renditions of real frontier murderers and thieves. In books as *Joaquín, The Terrible, The True History of the Three Bitter Blows That Changed an Honest Man to a Merciless Demon* (1881) by Joseph E. Badger, Jr., a fictional account of the career of Joaquín Murieta, society was blamed for producing criminals. The tone had scarcely changed decades later when Buck Jones portrayed Murieta in *The Avenger* (Columbia, 1931) or Dane Coolidge (q.v.) rendered his fictional account in *Gringo Gold* (New York: Dutton, 1939). Billy the Kid, alone, seemed to escape this idealization process, his behavior being justified in only one novel, Edmund Fable's *Billy The Kid, The New Mexico Outlaw: Or, The Bold Bandit of the West* (1881), but once Walter Noble Burns (q.v.) and, later, the movies came on the scene, they more than made up for lost time.

The cowboy really had to wait until Owen Wister's (q.v.) stories in *Harper's Weekly* before he emerged as a distinct hero type. True, Prentiss Ingraham created the first dime novel cowboy hero in 1887 writing about the supposed exploits of Buck Taylor, a star in Buffalo Bill's Wild West show, and, previously, Frederick Whittaker had written *Parson Jim, King of the Cowboys: or, The Gentle Shepherd's Big "Clean Out"* (1882), but these books were definitely ahead of their time and failed to interest many readers. Once, however, the Virginian, Lin McLean, and Scipio LeMoyne had made their impact in Wister's stories in the 'Nineties, there came a deluge even in the dime novels which persisted into the 'Twenties.

Harper's Weekly and *Harper's Monthly* were slicks and, from the start, the cowboy had a lively status in the slicks, however much he might concurrently appear in pulp magazines. *The Saturday Evening Post* had a particularly aggressive editorial policy concerning running Western stories and in the decade following the turn of the century numerous Westerns appeared in its pages by Emerson Hough (q.v.), Alfred Henry Lewis (q.v.), O. Henry (q.v.), and, toward the end of the decade, Rex Beach (q.v.). Many of Wister's *Harper's* stories were long enough to appear in two parts spread over two issues. With *The Line of Least Resistance* (1910) by Eugene Manlove Rhodes (q.v.) the first Western serial in four parts to appear in any mass circulation magazine, the *Post* initiated its policy of regularly featuring Western serials. Rhodes' novel *The Little Eohippus* (1912), run in the *Post* two years later, has the distinction of being the first cowboy-and-the-lady serial to appear in a slick magazine — the romance in *The Virginian* (New York: Macmillan, 1902) having never been a central plot ingredient in any of the fragments of the novel which Wister published prior to its appearance in book form.

Street and Smith and other dime novel publishers began, after the turn of the century, to introduce new lines of pulp magazines which frequently featured Western serials and stories and, presently, were devoted only to Western fiction. In 1919,

A representative cover from the New Buffalo Bill Weekly.

Street and Smith revamped the format of the *New Buffalo Bill Weekly* to *Western Story Magazine*, a bi-weekly. The first issue, dated 5 September 1919, contained, among others, a story by William MacLeod Raine (q.v.). Within a year *Western Story*'s circulation hit three hundred thousand per issue and it was made a weekly which it remained for the next twenty-five years.

The late 'Twenties and the 'Thirties were the boom period for Western pulp magazines. Doubleday published *West* and *Frontier*, as well as the higher class *Short Stories* — veteran Clarence E. Mulford (q.v.) frequently wrote for this last; the firm also issued in book form Western stories which had been previously serialized in a

series of *Four In One* volumes. Doubleday's commitment to the Western story continued unabated until the firm became one of the very few with a line of hardbound Western novels, publishing up to twenty-four titles a year under their Double D Western brand name.

Clayton House published *Cowboy Stories, Ace-High, Ranch Romances*, and *Western Adventures*. Of these, *Ranch Romances* lasted into the 'Sixties. Fawcett published *Triple-X Western*, but made its largest impact in the late 'Forties and 'Fifties with a broad line of Western comic books which, at one time, included the comic-book adventures of Tom Mix, Hopalong Cassidy, Monte Hale, Ken Maynard, and Gabby Hayes. Similarly, the Whitman Publishing Company which had begun during the 'Thirties to issue Little Big Books telling in words and pictures the storylines of films with Tom Mix, Ken Maynard, Buck Jones, and others, by the 'Fifties tried to repeat what Beadle and Adams had done with Buffalo Bill and issued a series of fictional adventures with Gene Autry, some of which were written by Lewis B. Patten (q.v.), to compete with Doubleday's "new" Hopalong Cassidy series written by Louis L'Amour (q.v.) under the name Tex Burns and Fran Striker's Lone Ranger books.

An ex-Clayton House editor, Harold Hersey, during the 'Thirties edited *Western Trails, Golden West, Riders of the Range*, and *Western Outlaws*, which, as most of the pulps, established a house style and a group of house names for the stories which were featured. Certainly one of the most ambitious publishers of Western pulps during the Depression was Ned Pines who hired Leo Margulies to edit *Thrilling Western, Thrilling Ranch Stories, Popular Western*, and *Texas Rangers*. A. Leslie Scott (q.v.), among others, contributed stories about Texas Ranger Jim Hatfield under the *Texas Rangers*' house name Jackson Cole (see House Names). *Dime Western*, from Popular Publications, was one of two pulps subscribed to by Franklin D. Roosevelt.

In the 'Thirties, Street and Smith added *Far West*, *Wild West Weekly*, and *Pete Rice Magazine*. However, the Old *Far West* should not be confused with the subsequent *Far West* which in the 1970s became the last surviving Western pulp magazine, which was only the then latest evolution of Leo Margulies who had himself become a pulp publisher. In 1969, Margulies tried to introduce a new Western pulp titled *Zane Grey's Western Magazine* with Zane Grey's (q.v.) two sons as advisory editors and, in addition to reprinting some of Grey's original fiction, it contained a host of new stories and a new series of Buck Duane adventures by Romer Zane Grey, Grey's eldest son, based on the central character from Grey's *The Lone Star Ranger* (New York: Harper's, 1915). The venture was not entirely successful, but it had to recommend it the fact that in the 'Teens and through the 'Twenties Zane Grey had been the most popular — and best paid — author of Western magazine serials, first in such periodicals as *Field & Stream* which serialized *Riders of the Purple Sage* (New York: Harper's, 1912), *Popular Magazine* which serialized *Desert Gold* (New York: Harper's, 1913), *Munsey's* which serialized *The Light of Western Stars* (New York: Harper's, 1914), *All-Story* which serialized *The Lone Star Ranger* and *The Border Legion* (New York: Harper's, 1916), and *Argosy* which serialized *The Rainbow Trail* (New York: Harper's, 1915). Grey then moved on to the slick markets where he could demand and receive $50,000 for serial rights to a novel, usually

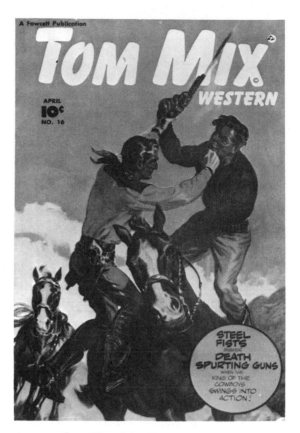

A cover from Tom Mix Western *comics.*

selling it to *Country Gentleman* or *Ladies Home Journal*, both Curtis Publishing periodicals, as was *The Saturday Evening Post*. It was because Grey was so well paid by these magazines that he increased his production to such an extent that his hardbound publisher still had a considerable backlog of novels which had been serialized but still had not appeared as books when he died in 1939.

All-Story was a weekly publication of the Munsey group edited by Robert H. Davis. After Grey had moved on to the slicks, Davis gave Max Brand (q.v.) a copy of Grey's *Riders of the Purple Sage* to read and suggested Brand try to duplicate it. Brand's serial *The Untamed* (New York: Dodd, Mead, 1949) was the result, an 85,000 word saga which began in *All-Story* in 1918. Brand continued to contribute heavily to the pulps, appearing in *Western Story Magazine* alone a total of 834 times if each installment of a serial is counted as an appearance. Reputedly Brand earned a million dollars from just *Western Story*, his accumulated word contribution coming to over thirteen million words in thirteen years. Brand's formula was quite succinct and amazingly successful: "Action, action, action," he once said, "is the thing. So long as you keep your hero jumping through fiery hoops on every page you're all right. The basic formula I use is simple: good man turns bad, bad man turns good. Naturally, there is considerable variation on this theme.... There has to be a woman, but not much of a one. A good horse is much more important."

Adventure, *Argosy*, and *Blue Book*, in addition to *Short Stories*, were publications somewhere between the pulps Brand wrote for and the slicks which were featuring Grey. Often authors began in the most primitive of the pulps and worked themselves up to these middling publications, if not all the way to *Collier's* or the *Post*. W.C. Tuttle (q.v.), Harry Sinclair Drago (q.v.), H.H. Knibbs (q.v.), Dane Coolidge, Eugene Cunningham (q.v.), Jackson Gregory (q.v.), and, later, Frank Gruber (q.v.) and Elmore Leonard (q.v.) belonged to this group. Conversely, there were others who were almost born for pulp writing — who were utterly incapable of a well-made plot or even a well-thought-out story — as Walt Coburn (q.v.), but whom pulp readers seemed to prefer for the very deficiencies which would have made them unacceptable to a more literate audience. At one point, Coburn had the distinction of having a pulp magazine named after him, so well-established had he become with pulp *aficionadoes*. Another, certainly, who enjoyed nearly the same reputation was Nelson C. Nye (q.v.).

By the late 'Twenties, Grey's excessive romanticism appeared adolescent to slick magazine readers who had, in the interim, become somewhat more sophisticated. Grey was soon superseded by Ernest Haycox (q.v.) who had begun writing for *Western Story Magazine* in the mid 'Twenties. By the late 'Twenties, Haycox was a regular contributor to *Short Stories* and *West* and by 1931 he had broken into *Collier's*. His sober heroes, subdued romance, and grim situations, coupled with his sensitive use of color and genuine poetic flair, comprise a wholly new tone which neither Grey nor his imitators could emulate. In the mid 'Thirties, while Eugene Manlove Rhodes' last novels were being serialized in the *Post*, Haycox was the most prominent Western writer in *Collier's*. Conrad Richter (q.v.), Stewart Edward White (q.v.), MacKinlay Kantor (q.v.), and S. Omar Barker (q.v.) were also concurrently writing for the *Post* or for *Ladies Home Journal*. By the mid 'Forties, Haycox was contributing himself regularly to the *Post*, followed closely by Luke Short (q.v.), another author who had come up from the pulp ranks and whose stories frequently challenged Haycox' for polish and precision. By the late 'Fifties, with Haycox having died in 1950 and Short having turned to paperback originals, the *Post* began carrying stories by Louis L'Amour (q.v.) who, in many ways, represented the perpetuation of their tradition.

With the demise of most of the pulps and slicks in the 'Sixties, the paperback original took over where they had left off and so, almost in a circle, in the course of a century Western novels were again complete under one cover as they had been in the days of the dime novel — except that, with inflation, they came to cost fifteen to twenty times as much.

There is, despite the enormity of the subject, very little published about either dime novels or pulp and slick magazines with particular reference to the Western. Henry Nash Smith devoted two chapters of *Virgin Land: The American West as Symbol and Myth* (Cambridge: Harvard University Press, 1950) to dime novels. Probably the best introduction to this area is *The Dime Novel Western* (Bowling Green: The Popular Press, 1978) by Daryl Jones, excellent in its survey but hopelessly unreliable in the conclusions the author drew from his exposure to dime novel literature. The book, however, is notable also for its bibliography. Specifically on the dime novels of Beadle and Adams is Albert Johannsen's *The House of Beadle and Adams* (Norman: University of Oklahoma Press, 1950) in two volumes and a supplement published in 1962.

Two very inadequate, if nonetheless entertaining, books have been devoted to the pulp industry, with chapters dealing with Western stories, Frank Gruber's *The Pulp Jungle* (Los Angeles: Sherbourne Press, 1967) and Ron Goulart's *Cheap Thrills* (New Rochelle: Arlington House, 1972). Robert Easton's book *Max Brand: The Big "Westerner"* (Norman: University of Oklahoma Press, 1970) is valuable for what it contains on Brand's work in the pulps.

Among story collections which give at least a feeling for pulp stories, Damon Knight edited *Westerns of the Forties: Classics from the Great Pulps* (Indianapolis: Bobbs, Merrill, 1971), which is adequate but not quite the equal of William Targ's earlier anthology *Western Story Omnibus* (Cleveland and New York: World, 1945) or Harry E. Maule's collection from the same year for the Modern Library titled *Great Tales of the American West* (New York: Random House, 1945) the Introduction to which gives the background and magazine experience of some of the contributors.

Besides such general collections, the reader is also referred to Philip Durham's re-issue of *Seth Jones* by Edward S. Ellis and *Deadwood Dick on Deck* by Edward L. Wheeler in one volume with an Introduction (New York: Odyssey Press, 1966) as examples of dime novels.

Six of Owen Wister's magazine stories have been re-issued in *The West of Owen Wister* (Lincoln: University of Nebraska Press, 1972) edited and introduced by Robert L. Hough. Fine examples of Ernest Haycox' shorter fiction can be found in *The Best Western Stories of Ernest Haycox* (New York: Bantam, 1960) comprising four previously hardbound collections and *Rawhide and Bob-Wire* (New York: Bantam, 1960) is a splendid Luke Short anthology. Louis L'Amour's slick magazine fiction can be found in the collection *War Party* (New York: Bantam, 1975). However, perhaps the best overall collection is to be found in *The Saturday Evening Post Reader of Western Stories* (New York: Doubleday, 1960) edited by E.N. Brandt which includes twenty stories originally published in the *Post* during the hey-day of the slick Western feature story. Two of them are long enough to constitute serials.

Finally, there is *The American West in Fiction* (New York: Mentor Books, 1982) with a lengthy General Introduction, Prefaces, and a total of twenty representative stories edited by Jon Tuska.

R

Raine, William MacLeod (1871–1954) Author of Western novels, short stories, essays, and non-fiction books, born at London, England of Scottish descent. In 1881, after the death of his mother, Raine immigrated with his father to Arkansas where he was raised. He attended Sarcey College in Arkansas and received his Bachelor's degree from Oberlin College in Ohio in 1894. After graduating, Raine traveled through the West, taking odd jobs on ranches. He settled for a time in Seattle, Washington, where he worked as a school principal. He tried to enlist in the Spanish-American War; however he had weak lungs and so was ineligible for service. Raine moved to Denver, Colorado in hopes that his health would improve, and here he worked as a reporter and editorial writer on *The Republican*, *The Post*, and *The Rocky Mountain News*. He began writing short stories and became a prolific contributor to such periodicals as *Argosy*, *Blue Book*, *People's*, *Popular Magazine*, and *Short Stories*. Raine switched to full-time free-lance writing and soon tried his hand at a novel. His early books were historical fiction with English backgrounds. Many of his Western serials and expanded short stories were eventually published in novel form. He married in 1905 and was widowed in 1922. He later remarried. He died of a heart attack in Denver.

A conscientious writer, Raine considered himself a craftsman rather than an artist and gained his reputation from his ability to depict ranch life accurately through character detail, dialect, and topography. His most outstanding characteristic as a Western author was his use of a Western code by which his heroes live. In all of Raine's Western novels the destiny of the frontier is determined by the high character and standards of his protagonists. In *The Big Town Round-Up* (Boston: Houghton Mifflin, 1920), a story set largely in New York City, the Western code of his hero is tested against the corrupt money men of the East. Raine was credited with being one of the first Western writers to show the sexual drives of his heroines. Although this is partly true, Raine consistently drew women as weak creatures whose virtue, above all else, must be protected. This was a main plot ingredient in *Wyoming* (New York: Dillingham, 1908), his first Western novel, *Mavericks* (New York: Dillingham, 1912), and *Sons of the Saddle* (Boston: Houghton Mifflin, 1938). Indians did not play an important part in his Westerns, but when they did appear they were viewed as an inferior, adolescent culture. In *Man-Size* (Boston: Houghton Mifflin, 1922), a story about the Canadian Mounties in the Montana Territory, a young girl, believed to be of mixed-blood, discovers she is white which makes her feel more acceptable.

Raine greatly admired Eugene Manlove Rhodes (q.v.) and wrote an unpublished article about Rhodes after he had spent some time with him. The idea of the corrupt politician as a villain which Rhodes stressed was often employed by Raine in his fiction. In *Riders of Buck River* (Boston: Houghton Mifflin, 1940), the hero, a one-time small rancher turned big rancher, is surrounded by corruption on all levels. Rhodes for his part considered Raine along with H.H. Knibbs (q.v.), B.M. Bower (q.v.), and George Pattullo(q.v.) among the writers who were telling the truth about the West.

Raine's formulary stories proved very popular. From 1920 on he wrote at least two books per year and was well publicized by his publisher. During World War I, 500,000 copies of Raine's Westerns were ordered for the British troops. W.H. Hutchinson in his essay "Virgins, Villians, and Varmints" which served as the Introduction to *The Rhodes Reader* (Norman: University of Oklahoma Press, 1957) commented that Raine's "popularity was so great that his English publishers bought his manuscripts sight unseen and, so Raine purportedly believed, did not bother to read them before printing. But Raine was a volumetric piker in the 'Western' game."

Raine's interest in gunfighters and sheriffs brought about the writing of two factually unreliable non-fiction works on the subject: *Famous Sheriffs and Western Outlaws* (New York: Doubleday, 1929) and *Guns of the Frontier* (Boston: Houghton Mifflin, 1940). He collaborated with Will C. Barnes on *Cattle* (New York: Doubleday, 1930), a succinct work on the history of cattle and ghost-wrote Billy Breakenridge's "autobiography" *Helldorado* (Boston: Houghton Mifflin, 1928). Raine wrote one Western under the pseudonym Austin Mac-Leod and edited an anthology of Western stories in 1940. Although his characters fail to come to life and his style is often turgid for the modern reader, he was a competent storyteller who wrote fast-paced, well-plotted stories, and his writing remained consistent throughout his career. His novel *High Grass Valley* (Boston: Houghton Mifflin, 1955) unfinished at the time of his death was completed by Wayne D. Overholser (q.v.).

William MacLeod Raine's Western novels are *Wyoming* (1908), *Ridgway of Montana* (1909), *Bucky O'Connor* (1910), *A Texas Ranger* (1911), *The Brand Blotters* (1912), *Mavericks* (1912), *Crooked Trails and Straight* (1913), *A Daughter of the Dons* (1914), *The Highgrader* (1915), *Steve Yeager* (1915), *The Yukon Trail* (1917), *The Sheriff's Son* (1918), *A Man Four-Square* (1919) [alternate title: *Arizona Guns*], *The Big Town Round-Up* (1920), *Oh, You Tex!* (1920), *Tangled Trails* (1921), *Gunsight Pass* (1921), *Man-Size* (1922), *The Fighting Edge* (1922), *Ironheart* (1923), *The Desert's Price* (1924), *Roads of Doubt* (1925), *Troubled Waters* (1925), *The Last Shot* (1926), *Bonanza* (1926), *Judge Colt* (1927), *Colorado* (1928), *Texas Man* (1928), *The Fighting Tenderfoot* (1929), *The Valiant* (1930), *Knife Through the Ace* (1930), *Rutledge Trails the Ace of Spades* (1930), *Beyond the Rio Grande* (1931), *Bad Man* (1932), *Under Northern Stars* (1932) [alternate title: *Bullet Ambush*], *The Black Colts* (1932) [alternate title: *Pistol Partners*], *Banded Stars* (1933), *The Broad Arrow* (1933), *For Honor and Life* (1933). *The Roaring River* (1934), *The Trail of Danger* (1934), *Border Breed* (1935), *Square-Shooter* (1935), *Run of the Brush* (1936), *Sorreltop* (1936), *To Ride the River With* (1936), *Bucky Follows a Cold Trail* (1937), *Sons of the Saddle* (1938), *On the Dodge* (1938), *Moran Beats Back* (1939) [alternate title: *Gunsmoke Trail*], *The River Bend Feud* (1939), *Riders of Buck River* (1940), *Trail's End* (1940), *.45-Caliber Law* (1941), *They Called Him Blue Blazes* (1941), *Justice Deferred* (1942), *The Damyank* (1942), *Hell and Highwater* (1943), *Courage Stout* (1944) [alternate title: *Rustler's Gap*], *Who Wants to Live Forever* (1945) [alternate title: *The Tough Tenderfoot*], *Clattering Hoofs* (1946), *The Nettle Danger* (1947) [alternate title: *Powdersmoke Feud*], *Challenge to Danger* (1947), *The Outlaw Trail* (1948) [alternate title: *The Bandit Trail*], *Jingling Spurs* (1950) [alternate title: *The Six-Gun Kid*], *Ranger's Luck* (1950), *Saddlebum* (1951), *Glory Hole* (1952) [alternate title: *West of the Law*], *Justice Comes to Tomahawk* (1952), *Dry Bones in the Valley* (1953), *Plantation Guns* (1954) [alternate title: *Arkansas Guns*], *Reluctant Gunman* (1954), *High Grass Valley* (1955) [completed by Wayne D. Overholser].

Raine's novel written under the pseudonym Austin MacLeod is *The Loom of the Feud* (1926).

Films based on William MacLeod Raine's Western fiction are *Face of Fear* (Fox, 1913) directed by W.J. Bauman [source unknown], *All on Account of Towser* (Vitagraph, 1915) directed by Ulysses Davis [source unknown], *Intercepted Vengeance* (Vitagraph, 1915) directed by Ulysses Davis [source unknown], *Through Troubled Waters* (Vitagraph, 1915) directed by Ulysses Davis [source unknown], *An Arizona Wooing* (Selig, 1915) directed by Tom Mix [source unknown], *Forked Trails* (Selig, 1915) directed by Tom Mix [source unknown], *Fighting for Gold* (Fox, 1919) directed by Edward J. LeSaint [based on *The Highgrader*], *Sheriff's Son* (Paramount, 1919) directed by Victor L. Schertzinger [source unknown], *The Big Town Round-Up* (Fox, 1921) directed by Lynn Reynolds, *Man-Size* (Fox, 1923) directed by Howard M. Mitchell, *Pure Grit* (Universal, 1923) directed by Nat Ross [based on *A Texas Ranger*], *The Man From Wyoming* (Universal, 1924) directed by Robert Bradbury [based on *Wyoming*], *Ridgway of Montana* (Universal, 1924) directed by Clifford S. Smith, *The Desert's Price* (Fox, 1925) direct-

ed by W.S. Van Dyke, *The Fighting Edge* (Warner's, 1926) directed by Henry Lehrman, *A Man Four-Square* (Fox, 1926) directed by Roy William Neill, *The Ridin' Rascal* (Universal, 1926) directed by Clifford S. Smith [based on *Mavericks*], *The Grip of the Yukon* (Universal, 1928) directed by Ernst Laemmle [based on *The Yukon Trail*], *Burning the Wind* (Universal, 1929) directed by Henry MacRae [based on *A Daughter of the Dons*], *Three Young Texans* (20th-Fox, 1954) directed by Henry Levin [source unknown], *The Man from Bitter Ridge* (Universal, 1955) directed by Jack Arnold [source unknown].

Randall, Clay. See Adams, Clifton.

Reardon, Dan. See Cook, Will.

Reese, John (1910–1981) Author of Western fiction born at Sweetwater, Nebraska. Reese's maternal grandfather was an itinerant frontier blacksmith whose stories gave his grandson the basis for many of his tales. Reese's father, an ex-Cavalryman, was a specialist in horses. "My earliest memories," Reese once said, "are of the Taylor ranch in Hall County, Nebraska, where they kept as many as fifty stallions, raised several thousand cattle, and up to 40,000 sheep." His first-hand knowledge of the country and its people proved invaluable to him. "I may be the last 'professional' writer alive who has 1.) ridden bucking horses, 2.) dehorned and castrated yearlings held on the ends of ropes dallied around saddles on good cutting horses, and 3.) talked to a horse Indian who has seen wild buffalo." Reese was of the opinion that "the 'noble red man' was a myth" and that "tribal life was hell," contrary to the notions of many.

At the age of 11, Reese was herding sheep. At 13, he was working as a farm hand. At 14, he was driving six head of horses tandem on a corn lister. His formal education was at Dunbar High School in Nebraska, from which he graduated in 1928.

By this time the Depression had already started for farmers and jobs were scarce. Reese wandered all over the United States and Canada looking for work and building up a collection of experiences from which to draw upon when he turned to writing. His first attempt to write for money came in the summer of 1932 when "I was persuaded to try the old *True Story, True Romances*, and *True Confessions*. For a while I was rolling in money, but I was still an amateur and quickly dried up." A new chapter began when Lowry Charles Wimberley accepted a short story for *The Prairie Schooner* and "did his best to make a writer of me." It did not happen at once, however, and a series of bread-and-butter jobs followed. He worked for the Writers Project, helped elect a lieutenant governor, and was given an office with the IRS as a reward. Eventually he started his own tax service.

One consequence of his tax work was acquaintance with an old pulp Western writer who urged him to try his luck in that field. The Armed Forces were ordering pulps by the ton and Reese went to work to help meet the demand. He found that he could turn out a 5,000 word short story in two to three hours, but for some time it was still necessary to work at a steady job and he spent four years as a reporter for the *Los Angeles Examiner*. Reese's first novel was

Sheehan's Mill (New York: Doubleday, 1943) — not a Western — and this was followed by *The High Passes* (Boston: Little, Brown, 1954), more than a decade later. Between these two books, Reese published an article in *The Saturday Evening Post* titled "Make My Next Dog a Mutt" which attacked the pure-bred dog racket. It brought him 2,000 letters, mostly furious, and the magazine twice as many. It also brought him an invitation to write a dog story for juveniles, which he did in *Big Mutt* (Philadelphia: Westminster Press, 1952); it sold 40,000 copies in hardcover and is still selling in paperback. After a long bout with illness he died in California, where he had made his home.

Reese's first Western novel was *Sure Shot Shapiro* (New York: Doubleday, 1968), but his best Western fiction unquestionably is contained in his trilogy, *Jesus on Horseback* (New York: Doubleday, 1971), which was subsequently published as three separate Double D Westerns: *Angel Range* (New York: Doubleday, 1973), *The Blowholers* (New York: Doubleday, 1974), and *The Land Baron* (New York: Doubleday, 1974). Among Reese's innovations was a series of books about frontier detective Jefferson Hewitt who made his debut in *Weapon Heavy* (London: Milton House, 1975).

Besides being an extraordinarily steady writer, Reese was an inventive plotter and had a fine ear for dialogue. As important as any of his writing skills, however, was his strong sense of the ridiculous. His Westerns are always funny, full of bizarre situations and peopled by unusual characters. An hilarious example of what he called a "modern" Western is *Omar, Fats, and Trixie* (New York: Fawcett, 1976). The humor is not always good natured. Long experience eroded any romantic illusions he may once have entertained and the laughter the book provokes is frequently satiric.

C.L.S.

A Good Day For a Hanging (Columbia, 1959) was directed by Nathan Juran [source unknown].

Reid, Thomas Mayne (1818–1883)

Author and editor of numerous pulp Western dime novels, born the son of a Presbyterian minister at Ballyroney, Ireland. Reid began studying for the ministry but, in 1840, he abandoned it and came instead to the United States. Once arrived in New Orleans, Louisiana, Reid pushed even further into the West, hunting and trading with Indians and even trapping along the Missouri and Platte Rivers. For a time he taught school in Nashville, Tennessee; then, in 1842, he went first to Pittsburgh, Pennsylvania, and on to Philadelphia. While in Pittsburgh, Reid published his first articles and poetry in the *Pittsburgh Morning Chronicle*. After living in Philadelphia for three years, Reid joined the staff of the *New York Herald* as a society editor. When the Mexican War broke out, Reid joined the New York Volunteers and was commissioned a Second Lieutenant, sailing with Burnett's regiment from New York to Vera Cruz in 1846. He was promoted to Captain by General Winfield Scott for bravery in storming the Chapultapec fortress. After the war ended, Reid lingered for a time in Mexico, and then returned to the United States in 1848–1849 during which time he wrote his first novel, *The Rifle Rangers* (1850), an exciting fictional account of the military campaign near Vera Cruz. Then, in 1850, he went to England where he was to remain for the rest of his life.

Reid's second novel, *The Scalp Hunters* (1851), is in retrospect his most memorable, notable for its eerie dream imagery and its introspective hero. Narrated in the first person by M. Henry Haller, the novel is set in the West from St. Louis, Missouri to Santa Fe, New Mexico and extending South from El Paso to Chihuahua. Among its characters is St. Vrain, who was a real-life Santa Fe trader. Haller earns his heroic reputation by riding a buffalo and is later saved from a death in quicksand by his horse, Moro. Thus Reid anticipated by more than half a century the glamorous stature accorded a hero's horse by Western films. The latter part of the novel is a captivity story, rescuing a beautiful girl from the Navahos, an almost mythological theme which has been widely varied since in Western fiction. At the conclusion, Haller marries a 12-year-old girl.

Ending a story by marrying off all the available characters became a convention fostered by Reid in his fiction. He also made frequent recourse to the theme of the heroine's weak brother caught in the clutches of a lecherous villain with designs on the imperilled heroine. All of Reid's dramatic stress was on action plots, and hence most of his characters, although generally unconvincing, were purely functional. He also indulged excessively in the convention of having many of his characters speak in dialect to the point, at times, where what they are saying is incomprehensible to a modern reader. Almost invariably he characterized the Indians as "the enemy," and he assumed, along with some of his contemporaries, outlandish notions about them, such as that the Pueblos and Navahos are descended from the Aztecs. However, Reid carried his racial bias only to the extreme of attributing what he felt to be the Indian's "inferiority" to cultural, rather than genetic, deficiencies. Reid was, if anything, even more harsh toward the Mexicans whom he characterized as vicious and debased, and his dislike for the Roman Catholic church prompted him in one novel, *The White Chief: A Legend of Northern Mexico* (1855), to show the priests as the principal culprits. It was, therefore, only to be expected that Reid would celebrate the spirit of Yankee imperialism which he firmly believed would save the Southwest from barbarism and the low-life savagery into which it had fallen. Alike with George Ruxton (q.v.), Zane Grey (q.v.), and Francis Parkman (q.v.), Reid attacked the Mormons for their polygamous beliefs.

Reid's preoccupation with being a naturalist, while it tended to lend local color to his narratives, also inspired him to write several books for young readers, among them *The Desert Home* (1851) and *The Boy Hunters* (1852), but they were more treatises on natural history and survival guides than entertaining fictions.

The only biographical work which has so far appeared on Reid is Elizabeth Reid's *Captain Mayne Reid: His Life and Adventures* (London: Greening, 1900), although several references to him can be found in Albert Johannsen's *The House of Beadle and Adams* (Norman: University of Oklahoma Press, 1950), Reid's principal publisher, and in the critical survey by Edwin W. Gaston, Jr., *The Early Novel of the Southwest* (Albuquerque: University of New Mexico Press, 1961).

Remington, Frederic (1861–1909) Artist, commercial illustrator, sculptor, and author of numerous Western tales and sketches, born at Canton, New York. Remington attended the Yale School of the Fine Arts 1878–1880 before he went to Kansas to take up sheep ranching. Although the area where he settled was definitely not the frontier, the isolation and the loneliness, particularly during the harsh winters, gave Remington many long hours to pursue his drawing and painting. Come the spring of 1884, Remington decided to sell his ranch and he became, for a brief period, a wanderer. He went first to Kansas City and then proceeded Southwest through Indian Territory into Arizona, returning to Kansas City in the late summer of 1884 whereupon he went into partnership in a saloon. When he discovered that his partners had cheated him out of his interest, he took up a pistol and decided to use a little frontier justice on them, being talked out of it only at the last moment — so deeply already had the ways of the wild West impressed him. In the fall of that year he returned East and married Eva Caten, a woman he had once unsuccessfully courted. The couple went to Kansas City, but within a year Eva returned to the East and Remington again set out for the Southwest. The separation was caused by financial distress; Remington was by this time virtually penniless.

In the summer of 1885 Remington went prospecting in the Pinal Range in Arizona Territory. Coincidentally, Geronimo broke loose from his reservation captivity and the Third United States Cavalry under General Crook took up the pursuit. Remington used the situation to advantage, sketching several Apache Indians on the San Carlos Reservation and three renegades who paid a hungry visit to his campsite one night. Harold

"Conjuring Back the Buffalo" by Frederic Remington.

McCracken, one of Remington's biographers, in his book *Frederic Remington: Artist of the Old West* (Philadelphia: Lippincott, 1947) pointed out that Remington never came within two hundred miles of Geronimo, but this did not faze Easterners, when, upon his return, with a full portfolio of Indian portraits, his sketches were instantly in great demand with magazines to be used as illustrations of the conflict between the Indians and the Cavalry. Remington's reputation was made almost overnight.

No less a one than Theodore Roosevelt (q.v.), who had just begun to publish the sketches which would constitute his book *Ranch Life and the Hunting Trail* (1888) in the *Century* magazine, asked for Remington to be his illustrator. Along with this commission, Remington himself turned to writing, often illustrating his own material, and in the 'Nineties published in magazine and then book form the stories and literary sketches contained in *Pony Tracks* (New York: Harper's, 1895), perhaps his most well-known book, and *Crooked Trails* (New York: Harper's, 1898).

For Remington, the meaning of the Western experience was the confrontation between man and a hostile physical environment. He was not quite the romantic that his friend, Owen Wister (q.v.), was and whose stories he frequently illustrated; and Remington's own tales are not obsessed, as were Wister's, with courtship of Eastern women in a Western environment. Nor was Remington a believer, as was Roosevelt, in the rugged life for its own sake. He was, however, more highly prejudicial than either, no matter how much he shared Wister's innate Eastern snobbery, and he set down his philosophy once in *Pony Tracks*: "Jews, Injuns, Chinamen, Italians, Huns — the rubbish of the Earth I hate — I've got some Winchesters and when the massacring begins, I can get my share of 'em and what's more, I will...." But, for all that, Remington was filled with contradictions; as much as he would rail at wilderness conditions, he felt drawn to them, and, as the years passed, his hatred for the industrial civilization of the East increased. Toward the end of the decade, Remington published four stories about one character in book form, *Sundown Leflare* (New York: Harper's, 1899), in which he had Sundown observe: "'White man mak de wagon un de seelver dollar, un de dam railroad, un he tink dat ees all dair ees een de country.'"

In what may well be his finest work, and his only novel, *John Ermine of the Yellowstone* (New York: Macmillan, 1902), Remington seemingly abandoned all his earlier prejudices and told a story singularly without romance of a white child raised by Indians who eventually joins the U.S. Army as a scout. Through Ermine's eyes the reader contrasts the Indian way of life with the "senseless mass of white humanity" always pressing further Westward from the East. Ermine is popular with the soldiers until he has the audacity to fall in love with a white woman, the Major's daughter, after which he is ostracized and, seeking vengeance against her fiancé, he is killed by an Indian scout seeking to impress the whites. It was a powerful idea, well ahead of its time.

In 1905, Remington summed up his disillusionment in a fantasy in which he wrote: "I knew the railroad was coming. I saw men already swarming into the land. I knew the derby hat, the smoking chimneys, the cord-binder, and the thirty-day note were upon us in a restless surge. I knew the wild riders and vacant land were about to vanish forever, and the more I considered

"When Winter is Cruel" by Frederic Remington.

the subject, the bigger the forever loomed." Near death, Remington cried out, "Cowboys! There are no cowboys any more!" Yet he himself had helped romanticize the West and because he had had such an influential impact, when others experienced the same feelings he had, what was manufactured to fill the void was the formulary Western and the cinema cowboy hero on his white horse, which, too, was not really the West, and certainly not what Remington decried as having vanished.

Pony Tracks with an Introduction by J. Frank Dobie, written and illustrated by Frederic Remington, has been re-issued by the University of Oklahoma Press. Also worth consulting, although many of the stories are identical, is *Frederic Remington's Own West* (New York: Promontory Press,

"The Broncho-Buster," a sculpture by Frederic Remington.

1960) written and illustrated by Frederic Remington and edited by Harold McCracken.

The most important recent book on Remington is Peggy and Harold Samuels' *Frederic Remington* (New York: Doubleday, 1982). In addition, reference should also be made to Robert Taft's *Artists and Illustrators of the Old West* (New York: Scribner's, 1953) for the coverage of Remington's years in Kansas, Harold McCracken's *Frederic Remington: Artist of the Old West* (Philadelphia: Lippincott, 1947), and G. Edward White's *The Eastern Establishment and the Western Experience: The West of Frederic Remington, Theodore Roosevelt, and Owen Wister* (New Haven: Yale University Press, 1968) for the interrelationships between these three men and their times, as well as Ben Merchant Vorpahl's generally excellent, *My Dear Wister: The Frederic Remington-Owen Wister Letters* (Palo Alto: American West Publishing, 1973).

Reno, Clint. See Ballard, Todhunter.

Rhodes, Eugene Manlove (1869–1934) Controversial Western novelist, essayist, and poet born in a log house at Tecumseh, Nebraska. The Rhodes

family, plagued by prairie fires, grasshoppers, and cyclones soon moved to Cherokee, Kansas, where Rhodes' father opened a general store. In 1881, the family moved again, this time to New Mexico where, for a brief period in 1890, Rhodes' father was made Indian agent for the Mescalero Apaches, but he lost the appointment due to his unwillingness to exploit the Indians for profit.

In 1889–1890, Rhodes attended the University of the Pacific at Stockton, California, but the lack of money forced him to leave after only two years. Returning to New Mexico, Rhodes engaged in a number of jobs from ranching, mining, and wagon freighting, to school teaching, road building, and dishwashing. As a teacher, when asked to take over a particularly unruly class, Rhodes stepped to the front of the room, unsheathed his side arm, and was able to conduct the session without interruption. However, when he applied for state certification to teach, he was turned down due to moral reservations as to his character. Thanks to Bull Durham tobacco, which offered books in a world classics library in exchange for coupons, Rhodes was able to further his education, and, in truth, he demonstrated the fact that the truest scholar is a self-taught man. For a time, he worked for the famous Bar Cross Ranch, although he avoided cows, preferring horse wrangling. His fellow waddies would recall, in years to come, how Rhodes always had his nose in a book when riding line and once even when trying to break an especially obstinate mustang by sitting on its head.

From his earliest recollection, Rhodes was convinced that he could write if given a chance. In 1896, Rhodes published his first work, a poem in *Land of Sunshine*, a periodical edited by C.F. Lummis. Rhodes published several more poems and in 1902 Lummis ran Rhodes' first short story, "The Hour and the Man," in *Our West*, another magazine he edited. Between the first poem and the first short story, one of Rhodes' poems had made its way East where it was read by May Davison Purple, a widow with two children. She wrote Rhodes a highly complimentary letter and after a long wait received a twenty-page letter in response. In July, 1899, Rhodes went by freight train East to meet his correspondent in person. Rhodes arrived, proposed, married her less than a month after his arrival, and then, four days after the wedding, penniless, left May in Apalachin, New York, where she lived, and returned to New Mexico in order to earn enough money to bring her and her children West, which he was able to do about half a year later.

It was by all accounts a strange marriage. After his death, May Davison Rhodes published *The Hired Man on Horseback: My Story of Eugene Manlove Rhodes* (Boston: Houghton Mifflin, 1938). Haphazard in construction, the book does nonetheless bring Rhodes to life in his element, and the descriptions of their early years together in New Mexico are surely its finest attribute. However, May Davison Rhodes was perhaps too strongly attached to her parents and too little prepared for the lonely and brooding way of life in Tularosa much less the isolation up at Rhodes' ranch in the San Andres mountains. After the birth of a son, May and the children returned East to live with her parents. Rhodes followed four years later. Although May quoted Rhodes as saying that he owed it to her that he stuck at writing at all, the truth of the matter is that being forced, because of her attachment to her parents, to live in the East and take up farming to support May, her children, his son with her and a daughter who died in infancy, as well as May's aging parents, Rhodes found himself in an unhappy predicament. To a friend he wrote these anguished words: "To write stories one needs some ease and *rest* when you are worn out. I am very tired, and yet I can write only at night." Rhodes' enlargement of the heart, which finally killed him, is generally blamed on a bout with influenza, but certainly the long hours he put in as a farmer followed by the equally long hours writing were a severe strain on his constitution. When it came to women, Rhodes subscribed to an excessively chivalric code and he fully expected his readers to believe that Jeff Bransford in *Bransford in Arcadia, or The Little Eohippus* (New York: Henry Holt, 1914) and Johnny Dines in *Stepsons of Light* (Boston: Houghton Mifflin, 1921) would sooner face hanging than implicate a woman, no matter how innocently, in their respective plights. It is therefore quite probable that Rhodes never complained to his wife about the anguish of his situation, but his best novels and stories were written during these years of exile and are permeated with a profound nostalgia for New Mexico.

Much of Rhodes' fiction was serialized in *The Saturday Evening Post* prior to book publication and the *Post* brought him to the attention of a wide and sympathetic audience. Rhodes' stories did not seek to undermine any of the *Post's* editorial prejudices — he never sought to characterize Indians and he never questioned the rightness of the American pioneering spirit. Indeed, for Rhodes, as he recorded in his Prologue to *Stepsons of Light*, the settlement of the West was "the greatest upbuilding of recorded time; and prime motive of the great migration was the motive of all migrations — the search for food and land. They went West for food. What they did there was to work; if you require a monument — take a good look!" Rhodes felt this way and he wrote his stories this way.

It was only when Rhodes' health was obviously failing and now that her parents were dead that May agreed to return with Rhodes to New Mexico, moving with him to Santa Fe in 1926. Among those who befriended Rhodes was author Mary Austin (q.v.), but times were hard and, in 1927, Rhodes moved to Alamogordo, and in 1931 he and May made the final move to Pacific Beach, California. "Not all the California sunshine could brighten the knowledge that we were old and broken and practically penniless," May recalled in her biography. "The fledglings were grown. They were gone. There were only a very lonely man and a very lonely woman, long, weary miles from the special lands we loved." The *Post* serialized Rhodes' novel *The Proud Sheriff* in 1932 and rejected his *Beyond the Desert* (Boston: Houghton Mifflin, 1934) because it was too verbose. Rhodes, who was destitute, wired the editors to inform them that he had only 48¢ and would revise it any way they wanted if they would send him some money. They wired him $100. Rhodes died of successive heart attacks, clutching his wife to him, and his body was transported back to the San Andres mountains where, in a remote spot, a marker was erected:

"Pasó Por Aquí"
Eugene Manlove Rhodes
Jan. 19, 1869 — June 27, 1934

The reference is to Rhodes' most memorable novel, of course, *Pasó Por Aquí* (Boston: Houghton Mifflin, 1927) and means "he passed this way."

It was Bernard DeVoto, in his essay "The Novelist of the Cattle Kingdom" which prefaces May Davison Rhodes' biography, who commented that Rhodes wrote "much the best dialogue put in the mouth of Western characters since Mark Twain (q.v.). The whole revelation of a man, perhaps the point of an entire story, may depend on the turn of a single phrase, and that turn may depend on an inflection which not the eye but the ear must catch. Yet the inflection is not missed: his Westerners tranquilly reveal themselves in authentic speech."

Rhodes chose for his villains the men who, historically, were the real villains in the West, in DeVoto's words, "the speculators, the bankers and manipulators, the mortgagees and monopolists, all the operators of the machinery by which the East systematically plundered its captive province...." Rhodes lived through that age that saw the very basis for the Homestead Act of 1862 brought to final defeat in the West. Frequently Rhodes had known outlaws living on his New Mexico ranch, in the old days, Sam Ketchum, Bill Doolin, Little Dick, Black Jack, two of the Dalton gang, and, unbeknownst to him, the Apache Kid. When, in one of his finest novels, *The Trusty Knaves* (Boston: Houghton Mifflin, 1934), he showed Bill Doolin to be less of a bandit than the Establishment which is planning a bank robbery, Rhodes knew what of he wrote, and he saw outlawry — although he would never have used these words — as disorganized class struggle, men in their confusion trying to survive among all the land-grabbers and Eastern capitalists who were exploiting them.

Eugene Manlove Rhodes' Western novels are *Good Men and True* (1910), *Bransford in Arcadia, or The Little Eohippus* (1914) [alternate title: *Bransford of Rain-*

Dust jacket from the original edition of Beyond the Desert *(Boston: Houghton Mifflin, 1934) by Eugene Manlove Rhodes.*

bow Range], *The Desire of the Moth* (1916), *West Is West* (1917), *Stepsons of Light* (1921), *Copper Streak Trail* (1922), *Once in the Saddle* (1927) [also containing *Pasó Por Aquí*], *The Trusty Knaves* (1934), *Beyond the Desert* (1934), *The Proud Sheriff* (1935).

Two collections of Rhodes' shorter writings have been edited by W.H. Hutchinson, who became executor of Rhodes' literary estate, *The Little World Waddies*, published privately by Hutchinson himself in a limited edition in Chico, California in 1946 and *The Rhodes Reader* (Norman: University of Oklahoma Press, 1957).

Films based on Eugene Manlove Rhodes' Western fiction are *Bransford in*

Arcadia; Or, The Little Eohippus (Eclair-Universal, 1914) [director unknown] remade as *Sure Fire* (Universal, 1921) directed by Jack Ford, *Within an Inch of His Life* (Eclair-Universal, 1914) [director unknown] [based on the short novel *The Line of Least Resistance*], *The Desire of the Moth* (Universal, 1917) directed by Rupert Julian remade as *The Wallop* (Universal, 1921) directed by Jack Ford [apparently so Rhodes could be paid twice for this property, the story on which this remake was based was given the title "The Girl He Left Behind Him" on both the copyright and release information], *West Is West* (Universal, 1920) directed by Val Paul, *Good Men and True* (Robertson-Cole, 1922) directed by Val Paul, *The Mysterious Witness* (Robertson-Cole, 1923) directed by Seymour Zerliff [based on *Stepsons of Light*], and *Four Faces West* (United Artists, 1948) directed by Alfred E. Green [based on *Pasó Por Aquí*].

"*The Fool's Heart*" (1915) was adapted for a two-act play by Charles Milton Newcomb in 1919 and was again adapted for televison by Ruth Woodman for *Suspense* on CBS-TV, 16 January 1951.

More notable than May Davison Rhodes' biography of her husband is W.H. Hutchinson's thorough and splendid *A Bar Cross Man; The Life and Personal Writings of Eugene Manlove Rhodes* (Norman: University of Oklahoma Press, 1956). The chapbook, *Eugene Manlove Rhodes: Cowboy Chronicler* (Austin: Steck-Vaughn, 1967), by Edwin W. Gaston, Jr., while unreliable as to plots in some cases and containing a paraphrase of the criticism of others, is recommended with these reservations as an adequate introduction to Rhodes for the uninitiated.

Richter, Conrad (1890–1968) Pulitzer Prize-winning novelist, short story writer, and essayist remembered primarily for his frontier fiction, born at Pine Grove, Pennsylvania. Growing up in the small farming community of Pine Grove was hard for the restless Richter and he spent many hours reading books. His father, grandfather, uncle, and great uncles had all been clergymen and it was intended that Richter should also go into the ministry, but, when he was 13, he turned down a scholarship and left preparatory school to attend high school in Tremont, Pennsylvania where his father's parish was at the time. He graduated from high school at 15, and for the next several years he worked as a teamster, a bank clerk, a farm hand, a timberman, and a subscription salesman. After reading a series of articles in the *Bookman* about newspaper men, Richter, at 18, decided upon a career in journalism. His first job reporting was for the Johnstown *Journal* and by the time he was 19 he was editing the weekly *Courier* at Patten. He later worked for the Pittsburg *Dispatch* and the *Johnstown Leader* before he accepted a job in Cleveland, Ohio, working as a private secretary. While in Cleveland his first short story, "How Tuck Went Home," was published in

1913 in *Cavalier*, a Munsey publication. Spokane, Washington, and the Coeur d'Alene region of Idaho where Richter had investigated a silver and lead mining venture several years previously provided the background for this tale of mining. His second story, "Brothers of No Kin," was published in *Forum* magazine in 1914 and was chosen as the best short story of the year in addition to being reprinted in several other periodicals. Editors soon began soliciting stories from Richter; however, he had married Harvena Achenbach in early 1915 and he needed a secure income. He decided to stick to business and write only in his spare time the kind of story that would command a decent price. He became involved working in the publishing business in both Reading and Harrisburg, Pennsylvania, until 1928. Also, for a short time, Richter published his own children's publication, *Junior Magazine*, for which he did the writing, editing, advertising sales, and copyrighting.

Between 1913 and 1933—Richter's apprenticeship period—he published more than twenty-five stories. Twelve of these were collected in *Brothers of No Kin and Other Stories* (New York: Hinds, Hayden, Eldredge, 1924). The stories, many of which have a rural setting, were undistinguished in that they were written in the popular style of that period with melodramatic plots, stereotypical characters, and trick endings reminiscent of the work of O. Henry (q.v.). During this period Richter also concerned himself with the philosophical problems of life and two book-length essays resulted before he moved to Albuquerque, New Mexico, in 1928 due to his wife's failing health—they were *Human Vibrations* (New York: Dodd, Mead, 1926) and *Principles in Bio-Physics* (Harrisburg:

Good Books, 1927). The enforced move to the Southwest proved advantageous for Richter's literary career because he decided to write the best historical fiction he could regardless of recompense. For five years Richter collected material on the Southwestern frontier from original sources, rare early books, newspapers, manuscripts, and from talking with surviving pioneers. Nine stories with Western settings were published in the *Ladies Home Journal* and *The Saturday Evening Post* between April, 1934 and January, 1936 and then collected in *Early Americana and Other Stories* (New York: Knopf, 1936), a collection acclaimed because of Richter's ability to blend realism and myth-making. The collective heroes of these stories, in which romance plays an important part and in which Indians appear only for dramatic purposes, are the family unit and the community.

The Sea of Grass (New York: Knopf, 1937) established Richter as a leading literary interpreter of the American West besides giving him financial security. The novel, which had been anticipated in his short story "Smoke Over the Prairie" (1935), was serialized in *The Saturday Evening Post* as were several of his later novels including *The Free Man* (New York: Knopf, 1943), a pedestrian story set in Pennsylvania around the time of the American Revolution, and *Always Young and Fair* (New York: Knopf, 1947), a period piece also set in Pennsylvania which was inspired by the spirit of the Theodore Roosevelt (q.v.) era. *The Sea of Grass*, written in the simple, poetic style at which Richter was so adept employs the familiar plot-line of cattlemen vs. nesters. The protagonist, Colonel Brewton, who personifies the pioneering spirit, raised much criticism for want of complexity; however Edwin W. Gaston, Jr., in his book *Conrad Richter* (New York: Twayne Publishers, 1965), stated that however "... lacking in complexity, Brewton still is more reflective than the stereotyped Westerner such as Zane Grey's (q.v.) Lassiter or Owen Wister's (q.v.) Virginian. In fact, Brewton—who stands somewhere between Walter Van Tilburg Clark's (q.v.) idealistic Arthur Bridges and his pragmatic brother Curt [in *The Track of the Cat* (New York: Random House, 1949)]—represents the best of the two extremes. One would have to search long, therefore, to find a more authentic character in Western fiction." It was authenticity about early life in America more than anything else that Richter strove for in his frontier fiction. *The Sea of Grass* in which the ranchers' open range is tamed by the farmers in their attempt to realize the agrarian dream is set in New Mexico during 1885–1900 and is told 25 years after the fact by a now young man who was but a child when the events took place and this kind of back-telling became a common Richter technique.

The Trees (New York: Knopf, 1940) was Richter's next book and the first in his epic trilogy about the settling of the Ohio frontier between the years 1790 and 1860. The trilogy, which also includes *The Fields* (New York: Knopf, 1946), Richter's fifth novel, and the Pulitzer Prize-winning *The Town* (New York: Knopf, 1950), Richter's seventh novel, is considered generally one of the better portraits of pioneer life. Richter depicted in these three books the Westering process and how the advancement of civilization places restrictions on the individual, thus showing both the benefits and drawbacks of progress. The trilogy was praised for both its central heroine, Sayward Luck-

ett, who personified the pioneering spirit of frontier women (and whose predecessor was Sayward Hewett in Richter's short story "The Rawhide Knot" (1938) and for his use of now forgotten dialectical expressions and folklore.

Richter's third novel, *Tacey Cromwell* (New York: Knopf, 1942), a mining story set in Arizona Territory about a brothel madam who wishes to attain respectability as does her gambler lover, seems forced and melodramatic in contrast to his two prior novels. Richter's third Southwestern novel, *The Lady* (New York: Knopf, 1957), which ran serially in *The Saturday Evening Post* and which has been compared to Willa Cather's (q.v.) *A Lost Lady* (New York: Knopf, 1927), an author whom Richter greatly admired, focuses on a lady of Mexican and English ancestry who is Richter's most complex heroine. Set in New Mexico, the conflict of the story is between cattlemen and sheepmen, the latter represented by Dona Ellen, the Lady.

In both *The Light in the Forest* (New York: Knopf, 1953), which was serialized in *The Saturday Evening Post*, and its companion novel, *A Country of Strangers* (New York: Knopf, 1966), Richter attempted to show life from the Indian point of view after having shown the Indian from the white settlers' point of view in books such as *The Trees* and *The Town*. Although Richter was sympathetic to the injustices done the Indians, he failed to understand the Indian way of thinking, simply because he could only view them as unmitigated savages.

Richter followed *The Light in the Forest* with another book on philosophy entitled *Mountain in the Desert* (New York: Knopf, 1955), a series of Socratic dialogues between a hermit and a number of students.

In 1960 he won the National Book Award for his autobiographical novel, *The Waters of Kronos* (New York: Knopf, 1960).

Literary historian John R. Milton (q.v.) said of Richter in his essay "The Novel in the American West" contained in *Western Writing* (Albuquerque: University of New Mexico Press, 1974): "Conrad Richter is, I think, a major and neglected American novelist who has suffered critically because his work is associated with the frontier and yet does not seem bound to it. *The Sea of Grass*, although a slight novel, portrayed the pioneer rancher in opposition to the encroaching farmer so well that it seems silly for anyone else to attempt the same theme."

Ringold, Clay, See Hogan, (Robert) Ray.

Roberts, Wayne. See Overholser, Wayne D.

Roderus, Frank (1942 —) Author of Western fiction in the formulary mode, born at Pittsburgh, Pennsylvania. Roderus was early disenchanted with formal education and never graduated from high school, although he was subsequently a department head in a school system of sixty thousand students. He wrote his first story at the age of five and knew what he most wanted to do. For nine years he worked as a newspaper reporter. When he was fired from a Midwestern newspaper, he decided to make the jump into fiction. Roderus' first Western novel was *Journey to Utah* (New York: Doubleday, 1976). It concerns a character named Stumpy Williams who, riding

through Colorado in the 1890s, comes across a girl afoot in empty country. Stumpy decides to help her and ends up being hunted by her brothers and finally jailed and accused of raping her. *The 33 Brand* (New York: Doubleday, 1977) and *The Keystone Kid* (New York: Doubleday, 1977) followed and were both nominated for Spur Awards by the Western Writers of America.

Roderus' fiction is notable for its projection of tarnished heroes who can readily gain a reader's sympathies and for the many cunning and suspenseful situations which these heroes invariably encounter and from which escape appears impossible.

Frank Roderus' Western novels are *Journey to Utah* (1976), *The 33 Brand* (1977), *The Keystone Kid* (1977), *Duster: The Story of a Texas Cattle Drive* (1977), *Home to Texas* (1978), *Easy Money* (1978), *Hell-Creek Cabin* (1979), *The Name Is Hart* (1979), *Jason Evers, His Own Story* (1980), *Sheep-Herding Man* (1980), *Cowboy* (1981), *Old Kyle's Boy* (1981), *The Rawhide War* (1981).

Rölvaag, O(le) E(dvart) (1876–1931) Norwegian-American novelist of the immigrant pioneer experience, born on Donna Island in Northern Norway, just below the Arctic Circle in a sod-roofed cottage that had belonged to his family for generations. The cottagers and fishermen that were Rölvaag's neighbors were strong and quick-witted, fond of story-telling and the local library was full of world literature that Rölvaag read as a boy. He went to common school, trudging fourteen miles a day, but he was never strong and was plagued by bronchial and heart problems that shortened his life. At 16 he started work as a fisherman, but a terrible storm the next year almost took his life and the prolonged exposure further undermined his health. After a particularly bitter winter, he decided to immigrate to the United States, but worked with the fleet for three more years until his uncle in South Dakota lent him the money for the trip.

Rölvaag left Norway in 1896 at the age of 20 with the equivalent of $1.50 in his pockets and his travel tickets. He went to live with his uncle in Elk Point, South Dakota, pictured in his first published book, *Letters from America* (Norway: American-Breve, 1912). So autobiographical was this series of episodes in novelistic form that Rölvaag insisted on using the pseudonym of Paal-Morck. It reveals his disillusionment with farm life where he dreamt of the Northern seas while feeding the cows and pigs. Although still learning English and older than most of the students, Rölvaag eagerly left farm life when he was accepted at Augustana Academy in Canton, South Dakota. In 1901 he transferred to St. Olaf College in Northfield, Minnesota. The college was run by Norwegian Lutherans and Rölvaag considered studying for the ministry, being deeply religious. But a systematic study of Norwegian literature, particularly Henrik Ibsen, turned him strongly towards becoming a writer. A first novel, written during this period, was never published but taught Rölvaag his craft. He graduated from St. Olaf in 1905.

Rölvaag became very active during the next decade, both in his writing and in his attempts to found organizations to preserve the Norwegian heritage in the United States. He was encouraged in his writing by a good reception given to *Letters from America* which, as most of his other works, deals with the immigrant Norwegian caught between two cultures and belonging to neither. He wrote in Norwegian which was not always translated into English immediately, for he had a wide following in Norway.

Rölvaag's greatest novel is *Giants in the Earth* (New York: Harper's, 1927), the first volume of his trilogy about an immigrant family. First published in Norway in 1924, once translated it became a Book-of-the-Month Club selection in 1927 and proved a success on both sides of the ocean. In it Rölvaag showed not the epic heroism of pioneering but the terror and loneliness of the immigrants who had to endure storms, frosts, prairie fires, and droughts in the wilderness as well as conflicts with their fellow men. The character of the lonely farmer's wife, who goes insane in her estrangement from the land, is well represented by Beret Hansa, who becomes a religious fanatic. After the death of her husband in a blizzard, Beret's life story continues in the second volume of the trilogy, *Peder Victorious* (New York: Harper's, 1929), in which she regains her energy and her life spirit. The hero of the story is, of course, her son and the narrative concern is with his Americanization and that of the small Norwegian settlement as it grows and becomes a Midwestern town. *Their Fathers' God* (New York: Harper's, 1931) completes the trilogy with the unhappy marriage of Peder and his Catholic wife, Susie.

P.O.

For further information see *Rölvaag: His Life and Art* (Lincoln: University of Nebraska Press, 1972) by Paul Reigstag.

Roosevelt, Theodore (1858–1919)

Twenty-sixth President of the United States of America (1901–1909), born at New York City, and often described as the patron saint of the West, because of his efforts to preserve the natural resources of his country. Roosevelt graduated from Harvard University and, for a time, studied law at Columbia University. Entering politics, he served two successive terms as a Republican in the New York state assembly (1882–1884). While an assemblyman, Roosevelt married and in 1884 he and his wife, Alice, were expecting the birth of their first child. Secure in his profession, the previous year, as an investment, Roosevelt had acquired a ranch in Dakota, and he intended to go on hunting trips there. Within two days of the birth of the child, both Roosevelt's wife and his mother died. In his diary, Roosevelt recorded that "the light has gone out of my life" and "for joy or for sorrow my life has now been lived out."

Throwing himself into his work, it was with even more pain that Roosevelt came to realize that his party was not inclined to reform and, somewhat disgusted with politics, he decided to retire to the life of a rancher. Carleton Putnam recorded in his book, *Theodore Roosevelt* (New York:

Scribner's, 1958), that "no man invests a fifth of his fortune in two ranches and writes of ranching, 'I shall make it my regular business,' if he is only seeking a stopgap. Roosevelt loved the West for the outdoor life it brought him and ranching because it gave that outdoor life a *raison d'etre*. In the West he could experiment with a literary career as well as business, the West itself providing a subject for his pen." And that is just what he did. He wrote *Hunting Trips of a Ranchman* (1885), and followed it with *Ranch Life and the Hunting Trail* (1888), *The Winning of the West* (New York: Putnam's, 1900), his monumental history of the opening of the West in six volumes, and a number of essays, many of which were collected in *A Book-Lover's Holidays in the Open* (New York: Scribner's, 1920). It was through these books, particularly the first two, that Roosevelt introduced to the East an image of the cowboy, the hired man on horseback, which, when augmented by the work of Frederic Remington (q.v.) and Owen Wister (q.v.), caused a heightened, if romanticized, enthusiasm for the West. "When drunk on the villainous whiskey of the frontier towns," Roosevelt wrote of cowboys in *Ranch Life and the Hunting Trail*, "they cut mad antics, riding their horses into the saloons, firing their pistols right and left, from boisterous light-heartedness rather than from any viciousness, and indulging too often in deadly shooting affrays, brought on either by the accidental contact of the moment or on account of some long-standing grudge, or perhaps because of bad blood between two ranches or localities; but except while on such sprees they are quiet, rather self-contained men, perfectly frank and simple, and on their own ground treat a stranger with the most whole-souled hospitality, doing all in their power for him and scorning to take any reward in return." Roosevelt, however, harbored a certain suspicion of Mexicans and also commented, in the same book, that "some of the cowboys are Mexicans, who generally do the actual work well enough, but are not trustworthy...."

Although he himself did not write fiction, he exerted a considerable influence on those who did, offering criticism and advice, as was the case with Stephen Crane (q.v.). When Crane wrote the short story "A Man and Some Others" (1897) in which an Anglo-American was surrounded and killed by a gang of Mexicans, Roosevelt wrote to him that perhaps someday Crane would write "another story of the frontiersman and the Mexican Greaser in which the frontiersman shall come out on top; it is more normal that way!" Similarly, when Owen Wister, a close personal friend of Roosevelt, published his story "Balaam and Pedro" (1897) and told graphically of how Balaam gouged out a horse's eye, Roosevelt, who called Wister Dan, commented, according to Wister in his book *Roosevelt: The Story of a Friendship 1880–1919* (New York: Macmillan, 1930), "I'm perfectly aware, Dan, that Zola has many admirers because he says things out loud that great writers from Greece down to the present have mostly passed over in silence. I think that *conscientious descriptions of the unspeakable* do not constitute an interpretation of life, but merely disgust all readers not afflicted with the hysteria of bad taste. ...When you come to publishing it in a volume, throw a veil over what Balaam did to Pedro, leave that to the reader's imagination, and you will greatly strengthen your effect." Wister did as Roosevelt asked, dedicating his book *The Virginian*

(New York: Macmillan, 1902), in which the story appeared in revised form, to Roosevelt and remarking that one page stood "newly written because you blamed it...." However, it did not strengthen the effect of the incident; to the contrary, it merely made Wister appear mincing. Yet it is a tribute to the moral influence Roosevelt exerted in his time, that as late as the film version of *The Covered Wagon* (Paramount, 1923), based on an Emerson Hough (q.v.) novel, the picture carried a dedication to Roosevelt.

What brought Roosevelt back to the forefront of political interest was not his unsuccessful bid for the mayorality of New York City in 1886, nor his becoming U.S. civil service commissioner (1889–1895) and president of the board of police commissioners of New York City (1895–1897), nor even his being assistant secretary of the Navy during the McKinley administration (1897–1898), but his urging war against Spain for imperialist and economic reasons. He resigned his office and helped organize the "Rough Riders," a group variously made up of rich Eastern adventurers and Western cowboys and a group which, in a way, typified the consensus of the nation which was achieved when Roosevelt became president after the assasination of McKinley. To immortalize the event in the popular imagination, Roosevelt hired Frederic Remington to paint "The Charge Up San Juan Hill," which was supposed to depict the decisive battle of the Cuban campaign, although Roosevelt led no troops up the Hill mounted on a war pony and brandishing his sword; it was, for its day, a semi-advanced form of political hype.

As a conservationist, Roosevelt supported the Newlands Act of 1902 which deployed monies received from the sale of

Western lands into federal irrigation projects. Roosevelt set aside numerous national park sites, Nature reserves, and protected wilderness areas. Although personally Roosevelt wrote in his *Naval War of 1812* (1882) of Thomas Jefferson that he was "perhaps the most incapable executive that ever filled the presidential chair," more charitably, and more aptly, Lawrence Clark Powell in his *Southwestern Classics* (Los Angeles: Ward Ritchie, 1974) remarked: "Since Jefferson, no president of the United States was culturally accomplished as Theodore Roosevelt, and none since has had such wide interests and attainments and intellectual curiosity." Because of Roosevelt's image of the West, coupled with that of Remington and Wister, the West was conceived during the first decade of the Twentieth century as a particular kind of civilization, rather than, as formerly had been the case, an alternate to civilization. "Thus in the minds of Eastern reviews," G. Edward White recorded in his book *The Eastern Establishment and the Western Experience* (New Haven: Yale University Press, 1968), "Roosevelt himself had evolved from a practical expert on cattle ranching and a teller of strange tales into first a chronicler of a phase of American civilization and finally a patriot who saw the legacy of a Western experience in some of the ideals of modern America." Roosevelt's memory remains as lasting as the land itself, which he served, for it is framed by forests and rivers, dams, orchards, and green fields, bird sanctuaries and game preserves, as well as those places of breath-taking beauty, Mesa Verde and El Morro, this president who once alarmed a cabinet meeting by exclaiming, "Gentlemen, I must tell you what just happened," and who then proceeded to describe two species of birdlife which had never before been observed in Washington, D.C.

The best among biographies of Theodore Roosevelt's early years is Edmund Morris' *The Rise of Theodore Roosevelt* (New Jersey: Coward, McCann, 1979). With special reference to Roosevelt's life as a rancher and his Western experiences, note should also be made of John Burroughs' *Camping and Tramping with Roosevelt* (Boston: Houghton Mifflin, 1907), Herman Hagedorn's *Roosevelt in the Badlands* (Boston: Houghton Mifflin, 1921), Lincoln A. Lang's *Ranching with Roosevelt* (Philadelphia: Lippincott, 1921), and William C. Deming's *Roosevelt in the Bunkhouse* (Laramie: Laramie Printing Co., 1927). A solid book on the inter-relationships between Roosevelt, Wister, and Frederic Remington is G. Edward White's *The Eastern Establishment and the Western Experience: The West of Frederic Remington, Theodore Roosevelt, and Owen Wister* (New Haven: Yale University Press, 1968).

Rushing, Jane Gilmore (1925 —)

Author of novels set in Texas, born at Pyron, Texas. Rushing was educated in Texas and received her Bachelor's degree and Master's degree from Texas Tech University. She worked as a newspaper reporter for several Texas-based papers and as a high school teacher before receiving her Doctorate in 1957 from Texas Tech University. She married in 1956 and in 1957–1958 was an instructor of English at the University of Tennessee in Knoxville. She was the recipient of several fellowships including the fiction fellowship to the Breadloaf Writers Conference in 1964.

As some other Texas women writers, especially Dorothy Scarborough (q.v.), Rushing was most at home writing about life in Texas. Her first book, *Walnut Grove* (New York: Doubleday, 1964), reflected her interest in the folklore and history of her home state. *Against the Moon* (New York: Doubleday, 1968), a contemporary story which focuses on the lives and loves of Texas women, won the Emily Clark Balch Award from the *Virginia Quarterly Review*. *Tamzen* (New York: Doubleday, 1972), set in West Texas in the 1890s, is concerned with the struggles between cattle ranchers and farmers over a disputed land area, Block 97. The lead character, Tamzen Greer, is one of Rushing's most memorable female creations. *The Rain Crow* (New York: Doubleday, 1977) traces the lives of three generations.

Rushing's generational novels have been highly praised and C.L. Sonnichsen in his book *From Hopalong to Hud: Thoughts on Western Fiction* (College Station: Texas A&M University, 1978) considered Rushing a "superior" writer.

Russell, Charles M(arion)

(1864–1926) Painter, sculptor, and illustrator born at St. Louis, Missouri, who in his later years, as Frederic Remington (q.v.) before him, turned to writing a series of short stories depicting the life and people of early Western life. Russell was sent to Montana to live under the guardianship of a sheepherder at the age of 16. This did not last very long, since at 17 Russell met Jake Hoover, a one-time mountain man, and for two years Russell lived with Hoover in the latter's cabin in the Pig-Eye Basin on the South Fork of the Judith River. In 1888, Russell went to live six months with the Blood Indians, a branch of the Blackfeet living in Alberta, Canada. Russell became a member of the tribe, his Blood name Ah-wah-cous (Horns That Fork, or Antelope). The Bloods urged him to remain with them, but Russell was restless and headed back for Montana.

Years later, Russell claimed that he was not a cowboy, but he made his living for some years doing range work. He also painted, trading most of his paintings to bartenders and saloon-owners to pay his bar bills or for credit; once in a while he would sell a painting for a grub stake so he could maintain himself in a cabin in the wilderness where he could paint without interruption. This all changed in 1896 when he married Nancy Cooper. Nancy Russell was a hard-driving, practical woman and she soon put Russell's painting on a firm commercial basis, getting him to swear off drinking in the bargain. There were annual trips to New York for exhibitions; she sought out movie stars of that era and William S. Hart, Harry Carey, and Will Rogers were soon counted among the Russells' friends.

Russell gained a considerable reputation as a storyteller and began writing and publishing his stories, first in newspapers and then in book form. *Rawhide Rawlins* (Great Falls: Montana Newspaper Alliance, 1921) was followed by *More Rawhides* (Great Falls: Montana Newspaper Alliance, 1925); but the best of the collections was published posthumously, *Trails Plowed Under* (New York: Doubleday, 1927). As Russell's paintings, these stories are concerned

An illustration by Charles Russell to accompany the words "out where the trails of men are dim and far apart" from B. M. Bower's The Lure of the Dim Trails *(New York: Dillingham, 1907).*

with the early West, scenes of wild life, cowboys, the Indian nations, and they have the ingenuous charm of the frontier itself. The Montana State Board of Education awarded Russell posthumously an honorary doctor of law degree "for greatest historic accomplishment in an artistic way of any person in the state."

Of the several books that have appeared about Russell, perhaps the most intimate portrait is to be found in *Recollections of Charley Russell* (Norman: University of Oklahoma Press, 1963) by Frank Bird Linderman edited by H. G. Merriam. Also recommended is *The Charles Russell Book* (Doubleday, 1957) by Harold McCracken for its many fine Russell reproductions.

Ruxton, George Augustus Frederick (1821–1848)

One of the most articulate and inspired of the Nineteenth-century travelers through the American West, born at Oxfordshire, England. When Ruxton was 7, his father moved the family to Broad Oak, an old rural estate about thirty miles Southeast of London. Ruxton's father, however, died soon after and Ruxton himself found going to school troublesome. He was finally expelled from the Sandhurst Military Academy and by 17 he had become a young adventurer, setting out for Spain to support the side of Isabella II. After being decorated by the Spanish government for bravery, Ruxton returned to England where he received a commission in the Ceylon Rifles and was transferred to the 89th Foot Regiment and sent to Ontario, Canada.

Inspired by his reading of the novels of adventure in the forests written by James Fenimore Cooper (q.v.), Ruxton's exposure to the Canadian wilderness only whetted his appetite for further exploration. Chucking his military career and selling his commission, as one could then do, Ruxton engaged an Indian friend, Peshwego, to act as guide and set out as a *voyageur* for the winter of 1843–1844 trekking through the frozen wastes of Ontario and Northern New York. In 1844, his trip completed, Ruxton returned to England, but not for long. Almost immediately he set out for Northern Africa and, when he encountered hostility among the natives, he returned to England and then set out for South Africa. After this last exploratory visit, Ruxton began to gain attention from the Royal Geographic Society in London.

Upon his return, Ruxton petitioned Her Majesty's Government for funding to continue his explorations. He was met with delays, despite the support of the Royal Geographic Society, and so he jumped at the chance, when it was offered him, to travel in North America. It was to become his Great Journey, an expedition that took him from the Southern coasts of Mexico through the Rocky Mountains and the plains of the American West, some three thousand miles. His record of the journey became a classic of its kind in Western American literature, *Adventures in Mexico and the Rocky Mountains 1846–1847* (1847). Ruxton began at Vera Cruz in August, 1846 and went Northward through Mexico City, through Silao, Agua Caliente, Durango, Chihuahua, El Paso, Socorro, Santa Fe, Taos, past the Spanish Peaks and down the Rockies to the Arkansas River and Pueblo. He wintered with an old mountain man, John Hawkens, and by hunting and exploring he came upon and set down the stories and legends and ways of men in a fashion that has proven enduring. He passed through St. Louis, Missouri, on his way back to England.

What followed was a burst of suprising literary activity which, beyond his *Adventures*, also included several interesting papers on various aspects of North American life. It was then he decided to attempt a more ambitious project and one for which he has been justly acclaimed, his imaginative and fictional but for all that highly literate and realistic *Life in the Far West* (1849). It is an episodic narrative that follows the experiences of two mountain men, Killbuck and La Bonté, notable for its wealth of incident, accurate portraits, descriptions of dress and of the struggle of men pitted against Nature and against each other, and for one more thing, what only the many days and weeks of solitude in the wilderness could have taught Ruxton: a sense of self-reliance that was both physical and philosophical. Perhaps because of his friendship with Peshwego, Ruxton came to espouse the Native American belief in the balance of Nature and, personally, he engaged in many Indian practices and beliefs, which seemed natural to him because he had been witness to the raw power of Nature and the littleness of man as had few men among his European readers proud of their carefully tended gardens and Nature poetry. Ruxton returned to the United States in 1848, but his health was broken by the previous hardships and he died of dysentery in St. Louis.

Life in the Far West subsequently became a primary source for later writers. Vardis Fisher (q.v.) borrowed the episode of the Indian passion for gambling and used it in *Mountain Man* (New York: Morrow, 1965). Harvey Fergusson (q.v.), as Mayne Reid (q.v.) in *The Scalp Hunters* (1851) and Stewart Edward White (q.v.) in *The Long Rifle* (New York: Doubleday, 1932) before him, borrowed the raid by mountain men on a Mexican fandango for his novel *Wolf Song* (New York: Knopf, 1927). Both Frederick Manfred (q.v.) in *Lord Grizzly* (New York: McGraw-Hill, 1954) and A.B. Guthrie, Jr. (q.v.) in *The Big Sky* (New York: Sloane, 1947) borrowed the episode of one man offering his carcass to another when both are starving in the wilderness. And so it continues.

As Neal Lambert put it in *George Frederick Ruxton* (Boise: Idaho State University Press, 1974), "the Western mountains and the men who lived in them were profound experiences for Ruxton. He saw with his eyes and felt in his bones a world that denied for man the assumptions about his importance and his nobility which give meaning and significance to his efforts."

For further information see *Ruxton of the Rockies* (Norman: University of Oklahoma Press, 1950) edited by LeRoy R. Hafen and the fine chapbook *George Frederick Ruxton* (Boise: Idaho State University Press, 1974) by Neal Lambert.

Ryan, Marah Ellis (1866–1934) An author best remembered today for her two lyrical novels about Indians of the Southwest, *Indian Love Letters* (Chicago: A.C. McClurg, 1907) and *The Flute of the Gods* (New York: Stokes, 1909), born Marah Ellis Martin at Butler County, Pennsylvania. Nothing is known about Ryan's educational background. In 1883, she married S. Erwan Ryan, who was an actor, and for a time Ryan herself pursued a career as an actress. She eventually turned to writing and her early work, both prose and poetry, was published under the pen-name Ellis Martin. Her first novel, *In Love's Domain* (1889), was published when she was 23.

In Ryan's early and very romantic novels set in the Northwest, she employed strong female characters. Throughout her Western fiction her love of Nature and admiration for people living on the frontier was boldly stated, and, in fact, quite often Easterners are portrayed as being snobs. In *Told in the Hills* (1890) a woman from Kentucky, after numerous adventures in the wilderness, decides to live in the Montana hills, rejecting "civilized life." In *That Girl Montana* (New York: Rand, McNally, 1901) the Western-raised daughter of a thief tries for a time to live in New York; however the restrictions placed upon a young girl in the East force her to return to the Northwest. Many interesting characters, often with secret identities stemming from some best-forgotten action or actions in their past, are incorporated into Ryan's complexly plotted stories. In such early novels as *Told in the Hills* or *Squaw Elouise* (1892), Ryan's treatment of Indians is very sympathetic.

In her book, *For the Soul of Rafael* (Chicago: A.C. McClurg, 1906), which is set in the Spanish period of California, Ryan followed Helen Hunt Jackson (q.v.) who in *Ramona* (1884) began the trend to portray Californios as being the best of the Spanish blood. According to literary historian Franklin Walker's book, *A Literary History of Southern California* (Berkeley: University of California Press, 1950), Ryan, subscribing to Jackson's school, specialized in writing about "hothouse Spaniards" which appealed to a wide, but uninformed, audience.

Indian Love Letters was one of the first books in which an Indian fell in love with a white—a storyline which was subsequently used by such writers as Harold Bell Wright (q.v.), Zane Grey (q.v.), Edgar Rice Burroughs (q.v.), Elliott Arnold (q.v.), and Jane Barry (q.v.). The book was written as a series of letters to a white woman from a Hopi Indian who has been educated in a white man's university; in them he describes the culture, religion, and environment of his people. In *From Hopalong to Hud: Thoughts on Western Fiction* (College Station: Texas A&M University Press, 1978), C.L. Sonnichsen stated that *Indian Love Letters* "... sentimentalized the Hopis hopelessly...." However, *Indian Love*

Letters' delicately written prose, which borders on poetry with its lyricism and graceful style, can certainly be enjoyable reading.

Although Ryan had never met an Indian, *The Flute of the Gods*, which followed *Indian Love Letters*, was considered a classic on Indian lore. Subsequent to its publication, Ryan began an intimate association with the Indians and spent two years living with the Navahos in Arizona and was the only white woman ever admitted to the inner council of tribal chiefs. Told from the Indian point of view, *The Flute of the Gods* is a dramatic story about the Southwestern Indians set in a region ranging from the Hopi village of Walpi in Northern Arizona (now the Hopi reserve) to the Tehua villages west of Santa Fe, New Mexico and to Mexico City during approximately 1528–1555. Ryan sought to recreate the early life of Southwestern Indians and included much Indian folk material in the novel. The main character is Tahnte, a fair-haired Tehua Indian with mystical powers who believes the Spanish explorers represent a threat to his people. The Spanish are drawn as terrible villains and included is the Span-

ish atrocity of burning 200 Indians at the stake as a part of a Christian crusade. This clash of religious beliefs is an essential part of the story. And as in Amelia Barr's (q.v.) *Remember the Alamo* (1888) and Mayne Reid's (q.v.) *The White Chief: A Legend of Northern Mexico* (1855), a Roman Catholic clergyman is a villain. Ryan extensively employed an abstract style in *The Flute of the Gods* which sought to imitate as closely as possible the rhythms and character of Indian languages.

Marah Ellis Ryan's novels with a frontier setting are *Told in the Hills* (1891), *Squaw Elouise* (1892), *That Girl Montana* (1901), *Miss Moccasins* (1904), *For the Soul of Rafael* (1906), *Indian Love Letters* (1907), *The Flute of the Gods* (1909), *The House of the Dawn* (1914), *The Treasure Trail* (1918).

Films based on Ryan's Western fiction are *Told in the Hills* (Famous Players, 1919) directed by George Melford, *For the Soul of Rafael* (Equity, 1920) directed by Harry Garson, *That Girl Montana* (Pathé, 1920) directed by Robert Thornby.

Sabin, Mark. See Fox, Norman A.

Sandoz, Mari (1896–1966) Historian, novelist, short story writer, essayist, and biographer whose literary focus was the Great Plains region, born at Sandoz Post Office, Sheridan County, in Northwest Nebraska. The daughter of Jules Ami Sandoz, who immigrated to the United States from Switzerland in 1881, and Mary Elizabeth Fehr, Sandoz grew up in the midst of the

later years of the cattleman-settler troubles. Her father, a surveyor and amateur horticulturist, was in constant danger of being shot by the hired killers of the ranchmen—her uncle had been shot in cold blood by one of the rancher's henchmen. Because her father spent all of his time pursuing his own interests her mother did most of the field and gardenwork so the responsibility of caring for her five younger brothers and sisters and the house fell on Sandoz. Although she was

Mari Sandoz

a thorough tomboy and knew how to trap and skin any animal, she could bake up a forty-nine pound bag of flour. As the people she would write about, Sandoz endured the hardships of frontier life, including witnessing prairie fires, cloudbursts, floods, and tornadoes, in addition to being struck by lightning, being snowblind for six weeks after being caught in a blizzard with her brother which left her permanently blind in one eye, and having her hair cut twice from a gun shot, once intentionally. Not all aspects of homestead life were so rigorous for she was taught a "wonderful at-homeness in the world and universe" and spent many hours sitting on a woodbox listening to old-time trappers, traders, hunters, and Indians talk about their adventures and travels in the early days which gave Sandoz a unique insight into a quickly vanishing era.

From the time she started school at age 9, where she made "the wonderful discovery that little black marks were the key to wonderful stories," Sandoz was writing. Despite the fact that her father did not believe in fiction, she sneaked books into the house where she read them in the attic.

At age 12, she had a story published in the Omaha *Daily News*. When her father found out that she was writing, he locked her in the basement and henceforth her early stories were signed with a pen-name. In 1913, after a total of four and one-half years of schooling, Sandoz passed the rural teachers' exam and began teaching in country schools which she did for seven years. When she was 26, she decided that she must have a college education and became determined to enroll at the University of Nebraska in Lincoln. She was finally accepted as an adult special, because she did not have any high school education, and for the next ten years she attended courses irregularly while holding part-time jobs working first in a drug laboratory and later as an English assistant, a proofreader, and a researcher of Sioux Indian history for the State Historical Society. She never obtained a degree—although in 1950 she received an Honorary degree from the University of Nebraska. However, this period allowed her to practice her writing skills. When her father heard she was given honorable mention in the 1926 Harper's Intercollegiate Short Story contest he sent her a one line note that read, "You know I consider writers and artists the maggots of society."

In the mid 'Twenties, Sandoz decided she would attempt to write a biography about her father. Although she was herself a character in the book and many of the incidents were based on first-hand observation, with the writing of *Old Jules* (Boston: Little, Brown, 1935) she learned the discipline of meticulous research by going through decades of newspapers, corroborating stories by endlessly interviewing people, and reading the 4,000 letters and documents her father had accumulated in his lifetime. (Although Jules Sandoz had disapproved of her writing, at the time of his death in 1928, he asked her to write down his story.) She later wrote about the book, that was three years in research and two years in writing, that "as I worked with the material, . . . it gradually dawned on me that here was a character who embodied not only his own strengths and weaknesses, but those of all humanity— that his struggles were universal struggles and his defeats at the hands of his environment and his own insufficiencies were those of mankind; his tenacious clinging to his dream the symbol of man's undying hope that over the next hill he will find the green pastures of his desire." Sandoz, as Charles Sealsfield (q.v.), chose for her characters, whether whites or Native Americans, representative figures who were not so much individuals but an entire people or group of individuals whose characterizations become manifest through a series of dramatic events.

The next book Sandoz worked on was *Slogum House* (Boston: Little, Brown, 1937), her first published novel and a book that had been on her mind for nearly a decade. By conscious design her first three novels were allegories. A staunchly independent person, Sandoz saw the irrevocable changes taking place in modern technological society and despised the parasitism that dictates the thought and life-style of an entire population and she addressed this idea in *Slogum House* although not as deeply as she did in her second novel, *Capital City* (Boston: Little, Brown, 1939), a modern story set in an imaginary city during the Depression. *The Tom-Walker* (New York: Dial, 1947) was her most difficult novel to write; she consumed over 9,000 sheets of paper in rough drafts. In it she traced the changes taking place in post-bellum America through three generations of the Stone clan who move West after the Civil War. A panoramic and often complex novel, unless one has a fairly extensive background in

American social history, *The Tom-Walker* contains a wealth of folk customs and commentary on financial expansion.

In 1941 and 1946, she served on the staff of Writers Conference at the University of Colorado and the University of Indiana respectively. Beginning in 1947 until 1956, she taught advanced novel writing at the University of Wisconsin in Madison during the summer sessions. In 1943, she moved permanently to New York City.

Her remaining five novels are best described as historical fiction, rather than novels of ideas as were her first three. *Winter Thunder* (Philadelphia: Westminster Press, 1954), an unabridged version of the short story "The Lost School Bus" which had appeared in *The Saturday Evening Post* in 1951, and *Miss Morissa: Doctor of the Gold Trail* (New York: McGraw Hill, 1955), deal with the feminine side of pioneering. *Winter Thunder* is about a woman schoolteacher and her seven pupils who are stranded in a blizzard. *Miss Morissa*—its only weakness being its title—is set in the North Platte River Valley during the 1870s and deals with a young woman doctor's efforts to become part of a small homesteading community situated in a cattle rancher's region. Based on a composite of three real women doctors, *Miss Morissa* is one of the few novels to treat with insight the role of the professional woman on the frontier.

Sandoz' consuming interest in the Plains Indians led her to write several classic non-fictional works about them. She made frequent trips to reservations renewing her contacts with survivors of the Indian wars and gathering information. Only two novels, however, told from the Indian point of view resulted, although many of her novels include Indians as characters since they were an integral part of the period she wrote about. *The Horsecatcher* (Philadelphia: Westminster Press, 1957), written for young readers although an adult can certainly appreciate the simplicity of style Sandoz employed when writing about Indians, tells the story of a young Cheyenne boy who wants to catch and tame wild horses rather than be a warrior and his eventual acceptance by members of his family and tribe. Her next novel was *Son of the Gamblin' Man* (New York: Clarkson N. Potter, 1960), a fictionalized account of John Cozad, a gambler and the founder of Cozad, Nebraska, and his son Robert Henry Cozad who became the world famous artist and teacher, Robert Henri. Her last novel, *The Story Catcher* (Philadelphia: Westminster Press, 1963), a juvenile told from the Indian point of view, won the Spur Award from the Western Writers of America and the Levi Strauss Award for Best Western novel.

She was more than a competent novelist. The magnum opus of the Sandoz canon is her Trans-Missouri series, a six-volume history of the Great Plains region. Sandoz worked on the project for thirty-seven years, beginning in 1927 and finishing in 1964. The series included her first book *Old Jules* in addition to *Crazy Horse: The Strange Man of the Oglalas* (New York: Knopf, 1942), a biography of the great Sioux war chief; *Cheyenne Autumn* (New York: McGraw-Hill, 1953) which chronicles the 1,500 mile trek of a small band of Cheyennes from Indian Territory to their homeland in 1878; *The Buffalo Hunters: The Story of the Hide Men* (New York: Hastings House, 1954), the story of the four great buffalo herds and their destruction; *The Cattlemen: From the Rio Grande across the Far Marias* (New York: Hastings House, 1958), an overview of the history of the cattlemen of the West from the time of Coronado through mid-Twentieth century; and *The Beaver Men: Spearheads of Empire* (New York: Hastings House, 1964) which deals with the early trappers and traders in the Seventeenth and Eighteenth centuries, chronologically the first book in the series. In writing these histories, Sandoz had wanted to come to an understanding of the effects that man had on a region, and, of course, the effects the region had in shaping man.

Three other non-fictional works were written: *These Were the Sioux* (New York: Hastings House, 1961), an appraisal of the Sioux people, their culture, customs, and wisdom, *Love Song to the Plains* (New York: Harper's, 1961), and *The Battle of the Little Big Horn* (Philadelphia: Lippincott, 1966). A miscellaneous collection of previously published pieces—short stories and articles written between 1925 and 1955—was published under the title *Hostiles and Friendlies* (Lincoln: University of Nebraska Press, 1959). On the thirtieth anniversary of *Old Jules*, a collection of excerpts from the Trans-Missouri series and *These Were the Sioux* in addition to several previously uncollected pieces were assembled in *Old Jules Country* (New York: Hastings House, 1965) which serves as an excellent introduction to Sandoz' non-fiction works.

Sandoz was awarded a number of honors during the course of her literary career including the National Achievement Award from the Chicago chapter of The Westerners for being the only author ever to have four of her books selected for the One Hundred Best Books on the West in a nation-wide poll. She was a lifetime member of the Nebraska State Historical Society and in 1961 was awarded the Western Heritage Award by the National Cowboy Hall of Fame.

Although Sandoz' work has enjoyed an avid readership and many of her books have been re-issued by the University of Nebraska Press and Hastings House, she has been neglected by literary historians. Because she had access to unique sources and interviewed many people, both whites and Native Americans, who are now dead, the authenticity of her books is questioned and sometimes even dismissed as unreliable. This is particularly true of her Indian studies. It must be said in her behalf, however, that she did not believe in the infallibility of man's memory and so she sought corroboration when possible for every story she was told before including it in any of her books. It has been said that if any person should have been born an Indian, it was Mari Sandoz. As the Plains Indians she knew and wrote about, she believed in a brotherhood with all things on earth and once said, "There are a few things in which I am deeply involved. Have you ever heard a prairie song lark rise into the clear thin air of the High Plains, spilling song golden as sunlight all around him? There are other things, too, that I cannot watch with detachment, things that anger me to the violence of my father. One is the sight of the earth exploited, and the other is the knowledge of man, red, white or whatever color, deprived of the right to walk in pride and dignity before all the world."

Cheyenne Autumn (Warner's, 1962) was directed by John Ford.

For further information see *Mari Sandoz, Story Catcher of the Plains* (Lincoln: University of Nebraska Press, 1982) by Helen Winter Stauffer, the first significant work on Sandoz and her writings.

Santee, Ross (1888–1965) Artist, essayist, short story writer, and author of Western fiction, born at Thornburg, Iowa. Of Quaker upbringing, young Santee lost his father when he was 3 and was reared by his mother and sisters. When he was 13, he moved with them to Moline, Illinois, and finished his high school years there. He liked hunting and fishing and he enjoyed drawing books out of the Moline Public Library, especially the works of Mark Twain (q.v.). Santee also spent time drawing but he disliked flowers and still life and, as a result, failed his high school art course.

Once he graduated, Santee enrolled in the Chicago Art Institute and studied to be a cartoonist. After four years of study, he sold his first drawing to *Collier's*. Going to New York City, Santee lost his interest in cartoons and spent his time painting scenes and people of that great metropolis. His sharp, simple style was recognized for its individuality, but the market for his work remained limited. Discouraged, finally, Santee joined his sister in Globe, Arizona, and there found his true center. He became a horse wrangler for the Bar F Ranch in 1915. He spent two years riding herd, living off the land, and helping with round-ups. Then he joined the U.S. Army, stationed at Camp Bowie, Texas. When he returned to Globe, Santee earned a living at the Old Dominion Smelter and Mine, which was nearby, and punched cattle part time.

In 1919, he went back again to the Chicago Art Institute, where an instructor encouraged him to try his luck again in New York. Santee rejected that proposal and resumed ranch life in Arizona. Then Frank Casey from the old *Life* bought several drawings and *Boy's Life* asked him to combine his sketches with some writing. Santee took up the suggestion and he began publishing stories in *Leslie's* and *Century* as well as exhibiting his Western sketches in the National Gallery in 1922. While on his way to this exhibition, Santee met and later married Eve Farrell. She typed his manuscripts, encouraged him, and shared his love for Arizona and the Southwest. Santee once told her: "Just forget every preconceived idea you've ever had about a cowboy, an Indian, or a Mexican, because you're going to meet the real ones now."

Although the Santees lived in Arden, Delaware, for some years, they returned to Arizona in 1936 where Santee served as director of the Arizona State Guide, part of the Federal Writers' project. After this, the couple returned to Delaware where they lived for the next twenty years and Santee wrote about and painted scenes of the West he had known. Globe and the Gila country naturally formed the setting for much of his fiction. It was his intent to tell stories about the people of the area, as accurately and as truthfully as possible. Other writers such as Edwin Corle (q.v.), J. Frank Dobie (q.v.), and Owen Wister (q.v.) had Santee illustrate their works.

Of his own books perhaps *Men and Horses* (New York: Century, 1926) captures best the hard work and loneliness of the Arizona cowboy. The short stories in this book deal with the cowboy's love for his horse, his isolation from home and family, his brand of humor, and his problems with women. In 1928 Santee produced *Cowboy* (New York: Cosmopolitan, 1928), probably the best known of his novels. It is the fictionalized biography of Shorty Caraway,

a young farm boy from East Texas who runs away to the West to learn to be a cowboy.

After *Cowboy*, Santee's writing took an interesting turn. In *The Pooch* (New York: Cosmopolitan, 1931) and *Sleepy Black* (New York: Farrar, 1933) Santee told his stories from an animal's point of view, that of a dog in a small town in Arizona in the former, that of a cow horse, rodeo bronc, and outlaw horse in the latter. *Apache Land* (New York: Scribner's, 1947) took yet another turn, being a series of sketches about Apache life, including a brief history of the various tribes. The book is perhaps also notable in that Santee accepted the Apaches as individuals and friends at a time when they had very little that was favorable written about them. Santee's two autobiographical books are *Lost Pony Tracks* (New York: Scribner's, 1953) and *Dog Days* (New York: Scribner's, 1955). Here as elsewhere his style is concise, direct, an intermingling of compassion and truth. In his work it is difficult to tell, as it is also with Andy Adams (q.v.) where fact leaves off and fiction begins.

D.M.-K.

For further information see Neal Houston's *Ross Santee* (Austin: Steck-Vaughn, 1968) and J.E. Reynolds' *The West of Ross Santee* (Van Nuys: J.E. Reynolds, 1961).

Scarborough, Dorothy (1877–1935) Poet, essayist, and regional novelist born at Mount Carmel, Texas. Scarborough lived for a time near Sweetwater, Texas, where her parents homesteaded. However, the greater part of her youth was spent in

Waco. She received her Bachelor's degree and Master's degree from Baylor University in Waco, where she taught English from 1905–1914. She became assistant professor in 1916. She attended the University of Chicago, Oxford University, and Columbia University, obtaining from this last her Doctorate in 1917 for her dissertation on *The Supernatural in Modern English Fiction* (New York: Putnam's, 1917) which was considered the most authoritative work on the subject for several decades. In 1923, Scarborough received an honorary Doctoral degree in literature from her alma mater for her work collecting mountain ballads and Negro folk songs. This folk material became an important part of her fiction and she was a charter member of the Texas Folklore Society. She contributed book reviews to the *New York Sun* and taught short story writing at Columbia University until her death after a short illness in New York City where she had lived since 1918.

Scarborough's first novel, *In the Land of Cotton* (New York: Macmillan, 1923), deals with the plight of the tenant farmer in Texas which was one of the first books along with Ruth Cross' *The Golden Cocoon* (New York: Harper's, 1924) to examine the subject. Scarborough saw the need for cooperatives and unions to protect the sharecropper from being exploited in the cotton growing regions of Texas. Two more books on the subject followed in what Scarborough came to call her cotton trilogy: *Can't Get A Redbird* (New York: Harper's, 1929) and *The Stretch-Berry Smile* (Indianapolis: Bobbs-Merrill, 1932). Although they are well-written novels, they do not have the power of Scarborough's most impressive work, *The Wind* (New York: Harper's, 1925).

Due to the tremendous success of the anonymous publication of Homer Croy's (q.v.) *West of the Water Tower* (New York: Harper's, 1923), *The Wind* was first published in 1925 anonymously as a publicity gimmick. However, by the end of 1925, when the book's sales did not reach Scarborough's expectations, she requested that her name be put on future editions. The appearance of the book brought hostile reactions from various groups in West Texas—the setting of the story was Sweetwater—including the West Texas Chamber of Commerce which felt Scarborough had deliberately maligned Sweetwater and exaggerated the arid climate of the region. Scarborough, who stated she was "convicted of realism in the first degree," responded by making clear that she was a loyal Texan. However, she was a novelist and did not feel it was her duty to promote the climate of West Texas. Despite the numerous complaints and letters from groups in Texas and other readers, *The Wind* received favorable reviews in other parts of Texas and throughout the United States.

The Wind had been anticipated in Scarborough's short story "The Drought" (1920), published in *Century* magazine and included, in a revised version, in *The Best Short Stories from the Southwest* (Dallas: Southwest Press, 1928) edited by Hilton Ross Greer. In the short story a drought brings about the ruin of a happy relationship between a newly married couple. Edna Ferber (q.v.) had been instrumental in encouraging Scarborough to write a novel about the strange effects of the Texas winds on humans. The story of *The Wind* is a study in defeat, showing the overwhelming effect the hot, dry climate and the impoverished life-style have on a young woman. The psychological drama is told through the point of view of Letty, an orphaned 18-year-old from Virginia who travels to Sweetwater to live with her cousin and his wife. Letty finds all aspects of pioneer life—the isolated environment of her lonely shack after she is driven into marriage, the other people she meets, and the wind which takes on human dimensions through Scarborough's skilful writing—an alien world. All aspects of her physical environment, including the well-researched folk material Scarborough incorporated into the storyline, contribute to Letty's emotional disintegration and final madness. In contrast to Letty, her cousin's wife exemplifies the strong pioneer woman who accepts the challenges of frontier life. *The Wind* ends tragically in the final section in which Letty, after being seduced by a cattleman whom she shoots in the midst of a violent sandstorm, runs into the sandstorm to her suicide. The film version of 1927 starring Lillian Gish was altered to end happily.

The Wind differs in various aspects from other authors of this period. Realist Hamlin Garland (q.v.) depicted the impact the social and physical ambience had on people but never permitted himself the completely pessimistic interpretation Scarborough employed in her novel. Also, the West is represented as a cruel and indifferent land in which people are only victims, in contrast to writers such as Zane Grey (q.v.), Emerson Hough (q.v.), Eugene Manlove Rhodes (q.v.), and Willa Cather (q.v.) who celebrated the triumph of the individual and the pioneering spirit. There are no heroes nor heroic deeds in *The Wind*.

As O.E. Rölvaag's (q.v.) *Giants in the Earth* (New York: Harper's, 1927), *The Wind* is important because it shows the woman's side of pioneer life. The majority of Western novels deals with men and their struggles, whereas books as *The Wind* attempt to show the negative effects the barren, sterile land could have on the human spirit and for that reason are an important contribution to our total understanding of the frontier experience.

The Wind (M-G-M, 1927) was directed by Victor Seastrom.

Schaefer, Jack (Warner) (1907—)

One of the most outstanding authors of Western fiction to emerge after World War II, born at Cleveland, Ohio. Schaefer's father, a lawyer, was an Abraham Lincoln scholar who knew American poet and Lincoln biographer, Carl Sandburg. Both of Schaefer's parents were avid readers and so, from an early age, Jack, too, read widely. In the late 'Twenties, Schaefer attended Oberlin College where his major interests were Greek and Latin classics and creative writing. Receiving his Bachelor's degree in 1929, Schaefer went on to do postgraduate work at Columbia University, specializing in Eighteenth-century English literature but finally giving it up as "a dull and stupid waste of time."

Schaefer then pursued a career working for the United Press as a reporter and office man. From 1931 until 1938 he was assistant director of education at the Connecticut State Reformatory while working, for much of the time simultaneously, as associate editor of the *New Haven Journal-Courier*, of which he became editor, 1939–1942. A number of editorial and newspaper jobs followed in the 'Forties, with the emphasis on editorial work since Schaefer had already then intentions of serious writing.

Perhaps Schaefer's most famous novel

is *Shane* (Boston: Houghton Mifflin, 1949) which was originally a short story that he expanded to serial length and which was accepted by *Argosy* in 1946 under the title "Rider from Nowhere." It took some time for him to find a hardbound publisher for the story, but once he did it became a perennial seller, being made into a highly successful and even classic motion picture, as a book eventually going through more than seventy editions in some thirty-one languages. It is perhaps worth noting that, as some other Western authors, Schaefer had never been West of Toledo, Ohio, when he wrote it.

The book is written with simplicity and clarity and for this Schaefer was inclined to thank both his work in journalism and his concentration on Latin grammar. Whatever the reason, Schaefer's style from that first short novel on retains these characteristics, combining them with an emotional richness and, in his later fiction, a sense of historical accuracy. *Shane* tells the story of a gunfighter who comes into a valley in the midst of a struggle between a cattleman and the homesteaders who would fence off the free range and put him out of business. The struggle can only and finally be settled through Shane's controlled violence, after which he must leave the valley. While there may have been nothing particularly new about this plot when Schaefer used it, what was refreshing was Schaefer's mythic and effective evocation of the frontier as akin to an allegory and as a background against which the story is told, as seen through the eyes of a young boy.

Jean Arthur (l.), Alan Ladd (center), and Brandon DeWilde (r.) in the film version of Shane *(Paramount, 1953) directed by George Stevens.*

The four years following publication of *Shane* found Schaefer writing a number of remarkable short stories and another excellent short novel, *First Blood* (Boston: Houghton Mifflin, 1953). The same year Schaefer published *First Blood* and an anthology of his short stories titled *The Big Range* (Boston: Houghton Mifflin, 1953), he also published what might be, critically speaking, his finest short novel, *The Canyon* (Boston: Houghton Mifflin, 1953). It is the story of a Cheyenne warrior seeking his own vision. Schaefer was being semi-autobiographical in writing it. Once *Shane* was in preproduction, he might easily have gone to Hollywood. He chose not to; instead A.B. Guthrie, Jr., (q.v.) worked on the screenplay. Schaefer moved to Santa Fe, New Mexico. "What I mean is: It was with *The Canyon* that I made my decision to keep right on with the furrow I had started to plow," he once explained it, "—to keep on with my somewhat lonesome attempt to prove that there is no reason why the attempt at least cannot be made to create literature out of Western material, to write only what I wanted to write and to please myself alone and not to fall into the trap of repeating myself, of doing the same kind of thing over and over just because a first one had been successful." Nor was it accidental that Schaefer had come to employ a Cheyenne as a point of view character and to tell his story in the word pictures of the Native American. He believed "the Amerinds in general (with some exceptions) were truly civilized and . . . we whites, better or ahead or whatever you want to call it only in our deadly emphasis on technology, were the invading barbarians."

Little Bear is Schaefer's Cheyenne protagonist in *The Canyon*. His is a spiritual quest for wholeness and only at the end of the story does he come to realize how complicated such a state is ever to achieve. Perhaps the only criticism that could be lodged against its outcome is that Little Bear's discovery is more comprehensible to a white man in the Twentieth century than it ever would be to a Cheyenne in the Nineteenth.

The Pioneers (Boston: Houghton Mifflin, 1954) was Schaefer's second collection of short stories. If taken in tandem with Schaefer's earlier collection, *The Big Range*, and his subsequent collection, *The Kean Land and Other Stories* (Boston: Houghton Mifflin, 1959), perhaps Gerald Haslam said it best in his chapbook, *Jack Schaefer* (Boise: Idaho State University, 1975), when he wrote that the "constant and accurate sense of the actual pioneers, whether they are in the foreground or in the background, makes [Schaefer's] frontier stories remarkably complete and compelling. There have been few better writers of short stories on the West than Jack Schaefer." Eventually Schaefer brought his short stories together in *The Collected Stories of Jack Schaefer* (Boston: Houghton Mifflin, 1966), an excellent companion volume for the similar compendium *The Short Novels of Jack Schaefer* (Boston: Houghton Mifflin, 1967).

Company of Cowards (Boston: Houghton Mifflin, 1957) is a novel which focuses on men in the military both during and after the Civil War, the psychological effects of cowardice, and the meaning of character. It is an interesting novel to contrast with stories with similar settings by James Warner Bellah (q.v.) and Ernest Haycox (q.v.). But, surely, of all Schaefer's later books the most outstanding is *Monte Walsh* (Boston: Houghton Mifflin, 1963), a novel that deals not with the cowboy myth but with *real* cowboys and calls to mind Andy Adams (q.v.), Ross Santee (q.v.), and Elmer Kelton (q.v.). It, too, was filmed, but the whole meaning of the novel was changed.

With *Mavericks* (Boston: Houghton Mifflin, 1967) Schaefer found himself to have come full circle. He was now dealing with the end of wildlife in the West, following the course earlier of the buffalo, indeed of a whole way of life. The story deals with the few remaining wild horses and the protagonist, Jake, can only lament: "We can remember 'em, I reckon that's all we've left ourselves able to do."

Henceforth, Schaefer turned to writing about animals, not humans, and, in his way, he was no longer able to romanticize characters as Shane. "Always," he commented, "I was writing about people, about us featherless bipeds who sum ourselves by genus and species as *Homo sapiens*. Any other creatures who crept in were stage furniture for the human drama. And then, as a writer, I came to a full stop. I had lost my innocence. I had become ashamed of my species and myself. I understood at last in full consequence that despite whatever dodges of motive and intent and personal activities I might cite . . . I was a contributing part of the heedless human onrush that was ruining the land I loved and forcing toward extinction ever more of my fellow creatures whose companion right to continued existence ought to be respected."

Films based on Jack Schaefer's Western fiction are *Shane* (Paramount, 1953) directed by George Stevens, *The Silver Whip* (20th-Fox, 1953) directed by Harmon Jones [based on *First Blood*], *Tribute to a Badman* (M-G-M, 1956) directed by Robert Wise [based on the short story "Jeremy Rodock"], *Trooper Hook* (United Artists, 1957) directed by Charles Marquis Warren

[based on an original screen story], *Advance to the Rear* (M-G-M, 1964) directed by George Marshall [based on *Company of Cowards*], *Monte Walsh* (National General, 1970) directed by William A. Fraker.

For further information see *Jack Schaefer* (Boise: Idaho State University Press, 1975) by Gerald Haslam.

Scott, A(lexander) Leslie

(1893–1974) Prolific author of very formulary Westerns under a number of pseudonyms, including Bradford Scott, Leslie A. Scott, A. Scott Leslie, and Jackson Cole (see House Names), born at Lewisburg, West Virginia. Scott attended Greenbrier Military Academy, the University of West Virginia, and the University of Virginia from which he graduated. While still in college, Scott sailed from the United States to England, India, and Singapore, working variously on a cattle ship, a pearling schooner, and other vessels.

Scott began writing Western novels for the pulp magazines in the 'Twenties, basing as much as he could on his wide and varied experiences. His settings included cattle ranching, at which he had worked while on his uncle's ranch in Texas; mining and civil engineering which he had studied at college and in graduate school; railroading, which he knew from having shoveled coal for the C&O along the New River and the mountain roads of Ohio and West Virginia.

In his lifetime, Scott wrote approximately 125 Walt Slade, Texas Ranger novels, all of them modeled on Eugene Cunningham's (q.v.) *Buckaroo* (Boston: Houghton Mifflin, 1933), which in turn was itself a variation of Dashiell Hammett's blood bath in *Red Harvest* (New York: Knopf, 1929). The way Scott had it worked out, each chapter would find Ranger Slade, usually joined by his friends, Estevan, a Mexican knife-man whose dialogue is generally confined to "my blade thirsts," and Sheriff Gene Putnam, battling it out with some of the master villain's minions. The average number of chapters is twenty-five, with at least two bad men dispatched per chapter. These bad men are described rather laconically as "ornery," which suffices for their motivation. The identity of the master villain is customarily concealed until about half way through, although he is conspicuous enough to be spotted by the average reader upon his introduction into the story. The action is tediously paced. Slade and his friends are either ambushed or ambush, which is followed by their adjourning to a cantina or a restaurant and eating, as if Scott would write a chapter and then break off for a repast. Slade has a horse called Shadow and his girl friend is Jerry Nolan who runs the Deuces Up dance hall and whom Slade likes best when she wears tights. Slade is called El Halcon, the Hawk, by the Mexicans, because of his acute hearing which can detect the villains' horses miles away and his super keen eyesight which, sometimes, is nearly telescopic. He is also a singer and in *Savage Gunlaw* (New York: Pyramid, 1971) he stops the action for a chapter to sing a medley of songs in a cantina, impressing everyone with his "great baritone-bass" Slade has a penchant for engineering and is always telling manufacturers and railroad men how to improve efficiency and the implication is that, when and if he retires, he will take up a career as an engineer.

Insofar as Slade is usually part of a triad

hero and his adventures consist primarily of killing villains he also falls into the trio Western category, founded by Clarence E. Mulford (q.v.) and refined by Eugene Cunningham and William Colt MacDonald (q.v.), but only Cunningham and MacDonald anticipated the number of deaths per book which Scott averaged. He wrote once of Slade, concerning the killings to his credit: "to his credit was right; anybody he was known to kill having a killing coming and over due." Scott's books lack even the modicum of characterization which was not true to this degree in the novels of his peers; his plots are virtually non-existent, save for the constant gun-play and violence. Yet, by the early 'Seventies, the Walt Slade series had sold over eight million copies and was clearly an adumbration of the works of Terry Harknett (q.v.) who further perfected plots of violence and death in his even more popular Edge series.

With the advent of the paperback revolution, Scott retitled many of his pulp serials (the books he wrote as Jackson Cole followed the Walt Slade formula) and resold them as original paperback novels, and he also continued to add new titles, right up until the final year of his life. In all, he wrote over 250 novel-length serials and novels, although not all of them were issued in paperback format.

A. Leslie Scott's Western novels as Bradford Scott are *Trigger Talk* (1956) [alternate title: *Sixgun Talk*], *Canyon Killers* (1956), *Border Blood* (1956), *Badland's Boss* (1956), *The Texas Terror* (1956), *The Texas Hawk* (1957), *Death Canyon* (1957), *Curse of the Texas Gold* (1957), *Powder Burn* (1957), *Dead Man's Trail* (1957), *Shootin' Man* (1958), *The Blaze of Guns* (1958), *Gun Law* (1959), *Texas Badman* (1959), *Texas*

Vengeance (1959), *Dead in Texas* (1959), *The Range Terror* (1959), *Holster Law* (1959), *Gun Gamble* (1960), *Guns of the Alamo* (1960), *Valley of Hunted Men* (1960), *Ambush Trail* (1960), *The Pecos Trail* (1960), *Lone Star Rider* (1960), *The Desert Killers* (1961), *Rangeland Guns* (1961), *Rangers at Bay* (1961), *Skeleton Trail* (1961), *Smuggler's Brand* (1961), *Gunsmoke on the Rio Grande* (1961), *The Masked Riders* (1962), *Gunsight Showdown* (1962), *Death Rides the Rio Grande* (1962), *Doom Trail* (1962), *A Ranger Rides to Death* (1962), *Guns of Bang Town* (1962), *Texas Devil* (1962), *Texas Rider* (1962), *Trail of Blood and Bones* (1962), *Gundown* (1963) *Gun Justice* (1963), *Ranger's Revenge* (1963), *The Rattlesnake Bandit* (1963), *Rustler's Guns* (1963), *Rustler's Range* (1963), *Hate Trail* (1963), *Gunsmoke Talk* (1963), *Death's Corral* (1963), *Outlaw Land* (1963), *Killer's Doom* (1963), *Bullets for a Ranger* (1963), *Outlaw Gold* (1963), *Trail of Guns and Gold* (1964), *Guns for Hire* (1964), *Horseman of the Shadows* (1964), *Death Calls the Turn* (1964), *Dead at Sunset* (1964), *Range Ghost* (1964), *Raiders of the Rio Grande* (1964), *The Ghost Trail* (1964), *Showdown at Skull Canyon* (1964), *Tombstone Showdown* (1964), *Trails of Steel* (1965), *Wasteland Rider* (1965), *West of Laredo* (1965), *Border Vengeance* (1965), *Bullets over the Border* (1965), *Death in the Saddle* (1965), *Thundering Guns* (1965), *Hot Lead* (1966), *Death on the Rimrock* (1967), *Bullet Brand* (1967), *Blood on the Moon* (1967), *Pecos Law* (1967), *Maverick Showdown* (1967), *Hot Lead and Cold Nerve* (1967), *Texas Death* (1967) [alternate title: *A Ranger Laughs at Death*], *Thunder Trail* (1967), *The River Raiders* (1968), *Death Tally* (1968), *Red Road of Vengeance* (1968), *Sixguns in a Bloody Dawn* (1968) [alternate title: *Death Rides the River Trail*], *The Sky Riders* (1968), *Haunted Valley* (1968), *Hard Rock Showdown* (1968), *Border War* (1968), *Outlaw Roundup* (1968) [alternate title: *Robber's Roundup*], *Lead and Flame* (1968), *Laredo on the Rio Grande* (1969), *Mountain Raiders* (1969), *Date with Death* (1969), *Bullet Justice* (1969), *Devil from Blazing Hill* (1969) [alternate title: *A Ranger to the Rescue*], *Hands Up!* (1969), *Rider of the Mesquite Trail* (1969), *Sixgun Doom* (1969), *Sixgun Talk* (1969) [alternate title: *Trigger Talk*], *Texas Blood* (1969) [alternate title: *Blood and Steel*], *Trail of Empire* (1969), *Curse of Dead Man's Gold* (1969), *The Sidewinder* (1969), *Death to the Ranger* (1970), *Death Whispers* (1970), *Ranger's Roundup* (1970), *Reach for Gold* (1970), *Ranger Daring* (1971), *The Ranger Wins* (1971), *Savage Gunlaw* (1971), *The Border Terror* (1972), *Spargo* (1972), *Border Daring* (1973), *Four Must Die* (1973).

Scott's novels as Leslie A. Scott are *Stranger in Boots* (1956), *The Avengers* (1956), *Ramrock Raiders* (1957), *Death's Harvest* (1967).

Scott's novels under his own name are *Tombstone Trail* (1960), *The Texan* (1960), *Arizona Ranger* (1960).

Scott's novels as Jackson Cole are *Gunsmoke Trail* (1955), *Gun-Blaze* (1955), *Gun-Runners* (1955), *Gun Town* (1955), *Texas Fury* (1955), *Trouble Shooter* (1955), *Two-Gun Devil* (1955), *Texas Fists* (1960), *Border Hell* (1961), *Buffets High* (1961), *The Death Riders* (1961), *Killer Country* (1961), *Land-Grab* (1961), *Massacre Canyon* (1961), *Outlawed* (1961), *Texas Manhunt* (1961), *Texas Tornado* (1961), *Thunder Range* (1961), *Trigger Law* (1961).

Scott, Bradford. See Scott, A. Leslie.

Scott, Leslie A. See Scott, A. Leslie.

Sealsfield, Charles. See Postl, Karl Anton.

Seelye, John (1931 —) Essayist, literary scholar, and novelist noted for one novel with a Western setting, born at Hartford, Connecticut. Seelye was educated in California, receiving a Master's degree in 1956 and his Doctor's degree in 1961, both from Claremont College. Most of Seelye's career was devoted to teaching and writing about American literature. He was a professor of English at the University of Connecticut from 1966 to 1974 and afterwards taught at the University of North Carolina at Chapel Hill.

During the 'Seventies, Seelye wrote dozens of essays and reviews for such periodicals as *The New Republic*, many of them critical but perceptive analyses of American popular culture. At the same time he published scholarly literary studies, *Melville: The Ironic Diagram* (Evanston: Northwestern University Press, 1970) and *Prophetic Waters: The River in Early American Life and Literature* (New York: Oxford University Press, 1977). These twin interests in popular American culture and classic American literature were employed in Seelye's novels. *The True Adventures of Huckleberry Finn* (Evanston: Northwestern University Press, 1970) recreates Mark Twain's (q.v.) beloved story, but this time, as Huck mentions in the Introduction, to satisfy supposed weaknesses in the original book as described by noted literary critics. *Dirty Tricks or Nick Noxin's Nobility* (New York: Liveright, 1973) playfully tells the story of

Watergate through the plot and moralistic style of Nineteenth-century Horatio Alger boys' novels.

The Kid (New York: Viking, 1972) is Seelye's only novel about the West. The locale and era of the story are common in formulary Westerns: an isolated fort in Wyoming in 1887. The story itself, however, deals with the eruption of violence when a blond adolescent and his gigantic black partner ride into the fort and becomes an unusual tale of guilt, innocence, and the ambiguity of justice, seemingly modeled on Herman Melville's short novel, *Billy Budd* (London: Constable and Co., Ltd., 1924). *The Kid* reveals that Seelye wrote fiction as an academic and scholar, rather than as a storyteller. The obviously contrived and author-manipulated direction of the story makes emotional participation almost impossible. Seelye himself said that he personally disliked formulary Westerns and never read them. On the other hand, *The Kid* is praiseworthy as an intellectual reflection on violence in American culture and as an allegorical restructuring of the themes of innocence and guilt so often explored in classic American literature.

J.N.

Seifert, Shirley (1888–1971) Author of Western historical fiction, Seifert attended Washington University in St. Louis, Missouri, where she received her Bachelor's degree. From 1917–1919, she taught history, Latin, and English at the high school level. In 1919, she worked as a secretary in the advertising section for the U.S. War Bond Organization in St. Louis. Her first short story was sold to *American* magazine that same year and for the next eighteen years she worked as a free-lance writer producing short stories for numerous periodicals, including *Delineator,* a woman's magazine which had once been edited by author Honoré Willsie Morrow (q.v.), and *The Saturday Evening Post.*

Seifert's first novel, *Land of Tomorrow* (New York: M.S. Mill, 1937), a story about life in Kentucky, ended her career as a short story writer and henceforth she devoted her full time to writing novels about various periods in American history. Seifert, who never married, viewed American history in terms of people and in her second novel, *The Wayfarer* (New York: M.S. Mill, 1938), she told the story of John Cotter, a real-life character who was born in New York. His brief career in the whaling industry in Massachusetts is recounted and his experiences in the West as a horse-breeder in the second half of the Eighteenth century.

Two historical novels, also set during the Eighteenth century, followed before the publication of *Those Who Go Against the Current* (Philadelphia: Lippincott, 1943) which is about Manuel Lisa, a Spanish-American who became one of the leaders in the drive to open up the Missouri River to the whites. A novel about the early life of Ulysses S. Grant, *Captain Grant* (Philadelphia: Lippincott, 1946), followed. *Down the Santa Fe Trail and into Mexico* (New Haven: Yale University Press, 1926) by Susan Shelby Magoffin who traveled the Santa Fe trail in 1846–1847 was the basis for Seifert's last historical novel set in the West, *The Turquoise Trail* (Philadelphia: Lippincott, 1950), as it would be for Elliott Arnold's (q.v.) *The Time of the Gringo* (New York: Knopf, 1953). The novelized version is in no way equal to the original source which is now an important historical document as well as being a Southwest classic. Seifert, in *The Turquoise Trail* as in all of her books, failed to elicit the reader's interest in her characters due largely to her own lack of investment of feelings in her creations. Nonetheless, her efforts in writing Americana were competent, well-researched projects, however superficial her characterizations.

Seltzer, Charles Alden (1875–1942)

Author of over forty formulary Western novels, born at Janesville, Wisconsin. Seltzer was educated briefly in public schools in Columbus, Ohio, where his family moved in 1876. While still quite young, he went to live on his uncle's ranch in New Mexico. Dressed in leather chaps and a sombrero, Seltzer, who was nicknamed "Rip," traveled throughout the West. In the late 1890s he returned to Ohio where he worked as a contractor, carpenter, and building inspector before he began to write Western fiction. For thirteen years he received rejection slips from editors upon submission of his manuscripts. During this period, his wife, whom he married in 1896, critiqued his work and tutored him, since his education had included only the modest fundamentals.

The publication of several short stories established a market for Seltzer in England and his first two books appeared in 1911: *The Range Riders* (London: Outing, 1911) and *The Two-Gun Man* (London: Outing, 1911). Seltzer continued to write at least one book a year until his death from a lingering diabetic illness which necessitated the amputation of his right leg one year prior to his death. His Westerns were quite popular and historian E. Douglas Branch in *The Cowboy and His Interpreters* (New York: Appleton, 1926) grouped Seltzer among the "aristocrats of cowcountry fiction," such as B.M. Bower (q.v.), William MacLeod Raine (q.v.), and Clarence E. Mulford (q.v.). Although not the craftsman that Raine was, nor the humorist that Bower was, Seltzer's books were well-plotted, action-packed ranch romances unique for the number of characters who are killed during the course of the story.

Seltzer's heroes are grim, quiet, and powerful men, who live by their own Western code and who are not above taking the law into their own hands. More often than not the latter causes a conflict between the hero and the heroine who, although she loves the hero, loathes his killings. In *The Range Boss* (Chicago: A.C. McClurg, 1917), the hero tells the heroine, an Easterner who has inherited a ranch, that: "'You'll shape up real Western—give you time,' he assured. 'You'll be ready to take your own part, without depending on laws to do it for you—laws that don't reach far enough.'" Every Seltzer hero takes his own part.

As Owen Wister (q.v.) and B.M. Bower, Seltzer in his early books often introduced an East versus West conflict by incorporating Eastern characters into his plots. In *The Two-Gun Man* a female writer goes West seeking local color for her stories which is quite similar to B.M. Bower's earlier book *The Lure of the Dim Trails* (New York: Dillingham, 1907). An Eastern cattle company in league with state officials in *The Trail Horde* (Chicago: A.C. McClurg, 1920) tries to force the local cattlemen to sell at a cheaper price by arranging a shortage of cattle cars at shipping time. In the tradition of Eugene Manlove Rhodes (q.v.), Seltzer's politicians and lawmen are often villains whom the hero must expose.

Charles Alden Seltzer's Western novels are *The Range Riders* (1911), *The Two-Gun Man* (1911), *The Triangle Cupid* (1912), *The Coming of the Law* (1912), *The Trail to Yesterday* (1913), *The Boss of the Lazy Y* (1915), *The Range Boss* (1916), *The Vengeance of Jefferson Gawne* (1917), *"Firebrand" Trevison* (1918), *The Man with a Country* (1919), *The Ranchman* (1919), *The Trail Horde* (1920), *"Drag" Harlan* (1921), *"Beau" Rand* (1921), *Square Deal Sanderson* (1922), *West!* (1922), *Brass Commandments* (1923), *Lonesome Ranch* (1924), *The Way of the Buffalo* (1924), *Last Hope Ranch* (1925), *Trailing Back* (1925), *Channing Comes Through* (1925), *The Valley of the Stars* (1926), *A Gentleman from Virginia* (1926), *Slow Burgess* (1926), *Land of the Free* (1927), *Mystery Ranch* (1928), *The Mesa* (1928), *The Raider* (1929), *The Red Brand* (1929), *Gone North* (1930), *A Son of Arizona* (1931), *War on Wishbone Range* (1932), *Double Cross Ranch* (1932), *Clear the Trail* (1933), *Breath of the Desert* (1934), *West of Apache Ranch* (1934), *Silverspurs* (1935), *Kingdom of the Cactus* (1936), *Parade of the Empty Boots* (1937), *Arizona Jim* (1939), *Treasure Ranch* (1940), *So Long, Sucker* (1941).

Films based on Charles Alden Seltzer's Western fiction are *The Boss of the Lazy Y* (Triangle, 1917) directed by Cliff Smith, *The Range Boss* (Essanay, 1917) directed by W.S. Van Dyke, *Trail to Yesterday* (Metro, 1918) directed by Edwin Carewe, *Fame & Fortune* (Fox, 1918) directed by Lynn F. Reynolds [source unknown], *The Coming of the Law* (Fox, 1919) directed by Arthur Rosson, *Treat 'Em Rough* (Fox, 1919) directed by Lynn F. Reynolds [source unknown], *Square Deal Sanderson* (Paramount, 1919) directed by Lambert Hillyer, *Forbidden Trails* (Fox, 1920) directed by Scott R. Dunlap [source unknown], *Firebrand Trevison* (Fox, 1920) directed by Thomas Heffron, *Rough Shod* (Fox, 1922) directed by B. Reeves Eason [based on *West!*], *Brass Commandments* (Fox, 1923) directed by Lynn F. Reynolds remade as *Chain Lightning* (Fox, 1927) directed by Lambert Hillyer, *Silver Spurs* (Universal, 1936) directed by Ray Taylor.

Seton, Anya

(1916 —) Author of historical-biographical novels with a Western setting, born at New York City and reared in Connecticut. Both of Seton's parents were writers. Her father, Ernest Thompson Seton, naturalist and author of outdoor classics, was the co-founder of the Boy Scouts. Seton, an only child, had an unorthodox unbringing, traveling extensively through Europe and the Far East. She was educated by private tutors and at Spence School in New York and later attended courses at Oxford University. She had planned to become a doctor and so studied medicine for a short time in Paris. However, she changed her mind and worked for a time as a nurse's aid and as a secretary in a mental hygiene clinic.

In 1938 she sold a short story to a newspaper syndicate for $5 and decided to write for a living. Her first book was *My Theodosia* (Boston: Houghton Mifflin, 1941). Her novels, in which romance plays an important part, deal with various phases of Americana. Two of her books were set in the West: *The Turquoise* (Boston: Houghton Mifflin, 1946) and *Foxfire* (Boston: Houghton Mifflin, 1951), the latter a goldmining story in modern-day Gila, Arizona. The writing of *The Turquoise* was determined by visits to her father's ranch in Sante Fe, New Mexico, and upon the advice of Mary Austin (q.v.) who a year before her death mentioned the forgotten legend about a New Mexican woman who lived on the slope of Atalaya. (Atalaya, a high peak of the Sangre de Cristo mountains in New Mexico, was once considered a sacred mountain by the Indians.) Years later Seton remembered Austin's words and sought out the story about "La Santa" from an old Spanish-American who had heard the legend when he was young. *The Turquoise* is the story of this woman, who sought respectability and wealth, only to return to her homeland, after spending many years in New York. Seton's respect for Indians and Indian culture is evident in her treatment of Navahos in *The Turquoise* and Apaches in *Foxfire*.

Seton strived to recreate the past as accurately as possible which she did by traveling to the places where her stories are set, as well as reading histories, journals, and books about people of those places. Her work, which she stated was largely influenced by the writings of Willa Cather (q.v.), is praised for her admirable ability to weave history within a well-told tale.

Foxfire (Universal, 1955) was directed by Joseph Pevney.

Shappiro, Herbert Arthur (1899–1975) and Shappiro, Budd (1928 —)

Herbert, born at New York City, began writing Western fiction under his own name and several pseudonyms, the most common one being Burt Arthur. Shappiro's son, Budd, also born at New York City, when he reached maturity, went into his father's business—mass-producing Western fiction—collaborating with him on several novels; and after his father's death, he rewrote several of their joint efforts. Some of these were indeed published as having been written by Burt and Budd Arthur, but many simply appeared under the more familiar name, Burt Arthur. Budd Shappiro himself could not distinguish which novels were joint efforts and which were not, although independently he wrote only two Western novels with a solo credit.

"My objective as a Western writer," Budd Shappiro once commented, "has always been the same as Burt's. We sought to entertain as many readers as possible as well as we could with adventure stories whose origins were uniquely American. We did not seek to deliver a message or a moral, only a manuscript on time and containing as interesting a yarn as we could concoct. My father spent much of his youth in Texas and some of the happiest times in my life have been spent in the West and Southwest...." Although these were certainly the same objectives shared by pulp writers of the old school, Nelson C. Nye (q.v.) and Walt Coburn (q.v.) among them, the Arthurs, especially in those books which were a collaborative effort, tended to have fewer mechanical and plot consistency difficulties than the standard pulp fare.

Herbert Shappiro's Western novels under his own name are *The Black Rider* (1941), *The Valley of Death* (1941), *Chenango Pass* (1942), *Mustang Marshal* (1943), *Trouble at Moon Pass* (1943), *Silver City Agents* (1944), *Gunsmoke over Utah* (1945) [re-issued as a Burt Arthur title in 1969], *High Pockets* (1946) [re-issued as a Burt

Arthur title in 1968], *The Texan* (1946), *The Buckaroo* (1947), *Boss of the Far West* (1948), [re-issued as a Burt Arthur title in 1969], *Sheriff of Lonesome* (1948), *The Long West Trail* (1948).

Herbert Shappiro's novels as Herbert Arthur are *The Killer* (1952), *Action at Spanish Flat* (1953).

Herbert Shappiro's novels as Arthur Herbert are *Bugles in the Night* (1950), *The Gunslinger* (1951), *Freedom Run* (1951).

Herbert Shappiro's novels under the name Burt Arthur, some of which have been rewritten by Budd Shappiro and some of which will be rewritten by Budd Shappiro, are *Lead-Hungry Lobos* (1945), *Nevada* (1949) [re-issued as *Trigger Man* in 1957], *Stirrups in the Dust* (1950), *Trouble Town* (1950), *Thunder Valley* (1951), *The Drifter* (1955), *Texas Sheriff* (1956), *Return of the Texan* (1956), *Gunsmoke in Nevada* (1957). In their original editions, these were solo performances by Herbert Shappiro. After 1957, when Budd Shappiro began collaborating, where known, his collaboration is noted; all novels, however, were nonetheless published under the Burt Arthur pseudonym and are *The Stranger* (1959) [with Budd], *Quemado* (1961) [with Budd], *Three Guns North* (1962) [with Budd], *Big Red* (1962), *Flaming Guns* (1964), *Ride a Crooked Trail* (1964) [with Budd], *Requiem for a Gun* (1964), *Sing a Song of Six-Guns* (1964), *Empty Saddles* (1964), *Two-Gun Outlaw* (1964), *Gun-Law on the Range* (1964), *Walk Tall, Ride Tall* (1965) [with Budd], *Gunsmoke in Paradise* (1965), *Ride a Crooked Mile* (1966) [with Budd], *Action At Truxton* (1966) [with Budd], *The Free Lands* (1966), *Action at Ambush Flat* (1967), *Outlaw Fury* (1967), *Duel on the Range* (1967), *Silver City Rangers* (1968), *Killer's Crossing* (1969).

Herbert Shappiro's novels, other than those above, which now bear the joint pseudonym with Budd Shappiro as having been written by Burt and Budd Arthur, are *Westward the Wagons* (1957), *Ride out for Revenge* (1957), *Three Guns North* (1961), *The Saga of Denny McClure* (1968).

Shirreffs, Gordon D(onald)

(1914 —) Author of Western novels which are always trying, in various ways, to break away from formulary trends while, nonetheless, preserving the brilliant precision of artfully constructed plots, born at Chicago, Illinois. Shirreffs attended schools in the Chicago area. During the Second World War, he was a Captain of Artillery. It was while serving in the U.S. Army at Fort Bliss, Texas, in 1940–1941 that Shirreffs, who had long been interested in Civil War history, became fascinated by the history of the Western states. Throughout the duration of the war, Shirreffs conducted Civil War research by mail and projected writing a Civil War history of the Southwest. After the war, he enrolled at the Medill School of Journalism at Northwestern University, which he attended for four years. It was not, however, until 1966 that he received a Bachelor's degree from California State University in history and a Master's degree in history from the same institution in 1973, long after he had established himself as a prolific author of Western fiction.

Using some of his research for his projected Civil War history, Shirreffs began writing fiction and *Rio Bravo* (New York: Fawcett, 1956) was his first published novel. "I tried," Shirreffs once commented, "to avoid the so-called 'standard,' or 'adult,' type Western in favor of well-researched fiction, based as closely as possible on actual occurrences and characters. The Western, in most cases, is highly fictionalized, with standard plots and characters greatly overdrawn, and repeated *ad infinitum*. I have always been amazed at how these almost identical characters and situations are constantly published and republished."

Shirreff's protagonists are usually ambiguous men, not all good and not all bad. His stories have an economic orientation and, as is historically accurate, his villains are usually the land speculators and Eastern investors who looked upon the West as a great Monopoly board which the lax laws permitted them to exploit and turn to their advantage. In the 'Sixties, most of his novels employed a vengeance/pursuit theme, with protagonists after a group of killers, removing them one by one, sort of one-man vigilantes, and *Quicktrigger* (New York: Ace, 1963) is definitely racist in its scenes of Indian carnage perpetrated by the protagonist. But Shirreffs' better books avoid such wearisome plot constructs, as in the case of *Voice of the Gun* (New York: Ace, 1962), or vary them in new and interesting ways, such as *Rio Desperado* (New York: Ace, 1962). His protagonists often have surprising depth and Shirreffs spent a good deal of time exploring human relationships. His women are strong, usually independent of men, and most of his characters have the sharply aggressive character so typical of the frontiersmen. When Shirreffs turned to a Cavalry story, as in *The Border Guidon* (New York: Signet, 1963), he wrote in the vein of James Warner Bellah (q.v.) and even Ernest Haycox (q.v.). Perhaps, beyond their precision and economy, Shirreffs' plots can be praised for their variety of characters and situations, frequent references to flora of particular regions, and the use of sunlight, rain, and other natural elements to create a haunting sense of mood which pervades his stories. His *The Gray Sea Raiders* (New York: Chilton, 1961) was awarded the Silver Medal of the Commonwealth Club of California for being the best young person's book written by a California author in that year.

Gordon D. Shirreffs' Western novels are *Rio Bravo* (1956), *Code of the Gun* (1956), *Arizona Justice* (1956) [first published under the pseudonym Gordon Donalds], *Range Rebel* (1956), *Fort Vengeance* (1957), *Gunswift* (1956) [first published under the pseudonym of Stewart Gordon], *Bugles on the Prairie* (1957), *Massacre Creek* (1957), *Son of the Thunder People* (1957), *Top Gun* (1957) [first published under the pseudonym of Gordon Donalds], *Shadow Valley* (1958), *Ambush on the Mesa* (1958), *Swiftwagon* (1958), *Last Train from Gun Hill* (1959) [a screenplay novelization], *The Brave Rifles* (1959), *Trail's End* (1959), *The Lonely Gun* (1959), *Roanoke Raiders* (1959), *Renegade Lawman* (1959), *Fort Suicide* (1959), *Shadow of a Gunman* (1959), *Apache Butte* (1960), *The Rebel Trumpet* (1960), *The Mosquito Fleet* (1961), *The Proud Gun* (1961), *The Gray Sea Raiders* (1961), *Ride a Lone Trail* (1961), *Hangin' Pards* (1961), *The Valiant Bugles* (1962), *The Border Guidon* (1962), *Tumbleweed Trigger* (1962), *The Haunted Treasure of the Espectros* (1962), *Rio Desperado* (1962), *Voice of the Gun* (1962), *Mystery of Lost Canyon* (1962), *Slaughter at Broken Bow* (1963), *Quicktrigger* (1963), *The Secret of the Spanish Desert* (1964), *Gunslingers Three* (1964), *The Nevada Gun* (1964), *Blood Justice* (1964), *The Hidden Rider of Dark Mountain* (1964), *Judas Gun* (1964),

Now He is Legend (1965), *The Lone Rifle* (1965), *Barranca* (1966), *Southwest Drifter* (1967), *The Godless Breed* (1968), *Five Graves to Boot Hill* (1968), *The Mystery of the Lost Cliffdwelling* (1968), *Showdown in Sonora* (1969), *Jack of Spades* (1970), *The Manhunter* (1970), *Brasada* (1972), *Bowman's Kid* (1973), *Renegade's Trail* (1974), *Shootout* (1974) [#2 in the *Gunsmoke* series published under the pseudonym Jackson Flynn], *The Apache Hunter* (1976), *The Marauders* (1977), *Legend of the Damned* (1977).

Films based on Gordon D. Shirreffs' Western fiction are *The Lonesome Trail* (Lippert, 1955) directed by Richard Bartlett [source unknown], *Oregon Passage* (Allied Artists, 1958) directed by Paul Landres [based on *Rio Bravo*].

"The Galvanized Yankee," a *Playhouse 90* production of 1958, was based on *Massacre Creek*.

Short, Luke. See Glidden, Frederick D.

Silko, Leslie (Marmon) (1948 —)

Poet, short story writer, essayist, and novelist of Native American, Mexican, and white descent born at the Laguna Pueblo. Silko grew up on the reservation and in Albuquerque, New Mexico. She was educated in Bureau of Indian Affairs schools and received a Bachelor's degree *magna cum laude* from the University of New Mexico where she had been elected to Phi Beta Kappa her junior year. She was an assistant professor at the University of New Mexico but also taught at the University of Washington and gave frequent papers and lectures all over the United States as well as being a mother.

Silko first attained national prominence when her short story "Lullaby" was selected by Martha Foley for inclusion in *The Best Short Stories of 1975* (Boston: Houghton Mifflin, 1975). Another story, "Yellow Woman," was included in Foley's *Two Hundred Years of Great American Short Stories* (Boston: Houghton Mifflin, 1975) and subsequently has been widely anthologized. "Lullaby" is told from the point of view of an old Navaho woman. "Yellow Woman" takes an ancient Keres myth and weaves it into a contemporary abduction story. The use of old traditions and oral tales and modern interrelationships, both Indian/Indian and Indian/white, is typical of Silko's style.

Nowhere is this melding of old and new more strikingly used than in *Ceremony* (New York: Viking, 1977), Silko's first novel, written with the help of a Rosewater Foundation-on-Ketchikan Creek, Alaska, artist-in-residence grant and a 1974 Writing Fellowship from the National Endowment for the Arts. In this novel, Silko used the ritual and power of storytelling for healing and communion. As many novels by Native Americans, this one demonstrates that the illness of Tayo, the protagonist, comes from the white world of World War II. Silko, however, placed some of the responsibility for evil/disease on the Indians themselves. The Japanese and the Laguna Indians are synonymous to Tayo as he hallucinates. Purification and ceremony help Tayo discover the logic rather than the confusion in the unity of all things. As the rituals themselves, the novel is interwoven with strands of poetry.

Silko has been anthologized frequently.

In addition to her own collection of poetry, *Laguna Woman* (New York: Greenfield Review Press, 1973), Silko's stories and poems may be found in *The Man to Send Rain Clouds: Contemporary Stories by American Indians* (New York: Vintage, 1974) and *Voices of the Rainbow: Contemporary Poetry by American Indians* (New York: Vintage, 1975), both edited by Kenneth Rosen.

P.O.

Silver, Nicholas. See Faust, Frederick.

Simms, William Gilmore (1806–1870) Popular author of historical novels of the Revolutionary War in South Carolina and "border" romances set on the Southwestern frontier of the 1820s and 1830s, born the second of three sons to William and Harriet (Singleton) Simms at Charleston, South Carolina. Disaster enveloped Simms' family in 1808 when, in rapid succession, his older brother, mother, and younger brother died, and his father's business failed. Leaving the 2-year-old William Gilmore in the care of a maternal grandmother, the elder Simms (whose hair had turned white in a single week) fled Charleston and settled initially in Tennessee before joining General Coffee's campaign against the Creek Indians in 1813 and later serving as an officer under General Jackson at New Orleans, Louisiana, and in Florida between 1815 and 1818. Meanwhile, William Gilmore Simms grew into a shy and precocious boy who loved books and preferred "musing in secret places" to joining in the games of his peers. Of these years he later wrote: "I had two brothers, both dead when I was

an infant. I grew up without young associates. I grew hard in consequence, hard perhaps of manner—but with a heart craving love beyond all other possessions." His formal schooling was brief, "worthless and scoundrelly." At 12 he was apprenticed to an apothecary for training as a physician. It was uncongenial labor, but he stuck with it for six years until an invitation from his father—who had finally settled and begun to prosper in Mississippi—offered escape and allowed him a year's sojourn on the Southwestern frontier during 1824–1825. Despite his father's urgings to remain in the West, where his gifts would bring quick financial success and "a Senate seat in ten years' time," Simms returned to Charleston, took up the study of law, and married his childhood sweetheart, Anna Malcolm Giles (who was already ill with tuberculosis). In 1827 he was admitted to the bar and appointed a city magistrate. In 1828–1829 he was editor and co-founder of the short-lived *Southern Literary Gazette,* and in 1830 he bought the Charleston *City Gazette,* a newspaper which he sold, heavily indebted, in 1832 shortly after his wife's death. While owner-editor of the *City Gazette* Simms made a second trip to the West, presumably to settle his father's estate in Georgeville, Mississippi.

After the failure of his publishing ventures, Simms turned to writing romances on American themes in the manner of Sir Walter Scott and James Fenimore Cooper (q.v.). *Martin Faber* (1833), the confessions of a condemned murderer, was followed by *Guy Rivers* (1834), his first border (frontier) romance. In 1835 Simms married Chevillette Roach, the daughter of a wealthy planter, and moved into her home at "Woodlands" in Barnwell County. He served in the South Carolina legislature 1844–1846. The Civil War was a shattering experience for Simms, leaving him in personal and financial ruin. His wife died in 1863 and "Woodlands" was burned by stragglers from General Sherman's army in 1865. Simms' attempts to re-establish himself as a writer failed. He died in Charleston.

Guy Rivers, set in the recently discovered Georgia gold fields, is the story of Ralph Colleton, a young, handsome, intellectual but headstrong Southern aristocrat who, prevented from marrying his cousin and disgusted with Carolina society, leaves for the Georgia frontier only to run afoul of a ruthless band of outlaws under the leadership of the notorious Guy Rivers. Rivers is a dark hero, a sort of shadow of Colleton. Once a brilliant lawyer, Rivers had turned to the frontier and a life of crime after being thwarted in love and career by essentially the same forces which drove Colleton into the wilderness. Despite its crudities of style and characterization, the book was a rousing success. Over the next ten years Simms produced three similar romances. *Richard Hurdis* (1838) is set in Alabama and based upon the infamous John A. Murrell gang, a "mystic brotherhood" of land pirates that had terrorized the Southern border in the early 1830s. In *Richard Hurdis* Simms explored frontier society and character more closely than in *Guy Rivers.* It is portrayed as a wild and barbarous land, an environment of gangsters, roving Indians, crass squatters and other riff-raff from the Eastern cities. A vagrant lot, they are inimical to the development of civilization. For Simms it was axiomatic that only settled peoples who have shouldered the discipline and responsibilities of permanence can produce civilization. The instinctive antagonism between the intelligent young hero, Richard Hurdis, and the criminal leader, Foster (Murrell), is that between culture and barbarism, or civilization and the frontier. Appropriately, Foster evades capture and moves Westward, his further villainies providing the framework for Simms' next border romance, *Border Beagles, Or a Tale of Mississippi* (1840), a rehash of the themes developed in *Guy Rivers* and *Richard Hurdis*.

In 1842 Simms published *Beauchampe*, a fictional reworking of the famous "Kentucky tragedy" of the early 1820s. A popular theme in Southern literature, it is the story of a young law student (Beauchampe) who married a frontier beauty (Margaret Cooper) only to discover that she had earlier been debauched and callously abandoned by a prominent local attorney (William Sharpe). Arrogantly refused when he challenges Sharpe to a duel, Beauchampe subsequently murders him and is himself condemned to the gallows. On the night of his execution, Beauchampe and Margaret commit suicide together in his jail cell. Simms considered *Beauchampe* to be his finest border romance. It was followed by *Helen Halsey* (1845), a frontier novelette, and, much later, *The Cub of the Panther* (1869) and *Voltmeier* (1869).

In addition to his frontier tales and Revolutionary War sagas, Simms also wrote two Indian romances, *The Yemassee* (1835), a story of the 1715 uprising of the Yemassees against the British colonists in South Carolina—probably his most enduring work of fiction—and *The Cassique of Kiawah* (1859), a romance of Indian warfare in South Carolina in 1685. He also published four short stories on Indian themes in *The Wigwam and the Cabin* (1845). While it is true that Simms larded these representative Indians with considerable praise, he roasted them nevertheless. While the Indians are described as "decidedly the noblest race of aborigines the world has ever known," Simms was always careful to emphasize the Indians' moral and intellectual inferiority to the white man. Ultimately, they are worse even than the Negro, for they cannot be made to settle and put to work. Simms argued that the early white settlers had flattered and spoiled the Indian as one would a talented and headstrong child. It would have been far better if they had been overrun by a ruthless, superior force, "parcelled off in tens, twenties and hundreds under strict task masters, (who) by compelling the performance of their natural duties—that labor which is the condition of all human life—would have preserved them to themselves and humanity." Simms believed that it was the Egyptian captivity that made the Hebrews great, just as individual genius is the result of strict discipline during childhood. The Indian had been ruined, therefore, by never being forced to settle and to work—if necessary, by the lash. This failing had predestined the Native American—the greatest of all aborigines—to corruption and disappearance. Unable to compete with the more rigorous whites, his only hope lay in his separation, his isolation in an Indian Territory far from the influence of white civilization with its debilitating mixture of virtue and vice.

During the 1830s and early 1840s Simms was considered one of America's greatest writers and compared favorably with Cooper and Washington Irving (q.v.). His stories were exciting and picturesque, his themes often sensational. But the crudity of his style and wooden characterizations have not lasted.

J.D.F.

The only collection of Simms' writings was published in the 1850s by J.S. Redfield (and, later, his successor W.J. Widdleton) of New York City. During the 1960s the Gregg Press issued reprints of several Simms' works as a part of its *Americans in Fiction Series*. Unfortunately, their selection did not include any of the border romances, but did contain *The Wigwam and the Cabin* (1845). *The Cassique of Kiawah* is not available in a modern edition, but *The Yemassee* was re-issued by Twayne Publishers. An important volume of Simms' essays, *Views and Reviews in American Literature, History and Fiction* (which contains a fine essay on Cooper), was edited by C. Hugh Holman (Cambridge: Harvard University Press, 1962).

Smith, Wade. See Snow, Charles H.

Snow, Charles H(orace) (1877–1967)

A prolific author of formulary Westerns who became immensely popular and far better known in Great Britain than in the United States where he lived and wrote, born at Lake County, California. Snow spent his early years in mining camps throughout the American West, principally in Nevada and Idaho, and then in Mexico, South America, and British Columbia. When he turned to writing, he drew on these experiences for background material. Snow married and in 1910 he went to the Napa Valley in California with his family. In 1914, at the age of 37, he was blinded in a mining accident and this seemingly brought his career to a close. In 1920, Snow began serving four years as a justice of the peace. It was also during this time that he published his first Western short story, "Stub-

The Thoroughbred Throwback." He followed this by writing exhaustively for the Western pulp magazines and even became a correspondent for two metropolitan newspapers.

It was Snow's practice to record his stories and from these recordings his daughter would transcribe and type the manuscripts. She would then read Snow the proofs and any changes that had to be made were then made. In all, Snow produced some 360 manuscripts of varying length, but it was not until *The Riders of San Felipe* (Boston: Hale, Cushman, 1930) that his novels began appearing in book form. Throughout the 'Thirties he published a wide assortment of Western novels under various pen-names as well as his own, but, beginning in the 'Forties, British publishers seemed more inclined to accept his books than American publishers and for the next two decades, up until the year he died in fact, his fiction won him a loyal and enthusiastic audience in the United Kingdom. As Walt Coburn (q.v.) and other pulp writers, Snow in his stories stressed action—some of it improbable—over any other literary consideration.

Charles H. Snow's Western novels published in the United States are *The Rider of San Felipe* (1930), *The Sheriff of Chispa Loma* (1931), *Don Jim* (1932), *The Silent Shot* (1932), *Tamer of Bad Men* (1932), *Stocky of Lone Tree Ranch* (1932), *Beyond Arizona* (1933), *The Cowboy from Alamos* (1933), *The Invisible Brand* (1933), *The Scorpion's Sting* (1933), *The Bandit of Paloduro* (1934), *The Gold of Alamito* (1934), *The Highgraders* (1934), *Hollow Stump Mystery* (1934), *Smuggler's Ranch* (1934), *Cardigan Cowboy* (1935), *The Sign of the Death Circle* (1935), *Six-Guns of Sandoval* (1935), *Argonaut Gold* (1936), *The Trail to*

Abilene (1937), *Trail of 56* (1937), *Border Feud* (1938) [alternate title: *Border Blood*], *Guns Along the Border* (1939), *Riders of the Range* (1939), *Outlaws of Red Canyon* (1940), *Sheriff of Yavisa* (1941), *Wolf of the Mesas* (1941), *The Brand Stealer* (1942), *Outlaws of Sugar Loaf* (1942), *Rebel of Ronde Valley* (1943), *Renegade Ranger* (1943), *Horsethief Pass* (1944).

Snow's American novels under the name Charles Ballew are *Red Gold* (1932), *The Gambler of Red Gulch* (1933), *One Crazy Cowboy* (1933), *Cowpuncher* (1934), *Texas Spurs* (1935), *The Treasure of Aspen Canyon* (1935), *Frontier Regiment* (1939), *Rim-Fire in Mexico* (1939).

Snow's American novels under the name Gary Marshall are *Flaming Six-Guns* (1934), *Raiders of the Tonto Rim* (1934), *The Watchers of Gold Canyon* (1934), *One Fightin' Cowboy* (1935), *Nevada Gold* (1937).

Snow's American novels under the name Ranger Lee are *Thundering Hoofs* (1937), *Rebel on the Range* (1938), *The Red Gash Outlaws* (1939), *Badland Bill* (1941), *The Bar D Boss* (1943).

Snow's American novel under the name H.C. Averill is *The Cowboy from Alamos* (1946).

Snow's American novels under the name Wade Smith are *Below the Border* (1952), *Dead Man's Saddle* (1955).

Snow's American novel under the name Dan Wardle is *Five Bars of Gold* (1955).

Sorensen, Virginia (1912 —) Author and short story writer, a majority of whose novels deal with various periods of Mormon history in the Western United States, born Virginia Eggertsen at Provo, Utah. Sorensen's great-grandparents went West with the Mormon pioneers and Sorensen recalled that in her childhood she "actually heard stories of the long trek and of the settlement of our town from people who had experienced it all." She was educated in public schools in Manti and American Fork, Utah, and attended the University of Missouri at Columbia where she studied writing before matriculating at Brigham Young University, in her home town, where she received her Bachelor's degree in 1934. From 1934–1939, she lived in Palo Alto, California with her husband, whom she married in 1933. During this five-year period Sorensen attended classes at Stanford University, where her husband taught, while raising two children and writing a three-act verse play about the legend surrounding Timpanogas, one of the highest peaks of the Wasatch range of the Rocky Mountains, and an unpublished novel. They were divorced in 1939.

Her first published book, an historical novel *A Little Lower Than the Angels* (New York: Knopf, 1942), is set in the Mormon settlement of Nauvoo, Illinois, during the 1840s and includes Joseph Smith as a character. The story, told from the female point of view, focuses on a woman who comes to live in Nauvoo with her husband. Sorensen's next three novels—*On this Star* (New York: Reynal & Hitchcock, 1946), *The Neighbors* (New York: Reynal & Hitchcock, 1947), and *The Evening and the Morning* (New York: Harcourt, Brace, 1949)—deal with the Mormons in the West, although *The Neighbors* which is set in Colorado has a number of non-Mormon characters. All three books have similar themes of man's relationship with his environment and the "problems of rootlessness." The books give rich presentations of Mormon communities, family life, and customs as well as being sensitive studies of the psychological workings of the characters. Sorensen rendered particularly understanding portraits of women who must function in a primarily male-oriented environment. Although a member of the Church of the Latter-Day Saints, as Vardis Fisher (q.v.) Sorensen was able to deal with Mormons and their beliefs somewhat impartially.

In 1946 she was awarded a Guggenheim Fellowship to Mexico where she intended to research the story about a Mormon apostate who had lived in Sonora, Mexico. She went to Guaymas and the surrounding areas where she visited the Yaqui Indian villages. *The Proper Gods* (New York: Harcourt, Brace, 1951) is a contemporary story about a Yaqui Indian who returns from service in World War II. The protagonist, who was raised in Arizona, returns to Mexico, the place of his birth, to be with his exiled family. His struggle to become part of the culture and way of life of his ancestors is the central conflict of the story although it is not as poignantly treated as is a similar conflict in N. Scott Momaday's (q.v.) *House Made of Dawn* (New York: Harper's, 1968). *Many Heavens* (New York: Harcourt, Brace, 1954) won high praise from the critics, although it is not her best book, and again deals with Mormons and the dilemma surrounding polygamy which had been abolished in the Mormon church in 1890. In 1954 Sorensen won a second Guggenheim Fellowship. She went to Denmark after which time she wrote her novel *Kingdom Come* (New York: Harcourt, Brace, 1960), a Mormon novel dealing with Danish converts.

An autobiographical story collection, *Where Nothing Is Long Ago* (New York: Harcourt, Brace, 1963), appeared before her novel, *The Man with the Key* (New York: Harcourt, Brace, 1974), a contemporary story set in Virginia. In the 'Fifties, she began writing juveniles and went on to win the John Newberry Medal from the American Library Association in 1957 for *Miracles on Maple Street* (New York: Harcourt, Brace, 1957).

Her work has been highly regarded for its simple, direct, and intelligent style and for her knowledge and understanding of the Mormon community in both the past and present. L.L. Lee and Sylvia B. Lee in their chapbook *Virginia Sorensen* (Boise: Idaho State University Press, 1978) wrote of Sorensen's work: "Her sense of place, community, and history, then, is Sorensen's vision, a vision that recognizes that the past is significant and always present, that society shapes us, and that a single place, not a mere series of places, is also part of being Western and being American. She has made the West *present*."

For further information see *Virginia Sorensen* (Boise: Idaho State University Press, 1978) by L.L. Lee and Sylvia B. Lee.

Spearman, Frank H(amilton)

(1859–1937) A novelist known during his lifetime for his exciting railroad stories, some of them with a Western setting, born at Buffalo, New York. Spearman was educated in public and private schools until he attended Lawrence College in Appleton, Wisconsin, with the intention of becoming a physician. Ill health, however, forced him to abandon his academic pursuits and at 20 he became a traveling sales-man. By the time he was 27 he had worked himself into the position of a cashier in a bank and by 29 he was president of the bank. It was in this capacity that he familiarized himself with the management and business practices of railroads, knowledge which was so expert that when he wrote *The Strategy of Great Railroads* (New York: Scribner's, 1904), the book was used as a text at Yale University.

Spearman's earliest fiction, contained in *The Nerve of Foley and Other Stories* (New York: Harper's, 1900), already utilizes railroad backgrounds for the dramatic action. Influenced by Owen Wister's (q.v.) success with *The Virginian* (New York: Macmillan, 1902), which was set in Wyoming, Spearman himself went to Cheyenne, Wyoming, where he stayed for two weeks and concocted the plot for what was to prove his most enduring novel, *Whispering Smith* (New York: Scribner's, 1906). Smith as he was drawn in the novel remains a fascinating character—the name "Whispering" having come about as a result of once losing his voice while suffering from a cold in Chicago. He is a trouble-shooter for the railroad. Upon publication, the novel became a best-seller and inspired an entire body of secondary literature about railroad detectives and trouble-shooters, from Ernest Haycox' (q.v.) *Trouble Shooter* (Boston: Little, Brown, 1937) to William Colt MacDonald's (q.v.) narratives about Gregory Quist.

Whispering Smith was written in an episodic style, covering a period of nearly four years although focusing on a group of main characters, and perhaps it was only natural that when Helen Holmes began starring in a series of chapter plays with a railroad setting Spearman was hired to script one of them, *The Girl and the Game* (Mutual, 1915). The next year his novel *Whispering Smith* (Mutual, 1916) was brought to the screen for the first time.

Although Spearman went on to write other novels, some of them Westerns, such as *The Mountain Divide* (New York: Scribner's, 1912), *Laramie Holds the Range* (New York: Scribner's, 1921)—certainly one of his best—*Hell's Desert* (New York: Doubleday, 1933), and *Gunlock Ranch* (New York: Doubleday, 1935), it was the creation of Whispering Smith which stayed in the public's mind. Spearman wrote a ten chapter serial as a sequel, *Whispering Smith Rides* (Universal, 1927), a year after *Whispering Smith* (PDC, 1926) had been remade, and in 1935 Spearman wrote an original screen story for *Whispering Smith Speaks* (Fox, 1935) which starred George O'Brien. The original novel was filmed a third time, *Whispering Smith* (Paramount, 1948), and then arrangements were made with Spearman's estate to update the character and make him a contemporary railroad detective in England on vacation before he is involved in a mystery in *Whispering Smith Vs. Scotland Yard* (RKO, 1952).

During his Hollywood days, Spearman became good friends with both H.H. Knibbs (q.v.) and Eugene Manlove Rhodes (q.v.), fellow Western writers. While he was alive, Spearman was frequently compared favorably to both Owen Wister and Rhodes, although, in retrospect, in view of his highly romantic view of the West, the railroad, and his penchant for varying the formulary ranch romance into a romance of the rails, perhaps H.H. Knibbs would make a better comparison. Spearman liked to people his novels with a great many background characters and he tended to explore character as much as he provided action narratives, so, in this sense, it would be just to say that he was definitely to be taken more seriously than many of his contemporaries, including Zane Grey (q.v.) whose novel *The U.P. Trail* (New York: Harper's, 1918) was more than a little indebted to Spearman's pioneering work.

Frank H. Spearman wrote the original screen scenarios for *The Girl and the Game* (Mutual, 1915) directed by J.P. McGowan [a fifteen chapter serial] and *Whispering Smith Rides* (Universal, 1927) directed by Ray Taylor [a ten chapter serial]. *Whispering Smith* (Mutual, 1916) was directed by J.P. McGowan, remade under this title (PDC, 1926) directed by George Melford, and (Paramount, 1948) directed by Leslie Fenton. *Whispering Smith Speaks* (Fox, 1935) directed by David Howard was based on an original story by Spearman whereas *Whispering Smith Vs. Scotland Yard* (RKO, 1952) directed by Francis Searle was based only on a character created by Frank W. Spearman. *The Runaway Express* (Universal, 1926) was directed by Edward Sedgwick [based on *The Nerve of Foley and Other Stories*].

Steelman, Robert J(ames)

(1914 —) Author of formulary Western fiction, born at Columbus, Ohio. In 1938 Steelman received a Bachelor's degree from Ohio State University and in 1939–1946 he worked as a civilian electronics engineer with the U.S. Army Signal Corps. After his discharge, he switched over to the U.S. Navy, also working as a civilian electronics engineer, from 1946 through 1969. Steelman's first Western novel was *Stages South* (New York: Ace, 1956), although it had been preceded by years of writing for Western pulp magazines, especially *Ranch Romances*. Steelman once commented: "My writing is largely of the Old West. I try hard to make my books authoritative and true to the times. Perhaps my principal aim is to do what I can to elevate the 'Western' to some literary significance, rather than see it condemned to a second-rate genre status." In Steelman's behalf, it should be said that this is very much the case with such books as *Portrait of a Sioux* (New York: Doubleday, 1976) and *Lord Apache* (New York: Doubleday, 1977), which, while still heavily formulary as to plot structure, do break away from convention in their poignant and memorable characterizations. But, unfortunately, plot structure is destiny and a formulary Western, no matter how well written, is still a formulary Western.

Robert J. Steelman's Western novels are *Stages South* (1956), *Apache Wells* (1959), *Winter of the Sioux* (1959), *Ambush at Three Rivers* (1964), *Cheyenne Vengeance* (1974), *Dakota Territory* (1974), *The Fox Dancer* (1975), *Sun Boy* (1975), *Portrait of a Sioux* (1976), *Lord Apache* (1977), *The Galvanized Reb* (1977), *Surgeon to the Sioux* (1979), *The Great Yellowstone Steamboat Race* (1980), *Man They Hanged* (1980), *The Prairie Baroness* (1981).

Stegner, Wallace (1909 —) Author of Western fiction, biography, history, criticism, born at Lake Mills, Iowa, while his parents (residing in Grand Forks, North Dakota, at the time) were visiting his Norwegian maternal grandfather. Stegner's fa-

ther was a wanderer and between 1909 and 1921 the young Stegner lived in North Dakota, Washington, Saskatchewan, and Montana as his restless and generally unsuccessful father searched for the pot of gold at the end of the rainbow.

In 1921 the Stegners moved to Salt Lake City, Utah, where they lived in twelve different houses in nine years. Stegner graduated from the University of Utah where his instructor in freshman English was Vardis Fisher (q.v.), soon to begin a long career as a Western novelist. According to Fisher, he gave the 16-year-old Stegner a chance to take a "D" in the course without attending classes so that he could do something more worthwhile, and Stegner accepted. However, Stegner's version is that he took two quarters of composition from Fisher and was then excused from the rest of freshman English. Of Fisher, Stegner said: "He was very influential upon me . . . he certainly took a can opener to my dim little mind."

Another influence on Stegner was historian Bernard DeVoto. After receiving a Master's and a Doctor's degree at the University of Iowa, and five years of teaching at Augustana College in Illinois, the University of Utah, and the University of Wisconsin, Stegner went to Harvard to teach composition. While there he was unwittingly caught in the middle of a debate between DeVoto and Sinclair Lewis, sympathizing with DeVoto but told (also sympathetically) by Lewis to get away from Harvard and the effete East and write great books in Iowa or Utah. The advice was good, but it might more appropriately have been given by DeVoto who considered himself a Westerner.

With six books already to his credit, including *Big Rock Candy Mountain* (New York: Duell, Sloan, 1943) and an excellent

historical narrative, *Mormon Country* (New York: Duell, Sloan, 1942), Stegner finally went all the way to California, to Stanford University's writing program, in 1945, where he stayed until retirement in 1971. He never forgot DeVoto, eventually writing his biography, *The Uneasy Chair* (New York: Doubleday, 1974). However, if any one man might be called Stegner's hero, it would be John Wesley Powell, military man, geologist, explorer of the Colorado River—a man of insight as well as action. Stegner told his story in *Beyond the Hundredth Meridian: John Wesley Powell and the Second Opening of the West* (Boston: Houghton Mifflin, 1954).

Stegner's work is almost evenly divided between fiction and non-fiction and each frequently reads as the other: the non-fiction is often given a narrative drive and an emphasis on character, while the fiction is usually informed by history. *The Preacher and the Slave* (Boston: Houghton Mifflin, 1950) was an attempt to bring biography into fiction and Stegner considered this his second major novel, *Big Rock Candy Mountain* being his first. But the critics did not approve; they remained silent. Perhaps in disappointment, Stegner did' not write another novel for eleven years. Then he turned to contemporary California for subject and setting in *A Shooting Star* (New York: Viking, 1961), *All the Little Live Things* (New York: Viking, 1967), and *Angle of Repose* (New York: Doubleday, 1971). The last of these is in some ways a thematic continuation of *Big Rock Candy Mountain*. Stegner's novel *The Spectator Bird* (New York: Doubleday, 1976) followed.

Perhaps his best evocation of the West is in *Wolf Willow: A History, a Story, and a Memory of the Last Plains Frontier* (New

York: Viking, 1962). As though one genre cannot cope with the Western landscape and its meaning, Stegner combined personal observation and reminiscence with fiction and history in his evaluation of the Northern Plains, particularly the other side of the Montana border in Saskatchewan. Vitality and change rub against stasis and permanence. Geometry shapes the major images of the land. And history is seen (as it is in Stegner's fiction also) as continuity, as a past with bridges to the present. Stegner's complaint about Western fiction was that it continues to celebrate the frontier and rarely, if ever, gets beyond the mythic and heroic past. He addressed this question, and many others equally pertinent, in his collection of essays, *The Sound of Mountain Water* (New York: Doubleday, 1969), especially in the controversial "Born a Square."

J.R.M.

The only book written about Stegner is *Wallace Stegner* (New York: Twayne Publishers, 1977) by Forrest G. and Margaret G. Robinson.

Steinbeck, John (Ernest, Jr.)

(1902–1968) Nobel and Pulitzer Prize-winning novelist and short story writer, essayist, newspaper correspondent, columnist, dramatist, screenwriter, noted for his atmospheric contributions to Western fiction, born at Salinas, California. Growing up near the ocean in the rich agricultural Salinas Valley, Steinbeck acquired a lifelong love for California landscapes and a passion for living outdoors. In high school he was not only a varsity athlete and president of his graduating class, but a writer for the school newspaper. Between 1920 and 1925 he attended Stanford University as a special student but never finished his degree, leaving college to work his way to New York City on a cattle boat. Failing to make his literary mark there other than as a newspaper reporter, he soon returned to California.

Steinbeck worked at a variety of jobs which gave him first-hand experience with the people and places that were to become characteristic of his best novels. Many school vacations were spent as a fruitpicker and ranchhand. Stints in the fish hatcheries and food processing factories, hod carrying, apprentice painting and construction work on Madison Square Garden when he was in New York, and hard labor with a road gang were among the ways he supported himself while trying to write.

Steinbeck is sometimes labeled a regional writer because California, especially the Monterey region, is the central landscape of all his major fiction as is the relationship between man and his environment, perhaps his most important theme. His first book, *Cup of Gold: A Life of Henry Morgan, Buccaneer* (New York: McBride, 1929), was not well received when it came out. Other "pirates" were attracting attention that year of the great stock market crash and resulting Depression. But Steinbeck was not to be deterred.

Tortilla Flat (New York: Covici, Friede, 1935) was the author's first success although Steinbeck was deeply disappointed in the public misunderstanding of what he was trying to do. His intent was to transpose the characters and themes of *Morte d'Arthur* (1469) by Sir Thomas Mallory to Monterey County. The knights of the Round Table were to become *paisanos*, descendants of the Spanish-Mexican-Indian inhabitants of the region. Lazy, irresponsible, and innocently drunk and gay, Danny, the leader of the revelers, Pilon, his friend, and other such characters as Terasina and Sweets Ramirez require a great stretch of the imagination to connect them to the ancient and legendary Britons. Hispanic-American critics have been severe with Steinbeck for his amoral and childlike characterizations of his Chicanos, who are picturesque and appealing but not very realistic.

Steinbeck's next novel, however, is quite different. *In Dubious Battle* (New York: Covici, Friede, 1936) is not only unromantic but goes beyond realism to naturalism in trying to show groups of men struggling against the overpowering forces of Nature and man's attempt to manipulate them. The work established Steinbeck as a master of social protest literature and a sympathizer with the poor working man. The story of the fruitpickers' strike and their defeat by the vigilantes hired by the landowners is a classic of Depression writing. In terms of Steinbeck's development, it led the way to his greatest novel, *The Grapes of Wrath* (New York: Covici, Friede, 1939), for which he won the Pulitzer Prize.

Here again, as in *In Dubious Battle*, Steinbeck was relentless in demonstrating the social and natural forces that beat down and destroy the ordinary small citizen. But the daily heroism of the common people, their dialects and habits, and their stoic acceptance of suffering are also knowingly depicted. Despite the violence which ends the book, the novel is a spiritual conquest for the Joads by virtue of their simple humanity and decent values. *The Grapes of Wrath*, an American classic in its own right, is populated with characters who have earned an immortality beyond its time. In these two novels, especially, Steinbeck subscribed to the theory that man is very much a part of the animal world and is fighting for his existence as part of an animal group in which he must merge his identity in order to survive. Out of this immersion comes a primitive force that can be called heroism, or an instinctual need to persevere.

One of Steinbeck's talents, as well as one of his drawbacks as a writer, was his frequent impulse to experiment with different types of work and with different literary forms. *The Red Pony* (New York: Covici, Friede, 1937), the story of a child, Jody, and his loss of innocence, was later rewritten as a film script for *The Red Pony* (Republic, 1949) directed by Lewis Milestone. Likewise his most famous play, the Broadway hit *Of Mice and Men* (New York: Covici, Friede, 1937), was first written out as a narrative story about the tragic friendship of two ranch hands. With *The Long Valley* (New York: Covici, Friede, 1938), a collection of short stories, Steinbeck brought his preoccupation with ordinary American characters, especially Californios, to a brief close.

Steinbeck's later work is not considered by critics to be as powerful or as inventive as his earlier work. *Cannery Row* (New York: Viking, 1945) and a sequel, *Sweet*

Thursday (New York: Viking, 1954), resemble *Tortilla Flat* in locale and characterization, but the primitives are more sentimental and less interesting. Similarly, *The Wayward Bus* (New York: Viking, 1947) is also uneven in tone. With *East of Eden* (New York: Viking, 1952), the history of three generations of a migrant Salinas Valley family, Steinbeck's popularity had begun to fall off. Perhaps it was because he was writing from New York City about the countryside he loved with nostalgia rather than direct contact.

P.O.

Screenplays on which John Steinbeck worked which employ a Western theme are *The Red Pony* (Republic, 1949) directed by Lewis Milestone, *Viva Zapata* (20th-Fox, 1952), directed by Elia Kazan, and films based on his fiction with Western themes are *The Grapes of Wrath* (20th-Fox, 1940) directed by John Ford, *Of Mice and Men* (United Artists, 1940) directed by Lewis Milestone, *Tortilla Flat* (M-G-M, 1942) directed by Victor Fleming, and *East of Eden* (Warner's, 1955) directed by Elia Kazan.

The Red Pony (NBC, 1973) was also adapted as a movie made for television.

Stephens, Ann S(ophia) (1810–1886)

Popular author noted for writing the first Beadle Western dime novel (see Pulp and Slick Western stories), born Ann Winterbotham at Humphreysville (Seymour), Connecticut. Stephens attended several schools in her home state. In 1831 she married Edward Stephens, who for two years published the *Portland Magazine*, a literary monthly, in which her first literary effort, a poem "The Polish Boy", was published. In 1837, after relocating to New York, she became an associate editor for *Ladies Companion*. In 1841, she joined the staff of *Graham's Magazine,* of which Edgar Allan Poe was editor at the time. Stephens, in addition, was contributing to numerous other publications. Her longest association was with *Peterson's Magazine* for which she served as co-editor for a time and principally contributed serials. She began her own magazine in 1856, *Mrs. Stephens' Illustrated New Monthly,* published by her husband, until it was later merged with *Peterson's.* Her first full-length book was *Fashion and Famine* (1854), a domestic tale which was adapted for the stage. More than twenty-five of her historical romances and domestic novels were serialized in *Peterson's* before being issued in book form.

In 1860, Irwin P. Beadle & Company paid Stephens $250 for the rights to reprint one of her early serials which was the first Beadle dime novel: *Malaeska: The Indian Wife of the White Hunter.* It became a bestseller. *Malaeska* was a tragic and moral tale (as were most of her stories) of an Indian princess married to a white frontiersman. Stephens continued to contribute dime novel tales, a form at which she became very adept, using the Far West and Indian romances as her two basic themes.

During the Civil War she compiled a *Pictorial History of the War of the Union* (1863). After the Civil War her stories continued to be popular and were brought out in a fourteen volume set in 1869 and a new twenty-three volume set was in the press at the time of her death.

Stevens, Dan J. See Overholser, Wayne D.

Stuart, Matt. See Holmes, L.P.

Suckow, Ruth (1892–1960) Regional novelist, poet, and short story writer, born at Hawarden, Iowa. Suckow's father was a Congregational minister and the family moved from one small Iowa parish to another during her childhood, giving her a deep sense of the people and the landscape of the state, all of which she subsequently used in her writing. Her mother was constantly ill and she and her older sister, Emma, grew up to be very independent; she was also close to her father, riding in a special seat on his bicycle when he made parish calls. She would sit in her father's study and write stories while he put together his sermons. In the rural towns and small cities in Iowa during that period the church was often the most important social institution and Suckow had an intimate view of local life.

Small and blonde, Suckow, as many other young women, was attracted to the stage and she left her studies at Grinnell College to spend a lonely year at Curry School of Expression in Boston, Massachusetts. She went to Colorado to help her mother nurse her sister who subsequently died of tuberculosis. Indeed, during her twenties, Suckow endured the deaths of her sister, nephew, and mother. Determined to become a writer, she majored in English at the University of Denver where she earned both a Bachelor's degree and a Master's degree, the latter in 1918. Her first published poem appeared in *The Midland* magazine that summer. In order to support herself when she finished school, Suckow worked first for an automobile guidebook company in Denver and then studied bee-keeping. She returned to live in her father's parsonage in Earlville, Iowa, and opened the Orchard Apiary, which was a successful enterprise though very hard and lonely work. In 1921 her first short story, "Uprooted," appeared in *The Midland* and she worked for half a year as an editorial assistant for that magazine. Meanwhile she was writing longer and longer pieces, several of which came to the attention of H.L. Mencken who published them in his magazine, *The Smart Set*. During this first period of her writing, her focus was on the development of a single Iowan's everyday life, depicted with vernacular speech and rural background. She wrote with a fresh and clear eye. She was quite productive, publishing at least ten or twelve pieces a year. Sixteen of her short stories were gathered together and published as *Iowa Interiors* (New York: Knopf, 1926); reviewers were inclined to compare her word pictures of domestic scenes to Dutch genre paintings.

With the serialization of her first novel, *Country People* (New York: Knopf, 1924), in the *Century* magazine, Suckow became an established professional writer. For the next ten years, she spent her winters in New York and Washington and her summers in Earlville. She met and married another Iowan writer, Ferner Nuhn, in 1929.

Country People, as many of Suckow's other works, deals with the conflict between generations of an Iowan family of German immigrants who accept the American success ethos. *Odyssey of a Nice Girl* (New York: Knopf, 1925), somewhat autobiographical, again studies German immigrants, but this time with the focus on a young girl's growing up in a colorless small town and dreaming that she is special and different. The second period of Suckow's writing takes off from this emphasis. For the next few works, although still keeping the Iowa setting, she explored the "new woman" of the 'Twenties, looking for self-fulfillment. It is in *The Folks* (New York: Farrar and Rinehart, 1934), her longest and possibly her best novel, that she shifted this viewpoint to a wider and more mature outlook, again going back to the various generations of a family and exploring the themes of continuity versus change.

Suckow is classified with other realists of this period, such as Sinclair Lewis and Sherwood Anderson. Her depiction of the Iowa "folk" has never been equalled. Her uncollected short stories and articles are still worth reading, as well as her other novels.

P.O.

Ruth Suckow's Midwestern novels are *Country People* (1924), *Odyssey of a Nice Girl* (1925), *Iowa Interiors* (1926) [short stories], *The Bonney Family* (1928), *Cora* (1929), *The Kramer Girls* (1931), *Children and Older People* (1931), *The Folks* (1934), *Carry-Over* (1936), *New Hope* (1936), *Some Others and Myself* (1952), *The John Wood Case* (1959).

For further information see *Ruth Suckow* (New York: Twayne Publishers, 1969) by Leedice McAnelly Kissane and *Ruth Suckow* (Boise: Idaho State University Press, 1976) by Abigail Ann Hamblen.

Sullivan, Reese. See Lutz, Giles A.

Swarthout, Glendon (Fred)

(1918 —) An author perhaps best known for his two novels with Western settings which have been made into films, *They Came to Cordura* (New York: Random House, 1958) and *The Shootist* (New York: Doubleday, 1975), born at Pinckney, Michigan. Swarthout received his Bachelor's degree from the University of Michigan in 1939, as well as his Master's degree in 1946, and his Doctor's degree from Michigan State University in 1955. During World War II he was enlisted in the U.S. Army where he rose to the rank of Sergeant and received two battle stars. Swarthout was associate professor of English at Michigan State University in East Lansing from 1951 through 1959 when he transferred to Arizona State University at Tempe. *The Shootist*, the story of a gunfighter who is aged and dying of lung cancer, was obviously written with John Wayne in mind and it was surely no accident that Wayne played the role in the film adaptation. It proved to be Wayne's last film appearance.

Films based on Glendon Swarthout's fiction are *Seventh Cavalry* (Columbia, 1956) directed by Joseph H. Lewis [source unknown], *They Came to Cordura* (Columbia, 1959) directed by Robert Rossen, *The Shootist* (Paramount, 1976) directed by Don Siegel.

T

Taylor, Robert Lewis (1912 —)
Newspaper correspondent, essayist, biographer, and novelist whose only novel of the West, *The Travels of Jaimie McPheeters* (New York: Doubleday, 1958), won the Pulitzer Prize in 1959, born at Carbondale, Illinois. Taylor received his Bachelor's degree from the University of Illinois in 1933. He worked as a newspaper reporter first for a weekly Carbondale paper and then from 1936–1939 for the *St. Louis Post-Dispatch*. In 1939 he joined the staff of *The New Yorker* where he worked until the early 'Sixties except for a stint as an officer in the U.S. Navy during World War II. He specialized as a profile writer with an interest in circus performers.

In *The Travels of Jaimie McPheeters*, Taylor combined his comic skills for creating oddball characters with intensive historical research about the Western emigration movement during the California gold rush period. The story of the 12-year-old Jaimie's adventurous trip from Louisville, Kentucky, to the California gold fields is told in the first person by Jaimie at the age of 17. Since Jaimie's speech is full of Kentucky idiom and boyish hyperbole, it takes on a humorous exuberance that several reviewers found comparable to Huck's dialect in Mark Twain's (q.v.) *The Adventures of Huckleberry Finn* (1884). The enthusiastic critical reception given *The Travels of Jaimie McPheeters* has somewhat dwindled, perhaps because the novel lacks truly epic scope, or perhaps because of inaccuracies in dealing with historical events and Native Americans. Yet the book has a wealth of happy characters.

J.N.

The Travels of Jaimie McPheeters (ABC, 1963–1964) was an hour-long television series with Kurt Russell as Jaimie.

Temple, Dan. See Newton, Dwight Bennett.

Thomason, John William (1893–1944) Author of Western fiction, a full Colonel in the U.S. Marines when he died and a career soldier, born at Huntsville, Texas. Thomason studied at several Southwestern universities before venturing to New York City in 1914 to study at the Art Students' League. He was commissioned a Second Lieutenant in the U.S. Marines in 1917. He was with the American Expeditionary Force during World War I and later saw service in the West Indies, Central America, China, and at sea. His first book, *Fix Bayonets* (New York: Scribner's, 1926), was declared at the time of its publication the first genuine American contribution to the art of the soldier's narrative. Thomason, in his literary career, turned occasionally to biography as with *Jeb Stuart* (New York: Scribner's, 1930), a biography of the Civil War cavalryman, but he proved equally adept at historical novels such as *Gone to Texas* (New York: Scribner's, 1936), set in the

Texas of the 1860s, and *Lone Star Preacher* (New York: Scribner's, 1941). This last is actually a collection of eight short stories dealing with episodes from the life of the Reverend Praxiteles Swan, a fire-eating Methodist minister who becomes a captain in the Texas infantry. These stories, due to their combination of military and historical ingredients, anticipated James Warner Bellah's (q.v.) perhaps more popular series about Fort Starke for *The Saturday Evening Post* in the late 'Forties.

Thompson, Gene. See Lutz, Giles A.

Thompson, Thomas (1913–) Author of formulary Western short stories and novels, born at Dixon, California. Thompson grew up in the Sierra foothills near Fresno, California, where he had a chance to know many working cowboys since it was the period when, according to Thompson, "they were still trailing sheep and cattle to the high pastures, bringing them down in the fall." His stepfather was a fan of Western pulp stories and Thompson himself was an avid reader in his youth; he read all the discarded pulp magazines which developed in him an interest in the formulary Western and which no doubt influenced his own subsequent Western stories. He attended Visalia High School and graduated from Heald Business College in San Francisco. Before turning to writing Western stories in 1940, Thompson worked as a sailor, a night-club entertainer, a male secretary, and a furniture salesman. After 1940 he contributed over 500 stories to pulp magazines and slicks such as *American Magazine, Collier's,* and *The Saturday Evening Post.*

His first Western novel was *Range Drifter* (New York: Doubleday, 1948). Several of his thirteen Westerns were serialized in magazines before being published in book form. *Gunman Brand* (New York: Doubleday, 1951) appeared in *Zane Grey Western Magazine, Shadow of the Butte* (New York: Doubleday, 1952) appeared in *American Magazine,* and *Forbidden Valley* (New York: Popular Library, 1955) appeared in *The Saturday Evening Post.* In the 'Fifties and early 'Sixties, Thompson wrote numerous teleplays for television Western series as *Wagon Train* (NBC, ABC, 1957–1965), *The Rifleman* (ABC, 1958–1962), and *Cimarron City* (NBC, 1958–1959). He worked as story consultant on the Western series *Temple Huston* (NBC, 1963–1964) and was for fourteen years associate producer and occasional scriptwriter for the popular Western series *Bonanza* (NBC, 1959–1973). He wrote one Western novel based on the Bonanza characters entitled *Bonanza: One Man with Courage* (New York: Media, 1966).

As the Western fiction of Clifton Adams, (q.v.) and Lewis B. Patten (q.v.) Thompson wrote well-plotted formulary stories. His knowledge of historical events and people were often woven into his storylines. In *Sundown Riders* (New York: Doubleday, 1950), set in Oregon, the events leading up to the Modoc Indian War of 1872–1873 led by Captain Jack supply part of the story's conflict. The Indians are portrayed as being manipulated and taken advantage of by land-hungry settlers. A white man, who is married to a Modoc woman, is torn between the Indian and the white culture although by the end of the story he decides to form an alliance with the Modocs. Thompson published two collections of short stories, *They Brought Their Guns* (New York: Ballantine, 1947) and *Moment of Glory* (New York: Doubleday, 1961). His short stories are less formulary and include some of his best character studies. In "Gun Job" (1953) an ex-sheriff is forced to take up his duties again as a lawman, despite his wife's protest, in order to protect a family of immigrants and their vision of America and the agrarian dream.

Thompson won the Spur Award from the Western Writers of America for Best Western Short Story in both 1953 and 1954. He also won the Levi Strauss Saddleman Award for "bringing dignity and honor to the legend of the West" in 1971. In 1977, he was awarded a lifetime membership in the Cowboy Hall of Fame. He was co-founder of the Western Writers of America and served as its president for two terms.

Thomas Thompson's Western novels are *They Brought Their Guns* (1947) [short stories], *Range Drifter* (1948), *Broken Valley* (1949), *Sundown Riders* (1950), *Gunman Brand* (1951), *Shadow of the Butte* (1952), *The Steel Web* (1953), *King of Abilene* (1953), *Trouble Rider* (1954), *Forbidden Valley* (1955), *Born to Gunsmoke* (1956), *Brand of a Man* (1958), *Bitter Water* (1960), *Moment of Glory* (1961) [short stories], *Bonanza: One Man with Courage* (1966).

Thompson wrote the screenplays to the Western films *Saddle the Wind* (M-G-M, 1958) directed by Robert Parrish and *Cattle King* (M-G-M, 1963) directed by Tay Garnett.

Thompson has contributed teleplays to the following Western television series: *Wagon Train* (NBC, ABC, 1957–1965), *The Restless Gun* (NBC, 1957–1959), *The Rifle-*man (ABC, 1958–1962), *Cimarron City* (NBC, 1958–1959), *Empire* (NBC, 1962), and *Bonanza* (NBC, 1959–1973).

Traven, B. (1890–1969) Believed to have been born Traven Torsvan at Chicago, Illinois, the son of Norwegian-Swedish immigrants, noted for *The Treasure of the Sierra Madre* (New York: Knopf, 1935) and other novels with a Western setting. Perhaps the most mysterious and secretive of American writers, Traven lived in Mexico City and wrote about the downtrodden, the wanderer, the seaman, and the Mexican Indian. Despite much international attention and a reward offered by *Life* magazine, Traven's identity remained unknown. There were many theories surrounding him. Some thought Traven was Jack London (q.v.); others that he was a black fugitive, an exiled member of the Industrial Workers of the World, and even a son of Kaiser Wilhelm II.

Traven pledged his German publishers to secrecy. He once wrote: "My personal history would not be disappointing to readers, but it is my own affair which I want to keep to myself. . . . I am in fact no way more important than the men who bind my books and the woman who wraps them and the scrubwoman who cleans up the office." He believed American publicity methods "reduced authors to the status of tight rope walkers, sword swallowers, and trained animals."

It is believed that Traven wrote in English and that his books were translated into German for the German publisher. The British editions were translated from the German but his American editions were published from his original manuscripts. For decades critics labeled him "America's great undiscovered novelist," but, in contrast, Traven was hugely successful in Europe. His books spanned over 500 editions in more than 36 languages but his American sales remained meagre.

Traven wrote with a sense of place and vernacular that rings with authenticity. In 1948 Traven, or an associate, responded to charges by critics: "On reading Traven one will find it some times not very easy. His style, his way to express himself, is now and then clumsy, cumbersome, twisted, mangled, and his English will frequently shock men and women of culture, although the ideas he wished to drive home are always clear. . . . Yet one must not forget that he has been a sailor for many years, that he has had to earn his own living and stand on his own two feet since he was 7. Until he was 35 [he] had no more than twenty-six days of education in grammar school. . . ."

The second novel by Traven to be published in the United States was *The Treasure of the Sierra Madre*, a tale of gold hunters and bandits in Mexico. Again, it appeared eight years after its original German publication. *The Bridge in the Jungle* (New York: Knopf, 1938) came nine years after the German edition. *The Rebellion of the Hanged* (New York: Knopf, 1952) was the last of Traven's books to have American publication by Knopf and for a long time it was the only American publication of a book from Traven's six volume series of jungle novels set in Mexico.

A reappraisal of Traven has come slowly. As a literary spokesman for the Mexican Indian, Traven was alone. He shed his coat of Americanism in the same untroubled fashion as the Indians who scatter the gold in *The Treasure of the Sierra Madre*. His is

the freedom of anarchy. Seldom has the call to arms been so moving as in the jungle novels which study the stresses and inequities leading to the Mexican Revolution. The spirit of revolt boils in Traven's prose. He was the master of outrage and observer of the terrible pace and need of redress. "The Indians knew," he wrote, "that there are gods and slaves, and that whoever is not a god can only be a humble and submissive slave. Between the two classes there was no other except that of a fine horse. But when the slave begins to be conscious that his life has become like that of animals, that it is in no way better than theirs, it is because the limits have been reached. The man loses all sense of reason and acts like an animal, like a brute, trying to recover his human dignity."

D.W.

The Treasure of Sierra Madre (Warner's, 1948) was directed by John Huston.

Turner, William O(liver) (1914—)

Author of Western fiction, born at Tacoma, Washington. Turner was raised in Evanston, Illinois, and graduated from Knox College in Galesburg, Illinois. He first began writing full time in 1955 and his first Western novel was *The Proud Diggers* (Boston:

Houghton Mifflin, 1954), published the year before. Turner lived in Iowa and North Carolina working as a newspaper reporter, advertising copy writer, public relations man, and trade magazine editor, before returning to the state of Washington. He also served in the U.S. Army during World War II.

Following publication of his first novel, Turner continued to write Westerns, attempting over the years to encompass as wide a scope of frontier history as he could. Where Turner dealt with Indians, as in *Blood Dance* (New York: Berkley, 1967), or in *Call the Beast Thy Brother* (New York: Doubleday, 1973), he used their presumed savagery (without mitigating circumstances, in most cases) as a conventional dramatic device, and, therefore, his novels tend to lack perspective. Turner's traditional Westerns, as *Shortcut to Devil's Claw* (New York: Berkley, 1977), are best read as purely escape and adventure fiction.

William O. Turner's Western novels are *The Proud Diggers* (1954), *The Settler* (1956), *War Country* (1957), *The Long Rope* (1959), *The Treasure of Fantan Flat* (1961), *The Highlander* (1963), *Destination Doubtful* (1965) [retitled: *Destination Death*], *Gunpoint* (1965), *Five Days to Salt Lake* (1966), *Ride the Vengeance Trail* (1966), *Blood Dance* (1967), *A Man Called Jeff* (1969), *Mayberly's Kill* (1969), *Place of the Trap* (1970), *Thief Hunt* (1973), *Call the Beast Thy Brother* (1973), *Medicine Creek* (1974), *Shortcut to Devil's Claw* (1977), *Kill Call* (1978).

Tuttle, W(ilbur) C(oleman)

(1883–1969) An author noted for his humorous Western novels and stories, often including detective story elements, born at Glendive, Montana Territory. Tuttle's father was a lawman and he heard many stories from him which he later incorporated into his Western fiction. "My education," Tuttle once remarked, "was all garnered in a Montana cow-town school, where you stayed until the seats got so short that you grew callouses on your knees. No graduation—you quit." Tuttle worked variously as a sheepherder, cowpuncher, salesman, railroader, forest ranger, and as a baseball player and team manager. In fact, from 1935 to 1943 he was the president of the Pacific Coast Baseball League.

Tuttle began free-lance writing for the Western pulp magazines in 1915 and published his first book of Western fiction five years later, *Reddy Brant, His Adventures* (New York: Century, 1920). Tuttle wrote his pulp stories under his own name and also as William C. Coleman and W.C. Coleman. An early association with the motion picture industry led Tuttle to write original stories for the screen or to have his pulp fiction adapted for two-reel films such as *The Man with the Punch* (Universal, 1922) which was an early Hoot Gibson vehicle. Buck Jones in particular was fond of Tuttle's stories and brought more than one of them to the screen, including Tuttle's *The Red Head from Sun Dog* (Boston: Houghton Mifflin, 1930) which formed the basis for one of Jones' better chapter plays, *The Red Rider* (Universal, 1934).

Tuttle may have borrowed his idea of range detectives from Frank W. Spearman (q.v.), but it was Tuttle who perfected this as a format for Westerns and thus influenced a number of later writers, such as William Colt MacDonald (q.v.) in his Gregory Quist books, as well as contemporaries such as

Clarence E. Mulford (q.v.). But for his somewhat unrealistic heroes, Tuttle's characterizations and his feeling for the West compare favorably with the fiction of H.H. Knibbs (q.v.) and even, at times, that of Eugene Manlove Rhodes (q.v.). A novel as *Thicker Than Water* (Boston: Houghton Mifflin, 1927), with its long prologue in which the reader meets a wide assortment of characters in a Western community, is fascinating until Hashknife Hartley and Sleepy Stevens come upon the scene with their formulary heroism. Both Hartley and Stevens were series characters of Tuttle's, as were Sad Sontag, Cultus Collins, and even Brick Davidson from *The Red Head of Sun Dog*, heroes who have continuing adventures through a number of books. In this way Tuttle was himself imitating Clarence E. Mulford, the latter having created his own saga of interconnected stories about the Bar 20 hands such as Hopalong Cassidy and Johnny Nelson. Such reciprocal influence between Mulford and Tuttle was due in part because they wrote extensively for *Short Story Magazine*.

In the 'Sixties, long after Tuttle had stopped writing, many of his earlier pulp serials were published in the United Kingdom in re-issues by W. Collins Sons & Co., Ltd. It is probably for this reason that Jenni Calder in her book *There Must Be a Lone Ranger* (New York: McGraw-Hill, 1974) singled out Tuttle and T.V. Olsen (q.v.) as among the better contemporary authors of Western fiction on the basis of stories Tuttle had first published in the 'Twenties. However the praise is warranted no matter what the case since it is precisely in the area of humorous Western stories where Tuttle was at his best.

W.C. Tuttle's Western novels are *Reddy Brant, His Adventures* (1920), *The Medicine Man* (1925), *The Flood of Fate* (1926), *Straight Shooting* (1926), *Sad Sontag Plays His Hunch* (1926), *Sun Dog Loot* (1926), *Thicker Than Water* (1926), *Rustlers' Roost* (1927), *The Deadline* (1927), *The Morgan Trail* (1928), *Hashknife of the Canyon Trail* (1928), *Hashknife of the Double Bar 8* (1928) [alternate title: *Arizona Ways*], *Hashknife Lends a Hand* (1929), *Law of the Range* (1929), *Hidden Blood* (1930), *Spooky Riders* (1930), *The Red Head of Sun Dog* (1930), *The Valley of Twisted Trails* (1931), *Mystery at the JHC Ranch* (1932), *The Silver Bar Mystery* (1933), *Loot of the Lazy F* (1933), *Horse-Shoe Luck* (1934), *Rocky Rhodes* (1934), *The Santa Dolores Stage* (1934), *Rifled Gold* (1934), *Tumbling River Range* (1935), *Hashknife of Stormy River* (1935), *The Turquoise Trail* (1935), *The Keeper of Red Horse Pass* (1937), *Bluffer's Luck* (1937), *The Wild Horse Valley* (1938), *Wandering Dogies* (1938), *Singing River* (1939), *Shotgun Gold* (1940), *Ghost Trails* (1940), *The Tin God of Twisted River* (1941), *The Mystery of the Red Triangle* (1942), *The Valley of Vanishing Herds* (1942), *Wolf Pack of Lobo Butte* (1945), *The Trouble Trailer* (1946), *Straws in the Wind* (1948), *The Trail of Deceit* (1951), *Salt for the Tiger* (1952), *Renegade Sheriff* (1953), *Singing Kid* (1953), *Thunderbird Range* (1954), *Mission River Justice* (1954), *The Shadow Shooter* (1955) [alternate title: *Road to the Moon*], *The Shame of Arizona* (1957), *Ghost Guns* (1957), *Danger Trail* (1958), *The King of Dancing Valley* (1958), *The Deputy* (1959), *The Rim Roder* (1959), *Silver Buckshot* (1959), *The Trail to Kingdom Come* (1960), *Outlaw Empire* (1960), *Dynamite Days* (1960), *Galloping Gold* (1961), *Gold at K-Bar-T* (1961), *Diamond Hitch* (1962), *Passengers from Painted Rock* (1962), *The House of the*

Hawk (1963), *Piperock Tales* (1963), *West of Aztec Pass* (1963), *Arizona Drifters* (1964), *Valley of Suspicion* (1964), *Double Trouble* (1964), *Stockade* (1965), *Double-Crossers of Ghost Tree* (1965), *Buckshot Range* (1966), *Montana Man* (1966), *The Payroll of Fate* (1966), *The Lone Wolf* (1967), *Lucky Pardners* (1967), *Me and Rudolph* (1968).

Films based on W.C. Tuttle's Western fiction are *Black Sheep* (Pinnacle, 1921) directed by Paul Hurst [based on the short story "Baa, Baa Black Sheep"], *Fools of Fortune* (American, 1922) directed by Louis Chaudet [based on the short story "Assisting Ananias"], *Peaceful Peters* (Arrow, 1922) directed by Louis King [based on the short story "Peaceful"], *The Sheriff of Sun Dog* (Arrow, 1922) directed by Louis King [based on the short story "The Sheriff of Sun Dog"], *The Man with the Punch* (Universal, 1922) directed by Ernst Laemmle [based on the short story of the same title], *The Devil's Dooryard* (Arrow, 1923) directed by Louis King [based on the short story of the same title], *The Law Rustlers* (Arrow, 1923) directed by Louis King [based on the short story of the same title], *Spawn of the Desert* (Arrow, 1923) directed by Louis King [based on the short story of the same title], *The Prairie Pirate* (PDC, 1925) directed by Edmund Mortimer [based on the short story "The Yellow Seal"], *The Border Sheriff* (Universal, 1926) directed by Robert N. Bradbury [based on the short story

"Straight Shooting"], *The Fighting Peacemaker* (Universal, 1926) directed by Clifford S. Smith [based on the short story of the same title], *The Wild Horse Stampede* (Universal, 1926) directed by Albert Rogell [based on the short story "Blind Trails"], *Driftin' Sands* (FBO, 1928) directed by Wallace W. Fox [based on the short story "Fate of the Wolf"], *The Cheyenne Kid* (RKO, 1933) directed by Robert Hill [based on the short story "Sir Peegan Passes"], *The Red Rider* (Universal, 1934) directed by Louis Friedlander [a fifteen chapter serial] [based on *The Red Head from Sun Dog*], *Rocky Rhodes* (Universal, 1934) directed by Al Raboch, *Lawless Valley* (RKO, 1938) directed by David Howard [source unknown], *The Fargo Kid* (RKO, 1940) directed by Edward Killy [source unknown], (Note: according to industry sources, during the years 1938–1940 Tuttle worked for the story department at RKO Pictures and, therefore, both *Lawless Valley* and *The Fargo Kid* appear to be original stories written for the screen), *Wildfire* (Action Pictures, 1945) directed by Robert Tansey [source unknown].

Hashknife Hartley (Mutual, 1950) was a radio series for one season, based on Tuttle's range detective, and starred Frank Morton in the role of Hartley.

Twain, Mark. See Clemens, Samuel.

Uriel, Henry. See Faust, Frederick.

V

Van Every, Dale (1896 —) Historian and author of Western fiction, born at Levering, Michigan. Van Every served in the Army ambulance Service from 1917–1919 where he achieved the rank of Second Lieutenant. He received his Bachelor's degree in history from Stanford University in 1920. From 1920–1928, he worked as an editor and correspondent for United Press in New York and Washington, D.C. Van Every followed his career in journalism with a fifteen-year stint in Hollywood as a screenwriter and a producer of drama and comedy films at Metro-Goldwyn-Mayer and Paramount studios. It was not until 1943, the year Van Every decided to become a fulltime free-lance writer, that he made use of his educational background in history and his first novel, *Westward the River* (New York: Putnam's 1945), appeared two years later.

The majority of Van Every's historical novels deal with the American frontier—West of the Appalachian Mountains and East of the Mississippi River—during the late Eighteenth century and early Nineteenth century, although his second novel, *The Shining Mountains* (New York: Messner, 1948), is set primarily in the Far West. "We are accustomed to imagine the West of the Indian fighter, the cowboy, the United States cavalryman," Van Every wrote in his Afterword to *The Shining Mountains*. "We cannot so readily envisage the earlier West before the covered wagon, with its special dangers, simplicities and rewards." Van Every attempted to recreate this period of history in the novel through use of his protagonist, Matt Morgan, an early version of the mountain man, and historical people as Meriwether Lewis and William Clark. The journals of Lewis and Clark, John Bradbury, Zebulon M. Pike, Thomas Nuttall, and James O. Pattie, all of whom were early explorers of the Far West region, were used for background material and local color.

The Ohio frontier was the subject of *Bridal Journey* (New York: Messner, 1950), as it was in his later books, *The Voyagers* (New York: Holt, Rinehart, 1957) and *The Scarlet Feather* (New York: Rinehart, 1959).

His fourth book, *The Captive Witch* (New York: Messner, 1951), deals with the opening of the West in 1779 and includes among its list of characters George Rogers Clark. The greatest earthquake known to have hit the North American continent served as background for *The Trembling Earth* (New York: Messner, 1953) which is set in Missouri. A collection of excerpts from five of his novels—*Westward the River, The Shining Mountains, Bridal Journal, The Captive Witch*, and *The Trembling Earth*—was the basis for Van Every's *Our Country Then* (New York: Holt, Rinehart, 1958) in which he wanted to give the reader an overview of American's first frontier. A brief essay preceded each excerpt to put it into its historical perspective.

In 1956 Van Every published *Men of the Western Waters* (Boston: Houghton Mifflin, 1956), an historical study of the making of America between the years of 1781 and 1794. In the early 'Sixties he began work on his four volume comprehensive history of the Westward movement. The tetralogy—*Forth to the Wilderness* (New York: Morrow, 1961), *A Company of Heroes* (New York: Morrow, 1962), *Ark of Empire* (New York: Morrow, 1963), and *Final Challenge* (New York: Morrow, 1964), this latter being compared to Theodore Roosevelt's (q.v.) *The Winning of the West* (New York: Putnam's, 1900)—focuses on outstanding individuals among the early pioneers in the Westward movement. His next book, *Disinherited: The Lost Birthright of the American Indian* (New York: Morrow, 1966), is a non-fiction work that examines the removal of the Five Civilized Tribes from the Southeastern region of the United States in the 1830s. *The Day the Sun Died* (New York: Little, Brown, 1971) also deals with Native Americans. The story centers around the Ghost Dance, the religious movement which spread throughout the Western Indian nations, beginning in 1889 with the vision of the Piute Messiah, Wovoka, and which culminated in the massacre at Wounded Knee on 29 December 1890. Van Every was sympathetic in his treatment of the Native American and included a mixed-blood girl and a white-educated Sioux among his characters. He took the liberty of making the artist-writer Frederic Remington (q.v.) a major character in the story. Remington had in reality covered the 1890 war for *Harper's* magazine, but as Van Every wrote in his Afterword to *The Day the Sun Died*, "there is no evidence that he took as active a part in the incidents of the campaign as the story has presumed."

Van Every's vast knowledge and in-depth research of frontier life and Native American culture along with his ability to recreate and bring to life various periods of American history through use of historical events and personalities, detail, and local color, make his books an important contribution to our understanding of the Westward movement. His works were highly acclaimed for their authenticity in recreating frontier life in addition to being entertaining and worthwhile reading.

W

Waters, Frank (1902 —) Considered by some critics and scholars to be the most distinguished Western writer of the Twentieth century, born at Colorado Springs, Colorado. Waters' mother was descended from an old Southern family and his father was a mixed-blood. As a child, Waters made frequent trips to a Ute Indian encampment where the dancing and the beating of drums seemed to be part of the pulsing of the human heart as well as of the earth itself.

At Colorado College in 1921–1924 Waters studied engineering and his first job was in the Wyoming oil fields. Then followed eleven years as an engineer with the Southern California Telephone Company, during which time he wrote his first novel, *Fever Pitch* (New York: Liveright, 1930), as well as *The Wild Earth's Nobility* (New York: Liveright, 1935), and the first drafts of *The Yogi of Cockroach Court* (New York: Rinehart, 1947) and *The Earp Brothers of Tombstone* (New York: Clarkson Potter, 1960).

He began to write full time in 1936, in Colorado, and then lived and wrote in Mora and Taos, New Mexico. With the exception of a few years during World War II, Waters lived in the Taos area, buying an adobe house at Arroyo Seco in 1947 and occupying it in the summers until he moved in during the winter of 1956–1957. The house was across a dirt road from Pueblo land, the scene of Waters' fictional triumph, *The Man Who Killed the Deer* (New York: Farrar and Rinehart, 1942), one of the best novels ever written about the Native American. Relatively neglected at first, it was resurrected by the University of Denver Press in 1951, reprinted again by Allan Swallow in 1954, grew in reputation through printings in Germany, Great Britain, and France, and finally emerged again in this country in paperback editions. It has since become a staple in college courses in Western American literature.

Psychologically, Waters was a Jungian, so that his methods involved the unconscious and its archetypal images. Jung himself, on a trip to America, visited the Taos Pueblo and was strengthened in the belief that true knowledge comes from the heart, intuitively, and not from the rational mind. In his fiction, Waters' search has been for unity, oneness, harmony, and those primal sources which have been scorned by modern civilization. A contemplative man, devout in his own way, Waters never worried about his lack of commercial success but remained quietly convinced of the rightness of his beliefs.

However, his novels are not tracts or sermons. Waters could tell a good story, relying heavily on personal family experience: in his Colorado mining trilogy, consisting of *The Wild Earth's Nobility, Below Grass Roots* (New York: Liveright, 1937), and *The Dust within the Rock* (New York: Farrar and Rinehart, 1941) which were revised and re-issued in one volume as *Pike's Peak* (Chicago: Swallow Press, 1971); and in sensitively portraying several ethnic groups in another trio of novels—mixed-bloods in *The Yogi of Cockroach Court* (New York: Rinehart, 1947), the Pueblo Indians in *The*

Man Who Killed the Deer, and the Spanish in *People of the Valley* (New York: Farrar and Rinehart, 1941). Maria del Valle of *People of the Valley,* although archetypal in her significance and function, is one of the great female characters in American fiction. Indeed, one of Waters' virtues as a novelist was his ability to create real and meaningful women, even though they usually serve as minor characters.

A reliance on the eternal earth was Waters' major concern, seen in Rogier's search into the heart of the mountain (in *Pike's Peak*), in Maria's preoccupation with all that crawls and grows upon the earth, and in the Pueblos' insistence upon the holiness of their particular mountain and its Blue Lake. *The Man Who Killed the Deer* was, in fact, an influential part of the long Pueblo struggle to have their sacred lake restored to them, which was finally done by an act of Congress in 1970.

J.R.M.

Although not a critical study, a good introduction to Frank Waters is *Conversations with Frank Waters* (Chicago: Swallow Press, 1971) edited by John R. Milton. Also suggested are *Frank Waters* (New York: Twayne Publishers, 1973) by Thomas J. Lyon and *Frank Waters* (Austin: Steck-Vaughn, 1969) by Martin Bucco.

Watts, Peter C(hristopher)

(1919 —) Author of Western fiction, under his own name and the pseudonyms Matt Chisholm and Cy James, born at Maida Vale, London, England. Watts was educated at a private school and attended art school. Finding it difficult to succeed with his second "serious" novel, Watts, who had studied North American Indians, decided to make use of this knowledge by trying his hand at a Western novel. He read books by Luke Short (q.v.), Frank O'Rourke, and Les Savage, Jr., all of whom Watts felt were good storytellers who drew well-rounded characters. After the publication of his first Western, written under the pen-name Matt Chisholm, *Halfbreed* (London: Panther, 1958), Watts began submitting a manuscript a month to his publisher. He continued to reside in London, although his major preoccupation was with the American West.

In 1963 he began the McAllister series, also written under the pen-name Matt Chisholm. The first book in this series of thirty books was *The Hard Men* (New York: Mayflower, 1963). Of Western heroes and his own Rem McAllister, Watts once said, "although a hero need not be whiter than white and though it is permissible for him to be something of a heller, his fundamental characteristics should be a kind that can be admired freely by a reader. As my hero, McAllister says: 'I never hit a woman— unless she deserved it.' A hero may be tough and mean, but he is never pretty. He must not betray a trust." So it is with Watts' heroes. Watts also wrote the Storm series and the Blade series under the pseudonym Matt Chisholm as well as two non-fiction books for young readers.

Under the pen-name Cy James he wrote the Spur series. When asked to write Westerns that fell into the "blood and soil" school of Terry Harknett's (q.v.) Edge series, Watts refused, stating he believed that Western writers have a responsibility to their readers and to themselves and should be able to "enjoy" writing about their creations. Under his own name Watts wrote two mainline fiction works and *A Dictio-*

nary of the Old West 1850–1900 (New York: Knopf, 1977) as well as a number of books under the pen-names Tom Owen and Duncan Mackinlock.

Peter Watts' Western novels as Matt Chisholm are *Halfbreed* (1958), *Hodge* (1958), *Riders at the Ford* (1958), *Hang a Man High* (1959), *Sutter's Strike* (1959), *The Saga of Trent Godden* (1959), *Blood on the Land* (1959), *Joe Blade* (1959), *Never Give Ground* (1959), *Wild Mustanger* (1959), *The Law of Ben Hodge* (1959), *A Posse of Violent Men* (1960), *Fury at Tombstone* (1960), *Pursuit in the Sun* (1960), *Prayer for a Gunman* (1960), *Hangrope for a Gunman* (1960), *Advance to Death* (1961), *A Rage of Guns* (1961), *Bitter Range* (1962), *Three for Vengeance* (1963), *The Proud Horseman* (1963), *The Hard Men* (1963), *Death at Noon* (1963), *The Hangman Rides Tall* (1963), *McAllister* (1963), *The Last Gun* (1966), *Cash McCord* (1966), *Spur to Death* (1966), *Hunted* (1966), *Gun Marshal* (1967), *Range War* (1967), *Indian Scout* (1967), *Apache Kill* (1967), *Kiowa* (1967), *Death Trail* (1967), *Gun Lust* (1968), *A Bullet for Brody* (1968), *High Peak* (1968), *Spur* (1968), *Three Canyons to Death* (1968), *The Trail of Fear* (1968), *Tough to Kill* (1968), *McAllister Justice* (1969), *Rage of McAllister* (1969), *Hell for McAllister* (1969), *McAllister Strikes* (1969), *Kill McAllister* (1969), *McAllister Rides* (1969), *McAllister's Fury* (1969), *McAllister Fights* (1969), *Gunsmoke for McAllister* (1969), *Blood on McAllister* (1969), *Hang McAllister* (1969), *McAllister Gambles* (1970), *McAllister Says No* (1970), *Shoot McAllister* (1970), *Trail of McAllister* (1970), *Stampede* (1971), *Hard Texas Trail* (1971), *Riders West* (1971), *McAllister Runs Wild* (1972), *Brand McAllister* (1972), *Battle of McAllister* (1972), *One Notch to Death* (1972), *One Man—One Gun* (1972),

McAllister Trapped (1973), *A Breed of Men* (1973), *Thunder in the West* (1973), *Battle Fury* (1973), *Blood on the Hills* (1973), *McAllister Must Die* (1974), *Vengeance of McAllister* (1974), *The McAllister Legend* (1974), *The Indian Incident* (1978), *The Tucson Conspiracy* (1978), *The Pecos Manhunt* (1978), *The Laredo Assignment* (1979), *The Colorado Virgins* (1979), *The Mexican Proposition* (1979).

Watts' novels as Cy James are *The Brasada Guns* (1961), *The Gun is My Brother* (1961), *The Violent Hills* (1961), *Death Rides Fast* (1964), *The Battle of Red Rock* (1964), *Ride the Far Country* (1964), *Hellion* (1964), *Hangrope Posse* (1965), *Gun-Rage* (1965), *Blood Creek* (1965), *Gun Hand* (1965), *Savage Horseman* (1966), *Man in the Saddle* (1966), *The Running Gun* (1966), *My Gun is Justice* (1966), *The Cimmaron Kid* (1969), *Longhorn* (1970), *Gun* (1971), *The Brave Ride Tall* (1971), *Blood at Sunset* (1972).

Wayne, Joseph. See Overholser, Wayne D.

Welch, James (1940 —) Native

American poet and novelist born at Browning, Montana. Welch was the son of a Blackfoot father and a Gros Ventre mother. His early education was at Blackfoot and Fort Belknap schools in Montana. He attended the University of Minnesota and Northern Montana College and eventually received a Bachelor's degree from the University of Montana. After doing manual labor, counseling in Upward Bound, and working as a firefighter, Welch moved onto a farm outside Missoula, Montana, to give himself more time for his writing.

Welch's poems, collected in *Riding the Earthboy 40* (New York: Harper's, 1971; revised 1975), are usually written in the first person and are characterized by a strong perception and animation of natural objects. The poems are filled with the loneliness of separation from friends and a longing to be part of the rhythms of Nature which Welch saw as the inheritance of his American Indian blood, but which he only seemed to experience momentarily. "Desperate is my song," he wrote in "In My Lifetime," "I run these woman hills, translate wind to mean a kind of life. . . ."

Welch's novel, *Winter in the Blood* (New York: Harper's, 1974), incorporates the same themes and many of the same images Welch used in his poetry. The title, for example, is taken from a line of "In My Lifetime."

The unnamed 32-year-old narrator/protagonist says, "I was as distant from myself as a hawk from the moon," and divides his time between laboring on a reservation farm belonging to his mother, aimlessly drinking or fighting in Montana small-town barrooms, and dreaming of the past, especially the death of his father and of his brother.

Reviews of *Winter in the Blood* praised the novel for its sharp, economic detail and sparse dialogue. Welch's barroom conversations are especially well done: the short, often disconnected phrases revealing the sad, spiritual distance between the speakers. The book also resembles N. Scott Momaday's (q.v.) novel, *House Made of Dawn* (New York: Harper's, 1969), in that both are stories of alienated native Americans—modern Americans who seek meaning in their lives through a discovery of their ancestral heritage. Welch, however, saw the regaining of such a heritage as less dramatically regenerative than did Momaday. Learning of the almost mythic past of his Blackfoot grandmother, the narrator of *Winter in the Blood* subsequently does no more than admit his love for his dead father and brother and acknowledges his need for love in his unhappy present life.

J.N.

Wellman, Paul I(selin) (1898–1966)
Novelist and historian of the West, born at Enid, Oklahoma. When Wellman was less than a year old, his parents relocated to West Africa. His father, a physician, practiced tropical medicine and his mother did mission work with the Bantus of Angola. Wellman actually spoke Umbundu before he did English. He remained in Africa another ten years before he was sent, together with his brother, to live with an aunt in Utah where he attended non-Mormon schools. His parents, totally incompatible, were divorced when he was 14. He later went to live with his mother in Cimarron, Kansas. His early historical works, *Death on the Prairie* (New York: Macmillan, 1934), *Death in the Desert* (New York: Macmillan, 1935)—concerned with the Indian wars — and *The Trampling Herd* (New York: Carrick and Evans, 1939), were an outgrowth of this period as well as his novels *Broncho Apache* (New York: Macmillan, 1936) and *Jubal Troop* (New York: Carrick and Evans, 1939). It was Wellman's good fortune to be exposed at a youthful age to the difficulties of human relationships in terms of his parents' problems and hence his dealings with sexual and romantic situations in his novels tended to be far more mature than the "true love" naiveté typical of formulary Western fiction. Wellman later combined his two histories of the Indian wars into a single volume, *Death on Horseback* (Philadelphia: Lippincott, 1947), which was a romantic, popular, but not altogether reliable account even in revision.

Wellman attended the University of Wichita in 1918 and in 1918–1919 he joined the U.S. Army. After World War I, Wellman worked for the next twenty years as a newspaper journalist. By the time he was employed by the *Kansas City Star,* he customarily worked all day at the paper and worked all night on his various books, bringing about a physical breakdown. His doctors told him that he must give up journalism or authorship and so, in 1944, Wellman resigned from the *Star* and with his wife and son relocated to Los Angeles. A two-year period working as a screenwriter, first for Warner Bros. and then for M-G-M, intervened before Wellman finally settled down solely to writing books full-time, working only in the morning hours. His novel *Angel with Spurs* (Philadelphia: Lippincott, 1942) was followed in the 'Fifties by a number of books which are notable for their strong characterizations, men as well as women, and their realistic plot situations, the most significant of which are *The Comancheros* (New York: Doubleday, 1952), *The Iron Mistress* (New York: Doubleday, 1954), and *Ride the Red Earth* (New York: Doubleday, 1958). Equally of interest is Wellman's second reworking of *Death on Horseback* for a two-volume history, *Indian Wars and Warriors, East* and *Indian Wars and Warriors, West* (Boston: Houghton Mifflin, 1959). Wellman was a friend to the Indian nations at a time when it was not fashionable to be one and anticipated the posture later historians were eventually to follow in treating the subject.

Paul I. Wellman's Western novels are

Broncho Apache (1936), *Jubal Troop* (1939), *Angel With Spurs* (1942), *The Bowl of Brass* (1944), *The Walls of Jericho* (1947), *The Iron Mistress* (1951), *The Comancheros* (1952), *Ride the Red Earth* (1958), *Magnificent Destiny* (1962), *The Buckstones* (1967).

Films based on Wellman's Western fiction are *The Iron Mistress* (Warner's, 1952) directed by Gordon Douglas, *Apache* (United Artists, 1954) directed by Robert Aldrich [based on *Broncho Apache*], *Jubal* (Columbia, 1956) directed by Delmar Daves [based on *Jubal Troop*], *The Comancheros* (20th-Fox, 1961) directed by Michael Curtiz.

West, Jessamyn (1902 —) Novelist, essayist, and short story writer who authored a number of stories set in the frontier era, born Mary Jessamyn West near North Vernon, Indiana. The Wests moved to Southern California in 1909, finally settling in Yorba Linda where West's father started a lemon grove. In 1914, a public library opened in Yorba Linda and West became a voracious reader of novels, poetry, and, according to A.S. Shivers in his book *Jessamyn West* (New York: Twayne Publishers, 1972), "a generous helping of socialism à la Jane Addams and Jack London (q.v.), . . . that helped make her sympathetic toward downtrodden minority groups, such as the 'greasers' (Mexican-Americans) in *South of the Angels* [New York: Harcourt, Brace, 1960]."

In 1919, after graduating from Fullerton High School, she enrolled at Whittier College, a Quaker school. Several unfortunate experiences concerning her writing and a composition instructor—experiences so devastating to West that she tried to commit

suicide—caused her to attend Fullerton Junior College in 1920. After returning to Whittier in 1921 she received her Bachelor's degree in 1923, the same year she married Harry Maxwell McPherson. Between the years 1924–1929, West worked as a secretary and a schoolteacher. She decided to further her education and, after attending a summer session at Oxford University in England, she matriculated in the graduate program at the University of California at Berkeley. Before taking her Doctoral orals, which had been delayed due to the illness of one of her examining professors, West was admitted to a sanitorium near Pasadena with a far-advanced case of tuberculosis in both lungs. Her condition was pronounced incurable. However despite the doctors' diagnosis West recovered, although she remained bed-ridden until 1945.

During this period of "horizontal life" West began writing stories. Her first story "99.6" was published in *Broun's Nutmeg* in June, 1939. Her early short stories were published in magazines such as *New Mexico Quarterly, Prairie Schooner, Collier's, Atlantic Monthly, Harper's Bazaar, American Prefaces,* and *Foothills.* Her first book, *The Friendly Persuasion* (New York: Harcourt, Brace, 1945), was a series of previously published stories about the Quaker couple Jess and Eliza Birdwell. The stories are set in Indiana and the book was, according to West, her "love poem to Indiana." The book with its vivid and sensitive depiction of external beauties of Nature and the back country of Indiana in the mid-1800s won West international fame and she began a life of teaching, writing, and traveling. The sequel to *The Friendly Persuasion, Except for Me and Thee* (New York: Harcourt, Brace, 1967), followed twenty-two years later and contained some stories which had been printed in magazines but also some unpublished stories about the charming Birdwell family. Her first novel, *The Witch Diggers* (New York: Harcourt, Brace, 1951), was about a "poor farm" in Southern Indiana and was highly praised for its grotesque and bizarre qualities.

West turned to her own childhood in Yorba Linda for the unified collection of previously published stories, *Cress Delahanty* (New York: Harcourt, Brace, 1953), about a young girl's bewildering adolescence. With *South of the Angels* West attempted a full-scale novel which was structurally more complex than any of her previous books. The story, which included over thirty characters, was set in 1916 in a small community Southeast of Los Angeles which had problems securing water for its agriculture. In *South of the Angels* West was able to evoke a strong feeling of the pioneering spirit reminiscent of the works of Willa Cather (q.v.). *A Matter of Time* (New York: Harcourt, Brace, 1966), a story set in modern California, followed. West also wrote two science fiction stories set in California.

West's novels *Leafy Rivers* (New York: Harcourt, Brace, 1967) which deals with the sexual awakening of a young women in the early 1800s and *The Massacre at Fall Creek* (New York: Harcourt, Brace, 1975) are both set in Indiana, although the former opens and closes in Ohio. *The Massacre at Fall Creek*, West's most ambitious historical novel, deals with the first white men in American history to be charged with first-degree murder for the premeditated massacre of nine Seneca Indians. West had read about the incident, which took place in 1824, years before and stated in the Afterword that, "over the years I remained haunted by the tragic events of the massacre

and the dread dilemmas they must have thrust upon whites and Indians alike; the more so perhaps because I had an Indian grandmother." The novel is sympathetic to the Native American and explores man's relationships with his fellow man and with the land.

A.S. Shivers perhaps summed up West's work best: "The realism of Miss West includes not only fidelity to physical detail and historical accuracy but to human psychology in the tradition of Henry James, whose critical observations she had read approvingly by 1949. She shares James' interest in fine consciences and in stylistic subtleties, but she never carries the cerebral distinctions and meanderings so far as to betray her into tedium."

Jessamyn West collaborated on the screenplay to *Friendly Persuasion* (Allied Artists, 1956) directed by William Wyler and on *The Big Country* (United Artists, 1958) directed by William Wyler.

For further information see *Jessamyn West* (New York: Twayne Publishers, 1972) by A.S. Shivers.

Westwood, Perry. See Holmes, L.P.

White, Stewart Edward (1873–1946) Prolific author of Western and adven-

ture fiction born at Grand Rapids, Michigan. The first years of White's youth were spent in a small mill town in Michigan, then one of the greatest of the lumber producing states. White spent his adolescence in California on a ranch, in the saddle much of the time. He entered high school in Grand Rapids in the third year, only to graduate at 18, president of his class and holder of the five-mile track record. White earned his Bachelor's degree from the University of Michigan in 1895. The next year, 1896, was divided between working for a packing house in Chicago, Illinois, at $6 a week and prospecting for gold in the Black Hills of Dakota. In the fall of 1896, White enrolled at the Columbia University Law School, but he did not finish, although in 1903 he received a Master's degree from the University of Michigan.

White's short stories were praised while he was at Columbia and he sold one of them for $15. He was further encouraged when *Munsey's Magazine* paid him $500 for serial rights to *The Westerners* which appeared in book form in 1901. White went to work for McClurg's in Chicago, a bookstore operated by a publishing house, selling books for $9 a week. He left to try lumberjacking in the Hudson Bay country, writing in his spare time. He composed *The Blazed Trail* (New York: McClure, 1902) in the early hours of each morning and was reassured when he showed it to his stern foreman only to have the foreman stay up until four in the morning to finish it.

In April, 1904, White married Elizabeth Grant of Newport, Rhode Island, and the couple spent their honeymoon camping and hunting through Arizona, and went on to undertake similar journeys in 1906 to California and Wyoming. The outgrowth of the time spent in Arizona was *Arizona Nights*

Cover of Stewart Edward White's classic book Arizona Nights *(New York: McClure, 1907).*

(New York: McClure, 1907), which remained White's personal favorite among his works, along with *The Silent Places* (New York: McClure, 1904); in fact, "The Rawhide," the longest of the short stories and sketches in *Arizona Nights*, White continued to regard as his most coherent piece of work.

White followed the example of Theodore Roosevelt (q.v.) and went to Africa from which emerged a wealth of stories and novels. Eventually he came to settle in Santa Barbara, California, then moving upstate to Burlingame, doing historical research in the library at Stanford University. By the time White came to write his autobiography, *Speaking for Myself* (New York: Doubleday, 1945), he had fifty-three books to his credit, more than half of them with a Western or Far North setting. As Jack Schaefer (q.v.) put it in his anthology *Out West* (Boston: Houghton Mifflin, 1955), "inevitably, with such output and such range, the work is uneven. But Stewart Edward White has covered American pioneering, and particularly Western phases of it, in fiction and non-fiction, more thoroughly than almost any other writer." White himself attached no special significance, apparently, to this effort. In *Speaking for Myself* he had this to say: "Writing is a good job. And in making that statement I am not referring to the fact that it is sometimes well paid, or that a man's time is his own to arrange as he pleases, or that he can live where he chooses, or that it makes for fame. Writing is a good profession because it is a friendly profession; it makes friends. And friends are good things to have, even if you never see them; yes, even if you never hear of them. I am just enough of a mystic to believe that the establishment of even unknown bonds of affinity is somehow strengthening to the soul."

Writing about *Arizona Nights*, Lawrence Clark Powell in *Southwest Classics* (Los Angeles: Ward Ritchie, 1974) commented that "by including folklore, tall tales, and cowboy lingo, White was closer to Gene Rhodes (q.v.) than to Zane Grey (q.v.). His story of buried treasure in Baja California anticipated [J. Frank] Dobie's *Coronado's Children* [Dallas: Southwest Press, 1930], and in the novelette 'The Rawhide,' which crowns *Arizona Nights*, he foretold Conrad Richter's (q.v.) *The Sea of Grass*

[New York: Knopf, 1937] and Willa Cather's (q.v.) *A Lost Lady* [New York: Knopf, 1923]."

Stewart Edward White's Western and Far North novels are *The Westerners* (1901), *The Claim Jumpers* (1901), *The Blazed Trail* (1902), *Conjuror's House* (1903), *The Silent Places* (1904), *Arizona Nights* (1907) [short stories], *The Riverman* (1908), *The Rules of the Game* (1909), *Gold* (1913), *Gray Dawn* (1915), *Rose Dawn* (1920), *The Killer* (1920), *On Tiptoe* (1922), *Skookum Chuck* (1925), *Secret Harbour* (1925), *The Long Rifle* (1932), *Ranchero* (1933), *Pole Star* (1934) [with H. De Vigne], *Folded Hills* (1934), *Wild Geese Calling* (1940), *Stampede* (1942).

Films based on Stewart Edward White's Western fiction are *The Westerners* (Hodkinson, 1919) directed by Edward Slomen, *The Call of the North* (Paramount, 1921) directed by Joseph Henabery [based on *Conjuror's House*], *The Killer* (Pathé, 1921) directed by Howard Hickman remade as *Mystery Ranch* (Fox, 1932) directed by David Howard, *The Gray Dawn* (Hodkinson, 1922) directed by Eliot Howe and Jean Hersholt, *Arizona Nights* (FBO, 1927) directed by Lloyd Ingraham, *Under a Texas Moon* (Warner's, 1930) directed by Michael Curtiz [based on the short story "Two-Gun Man"].

In addition to White's own rather gossipy and scarcely chronological autobiography, *Speaking for Myself* (New York: Doubleday, 1945), an excellent study can be found about White's life and work in *Stewart Edward White, His Life And Literary Career* (Los Angeles: University of Southern California, 1960) by Edna Rosemary Butte.

Wilder, Laura Ingalls (1867–
1957) Author of the "Little House" books
for juveniles which serve as useful documents in our understanding of what everyday life was for pioneer women, born Laura
Ingalls in a log cabin at Lake Pepin, Wisconsin. The nomadic Ingalls family did not
remain in any one place for more than a two-
year period until 1879, when they finally
settled permanently in De Smet, Dakota
Territory. In 1885, after a period of teaching
school, Laura married Almanzo Wilder, a
homesteader living in the De Smet area. In
1894, Wilder's husband built a home by
hand in the Ozarks region of Missouri,
which Laura later called Rocky Ridge Farm
and which became a permanent nonprofit
exhibit in Mansfield, Missouri. Wilder began her writing career by contributing a
column, "As a Farm Woman Thinks," to a
local newspaper.

Feeling a profound loss over the deaths
of her parents and sister, Wilder wrote her
first book, *The Little House in the Big
Woods* (New York: Harper's, 1932), an autobiographical account of her early family life
in Wisconsin, which was very successful.
She quickly followed it with *Farmer Boy*
(New York: Harper's, 1933), the only novel
in which Wilder does not appear as a character, which is about her husband's boyhood in upstate New York. *Little House on
the Prairie* (New York: Harper's, 1935) continues the story of her first novel and is set
in Kansas during 1869–1871 after the Ingalls family journeys Westward by covered
wagon. *On the Banks of Plum Creek* (New
York: Harper's, 1937) tells about Wilder's

adventures with her pioneering family in
the wheat field region of Minnesota during
1874–1876. In *By the Shores of Silver Lake*
(New York: Harper's, 1939) the Ingalls family takes up homesteading in the Dakota
Territory. The extremely hard conditions of
the winter season of 1880–1881 in the Dakota Territory are covered in *Long Winter*
(New York: Harper's, 1940). In *Little Town
on the Prairie* (New York: Harper's, 1941),
Wilder is 15 and working in town to help get
her sister Mary, who is blind, through college. The last book published before
Wilder's death, *These Happy Golden Years*
(New York: Harper's, 1943), is about the
period when Wilder was 16 and in order to
teach school is forced to board with the
Brewster family who lives on an isolated
land claim. The character represented by
Mrs. Brewster, who suffers from depression
and melancholia due to the extreme conditions of the harsh and isolated environment,
stands in direct contrast to other female
characters, as well as Wilder herself, who
accepted the challenges of pioneer life.

Rose Wilder Lane (q.v.), Wilder's
daughter who also became a writer, discovered a manuscript, written in pencil on a
school tablet as all of Wilder's manuscripts
were, after Wilder's death. The posthumous
novel, *The First Four Years* (New York:
Harper's, 1971), deals with Wilder's early
years of marriage to Almanzo (Manly in the
book). The book, as the others in the series,
shows the hardships and deprivations the
newlyweds encountered including bliz-
zards, loss of crops due to hailstorms, periods of extreme heat, and grasshoppers, a fire
which destroys most of their possessions, a
bout with diptheria which leaves Wilder's
husband partially paralyzed, and the loss of
a son shortly after birth. Wilder also depicts

in all of her stories the joys and love shared by the early pioneers in their devotion to each other in their attempt to realize their agrarian dream. The books show the great integrity and strength the early pioneers, especially the women, had in the face of frontier adversity. As Willa Cather's (q.v.) pioneer stories and Lucia Moore's award-winning novel, *The Wheel and the Hearth* (New York: Ballantine, 1953), Wilder's "Little House" books are a celebration of the pioneering spirit of yesteryear. In her later years Wilder said about her books in an open letter to her readers, "the way we live and our schools are much different now, so many changes have made living and learning easier. But the real things haven't changed. It is still best to be honest and truthful; to make the most of what we have; to be happy with simple pleasures and to be cheerful and have courage when things go wrong."

The television series *Little House on the Prairie* (NBC, 1973–1982) is based on Wilder's "Little House" books.

For further information see *Laura* (Chicago: H. Regnery, 1976) by Donald Zochert.

Wister, Owen (1860–1938) An author who made the cowboy a popular hero among Eastern readers with his novel, *The*

Virginian (New York: Macmillan, 1902), born at Philadelphia, Pennsylvania. Wister was educated at St. Paul's, Concord, New Hampshire, and attended schools in England and Switzerland. He graduated from Harvard in 1882 with honors, having majored in music. Among his acquaintances at Harvard was the man who probably would have more influence on him than anyone else, the future Rough Rider, rancher, and President of the United States, Theodore Roosevelt (q.v.). While still an undergraduate, Wister wrote a story "The New Swiss Family Robinson" which was published in the *Lampoon*. Following graduation, Wister continued his music studies for two years in Europe. At his father's insistence, Wister returned to the States in 1884 and became a clerk at the Union Safe Deposit Vaults in New York City. Wister was also a founder of the Tavern Club of Boston of which American novelist, William Dean Howells, was the first president. It was Howells who recommended that Wister not publish a novel he wrote in collaboration with his cousin, Langdon Mitchell, titled *A Wise Man's Son*, because it was supposedly too realistic and too shocking for the American reading public.

A nervous breakdown prompted Wister's physician to suggest he go to Wyoming for a sojourn, which he did in 1885. It was the first of fifteen trips West which Wister would make over the next ten years, initially for his health, and then to find material for his fiction. During the years 1885–1888 Wister attended Harvard Law School and, upon graduation, became a member of the Philadelphia Bar Association, affiliating himself with attorney Francis Rawle's office. In 1891, after having returned to Wyoming for the fifth summer in search of health and big game, Wister wrote his first two Western stories, "Hank's Woman" and "How Lin McLean Went East," published in 1892 in *Harper's* magazine and for which he was paid $175. The stories proved so popular with readers that by 1893 Henry Alden, the editor of *Harper's,* worked out a contract with Wister whereby the magazine would finance him on a trip throughout the West, promote the stories, and engage Western artist and author, Frederic Remington (q.v.), to do the illustrations. It was through this collaboration with Remington that a friendship developed between the two men that was to have long range significance on the way in which the West was conceived by the Eastern Establishment and which has been narrated in some detail in Ben Merchant Vorphal's book, *My Dear Wister: The Frederic Remington–Owen Wister Letters* (Palo Alto, California: American West Publishing, 1973), and, in more scholarly terms, and taking more fully into account Theodore Roosevelt's impact on both men, by G. Edward White in *The Eastern Establishment and the Western Experience* (New Haven: Yale University Press, 1968).

It has been said that through writing almost exclusively for magazine publication Wister unduly limited himself and his ability to be experimental and daring in his fiction. While this may or may not be true, it is very evident that Wister was primarily a short story writer and neither of his novels with Western settings are quite that, being rather series of short stories loosely connected by narrative bridges. Wister's fundamental instincts were those of an Eastern snob, a frame of mind from which he never escaped, although he was utterly determined to remain wholly faithful to his sources and to describe actual events he had seen in the West. In his first collection of stories, *Red Men and White* (New York:

Harper's, 1896), Wister revealed a condescending attitude toward the Indian nations which he was to maintain throughout his Western writings. This was coupled with a disproportionate admiration for veteran Indian fighters as General Crook who, Wister felt, knew better how to deal with the Indians than Easterners who were "rancid with philanthropy and ignorance."

Vorphal in *My Dear Wister* reprinted Wister's essay "The Evolution of the Cow-Puncher" which Wister first published in 1895. In it Wister set forth his vision of the cowboy as a modern incarnation of the medieval knight of romance. "Destiny tried her latest experiment upon the Saxon," he wrote, "and plucking him from the library, the haystack, and the gutter, set him upon his horse; then it was that, face to face with the eternal simplicity of death, his modern guise fell away and showed once again the medieval man. It was no new type, no product of the frontier, but just the original kernal of the nut with the shell broken." There was almost no basis for this in reality. It was a preconceived notion Wister took with him from the East and projected onto the cow-puncher. But it was a notion that struck the fancy of the East. Other Easterners soon began to take over Wister's imagery, some of them as Clarence E. Mulford (q.v.) writing books about the West for seventeen years before ever going there, others as Zane Grey (q.v.) imbued with all the romance but going West on visits to get descriptions of Nature as a backdrop for glamourous fantasies of knight errantry.

Wister's first Western "novel" was *Lin McLean* (New York: Harper's, 1897), consisting of six short stories which he strung together about the same central character. As Specimen Jones, the horse soldier Wister had first introduced in *Red Men and White,*

Artist Frederic Remington's conception of Owen Wister's Lin McLean.

Lin McLean is more a Westerner, and therefore less an Easterner's conception of a Westerner, than any of Wister's later creations, including the far more well-known Virginian.

In the novel, Lin falls in love twice, the first time with Katie Lusk, a hash-slinger from Sidney, Nebraska, who, it turns out, has a husband still living from whom she has never been divorced and to whom she returns once he has money again and Lin has lost his money. The second romance is with the wooden, lifeless, perverse Jessamine Buckner, a girl from Kentucky who is characterized by her unrealism when she is introduced—her brother is a convicted thief which fact she steadfastly refuses to acknowledge—and she retains this posture throughout the book to the end. Vorpahl may well be justified in his opinion that in *Lin McLean* Wister created two Lins: ". . . a 'real' one—made of foggy, sentimental stuff—to marry Jessamine Buckner, and another one—fickle, adolescent, sexually attractive, with a mean streak and a killer instinct—to cohabit with Katie Lusk. The former Lin had little but a certain questionable innocence to recommend him. The latter was no 'real' American, but he moved with real verve, spoke with a real edge and generated a real excitement."

It would seem that Wister's own peculiarities constantly interfered with his desire to describe the West and its people as they really were. Romance and marriage in his novels, as in some of his stories, served only to emasculate his cowboys, to make them docile Easterners concerned more with personal ambition, accumulation of wealth, and achieving what would be considered status by Eastern standards, rather than luxuriating in their freedom, the openness and emptiness of the land, and the spontaneity of its inhabitants combined with the West's utter disregard for family background and education. To make his cowboys acceptable heroes to *himself*, as well as to his Eastern readers, Wister felt compelled unconsciously to provide them with Eastern values, and it is for this reason that his stories always fail truthfully to depict the real clash between East and West which has always existed.

The Jimmyjohn Boss and Other Stories (New York: Harper's, 1900), Wister's next story collection, contains a substantially revised version of "Hank's Woman," his first story, which significantly altered the focus from Lin McLean, in the earlier draft, to the Virginian, who was more Wister's kind of Westerner and, by Wister's own admission, a composite prototype, rather than, as Lin, based on an actual person. *The Jimmyjohn Boss* also contains Wister's long story, "Padre Ignazio," a tale of a European priest working in a California mission, which, if highly romanticized, is still one of the finest stories Wister ever wrote.

In his political and social philososphy, Wister was a Progressive and what has come to be called a social Darwinist, meaning that he believed in a natural aristocracy, a survival of the fittest—the fittest being those who measured up closest to his Eastern values. In *The Virginian*, which became a best-seller the month it was published and which has never been out of print since, Wister put this philosophy into the Virginian's mouth when the Virginian tells the narrator, ostensibly Wister: "'Now back East you can be middling and get along. But if you go to try a thing in this Western country, you've got to do it *well*.'" Yet, at the same time, in his notebooks, which were subsequently published as *Owen Wister Out West: His Journals and Letters* (Chicago: University of Chicago Press, 1958), edited by his daughter, Fanny Kemble Wister, Wister lamented the sloth which he felt the West induced in people and it was this lamentation which led to his eventual disillusionment with the West after 1911 and his refusal ever to return there. Wister's only defense against this, apparently, was through exalting his heroes.

Wister had run an earlier version of a chapter from *The Virginian* titled "Balaam and Pedro" in *Harper's* and told in explicit detail how Balaam gouged out the eye of a horse. Theodore Roosevelt, who fancied himself a literary critic, chided Wister for what he felt was a slip in good taste. Wister, intent on retaining Roosevelt's favor, deleted the offensive passage when *The Virginian* was published in book form and even mentioned the deletion in his dedication of the novel to Roosevelt.

There are three basic plots in *The Virginian*. The first deals with the Virginian's conflict with Trampas, established early in the narrative when, in a poker game, Trampas calls the Virginian a son-of-a-bitch—although Wister only implied the epithet by means of a dash—and the Virginian replies with the now famous line, "'When you call me that, *smile*!'" The second conflict is the Virginian's prolonged and belabored love affair with the Bear Creek schoolmarm originally from Bennington, Vermont, Mary Stark Wood, known as Molly. The third conflict is the Virginian's personal rise from being just a footloose cowhand to being foreman on Judge Henry's Sunk Creek Ranch and finally, following his marriage to Molly, the judge's partner. All three con-

Walter Huston (l.) as Trampas and Gary Cooper (r.) as the Virginian in The Virginian *(Paramount, 1929) directed by Victor Fleming.*

flicts are highly Wisterized, which is to say stylized and romanticized.

Wister's heroines, Jessamine Buckner and Molly Wood, are both perversely repelled by the prospect of marital commitment, and both tend to wear poorly on readers. This is above all an indication of how much Wister had changed in the intervening years. When Molly Wood made her first appearance in a Lin McLean story in *Harper's* in 1893, "The Winning of the Biscuit-Shooter," Wister had Lin remark: "'I'm glad I was not raised good enough to appreciate the Miss Woods of this world . . . except at long range.'" In the final version of *The Virginian*, Lin is one of Molly Wood's rejected suitors!

Wister next published *Members of the Family* (New York: Macmillan, 1911), again a collection of short stories, many of them featuring Scipio LeMoyne, whom the Virginian had hired as a cook in *The Virginian*, and of which the first story, "Happy Teeth," featured the Virginian. But what had changed most was the tone.

His last collection of Western stories, *When West Was West* (New York: Macmillan, 1928), was published the same year as Macmillan issued his collected works in eleven volumes. The title itself conveys how Wister felt that the West had vanished, even that of it which he had known, and his stories are shot-through with his feelings of nostalgia and disillusionment. Most of them had been run in *Cosmopolitan* and reflect the kind of cynicism then made popular and typified by the short stories of W. Somerset Maugham, a regular *Cosmopolitan* contributor, as, for example, Wister's "Skip to My Loo" which tells of a man returning home who decides to spend a night with a whore before seeing his wife only to discover that the whore *is* his wife. The last story in the collection is fitting. Titled "At the Sign of the Last Chance," Wister described how one night a group of cowboys in a poker game come to the realization that their time was over and take down the sign of the saloon and bury it in remembrance of a West that was once but is no more.

Roosevelt: The Story of a Friendship, 1880–1919 (New York: Macmillan, 1930) was Wister's last book, a semi-autobiographical tribute to the man who had so overshadowed his life and whose Progressive Republicanism had so inspired Wister's social thought.

The Virginian was produced four times under the original title (Paramount, 1914) directed by Cecil B. DeMille, (Preferred Pictures, 1923) directed by Tom Forman, (Paramount, 1929) directed by Victor Fleming, and (Paramount, 1946) directed by Stuart Gilmore. *A Woman's Fool* (Universal, 1918) directed by John Ford was based on *Lin McLean*.

The Virginian also served as the basis for a long-running television series (NBC, 1962–1970) although the character of Trampas was changed to that of one of the "good guys." In 1970 this series was retitled *Men from Shiloh* but still with James Drury in the role of the Virginian, playing for a single season. Several of the TV episodes were released overseas theatrically, including *The Devil's Children* (1963), *The Final Hour* (1963), and *The Brazen Bell* (1966), testifying to the persistent popularity of Wister's cowboy creation.

Women on the Frontier Women, by and large, are minor characters in Western novels. Their contribution to the plot is negligible for their major purpose in the story is as the "romantic interest." The Western heroine stereotype is the embodiment of purity, beauty, and wholesomeness. She is usually single and helpless; if she is married, she is depicted as passive and long-suffering. The myths surrounding the "weaker sex" on the frontier proliferated by books (and films) have hopelessly distorted the true role of women in the West. Beginning in the Nineteenth century the American West was defined by historians and theorists as a masculine experience and so it has remained over the years despite the contrary evidence to be found in journals, letters, diaries, and reminiscences written by women who lived in the West.

GENERAL HISTORIES

The role of women in the settlement of the Western frontier is unfortunately a neglected area. Women are virtually excluded from the standard books about this period of American history. One hundred years of historical research have produced less than a dozen historical studies about frontier women. The two best books are *The Gentle Tamers* (New York: Putnam's, 1958) by Dee Brown, a popularized treatment of the subject, and *Frontier Women: The Trans-Mississippi West 1840–1880* (New York: Hill and Wang, 1979) by Julie Roy Jeffrey, a scholarly approach, notwithstanding its having been written for a general audience. Although entertaining and filled with both facts and trivia, Brown's book fails in that it is not synecdochical, that is, he does not come to any far-reaching or generalized conclusions in terms of the relationships between frontier women, the region in which they lived, and the ideologies in which they thought or which influenced the

way they thought. Whereas, having made use of both published and archival firsthand accounts, Jeffrey's *Frontier Women* not only adds to our comprehension of pioneer women by focusing on the agricultural frontier, the mining frontier, the urban frontier, and the Mormon frontier, but also to our understanding of Western history through her firm grasp of the Nineteenth-century milieu.

For those interested in a Nineteenth-century view of frontier women William W. Fowler's *Women on the American Frontier* (1878; Collectors Editions, Ltd., 1970) is a good place to begin although it is often maudlin in its treatment.

Minority women suffer from even more neglect by historians. There are no general histories about black or Hispanic women in the West. However, the role of Native American women in Indian mythology and within various North American Indian cultures is examined generally in *Indian Women of the Western Morning: Their Life in Early America* (New York: Dial, 1974) by John Upton Terrell and Donna M. Terrell.

Much more historical research than has so far been published on this subject must be undertaken.

COLLECTIONS OF BIOGRAPHICAL SKETCHES

Throughout history there has been a fascination with women of easy virtue. This is no less true in the history of the American West and there is an enduring myth that the frontier was populated by prostitutes and women of questionable reputation. The lives of sporting-house women, unscrupulous women in search of wealth and power, and gun-toting cowgirl queens have provided writers with material that is told and retold in books about frontier women. These infamous adventuresses are the focus of Harry Sinclair Drago's (q.v.) *Notorious Ladies of the Frontier* (New York: Dodd, Mead, 1969) which includes biographical sketches on the two most famous written-about cowgirl queens, Calamity Jane and Belle Starr, and is generally more reliable in terms of historical and biographical facts than are Brad Williams' *Legendary Women of the West* (New York: David McKay, 1978) or Duncan Aikman's *Calamity Jane and the Lady Wildcats* (New York: Holt, Rinehart, 1927).

For those interested in less scandalous, more common frontier women a number of collections are available. The best is *Women of the West* (Millbrae, California: Les Femmes, 1976) by Dorothy Gray in which the lives of nineteen women are each examined in an historical framework. Also recommended is *The Women Who Made the West* (New York: Doubleday, 1980) edited by the Western Writers of America, although these biographical sketches of fifteen frontier "heroines" are stylistically of varying quality.

AUTOBIOGRAPHIES AND BIOGRAPHIES

Since there are so few secondary sources that eschew the stereotypical images of frontier women popularized in fiction, primary sources are indispensable in a study and analysis of frontier women. Certain of the following first-hand accounts are frequently available from reprint houses and university presses.

ARMY LIFE Accounts of Western frontier Army life rarely take into account the fact that women were present, yet women who traveled from fort to fort with their husbands did, upon occasion, write about their experiences. Elizabeth Custer's trilogy— *Boots and Saddles* (1885; Norman: University of Oklahoma Press, 1961), *Tenting on the Plains* (1887; Norman: University of Oklahoma Press, 1971), and *Following the Guidon* (1890; Norman: University of Oklahoma Press, 1966)—is the best known. Unfortunately, instead of writing about the Army from the woman's point of view, Custer spent most of her time in all three books white-washing and glorifying the life and career of her husband, George Armstrong Custer. Perhaps the best books on what Army life was for women are *My Army Life* (Philadelphia: Lippincott, 1908) by Frances Carrington and *Vanished Arizona: Recollections of My Army Life* (Philadelphia: Lippincott, 1908) by Martha Summerhayes. Summerhayes' book, considered by many historians to be a classic of the Southwest, is particularly valuable for its appreciation of Mexican and Indian culture in Arizona during the 1870s.

RANCH LIFE "Among hundreds of books written by and about range men," wrote Southwest historian J. Frank Dobie (q.v.), "there are hardly a dozen valid ones concerning women." Dobie considered Agnes Morley Cleaveland's *No Life for a Lady* (Boston: Houghton Mifflin, 1941) and Nannie T. Alderson's *A Bride Goes West* (New York: Farrar and Rinehart, 1942) written with Helena Huntington Smith two "ranch life" classics. Cleaveland's portrait of growing up on a New Mexican ranch and Alderson's depiction of ranching in Montana in the 1880s are both told in a highly humorous anecdotal style. Of almost equal interest is *Women in Levis* (Tucson: University of Arizona Press, 1967) by Eulalia Bourne.

Bourne was a schoolteacher and rancher in Arizona whose love of children was superseded only by her love of bovines.

MINING LIFE The mining frontier of the American West was one of the few places where a woman was in fact a *rara avis*. However, women did eventually make their way into even this strictly masculine environment and several have left records about mining life as it affected women. Most historians agree one of the classics in the area is Louise A.K.S. Clappe's *The Shirley Letters* (San Francisco: Grabhorn Press, 1922) written from the gold fields of California in 1851–1852. Clappe's letters have been cited as the basis for several of Bret Harte's (q.v.) mining camp stories. Anne Ellis' book, *The Life of an Ordinary Women* (Boston: Houghton Mifflin, 1929), is a marvelous portrait of girlhood, young womanhood, and motherhood in the mining camps of Colorado where life was for so many a constant struggle. Also noteworthy is *Let Them Speak for Themselves; Women in the American West* 1849–1900 (Hamden, Connecticut: The Shoestring Press, 1977) edited by Christiane Fischer, a collection of autobiographical writings by women, many of whom wrote about and from mining camps.

PIONEER LIFE Elinore Pruitt Stewart left Colorado in 1909 to become a homesteader in Wyoming. She was a natural born storyteller and in her two books—*Letters of a Woman Homesteader* (Boston: Houghton Mifflin, 1914) and *Letters on an Elk Hunt by a Woman Homesteader* (Boston: Houghton Mifflin, 1915)—Stewart recreated her experiences and the people she met with both humility and humanity. The story of Barbara Jones, mother, homemaker, nurse, storekeeper, and teacher is told in

Ma'am Jones of the Pecos (Tucson: University of Arizona Press, 1969) by Eve Ball, who brought validity and recognition to oral history as a means of studying the American West. A modern-day pioneer story is told in *Home Below Hell's Canyon* (New York: Thomas Y. Crowell, 1954) by Grace Jordan, the mother of a family that went to live in Idaho as a self-sufficient unit during the Depression years.

OVERLAND TRAIL The contributions to overland emigration made by women are slowly gaining recognition from historians as John Mack Faragher in his study *Women and Men on the Overland Trail* (New Haven: Yale University Press, 1979). Firsthand accounts by women who shared in the four-month, or more, test of courage are available. *By Ox Team to California: A Narrative of Crossing the Plains in 1860* (Oakland: Oakland Enquirer Publishing Co., 1910) by Lavinia Honeyman Porter, *Across the Plains to California in 1852* (New York: New York Public Library, 1915) by Lodisa Frizzel, and *A Frontier Lady: Recollections of the Gold Rush and Early California* (New Haven: Yale University Press, 1932) by Sarah Royce are good places to begin for those interested in the subject. Many women did not want to leave their homes, families, and friends, and this side of the story is told by the great-granddaughter, Beatrice L. Bliss, of one who did not want to go in *Mary Vowell Adams: Reluctant Pioneer* (Myrtle Creek: Oregon: The Mail Printers, 1972). A brief diary of an overland trip is contained in *Mountain Charley* (1861; Norman: University of Oklahoma Press, 1968) by Mrs. E.J. Guerin who for thirteen years dressed as a man and worked at "men's" jobs while searching for the slayer of her husband.

AMONG THE INDIANS   For various reasons a great number of women found themselves living among the Indians and the accounts left by them add to our knowledge and understanding of multi-cultural relationships in the West. *Desert Wife* (Boston: Little, Brown, 1928) by Hilda Faunce, who lived on the Navaho reserve with her trader husband, should be supplemented with Elizabeth Ward's *No Dudes, Few Women: Life with a Navaho Range Rider* (Albuquerque: University of New Mexico Press, 1951). Ward took a greater interest in Navaho culture than did Faunce and thus Ward's view is not as one-sided. Mary Ellicott Arnold and Mabel Reed served for two years as governmental field matrons to the Karok Indians of Northern California. They came to appreciate, and to some extent to prefer, many aspects of Native American culture and their experiences are told in a wonderful book, *In the Land of the Grasshopper Song* (New York: Vantage Press, 1957).

MINORITY WOMEN   A fascination with the warrior image in Indian culture has contributed to a lop-sided view of Indian life. A good place to begin for those interested in the Native American woman's story is *Pretty-Shield: Medicine Woman of the Crows* (New York: John Day, 1932) as told to Frank B. Linderman. Indian women of the Southwest are best represented in books as *A Pima Past* (Tucson: University of Arizona Press, 1974) by Anna Moore Shaw, *Me and Mine: The Life Story of Helen Sekaquaptewa* (Tucson: University of Arizona Press, 1969) as told to Louise Udall, and *Yaqui Women: Contemporary Life Histories* (Lincoln: University of Nebraska Press, 1978) by Jane Holden Kelley.

The role of Hispanic women within their culture is told in *We Fed Them Cactus* (Albuquerque: University of New Mexico Press, 1954) by Fabiola Cabeza de Baca.

CRITICISM

The images of women in the works of Western writers as Mari Sandoz (q.v.), Willa Cather (q.v.), Virginia Sorensen (q.v.), and Conrad Richter (q.v.) are critically dealt with in *Women, Women Writers, and the West* (Troy: Whitson, 1979) edited by L.L. Lee and Merrill Lewis. The nineteen essays in this collection, the first of its kind, explore the works of women writers who have dealt with the Western experience in their writings, examine materials contained in various journals and diaries by women, and critique the changing images of fictional female characters in Western fiction written by both men and women.

Wright, Harold Bell (1872–1944) Popular writer noted for combining religious notions with stories employing a Western setting born at Rome, New York. Wright's mother died when he was 10 and his father put him out to work on a farm. Wright's only schooling was at a country school. As an adult, he entered the preparatory department at Hiram College in Ohio, but left after two years due to illness and exhaustion. He went to Missouri and became interested in the backwoods people, preaching in a schoolhouse on Sundays. With neither college nor seminary training, Wright was a pastor for ten years in various rural churches. When his health compelled him to give up his self-appointed ministry, he ventured into the Ozark mountains to recuperate and, while there, wrote his first

Western novel, *The Shepherd of the Hills* (Chicago: Book Supply Co., 1907). This book's success henceforth determined his life's work. After completing a second non-Western novel, Wright moved to the Imperial Valley in California and wrote what was to become his most famous and popular novel, set in the Colorado desert, titled *The Winning of Barbara Worth* (Chicago: Book Supply Co., 1911).

By 1916, Wright went to the Arizona desert to wage a bout with tuberculosis, which had plagued him much of his life, and was successful. Wright, as Zane Grey (q.v.), attributed to the West the powers of a spiritual as well as a physical restorative agent, and this was nowhere more obvious than in his novel *When a Man's a Man* (Chicago: Book Supply Co., 1916).

Wright's fiction throughout was scented with a heavy sentimentalism and managed, albeit somewhat adroitly, to narrate fictional events in terms of didactic sermonizing that had a wide appeal to a vast number of people who generally did not read anything. In his favor it can be remarked that Wright gave a sympathetic portrait of the solitary Apache, Natachee, in *The Mine with the Iron Door* (New York: Appleton, 1923). Wright's popularity was further enhanced by the high-quality motion picture versions of his works, films in which the sermonizing was kept at a minimum and story values were stressed.

Films based on Harold Bell Wright's Western fiction are *The Shepherd of the Hills* (Wright, 1919) which was produced, written, and directed by Wright himself remade under this title (First National, 1928) directed by Albert Rogell, and (Paramount, 1941) directed by Henry Hathaway . *When a Man's a Man* (First National, 1924) was directed by Edward F. Cline who also directed the remake under this title (Fox, 1935). *The Winning of Barbara Worth* (United Artists, 1924) was directed by Henry King. *The Mine with the Iron Door* (United Artists, 1936) was directed by Sam Wood remade under this title (Columbia, 1936) directed by David Howard. Film producer Sol Lesser whose Principal Pictures produced *When a Man's a Man* for Fox release and *The Mine with the Iron Door* for Columbia release in the mid 'Thirties also adapted four non-Western stories by Wright and made Westerns of them in *Wild Brian Kent* (RKO, 1936) directed by Howard Bretherton, *Western Gold* (20th-Fox, 1937) directed by Howard Bretherton, *It Happened Out West* (20th-Fox, 1937) directed by Howard Bretherton, *Secret Valley* (20th-Fox, 1937) directed by Howard Bretherton.

Wynne, Brian. See Garfield, Brian.

Wynne, Frank. See Garfield, Brian.

Zorro. See McCulley, Johnston.